A RUSSIAN CULTURAL REVIVAL

A
RUSSIAN
CULTURAL
REVIVAL

A Critical Anthology of *Emigré* Literature before 1939

TEMIRA PACHMUSS

editor and translator

THE UNIVERSITY OF TENNESSEE PRESS / KNOXVILLE

Subventions from the National Endowment for the Humanities, Washington, D.C., and the Research Board of the University of Illinois at Urbana-Champaign toward publication of this volume are gratefully acknowledged.

Library of Congress Cataloging in Publication Data

Pachmuss, Temira
  A Russian cultural revival.
   Includes bibliographical references and index.
   1. Russian literature—20th century—Translations into
English. 2. Russian literature in foreign coun-
tries—Translations into English. 3. Russian literature—France. 4. English litera-
ture—Translations
from Russian. I. Title.
PG3213.P3   891.7   80-20670
ISBN 0-87049-296-9
ISBN 0-87049-306-X (pbk.)

*To the memory of
my sister Nina*

Contents

A Russian Cultural Revival

Contents

Preface

Among the few books concerning Russian *émigré* literature, the best and most comprehensive is Professor Gleb Struve's *Russkaya literatura v izgnanii* (Russian Literature in Exile).[1] Several earlier publications dealt with the problems of Russian *émigré* life but touched upon literary themes only peripherally, if at all. Among them are Hans von Rimscha's book, *Russland jenseits der Grenzen, 1921–1926*[2]; A. V. Amfiteatrov's review, *Literatura v izgnanii* (Literature in Exile)[3]; W. Chapin Huntington's publication, *The Homesick Millions: Russia-out-of-Russia*[4]; Sir John Hope Simpson's *The Refugee Problem: Report of a Survey*[5]; and *La Russie en exil*[6] by Jean Delage. Several brief references to *émigré* Russian literature may be found in Marc Slonim's *Modern Russian Literature: From Chekhov to the Present*.[7]

Gleb Struve's publication was followed by Ludmila Foster's *Bibliografiya russkoy zarubezhnoy literatury, 1918–1968* (Bibliography of Russian *Emigré* Literature, 1918–1968),[8] Michèle Beyssac's *La Vie culturelle de l'émigration russe en France: chronique (1920–1930)*,[9] as well as by two volumes of instructive and well-chosen essays and articles compiled and edited by N. P. Poltoratzky, *Russkaya literatura v emigratsii: sbornik statey* (Russian Literature in Exile: A Collection of Articles)[10] and *Russkaya religiozno-filosofskaya mysl' XX veka* (Russian Religious-Philosophical Thought of the Twentieth Century).[11]

As is evident from the titles cited, the major publications concerning Russian *émigré* literature are in Russian,[12] and thus for the most part inaccessible to the English-speaking reader and critic. Moreover, this area now boasts only a few specialists, and much remains to be explored in depth.[13] Only three or four American universities offer courses in Russian *émigré* literature, due basically to the lack of pertinent materials not only in English, but even in the original language. The works of D. S. Merezhkovsky, Mark Aldanov, and Vladimir Nabokov, translated into English as well as into other languages, are among the few gratifying exceptions. To these belongs also a collection of Zinaida Hippius's short stories, published in 1972.[14]

Aware of this neglect of Russian literature in exile, Professor Heinrich Stammler—a widely acclaimed specialist on Merezhkovsky, V. V. Rozanov, and several important Polish literary figures—advised me: "An anthology of Russian *émigré* literature is badly needed, especially now, after the publication of the two analytical volumes dealing with this matter, under Nikolay Poltoratzky's auspices, by the University of Pittsburgh Press." Indeed, the works of Russian *émigré* writers have yet to find their deserved audience of appreciative, sympathetic readers and scholars. This volume, therefore, is intended to fill the gap in the exposition and analysis of Russian *émigré* literature in English translation.

Without claiming to be comprehensive, *A Russian Cultural Revival: A Critical Anthology of Emigré Literature before 1939* offers an overview of the *émigré* literary scene in Paris during the 1920's and 30's. It brings into focus the various literary genres, aesthetic credos, and individual artistic methods which reveal the nature and substance of the Russian cultural world in exile. The major emphasis here falls on the period 1923–39, considered the apogee in the literary activity of the so-called first emigration. Many masterpieces were written during this time, which was marked by Ivan Bunin's receipt of the Nobel Prize for literature in 1933. Bunin's novella "Mitina lyubov' " (Mitya's Love), the short story "Solnechny udar" (Sunstroke), and the novel *Zhizn' Arsenyeva* (The Life of Arsenyev), Alexey Remizov's *Obraz Nikolaya Chudotvortsa* (The Image of Nikolay the Miracle Worker), Boris Zaytsev's novel *Dom v Passy* (The House in Passy), Ivan Shmelyov's novel *Nyanya iz Moskvy* (The Nanny from Moscow), Merezhkovsky's historico-religious writings, and also Mark Aldanov's historico-philosophical works all appeared during this period. Numerous collections of poetry—those of Zinaida Hippius, Marina Tsvetaeva, Vladislav Khodasevich, Georgy Adamovich, Georgy Ivanov, Nikolay Otsup, and Bunin, to give only a few examples—were published between 1923 and 1939. Several young writers also made their debuts in the Russian press abroad. These fresh beginnings, viewed against the background of lost dreams and nostalgic aspirations among the exiles, constitute one of the most remarkable and at the same time most pathetic chapters in modern history.

The selection of works for this volume was made largely under the tutelage of V. V. Weidlé, an erudite historian of Russian art and literature and himself an *émigré* writer. It was decided, however, that this selection should not be strictly confined to the 1923–39 era. Therefore, some works date back to the second decade of our century, whereas others have appeared since World War II. These exceptions were made on the basis of the following considerations: first, some of the earlier works were felt to be more representative of the individual author's artistic craftsmanship than those written between 1923 and 1939; second, I wished to emphasize the frequently modernistic themes and style of the work, rather than its chronological place; third, this volume seeks to show the continuity of Russian literature ensuing from the *émigrés'* effort to maintain a viable Russian cultural tradition abroad, despite difficulties of doing so through many years of exile. Since the major works of Merezhkovsky and Vladimir Nabokov have been translated into English and are readily available,[15] none of them are included here. Mark Aldanov is represented by a single fragment from one of his novellas. My aim has been to provide an arena for the reader's discovery of still little-known but truly gifted *émigré* artists, and to encourage further explorations into this unique literary legacy. Unfortunately, because of space limitations, several important writers have been omitted, such as Nikolay Nikolaevich Turoverov, who wrote poems about the Russian Cossacks, and Georgy Peskov (pseudonym of Elena Al'bertovna Deysha), a brilliant short story writer. However, since both of them published in Estonia and Latvia, they will be included in my forthcoming book, *Russian Emigré Literature in Finland and the Baltic States, 1921–39*. Nina Nikolaevna Berberova, a short story writer and critic, is represented here by only one poem. The reader interested in her works may find valuable information in her book *The Italics Are Mine*.

Included are samples of fiction, literary criticism, reminiscences, travel notes, one-act plays, and poetry. Each writer is provided with a concise biblio-biographical introduction and a critical exposition on his works. The index to the volume includes the names of all writers and works contained herein, as well as the names of journals, periodicals, and newspapers mentioned. Due to the lack of critical material in English, information from various Russian literary sources is offered here, in condensed formulations, in the introductions to the individual writers.

In presenting only selected works from the much larger context of Russian literature in exile, I am quite aware of the necessary limitations of my book. This subject awaits a more detailed study and a more comprehensive anthology. I have attempted to accomplish here at least a part of this immense task, since most of the materials which follow are unknown to most students of Russian literature. This may well be their first introduction to the extraordinary verse of Dovid Knut, Anna Prismanova, or George Ivask, or to some of the finest writings of Remizov, Yury Fel'zen, and Gaito Gazdanov—an introduction to belles-lettres which testifies to the vital diversity of its literary genres, to experimentation in prosody, to an aesthetic rebellion against the prescribed artistic norms of their native land, and to the literary ferment in the life of "Russian Paris." It is my sincere hope that, thanks in part to new vistas opened by this selection of artistic works, the reader will be better prepared to appreciate the Russian contribution to world literature outside the Soviet Union, and more able to relate it to present-day ideas, dilemmas, and values. Russian *émigré* literature deserves this effort.

This work was not undertaken for the sole benefit of students of Russian literature; nor is it expressly geared to those unacquainted with Russian *émigré* writings. It is also intended for those readers who wish to increase their understanding and to broaden their view of the European avant-garde, but who lack essential facts concerning Russian achievements in this area of modern literature. The contemporaneity of Russian *émigré* literature, its stylistic experimentation, and its philosophical and psychological content are clearly of far-reaching significance within the international context of the twentieth-century avant-garde experience. The *émigré* phenomenon is not merely an isolated though interesting addendum to contemporary literature, but is organically linked to its development. This can be seen, for example, in the works of Vladimir Nabokov. I hope the present anthology will help to remove some of the superficial linguistic (and perhaps even political) barriers surrounding the edifice of Russian art and literature in exile, at least in the eyes of many Western readers.[16] The anthology may also serve as a source of reading material for courses in contemporary Russian literature taught at colleges and universities in the West, and thus may inspire interest in an area too frequently and most undeservedly overlooked.

All of the English translations were done especially for this anthology. They attempt not only to convey the literal meaning of a poem, but to illustrate its poetic qualities as well—its particularly striking images, its individualistic use of colors and fragrances, or its sonority. In other words, the translations attempt to reflect that fragile essence of poetry which is most easily (and often unavoidably) distorted or lost in translation. In many instances it was not possible to convey the exact nature of the original sound instrumentation, innovative meter, rhythm, "weight" and accent of words in relation to one another. However, references are provided for the reader who wishes to make a closer aesthetic evaluation of the artist's themes and craftsmanship by examining the original Russian texts. Whenever possible, citations are to original editions, rather than to subsequent anthologies. Unfortunately, although various collections of poetry were checked and rechecked, several places and dates of original publication proved most difficult to ascertain. References to the original sources of the selections are given in brackets next to the general citation of source text.

To the usual difficulties one encounters in translating from Russian into English—specifically due to the emotional and semantic richness of the Russian language, its abundance of diminutives, and its conciseness—may be added the "impalpable quality," as it were, of each writer's literary style. There is often a certain reticence about finishing a thought or fully expressing an idea behind words or images, especially those concerning color and fragrance. Other works present a linguistic challenge, for example, those of Remizov, whose neologisms, "word-weaving," and re-creation of the medieval style, whether in ancient or modern context, were especially diffi-cult to render. A painter *manqué*, Remizov enhanced his highly fanciful style by adding his own sketches. The ornamental quality of his style is partially lost in translation. As a result, he, like many other Russian avant-garde writers in exile, has failed so far to achieve notice commensurate with his importance to modern literature. I hope this anthology will make at least an initial step toward bringing these authors well-deserved recognition.

The translation of Russian substandard, dialect, and slang expressions, as well as Russian-Yiddish phrases, also presented certain difficulties. Together with broken sentences, *Verfremdung* effects, and speech distortions, such can only be approximated by foreign equivalents. Consequently, some passages required explanation. Others, most unfortunately, acquired a melodramatic character; still others became somewhat distorted due to a change in emphasis. In some places a word or expression not in the original was added for the sake of clarity.

The transliteration of Russian names and titles follows standard rules, with a few exceptions to allow for more commonly accepted spellings. Any italics found in the texts are in the original sources.

The anthology consists of two parts, prose and poetry. The works of some authors who excelled in both appear in the prose section. The individual writers are presented in a sequence largely determined by chronological means, based on their first appearance on the literary scene. Another ordering factor has been the artistic visibility of certain authors. Lidiya Chervinskaya and Anatoly Steiger follow one another because their verse, taken together, elucidates the "Parisian note" technique. Georgy Ivanov and Irina Oboevtseva, as well as Alexander Ginger and Anna Prismanova, appear side by side because they were married, even though their respective poetry is altogether different in its poetic design and tenor.[17]

While preparing this volume, I was fortunate enough to have the advice and support of a number of people who deserve my warmest thanks. The late Professor V. V. Weidlé, T. A. Velichkovskaya, S. P. Zhaba, Yu. K. Terapiano, the late G. V. Adamovich, the late V. A. Zlobine, all of Paris, the late I. E. Saburova and the late D. I. Klenovsky of Munich and Traunstein, respectively, answered many of my inquiries and supplied me with valuable information. A large part of the research and translation for this book was made possible through my appointment as an Associate of the Center for Advanced Study at the University of Illinois during the spring semester, 1977. This assistance is herewith gratefully acknowledged. I also thank the University of Illinois Graduate Research Board, the Library, the Russian and East European Center, and the Department of Slavic Languages and Literatures, all at the University of Illinois, for various grants given in support of research, final preparation of the manuscript, and acquisition of necessary source material. Finally, my sincere thanks go to L. H. Miller, Special Languages Librarian at the University of Illinois, and to Heinrich Stammler, George Ivask, Edward Napier, and Roberta Goldblatt for their invaluable assistance.

Naturally, I assume full responsibility for all factual information and interpretation.

Temira Pachmuss
Urbana, Illinois

July 1980

Great care has been taken to trace the copyright holders of all works presented in this volume. Permission has been requested even in those cases where a claim could hardly be substantiated. Special gratitude is expressed to the following poets, writers, and critics (and their literary heirs) who permitted their works to be included in my English translations: Lidiya Chervinskaya, Igor' Chinnov, N. V. Codray (for Alexey Remizov), Ives Gentil-homme (for Ivan Shmelyov), Gillès de Pelichy (for Anatoly Steiger), Basil Ginger (for Alexander Ginger and Anna Prismanova), Dr. M. Greene (for Ivan Bunin's four poems and two short stories), E. F. Jellatchitch (for Yury Mandel'shtam), Yury Ivask, M. D. Krachkovskaya (for Dmitry Klenovsky), Ivan Makovsky (for Sergey Makovsky), Victor Mamchenko, Irina Odoev-tseva (for Georgy Ivanov's as well as her own poems), T. A. Ossorguine (for Mikhail Osorgin), Valery Pereleshin, A. Polonski (for Mark Aldanov), N. V. Reznikova (for Alexey Remizov), Irina Saburova, T. Smolensky (for Vla-dimir Smolensky), N. B. Sollogub (for Boris Zaytsev), N. D. Tatishchev (for Boris Poplavsky), Yury Terapiano, Tamara Velichkovskaya, and the late V. V. Weidlé. The Agence Hoffman, Paris, has granted permission to reprint the four poems by Ivan Bunin.

NOTES

1. Gleb Struve, *Russkaya literatura v izgnanii* (New York: Chekhov, 1956).
2. Hans von Rimscha, *Russland jenseits der Grenzen, 1921–1926* (Jena, 1927).
3. A. V. Amfiteatrov, *Literatura v izgnanii* (Belgrade, 1929).
4. W. Chapin Huntington, *The Homesick Millions: Russia-out-of-Russia* (Boston, 1933).
5. John Hope Simpson, *The Refugee Problem: Report of a Survey* (London: Royal Institute of International Affairs, 1939).
6. Jean Delage, *La Russie en exil* (Paris, 1930).
7. Marc Slonim, *Modern Russian Literature: From Chekhov to the Present* (New York: Oxford Univ. Press, 1953).
8. Ludmila Foster, *Bibliografiya russkoy zarubezhnoy literatury, 1918–1968* (Boston: Hall, 1970).
9. Michèle Beyssac, *La Vie culturelle de l'émigration russe en France: chronique (1920–1930)* (Paris: Presses Universitaires de France, 1971).
10. N. P. Poltoratzky, *Russkaya literatura v emigratsii: sbornik statey* (Pittsburgh: Univ. of Pittsburgh Press, 1972).
11. N. P. Poltoratzky, *Russkaya religiozno-filosofskaya mysl' XX veka* (Pittsburgh: Univ. of Pittsburgh Press, 1975).
12. Nina Berberova's much-disputed book, *The Italics Are Mine* (New York: Harcourt, Brace, 1969), is largely about herself and lacks objective references to other Russian writers in exile. The anthology *The Bitter Air of Exile: Russian Writers in the West, 1922–1972*, ed. Simon Karlinsky and Alfred Appel, Jr. (Berkeley: Univ. of California Press, 1977), was originally published as "Russian Literature and Culture in the West: 1922–1972," *Triquarterly 27* (Spring 1973) and 28 (Fall 1973). In his short preface Karlinsky says, "Some of the more famous names are not included; a few rather obscure ones are" (p. 8).
13. Several monographs in English deal with individual writers, such as Zinaida Hippius, Marina Tsvetaeva, Ivan Bunin, Vladimir Nabokov, Mark Aldanov, and D. S. Merezhkovsky.
14. *Selected Works of Zinaida Hippius*, tr. and ed. Temira Pachmuss (Urbana: Univ. of Illinois Press, 1972). Any Barda compiled a bibliography of Hippius's works in Russian entitled *Bibliographie des oeuvres de Zénaïde Hippius* (Zinaida Gippius, bibliografiia) (Paris: Institut d'Etudes Slaves, 1975). Among several doctoral dissertations on Zinaida Hippius, written in this country and elsewhere, the following deserve mention: Nina Awsienko, "Symbols-Ideas in Hippius' Poetry" (Univ. of Illinois, 1973), and William Edward Napier, "The Love Ethic of

Zinaida Hippius" (Univ. of Illinois, 1974). Nicholas Barmache compiled *Mikhail Andreevich Osorgin: bibliografiia* (Paris: Institut d'Études Slaves, 1973). Recent doctoral dissertations on *émigré* literature include D. M. Fiene, "The Life and Work of M. A. Osorgin, 1878–1942" (Indiana Univ., 1973); Roger Muir Hagglund, "A Study of the Literary Criticism of G. V. Adamovič" (Univ. of Washington, 1967); Antonina Licharev de Yackovlev, "Bunin's Prose Writings in Exile" (Univ. of Illinois, 1967); Elizabeth Malozemoff, "Ivan Bunin as a Writer of Prose" (Univ. of California/Berkeley, 1938); Margaret Ann Troupin, "Marina Cvetaeva's 'Remeslo': A Commentary" (Harvard Univ., 1974); L. D. Majhanovich, "Vladimir Nabokov-Sirin: The Early Prose—A Commentary on Themes, Style, and Structure" (Univ. of Illinois, 1976); Sona Aronian, "The Dream as a Literary Device in the Novels and Short Stories of Aleksej Remizov" (Yale Univ., 1971); Renate Schilk Bialy, "Devices for the Incongruous: A Study of A. M. Remizov's Prose" (Univ. of California/Los Angeles, 1974); Sarah Adalene Predock Burke, "Salient Features in the Writings of A. M. Remizov" (Univ. of Texas/Austin, 1966); Andrej Kodjak, "The Language of Alexej Remizov" (Univ. of Pennsylvania, 1963); Olga Gromov Sorokin, "Ivan Šmelev: His Life and Work" (Univ. of California/ Berkeley, 1965); Edythe Charlotte Haber, "The Works of Nadezda Aleksandrovna Teffi" (Harvard Univ., 1971); Elizabeth B. Neatrour, "Miniatures of Russian Life at Home and in Emigration: The Life and Works of N. A. Teffi" (Indiana Univ., 1972); Paul Victorovich Gribanovsky, "Boris Zaytsev i ego 'Putniki' (Boris Zaytsev and His Wanderers)" (Univ. of Washington, 1968); Ariadne Shilaeff, "The Fictionalized Biographies of Boris Zaitsev" (New York Univ., 1969).

15. The following books by D. S. Merezhkovsky, in English translation, are available from the University of Illinois Library at Urbana-Champaign: 1) English translation of *Rozhdenie bogov: The Birth of the Gods*, tr. Natalie Duddington (New York, 1926). 2) English translation of *Smert' bogov* (part I of *Khristos i antikhrist: trilogiya*): *The Death of the Gods*, tr. Bernard Guerney (New York, 1929), and *The Death of the Gods*, tr. Herbert Trench (New York, 1901). 3) English translation of *Voskresshie bogi: Leonardo da Vinci* (part II of *Khristos i antikhrist: trilogiya*); *The Forerunner* (London, 1902), "sole authorized translation from the Russian." Also *The Romance of Leonardo da Vinci*, tr. Bernard Guerney (New York, 1928), and *The Romance of Leonardo da Vinci*, tr. Herbert Trench (New York, 193?). 4) English translation of *Pyotr i Alexey* (part III of *Khristos i antikhrist: trilogiya*): *Peter and Alexis* (London, 1905), "sole authorized translation from the Russian." Also *Peter and Alexis* (New York, 1906), "sole authorized translation from the Russian," and *Peter and Alexis*, tr. Bernard Guerney (New York, 1931).

Nearly all of Vladimir Nabokov's works are available in English. Those still unavailable include early short stories and poems published in various Russian literary journals and newspapers in Estonia, Latvia, and Finland, 1923–36. They will appear in my forthcoming book, *Russian Emigré Literature in Finland and the Baltic States, 1921–1939*.

16. Unfortunately, in Soviet scholarly and critical writing, the works of these authors are seldom mentioned; as a consequence, their names are virtually unknown to the Soviet reader. The religious or mystical views of the Russian *émigré* writers, their individualistic or pessimistic attitudes, and their surrealistic imagery are officially ignored in the Soviet Union. A few exceptions are made when their works denounce life abroad, or when they may be used as testimony to the *émigré* writer's patriotic moods and nostalgia for his native country. But even in such cases the censors may abridge or alter original texts.

17. I could not satisfy the requests of several widows of deceased authors to present their husbands' works in accordance with the "friendly" or "unfriendly" divisions within "Russian Paris."

Sources

Literary Questions	*Literaturnye voprosy*
The Loyalist	*Blagonamerenny*
Milestones	*Vyorsty*
Native Fields	*Rodnaya niva*
The New City	*Novy grad*
The New Direction	*Novy put'*
The New Fields	*Novaya niva*
The New Gazette	*Novaya gazeta*
The New House	*Novoselye*
The New House	*Novy dom*
The New Life	*Novaya zhizn'*
The New Review	*Novy zhurnal*
New Russia	*Novaya Rossiya*
The New Russian Book	*Novaya russkaya kniga* (originally *Russkaya kniga* [The Russian Book])
The New Satyricon	*Novy satirikon*
The New Ship	*Novy korabl'*
New Time	*Novoe vremya*
The New World	*Novy mir*
The News	*Novosti*
The North	*Sever*
The Northern Herald	*Severny vestnik*
Numbers	*Chisla*
The Oven Prong	*Ukhvat*
The Petersburg Herald	*Peterburgsky glashatay*
The Phoenix	*Fenix*
La Renaissance	*Vozrozhdenie* (a newspaper in 1925–40; a journal since 1949)
The Road	*Put'*
Russia	*Rus'*
Russia Illustrated	*Illyustrirovannaya Rossiya*
Russian Annals	*Russkie zapiski*
The Russian Archive	*Russky arkhiv*
The Russian Book	*Russkaya kniga* (later renamed *Novaya russkaya kniga* [The New Russian Book]
The Russian Contemporary	*Russky sovremennik*
The Russian Past	*Russkaya starina*
Russian Thought	*Russkaya mysl'* (a journal in 1921–27; a newspaper since 1947)
The Sail	*Parus*
Satyricon	*Satirikon*
A Small Flame	*Ogonyok*
Sofia	*Sofia*

The Star	*Zvezda*
The Sword	*Mech* (appeared as a journal until issue 20, 1934; then, as a newspaper)
The Theatre	*Teatr*
Theatre and Art	*Teatr i isskustvo*
The Voice of Life	*Golos zhizni*
The Voice of Russia	*Golos Rossii*
The Will of Russia	*Volya Rossii* (a newspaper in 1920–21; a journal since 1922)

NEWSPAPERS

Churaevka	*Churaevka*
The Common Cause	*Obshchee delo*
Dawn	*Zarya*
Days	*Dni*
For Freedom	*Za svobodu* (until 1921, *Svoboda* [Freedom])
Freedom	*Svoboda* (renamed *Za svobodu* [For Freedom] in 1921)
Gun-bao	*Gun-bao*
The Kharbin Times	*Kharbinskoe vremya*
The Latest News	*Poslednie novosti*
The Lighthouse	*Mayak*
Literary Gazette	*Literaturnaya gazeta*
The Modern Word	*Sovremennoe slovo*
The Mouthpiece	*Rupor*
The New Russian Word	*Novoe russkoe slovo*
New Time	*Novoe vremya*
Our Path	*Nash put'*
La Renaissance	*Vozrozhdenie* (a newspaper in 1925–40; a journal since 1949)
The Rudder	*Rul'*
Russian News	*Russkie novosti*
The Russian News	*Russkie vedomosti*
Russian Thought	*Russkaya mysl'* (a journal in 1921–27; a newspaper since 1947)
The Russian Voice	*Russky golos*
The Russian Word	*Russkoe slovo*
Speech	*Rech'*
The Stock Gazette	*Birzhevye vedomosti*
The Sword	*Mech* (appeared as a journal until issue 20, 1934; then, as a newspaper)
Today	*Segodnya*

Unity	*Edinenie*
The Will of Russia	*Volya Rossii* (a newspaper in 1920–21; a journal since 1922)

Collections And Anthologies

Anchor: An Anthology of Emigré *Poetry*	*Yakor': Antologiya zarubezhnoy poezii*
Collection of Poems (The Union of Young Poets and Writers; Paris, 1929–1931), Books I-V	*Sbornik stikhov (Soyuz molodykh poetov i pisateley;* Paris, 1929–1931), Knigi I-V
Concord: From Contemporary Russian Emigré *Poetry*	*Sodruzhestvo: iz sovremennoy poezii russkogo zarubezhya*
Convolutions	*Izluchiny*
Crossroads	*Perekryostok*
Gumilyov's Collection	*Gumilyovsky sbornik*
In the West: An Anthology of Emigré *Poetry*	*Na Zapade: antologiya zarubezhnoy poezii*
The Island	*Ostrov*
Literary Review: A Free Collection	*Literaturny smotr: svobodny sbornik*
Literature Abroad: A Collection-Anthology of Works of New Emigré *Writers, 1947–1957*	*Literaturnoe zarubezhye: sbornik-antologiya proizvedeny pisateley novykh emigrantov, 1947–1957*
The Muse of the Diaspora: Selected Poems of Emigré *Poets, 1929–1960*	*Muza diaspory: izbrannye stikhi zarubezhnykh poetov, 1929–1960*
The Pearls of Russian Poetical Works: Selected Poems from the End of the 18th Century to Our Time	*Zhemshchuzhiny russkogo poeticheskogo tvorchestva: izbrannye stikhotvoreniya ot kontsa 18-go veka i do nashego vremeni*
The Relay Race: A Collection of Russian Emigré *Poetry*	*Estafeta: sbornik stikhov russkikh zarubezhnykh poetov*
The Russian Collection: Book I	*Russky sbornik: kniga I*
Russian Emigré *Literature: A Collection of Articles*	*Russkaya literatura v emigratsii: sbornik statey*
To New Horizons	*K novym dalyam*

A RUSSIAN CULTURAL REVIVAL

Introduction

More than half a century has passed since the tragic exodus of many of Russia's most eminent writers, critics, philosophers, scholars, and statesmen in the wake of the October Revolution of 1917 and the ensuing Civil War. Paris soon became the *émigré* capital of Russian culture, art, and literature. Several other important *émigré* centers emerged throughout Europe in the early 1920's—Berlin, Prague, Warsaw, Belgrade, Sofia, Riga, Helsingfors, and Revel'—but the tone of Russian belles-lettres was set by the Russian intellectual community in Paris. Short stories, tales, travel notes, memoirs, novels, and lyrical poetry dominated Russian literature in Western Europe; freedom and a Christian optimism were its basic tenets.

There were many newspapers, literary journals, and almanacs in which Russian writers could publish their works. Russian-language newspapers, such as *The Latest News*, *The Common Cause*, and *La Renaissance* in Paris, and *The Rudder* (Berlin), *Days* (Berlin; from 1925, Paris), *Today* (Riga), *For Freedom* (Warsaw), *New Time* (Belgrade), *The Will of Russia* (Prague, 1920–21), *Russia* (Sofia), and *The New Russian Word* (New York), provided a forum for *émigré* creative endeavors. For the most part, these newspapers maintained a high cultural level, as did the many Russian journals and almanacs published in Paris—for example, *Contemporary Annals*, *Russian Thought*, *Milestones*, *The Link*, *The Window*, *Russia Illustrated*, *Numbers*, *Future Russia*, *Russian Annals* (Paris-Shanghai), *Encounters*, *The New City*, the almanac *The Circle*, *The Russian Book* (later renamed *The New Russian Book*; Berlin), *The Loyalist* (Brussels), *Innovations* (Tallin), and others.[1]

Some of the more illustrious writers living in Paris from the beginning of the 1920's were Mark Aldanov, Konstantin Bal'mont, Ivan Bunin, Don Aminado, Zinaida Hippius, Alexander Kuprin, S. K. Makovsky, D. S. Merezhkovsky, Sasha Cherny, Lev Shestov, and Nadezhda Teffi. All of them left the Soviet Union when they realized that the new government was determined to control and direct the themes, plots, and artistic techniques of their present and future works. In 1920–23 they were joined by Georgy Adamovich, Boris Zaytsev, Georgy Ivanov, Nikolay Otsup, Alexey Remizov, Vladislav Khodasevich, Marina Tsvetaeva, Ivan Shmelyov, Irina Odoevtseva, and Mikhail Osorgin, and by such noteworthy philosophers, scholars, and statesmen as Nikolay Berdyaev, N. O. Lossky, Fyodor Stepun, B. P. Vysheslavtsev, Semyon Frank, Sergey Bulgakov, Anton Kartashev, Mark Vishnyak, Pavel Milyukov, V. D. Nabokov, Pyotr Struve, and

Ilya Bunakov-Fondaminsky. The Soviet writer Evgeny Zamyatin moved to Paris in 1931. Vyacheslav Ivanov settled in Italy (1924), Igor' Severyanin in Estonia, and Mikhail Artsybashev and D. V. Filosofov, the Merezhkovskys' intimate friend of many years, in Warsaw.

The literary reputation of the so-called older generation of poets and fiction writers had already been established in Russia. But the "younger" generation of *émigré* writers—among them Alexander Ginger, Dovid Knut, V. Sirin (Vladimir Nabokov), Boris Poplavsky, Lidiya Chervinskaya, Anatoly Steiger, Victor Mamchenko, Anna Prismanova, Antonin Ladinsky, Vladimir Smolensky, and Yury Terapiano—developed their talents and emerged as significant artists outside Russia, by and large apart from the influence of their Russian mentors. However, several of the older writers (Bunin, Hippius, Georgy Ivanov, Khodasevich, and Adamovich, for example) were very much involved with the Russian "Bohemians of Montparnasse" and urged them to master the Russian language and rules of prosody. Zinaida Hippius, furthermore, was instrumental in establishing two literary journals, *The New House* and *The New Ship*, in which the younger writers—Nina Berberova, Terapiano, Steiger, Yury Fel'zen, and Vladimir Zlobine, to name a few—could publish their works. Another outlet for the young writers was provided through a yearbook of the literary group *The Circle*, initiated by Ilya Bunakov-Fondaminsky. These "aspirants" were instructed in the art of writing by Hippius, Adamovich, and Khodasevich, while Bunin held symposiums at his residence which were attended by members of the "new generation." In fact, Galina Kuznetsova and Leonid Zurov may be referred to as Bunin's disciples in art.

Among these literary groups perhaps the most important and sophisticated was The Green Lamp, an *émigré* literary and philosophical society founded by Zinaida Hippius and her husband, D. S. Merezhkovsky. Its president was Georgy Ivanov, and its secretary, Zlobine. Not only literary matters, but also religious and political questions were raised and debated during the meetings of this society. Terapiano, one of the constant attenders at the Merezhkovskys' Sunday salon, described the founding of The Green Lamp:

> The Merezhkovskys decided to create something like an "incubator of ideas," a kind of secret society in which everybody would "conspire" with regard to the most important questions discussed at the "Sundays" by transforming them into public discussions, so as to "build a bridge" for spreading a "conspiracy" among wider *émigré* circles. During the first years of its existence the audience of "The Green Lamp" was very sensitive, very nervous. Exchanges of opinion between the older and younger generations sometimes became heated arguments; speeches were interrupted by utterances from the audience. But behind all this throbbed real life, [. . .] despite the fact that the themes at the first meetings were intentionally abstract.[2]

4

The first meeting of The Green Lamp (February 5, 1927) opened with speeches by Khodasevich and Merezhkovsky on the objectives and goals of the new society. Reports were made by M. O. Tsetlin on "Literary Criticism," Hippius on "Russian Literature in Exile," Bunakov-Fondaminsky on "The Russian Intelligentsia as a Spiritual Order," and Adamovich on "Does Poetry Have a Goal?" These subjects testify eloquently to the spiritual and intellectual aspirations of the *émigrés* in Paris, as well as to their desire to actively shape the future of Russian culture and literature.

The Green Lamp was an offshoot of the Merezhkovskys' famous Sunday *soirées* frequented by the Russian intellectual elite—Professor V. N. Speransky, Berdyaev, B. P. Vysheslavtsev, K. V. Mochul'sky, S. K. Makovsky, Teffi, Lev Shestov, Mark Aldanov, Remizov, Bunin, Shmelyov, and Boris Zaytsev. The former head of the provisional government, A. F. Kerensky, and the former minister of Russian Orthodoxy in Kerensky's cabinet of ministers, A. V. Kartashev, also attended several of these Sundays. From the younger generation were Adamovich, Georgy Ivanov, Odoevtseva, Terapiano, Khodasevich, Nikolay Otsup, Dovid Knut, V. V. Weidlé, Ladinsky, Chervinskaya, Yury Fel'zen, and others. These Sunday salons became cultural events of great significance to the *émigrés*. Discussions centered on poetry, philosophy, religion, and metaphysical concepts stimulated a lively interchange of ideas. The Holy Trinity, love, life and death, the Third Testament, Vladimir Solovyov, Kierkegaard, Hegel, Nietzsche, and Marx were among the topics discussed. The guests also analyzed and evaluated the latest ideas arising in belles-lettres, periodicals, newspapers, and the various literary *soirées*.

Among other important events in the cultural life of "Russian Paris" was the First Congress of Writers in Exile, organized in 1928 under the auspices of the Yugoslavian government. Writers and journalists from various countries were received in Belgrade by King Alexander, who honored several Russian authors, among them Merezhkovsky and Hippius, with the Order of St. Sava. A special publishing commission attached to the Serbian Academy of Sciences, under the title of "The Russian Library," began to publish the works of Russian writers residing in Western Europe: Bunin, Hippius, Kuprin, Merezhkovsky, Shmelyov, Remizov, Bal'mont, Amfiteatrov, Teffi, Igor' Severyanin, and others.

An invaluable, wittily written record of all of these manifold activities may be found in Zinaida Hippius's 1939 draft of an unfinished essay, "Istoriya intelligentskoy emigratsii: skhema 4-kh pyatiletok" (A History of the Intelligentsia in Exile: A Sketch of Four Five-Year Plans).[3] Hippius divided the "Russian history" of the *émigré* intelligentsia into four phases: the First Five-Year Period, 1920–25; the Second, 1925–30; the Third, 1930–35; and the Fourth, 1935–39. For each she presents a detailed picture of literary events (meetings, *soirées*, discussions, and conflicts), as well as a detailed account of various publishing efforts. Hippius adds her own observations and draws conclusions about each period. For example, she characterizes the First Five-Year Period (1920–25) as a time when the "older generation, old and new (post-revolutionary) *émigrés*, politicians, writers, and others were closely united against their common enemy, Bolshevism." This period was also the beginning of Russian newspapers and journals in exile: "Among those initiated were V. L. Burtsev's *The Common Cause*, *The Latest News* (later headed by Milyukov), *Contemporary Annals*, *Russia Illustrated* (beginning under the editorship of S. L. Frank and ending under that of M. P. Mironov), M. S. Tsetlin's *The Window* (and their literary meetings in his apartment), as well as Pozero-Chaykovsky's Russian Publishing House." In addition, societies, conferences, meetings, and unions were organized. "The Russian emigration then included Bunakov-Fondaminsky, M. O. Tsetlin, Bunin, Kuprin, N. K. Kul'man, I. I. Manukhin and his wife T. I. Manukhina, A. M. Remizov, M. Aldanov, and Alyoshka Tolstoy." Several of these people wrote for *Mercure de France* and other French periodicals and journals as well.

One important question at the time concerned a "political reconciliation" with the Soviet Union. Hippius and Merezhkovsky censured Berdyaev's suggestion that the Russian Church abroad should become a mediator between the Soviet government and Russian Orthodox believers, or that it should help create harmony between the "Kingdom of Caesar" and Russians in exile. The poet scorned Berdyaev's journal *The Road*, with its "conciliatory position," and E. E. Lazarev's journal *The Will of Russia*, an organ of the "left wing" of the Socialist Revolutionary party under the editorship of V. I. Lebedev, M. L. Slonim, and V. V. Sukhomlin. *The Will of Russia* refused to accept *émigré* writers as sole representatives and keepers of national culture, instead devoting its main attention to new Soviet literary publications. The critical section of the magazine reviewed systematically all literary events in the USSR. The Merezhkovskys' relations with *The Will of Russia* were, therefore, far from cordial, for they felt that the journal was flirting with the Soviet Union.[4] They also objected to another Russian journal, *Milestones*, edited by D. P. Svyatopolk-Mirsky, P. P. Suvchinsky, and S. Ya Efron (Marina Tsvetaeva's husband). Its "Evraziystvo" (Eurasianism, an ideological and political movement of the 1920's and 1930's among Russian *émigrés*) was unpalatable to Hippius and her husband, because it emphasized the Asiatic factors in the making of Russia and Russian culture, and it advocated an "Exodus to the East." *Milestones'* main thesis, that the Russians should stand "face to face with Asia, having turned their backs toward Europe," was against the Merezhkovskys' fundamental beliefs. Hippius particularly inveighed against the journal's "politics of appeasement" with the Soviet government; the idea that Russian literature abroad should be linked to Soviet literature and Soviet socialism was altogether alien to her.[5] She engaged in spirited polemics with E. D. Kuskova, S. N. Prokopovich, and A. V. Peshekhonov, who pleaded for better understanding by Russian *émigrés* of the new political, economic, and cultural realities in the USSR. Kuskova's call for an end to the "civil war" between the *émigrés* and the Soviet government was unacceptable to Hippius.[6] She was also angered by P. N. Milyukov's theory on the "evolution of Bolshevism." According to this theory, the Russian intelligentsia in exile should not be actively engaged in opposing Bolshevism. No intervention would be necessary, Milyukov claimed, for Bolshevism would, in due time, change of its own accord. The Merezhkovskys, on the other hand, had always hoped for immediate military intervention.[7] Hippius opposed yet another group of Russian *émigrés*, *Smenovekhovtsy*, whose weekly journal, *The Change of Landmarks*, was edited by Yu. V. Klyuchnikov. Its appeal to Russians abroad to consider themselves "conquered by the Soviet government" was, of course, ridiculous in her eyes.[8] These developments in the late summer and fall of 1925 were considered by many *émigrés* as an alarming conspiracy originating in the Soviet Union; thus it is not surprising that some Russian writers in Paris, such as Mikhail Osorgin, with his idea of a "spiritual return" to Soviet Russia, were criticized in Russian *émigré* journals and newspapers. Vladislav Khodasevich and A. F. Kerensky openly opposed Osorgin's views, and Hippius was always at loggerheads with him, as is evident from her correspondence with Georgy Adamovich and Greta Gerell.[9] Osorgin's lecture on March 1, 1924, in which he advised young Russians in Paris to return to Russia to participate in the destiny of their homeland, was condemned by all *émigré* circles. Henceforth, he was considered pro-Bolshevik by many Russian readers in the West.

Hippius accounts for the Second Period (1925–30) by describing the activities of the older and younger generations, M. M. Vinaver's *The Link*, the Sunday *soirées* of the Merezhkovskys, the meetings of The Green Lamp, the journals *The New House*, *The New Ship*, *Milestones*, and *Numbers*, Kerensky's newspaper *Days*, the collection of poetry *Crossroads*, and other associated events, such as the literary group *Kochevye* (Camp of the Wanderers), headed by Marc Slonim, and its fortnightly journal *The New Gazette* (its contributors were little known or completely unknown). In the Third Period (1930–35) Hippius bewails the gradual demise of the Parisian-Russian literary journals and hopes for the regeneration of Russia. Particularly instructive is her delineation of the period 1935–39 and her thoughts on the impending conflict between Stalin and Hitler, the politically oriented flight of S. Ya. Efron to Moscow, the growing skepticism and "literary passivity" of "ex-young" (as she labeled them) Russian writers, and the emergence of I. I. Bunakov-Fondaminsky's *The Circle* (in collaboration with Nikolay Berdyaev, G. P. Fedotov, E. Yu. Skobtsova [Mother Mariya], K. V. Mochul'sky) and its yearbook. "All conferences, meetings, and societies are replaced by *Vechera poezii* [Evenings of Poetry], during which multitudes of 'poets' recite their own works," quipped Hippius. The "ex-young" writers viewed the "international scene with alarm and apathy (where are we to go and *with whom*?)." The older generation did not voice any opinion, but "distrusted each and every being." It was impossible at that time to form any new ideological or literary groups. "No one wished to write, since literary works were considered purposeless and meaningless." The ominous presence of Hitler and Stalin and the threat of impending war preyed on the minds of the Russian exiles.

However subjective and humorous Hippius' interpretation of the Russian-Parisian atmosphere and literary events of those years of exile may be, her "History" nonetheless has considerable historical and literary significance and is a welcome addition to those few works devoted to Russian literature in the West. Nothing has been written on this subject in the Soviet Union; no bona fide discussion of the artistic, political, and philosophical views of Russian émigré writers has yet been permitted there.

The Russian intellectual community lived in close contact with French literature throughout the period 1920–39, and beyond. Although there was no significant "cross-pollination" between the literature produced by older Russian writers and French literature, the situation was different with the younger Russian writers who had been intellectually and artistically nurtured in the West. Poplavsky, Yury Fel'zen, and Gaito Gazdanov eagerly availed themselves of the rich Western literary tradition, as well as of its radical innovations. Western experimentation echoes in the declamatory intonation of Dovid Knut's early poems; irony and the grotesque appear in the later poetry of Georgy Ivanov and Khodasevich, the representatives of the "middle" generation; bizarre and surrealistic visions, even features of Dadaism, crop up in the creations of Poplavsky; enraptured "sound and color chains" and emphasis on verbal mastery are characteristics of Ladinsky's verse; philosophical meditations and lengthy discourses on psychological entanglements play a role in the works of Yury Fel'zen; verbal play, archaisms, different levels of diction, puns, neologisms, "nonsense" language, and whimsical word-play highlight Remizov's new ornamental patterns with their almost hypnotic combinations and recombinations of phrases. The early prose of V. Sirin, with his distinct penchant for fantastic impressionism, also belongs to this creative explosion. It indicates a partial break with that literary conservatism of the nineteenth century which characterized the works of some of the older representatives of Russian poetry and belles-lettres. Echoes of Russian Symbolism, Acmeism, and Futurism could also be heard in the works of both generations. There is indeed ample evidence of a common striving toward innovation. Russian émigré literature was unquestionably neither static nor irretrievably chained to its "mother" culture in Russia, as has been incorrectly suggested by some scholars.[10]

The Russian émigré intellectual community in Paris created a "conspiracy" of sorts, to use Terapiano's apt expression—a positive "conspiracy" to sustain and further the development of Russian (as distinct from Soviet) culture. Serving as the center of an underground web connecting various émigré intellectual communities throughout the world, Russian artists, writers, musicians, scholars, and philosophers in Paris have maintained their native lines of communication, even while living in close contact with alien cultures. These links have fostered creative ferment in all areas of art and knowledge and have helped establish a uniquely Russian *émigré* culture, one distinct from (though not oblivious to) its nineteenth-century progenitor and from neighboring twentieth-century Western European cultures.

Russian *émigré* literature, while unique in some respects, may also be considered part of a larger phenomenon, almost a tradition, of expatriate writing: Americans in Paris; Germans and Frenchmen in exile during the Nazi period. Carson McCullers (1917–67), the American novelist, lived and worked in Paris (1950–55) on her novel *Clock Without Hands* (1961), on a play entitled *Square Root of Wonderful* (1958), and on some poems. F. Scott Fitzgerald (1896–1940), eager to experience a deep spiritual change, went to France (1924–30), where he completed one of his most widely acclaimed novels, *The Great Gatsby* (1925), and worked on *Tender Is the Night* (1934), both delineating the confusion and glitter of America in the 1920's. Henry James (1843–1916), the noted American novelist and critic, became a British citizen in 1915 in protest against U.S. neutrality in World War I. From 1872 to 1874 he resided in Italy, where he wrote his first important novel, *Roderick Hudson* (1876). In 1876 he settled in London, where he published *Daisy Miller* (1879), among other works. Another distinguished American, T. S. Eliot (1888–1965), became a British subject in 1927, and in England his most celebrated works appeared. Sylvia Plath (1932–63), an American poet, also went into self-imposed exile in England, where she published her novel *The Bell Jar* (1963) and several collections of poetry.

England also harbored some French writers, for example, André Maurois (pseudonym of Emile Herzog, 1885–1967), a novelist, biographer, and historian. Opposed to the Nazi occupation, he lived in England and the United States during World War II. Wystan Hugh Auden (1907–73), an English poet, established himself in Spain, and in 1938 he traveled on to the United States, becoming an American citizen in 1946. *For the Time Being* (1945) and *The Age of Anxiety* (1947) were written during this period. The controversial English novelist and poet D. H. Lawrence (1885–1930) spent much of his life in Italy and New Mexico. He analyzed the ills of modern civilization as the results of atrophied human emotion, and uninhibited passion as a revitalizing force became something of a mystical ideal for him. This philosophy—not shared by many of his contemporaries—dominates *The Rainbow* (1915), *Women in Love* (1920), *The Plumed Serpent* (1926), and particularly *Lady Chatterley's Lover* (1928).

The advent of the Nazi regime made an exile out of Thomas Mann (1875–1955), who escaped to Switzerland and later to the United States. He became an American citizen in 1944 and participated in the fight against fascism. In 1952 he returned to Switzerland. During his *émigré* years, Mann wrote of the biblical exile in his trilogy *Joseph und seine Brüder* (tr. *Joseph and His Brothers* [1933–43]: *The Young Joseph* [1935], *Joseph in Egypt* [1938], *Joseph the*

Provider [1945]). Bertolt Brecht (1898–1956), the German poet and play-wright, having been converted to Marxism in the winter of 1928–29 and exiled from Germany in 1935, escaped to Denmark and then (1940–41), via Sweden, Finland, and the Soviet Union, to California. His anti-Nazi plays include *Der aufhaltsame Aufstieg des Arturo Ui* (1941), *Furcht und Elend des Dritten Reiches* (*The Private Life of the Master Race* [1944]), and *Mutter Courage* (*Mother Courage* [1941]).

One salient characteristic of every literature in exile, especially political exile, is its orientation toward the past. *Emigré* literature adheres to the traditions of yesterday because they provide a certain stability within an alien and largely unfriendly world. This hold on the past is especially evident in those German writers who fled the Nazi regime, and in the numerous Russian writers, poets, and philosophers who hurried to leave their home-land after the Bolshevik Revolution in 1917.

This book is a tribute to those Russian writers in exile whose works so graphically illustrate the widely divergent attitudes and philosophies preva-lent among the Russian intellectuals in the early 1920's and reveal their search for new artistic forms and expression. Like the Russian modernists at the turn of the century, these writers advocated freedom from the prevailing norms and rebelled against the dogmatic treatment of art made fashionable by Belinsky, Chernyshevsky, Dobrolyubov, Pisarev, and their disciples in the Soviet Union. In protest against the nineteenth-century radicals and their twentieth-century heirs, who had imposed upon the arts a civic and mate-rialistic ideology, the *emigré* writers openly avowed idealism, Christian op-timism or Christian resignation, and a mystico-ethical *Weltanschauung* which was entirely their own.

Individual representatives of Russian literature and culture in exile often differed in their personal aesthetic and philosophical allegiances. However, they shared certain characteristics: an opposition to any coercion in artistic creation, whether in content or in form; a mood of nostalgia and anguish; a longing to return to their native land; and a conscious participation in the crystallization of a culture reflecting their unique experience in exile.

NOTES

1. For more information regarding the Russian press, see Struve, *Russkaya literatura v izgnanii*; Foster, *Bibliografiya russkoy zarubezhnoy literatury, 1918–1968*; Temira Pachmuss, *Intel-lect and Ideas in Action: Selected Correspondence of Zinaida Hippius* (Munich: Wilhelm Fink Verlag, 1972); Emmanuel Shteyn, *Poeziya russkogo rasseyaniya, 1920–1977* (Ashford, Conn.: Izd. Ladya, 1978); V. Krylova, *Russkaya biblioteka: bibliografichesky byulleten' (sovetskaya i zarubezhnaya literatura)* (München, August 1955); M. Shatoff, *Bibliografichesky ukazatel' russkoy pechati za rubezhom* (New York, 1959–67); *Entsiklopediya russkikh pisateley*, comp. I. Ignatov (State College, Pa., 1972); Fiene, "The Life and Work of M. A. Osorgin, 1878–1942."

2. Yu. Terapiano, *Vstrechi* (New York, 1953), pp. 46–47.

3. Published with an introduction by Temira Pachmuss in *Russian Language Journal* 26 (1972), no. 93, pp. 3–13; nos. 94–95, pp. 3–19.

4. For further reference, see Marc Slonim, "Volya Rossii," in N. Poltoratzky, *Russkaya literatura v emigratsii*, pp. 291–300.

5. For more information, see Pachmuss, *Intellect and Ideas in Action*, pp. 141–169.

6. *Ibid.*, pp. 168–179.

7. *Ibid.*, pp. 168–170.

8. Struve, *Russkaya literatura v izgnanii*, pp. 30–40.

9. Pachmuss, *Intellect and Ideas in Action*, pp. 338, 352, 363, 593.

10. See, e.g., John Glad, "The American Chapter in Russian Poetry," *Russian Language Journal* 30, no. 106 (Spring 1976): 173–184.

Ivan Bunin (1870–1953)

Ivan Alexeevich Bunin, the first Russian Nobel Prize laureate in literature, left Russia in February, 1920, via Odessa, Constantinople, Sofia, and Belgrade, arriving in Paris the same year. Later he moved to Grasse, often returning to the French capital, where he died at the age of eighty-two.[1] While he published many works in exile, his literary reputation had already been established in Russia. His masterpieces include "Gospodin iz San Frantsisko" (The Gentleman from San Francisco; Moscow, 1915), *Chasha zhizni* (The Cup of Life; Paris, 1921), "Mitina lyubov' " (Mitya's Love; Paris, 1925), *Grammatika lyubvi: izbrannye rasskazy* (The Grammar of Love: Selected Short Stories; Belgrade, 1929), *Zhizn' Arsenyeva* (The Life of Arsenyev; Paris, 1930), *Bozhye drevo: miniatyury* (The Tree of God: Miniatures; Paris, 1931), *Petlistye ushi: rasskazy* (The Knotted Ears and Other Stories; New York: Chekhov, 1954), among others. Bunin's book of poetry, *Izbrannye stikhotvoreniya: 1900–1925)* (Selected Verses: 1900–1925), appeared in Paris (1929).

Bunin's stories are simple and free of bias—a very refreshing feature in Russian belles-lettres at a time when writers considered it not merely a convention, but a matter of duty and responsibility to include a personal evaluation of the issues presented in their works. As a fiction writer, Bunin is primarily interested in portraying nature, people, and events, rather than in interpreting and analyzing them. His descriptions are slow, detailed, and meticulously accurate. Bunin's sensitivity toward color, sound, and line makes him an impressionistic artist. His landscapes abound in personified epithets, lyrical and symbolic undertones, "impressionistic flickering lights,"[2] digressions, and metaphors. His fiction is free of contrived plots, its style is lucid, its scenes are true to life. Though lacking well-developed plots and denouements, his stories have profound meaning. The works of a skillful craftsman, their poetic elements are carefully controlled. He may be referred to as a writer who continued the classical tradition in Russian literature; his tone is impersonal, and there is a classic rigor in the structure of his works. Bunin was not influenced by Dostoevsky (unlike the Russian Symbolists, or even Gor'ky and his "Pleiad"), nor did the Russian *Sturm und Drang* period have any visible effect upon him. Deliberately abstaining from proselytizing (in the vein of Gor'ky, for example) Bunin merely presents, clearly and impersonally, the object of his interest. He never attempts to solve the "burning questions of the day," and he shuns artificiality, rhetoric, and melodrama. According to Zinaida Hippius, Bunin combines "the honesty and purity of a [real] writer with the most refined artistic taste."[3]

In his portrayal of the Russian peasant, Bunin avoids the tradition of those nineteenth-century Russian humanitarian writers who extolled the alleged meekness, holiness, and inborn wisdom of the Russian peasantry. He depicts peasants as thieves, drunkards, swindlers, shameless liars, and murderers. The mood, form, and subject matter of his short story "Nochnoy razgovor" (Conversation at Night, 1911) resemble Turgenev's "Bezhin lug" (Bezhin Meadow); yet Bunin's almost cruel portrayal of the Russian peasant surpasses even Chekhov's "Muzhiki" (The Peasants) in its gloominess.

His vision of the world has "double outlines." On the one hand, it is a world of beauty, joy, and love of life; on the other, a world of repulsive, tedious, and hopeless chimera. Love is an evanescent feeling which cannot endure, for death is the one true reality. Therefore nothing is worth emotional involvement. Human life is devoid of meaning, for everything will eventually turn to dust. The catastrophic consequences of sinful flesh are portrayed in "Mitya's Love." Mitya is defeated by his concupiscence; he is condemned to suicide by his sexual drive. Bunin's pessimistic outlook is also reflected in *The Life of Arsenyev*, where he not so much portrays life as attempts to fathom its meaning through its earthly manifestations, beautiful yet doomed to decay. He spares no effort to create an impression of the world's fragility and gradual disintegration. In his conception life lacks all positive ideals; the world is ruled by the merciless law of nature which reduces human beauty and joy to death and insignificance. Man is therefore subjected to an inescapable solitude and the tyranny of fate.

Bunin appears to share Tolstoy's hostile attitude toward culture and civilization, and, like Leonid Andreev, Mikhail Artsybashev, and Sergey Sergeev-Tsensky, he depicts life as vanity, madness, and horror. He uses some of the favorite themes of Russian "decadent" literature, among them murder and suicide. In his writings, suicide becomes a purely literary device, a traditional ending to a narrative or a drama. His work may be described as a beautiful requiem for a Russia that has passed, taking with it peace, tranquility, and scenic grandeur. The success of Bunin's fiction springs from his accomplished style and aesthetic rendering of atmosphere, from his sense of artistic restraint and equilibrium, from his sensitivity to nature, and, finally, from his poetic detachment concerning the issues raised. Zinaida Hippius gave the following pertinent summary of Bunin's artistic method: "He is a writer of acute vision. A profound, obstinate, and powerful love for the essence of life, for its meaning and its sacred mystery is his most prominent characteristic. Another is an irreconcilable and active hatred for the impurity and falseness which tend to envelop human life. In his hands he holds a powerful weapon—his magic words."[4]

Bunin proved himself an accomplished writer of artistic miniatures, as well as of lyrical poetry. His verse is solemn and simple, permeated with the persona's moods, reflecting his thought amidst beautiful, nostalgic nature. Weidlé, Yury Ivask, and many others insist that Bunin's lyrical power is revealed in his fiction alone. His poems seem to lack that lyrical flame which contains the essence of his prose. This does not mean that Bunin's lyrics are inferior to his fiction. He is a typical representative of Russian Apollonian poetry, writing in the vein of Pushkin and Batyushkov. There is a simplicity and economy in his verse, with delicate water colors, pensive moods, small yet expressive sketches of Russian nature, and the persona's sad smile at the ever-receding Russian past. In meter and rhythm, however, these poems are rather monotonous and lacking in ardor. Nevertheless, Bunin's prose is so overpowering in its artistic polish and expressiveness that it is difficult to give an impartial judgment of his overall achievement in lyrical poetry.

NOTES

1. For more information on Bunin's life, see Vera Nikolaevna Murovtseva-Bunina, *Zhizn' Bunina: 1870–1906* (The Life of Bunin: 1870–1906; Paris, 1958).
2. T. M. Bonami, *Khudozhestvennaya proza I. A. Bunina: 1887–1904* (Vladimir, 1962), p. 90.
3. "Literaturnaya zapis'. Polyot v Evropu," *Sovremennye zapiski*, 18 (1924): 128.
4. "Tayna zerkala: Ivan Bunin," *Obshchee delo* no. 304 (1921).

IN THE COUNTRY

FROM: *Povesti, rasskazy, vospominaniya* (Novellas, Short Stories, Reminiscences; Moscow: Moskovsky rabochy, 1961). First published in *Detskoe chtenie* (Readings for Children) (Moscow) No. 1, January. 1898.

When I was a small boy, it always seemed to me that spring began along with the Christmas holidays. "December—now that's winter," I thought. The weather in December is, for the most part, severe and gray. It grows light slowly. From morning on, the city is drowned in a gray, frosty fog, while the trees are clothed in thick hoarfrost, lilac colored; the sun can't be seen the entire day, and only in the evening might you notice its trace in the mute-red sunset lingering long in the heavy western mist . . . Yes, this indeed is winter!

I would wait for Christmastide impatiently. When, toward the end of December, as I hurried in the mornings to school, I saw the shops full of hundreds of shiny toys and decorations ready for Christmas trees; when I saw at the market whole carts of little green trees cut down for the holidays, and in the meat section whole mountains of frozen pigs' carcasses, suckling pigs and poultry, slaughtered and plucked, I would say to myself with joy: "Well, the holiday's really close now! Soon the dead of winter will end and things will turn to spring. I'll go to the country for two whole weeks, and there meet the start of spring."

It seemed to me that only in the country could one even notice that spring was beginning. It seemed to me that truly bright, sunny days existed only there. And it's true—in the city we forget about the sun, seldom see the sky. We are more fond of billboards and the walls of buildings.

So, finally, the long-awaited happy day arrived. In the evening a bell suddenly rang in the hallway of our apartment. I ran headlong into the entrance hall and bumped against a tall man in a raccoon coat. The collar of this large coat and the cap on the head of this tall man were covered with hoarfrost.

"Papa!" I squealed ecstatically.

"Get away, get away, I'm cold," father said gaily. And indeed, he smelled pleasantly of frosty freshness, snow, and the wintry air.

I wouldn't leave my father's side. Never had I loved him as I did on such an evening; never did I fall asleep so sweetly!

I fell asleep, filled with dreams of the next day's journey to the country. And it was truly a festive journey. The train ran quickly among the even, snowy fields; the car was illuminated by the morning sun. Swirling puffs of white smoke swam before the windows, falling smoothly and spreading over the snow along the road, while wide shadows walked across the train car. Because of this the sunlight seemed to disappear, then to burst anew through the windows in bright, amber stripes . . . Even the throngs of people in the car, the crowding, and noise were gay!

Now a solitary, familiar station appears among the empty fields. How quiet it is in the fields when the rumble of the train has passed! Curling up in the back of the sled, you close your eyes and sway slightly; you hear the bell pealing out above the three horses harnessed in their troika, how the runners screech and knock against bumps. The lead horse ambles; the lean trace horses, first snorting a bit, then breaking into a gallop, churn up a ball of snow at the front of the sled, while very quickly the long whip of the coachman curls snake-like around the sled. You turn around—and it seems that the strip of road is slipping out from under the runners and scurrying back into the flat snowy field . . .

And afterward—moving at a slow walk across the drifting meadows, under precipices overhung with heavy snows! The crests of the snowy cliffs curl inward like enormous shells. Their clear, cold outlines are distinct and sharp against the sky; from below, the sky seems a deep, dark blue! The trace horses play while trotting, gobbling snow in their mouths and spitting it aside . . .

"Stop fooling!" the coachman angrily shouts, cracking his whip—and again the runners knock against the bumps, and the little bell bursts forth piercingly under the rhythmically swaying arc . . .

Meanwhile, the short day is already fading. Lilac clouds have risen from the west, the sun has dipped into them, and a quiet, wintry evening falls. Above the darkening snows the frosty mist of night rises to the east. Ahead the snowy road merges with it, and a deathly silence reigns over the steppe. Only the runners quietly squeak along in the snow, and now and then the little bell rings out pensively; the horses trot in step. Yellow buntings fly noiselessly past them along the road . . . A peasant in a low, wide sledge pulls up just behind us somewhere along the crossing, and I feel on the back of my head the regular warm breath from the frost-covered muzzle of his shaggy, short, and stocky horse trotting behind our sled.

"Don't get on top of us!" The voice of our coachman rings out intermittently in the deathly silence of the field.

And the peasant also shouts something, jumps out while his sledge goes skidding, and again, on the run, tumbles sideways into his sledge.

Everything around us grows darker and darker, and it's already night as we drive into the familiar village. The night is dark, but starlit. Small stars shiver with sharp, blue flames; the large ones sparkle with the iridescent glitter of multicolored gems. Here and there in the village, windowpanes still glow red in dimly darkening huts . . . In the clear, frosty air the creak of a gate or the howl of a little dog echoes loudly . . .

And a sensation of deep satisfaction and peace fills your soul when, at last, you slowly drive up to a snowdrift before the porch of a small, well-lit, and warm country home!

"So where is this spring?" you are asking.

Isn't this joyous feeling which has filled the soul because of this whole, merry, sunny day of journeying into the country—isn't it much like spring? Wasn't it with a springlike sensation that I opened my eyes, awakening the next morning in the nursery?

From early morning, a blue semi-dusk always pervaded the large rooms of our old house. This was because the house was surrounded by a garden, and the window glass was painted over from top to bottom by a frost of silvery palm leaves and ferns in patterns of mother-of-pearl. Even before tea I managed to scurry through all the rooms, look over all these drawings which the frost had made during the night, and even to spend some time in the small entrance hall where the skis were standing.

"Papa, I'm going to go skiing around a little," I timidly said to my father just after tea.

Father looked at me intently and answered, smiling: "Oh, you, such a savage! A real wild nomad! It's still cold, you know; you'll freeze your nose off!"

"I'll only be a minute . . . "

"Well, if that's the case—hurry off!"

"I'm a wild nomad, I'm a wild nomad!" I shouted, jumping up with joy and hurriedly preparing for the outing.

Sharp, frosty air plucks and snatches at everything when you step out of the house. Beyond the garden, dawn is still glowing coldly. The sun has only just popped out from beyond the snowy field like a fiery ball; yet the whole picture of the village already sparkles with the bright and wonderfully tender, pure colors of a northern morning. Puffs of smoke show crimson and slowly disperse above white roofs. The garden is clothed in silvery hoarfrost . . . That's just where I need to go! So, standing on my skis and surrounded by the hounds, I hurried to plow into the depths of the thicket where one could get buried up to his head in the snow.

"I'm a wild nomad!" I shouted to the dogs, heading across the downy snow toward the drift beneath the garden.

There a dense and thick hoarfrost covered the old broom groves until midday. It's so thrilling to shake it loose and to feel its cold down sprinkle over your face! It's even more thrilling to watch the workers on the pond make holes in the ice and pull enormous blocks out of the water with hooks. As if they were squares of bright, mountain crystals, the ice blocks shine in the sun, twinkling with green and blue tints . . .

Toward dinnertime the sunny day really bursts forth. Drops of water fall from the overhang of the roof. The pits and bumps of the road along the old village pasture shimmer like an elephant's ivory tusk.

"Spring, spring is near!" you think, as you shade your eyes from the sun's caress.

And all day you want to stay outside and never come in! Everything pleases you. Whether you go by chance to the cattle shed where the melancholy cows, sighing deeply now and then and heaving their sides, doze near the crib; and the horses, grown lean from the winter, wander, while the lambs huddle in the pen; or whether you walk to the threshing floor and hear along the way how the sparrows romp and chirp in the acacia bushes, how suddenly their whole noisy flock takes off and, like the rain, sprinkles onto the roof of the threshing barn—everything pleases you . . . While on the threshing floor, in the safety of the haystacks and walls of straw, blocked up with snow, it's especially cozy. It's good to lie around under the sun on the chaff, in the straw which smells so pungently of snow and mice!

The entire holiday passed for me in the enchantment of these sunny days, these bright dreams of approaching spring. You'll forget the lessons, you'll even forget the skis, and you'll spend all your time sitting in the sunlit hall, forever gazing at the distant, snowy fields which already glisten with the spring-like golden mica of a firm, frozen snow crust.

"Well, don't be sad, do you hear?" said father when they were finally preparing me to go back to the city. "Now you won't even notice the coming of spring. In about two months it'll be Easter, and then summer. You'll come back then—I'll give you a foal to ride, we'll ride together, and go after quail . . . "

I was sorry to leave my family home, but I quite agreed with father. Soon now it'll really be spring!

"You know, Papa, it's true, it simply smells of spring!" I said, too, as we sat down in the sledge in the morning, rolled through the gateway across a high snowdrift, well packed with yesterday's snowstorm, and deeply inhaled the fresh wind which smelled of new-fallen snow.

"Do you like spring?" father asked with a smile.

"I like it, Papa! Very much!"

"And do you like the country?"

"Of course, I like it . . . "

"That's good," father added. "When you grow up, you'll remember that man should live close to nature, love his native fields, the air, the sun and sky . . . It's not true that it's boring in the country. There's much poverty in the country—that is true; and it means that one must work at things that will lessen this poverty—help the country people, labor with them and for them . . . one can live well in the country!"

"True, true!" I thought. "It never so much as smells of spring in the city. But here it does. And the ice holes over there already blackened, begun to thaw out . . . "

We are riding through a large village above a river, and I rush to get my fill of all the village sights.

Around us dirty roofs are black amid the drifts; but soon the drifts will melt, and even these poor houses will be clean and gay. Even now there's gaiety in them, especially in these brick ones, where the well-to-do families live. And with what pleasure I entered just such a house when we stopped to feed the horses!

It's always damp in the brick houses of well-to-do peasants. Charcoal fumes hang in a greenish haze in the warm air; on the floor—wet straw; yet there is always a delicious smell of bread rising. There are many people. And everyone is at his work. One jerkily drones with a bowstring; another beats and raises a downy white "billow"; yet another mends a yoke, with a sudden decisiveness pulling apart the waxed end, the part threaded through the leather, in different directions. Meanwhile an experienced man, a tailor in a waistcoat dotted with needles and a skein of threads around his neck, enter-tains everyone with old wives' tales. Sitting hunched up on a sawhorse—one leg under him, while the knee of the other is raised almost to his face—and contriving to hold the edge of the cloth or the sheepskin with the large toe of his bare foot, he sews intently, never once falling into silence, pensively smiling with gay, wise eyes, tossing the hair off his forehead and threading the needle in the light. And everyone looks at him in a friendly way. He is at ease everywhere, even with the children, whom he rocks in his arms in the

18

evenings. He lets them grab him by his beard, and then suddenly gnashes his teeth, snaps like a dog, and snatches the child's tiny hand with his mouth. In response, the child, having awaited his "prank" with a palpitating heart, gleefully jumps up and bursts into prolonged laughter . . .

This isn't the first time I've seen him, and now I look at him with deep curiosity. But it's time to go. We say goodbye to our host and walk out onto the porch. The host, who leads us out, stands on the porch in a cap but only in shirtsleeves, looks at me, and says with a smile:

"Well then, young master, it means—from now until spring in the city?"

"Until spring," I say, "but it'll be spring soon, you know!"

"Soon, soon!" the peasant agrees.

Again we ride past black village huts, across hillocks, where youngsters sled down on "ice chunks," across meadows where rook nests sway in tall willow thickets. Around the frozen bumpy edges of the ice holes, peasant women briskly wash linen in the icy, dark water and shrilly exchange remarks . . .

But the village has also ended. Ahead are only fields, a white sheet of downy snow. How much of it has piled up in the hollows during the night! . . . Again the wind has risen in the fields; it carries the horses' manes and tails to one side. The road is difficult, but the horses are becoming restive; it's as if they like the wind and the spaciousness of the fields, and they quickly carry us forward . . . The sky is completely covered with clouds; a small forest darkens in the distance.

"The thaw has begun," I think.

And I imagine how these gray days will go on now for a long time, even while the past year's wormwood dolefully rocks in the wind at the bounds of the deserted steppe. But still, spring is near! Soon this very wind will be warmer, and when March arrives, gay and noisy, it'll trip through the birch forests in the brilliance of the spring sun, arousing nature from her wintry sleep. And later, floods will thunder down through ravines, birds will fly back from the distant south, the fields will turn green . . .

How good it is in the fields!

A BENEFIT PERFORMANCE

FROM: *Sobranie sochineny* (The Collected Works; Moscow: Izd. khudozh. literatury, 1966), V. First published in *The Latest News*, No. 3199, December 25, 1929.

In Moscow—well, let's say, on Molchanovka—lives "a former actress of the Imperial theaters." Single, quite aged, broad-faced and wiry. She gives singing lessons. And this is what happens to her every year in December.

Once on a Sunday—we'll set it on a very frosty, sunny morning—a bell rings out in her entrance hall.

"Annushka! They're ringing!" she anxiously cries out from the bedroom.

The cook runs to answer the door—and is actually taken aback, so brilliant are the elegant guests: two young ladies in furs and white gloves, and a student, a dandy, their escort, thoroughly frozen in his light overcoat and thin shoes.

The guests wait for a rather long time in the cold living room bathed in amber through the frosty patterns on the windows. Then they hear the brisk steps of the hostess and quickly rise to greet her. She is very nervous—she knows what this is all about—and has heavily powdered her face and perfumed her coarse and bony hands . . .

"Good Heavens, excuse me, ladies and sir, it seems I've made you wait," she says with an enchanting smile and the ultimate of high society ease, entering quickly and overcoming her palpitating heart with difficulty.

"It is for you to excuse us for the disturbance." The student interrupts her with gallant deference, bowing and kissing her hand. "We appear before you with a zealous yet most humble request. The committee for the organization of the traditional literary-vocal-musical *soirée* on behalf of the needy pupils of the Fifth Moscow High School have entrusted us with the honor of petitioning you for your benefit performance in this *soirée*, which will take place on the third day of the Christmas holidays."

"Ladies and gentleman, if it's possible, spare me, please!" she begins enchantingly. "The fact is that . . . "

But the young ladies beg her so amicably, so ardently, and in such a flattering fashion that she doesn't succeed in making even this weak attempt to refuse, to decline . . .

After this, three whole weeks pass.

And for the entire three weeks Moscow works, trades, enjoys itself; but amidst all its most varied matters, concerns, and enjoyments, Moscow secretly lives for only one desire—the anticipation of that illustrious evening, the twenty-seventh of December. Numerous posters of every color and size blaze on all its streets and crosswalks: *The Lower Depths, The Bluebird, Three Sisters;* Shalyapin in *The Mermaid,* Sobinov in *The Snow Maiden;* Shor, Craine, and Erlich; the opera of Zimin, a *soirée* of Igor' Severyanin . . . But now everyone's attention is drawn only to that small poster on which is boldly printed the name of the benevolent participant of the literary-vocal-musical *soirée* on behalf of the needy students of the Fifth Moscow High School. As to the participant herself, she remains at home continuously, working without respite so as not to disappoint Moscow's expectations. Endlessly she selects what to sing, tests her voice from morning till evening, studies first this, then that . . . the days pass unusually quickly, and the approaching day is already pushing her into a state of terror: that dreadful twenty-seventh of December will be here before one can scarcely turn around!

She has discontinued giving lessons, doesn't receive anyone, and doesn't even leave the house, afraid of catching bronchitis or a head cold. With exactly what selections should she appear before her audience? The public has no idea how difficult this decision is, even for the most experienced artist! How much feeling one must display here, how much taste, tact, experience! However, after long and tiring doubts and hesitations, she settles the matter by keeping her old, unchanging repertoire. Again she goes through three works—one French, sad and tender, bewitching, like a lullaby, yet concealing within it the enormous passion, force, and pain of a loving woman's soul, madly desiring but sacrificing happiness; the second—full of all the brilliance of a coloratura and Russian daring; and then her crowning glory, "I would kiss you, but I fear the moon might see us," with which, as always, she could make an especially brilliant display, executing it "with fervor," playfully, youthfully, and ending it on such an desperately high-pitched and triumphant note that the entire hall would tremble with applause. In addition, she prepares twelve works for encores . . . The days keep flashing by, and there is a certain feeling growing in her soul as if the hour of her execution were approaching. Nevertheless, she works and works. And so the last, the fateful day arrives!

On the morning of the twenty-seventh of December, her strength is stretched to its very limits. There is still one rehearsal in the morning, but it's already the final dress rehearsal. She sings as if she were already on stage—in full voice, with all her artistic expressiveness. She goes through her entire program with her accompanist. And she feels that her work has not been in vain! Yet, all the same, who knows what awaits her tonight? Triumph or fiasco? Her face is ablaze, her hands are like ice . . . After the rehearsal she goes to her bedroom, undresses, and lies on the bed. Annushka brings her something quite unusual—some caviar, cold chicken, and port. In this manner, on the day of the performance, all great actresses have breakfast. Having snacked, she gives orders to draw the blinds, to leave her alone, and to keep complete silence in the house, while she closes her eyes and lies in the dark, motionless, trying not to think about anything, not to be upset by anything, one hour, two, three—right up to six o'clock in the evening. At six she jumps up: the shrill bell sounds in the entrance hall. The hairdresser!

With a pounding heart, with burning ears and cheeks, she pours out with an icy hand all forty drops of tincture of etheric-valerian and, in a robe, with her hair let down, like a virgin whom they have come to prepare for immolation, she seats herself before the mirror. The hairdresser enters, warming his hands above the gas stove in the kitchen as a preliminary, and says encouragingly:

"Gorgeous weather! Fairly cold, but gorgeous!"

He works meticulously and slowly, feeling that he is himself a participant in the forthcoming presentation, completely understanding and sharing her artistic excitement, being himself of an artistic nature. His light and casual conversation and, in general, his entire experience in such matters, as well as his firm belief in her forthcoming success, calm her little by little, returning strength, courage, and hope to her . . . but when he finishes his work and, looking it over from all sides, is certain that nothing more need be done to improve this splendid creation and styling, he leaves. While the clock in the dining room slowly strikes seven, her heart again begins to sink. At eight-thirty they will come for her!

Then eight o'clock strikes, but she is still not ready. She again pours out the drops—this time Hoffmann's valerian—puts on her best lingerie, applies rouge and powder . . . At half-past eight the bell rings out. She is thunder-struck—they've come! Annushka runs to the entrance hall. Because of the excitement she, too, is not herself—she's unable to open the door immediate-ly . . .

They—this time, two students—have come in a huge, ancient, rented carriage, harnessed to two gigantic jades. They are dandies, too, and not wearing rubbers. Their feet are numb from the frost. In the living room, where the odorous kerosene lamps burn dimly, it is cold, as always. They patiently sit in their dress coats, shining with their smoothly combed heads, sweet smelling with their pomades and brilliantine, with large white satin bows on their chests—like two best men. They sit silently, waiting politely and steadfastly, and looking at the closed doors on both sides of the room. They also look at the frost-covered windows which sparkle with small blue and red lights, at the piano, at the portraits of great male and female singers along the walls; they listen to the ringing and rumble of streetcars remotely beyond the windows, to Annushka's and the actress's own nervous steps behind the doors . . . A quarter of an hour passes, half an hour, forty minutes . . . Suddenly one of the doors unexpectedly flies open. As if at someone's command, they leap from their seats, while the actress, wearing a charming and unconcerned smile, strides quickly toward them.

"Good Heavens, pardon me, gentlemen. It seems I have made you wait . . . Is it time for us to go? Well, then, let's go, if you please. I'm ready . . ."

Burning on her cheekbones are two crimson spots, visible even through her rouge and powder. Her mouth smells of lily-of-the valley drops, her hands, of lotion; her ethereal dress, fashioned from smoke-colored gossamer, is scented with perfume. She resembles Death, in regalia for a ball. Something of black lace, Spanish-looking, adorns her high and sophisticated coiffure—her gray hair curled and fluffed from every side. A fur of curly white goat-skin lies across her bare shoulders and enormous clavicles . . . The students dash after her into the entrance hall. The one who is taller and thinner grabs her overshoes and, deftly kneeling, slips them adroitly over her black satin pumps with the diamond buckles. He smells the odor of mice from under her arms as she bends down to help him and, at the same time, to modestly pull down the hem of her white lace-edged pantaloons . . .

She first sang about the meeting of a cloud with thunder; next, about refuge . . . "into this refuge the Lord hath guided us," and, with particular brilliance, "I would have kissed you . . . " A small critical elderly man in the first row let out a caustic giggle when she sang these words, and even shook his head. His action was not in the least ambiguous: "No, thank you! Please, don't kiss . . . " Nevertheless, he made a fool of himself, for the actress was a tremendous success. She was called back on stage repeatedly, and they forced her to sing an encore—especially those tactful youths who were standing in the aisles, shouting frantically, and clapping their cupped hands with a horrifying resonance.

POEMS

THE COCK ON THE CHURCH CROSS

FROM: *Yakor': antologiya zarubezhnoy poezii* (The Anchor: An Anthology of *Emigré* Poetry; Berlin: Petropolis, 1936), comp. G. Adamovich and M. Kantor. First published in the almanac *Medny vsadnik* (The Bronze Horseman) (Berlin, 1923), Book 1.

> He glides, and floats, and scurries like a skiff
> And, oh how high, above the earth!
> The heavens retreat behind,
> But he goes forth—always singing.
>
> He sings that we're alive,
> That we shall die, that day after day
> The years go by, and ages flow—
> Just like a river, like the clouds.
>
> He sings that all's deception,
> For it's barely a moment that fate allows
> A father's house, a beloved friend,
> A home with children, and grandchildren.
>
> He sings that he holds his ark
> On the path to a magic realm,
> That only death's sleep is eternal,
> And God's temple, the cross, and he.

November 12, 1922

23

IVAN BUNIN

TEFFI[1]

FROM: *The Anchor: An Anthology of Emigré Poetry* (see above).

I began a little ditty,
But hadn't the strength to sing it.
A hunchback crawled up a narrow ladder
And extinguished the sun . . .

Through darkened alleys
Christ was walking yesterday—
He kept asking after someone,
And, for someone, He carried something . . .

Through the window I dared not look—
They'll see me—swear at me! . . .
I'm rocking—black-nosed and webfooted
Little hunchbacks . . .

Blue tulips are blooming
In the azure lands . . .
There, someone on a little flute
Will sob through my song!

———————

FROM: *The Anchor: An Anthology of Emigré Poetry.*

My sun, you'll not warm me,
Try as you will,
You burn too serenely—
I desire too intensely!

My heart, you'll not hear me,
Try as you will,
You beat too loudly—
I call too shyly!

My happiness, you'll not console me,
Try as you will,
You'll lie too delicately—
I'll know too bitterly!

24

My beloved, you'll not love me,
Try as you will,
I burn too brightly—
You'll take it all too simply!

FROM: *K novym dalyam* (To New Horizons; Stockholm: Northern Lights, 1921).

That star which floated in the dark water
Under the tangled brush in an overgrown garden—
That little flame, which twinkled in the pond till dawn,
I'll never find in the heavens now.

And to that village, where I passed my youth,
To that old house, the house of my first songs,
Where in my youth I awaited happiness and joy,
I'll never, never return!

NOTE

1. Nadezhda Teffi, a Russian writer, was fond of inventing hilarious mystified ditties, sketches, and scenes. It is to Teffi's ability as a humorist that Bunin dedicates his poem.

Zinaida Hippius (1869–1945)

Zinaida Nikolaevna Hippius was an influential poet of the early Symbolist movement, characterized by distinct metaphysical leanings. She was born in Belev (District of Tula), the elder daughter of the super-procurator of the St. Petersburg Senate, who was later chief judge in Nezhin (District of Chernigov). With the exception of the few months spent at the Kiev Institute for Girls (1877–78), and later in the Fisher private classic school in Moscow (1882), Hippius received her education at home. She was taught literature, music, history, mathematics, dancing, and horseback riding. Her French, English, and German governesses taught her foreign languages, which she spoke quite well. An avid reader, she surprised her tutors from the Gogol' Lyceum at Nezhin with an excellent knowledge of Russian literature, particularly of Turgenev and Gogol', although her favorite author was Dostoevsky.

Hippius began to write poetry very early. Her first poems, which appeared in *The Northern Herald* in November 1888, were somewhat Nadsonian in tone. Her interest in Nadson was short lived, however, and after 1888 her verse was entirely different in manner and content. When she arrived in St. Petersburg shortly after her marriage to D. S. Merezhkovsky in Tiflis in 1889, Hippius came to know Lev Tolstoy, Chekhov, Leskov, Vladimir Korolenko, Apollon Maykov, Alexey Pleshcheev, Yakov Polonsky, Bal'mont, N. Garin, Maxim Gor'ky, the celebrated pianist and composer Anton Rubenstein, the super-procurator of the Holy Synod Pobedonostsev, the poet Minsky, and other illustrious writers, musicians, and artists of the northern capital.

Active in promoting new forms of art and a view of Symbolism permeated with religious philosophy in poetry, Hippius also distinguished herself as a prolific poet, fiction writer, playwright, essayist, and critic.[1] In Renato Poggioli's estimation, Hippius became "the uncrowned queen of the literary life"[2] in St. Petersburg. "Clever and beautiful," Poggioli continued, "she acted not only as the Sybil but also as the Sylphide of the philosophical and religious circle that formed around her husband and herself."[3]

For Hippius, literature was a profound spiritual experience. The central theme of her creative work is the spirit and its efforts to regain the supreme harmony between love and eternity, love and death, the miraculous and the real. In her eyes, literature was a means of embodying for humanity the unity of the transcendental and the phenomenal. Art is that source which generates beauty, refinement, morality, and religious thought. Challenging the social and ideological approach to art, she insisted on paying more respect to universal culture and the mystery of aesthetic beauty and harmony. More consideration should be given to the eternal properties of art—the love of God, Christian ethics, poetry of feeling, and elevated thought. Philosophical and religious matters were the basis of Hippius's *Weltanschauung*, and, like other Russian Symbolist writers, she separated the empirical world from a spiritual world of mysterious significance and immanence. Her poetry and fiction reflect an anti-positivistic, dualistic view of life: a world divided between the realm of physical phenomena and a higher, eternal reality, indivisible and intangible. Hippius's own law in art was formulated in an aphorism: "Art should materialize only the spiritual." Art reveals the Divine Spirit; in art the Divine Logos assumes a human image; the purpose of art is to promote the moral and spiritual development of human beings. These tenets comprised the essence of Hippius's metaphysical outlook throughout her life. Her poetry presents her spiritual experiences in imagery that is strikingly, uncannily concrete. Colors, sounds, images, and moods blend in the eerie spectre of Hippius's universe, a physical and emotional void instilling mystery and dread. These moods, however, are always counterbalanced by idealistic strivings and an ardent faith in God and His Mercy. In essence, these poems are spiritual psalms, reminiscent of devotional hymns or chants in praise of God, such as the "Gloria in Excelsis."

Zinaida Hippius began her artistic career as a poet of aestheticism and aristocratic aloofness from the coarse and obstreperous crowd. She voiced a longing for an ideal vision of the universe, for "that which is not of this world." At the turn of the century, however, the tenor of her work changed—she became conscious of her personal will, determination, strength of intellect, and individual calling. She came to advocate an "apocalyptic" Christianity which believed in the Second Coming of Christ. She wished to participate in the creation of the new man, whose spirit would be enlightened and dignified, and whose flesh would be transfigured and ennobled.

Hippius's voluminous prose is also remarkable and deserves close attention by students of contemporary literature. Her early narratives resemble medieval novelettes in their mysticism, verbal refinement, craftsmanship, sophistry, and wry humor. She frequently treated psychological problems—her own and those of her characters—by way of introspective analysis, presenting entangled feelings of guilt, self-deprecation, and spiritual crises. Her preoccupation with the "burning questions of the day" and her technical polish and sophistication made her a fashionable and important writer in pre-revolutionary belles-lettres. The first two volumes of Hippius's stories, *Novye lyudi: rasskazy* (People of Today: Short Stories, 1896) and *Zerkala: vtoraya kniga rasskazov* (Mirrors: A Second Book of Short Stories, 1898), imply a rejection of conventional ethical concepts and norms of behavior. Her protagonists advocate the Nietzschean philosophy of egoism and the pursuit of personal happiness at the expense of social considerations.

27

Religious divination, reflections on beauty and harmony, social concepts, and the preaching of neo-Christianity and ecumenity (*sobornost'*) are the concepts intrinsic to *Tretya kniga rasskazov* (The Third Book of Stories, 1902) and, especially, *Aly mech: rasskazy* (The Scarlet Sword: Short Stories, 1906). Here we find Hippius's rejection of Pisarev's and Chernyshevsky's treatment of social ideas in art and her insistence on the mystery of aesthetic beauty and harmony. Her polemics with the Russian radical critics' "latest" ideas on the "profits" and "usefulness" of literature, and their negation of the soul, are presented in "Vne vremeni—stary etyud" (Outside of Time—an Old Etude). In *The Scarlet Sword* Hippius upheld her belief that heaven, earth, and man sustain one another, and that together they form one inseparable whole.

In *Chernoe po belomu* (Black On White, 1908), the fifth book of Hippius's stories, the reader finds references to the important themes in Russian belles-lettres at the time. She dwells, for example, on the critical portrayal of the basic indifference and complacency of people toward love, toward spiritual friendship, and even toward death—a view which she shared with Chekhov. And in *Lunnye muravyi: shestaya kniga rasskazov* (The Moon Ants: A Sixth Book of Short Stories, 1912), psychological and religious considerations, as well as the themes of spiritual metamorphosis and exaltation, are again in the foreground. Hippius never relinquished her premise, formulated at the turn of the century: that art is real when it guides the reader toward the spiritual and stimulates his search for God.

Hippius and Merezhkovsky left St. Petersburg on December 24, 1919. In Poland they, together with Boris Savinkov and General Glazenap, tried to organize a military opposition to Bolshevism, but President Pilsudski's peace with Bolshevik Russia put an end to their "Russian cause" there. They left Warsaw on October 20, 1920, and went to Paris via Wiesbaden.

Hippius continued her literary activities in France, contributing poems, short stories, articles, and essays to various literary journals. In 1925 she published her reminiscences, *Zhivye litsa* (Living Portraits), and, in 1938, she initiated the publication of a group of articles and short stories under the title *Literaturny smotr: svobodny sbornik* (Literary Review: A Free Collection). The volume of her poetry entitled *Siyaniya* (Radiances) came out in the same year. The latter reveals that in exile Hippius retained full control of her former skill in versification. She upheld her interest in experimenting with metrical structure, rhyme, and poetic imagery. All of them manifest the poet's unique personal and metaphysical perception of the world and her particular emphasis on the importance of the individual and the significance of intuitive and spiritual revelation.[4] Her verse of the emigration period continued to express a sorrowful recognition of the insurmountable chasm between the two realms, the lofty and lowly. Fatigued and out of touch with immediate realities, Hippius died a lonely death on September 9, 1945.

NOTES

1. For more details, see Temira Pachmuss, *Zinaida Hippius: An Intellectual Profile* (Carbondale: Southern Illinois Univ. Press, 1971).

2. Renato Poggioli, *The Poets of Russia: 1890–1930* (Cambridge: Harvard Univ. Press, 1960), p. 111.

3. *Ibid.*, p. 112.

4. For more information about Hippius, one of the most original and sophisticated poets in the history of Russian literature, see Oleg Maslenikov, "The Spectre of Nothingness: The Privative Elements in the Poetry of Zinaida Hippius," *Slavic and East European Journal*, n.s. 4 (1966): 299–311, and "Disruption of Canonical Verse Norms in the Poetry of Zinaida Hippius," *Studies in Slavic Linguistics and Poetics in Honor of Boris O. Unbegaun* (New York, 1968), pp. 89–96; Temira Pachmuss, *Z. N. Hippius: Collected Poetical Works, Vol. I: 1899–1918; Vol. II: 1918–1945* (Munich: Wilhelm Fink Verlag, 1972), and Olga Matich, *The Religious Poetry of Zinaida Gippius* (Munich: Wilhelm Fink Verlag, 1972). A volume of Zinaida Hippius's short stories entitled *Selected Works of Zinaida Hippius*, tr. and ed. Temira Pachmuss (Urbana: Univ. of Illinois Press, 1972), and a volume of Hippius's diaries entitled *Between Paris and St. Petersburg: Selected Diaries of Zinaida Hippius*, tr. and ed. Temira Pachmuss (Urbana: Univ. of Illinois Press, 1975), may serve as further examples of the poet's experiments in prose.

POEMS

RAIN

All selections cited here are included in Temira Pachmuss, *Z. N. Hippius: stikhotvoreniya i poemy* (Z. N. Hippius: Collected Poetical Works, Vol. I: 1899–1918; Vol. II: 1918–1945) (Munich: Wilhelm Fink Verlag, 1972).

> Nothing matters: fires, searing heat,
> It's all over — and it's all different:
> The low clouds drizzle gray.
> Oh, you sweet rain! Rustle! Rustle!
> Your murmuring's dear and close to me
> Like quiet tears of the soul.

> 1936

THE FROG

> Some frog (who cares which one!)
>   Sings beneath the black-swollen sky
> Pensive, insistent, on and on . . .
>   What if it speaks of — the essence?

And what if suddenly, comprehending his language,
  I were to change, and everything were to change;
And I'd perceive the world afresh,
  And something new in the world would open to me?

With chagrin I slam the window:
  It's all the mirage of a southern night
Of tormenting insomnia-dreams . . .
  Some frog? What drivel!

1926

MODERATION

There's always something lacking —
Or something in excess . . .
As if all things had an answer —
With the final syllable missing.

Something completed — but not quite right,
Irrelevant, unstable, precarious . . .
Each sign incorrect,
Each decision — an error.

The moon slithers across the water,
But its path is a golden lie . . .
Everywhere, excess and loss.
Moderation — is only with God.

1924

NEVER READ POEMS ALOUD

Never read
  Poems aloud.
If you do — then beware:
  Their spirit will fly away.

Like skeletons they will lie,
  All white and gray . . .
Who'll testify
  These were poems?

The music of words
  Loves muteness.

30

The noise of a voice destroys
The soul of a poem.
[published posthumously, 1961]

PERHAPS

This strange world alarms me so!
The longer I live — the less I grasp.
There are no answers. Just one: perhaps.
And the most sincere, direct one: I don't know.

No answers come to my pensive alarm.
But why does it increase with every day?
How did it first begin? From where did it come?
                                        Somewhere—
I don't know where—there are answers . . . perhaps?

1937

THE ANCIENT, THE OLD, AND THE YOUNG

The ancient, the old, and the young
Committed the very same sins.
Berberovas, Zlobines, Bunins
Began to recite their poems.

The same misfortune befell
The wise, mediocre, and stupid,
Khodaseviches and Otsups.

What yardstick can measure my grief?
Oh, let me, please, let me believe
That all this won't last forever!

Into the staid Green Lamp
They came, all in a lump —
Georgy Ivanov with Irene,
Yurochka and Tsetlin,

And, decrepit in days, Hippius —
All, bursting in with their poems,
To the misfortune of all Green Lamps.

31

What yardstick can measure the poets?
Oh, let me, please, let me believe
Not only in iamb and trochee.

It's commencing; well, here it goes:
Imperious, Otsup arises.
Merezhkovsky, Ladinsky melt
In a single heavenly tangle.

Like an ancient Hebrew kid,
Knut sobs out a biblical poem
And stands there, weeping and weeping . . .

What yardstick can measure my fright?
Oh, let me, please, let me believe
The whole audience won't fall asleep.

1937

OUTSIDE OF TIME: AN OLD ETUDE

". . . Sun, stand thou still . . ."
Joshua 10:12

From: *Aly mech: rasskazy* (The Scarlet Sword: Short Stories; 1906).

In the spring of that year I absolutely did not know where to go. I simply had not the strength to spend the summer in Petersburg, a few months in the Swiss Alps seemed like the height of boredom, and there was no way I could go to Peterhof, my usual summer residence, as I had been having a fight with my cousin Nina. We weren't really fighting, just "needling" one another. She exploded at me because I had made some comment or other about the ignorance of her patrons—Baron Nord, Coco Spesivtsev, and the others. She was upset about that and, since I would not renounce my opinion and had no desire whatsoever to ask for her forgiveness (I'm sick to death of eternally begging forgiveness!), Cousin Nina and I drifted apart, and there was no way I could settle at Peterhof. That very Baron Nord and Coco Spesivtsev would have laughed behind my back if they had found out that I was so dominated by this woman.

I stopped seeing my cousin—which would have made me feel extremely good, if only I hadn't had to worry about where to spend the summer.

32

My uncle, an old bachelor, sickly but cheerful, whom I visited in Tsarskoe, exclaimed upon hearing my complaint:

"Do you know what my advice to you is? Go visit our relatives in Osokino, the Levonins. You won't regret it. It's a remote corner, I confess; it's sixty *versts* from the nearest town, I don't know the roads or the area, I've never been there, but they've been asking me to come for twenty years already . . . Certainly you'll like it. Take your paints along, your canvas, and all of your art materials. I tell you, the country, even for a dilettante artist like yourself, is a real treasure . . ."

I let my uncle's caustic remark about my dilettantism pass, and, fascinated with the idea, inquired:

"What Levonins? How are they related to us? Wouldn't it be embarrassing for me, a stranger, to go there? How big is the family?"

Surprisingly, my uncle did not go into detail. He merely said, smiling, that there wouldn't be any embarrassment since, I'm still a "relative," albeit distant; that he would write a letter to them today about my visit, that the family consisted of two "girls," Polina Vasilyevna and Adelaida Vasilyevna. He gave me a detailed itinerary and advised me to pack as quickly as possible.

"How can I go and stay with two young ladies? Or are they old maids? No, uncle, I'd die of boredom if that were the case!"

"I won't say a word," my uncle cut me off. "Go on—you'll see for yourself. I'll write to them about you today."

Not even three days had passed when I, with all of my amply heavy baggage (my "art materials" alone took up considerable space), in a disgusting car and on a provincial railway, approached the district town, where I had to take another road to get to my newfound relatives. It was early morning. I had hardly slept at all, so I was in a rather foul mood.

"It just never ends," I grumbled, looking out the window at fields and copses rushing by. "Imagine—on a country road for sixty *versts*! A journey to the very edge of the world! And all for some sort of nightmarish spinsters! How can I be related to them? It's all my uncle's invention! They'll probably even want me to call them auntie and respectfully kiss their hands! I can hardly wait!"

I was irritated, too, because there was nowhere for me to dress. I'm used to dressing with extreme care. An appealing exterior—the result of good bearing—wins a great deal, and I knew that my appearance was pleasant. Cousin Nina, in her nicer moments, would say: "The main thing I like about you is that you are not simply a *beau garçon*. You've got something . . . something . . . *de la poésie* . . . understand?"

What else! I understood that perfectly. I rather liked myself on the whole, and was happy being me. Age thirty, tall, golden hair thrown back, independent, wealthy, completely free, talented, and inclined toward painting

. . . Only in this last point was there something which I did not completely like—but more about that later.

It was already a quarter to eight when the slow train finally came to a stop in the station. I was confronted by a yellow wooden depot with a fence of the same color, behind which showed the puny trees of the parterre around the station, a plank platform with a stooping gendarme in a canvas suit, and a small group of coarse peasants. Their backs were bent under gray sacks, and their faces expressed confusion and disbelief.

The porters didn't even show up. Somehow I crawled out of the car and made my way to the station, dragging along all of my suitcases and packages. In the buffet (where they gave me some hideous coffee) I found an efficient lackey whom I asked to hire a horse for the trip to Osokino.

"Where would you like to go?" the lackey asked me.

"To Osokino, sixty *versts* from here. The Mademoiselles Levonin. Really, you don't know them?"

"Osokino? I've heard of it . . . But it is very far . . . Not very many of the gentlefolk go there. If I may say so, you won't find a driver so experienced . . . That is, one travels with his own horses there . . ."

"Well, please ask around, my good man. It's necessary that I find someone."

After a considerable interval of time a driver was presented to me. A carriage or a surrey, I don't know—all I can say is that it was some tall, frightful thing with no springs. Two scrawny nags in stringy traces stood with heads lowered. The coachman, an austere peasant, gloomy and venomous, demanded an unbelievable price of me, which I gave him right away.

I was really beginning to be afraid.

They brought over my suitcases and we started off. The carriage bounced along the incredible road through town. A white cathedral with a golden cupola, a municipal boulevard, some office or other, rows of wooden stores in which wheels, soap, and bagels were sold, the market square with a few carts (since it was a weekday) and some trampled black straw—all flashed by. Simple houses, clean and tiny, were followed by dark little shacks with opalescent glass windows stuffed in places with rags. Finally a pub with a blue sign and a little wooden porch disappeared from sight—and we left the town behind. The highway stretched out to the right, but we turned off right away onto a country road. I finally caught my breath, but I couldn't even enjoy the wonders of the city from the top of my carriage, it jolted me about so. I came to myself only when we got onto the country road. Open spaces passed by, the June sun, rising higher, was growing rather hot.

"Listen," I began, turning to the sullen peasant. "Do you know the way?"
"Yes."
"You mean you've been to Osokino before?"
"Yes, I've been there."
"What do you think: Is it nice there?"

34

"Yes, it's nice."

"What about the ladies?"

"They're all right."

There was no possibility of continuing such a conversation. An acquaintance of mine, a student, once told me that one often encounters melancholia among these people, and that they always end up committing suicide. I thought that my driver would probably commit suicide.

We entered the forest, and from then on the road seemed to become lost within it. The trees grew smaller, almost turning into bushes, and I glanced along the tops of young birch trees and tiny asps, trembling with each and every little thin-stemmed leaf—when, all of a sudden, walls appeared near the road, and that very road, little-traveled, green and damp, would recede farther, fading away in the shade of the straight, tall trees, the tops of which shone in the sun. I leaned back. The green branches met above the road, not letting the sun penetrate. The green forest thickened on the right and on the left, with not even a ray of light shining through. The road grew softer still, and damp, and was covered with moss. Sharp, languid fragrances seized me. It smelled of earth, the leaves of berry bushes, last year's decayed leaves, and the fresh, loose bark of the birch trees. The air was damp and cool. I breathed quickly, delighting and marveling at the unusual, animated aroma. A happy, unsuspecting bird whistled, not too loudly, but clearly; it would finish its short little song—and then begin again on the same note. I heard a cuckoo nearby, very close. I started. The bird also became frightened, hearing the soft noise of the wheels along the moss-covered road, and immediately fell silent.

It seemed as though I'd fallen into some mysterious world. How strange it seemed! Here there were trees, moss, grass, sky, and air. There were trees, moss, grass, sky, and air in Peterhof, too. Nevertheless, I felt as if I were seeing all of this for the first time. Even my disposition changed, and my thoughts became more serious, quieter, and simpler.

The road just kept going; my coachman was silent. The carriage swayed now only gently. I made myself comfortable and gradually fell asleep.

"There it is: Osokino. You can see it from here."

The sun had already fallen to the horizon when, after a day of travel with a two-hour stop to feed our horses in some dirty little hamlet, the peasant turned to me and pointed straight ahead with the handle of his whip.

"What? Where is it?" I asked, raising myself up in the carriage.

We had left the forest. Now vast, endless fields of grain and meadows stretched out to the left, while on the right, a long lake, hemmed in by dark rushes, shone in the sun like liquid tin. We got to the top of a small hill, and I saw clearly the white manor house, a large stone building with a mezzanine. The leafy trees of the garden loomed dark from behind. In front, on the grounds, I could distinguish grayish-colored storehouses, sheds, various outbuildings, and a lane running through trimmed acacias. On the right, at a considerable distance from the house, beyond the hill, shone the cross of a small church. Some other structures could just barely be made out beyond that.

Our horses hastened along, a little happier, sensing a respite. The tall, thick rye fluttered now at the very edge of the road. Every stalk bent its long head. The glossy strips of rye undulated slowly along the wide expanse of the fields.

I was looking at the grain when suddenly, on the horizon, I saw something white. I am a little shortsighted, but we drew closer, and I was able to discern the shapely figure of a woman in a pastel dress, which seemed a little strange to me; why, I was unable to say. Something about it was uncommon, though not uncomely. I could not make out the woman's face. She was rather far away, and I noticed that she was wearing a wide round straw hat with a black ribbon around the crown. The hat cast a shadow on her face, and the ends of the ribbon fluttered lightly in the breeze. This hat, too, seemed a little strange to me. I remembered that hats of such design are called *bergerka*. My cousin Nina explained it to me when I went to the final *bal masqué* one day last winter.

I was about to stop, assuming, not without some basis, that this was one of the inhabitants of Osokino. My coachman, however, clicked his tongue, and we darted down the hill, quickly finding ourselves at the gates of the estate.

An old man, the watchman most likely, was already slowly opening the gate. A whole pack of dogs dashed under the wheels. My carriage pulled right up to the portico.

I have to admit, it was very embarrassing for me. I felt guilty of something before my unknown hostesses. I awaited them eagerly, having cast off all my expectations beforehand and having decided not only to call them auntie but to kiss their hands as well. I was ready to make even greater sacrifices.

But the ladies of the house did not appear. An old servant in pea-green livery, with a kind, very gentle face, ran out to meet me. (I don't know why, but he reminded me of Aksakov's *Bagrov's Grandson*.[1] It sometimes happens that something will unfailingly call to mind something else, apparently totally unrelated. No matter how much you look, you will never find the connection.) He was followed by maidservants, again not in the least bit young. One friendly, gray-haired chambermaid really struck me; she was dressed rather in the manner of a young *soubrette*, namely, in a light calico dress, a short apron with tiny pockets, and a little white cap.

All of them rushed to kiss my hand. I was dumbfounded and I blushed, but I did not protest.

"If you please, sir, if you please," the gentle old man kept saying, while my bags were being taken from the carriage. "We've been waiting for you, and here you are. We thought you wouldn't come on such a dreary day as today, a

Monday. Miss Adelaida Vasilyevna is here, in her room, but Polina Vasilyevna has gone out for a walk. If you please, everything is ready for you on the mezzanine. If something is not quite right—the ladies said that you could move downstairs."

I liked everything on the mezzanine very much, however. There were two large rooms, a study and a bedroom. One room had a balcony facing the garden where a second small lake shone near a hill through the foliage of the trees; the other room faced the side of the courtyard, the fields, and the larger lake. The ceilings were a little low, and the furniture was not altogether comfortable—upholstered damask, and bulky—but I liked the furniture with the straight backs. Having just barely looked around, I began to wash, to put away my things, and to change clothes. The old man, who was called Finogen, left, saying that it would soon be time for tea and dinner.

Without my being aware of it, it had grown dim in my room, and the twilight had already turned into night when I, now completely dressed, heard a knock at the door.

I expected it to be Finogen again, but instead that same chambermaid whom I had noticed on the portico entered.

"Dinner is ready, sir," she said with a slight grimace, crossing her arms underneath her little apron. "Oh, good heavens, your carousel lamp isn't even lit!" She went quickly up to the table between the windows, where I had earlier noticed a large porcelain lamp. Actually, I hadn't had a chance to look over my "study"—that is, the room facing the side with the garden—as I'd spent all my time in the bedroom.

The lamp was beautiful, Saxon, it seems; but it burned oil, not kerosene. (The chambermaid had not made a mistake when she said "carousel.") You have to tighten these lamps every quarter of an hour, as I discovered, or else they go out.

"What's your name, dear?" I asked the chambermaid as she was fussing with the lamp.

"Me, sir? Nadya. I work for Polina Vasilyevna. Antonida serves the older lady, sir. Polina Vasilyevna knows of your arrival at the estate. She was walking in the fields, sir."[2]

"Oh, so that was Polina Vasilyevna? In the light dress?"

"That was her, sir. She likes very much to go for a walk at sunset."

"Listen, Nadya . . .," it was a little embarrassing for me at first to call such a venerable person "Nadya," but I quickly got used to it, all the more because her face, all in small wrinkles, looked so fresh, dear, and kind from under her gray hair and the frill of her coquettish little cap. "You see, Nadya, I came so unexpectedly. It's rather embarrassing for me . . . I don't know your mistresses . . ."

"Oh, what do you mean! The ladies are so glad you're here! Konstantin

37

Dmitrich (that was my uncle) wrote that you're an artist. You're our ladies' cousin, it seems they said. I'm kind of glad, too, our ladies will have a nice time, they need a little social company . . ."

The reddish light of the lamp fell in a round spot on the table. I raised my eyes to the now illuminated part of the wall between the windows—and came to a standstill for a second. A small, round portrait, not clearly distinguishable against the off-white wallpaper, was glowing faintly there. My eyes could not tear themselves away from it, although it was simple and pale. The thin, twisted frame shone dimly. A young lady in a muslin dress, with ash-blonde hair curled around her ears in the old style and large, very blue, puzzled eyes had been portrayed there in pale pastels and transparent shades of pink against a white background. I don't know what kind of unknown charm there was in this simple, gentle face, but my chest contracted as if in pain—and I looked at the miraculous pastel, trembling, almost in reverence and torment.

"Who is that?" I asked involuntarily and timidly, pointing to the portrait.

"That?" Nadya was already preparing to leave the room. "Oh, good heavens, the year before last Adelaida Vasilyevna lived in this room, so she hung up that portrait and it has stayed there. I didn't even notice . . ."

"But who is it?"

"Why it's our young mistress, Polina Vasilyevna. The late master, her papa, painted her. He painted very well, they say, and he portrayed her completely like herself . . . But come to dinner, sir, if you please, the ladies are in the dining room . . ."

Nadya disappeared. With an effort, I tore myself away from those enormous blue eyes in the portrait, walked up to the door and, on the threshold, looked back again, as if afraid that "she" might leave. Finally, I opened the door and quickly went downstairs.

I don't know what I expected when it was time to meet my hostesses, and I don't remember what I was thinking about while going down the stairs. The dining room was a spacious room with dark oak furniture and a table which, illuminated by two candelabra in which wax candles were burning, stood set for dinner in the center of the room. In the faint glimmer of the candles I suddenly caught sight of the tall figure of a woman, very thin, standing with her back to me. It seems she was setting a bouquet of cornflowers on the window. She turned around at the sound of my footsteps. My heart pounded violently—and stopped for an instant. What was this? A muslin dress with a high bodice and a billowing skirt, a pale complexion, ash-blonde hair, curled low on the ears . . . But I had already collected myself. In front of me stood my hostess, the "young lady." She smiled prettily and shyly and, without giving me her hand, curtsied to me, blushing. Her tiny face, thin and longish, all in small, delicate wrinkles, radiated coyness and delight. Her hair, too, was light; it was streaked imperceptibly with gray. Her hands, somewhat dried and yellowish, in black mittens, clutched the bunch of cornflowers. The "bergerka" lay on a chair—it suited her extraordinarily well in this strange dress with its high, promontory bodice and short sleeves.

"Polina Vasilyevna . . . ," I began.

Polina lowered her familiar blue eyes and again laughed gaily.

"*Soyez le bien venu, Monsieur Georges,*" she said with a slight burr. "That is correct, is it not? You are called *Monsieur Georges*? You are our cousin, but my sister and I have decided to call you *Monsieur Georges*. That's better . . . more comfortable somehow. Will you allow me? Sister dear! Adele! Come quickly."

I turned to meet Adelaida Vasilyevna, who was just then entering. She was shorter than her sister, not quite so thin, although even she was corseted. Her dark dress, also with a high bodice, was covered above with a pelerine cape and a delicate frill. Her completely white hair was combed smoother and her face, wrinkled like her sister's, seemed however to have more of a yellowish tinge. She was probably about three years older than Polina. For some reason, I remember, the material of her dress struck me—thick brown silk, like bast, embroidered with tiny, satiny flowers. I remember too that, for a long time when I was a child, I'd seen in Grandmother's trunk a disassembled coat just like this dress.

Only Grandmother's coat and the trunk smelled especially sweet and sharp. I had called the smell "centennial," and it seemed to me that Adele's dress must have smelled like that.

I noticed right away that Adele treated her sister as an older woman would treat her favorite spoilt little baby. She reprimanded her gently for taking such a late walk. Polina made an excuse and then made a face as though she were angry. It was clear, by the way, that there was profound harmony between the sisters.

With a hearty appetite I ate an excellent country dinner and tried to maintain a conversation, but in the depths of my soul I was confused and couldn't find the right tone at all.

"So you never leave the country?" I asked Adelaida.

"No, we left society. And as long as we are not bored . . . Polina studies music and I take care of the house a little . . . It's nice, you know, to lock yourself up in the middle of nowhere. Petersburg with its parties, concerts, and gatherings wearied us long ago. Isn't that right, Polina?"

"Oh Adele, you know I never get bored. I love the fields so much, and the flowers, and going for walks . . . And loneliness always . . . says so much to my heart. . ."

"How is Konstantin Dmitrich?" Adele asked me about my uncle. "Is he still as naughty as ever? Oh, he is a horrible madcap! He's the most unbearable of the young rakes, that's for sure! But I have forgiven him everything for his indefatigability. Just let some interesting little party get going, a *partie de plaisir**, and he's the first one there."

I was about to open my mouth to say that my uncle, Konstantin Dmitrich, had been paralyzed and bald for a long time and, living strictly in Tsarskoe, ran around less than anyone. But it somehow did not get said, and I remained quiet.

"And do you paint?" Polina asked.

"Yes, a little . . ."

"Oh, how I enjoyed last time the painting of that . . . famous . . . What is his name, Adele? You know, that new one?"

"I don't remember . . . Oh yes, a beautiful portrayal. He will succeed. Do you like music? Polina can sing for you sometime . . ."

"Oh no, Adele! I've been singing completely off key lately."

Having inquired as to my interests in literature, the sisters decided to entertain me with that theme, too. It appeared that they had a whole library, to which Polina promised to escort me tomorrow.

"Adele reads very little," Polina complained. "Whereas I—always, always with a book, float away to unknown countries . . . Among the Russians there are no writers who really uplift the soul. One young writer began fairly well. Her name was Evgeniya Tur, have you read her? I have just finished 'The Niece.' As for the poets—perhaps only Zhadovskaya . . ."

"You mean you don't care for Druzhinin?"

"Him, for . . . *une dame qui a quitté son mari*?† No, no, that's terrible!"

Polina even flared up, gesturing in disapproval.

"You mean you don't even like Pushkin?" I asked.

"Yes, Pushkin . . . Of course . . . *Entre nous soit dit*‡: that critic, you know which one, a priest's son, I think, seems nevertheless to be right about one thing: there is not enough elevation in Pushkin. I don't share the opinions of that critic at all, or of all the newest views on utility, the negation of the soul, etc. No, no, it's horrible! But he had some credible remarks concerning Pushkin. What is he writing now? Adele, Adele," she cried, not giving me time to answer, "do you remember when we met Gretch? Tell me, do you ever see Gretch in the literary circles?"

"He's dead," I said finally.

"Oh, my heavens, what happened to him? How sad!"

Our conversation dragged on. And, strange as it may seem, after a little while I was refuting Pisarev and Dobrolyubov with such ardor, as if their articles had just come out and I were to enter into polemics with them the next day in a journal. Old images long forgotten, almost unknown, arose in my soul. I was going to discuss the fact of the emancipation of the serfs—my

*a pleasant little *soirée*
†a woman who has left her husband?
‡just between us

hostesses held different opinions on that subject—when all of a sudden I noticed that it was late and time to go to bed. Adelaida was restraining a yawn, but Polina listened to me and nervously picked at her mittens.

I bowed again ceremoniously, and received in answer two curtsies and pleasant smiles.

I went directly to my bedroom, climbed up on the extremely high feather bed and, in spite of the hot weather, fell asleep right away. I dreamed about Gretch rising slowly from his coffin, which he shared with Bulgarin for some reason, making a most malicious fist both at me and at Polina, with her mittens on, attired moreover in a muslin dress, from whom I was supposed to remove some sort of spell. I got excited, cried out, moaned, but nothing happened. Polina kept on nodding to me, sadly and languorously. And then it wasn't Polina anymore, but someone with a pale, delicate face and large, indecisive eyes . . .

I was sitting in the garden above the lake, trying in vain to depict in oils the narrow leaves of the willow and the patches of sunlight below it, reflected in the water—when someone tapped me on the shoulder with an umbrella.

I looked around. Polina was standing behind me in her *bergerka* and black mittens. With two fingers she lifted her light dress slightly and, from under the frill, her foot showed, in a white stocking and a prunella slipper with straps.

"You're here, *Monsieur Georges*. I was walking through the garden and all of a sudden I saw—you . . . How nice, how nice!" she continued, glancing at my drawing which didn't look like anything. "Yes . . . you are an artist!" she affected a most curious expression, shook her head coquettishly, and her wrinkled face became smaller yet. "Would you like me to take you to the library? I have the key. I've been promising you for a long time. You've tired of painting . . . It's so hot now . . ."

I agreed happily. I had not even seen the house of Osokino properly. And I really had no desire to paint a landscape. I had other plans . . .

We entered the cool, spacious rooms. Everything was both surprising and agreeable to me. Surprising, however, only at first. Later, by contrast, it all began to seem familiar, native, as if I had always lived here and as if it were impossible to live in a different way. A large room with straight divans under slipcovers, a parlor with stoves in two of its corners and a door out onto a terrace; a cloudy mirror in a gilded frame, a mahogany dresser in the style of a chiffonier on top of which stood blacker-than-black busts of Voltaire and Savonarola; discolored paintings, speckled with tiny little cracks, oval lifesize portraits of some people in cuffs and ruffled shirts, with tufted hair on high foreheads and lifeless facial expressions. On the furniture there were endless embroidered cushions, most likely homemade. The light, square room was more cheerful than the others. A tiny yellowed piano on four small legs took shelter here near the wall.

"I sometimes sing here," Polina said, lowering her eyes. "My sister accompanies me."

The library turned out to be a fair-sized room, filled with bookcases.

"Here, I'll leave the key with you, *Monsieur Georges*," Polina said, curtsying. "I don't want to bother you. Here, in this cabinet, there are the magazines. There are some humorous ones, too. My sister and I often take one volume or another and look it over when we want to laugh a little. It's filled with such terrible epigrams on our society . . ."

She left. I opened the cabinet. Dust from the long-untouched piles of books fell into my eyes. The books smelled of rotten print, dried paper, old leather, and mustiness. And what wasn't here! French books from the beginning of the century with poorly printed texts and colored pictures, all of them of some women with umbrellas and cavaliers in blue caftans. There were Russian books, too—an old edition of Pushkin, a songbook, instructions on jam-making, and a home encyclopedia of medicine (in which, by the way, it advised that one should never lean one's stomach against the table after dinner, "for fear that from this bad consequences might arise"). In the magazine cabinet I found copies of *The Contemporary* for several past years, with uneven pages stuck together. *The Spark* nourished its wit on ladies in crinolines and on Askochensky, who was unknown to me, much to my shame. I fell upon *The Contemporary* but soon tired of it because I didn't understand anything. I started in on the French books and got so carried away that they could barely manage to call me to dinner. The collection of French engravings had so delighted me that I became even more friendly toward *The Contemporary*, and that evening Polina and I had a heated discussion about one of the stories, which she, as it turned out, had also read.

It was raining, a cold drizzle, typically autumnal. However, it was warm and light in the room. The samovar sang liltingly on the table, wax candles cast a soft light on Adelaida's white hair as she bent over her work, and on the paper of the album in which I had drawn a landscape with two huge trees near a stream. The album belonged to Polina. It had kept me very busy. It was bound in leather, though that binding was falling off with age; there were yellowed pages on which doves were drawn, bushes, roses, and verses written in yellow ink, maxims and madrigals, for the most part in refined French. It had most likely been many, many years since anyone had written in this album. For the first minute it was terrible and shameful for me to touch these pages, as it is shameful to write something with a soft pencil on the half-rotten cross of a grave. But Polina looked on my hesitation perplexedly, and so I set to work, already taking delight myself, vanquished by all of these innocent verses and roses and by Polina's entreating voice. I could never, by the way, refuse her anything.

"You know, Polina," the elder sister suddenly interrupted the silence, "you should sing something. It's a rather boring evening. And *Monsieur Georges* has not yet heard you."

Polina blushed terribly and, for the first time, looked at me with such faith, devotion, and even happiness, that I was embarrassed. I thought she did not want to sing and was asking me to decline Adele's offer; but to my amazement she, posing ever so slightly, stood up gracefully and walked to the corner. Adele, bustling gaily, immediately followed and sat down at the piano, while Polina looked for her music. I found a place for myself in the corner, near a table on which an oil lamp was burning, and became absorbed in my sketching.

With the first notes of the song, however, my pencil stopped, and I froze. It would be impossible to describe the sound, impossible to convey in words a notion of the noise, the pitch, the harmony—or, rather, the dissonance. I will only say that for the first time since my arrival at Osokino, regardless of all the surprising, strange things, for the first time an uncontainable laughter, hysterical and morbid, rose in my throat. I thought, if only I were free, I would have laughed, laughed to tears, to shouting. I would even have howled and moaned uncontrollably. The tone of the piano was not even close to the sound of a quivering string, but sounded rather like the subterranean howling of a dying animal. Polina's voice wheezed on the low notes and cracked on the high ones—not drowning out the accompaniment, however. But after the first unexpected sounds, I opened my eyes and looked around. Adele's face was serious and intent; I noticed some of the female domestics in the doorway—and not one of them was smiling. On the contrary, they were all listening attentively and, it seems, with pleasure. The sounds continued. I listened and grew accustomed to them. I even began to comprehend exactly what she was singing. Then, finally, when the very sharpness of the sounds, the screeching and howling ceased to amaze and disturb me, my shattered nerves calmed down, and the smell of something distant, almost immemorial, shrouded, drifted to me, and compelled me to pay attention. The tune changed, straining and bursting, as I kept trying to remember, to remember . . . right now, this very minute . . . Desultory images floated before me. A hall, large and rather dark . . . a candle on a piano . . . I am somewhere up high, my head is above the light curls of a woman sitting at the piano and singing. Her face is very white, her lips pink. I have been told that I had a stepsister, sixteen years older than I, who died young, a girl of remarkable beauty. They would carry me into the hall when she sang. I was probably about three years old. I loved her singing madly, and since that time I had never again heard this melody. It was so long ago that I was dumbfounded that I could even remember—and I was excited as never before. The further back the memory went, the more magical it was. It seemed that I was hearing the voices of another world.

Polina noticed my unrest and suddenly became terribly confused, al-

43

though she shone with satisfaction at the same time. She was about to sing another song when I asked her to repeat the same one. I couldn't make out the words and would have liked to go up to the piano and look at the music, but then I changed my mind. Let my memory fly away, freely and at will, just as lightly and unexpectedly as it had come. It had slipped out of the shadows for a moment, and it would hide again—who knows, maybe forever. I said nothing to the sisters. I wanted to retain all of this for myself alone.

I don't know why on this evening the delicate face of the portrait with its blue eyes persistently haunted my imagination. I rarely looked at the portrait, as if afraid that it would lose its power over me; but I remembered it and thought of it the whole time. Polina, as she was singing for the second time, accompanied herself. I saw her shapely figure from behind, her ash-blonde hair, with its low coiffure. I didn't even hear the harsh sounds anymore, and little by little it appeared to me that this was not Polina at all. Rather, it was that pale girl, and she was singing this song so dear to my heart not now, but in some infinitely remote time which had become the present.

When we parted, I kissed Polina's dried and yellowed hand, which had no glove on it this time. It seemed to me that her hand was trembling. I don't know how, but I managed to mumble a request which I had been wanting to make for a long time, but which I for some reason hadn't dared to express:

"Polina Vasilyevna . . . There, in my room, I accidentally . . . your water-color portrait is a marvelous work. Will you allow me to make a copy?"

A hasty and excited permission was granted—I wasn't paying attention and almost did not hear what phrases were used. I was happy. If I only can! Will I be able? I nearly ran upstairs, and I looked at "her" for a long time in the light of the carousel lamp. She looked at me too, directly and questioningly, with her unsmiling eyes.

We sat on the wide terrace, finishing our after-dinner tea. The evening, descending upon the meadows, was clear, quiet, all golden-yellow. Warmth, but not heat, enveloped me, fragrant and caressing. In the garden it was completely dark already, but the long rays of the sun still lingered over the meadows. Grasshoppers chirped busily in the grass. The air was so clear and clean that the sound of the wheels of a carriage far, far away could be heard. I didn't feel like talking; rather, I wanted to breathe, to live.

I don't know how much time had passed since I had come to Osokino. The days came and went; I had lost track and didn't even want to count them. I only knew that the hay had been mowed long ago, that the rye had already turned yellow and bent to the ground, and that frequent winds had started to ripple the water of the large lake. But the lake stood motionless now, as if asleep. The skies paled. On the horizon, from the east, low, round clouds gathered and spread slowly and subtly, changing color.

"Adelaida Vasilyevna," I directed myself to the elder sister, who sat quietly and who had seemed sad to me all day. "Why are you so pensive? Guess what I was thinking? I was thinking that I don't even know what the date is today, what month it is, how long I've been here with you . . ."

Adelaida laughed, gesturing with her arms.

"Why, what do you have to know that for, *Monsieur Georges?* We've lived like that for a long time. We know the days of the week, the church bells ring on Sunday, but the date, whatever do we need that for? We have no dealings with our neighbors; there isn't even a village nearby. Our people go to town when necessary, but there is nothing for us in town. We have our own provisions. We have a library, a piano . . . A steward looks after our domestic affairs, he lives far away, and when he comes he only wants to give me bills . . . But I don't bother with him. God help him. Should I worry about this myself? No, we decided once and for all to leave society and are not about to change that. Winter, spring, summer . . . and then, winter again . . . It's nice to live in the backwoods, to forsake voluntarily the petty cares and squabbles of the world . . ."

"But you can never keep track of the days," I said. "They all look alike, as if they were all one day." Adele smiled and shook her snow-white head.

"Alike? What do you mean alike? There—do you see those clouds, the light ones, beyond the meadow? They look very much like yesterday's and tomorrow's, and like many other clouds which have been and will be. It's as if they were all one cloud. Nevertheless, they are not yesterday's or tomorrow's, and they are all different. So should a person's days all be different and yet always alike, now, then, and eternally, until the end of the world . . ."

I looked at Adelaida in wonder. This was the first time she had talked to me so—seriously and wistfully. I shifted my eyes to Polina. She sat quietly the whole time, with lowered eyelids. The expression on her sweet face seemed changed to me, troubled and sad. Lately we had been together almost constantly. We would go for walks, read, and talk. I loved to talk with her. There was something simple, almost childlike, in her speech, sometimes sly, sometimes enigmatic. It was as if I were reading a book in which the letter "T"[3] was still printed with three strokes, and I myself were becoming the hero of that book. Besides that, she would divert me from my sorrowful thoughts—the copy of the portrait was not getting on well at all. Occasionally I was surprised—could I really hope to copy "her"? After all, she was unique . . .

"What's the matter with you, Polina Vasilyevna?" I inquired, taking her hand. "Are you ill?"

Suddenly, to my amazement, Polina pulled her hand away, jumped up quickly, and ran out. I seemed to hear a restrained sob, but I wasn't sure. Adelaida also stood quickly and followed her sister. I was left alone in my bewilderment and sorrow.

The reddish moon rose late and cast a light on my window sill. I sat in my study without lighting the candles. I knew that "she" was here, and that if it were light I would look at her all the time. I didn't want that.

It was dark and still in the garden. The glow of the moon, not yet bright, shed hardly any light on the little meadow in front of the house. A dampness came up from the lake. The trees were still, black as ink, as if they were not sleeping, but dead. I heard a knock. I was surprised. I thought it was late already. However, my watch hadn't been running for a long time.

I recognized Nadya, but she seemed a little strange to me. Without saying a word, not surprised at the darkness, she walked up to me and thrust a small scrap of paper right into my hand.

"What is this, Nadya?"

"From the young lady," Nadya answered in a whisper.

"From Polina Vasilyevna? Is she not well?" I cried.

"Shhh . . ." Nadya whispered again, placing her finger to her lips. "Read it, please."

I didn't even notice exactly when she disappeared. What was all this mysteriousness? I lit the lamp and opened the note, which had been sealed with wax. In large, uneven handwriting and with errors in spelling, the note stated:

"*Monsieur Georges, je suis folle, je rougis de mon audace, mais je vous supplie à genoux de me pardonner. Vous êtes un noble coeur. Venez dans une heure en bas, tout près du lac—vous savez? où est le vieux banc. J'ai à vous parler. Je vous dirai tout. Pauline.*" §

The French was terrible, but poor Polina could scarcely have written such words in Russian. I read and reread the note, beside myself with horror. I hadn't managed to come to any conclusion yet—when again someone knocked at the door. It wasn't even a knocking; rather, it was as if someone were scratching at the door, not daring to open it. With the note in my hand, I went to the door and threw it open. Adelaida stood there.

"Good Lord, Adelaida Vasilyevna, is that you? Come in, please."

She came in, looking around, confused by the unfamiliar thought that she was in a young man's study, and seemed ready to run out any second. Her nervousness overcame her. She fell into an armchair and her tears overflowed.

I was terribly frightened. Finally she calmed down a little and started talking hurriedly:

"*Monsieur Georges* . . . I understand . . . This nocturnal rendezvous might surprise you . . . but I could not . . . I must save . . . prevent . . . Lord," she cried, seeing the note in my hand, "I thought so, there's her note!"

I threw down the note and did not know what to do, confronted by the

---

§I am beside myself, I blush from my audacity, but I want to implore you on my knees to forgive me. You have a noble soul. Come down in one hour, right down to the lake—you understand?—where the old bench is. I have to speak with you. I will tell you everything.

sincere tears of this kindly woman with her white hair and honest (now completely aged) face.

"You understand, *Monsieur Georges*, you know everything. She loves you . . ."

"Who?" I cried. "Polina Vasilyevna?"

It was as if my eyes were opened. And strange—an unexpected, fervent, joyous wave swept over my heart. "She loves me! Polina loves me . . ." The candle burned on the table without flickering. Adelaida Vasilyevna sat in the armchair. And from the wall, up above, those large blue eyes looked at me, filled with tenderness.

Adelaida Vasilyevna did not notice my agitation.

"I know, you have an honest heart, *Monsieur Georges*. Do understand her. She tore herself away from the temptations of the world early; she has always had a passionate soul . . . You were so kind to her, you read and talked, and then that portrait . . . (I shuddered, but she did not notice.) You liked her, in a word . . . But you, after all . . . You . . . cannot . . . be serious about this?"

She gasped for breath, but then regained control of herself and continued:

"I ask you now . . . Have pity on her, on us . . . I've always been a mother to her, I won't allow . . . To be blunt, leave tomorrow, don't see her," she finished and folded her hands, entreating me.

I remained silent. I had not the strength to speak. I had already composed myself, but my heart ached intolerably. Adelaida Vasilyevna took my silence for consent.

"I haven't been mistaken about you, *Monsieur Georges*," she stated solemnly, arising from the armchair. "You will leave, I see, and I appreciate it . . . Besides, it would be impossible," she added, as if to herself. "I'll make arrangements . . . There will be a horse at dawn . . . If any of your things are left behind, we'll send them. Have I your word of honor, *Monsieur Georges*, that you will leave?"

I was still unable to speak. I nodded.

"And . . . you won't see her?"

I again nodded. Adelaida Vasilyevna suddenly hugged me tightly, with her arms around my head, as a mother would embrace her child, and kissed my forehead. Then, probably ashamed of her unexpected action, she slipped over to the door and disappeared.

I sat in the armchair near the open window. The moon rose higher and shed a silver light on the grass and on the tips of the lindens and maples. The crickets fell silent. A night bird languished in solitude among the reeds near the lake. Something white seemed to appear before me, flashing behind the trees. It was Polina . . . "She loves me . . . She is waiting for me, yet I do not join her. Who is Polina? Does it even matter? It was that same Polina with curly, light hair and gentle eyes. Why don't I join her? Don't I really love her?"

I looked at her pale eyes—and it seemed to me that there was bitterness and reproach in them. The longer I looked, the more unbearably my heart ached.

The time passed. I hadn't noticed that the moon had set, that it was beginning to grow light, that the garden was becoming gray and lifeless. The snorting of horses woke me from my trance, but not completely. Mechanically I stood up, dressed, barely realizing what I was doing, grabbed a suitcase, threw some things into it and, preparing to leave, stopped for the last time before the portrait. For the last time her eyes looked at me with wonder and infinite injury. I moved closer, touched her pink, almost rose-colored, half-opened mouth with my cold lips—and left.

It was barely dawn; it was gray in the forest, damp and eerie. The wheels hummed softly. The trees bent their cold branches, and large, quiet drops of dew fell to the ground. I cried silently and bitterly, and pain, like a rigid hand, gripped my heart. I cried because I loved Polina so.

1895

THEY ARE ALIKE

". . . Have I not chosen you twelve?
But one of you is a devil."

JOHN 6:70

FROM: *Lunnye muravyi: shestaya kniga rasskazov* (The Moon Ants: A Sixth Book of Short Stories; 1912)

The overturned heavenly dome was not azure, not even blue, but a thick lilac—from the sultry heat and the yellowness of the hilly plain which stuck its edges into the firmament. These edges, where they joined the canopy of heaven, became dark and gray. Almost in the middle of this lilac vault stood the sun. It appeared to be not a luminary, but a fiery hole through which the flaming rays of some imaginary world burst forth. The rays fell to the earth, hot and heavy, crushing, strangling, and illuminating it with an extraordinary radiance. The earth ceased its breathing, dying in the glory of the heavy glare.

A group of pilgrims was walking single file, close to one another, along the highway beside the fields of yellow wheat. The highway meandered through the hills, from the lowest settlement to the one up on the hill. One could see far and wide, and both settlements were visible, or maybe they were towns. Both of them were white and flat, and they sparkled in their whiteness, like two diamonds. The sun devoured and oppressed the highway. Some scattered, dwarfish, crooked trees, casting short, knotty, dry shadows onto the yellow dust, grew here and there amidst the fields of wheat.

48

The pilgrims walked silently, slowly, somewhat bent under the weight of the sun. They were dressed in long yellow and white and white and gray garments, the tops of which covered their heads and shadowed their faces.

They walked close to one another. At some distance from them a woman was walking. They had been walking for a long time and were tired; the woman had been following them for a long time, too. They seldom turned around, and perhaps the woman thought that they had not seen her following them. She kept away from them; she never came up close, yet she continued to walk.

The pilgrims carried neither staffs nor bags. However, one of them held something bulky, with sharp corners, under the folds of his yellow garment.

There, where the road ascended, stood three gray trees with very short shadows. Large white stones lay beneath them.

"Teacher, let's rest here," said one of the pilgrims, tall and lean, lifting the cover off his face a little. He was old and bald. His rounded eyebrows above his kind, pale eyes, raised as if in astonishment, formed symmetrical wrinkles on his brow.

"Rest! But there is no water or shade here! Wouldn't it be better to rest after we arrive in the town? You do grow tired very quickly, Jacob!" objected another pilgrim, dressed in yellow, the one carrying the box under his garment.

Jacob would probably not have insisted, for he was meek. But at that moment a third pilgrim, a boy without a beard, with a delicate face and curly hair, likewise threw the cover off his head and said:

"Oh, if we could only rest a little! We're so tired! What do you say, Teacher?"

The one whom they addressed as "Teacher" came up to a white rock under the tree and sat down. The man in yellow therefore no longer objected; he also sat down on one of the rocks, directly opposite the Teacher.

The curly-haired boy sat on the ground near the Teacher's feet. Silence ensued, from the intense heat and the weight of the air.

One of the pilgrims, neither old nor young, with a goatee and quickness in his movements, shielded his eyes with his hand and looked with great interest at the road.

"Why is this woman following us? She has been following us for a long time, yet she has not approached us even once. What does she want?"

"Maybe she is ill. Indeed, there are many people who come to see the Teacher," Jacob answered.

The curious pilgrim, however, was not satisfied.

"No, she is young and healthy. I noticed her when we were still over there on the bank of the river. She stood and watched, but she did not approach us. She was not listening to us—she only watched us. Look how angry her face is!"

"It would be much better if women stayed at home, spinning and thinking

49

how to help the poor," said the pilgrim with the box, who was sitting opposite the Teacher. This pilgrim, too, started to observe the woman closely. She was moving directly toward them, very slowly but resolutely.

The pilgrim eyed her for a long time, and suddenly a thin shadow fell over his face. His face was young and dark, with a straight, short nose; his lips were red and compressed; his eyes, which resembled the sky, were dark, almost black; his dark, soft hair, curling gently, fell onto his forehead; his soft, black beard had hardly any curls. It seemed that a man with such a face could never smile. In fact, he never did smile. He was entirely dark, and yet bright at the same time. His garment, too, was almost bright yellow.

When the woman began to approach them, he turned away indifferently and lowered his bold, dark eyes.

The woman did not come close to them, but stopped near the last tree, leaning her head against it. She was silent. From under her lowered gray hood one could see her strange, passionate eyes.

The pilgrims were likewise silent for a while, looking at her. The dark pilgrim did not raise his eyes and did not stir. Finally the pilgrim with the goatee, who could barely remain seated because of his curiosity, said as if to himself:

"What a bore! She keeps on pestering us. Should I ask her what she wants?"

He stopped. Since everyone else was silent, he continued, now addressing the woman:

"Do you need something, my good woman? You keep on following us . . ."

The woman moved away from the tree and said in a low, wavering, indistinct voice:

"I . . . wish to speak to your Teacher . . ."

"To the Teacher? Why, then, didn't you come up to us on the bank when the others were there? Are you ill? Where are you from? Who are your parents?"

The woman became confused, frightened, and did not know which question she should answer first. Then she said timidly:

"I'm from over there . . ." she made an indefinite motion toward the east. "My parents . . . he knows," she said suddenly, firmly, even angrily, and suddenly pointed at the dark pilgrim. "I am not ill. I wish to speak with your Teacher."

The curious pilgrim laughed good-naturedly and joyously:

"Oh, you know her then?" he asked the dark man with animation.

But the dark man neither spoke nor stirred.

"I have to speak with your Teacher," the woman repeated urgently. She threw off her cloak and looked straight ahead, no longer timid. However, she was not looking at the Teacher, as if avoiding his glance; nor was she looking at the dark pilgrim who had known her. She was looking at the disciple with the goatee who was talking to her. She was very young, perhaps fifteen or sixteen, with a narrow, golden-brown face and huge, dark, angry eyes.

The curious pilgrim shook his head.

"You know not what you ask, my good girl. Go home. You cannot speak with the Teacher. The Teacher never speaks to women."

"Yes, go home," Jacob chimed in, wiping his bald head. "Why pester us? You are not ill. Go home."

But the girl would not move.

Two of the disciples who had been silent—one with long hair, and another with curly hair, smiling, and with alert eyes—rose slowly. The one with long hair said:

"This is not good. Let her leave us."

The girl became frightened and almost cried out:

"I have to . . . I must talk to the Teacher . . ."

The disciples all started talking at once, but at this moment the Teacher motioned with his hand, having freed his arm from under the folds of his garment. The disciples fell silent, seeing that he wanted to listen to the girl. They were astonished, yet they remained silent.

The girl also understood this gesture. She suddenly became frightened again, clenched her teeth, and looked for the first time at the One whom she had been following for such a long time.

He was sitting on the white rock under the tree. His eyes resembled the sky—only they were lighter, almost like the sun. It seemed that he never smiled, but he did smile sometimes. His smile was so unbelievably beautiful, such a joy of joys, that no one who saw it could believe that he had actually seen it, and would forget that he had seen it. Each time this smile was the first and the last one, ineffable, and there were no words which could recall it. Now he was not smiling. He was sitting there all luminous, but not bright. He was quiet, and his garment was lighter than that of the others. It was almost white.

The girl did not lower her eyes. At first she was silent, but later she said, as though with an effort:

"I wanted to talk to you, Teacher . . ."

She stopped again, but then continued more boldly:

"Everyone says that you know everything, and that your judgment will be in accordance with the truth and with the law. I wanted to ask you . . . Let one of your disciples go with me. That one."

She turned a little and pointed at the dark pilgrim.

"Him," the girl reiterated. "If you know everything, then you also know he is betrothed to me. Of our kin, he is the person closest to me. I am the only daughter in my father's house, and he should become one of our family. Our betrothal had taken place, and there was harmony between us, and he was saving the money for a house, and together we bought some sheep and other

51

animals. I was his betrothed; no one but he can come to me. How can I fulfill the law of my ancestors if he leaves me? If only you could see my parents' grief! Take pity on me, let him go with me! Don't you have enough disciples? People follow you in crowds! He hasn't come back home, to our roof, since he heard about you; he heard you and he left, and only from the people did I learn that he follows you everywhere, that he carries a box with money for the poor, and that only once did he return to our town, with you, and then he left again, with you. I saw you and followed you. Do let him go with me. Command him and, if he does not obey you, may he be accursed by God as a violator of the law."

The disciples all started talking at once, and their murmuring interrupted the words of the girl.

"What's this! What's this!" exclaimed Jacob, who was frightened. "What a way to talk! How can you say such things to the Teacher? You don't even know what you are asking! The Teacher has ordered us to leave our homes, our wives, our children, and to follow him. And you want him to order one of his disciples, who has stayed with him, to return to you?"

"Be silent, old man!" the girl interrupted him. "You have lived your life according to the law; now you are throwing away the rest of your life. But what about me? I haven't left anybody—but I have been left. I have not yet lived—but I must die. I am the only daughter of my father; he won't see his grandchildren, for I shall die like the grass, trampled down, like a young tree which has not borne fruit. Our kin will be reduced to dust and, like dust, will be scattered in the air. The Teacher does not want this! He has not come to deprive a mother of her children!"

The curly-haired disciple with sharp eyes, with doubt in his searching look, said with a smile:

"One should investigate to see if everything is really as you describe it."

"Then investigate! Judge! Examine! Put my words to the test! Oh, how well I know your kind! There were two of your brothers there. Where is your brother now? You put everything to the test; you investigate everything; there is no truth as far as you are concerned! Why do you follow the Teacher? Are you testing his truth? If you don't believe me, then ask him," she added, pointing to the dark man. "He is here. He knows that what I am saying is the truth."

"The girl is not acting against her conscience," said the curious pilgrim with some condolence and turned to the dark man:

"So, you have abandoned her? And have followed the Teacher? What do you plan to do now? What will you do?"

The dark man, not raising his eyes, answered with some difficulty:

"I shall do everything the Teacher will command me to do. He knows my path."

All eyes turned to the Teacher. They were waiting for him to reply.

The Teacher was silent.

52

The girl, seeing that he was silent, began again to implore him, reaching out her arms:

"Let him go! I beg you—return him to me. You have so many other disciples! The law, given to us for eternity by our ancestors must be fulfilled! It must be fulfilled!"

The boy with the delicate face, sitting at the feet of the Teacher, said quietly, as if sighing, while looking ahead:

"The time and the age must be fulfilled. The law must be fulfilled, too . . ."

The girl spoke again, but the Teacher remained silent. Then she cried out in despair:

"You don't want to let him go? You don't hear me! Do you think he loves you? I know that he is following you not out of his love for you!"

Jacob, and everyone else after him, looked at the dark man. He said nothing, but a sorrowful expression had changed his entire face. And it was clear that he did love the Teacher.

The girl, however, noticed nothing.

"You know, when he hadn't seen you yet, when he had only heard of you, he had already decided what he would do. You are a prophet; people listen to you, and they talk about the deeds which you perform. Your fame precedes you because of your deeds—and so he thought . . . he who is now sitting here in silence, 'Am I not likewise a prophet? Do I not have the same power?' Because," the girl stopped here, for she was nervous and angry, "because they had whispered to him that he resembles you like a twin . . . That both of you have one and the same face."

Having cried out these words, the girl looked intently at the Teacher and fell silent at once. She stood there with her voice broken and her eyes wide. She appeared not to believe the words which she had just uttered; it was as if she had said them against her own will. And now, having looked at the Teacher, she was stupefied with fear and a new despair. The disciples rose in astonishment and looked at the men who were sitting opposite one another, at the dark man in his yellow garment—and at the Teacher.

They did resemble one another, like twins. But one was completely dark, whereas the other was completely light. One was vibrant; the other, serene. Moreover, there were two different expressions of silence on their faces.

Horror, jealousy, and disgust overwhelmed the disciples—vaguely in some, and distinctly in others. Only the young disciple, in his thoughtless tranquillity and trust, leaned his head against the Teacher's knees.

The Teacher closed his eyes. Then he opened them, looked at the girl—and smiled. With this smile any resemblance between the dark man and the Teacher disappeared. His smile was such a great joy that none of those who saw it could believe they had actually seen it, after it died away. However, the girl and everyone around her were no longer afraid. It was as if someone kept on repeating to their souls which had been disturbed and were gradually calming down, "All is well. You see, all is well."

53

With tears of bewilderment on her long eyelashes, the girl took a few steps forward and then suddenly fell to her knees.

"Lord," she said humbly, smiling through her tears, not knowing why herself. "My Lord! Forgive my foolishness. I know nothing—you know everything. I thought I needed the man whom you took away, who had promised to become my husband. No; you have not taken him away—I am giving him to you, if you need him. You know the path and the law. I know only that I wish not that which I desire for myself, but that which you desire. Take him if you need him." And she prostrated herself before him on the ground, as if before God.

The Teacher rose, as did all his disciples. The dark man also rose, but he did not approach the Teacher; he remained standing at some distance.

The Teacher put his hand on the girl's uncovered head.

She did not dare to kiss his hand—she merely pressed her lips against the folds of his robe. Then the Teacher left her, going up the hill. His disciples, hurriedly adjusting their garments, followed him in a close group. The boy with the delicate face was walking closer to the Teacher than anyone else. The curious pilgrim with the goatee pushed his way to him; they were followed by Jacob and the others. The dark man was behind them. The box weighed heavily on his arm. The Teacher had not let him go away. The dark man now felt how frightfully distant he was from the Teacher, and that between them stood—Sorrow. However, he was probably not the only one who felt this way, for even the curious disciple, always jealous and restless, now turned and looked at him without passionate displeasure or envy, but only with a sympathetic sadness.

The oppressive sun beat down upon the dark man's shoulders. Bending under its fiery rays, as if under sharp whips, and supporting the box, which also weighed him down, he dragged himself along, ascending the stony path. The Teacher's white robe sparkled, blazing in the distance, almost on the summit of the hill.

Down below, leaning against the tree and following them up the road with her eyes, stood the happy girl, with tears on her eyelashes. As before, she knew nothing, but her new, nameless joy remained with her.

NOTES

1. S. T. Aksakov, *The Childhood of Bagrov's Grandson* (1858), a semi-biographical work reflecting manor life on the steppes in the 1790's.

2. "She was walking in the field, sir." Here Nadya uses the plural form of the verb, although the reference is to a single subject—a means of showing the respect, and old-fashioned in usage.

3. Reference is made to the old printed form of the Cyrillic "T."

Alexey Remizov (1877–1957)

Alexey Mikhailovich Remizov, one of the most versatile and original Russian writers of the twentieth century, was the son of a merchant. He was educated at the University of Moscow, where he studied natural science, but was expelled in 1897 for radical political activities and exiled to Penza, and later to Vologda— provincial centers which appear in some of his earlier works. In 1904 he was allowed to move to St. Petersburg, where he and his wife, Serafima Pavlovna (née Dovgello), became friends of Zinaida Hippius, who often helped them in their "desperate straits" (in Hippius' words). They seemed to have financial problems all their lives; according to Georgy Adamovich, "Remizov's style was to be a beggar."

Remizov traveled much through Russia, made several religious pilgrimages, and spent time in monasteries. Like most Russian Symbolists, Remizov at first believed that the Revolution would purify Russia and prepare it for its impending spiritual metamorphosis. But he soon grew disillusioned, and was given permission to go abroad for reasons of health. In 1923 he settled in Paris, where he contributed to various literary journals and newspapers. His major works written in exile include *Pyataya yazva* (The Fifth Pestilence; Berlin, 1922), *Vzvikhryonnaya Rus'* (Frenzied Russia; Paris, 1927), and *V rozovom bleske* (In a Rosy Glow; New York, 1952). He was also the author of poetry collections, for example, *Mechty yunosti* (Dreams of Youth; St. Petersburg, 1910) and *O sud'be ognennoy* (Of Fiery Fate; Petrograd, 1918). His early novels, published in Russia, *Prud* (The Pond, 1907), *Chasy* (The Clock, 1908), and *Krestovye syostry* (Sisters of the Cross, 1910), are harrowing portrayals of life in Russian provincial cities. Man appears in them as merely the plaything of evil destiny. A grotesque, extravagant, and ornate style characterizes some of these early writings, although others among them tend toward naturalism and, strangely enough, achieve symbolic significance. Remizov named as his literary ancestors Gogol', Leskov, and Dostoevsky. From the latter came the concern for humiliation and suffering so typical of his earlier writings. From Gogol', Vladimir Dahl, and Leskov he inherited his preoccupation with the nuances, syntax, and intonation of Russian colloquial speech, and the semantic possibilities of a language rich in archaic and dialect forms and folk expressions, neologisms, and a unique syntax. In these attempts he followed the lead of Leskov, with his interest in fantasy, folk legends, and popular religion, both Christian and pagan. Saturated in these popular elements, Remizov's style developed into a grotesque, multi-layered speech pattern, with abundant proverbs, puns, quips, allusions, folk etymologies, and borrowings from foreign languages. This unique emphasis on stylistic effect makes Remizov, along with Andrey Bely, a master of Ornamentalism, a trend which developed out of Symbolism and prevailed in Russian belles-lettres from 1912 to the 1920's. Remizov does not stress psychological characterization, although dreams play an important part in all his work. (In fact, he has many remarkable recordings of his own dreams and hallucinations.) Fairytales and religious legends are especially congenial to Remizov, because in them his poetic prose, stylistic mannerisms, grotesque imagery, and whimsical imagination can be given free rein. He often animates material things and envisions the uninterrupted unity of past, present, and future. Some of his stories abound in demons, fairies, fantastic animals or beasts, and madmen; other emphasize the ideals of sympathy, understanding, humility, and charity. His works manifest a curious, frequently surrealistic blend of different genres and varied styles, providing excellent examples of his rhythmic prose, verbal repetition, and visual design.

Remizov was firmly convinced that only through dreams can man fathom the mystery of other worlds and mystical powers that influence the world of finite experience. He presents the magic power of the universe through a variety of myths, with no clear distinction between empirical reality and dream, or what lies beyond the dream. His unique concept of the world, together with his experimentation with the lexical, phonetic, and intonational depths of the Russian folk language, enabled Remizov to create a completely new style of fiction. And he protested what he called the deformation of the original Russian language by German grammar with its pedantic, orderly rules.

However, Remizov was also capable of simple, straightforward narrative, as in the stories about his wife *Olya* (1927) and *In a Rosy Glow*, mentioned above. In these works the reader can sense the author's compassion, especially for the defenseless and limited little man. Yet even there Remizov's basically pessimistic *Weltanschauung* is perceptible: life is grotesque, insane, and man's only salvation lies in self-abnegation and humble acceptance of a dismal fate, for he cannot struggle against it. These works have complex thematic patterns and stylized characters.

Remizov's personal and literary eccentricities were also manifest in his lifestyle. An outstanding student of Old Russian manuscripts, he practiced the florid and beautiful old-style calligraphy, even writing letters to his friends in this whimsical manner. Or, fascinated with everything eccentric, he organized a mysterious Grand Federation of Apes, of which he himself was secretary. (He issued exquisitely written Charters of Membership for other Russian writers he considered worthy of this honor. The Charter bore a seal of the Grand Federation of Apes, prepared by Remizov and signed with the "very own tail" of the Apes' Tsar Asyka.[1])

At the turn of the century Russian avant-garde journals eagerly published

Remizov's stories. Many writers, among them Alexander Blok, Andrey Bely, Fyodor Sologub, Vasily Rozanov, Vyacheslav Ivanov, and the Merezhkovskys, were the Remizovs' intimate friends; they praised his publications and admired his peculiar, often eerie poetic universe. In exile, Lev Shestov, Nikolay Berdyaev, Dmitry Svyatopolk-Mirsky, and Marina Tsvetaeva, as well as the writers and poets of the younger Russian generation abroad, continued to applaud his works. Among his close friends in Paris were Sofiya Pregel', Count Józef Czapski, Boris Zaytsev, Sergey Makovsky, and Victor Mamchenko. They helped the Remizovs in times of financial crisis and illness.

Remizov's ornamentalist tendencies influenced Zamyatin, Prishvin, Yury Olesha, and Pil'nyak and, through them, several Soviet writers, including Babel', Bulgakov, and A. N. Tolstoy. His experiments in style, his world outlook, and his interest in contemporary man and the latest Western European concerns in art and culture were curiously combined with a fascination for pre-Petrine Russian, and became a source of lasting inspiration for these and other Russian writers.

NOTE

1. See more about Remizov (on himself) in *Novaya russkaya kniga* (The New Russian Book), no. 9 (1921).

ESPRIT
HISTOIRE-SALADE
SKAZ-VYAKANYE

FROM: *Sovremennye zapiski* (Contemporary Annals) 23 (Paris, 1925).

ABOUT HIM HIMSELF

I found him in the kitchen in a box under the oven—in the coals. He was lying in a corner—so delicate, with two arms, three legs, as it should be; and nearby there was a pine cone. The cone was dilapidated; I had burned it in the fireplace. I put him on a silver plate—on the wall; he was so delicate, with two arms, three legs, as it should be. And I noticed: often at night a feeling of ennui would pervade the room. I would look at the wall—there he was, so delicate, two arms, three legs; for some reason he wasn't gay. And I wasn't gay either. Or was it because of the pine cone? "Are you sad about the pine cone?" I tried to begin a conversation—he wouldn't answer; he was sulking. Thus came spring, and then we didn't need coal anymore. I cleaned out the fireplace, went to the kitchen, rummaged a bit in the box beneath the oven—perhaps there was another cone left? No, only a fluffy little feather, and nothing more. The chestnut tree below my window had bloomed (that's why our street was *Villa Flore*, because of the chestnut tree!).

In the evenings, when the electricity burned in the house and light streamed out all the windows from each floor, the chestnut stood like a Christmas tree—a thick, tall fir dressed in snowy-white lights—

> Christmas song—Christmas song
> water-nymphish
> willowish
> lily

You couldn't tear yourself from the window.

But still he was unhappy! "I'll get you a cone!" And I saw how he cheered up—he swam with his arms. I commanded, "Bring me a cone!" From the Ocean, together with three claws (one big, the next a little smaller, the third really tiny—the size of a fingernail) and with a blistered branch of seaweed, there also arrived my promised cone. I placed it on his silver plate and hung it up; it was a cedar cone, succulent, strong—enough for the whole winter. "Here you are!" And everything calmed down. He remained calm both before the cock's crow (in our yard we had a henhouse; a cock lived there!) and even while the cock crowed; peace and quiet. He had calmed down.

He was called *esprit*, but in Russian his Russian forest name was *Koryabala*.

A learned spiritualist once visited me and noticed him on the wall—

"Where," he asked, "did you get this? This is like something from a photograph by Richet—it's a materialized spirit!"

And I replied: "Yes, that certainly is a spirit—*esprit*, in Russian *koryabala*."

ABOUT THE LITTLE MOUSE

A little mouse took up residence in our kitchen. She caused a lot of problems. But we didn't touch her—we felt sorry for her. Indeed, she had nothing to eat in our place—she was really an odd one. Dinner's leftovers I locked in the cupboard. Very seldom was anything thrown away. I looked for her little burrow—under the oven in the same corner behind the cone box, where I once found my *esprit*. There into her little burrow she dragged paper and all sorts of crumbs and old crusts. You'd come into the kitchen at night to put the tea kettle on the stove, and she—swish!—only a little tail, like a whisker—chik! There was only one danger: that the little mouse, if she couldn't get enough food, would move on to the books—our books would be lost! And even though you'd often remember that there was a little mouse—

"danger!"—still you didn't want to touch her. So we got used to it. The little mouse lived comfortably in the kitchen.

Through the wall—

un petit piège pour une petite souris—
a little trap for a little mouse!
une tapette à souris pour attraper—
a snap trap—to catch our mouse!
une souricière—
a mouse trap!
un attrape-souris—
a contraption!
je vais la piger cette souris—
saying, "I'm going to catch this mouse!"
à la bonne heure! c'est bien—
"well, it's about time!"

And the most frightening:

mort aux rats—
death to rats!—such terrifying poison!

Through the wall, I often heard it—this conversation about our little mouse.

So I figured it out—the little mouse lived with us, but ate with our neighbors. Well, good for her!

Once Serafima Pavlovna went to the Sea-Ocean to the good sorceress Flory (*Fleury*) for some seashells and pebbles, and also for a cone for my *esprit*. She ordered me: "You must eat absolutely every day, and at night not sit up too long, but go to sleep when the cock starts to crow!" The very first evening I was left alone, I sat down to my work. My work was sorting out words, like pebbles, and stringing word-shells—that is, composing, "mastering the material," with all the piercing awareness of the tug of paper, pen, and ink! At a late hour I turned from my table to the mirror—next to the mirror over the fireplace was a clock which struck the hour—to look at the time. And I saw—really close to me, right in a ray of light—a little mouse sitting on the rug and preening herself behind the ear with her little paw, working so diligently. I thought, "There's a clever one. She wants me to notice her!"

I was so happy to see her. I had been left alone; the little mouse understood this and came out—to watch over me. I greeted her. But neither my speech nor my movement when I had turned around to look at the clock frightened the little mouse. The little mouse still remained seated on the rug—her most delicate lips pursed, her ears perked sharply, her tiny tail swishing. And on

59

the next day, and the third—as soon as night came, the little mouse would sit with me, and keep watch.

I began to watch for the little mouse.

Once, after dark, the rain forced Shletser into my house. Actually, not so much the rain, but rather our common passion: we spent many evenings together at the Diaghilev ballet, and for me the beginning of the summer was infused—transfixed—with the music of "The Wedding Night" (*Noces*) of Stravinsky, and my eyes were painted by Picasso. Shletser, on the other hand, no longer walked, but tumbled like an inchworm under the influence of "The Blue Train" (*Le Train Bleu*). We conversed only about these matters. And, too, about quarter-toned music.

Well, my little mouse was shy about staying in Shletser's presence. I saw her run—she was worried—either to the clock on the fireplace, or into the corner by the radiator, or behind the shelf among the books.

"What's that?" he said. "Did the light flicker, or was it a mouse?"

"Why," I replied, "would we have mice? We don't have mice. You're seeing things!"

The following day, also in the evening, Mochul'sky and Prince Mirsky came. The conversation was about style—about our great, strong Russian style with its rigid rhythm.

Mochul'sky was talking. The Prince, as usual, was sitting like a lion, in sullen silence.

Suddenly he bared his teeth!

"You have mice—!"

But even at this point I didn't betray my little mouse. I knew quite well it was she—this hour was precisely the time for her guard duty.

"Now, really," I said, "where could mice come from in here! That was the light flickering!"

So every evening for a whole week the little mouse watched over me.

Then I received a letter from the Sea-Ocean: tomorrow Serafima Pavlovna would be home. I received the letter during the day, and that evening the little mouse disappeared. The little mouse left and hasn't shown herself since. She understood! She went back to her little burrow; she had done her duty!

What a clever little mouse! She watched over me while I was alone; she traced patterns in space, like my letters on paper. She was my guardian and the living shadow of my thoughts.

DIE HEILIGE MAUS

Not far from Munich, on the banks of the Ammersee on the "holy mountain" of Andechs, there stands a monastery, *Kloster Andechs*. Many times during our first winter in Berlin I looked for notations on the calendar *(Marianischer Kalender)* about "Holy Germany." Even here in Germany I wanted to find the little paths along which wander the suffering and disconsolate, those who have lost hope for consolation from other people, those who have surrendered themselves to despair in our sinful world, who wander in search of a miracle, seeking out a holy place which has been sanctified by faith throughout the ages. How terribly joyful I was when, not even thinking of it, I found myself right in the most sacred place in "Holy Germany."

We were living nearby, in Breitbrun on the Ammersee, and went there on foot. As we were walking through the forest, I came across a dry branch lying on the road. It looked, well, just like a winged lizard. But this was a good sign: "The word *Andechs* comes from *Eidechse* and *die Eidechse* means lizard, a twisting lizard." I picked up the branch, and we climbed the holy mountain. Quietly and lazily the convoluted path led us right up to the walls. It was an ancient monastery. There was a holy spring; it also had relics, a school in honor of our Nikolay *(St. Nikolausanstalt)*, and a famous brewery *(Kloster-Brauerei)*.

A monk led us to the sacristy. What relics were not to be found there!—nails from the Crucifixion, a thorn from the Crown of Thorns, the cassock of Nikolay the Consoler. The pilgrims followed the monk, listened, stood in wonder, and kissed the relics. And then I noticed something—and I couldn't believe my eyes—*das Bild des heiligen Mäuschens*, the icon of a holy mouse!

The monk became more lively and began to tell us about the mouse, to explain this veneration of a mouse and how it came to be among the "blessed."

This is how it happened. Heathens, either Swedes or Hungarians, had started to ravage the monastery, so the monks hid their treasures in the church beneath the floor. Among these treasures was a tabernacle *(Monstranz)* with the Blessed Bread and Wine *(Hostie)*. This Eucharist was miraculous—in answer to their prayers for a sign to convince the unbelievers, the bread was changed visibly and tangibly into the Body of Christ. A hundred years passed. When everything had become peaceful again, and the destroyed monastery had been rebuilt, a legend circulated about the treasure; but where it was hidden, no one remembered. The monks thought about this a great deal but couldn't come up with anything.

"Once during Mass," the monk related, "they saw a little mouse come out of the altar; in his tiny paws he held a small scrap of paper rolled into a tiny scroll. Well, they didn't touch the little mouse, but they took the scrap of writing. And when they looked to see what was written there, they were dumbfounded—it was about the treasure! Immediately they took up the floor, just at the place where the little mouse had been sitting—and found everything, the Tabernacle and the miraculous Bread and Wine."

> *Eine Maus zeigt durch den Zettel an,*
> *Wo man das Heiligtum finden kann.* *

* A mouse announces through a note where one may find the holy relic.

The pilgrims listened to the story of the little mouse—what a smart little one!

The monk walked on—and I noticed everyone bowed and kissed the icon of the mouse. The moustachioed one was painted sitting, his tail like a tiny string. Even I bowed to *die heilige Maus!*

I remembered the little holy mouse because I've just been speaking about my own—the one who watched over me for seven nights!—and also because A. S. Eliasberg climbed the holy hill of Andechs with us, and it was difficult for him; he had a weak heart. Just now I found out he is no longer in this world—his heart couldn't stand this sinful earth any more! How well he knew the Russian language. And he loved Russia's speech, her shores, as others rarely do.

GESPENST†

I didn't find him anywhere, he came all by himself—

During the day, on Saturday, Scholz arrived—I remember he came from Riderau (Riderau is also on the Ammersee, as is Andechs)—and in the evening, Kaiser and Osipov. But the next morning spring arrived!—through the window came the Sunday bells from Moabit (across the Lessing Bridge from Old Moabit), and from Tiergarten came the earthy smell of the bursting trees and the muffled tolling of the bells of *Gedächtniskirche*, with their green aura of spring, and you couldn't tell whether you were in Moscow or Berlin. Then a little bell rang—the telephone! I went over to it and saw lying on the telephone book, near the small toylike telephone, an indescribable sort of stuffed toy animal—pitch black, an ear and an eye, and all tails . . . soft! When Elya and El'za saw it—

"Ah!" they exclaimed at once. *"Das ist ein Gespenst.* (Why, that's a geshpenst!)"

"Geshpenst!" Well, of course, this was more obvious to them—their eyes were still clear, they hadn't been beaten down by life's trifles; indeed, they had as yet counted only ten springs in all their lives.

But I was convinced that neither Rudolph Scholz, the Tolstoyan, nor Rudolph Kaiser, the philosopher and editor of *Die neue Rundschau*, nor Osipov—our "Keeper of the Keys of the OGMCF" (i.e., the Keeper of the Keys of the "Order of the Great Monkey's Chamber of Freedom"),[1] none of them could have stuck him in my house.

†The ghost

Yes, he came all by himself—the *Gespenst*!

The geshspenst (ghost, apparition) was like a brother of the *esprit!*

Only I knew nothing of the *esprit* then; we were living in Berlin, on Lessingstrasse, and I was called, in the German manner, *Remersdorf*. So Frau Karus, who came to us in the mornings to clean the rooms, called me Remersdorf, and following her example so did all the little children—the shoemaker's daughter and all her brothers, and the children of the proprietor of the coal shop where we bought our briquets, and the doorman's little girl, and all their companions and friends and acquaintances—from Tiergarten to Old Moabit, and even over there in Charlottenburg around Kirchstrasse, where we used to live. They'd stand under the window—our apartment was above a *Drogerie* (a drugstore), on the second floor, the windows were open, my whole magical room was like, well you can't imagine—a flock of them would stand there and shout: *"Herr Remersdorf!"* until you peeped out as if you were a geshpenst yourself. But I only learned of the *esprit* on Villa Flore, when from Remersdorf I unexpectedly and quite surprisingly turned into Remoz. I think I represent the interrelationship entirely correctly and with complete visual clarity:

$$\frac{\text{Remersdorf}}{\text{Alexis Remoz}} = \frac{\text{Gespenst}}{\text{Esprit}}$$

In the evening with the electric lights on, my room became—to the outsider looking in—a magical kingdom. A spider, a spider directly above my table, would lower his threads into all the corners, and by these threads he would draw his victims to him—small toy beasts—lions, rhinoceroses, wolves, zebras, horses, cows, buck and nanny goats, deer, pigs, foxes, frogs, hares, cocks, dried flowers, leaves, little twigs, roots, stars, and the nephew of the little *Untergrundick* (metro worker) who helped the little *Untergrundick* check the tiny screws in the metro at night, swarthy like the geshpenst, and totally entwined with thin, tail-like wires, but his eye was like a small lantern; and of course the geshpenst himself was there. These victims of the spider, the nephew, and the geshpenst—they all attracted the children.

When, after prolonged outcries, I would invite them in for a moment and the flock noisily rushed to me, how many tiny hands stretched out toward these sacrificial threads!

"Pferdchen! Pferdchen!" (A little horsie! A little horsie!)

And each time I'd say:

"Zu Weihnachten." (For Christmas.)

More than once I heard Frau Karus explain that, if we started to take away the little horses every night, then there would be nothing left for the spider. But if we did this on Christmas, that would be a different matter—that would be *das Geschenk* (a present).

From outside, you could also see a section of the living magical wall, the wall opposite my table—you'd see there:

—through the skeleton of a fir tree—clearly visible!—the tail of Baba Yaga and flying with her a pine cone, and behind the pine cone a wind spirit;

—Misha the Bear with a pole and on skis, prancing along clear fields from forest to forest, fearing no one;

—a winged lizard—with jasper eyes (the same one I had found on the way to Andechs); it was lying on the road in the dried leaves;

—a *Zwerg*‡ *(razeter)* in a red cap—a troll gardener, and that's why he had a watering pot in his hands;

—cocks and hens pecking the ground, twitching their tail feathers;

—the little *Untergrundick* (in French, the *metro* worker);

—a gray duster, the kind which kicks up dust in the street, with automobile tires on its feet;

—a lumberjack, a mossy old grandfather;

—a flying black cat;

—a small tinkling bell;

—a little cobblestone devil in red with a fork;

—a scurrying little devil in black;

—a delicate little monkey tiptoeing along, while looking over his shoulder;

—a silver Star of Bethlehem flying, like a tail, above Baba Yaga;

—four Michels—four honey cakes;

—the fifth, with "Michel" written in the center with white sugar, like the little grunting piglets at the honey cake fair;

—a small cock popping out of a tiny house: he cock-a-doodle-doos and disappears;

—an apelike court chamberlain in a crown—"the Court Chamberlain of the OGMCF";

—and, at the foot of the court chamberlain, a male donkey (on a little thread) prancing;

—a jumping froglike *Hampelmann;* §

—a hare—*Schneehase*—white, like snow;

—a black pigeon coop made on one small twig;

—two broken Michels—really terrible!

—a mouse and a mouse's boat;

—a monkey flag *(Affenfahne)*;

—a white Duck *(Shumka)*, "the one eaten by the wolves";

—a tiny quail and a little yellow bird;

—"the meetings of dawgs";

—tiny whistles: a delicate, long flute, and a little birdlike flute, a rattle from Schwarzwald, two bird beaks, the London-Svyatopolk-Mirsky

‡dwarf
§jumping jack

pipe (Prince D. P. Mirsky—plenipotentiary from the OGMCF in London);
—a Bavarian clay pipe;
—and a quarrelsome *fetyuch* (from the French, *la fétuque*).

The children would stand beneath my window in a flock, bewitched. Passersby would glance in.

But of all the children, Elya and El'za clung to the little toys the most often and with the most affection.

During the first year of our Berlin existence, after leaving Russia, when, as in Russia, all these sundry . . . geshpensts had just begun to appear and creep onto my wall, already on Kirchstrasse, Elya and El'za had adopted them at first glance as their own—and me along with them.

I remember how a man from the central *troika*[2] of the housing division came—we as foreigners *(Ausländer)* had the right to two rooms from the landlord—he looked and immediately sized me up: *der Naturforscher* (a researcher in the natural sciences). But El'za greeted both me and the *Feuermännchen* (the little fireman, who was also a *Zwerg*, a dwarf) and, when she said goodbye, she even tousled the beard of the little axe-twirler *(Kolovyortysh)*, as if bidding farewell. The next time she brought Elya. However, Elya exchanged greetings with the *Feuermännchen* nose to nose.

Elya was the daughter of the laundry man; El'za—I don't know.

Elya was as fair (as rarely occurs) as steppe grass, but El'za appeared dark, when, with eyes like saucers, they would both look, head to head, at my wonders.

Elya was headstrong; she even knew French, *la vache* (cow). El'za spoke so softly, and her eyes were so sorrowful. Elya explained to me that El'za was very poor, often ill, and she had not one single toy—this happened while we dragged Peter to Charlottenburg *Schloss* for "a stroll" (Peter was a cat, their mutual darling), and we were having such a gay time that Elya "let herself go." But El'za—

I had gone outside to have a smoke and saw the children coming in a crowd, dragging something and shouting; they'd stop a bit, then begin again shouting the whole length of the street. I ran after them—"What's this?" They shouted, "Peter! Peter!" And they showed me—I saw the cat wrapped in a rag with a little ribbon. "Where are you going?" *"Nach dem Schloss spazieren!"* (To the *Schloss* for a walk.) And again they started shouting. I followed them.

It was an extraordinary thing—I had noticed that even here in Paris both adults and children would often stop me: "What time is it?" But this is my misfortune. Calculations are impossible for me; I always get confused about numbers in a foreign language—and here, it seemed as if on purpose, they'd ask me . . . At that time I still carried a watch. I'd take out my watch, look at it, and speak in measured tones, with great deliberation *(langsam— doucement)*[||]. God only knows what I'd answer sometimes.

Through the cat, as I walked to the *Schloss* with the gang; and through that watch—that's how I got to know everyone. I had lots of little friends in Charlottenburg. And they never laughed at me and no longer shouted after me *"Ausländer!"*

When we moved to Lessingstrasse, we had no telephone for a long time, although as Russians we were accustomed to having one. It always seemed that something was lacking; we were bored, and then a certain kind of sorceress named Kuku presented us with a teeny toy telephone. When the real one was installed, we left the toy one standing next to it.

Elya would come for the laundry or return it, and El'za was always with her. They'd greet the *Feuermännchen* and the little axe-twirler, *Kolovyortysh*, quickly gulp down some sweets (I always saved some cookies for them), examine the spider and all the spider's threads with their victims, have a look at the magical wall with Baba Yaga, and then head for the toy telephone, and talk to each other for a long time. They liked the telephone very much.

One morning Frau Karus was straightening the room, and I noticed her glance at something, look around, and then start searching.

"Where's the telephone?"

"Why over there," I said, "by the telephone!" I knew which telephone she had in mind.

"It's not here!"

"Look carefully; perhaps it fell under the book shelf?"

"Nothing's here!"

"Where could it have gone?"

"Someone's taken it!"

But who could have taken it? Yesterday evening Lev Shestov was here; he'd just come from Paris, but he wouldn't want a telephone just for that reason. Paris—a telephoneless city! Polyakov-Litovtsev had dropped in; he had looked attentively at the telephone. I noticed that. But why would he take away my telephone, when in fact he'd come to bail me out of my predicament—tomorrow was the deadline to pay for the apartment! Osorgin had also been here; in an offhand manner, he flipped something in his hands. Perhaps Osorgin put it in his pocket accidently? No, he has no desire for such a thing; if he did . . . he'd want a wireless one! The matches had disappeared!

[||]slowly-gently

But that's Berdyaev—these smokers always do that! I didn't tell Frau Karus about Berdyaev. I said something completely different:

"Matches are not a telephone and no one would take the telephone. It's probably lying around right here somewhere. I'll look for it myself."

But it suddenly dawned on Frau Karus:

"I bet those naughty girls took it from you! I'll get to the bottom of this."

Frau Karus was very upset and, though continuing her cleaning, she couldn't calm down.

"If they're starting to snatch phones now," she stood still with her broom while her lips trembled, "by the time they're twenty, they'll clean out the whole house!"

Frau Karus was thrifty, reasonable—"God-fighting" (that's from "God-fearing"; "God-fighting" is how a certain old German lady in Petersburg once characterized herself).

Frau Karus was totally unable to reconcile herself to the Kaiser's abandonment of Germany during the Revolution; but above all she could not forgive the Kaiser for remarrying. By birth she was from the Mazursky Lakes, but she had lived her whole life in Berlin. She had not forgotten her native swamps and could not forgive the fact that so many Russians had been drowned there during the war. And whenever she recalled this, she would assume a threatening expression—she'd stand like that with her broom, and her lips would start to tremble. She loved huge funeral processions—she took part both when the murdered Turkish ambassador was buried and when they carried Vorovsky into Berlin. And, unlike the others, she believed in Spirits—in *Zwerge;* she would look tenderly at the *Feuermännchen*, and sometimes she might even tweak his nose. True, she was indifferent to the little axe-twirler *Kolovyortysh*, yet she'd never offend him! The *Feuermännchen* was from the very heart of Germany, which had revealed Christmas to the world—indeed, nowhere else in the world is there such a Christmas Eve as *die Weihnachten*, just as nowhere else is there such a beautiful Easter as in Russia!

The *Feuermännchen* was a real German (he worried about the temperature and the electricity), whereas the axe-twirler *Kolovyortysh* (a witch's servant) was from the Murom Forest. And for thirty years now, summer after summer, early in the evening on St. John's Eve Frau Karus had gone out of the town to Toybits, and there in the circle around a fire she would dance the witch's dance *(der Hexentanz)* at midnight.

Usually, as I have noticed here, though it's true that it's only been a short time—during the three years of my life in this ancient non-

Russian land—they somehow don't believe very much in spirits or in *Zwerge*, or even in *razetery*.

We went to Oberammergau for the Passion Play *(die Passionsspiele)*, but no empty rooms were available, so we stayed in Unterammergau in a hut where they accepted overnight lodgers. In the morning we were waiting for a train; I was sitting with the landlady on a little bench, but my eyes were on the mountain.

I asked: "So the mountain spirits don't trouble you?" She smiled. "The *Zwerge?*" I said.

And again she smiled—or did she remember something?

"No," she said, "there are no more spirits, and there are no more *Zwerge*. There is only one Russian prisoner-of-war here; he is peaceful."

And as regards Karlsbad: "The summer is rainy, it drizzles from morning on—if only the sun would break through just a little!" One day I said to Fräulein Mary who was cleaning our room: "If only you could go to the mountain, you could ask the sorcerer: 'When will it be clear?' "

But she answered: "There are no more sorcerers anywhere!"

"Of course," I thought, "if there are no spirits or *Zwerge*, then why should there be any sorcerers?"

"But do you know," I said, "some scientists are watching that red star through a telescope from your Bohemian Mountains, where, so you say, there are no more sorcerers? But a resident of that red place—a Martian, there is only one such on the whole earthly globe, and he's living in Moscow, Victor Shklovsky—he told me that on that red star there was such embitterment for lack of even a gulp of water (and you yourself understand what thirst is), that they began to invent ways of getting water, saving water, and they greatly excelled in science and built such excellent machines. And so the most common engineer, someone just like our neighbor, was turned into a sorcerer, and the spirits, the *Zwerge*, appeared again; that is, they were seen again—indeed, they hadn't gone anywhere! Well, of course they were electrical *Zwerge*, entwined in wires." Fräulein Mary listened and was amazed: "If only a woman would come from Mars to Karlsbad!" If an American girl had given her a green sweater, then a Martian girl would probably give her a whole dress! I thought to myself, "Well, perhaps all this is just as it should be," I thought, "that at a particular stage of development in the human soul it is entirely hygienic for the soul to retreat from superstition—old beliefs and prejudices—from all that which is called superstition, which weakens the human will, blinds man, holds him in constant fear; indeed, sometimes the hands must be unbound so that everything might vanish—spirits and

Zwerge—to leave man in his freedom with his brain, to arouse in this way his energy. He would be pushed into independent action by arithmetic—by the four rules leading to the chain rule—by arithmetic which leads to mathematics—to higher mathematics, and a whirlwind of infinitely small differentials would splash over there—and then they would appear again, the spirits and *Zwerge*, but you wouldn't be frightened, nor feel persecuted; no, on your head there would be a cock's crown, in your right hand a three-tailed lash, in your left a wreath, but your legs would be like a serpent's—and it is no accident that in the most mathematical city in the world, in Paris, there is the Richet Institute where they photograph spirits—

No, it is not because the Mazursky Lakes are not the Bohemian Mountains, or because they are closer to bewitching Lithuania, that every summer on St. John's Eve Frau Karus, with all her emotions and faith in the purifying fire, prances in a circle around the blaze.

In the evening Frau Karus appeared unexpectedly.

She had found out—El'za had taken the phone.

"But tell me what you know of this, because Elya's father is asking me." He's found that she had the geshpenst; she brought him to her father on Easter, showed him, and assured him that Remersdorf had given the geshpenst to her as a present. But now the father has become suspicious; he told her: "You won't move from that spot till you confess!"

Frau Karus pronounced these words with the same feeling as when she was threatening someone or other with her broom, when she remembered her native Mazursky swamps where so many Russians had been drowned.

I looked at the Spider, where, I recalled, the geshpenst hung on a thread—there was no geshpenst.

"No, I didn't give the geshpenst to Elya."

The bell rang—the toymaster Smirnov.

Toys—he heaped the whole table with multicolored tin whistles from Vyatka.

We turned on the lights, and I became engrossed in horses and goats. It was more miraculous than usual: the north—Russia—was depicted, and on top of the silver and snow different mosses shone brightly—multicolored, like the fires of a northern night.

Frau Karus had gone; she somehow left unnoticed. I hadn't even had time to grasp the situation.

"Perhaps it would have been better to say I gave her the geshpenst! And the next time Elya came, I could explain to her that, if she had asked, I would certainly have given her the geshpenst. But now—'You won't move from that spot till you confess!' And there was also Frau Karus—'Remersdorf didn't give her the geshpenst!' "

The thought flashed through my mind and vanished into the multicolored whistles from Vyatka and Smirnov's tales about Nestorych, the grandfather sorcerer.

NESTORYCH

Nestorych was an old man over eighty, erect, lanky, and he had a long beard, white with green patches, and he always wore a long coarse linen shirt to his knees, belted with a plait—except at Mass, when he wore a little belt with a prayer on it. In winter, he wore a rabbit hunting cap; in summer, a hat with a sheaf of buckwheat on it; and when the old man walked near the beehives, the bees would sit on his buckwheat. His boots were smeared with tar, and he'd only put on trousers the time he'd gone courting.

His house was way up on the mountain; he had a garden and bees there. And at the foot of the mountain there was a small stream; in the stream there were gudgeon; so during Lent there was fish chowder. Nestorych had been serving as a deacon for fifty years. On Sunday at Mass he wore a red ribbon as wide as a towel on top of his coarse linen shirt—and on it a gold medal "For diligent service." His old woman was called "Ba." That's what the old man called her, so that's what the other people called her behind her back. As dry as a dried-out fir and silent as a deaf-mute. However, if something crossed her—"I'll leave!" and she'd sock him on his bald head. "That's Ba for you!" the old man would say, and nothing more, for they'd been together for an eternity, and without the old woman a stove wasn't a stove to him, and warm wasn't warm.

On Sunday, Nestorych would return home after the service, go into the house, and, as his first task, wish the old woman a good holiday. "Well, Ba, let's have dinner." Then the old woman would show him what kind of cheese tarts she had prepared for the cabbage soup, and what kind of cabbage soup there was, or the buckwheat *kasha* with sugar and Lenten oil, and the baked apples for a tastie and, of course, the *kvass*! The old man ploughed and worked in the church and in the garden and with the bees, and went fishing: however, at home the old woman reigned; it was her kingdom—"Ba!"

In the lefthand corner under the icons there was an ancient mahogany chair; the whole back of the chair and its sides were hung thickly with bast strings. They'd buy ring-shaped rolls for themselves, and the old man himself would always untie the string from which they hung and attach it to the chair—to keep things tidy and for emergencies. In his long coarse linen shirt, with the gold medal on its red ribbon, Nestorych would sit in the corner on his bast-covered mahogany chair; he looked so dignified that, if you dared talk drivel, he'd cut you down with a glance—so severe was he. "Listen, brother, you can't feed me with your promises!" he'd say, but his voice was scratchy, like the snow under sledge runners. And he'd look at you—like frost!—you wouldn't forget it your whole life long. You'd swear not to feed trusting people with kind, empty words. "This is a rotten habit," squeaked the old man, "worse than any drunkenness; when a drunkard drinks, he hurts himself, but this infamy—these promisers—they always bring glory to themselves, and for the other guy—fooey!" Because of his stern expression and straightforward words, Nestorych was feared—feared, but respected.

For a hundred *versts* and farther, all the way to Kaluga he was trusted; the settlement was well-traveled, many were always going here and there on business—both to Kaluga and from Kaluga. And whatever you'd leave with him, it would always be as safe as if it were his own. And what didn't they leave with him! He had trustworthy hands.

Nestorych taught the children to read and write, but in his own way, sing-song—*az-ba-ba, vedi-az-ba, glagol'-az-ga*. But when the schools were opened, he quit teaching and spent all his time with his bees and at church services. It was then that the rumor spread—he was a sorcerer! And he was an honest-to-goodness sorcerer; indeed, could an ordinary person do such things? He could cast a spell on blood, and he knew the word to cure you from snakebite; and if someone had a toothache, he'd put a little piece of paper with a prayer written on it on the tooth, and the pain would disappear.

But this was the main reason for this rumor spreading and growing, and why everyone began to obey Nestorych and fear him as a sorcerer: once some children stole into his garden to shake down the pears; the old man looked around—no pears.

Who—whose children? But it was easy to find this out, because everyone knew everyone else, and the mother of the children happened to pass by.

"Are those your children?"

"They're mine."

"Bring them here to me!"

She went to fetch them. "Now you'll be punished for your stealing!" she called to them. They ran up to him barefoot—three boys and three girls. They howled: "We found them under the tree!"

"Like hell! You dared to steal my pears, stay here!"

They stood there and were even afraid to howl.

The old man went into the house, got a strong thread. He led all the children to the porch and tied them to it.

"Whoever breaks this—and it's very easy to break—will have nothing but trouble!" And he held them with that thread for about three hours—three hours as if they were rooted to that spot; they didn't even move.

After this—never mind actual stealing, they were afraid even to think about such a thing when reminded of Nestorych. And not only children—what's it to children; to them it's like water off a duck's back—but grown ups, big people.

"If," they said, "he would do such a thing to the children, then what's in store for us—he'll do something even worse to us." It was from this incident that the rumor spread, and not only there, in Kaluga, but to Moscow itself—he was a sorcerer.

I accompanied Smirnov to Klopstockstrasse; at the corner we stopped by a wine shop, sat down, each drank a small glass of tarragon wine—and toasted Nestorych. Then I returned home and immediately went to bed.

The next day I had to get up a little earlier and go to Alexanderplatz, to the *Polizeipräsidium*# for our "yellow ticket" *(Personalausweis)***—every three months we had to renew our residence permit—and this was always terrifying for me. There were some fortunate ones who had managed to obtain this permit "forever," "no expiration date," "from now on indefinitely . . ."—*(bis auf weiteres)*,‡ but I hadn't managed this, and every three months I waited in fear and trembling to receive the "yellow ticket"; never with confidence, but on the contrary, always prepared not only for refusal, but even for deportation . . . There had already been such cases.

I don't know if it was from the tarragon wine or the hopeless anxiety before going to the *Polizeipräsidium*, but I fell asleep immediately.

And suddenly it was as if something bumped me; I remembered something through my sleep—I remembered the telephone, Elya, El'za, Frau Karus, the geshpenst—

I got up, turned on the lights, and went to the Spider; from the Spider my eyes moved along the threads and I suddenly saw—way back in the "buffoon's corner," by the London-Svyatopolk-Mirsky pipe—the geshpenst:

the geshpenst was hanging on a thread.

#Police Headquarters
**personal identity card
‡until further notice

And I recalled clearly how on Easter I had crawled onto a chair and with a small pair of scissors had cut down the nephew of the little *Untergrundick* and given him to Elya.

But the "nephew," although he also had a tail and was swarthy, wasn't the geshpenst at all! What sort of geshpenst had Elya's father found in her toy box among the little ribbons, Christmas tree stars, and sundry sugar angels? And what geshpenst had Elya shown him, saying that Remersdorf had given it to her for Easter? I gave Elya the "nephew"! Perhaps Elya's father mistook the "nephew" for the geshpenst—after all, he was also swarthy, had a tail, and his eye was like a little lantern!—even Elya herself—But Frau Karus had gone there and said: "Remersdorf didn't give her the geshpenst!"

I glanced again at the Spider, at his sacrificial threads—the geshpenst hung on a thread, but the "nephew" wasn't there—

of course, I had cut down the "nephew" that time and given him to Elya, but Elya had passed him off as the geshpenst!

Again I turned off the lights. I lay down.

But I couldn't fall asleep anymore.

What have I done? I've slandered her. "You will not move from that spot till you've confessed!" But I had actually given him to her. "No, Remersdorf didn't give him to her." Then it must be she stole it. Elya "stole" the geshpenst, or the "nephew"—what's the difference; it was the one I had given her as a present. Of course, when you deal like that with an adult, when you slander him—but we've grown used to everything; of course it's unpleasant, but after all, from a grown up you can expect anything, even the most outrageous act—even slander, the most outrag . . . but Elya—she's only counted ten springs in her life, and to have such a black shadow on her soul from now on—slander! And what's more, she didn't ask me; I crawled up on the chair myself, cut down the "nephew" with a little pair of scissors, and gave him to her. I saw how much she liked him, and she carried him home in her arms like a kitten, like Peter, kitty-kitty. And then I denied I had given him to her. "Remersdorf didn't give him away." Well, then it must be she stole it. How could I have done that . . . a grown up . . . Now she'll no longer be faced with a toy, but a real geshpenst, the most terrible of monsters, the kind you only see in your dreams. Or—what about the next time someone actually *does* give you something? Will you have to give a receipt, as if you were accepting laundry, a receipt that this is a present, or else they might—and you can always expect this!—say: "I didn't give it away, she stole it"? No, no, it would be better to avoid people altogether, to hide somewhere. "I didn't give it away. How is it then—?"

After I had imagined all this, not only couldn't I fall asleep—or even find a place for myself; I couldn't even lie comfortably, and kept tossing from side to side.

73

I lit a match and looked at the clock—two o'clock.

Two o'clock! Frau Karus had left at eight; six hours must have passed since the girl entered the darkness of her first burning, black feeling—of slander.

But what can I do?

I suddenly asked myself:

"How would Baltrushaitis act?"

Or was it because Baltrushaitis was a Lithuanian, the gloomiest and most silent—

"Baltrushaitis would, despite it being nighttime, go to Kirchstrasse, where Elya lives . . ."

I stopped.

"But how would I get into the apartment? Berlin isn't Moscow or Petersburg. Now in Moscow or Petersburg you can ring the doorman at any time of night, and the doorman will open up; of course, you give him a tip, and ring the apartment, wake up the father—it can't be helped!—and tell him everything, carefully explaining about the geshpenst, that the 'nephew' is not the geshpenst, and that I did give Elya the 'nephew' but not the geshpenst. And if Elya isn't sleeping, and she probably hasn't fallen asleep with this darkness on her soul, indeed her very first—let's put her mind at ease. But there are no doormen in Berlin, and you can't get into the lobby even by knocking—this is a common occurrence; who hasn't run into trouble by forgetting the key to his apartment!—and even if you whistle under the window, it's still in vain. If this signal, however, had been agreed upon, then they would open the door even at three or four; but without this agreement—why should they? I myself wouldn't open up—if there's someone whistling, he's probably whistling to the neighbors!—that's what I'd think, and that's what everyone would think. Most likely even Baltrushaitis wouldn't be able to do anything; all he could do is wait—"

I don't know how I waited till morning.

I didn't doze for a minute the whole night. Having consoled myself with Baltrushaitis, that is, that even he would be powerless to do anything were he in my place, and considering myself justified in not getting up, and still fidgeting in bed, I started to reconstruct everything from the very beginning, from Easter, when I gave away the "nephew." I now had no doubt that it was the "nephew," but Elya and her father had mistaken him for the geshpenst.

I was the first to arrive at the *Polizeipräsidium*. There were no lines. And I received my yellow ticket without any delay or waiting. But this didn't gladden me a bit! Whereas at such moments I usually felt independent and secure in my legal rights—for three additional months I wouldn't be deported from Berlin, and in a predicament I could always show this yellow ticket.

From there I had to go to register at our Tiergarten police station. I took the city railroad, and it was odd that everything was the same as always—in the cars they were eating sandwiches on which there was not a trace of butter, but between the slices of gray bread there was something greasy and gray— disgusting!—lard. As always, the train was moving very fast, and during the quick stops some people would push their way out of the car, while others would squeeze into the car. The agony of the previous night had receded, but something else tortured me: How would I face Frau Karus, how would I tell her—? I was frightened. I deliberately did everything slowly, to put off the meeting, but it came about very quickly. Completely oblivious, I reached my stop in no time and very quickly approached the police station.

There, with no delays at all, they skillfully pulled a small pink and green card from a little box, checked it, and put it back in the small box: "*Es ist erledigt*" (it's ready)—we may live three more months in peace—for three months we have the right to reside here. How happy I would have been if—

Slowly I walked home.

If I had had the contract with me, I would have stopped by the *Drogerie* and paid the landlord for our apartment—I had had the money since the day before yesterday; as I've already said, Polyakov-Litovtsev dropped in and helped me out. Yes, at any other time there would have been another happy moment—the third: the police, the station, the landlord. Still another month of life! I always wanted so much to live! I felt this especially when the deadline would come to pay for the apartment, but there was nothing to pay with, and you'd wait for a miracle. Of course, anything could happen, and there could be one fine day—why should I close my eyes to it, when no miracle would happen—and then . . . But this time I had the money, I had even dragged it to the police with me, only I didn't have the contract. What a shame! I'd forgotten the contract!

I climbed the stairs to my door even more slowly.

At the door I took out my watch—"Let me see!"— and behind me was Frau Karus; I sensed this and turned around:

In fact, it really was Frau Karus; her expression was unusually solemn—in her hands she held the telephone. It was indeed the teeny toy one, smaller than the smallest Lilliputian match box, nevertheless as important as the Charlottenburg *Schloss* itself!

"Frau Karus," completely crushed, I couldn't find the words.

"She confessed! Elya confessed!"—Frau Karus told me solemnly, in hushed tones.

We went into the apartment together and headed straight to my room.

"Frau Karus," I began in confusion, "the geshpenst—"

"She confessed! I came to her father. But she had already confessed— 'When Remersdorf left the room, I crawled onto a chair, and with a little pair of scissors I cut down the geshpenst.' Tomorrow both of them are coming to ask your pardon and to bring back the geshpenst."

75

"Frau Karus, I gave it to her!"

Frau Karus was shaking her head with displeasure:

"If they start now . . . then at twenty . . ."

"Frau Karus—"

I didn't know what else to say. I realized—no, no matter what, she wouldn't believe me. She thought I wanted to protect the child, and in her opinion that was definitely not the thing to do—"because if they start to drag off geshpensts at ten, then at twenty—"

I took the scissors, crawled onto the chair, and began cutting off of the Spider whatever I chanced on—horses, cows, deer, foxes, frogs, stars. I collected two full boxes.

"Frau Karus, take them to the girls! This is for Elya and this—for El'za. And here are the little slippers!" I remembered Elya liked them very much, and so I cut down the tiny magic red slippers; I also cut down the warm fluffy monkey, bobbing on a slender little thread, "the monkey's for El'za, the little slippers—for Elya."

"Ach!" Frau Karus seemed to blossom all over, "*wunderschön!*" (wonderful)—and her eyes became extraordinarily kind, "wonderful!" She looked at me good-naturedly.

And my heart began to leap—from some kind of sudden freedom. With precisely this look she had lifted from me that blackness—that chain—that night.

"Actually, Frau Karus, you were confused about that geshpenst; the nephew was not the geshpenst, and I made a mistake. I'll show you right now—next to the London-Svyatopolk-Mirsky pipe, over there—he's hanging there on a tiny thread, I saw him during the night!"

Frau Karus squinted—she couldn't see very well.

I looked—he was nowhere to be seen. Next to the London-Svyatopolk-Mirsky pipe there was no geshpenst—the geshpenst had disappeared.

CHRIST'S GODSON

FROM: *Skazki russkogo naroda, skazannye Alexeem Remizovym* (Fairy Tales of the Russian People as Told by Alexey Remizov; Berlin, 1923).

The couple lived in poverty, in such dire need that it was actually impossible to invite anyone to visit. Nevertheless, everyone has his own holy day, and without a holy day life—which is cruel to begin with—would lack all light.

A son was born. He had to be christened, but there was no one to ask to be godparents.

If you're wealthy and have power—everybody comes to you. But to the poor—who is attracted by rags?

There sat Ivan and Marya.

"What shall we do with the child?"

Well, grumbling won't help, either.

A pilgrim was passing through.

"Let's call in the pilgrim; the pilgrim won't refuse!"

But when they looked at his face, it was actually terrifying—his nose was missing and, like death itself, his teeth were bared in a hideous grimace.

"What shall we call the baby?" Marya said, already unhappy.

What choice was there? Only to suffer it—one couldn't very well leave the child unbaptized either.

"Let's call him Job—Job, my godson," replied the pilgrim meekly.

It was clear, he too spoke not joyfully, but with sadness.

Who really knows:

> wherefore and why things happen to a man—why
> you come into this world and everyone flees from you?

So they baptized him; they named the baby Job, as his godfather had said. And they felt sad.

"Let's ask," Ivan said to Marya, "our godfather to stay with us for just a bit."

They turned around, but he was nowhere to be seen—as if he'd never been.

Job grew up and began asking his mother and father where and who his godfather was.

They didn't want to tell—why remember?

They no longer lived in the same way. Things had gotten better, it had become bright and gay in their home—it seemed that good fortune had come with Job.

But Job kept insisting, "Tell me, tell me."

"We were living in poverty," his father said. "No one would visit us, and we couldn't, in good conscience, invite anyone. When you were born, there wasn't even anyone to ask to be a godparent—who would come to such poor people! Some pilgrim agreed. We baptized you, and since that day he's disappeared; we've never seen him again."

"How I would like to see him!" Job dreamed. "On Easter Sunday, when everyone walks from the church exchanging blessings with his godfather, I have no one."

"You stupid little thing," his mother said, "it'd be better to exchange blessings with a dog—your godfather was disgusting!"

At Easter matins Job stood in the church.

Everyone went and exchanged blessings; only he stood and approached no one.

And then someone came up to him—stopped before him.

"Christ is risen, my dear godson!"

"Truly He is risen."

Job rejoiced—he had found his godfather.

His godfather took him by the hand and led him—not out of the church, but inside the church, upwards, through the air—into the heavens.

———————

His mother and father cried—they had lost their son.

They sat at the table to break the Lenten fast. There was no Job; Job had disappeared.

"Did you see our son at matins?"

Everyone said, "We saw him exchange blessings with his godfather, and together they left the church. They were a match for each other—both young, the same age."

"Then it must have been some rogue who took him away—his godfather was disgusting, old; he had no nose."

———————

For a year Job had been gone.

For a year not a thing was heard of him.

The old couple grieved for their son. They couldn't accept it—he had disappeared!

But one must learn to accept misfortune:

> misfortune comes not without reason, just as there is nothing in life
> that is without purpose—both sickness and disasters; only, is there no
> one who knows and will tell, why and wherefore such things exist?

The following year, at the very same Easter matins, as people were about to go and exchange blessings, Job, as if awakened from a dream, was standing right there, next to the pillar, in the same place he had stood before.

The mass ended. Job went home.

"Christ is risen, my parents!"

When the old couple looked—they saw Job, their son.

"Truly He is risen!"

They burst into tears—they hadn't expected, hadn't hoped for him.

"Truly He is risen!"

They began to question him. Where had he been? Where had he vanished to? And for a whole year!

"It wasn't a year; only three hours. And tomorrow I'm going again."
"But where will you be going?"
"To Mark, the rich man. I must bring him a money box from my god-father. You see, I found my godfather, and it's my godfather I've been with."
Early, even before the sun had risen, Job began to take his leave.
But they wouldn't let him:
"Spend just one little day with us!"
He left.

Job went to Mark, the rich man.
Mark was sitting at the window, rocking his parents in a cradle. They were old and couldn't walk.
"Mark, take this money box, feed your parents. This money is for bread for you."
"I have no need of gold—the rich will take it from me, the courts will punish me."
Mark returned the money to Job.
And Job left that poor one—Mark, the rich man.

Job went along the road.
Some people were stacking wood.
"God help you, good people!"
"Oh, dear little brother, we have no mittens on our hands and, as you can see, we're without boots; we're naked and barefoot, our clothes are torn all over and our strength is gone from hunger. Ask the Lord God, will we suffer long?"

Job went further.
Some women were drawing water—from one well into another they poured the water with buckets.
"God help you, good people!"
"Oh, dear little brother, the skin has peeled off our hands, we're frozen. Ask the Lord God, will we suffer long?"

Job went further.

A house stood there; under its corner—an old woman. The old woman was holding the house up on her shoulders.

"God help you, good person!"

"Oh, dear little brother, it's broken my whole back. I hold this weight day after day all by myself. Ask the Lord God, will I suffer long?"

Job went farther.

A pike was lying on the road—how its eyes bulged, its mouth gaped! Job took pity on the pike.

The pike spoke to him:

"Oh, dear little brother, I cannot go without water, and I so want to swim! I can't live on land. Ask the Lord God, will I suffer long?"

Job came to a cave.

"Good day, godfather! I almost didn't find you."

"But where have you been?"

"I've come from Mark, the rich man."

"You've crossed the whole globe."

"Mark did not take the gold; the rich, he said, would take it from him, the courts would punish him."

"Take him some bread."

"And while I was traveling, I came across some people; they were stacking wood—they suffered greatly, their clothes were torn, and they were hungry."

"Let them stack forever; why did they steal the wood? By their offense, by their slander, by their callous hearts they took the warmth from the hearts of others."

"I met some women; they were pouring water from one well into another. They were frozen."

"Let them pour forever. Why did they thin the milk with water? They cheated, they deceived the hearts of others!"

"I also saw a pike; the pike was lying on the road. It was cracked all over, from thirst its mouth gaped, and it begged for the sea."

"Greedy, cruel, let it spit out forty ships! Then it can go to the sea!"

Job wished to go right away and repeat the words of his godfather to all those tortured ones. They awaited him, there on the road.

"My kind godson," the godfather stopped him, "the Tsar beyond the Mountains has a daughter, the tsarevna Magdalene; take Magdalene for your wife. I myself will marry you."

80

Job took his leave and went from the cave back along that very same road.

Job came to the pike.
It rejoiced:
"Well, what am I to do, dear little brother?"
"If you spit out the forty ships, you will be free in the sea!"
The pike spit out ship after ship—all forty ships, and once more swam in his sea.

Job came to the old woman, who was holding the house on her shoulders.
"Well, what am I to do, dear little brother?"
"Suffer forever."
The old woman began to cry:
"—forever, how long is that?"

Job came to those who were pouring water from one well into another.
"Well, what are we to do, little brother?"
"Suffer forever."
The unfortunate ones began to tremble:
"—forever, and will there be no end?"

Job came to those who were stacking wood, hungry, with their clothes torn.
"Well, what are we to do, dear little brother?"
"Suffer forever."
And their arms fell to their sides:
"—forever."

Job came to Mark, the rich man.
"Mark, here is some bread for you."

"I don't want it; I don't need it—my parents have died."
Job put the bread on the table for the poor one—Mark, the rich man.

His mother and father were hurt. Their son didn't live with them.
"We didn't raise you so that we'd never see you at home!" And they were
very sad:
"There won't even be anyone to close our eyes."
A pilgrim, like his godfather, Job traveled a difficult path:
    there's so much joy in the world, and yet
    in the world just as much unendurable torture.
Can it be there is no end?
Suffering—forever?
And is there no power that can free us?

Job spoke to his father and mother:
"The Tsar beyond the Mountains has a daughter, Magdalene. My god-
father has betrothed me to Magdalene."
His father and mother cried out in horror:
"To Magdalene! She lies rotting, terrible to look at; they even give her food
through the window—a stench rises from her."
Job did not listen.
He did not heed their words:
"Magdalene will be my wife."

Job asked:
"May I see the tsarevna?"
"Oh, my dear little brother," the tsaritsa said, "you cannot go to her—a
stench rises from her."
"Never mind, let me—I am taking her as my betrothed."
"How can you take her!" the mother wept, "the unfortunate one."
Job went into the tsarevna's room.
The tsarevna lay there—forever without hope.
She raised her eyes hopelessly.
No one had ever yet asked for her, and in her heart all pleadings were
covered with scabs.
"Arise, Magdalene, it is I, Job, your betrothed!"

And Job took her by the right hand, like a bride.
Suddenly, like a fire, a flame flashed hotly.
Magdalene arose, immaculate as a bride.

On Ascension Day Job led his bride into the church.
There his godfather married them—Job and Magdalene.
And he led them—not out of the church, but inside the church, upward,
through the air—into the heavens.

FAITH IN NIKOLAY

FROM: *Zveno* (The Link, no. 2; Paris, 1928).

Before Baty there was in Rus' a certain Nikolay: Nikolay "the Wet."
In Kiev, at St. Sophia's, on the inner balcony (the one set aside for the choir), stands this image: Nikolay enveloped in a green chasuble, as green as the stained glass of St. Nicolas in the Chartres Cathedral.
During the transfer of the sacred remains of St. Nikolay from Lycian Myra to Bari, they were carried across the sea, and his grace permeated the entire world. At both ends of the earth a miracle occurred: in Nantes the Prince of Bretagne (the boy Conan) was miraculously healed, and on the Dnieper a dear little boy, Vanya, began to recover.
The father of Conan was Alain Fergean,
the second Duke of Bretagne from the
House of Cornwall, his mother Hermangard;
the Abbey of St. Nicolas is in Anges, one of
the most revered holy places in Western
France. The parents of Conan took a
vow to go to this Abbey and consecrate themselves
and their children to St. Nicolas.
Only a miracle could save Conan.
And, when the name of St. Nicolas was
spoken over the dying boy, the fading
"three-thousand-year old" eyes of the
Celtic boy suddenly sparkled, and he
began to speak of the sea. He told of
how he was gathering little cockleshells
on the shore and that an old man

approached him, took his hand,
and led him across the waves,
and that the waves sprinkled his face . . .

While his mother was sailing across the Dnieper, she dozed off; at that moment Vanya fell into the water and sank to the bottom. She returned home without having recovered him. But that night they saw an old man walking on the water near the St. Sophia side, and at his feet the river bottom rose up; he stooped and caught a small boy, took him into his arms, and carried him to the shore. He brought him to St. Sophia itself, and laid him on the inner balcony therein—it was warm there. Vanya came to and gulped the air like a tiny fish.

This was the first miracle in Rus'—the one of Nikolay "the Wet."

And the very same Nikolay, in a chasuble of seaweed, appeared on Lake Il'men' on the Island of Lipno. The water from this icon healed Mstislav, the son of Vladimir Monomakh. The icon was placed in Novgorod in the church on the *dvor* [estate] of Mstislav's grandfather Yaroslav, and around the icon was engraved the miracle of Mstislav, and it was called Nikolay Dvorishchensky or Lipinsky.

After Baty there were three Nikolays in Rus': Nikolay Mozhaysky, Nikolay Zaraysky, and Nikolay Velikoretsky.

And all the other Nikolays—there isn't a corner of Russia where his image does not exist—all the innumerable Nikolays, named after the place of their first visitation—Nikolay of the Seven Little Meadows, Nikolay of the Flood, or of the Drought; or for their miraculous powers of intercession—Nikolay of the Matchmakers, Nikolay of the Warriors; or the place where they dwelt— be it a street, a settlement, a district, a town, a region—Nikolay Myasnitsky, Nikolay Baturinsky, Nikolay Ipatovsky, Nikolay Korel'sky, all of them are either Mozhaysky, or Zaraysky, or Velikoretsky.

In these three forms, these three icons, Nikolay appeared in Russia:
as the leader and builder of the Russian lands—
the terrifying Nikolay Mozhaysky; as a spiritual mentor
and miracle worker—the winged Nikolay Zaraysky; as a man
of pity and forgiveness, before whom one was not at all
terrified, but rather ashamed—the kind Nikolay Velikoretsky.

The most widespread purely Russian image of Nikolay (whose representation has very little, if almost nothing at all, in common with the Nikolay of Lycian Myra) is the carved "Nikolay Mozhaysky": a heavy-set, stern, terrifying man, standing rigidly, in one hand a sword, in the other a tiny church surrounded by a wall—a kremlin. Five perpetual icon lamps stand before him. The gunners had seen him on the outskirts of Kazan' during the night of the Taking of Kazan', and he appeared to Yermak in the Siberian Kingdom. In the same form he stood at the Gates of Nikolay in Moscow, guarding the Russian heart—the Kremlin. Napoleon, abandoning Moscow, ordered these gates torn down and the tower blown up; only a pile of bricks remained! But he wasn't touched, and his lantern was unbroken. Recently, on the anniversary of May Day, draped with all kinds of red rags, it gave forth such a gigantic flame that everything was burned away in a flash, not one little banner remained, no "Internationale," as if they'd never existed. All the tsars, "the great lords," from Tsar Ivan and even Peter, all would go to bow before him in Mozhaysk.

The same one with the sword and kremlin, Mozhaysky, under the name "Radonsky," stands in the Church of Nikolay Ugresh outside Moscow. He appeared to Dmitry Donskoy before Kulikovo. And at the sentry posts of the outlying monasteries, Mozhaysky is everywhere; only there he is called "Nikolay of the Warriors." All of Siberia pays homage to Mozhaysky, the Muscovite, his lips stained with the blood of martyrs to the Russian God.

By order of the VIIIth Ecumenical Council, carved depictions of saints were forbidden ("they're worshipping sorcerers"), and the Synod Edict of 1723 decreed the removal of all carved and "sitting" images. Many such images were taken out of the Russian churches, but he was not touched.

Another Nikolay, brought from Korsun' from the Church of the Apostle Jacob as a miraculous icon, was "Nikolay Zaraysky." Like the Nikolay of Lycian Myra, he is holding his hands in a position of blessing and carries a Gospel. Since his hands are not pressed to his chest, but extended, and because of the way they raise the front piece of his chasuble (*philoni*), he seems to have wings. Framing the image are his miraculous deeds, and in the center—the expulsion of a demon from a well. His fame extends from the time of Baty—from the story of Princess Yevpraksiya of Ryazan', who at the news of the death of her husband threw herself and her son from a turret. But his highest glorification came during the Troubled Times. Enveloped in a metal setting and a chasuble—a gift from Vasily Shuysky—he stares out, like a spectre; and it is both terrifying and awe inspiring to look upon him, the Miracle Worker.

The third Nikolay is found in Vyatka—"Nikolay Velikoretsky." A half-length portrait, with his arms close to his body, he is depicted in a pose of blessing, holding a Gospel. This one is more of an ordinary human being, a "supernumerary priest," with the face of a simple man, a "peasant," with miracle-working eyes, in the depths of which all man's misfortunes and uncertain fate disappear and from which flows the warm light of compassion—Nikolay "the Kind." The favorite image of Ivan the Terrible, who frequently stayed in Moscow, it was brought from Vyatka. A copy of it is next to Vasily Blazhenny in the Pokrovsky Cathedral. Yet it was called neither the Pokrovsky Cathedral icon nor the Vasily Blazhenny icon, but by the beloved name Nikolay Velikoretsky.

Every Nikolay has his own area of intercession and each his own prayer:

> The Terrible Nikolay Mozhaysky allows no
> offense to the Russian land and rewards the
> just, while punishing the guilty;

the winged Nikolay Zaraysky grants
whatever miracle is requested of him;
the kind Nikolay Velikoretsky will not turn you away,
even the lowliest; he accepts and comforts all.
                    Mikola, Mikola the Holy One—
                    Mozhaysky, Zaraysky,
                    Traverser of Seas,
                    Confessor of Lands.
                    Even the pagan hordes
                    know Mikola,
                    and offer to Mikola
                    bright candles of wax,
                    on the eve of the honey harvest.
                    Glory to him, the Light,
                    glory to him—and strength
                    throughout all his lands,
                    throughout the whole Universe—
                    glory now and forever,
                                Amen!
In this manner children used to praise Nikolay on St. Nikolay's Day, as we
now praise Christ's birth on Christmas.

There was circulated in Rus' a saint's life of Nikolay the Miracle Worker,
which is not found in any *Minei*, in Greek or in Latin. Into Russia came the
story of the Syrian saint's life "Nikolay the Wanderer," connected with the
cult of the Archangel Michael. In this most remarkable saint's life the three
images of Nikolay—Mozhaysky, Zaraysky, and Velikoretsky—merge.

This saint's life—"Nikolay the Wanderer"—was the cornerstone of the
Russian belief in the miraculous image of Nikolay.

Little was known in Rus' from the canonical saints' lives already recorded
in books. The "consecration" of Ariah was undoubtedly known, because in
the Patriarchal Sacristy there is preserved a white omophorin with red
tassels, taken from the Holy One at Nicea after his consecration; the miracle
of Vasily (*Thauma de Basilio adolescente*)—the blind gave praise to this miracle;
the deliverance from death of three unjustly condemned military leaders
(*Praxis de stratilatis*); the miracle of the three sisters, endowed with gifts by
Nikolay, (*Praxis de tribus filiabus*)—this was especially praised by Thomas
Aquinas and is beloved by us in the town of Moscow, as depicted in the icon
of Nikolay Gostunsky which was painted during the reign of Ivan the Great,
and there wasn't a single bride in Moscow who wouldn't go to pray to
"Nikolay of the Matchmakers"; the miracle of the rug (*Thauma de stromate*), as
evidence of the unusual kindness of the Holy One toward the ultimate

sacrifice of the poor; the miracle of the three icons (*Thauma de patriarcha*): these icons were preserved in the Great Uspensky Cathedral—the Savior, the Mother of God, and Nikolay, and according to legend the Patriarch of Tsar'grad called Nikolay "the Holy One of the Peasants," i.e., of lower-class origins—a miracle especially favored by Ivan the Terrible; the miracle of the three merchants "drowned by pagans" (*Thauma de tribus Christianis*)—a supernatural tale which disregards all physical laws.

More often, local miracles were mentioned—all kinds of "new intercessions," i.e., cures (according to Russian custom, to intercede and to heal are one and the same), or such miracles as were immortalized by the monastic iconographers. All who have been to the Tereben'sky Monastery (the settlement of Terebeni in the District of Vyshnevolotsk), can, of course, recall the miraculously vivid *letopis'* on the walls of the Cathedral:

1657—the miraculous deliverance from fire of the Cathedral, in which stood the ancient miracle-working icon of the Holy One—Nikolay;

1664—a repetition of the same miracle;

1705—the miraculous cure of a woman from an eye disease;

1707—the miraculous cure of a master tailor, who had been punished by a disabling ailment for robbery and who had repented;

1709—the cure of the son of a military leader of Ustyuk, who had suffered from seizures;

1712—the Holy One Nikolay returned to her home a maiden who had been missing for a long time;

1802—the miraculous cure of Mme Glikeriya Fyodorovna Kozlyanova's peasants of the settlement of Pkhov of their illness;

1804—the landowner Ruminov from Bezhetsk is punished, because during a Bezhetsk religious procession in the city of Bezhetsk he uttered insolent and vile words and, upon his repentance, was cured in full view of everyone;

1815—the cure of a person with weakened hands and legs in the city of Bezhetsk on the river Mologa.

However, more than any of the recorded miracles and "intercessions," the Russian land abounded in miraculous fairytales about Nikolay—tales which sweetly scented and illuminated that land with their warmth, compassion, and grace. This faith in Nikolay entered the soul of the Russian people—they were born into this world with it, and the triple image of Nikolay has merged into the one image of their fate—

Nikolay still walks among the groves—

Glory to him.

He still seeks the unfulfilled—

Glory to him.

That which is unfulfilled, unredeemed—

Glory to him.

87

Nikolay still wishes to fulfill—

Glory to him.

And he whom we have glorified, blessings to him—

Glory to him.

To whomever he appears, that one's plea will come true—

Glory to him.

It will soon come true; it will not be forgotten—

Glory to him.

And to understand to what extent this faith was still strong and relied upon in Russia—the genuine Russian faith in Nikolay—I will relate one recent occurrence in Moscow, to which I myself was an involuntary witness.

There lived in Moscow a contractor named Myslin.[3] Or, as the simple people, the servants and janitors, called him, "Smyslin."[4] He also ran a little shop, a food store; he was a merchant. In height, he was close to Peter the Great; but his stomach bulged, it stuck out of its own accord, like an iron beneath his floor-length frock coat. The growth on his face was sparse, like a mammoth's, but his head was slicked down; he had the hair of a horse, streaked with gray, cut as if a bowl had been put on his head. He revered the past, was a church elder and a big wheeler-dealer, this Smyslin. He had all sorts of business deals with his neighbor. His neighbor was the factory owner Lev Semyonych or, as Myslin called him in the Russian way, Lyon[5] Silenych;[6] in appearance he was, well, like Myslin, only the exact opposite—thin, short, a massive beard, but with a head as bald as a little knee. And there was a deep friendship between them. Lev Semyonych captivated Myslin with his efficiency and orderliness. There was always an accurate inventory and never any substitutions, and everything would be accomplished exactly as he promised; he was agreeable, not a procrastinator; he had a great understanding of business affairs, loved his work, and it was a pleasure to do business with such a fellow. He was, moreover, a good person. Myslin was so taken with his neighbor that he held him up to everyone as an example, and he always managed to mention his neighbor, even when it was inappropriate. There was only one misfortune: Lev Semyonych was a Jew.

What if, let us say, Myslin had on his soul all sorts of evil deeds? What if he still had some things to repent, and if (although approaching the end of his life), feeling no embarrassment before his grown sons and the memory of his late wife, he married again—a really young little thing—and was so stupified by this event that he talked to everyone only of his marriage—how shameful!—praising the youth of his wife or, as he himself expressed it, "Nastya— she's like the Priestly gates!" But what if, even in his fallen obduracy, he still

88

kept in mind and firmly believed that he could not approach death without repentance (he was, after all, a church elder, and summoning the priest for any whim at all would not cost him anything), and besides he had put things in order for his soul beforehand (he had had his name entered in the Book of Prayers in Memory of the Dead and in the Church)? And what then if he still believed that, even if he misbehaved, God would help him in these matters and would give him another chance, and he—Myslin's soul—would find a little place in the heavenly kingdom (they'd set aside some corner in the fresh air with the righteous men for him to rest in peace)? Whereas here we have Lev Semyonych. He leads a conscientious life and doesn't bother with these inanities. His sons work with him in the business, and he provides for his daughters, and his home is clean, completely orderly; yet his place in the next world is clear—he'll go to hell. No matter what, to hell—in the very hottest part he'll be forced to collect burning cowberries with his bare hands or, sunk in a Moscow river ice hole, he'll catch frogs with his mouth for the devils.

But what if, let's say, God forbid, Myslin dies without absolution? And, what's more, what if he's deceived by his sons who don't fulfill his wishes about his soul, and he has to make do with Tartarus? And they would shut him up to boil in a pitch pot—again, it still won't be at all like the place where Lev Semyonych must go, because he, Myslin, was baptized, and nowhere in the Scriptures does it say anything about co-mingling. It says, "They are many abodes," but it could be one will be forced to suffer in solitude and will never share a word in one's misfortune with a companion.

According to the law, that's what must happen. Myslin believed in the law and had no doubt about it. It wasn't that he refused to be reconciled to his fate, but that he was looking for whatever means his faith might provide by which even the Jew Lev Semyonych might find a place in the heavenly kingdom. And even if both of them were destined for pitch-black hell, they would at least be able to crawl into one pot to boil together.

Precisely here that Russian faith—that faith in Nikolay—who is not exactly above the law, but . . . who can himself, if you will, make certain accommodations in the law, and in whom one cannot help but believe—throbbed through Myslin's entire being, from his mammoth head to the coal iron of his gluttonous belly.

I had to go and see Lev Semyonych about some matter or other. I found Myslin there. I had met him several times at Lev Semyonych's, but this time his unusual solemnity amazed me—he didn't even notice me.

"Lev Semyonych," Myslin said, "I understand that you, as a Jew, will not acknowledge Christ—that's as it should be," and, craning his mammothlike head while sucking in the whole of his coal iron tummy, he said: "Lev Semyonych, I understand, but . . . how about Nikolay the Intercessor . . .?"

JACOB BETRAYED: A BELOVED MOSCOW LEGEND[a]

FROM: *The Link;* no. 5 (Paris, 1928)

In Constantinople, during the reign of Empress Irina, there lived a photographer named Jacob. Before taking up photography, Jacob had had many varied professions. It wasn't that all of his jobs failed, but that they had their own destined lengths of existence; when its time approached, each job would stop dead. So what could one do but start another?

Jacob got a job in a factory in Alexandria and had just begun to settle in when a friend wrote from Rome: "Come here, Yasha, there's a place in the technical section." Jacob was a long time in deciding, but his friend described life in Rome so insistently and temptingly that he couldn't argue. So Jacob moved from Alexandria to Rome. And everything was fine—even the job "in the technical section" was good. But an order was issued: check the ranks of workers to see that each definitely held a Roman passport, and whoever didn't should be purged. Jacob had an Alexandrian passport, and so they removed him. Jacob moved back to Constantinople, looked around for a new job, passed the driver's test, and opened a driving school in partnership with a certain Greek. At first things went very smoothly. There were lots of students, and even a captive Saracen Aga signed up. But then for some reason everything just fell apart, and gradually it all came to nought. The school had to be closed, and they demanded such a tax that he hadn't the slightest idea how or when he could pay it. Jacob undertook to raise chickens just outside Constantinople. He established an egg factory and sold chicks. But somehow

[a] In the tenth and eleventh centuries in Byzantium there were three well-known Greek legends on the theme "a trust betrayed," in which thieves plunder property under the protection of the icon of a saint: *De imagine Nicolai in Africa* (the saint intercedes for the Saracens under his protection), *De pastore fure* (a saint makes a poor shepherd, who has robbed a lowly monk guarding a chapel, see the error of his ways), *De imagine cruenta* (in which the purity of the monastic life is revealed to overly conceited monks through a deception). In the twelfth century there appeared simultaneously in France and in Russia a legend on the theme "guarantee, fraud, punishment." In France it was called *Juif volé* (a Christian deceives a Jew); in Russia, "Concerning a Polovtsian, Who Was Given Bail by a Certain Christian, and His Atonement to Saint Nikolay for His Deeds: (the pagan deceives the Christian)." From the collections *Legenda aurea*, *Jacobus de Voragine* and *Speculum historiale*, *Vincent de Beauvais*, the legend of the defrauded Jew evolved in the fifteenth century into a miracle: *Miracle de Monseigneur saint Nicolas d'un juif prêta cent écus à un chrétien à XVIII personnages*. The very same legend was circulated from the fifteenth century in Russia as "The Miracle of Saint Nikolay Concerning the Money Lent by a Jew to a Certain Christian" and became, in Moscow, a miracle as beloved as the miracles of "the carpet," "the three icons," and "the three merchants." But they forgot about the "Polovtsian"; and, in fact, what kind of moral could that story possibly hold—a pagan, not believing in the icon before which he was forced to swear, after having taken such an oath, deceived his persecutors? "The Polovtsian" is interesting as an intrusion of the image of Nikolay into the chivalric world and as the first appearance of the image of "Nikolay Mozhaysky," the leader and defender of the Russian land before Baty.

the eggs failed, too—instead of chicks, God only knows what hatched, something like flying mice, and no one would buy them. He gave up the chickens and took up rabbits. Everything was going well, but again something happened: either he had overfed them, or they didn't eat enough—all the rabbits died; only tails and paws were left. For half a year Jacob sold foxes; he would have sold every last one, but there were a lot of middlemen, and each tried to take advantage just a little. So they pushed the foxes to such a price that for the same amount one could buy a live elephant. Jacob put his foxes in mothballs until a better time and went to learn photography from the renowned Byzantine photographer Agapit.

Agapit was a sensible and conscientious teacher. He taught Jacob to photograph all types of landscapes and busts and graduated him with a diploma, bestowing the title Master of Photography.

Jacob opened his studio—at first a small one, to take snapshots for passports—and really filled the orders quickly. All was going well. He moved into a larger building on a busy street, photographed the most famous Byzantine poets and musicians, exhibited them in the shop window, and became famous himself. He pulled the foxes out of mothballs and made a coat for his wife for New Year's, and from the leftovers he decked out all his children—some in the paws, and others in the tails.

His teacher Agapit once dropped in on Jacob for a cup of tea and mentioned, in passing, that his business was doing poorly and that if Jacob would lend him a hundred francs he would be very grateful. That he would repay the money on time, Jacob had no doubt—during his studies Jacob had seen and was still aware of Agapit's genuine piety and reverence for the blessed saints, most of all for Nikolay:

"As Nikolay is my witness."

Jacob had actually heard a great deal about the many miracles surrounding Nikolay while studying under Agapit. So now, when Agapit swore on Nikolay, he trusted him and had no doubt that Agapit would keep his word and not deceive him.

"Agapit Semyonych, here's your hundred francs!" Jacob placed one hundred paper notes before Agapit.

Agapit put the money in his pocket, drank his tea, and with that the affair was concluded.

And so time passed, unnoticed in the flurry of business. And just as everything usually began well for Jacob and was then followed by some disaster, so it was with the photography. All the negatives he had in stock, down to the last one, were somehow scratched; and, as had once happened with the eggs, problems began to crop up with the pictures. He would photograph a pleasant face, but when it was developed—he'd be ashamed to show it. The photos would turn out with all sorts of flattened skulls and outrageous noses; the clients were offended. It was very difficult for Jacob—he had to replace his entire inventory and take the materials on credit.

When Agapit's due date approached, Jacob waited. Right now was a most opportune time for him to be reimbursed.

Agapit not only did not come with his payment, nor contact Jacob, but he began to avoid him. He'd see him on the street, dash to the other side, and walk by, turning away as if looking for a house number. Jacob had to go to Agapit himself. Perhaps he forgot? Everyone forgets; sometimes even the right word pops out of one's memory. The more so with money!

But Agapit said:

"A hundred francs! Excuse me—I gave them back to you."

Jacob didn't even manage to ask "when," since the other had already named the date.

This greatly grieved Jacob. He couldn't understand. How was it possible that such an accurate man as he had always known Agapit to be, a religious man—how could he so easily transgress his faith? Indeed, he had sworn! He had called to witness a saint, in whom he had faith and whom he venerated. Jacob's heart was crushed; everything in him began to throb—he felt battered by thousands of fists. No, such people must learn a lesson—that there's justice in this world, and a swindler must be shamed and punished!

Jacob took his complaint to court.

But Agapit thought to himself: so what? There isn't any receipt, and what of the oath? Jacob is of another faith; the promise of Paradise isn't offered to him, and I won't be faced with answering for him in the next world. Besides, what's a hundred francs to Jacob? His business is good. Why, he had a fox coat made for his wife, and who doesn't know what the price of fox is now—as much as a live elephant! Even all his children are decked out with little tails and paws—that isn't just for advertising, they're not given away free of charge. And besides, even if it were so pressing, and I really ought to give him the hundred francs—because he had to make an urgent payment or something—he'd get along anyway; he'd be helped, he's not like us; a person like Jacob, such a skillful master, isn't just ignored. Well, even if—we're all human, and every man can be either an angel or a scoundrel!—even if no one helps him, he can still get himself out of a jam. No matter what life may have just dealt him—one minute it throws him down, he gets up; the next it turns him upside down, he rights himself. Jacob won't fail, and these hundred francs mean nothing to him; whereas I, Agapit, could really use them right now. Business is going poorly.

———————

On the appointed day Agapit and Jacob were summoned to court.

Agapit testified that he had repaid the money, a hundred francs. Jacob said he had not. But he could not produce a receipt, none at all. Why, he was asked, was there no receipt? Jacob said, because he had trusted Agapit even without a receipt. He had trusted him because Agapit had called Nikolay to witness—Agapit was a pious man and had faith in and reverence for the saint, and his faith was stronger and more reliable than any receipt; how could he not trust him! The court said, "Bring in the icon of Nikolay the Miracle Worker, and let Agapit swear that he repaid Jacob—and we will believe him."

They brought in the image and set it down. All awaited the outcome. Would Agapit refuse, or not? Who was right—Agapit or Jacob? Agapit did not refuse. He was ready to swear three times over.

Agapit had with him his portfolio. In the portfolio with the finished photographs and photographic plates were two hundred-franc paper notes. While standing before the icon to swear, he addressed Jacob:

"Colleague, take my portfolio, as it is inconvenient for me to hold it right now."

Jacob took the portfolio from Agapit.

Agapit, raising his hand to make the sign of the cross, swore—he had repaid the amount of one hundred francs in paper notes to Jacob, and had added a hundred in recompense for his trust.

Well, what can one say? Who's right? The matter was clear.

A decision was rendered—Jacob must not demand the amount of one hundred francs from Agapit, and must pay the court costs.

Jacob, returning the portfolio to Agapit—"Hold your own things!"—from outrage and bitterness, could not find words to express his feelings. "Can this be so? If it's man's nature to be unjust, I guess it really is possible that a man can do that over there"—and he pointed to the image and then upward—"and up there it would remain unpunished? Will Agapit be pardoned? What about the saint, in whose name Agapit swore? Can it be he'll ignore this offense and not intercede?"

And humbly taking from his wallet the amount he was ordered to pay the court, he gave it to the bailiff and walked out behind Agapit.

Court was adjourned. With that, the matter was ended.

With his portfolio under his arm, feeling self-satisfied, Agapit walked out of the court. He walked out with honor. Right or wrong, success does reassure one. Even if you're nothing, publicly it will be said of you that you're something—indeed, you'll feel, thank God, like you're something. Having grown a head taller, Agapit walked along the street and everyone stepped aside for him. In a moment he'd jump on the bus and then be home. If only the bus would come sooner!

Agapit looked back. How crushed Jacob looked, as he trudged along, and how the poor man had fallen behind, although they'd left together! But who was that? Some monk; no, he's wearing a judge's robes, a judge was helping him along. It seemed to Agapit that this monk or judge raised his hand and threatened him. And he lost all his enthusiasm. "Threaten me!" he said angrily, "go ahead, threaten me!" and began to hurry on. Perhaps it would have been better to wait there, but for some reason he went on; besides, it wasn't very far to the next bus stop. Again he looked back—but the same two were pursuing him, and Jacob was not at all as weak as before, while this judge, it was now clear, was an old man. He leaned over and was saying something, advising Jacob—"Complain?" "It wouldn't do any good!"—and again he raised his arm and threatened Agapit.

And, as if he'd been hit in the head, Agapit rushed across the street—over there the bus was coming; if only he could manage to reach it! Suddenly he felt as if some blind force was pushing him on the shoulder. He made an enormous effort to pull away, but couldn't. He fell on his back, saw before his very nose a metal bumper, and simply said to himself, "The end!" And it was indeed his end.

People shouted:

"The photographer Agapit has fallen under a car!"

The car stopped.

They dragged Agapit from underneath—no signs of life, dead!—and laid him on the sidewalk. The torn portfolio lay beside him, and from it stuck out photographs and photographic plates and two hundred-franc notes.

Jacob approached the scene.

"Here's your money!" they said to him. "We all came from the court; we all know—the swindler has been punished."

But Jacob didn't take it—he didn't need this money.

"If it was the saint in whose name Agapit swore, if it was Nikolay who punished him this way for me—because he deceived a man!—then let him resurrect Agapit, God be with him!"

And as soon as Jacob said, "God be with him!" Agapit moved, wiped his face with his hand, and stood on his feet. At this, everyone moved away.

Only Jacob remained.

When he saw Jacob and the crowd looking at him, Agapit understood everything.

"Here's your money," he said to Jacob, "take it with you!" And he bent down to pick up his portfolio.

But Jacob remained silent and the crowd pressed even closer, awaiting something.

"I have deceived you."

At that point Jacob took him by his hand and, shielding Agapit with his body, led him out of the crowd.

Jacob took him all the way home. On the way Agapit told him how he'd seen Jacob, and how Jacob had come out of the court betrayed and defenseless, and with him an old man. It was this man who had righted the wrong done to Jacob.

"That was Nikolay."

And from that time the two famous Byzantine photographers, Agapit and Jacob, became great friends. They would drop in on each other for tea and, in difficult times, always helped each other.

NOTES

1. Here Remizov gives a word created from the initials of his "Order"; it is a parody of the Soviet system of bureaucratic abbreviations.
2. Remizov parodies Soviet bureaucracy by using this term.
3. From the Russian *mysl'*, thought.
4. From the Russian *smysl*, sense.
5. From the Russian *lyon*, flax.
6. From the Russian *sil'ny*, strong.

Marina Tsvetaeva (1892–1941)

Marina Ivanovna Tsvetaeva, one of the most gifted and original twentieth-century Russian poets, was born in Moscow. She left the Soviet Union in 1922 and went to Berlin, Prague, and finally Paris. In 1939 she returned to Russia, dying two years later. She has since been "posthumously rehabilitated."[1] Her poetry is spontaneous, impetuous, full of passion and fire. She specialized in unusual and intricate rhymes and complex sound effects. Much of her poetry has a folk inspiration; for example, *Vyorsty* (Milestones; Moscow, 1922), *Tsar'-devitsa: poema skazka* (The Royal Maiden; A Poem-Fairytale; (Berlin, 1922), and *Molodets: skazka* (A Fine Fellow: A Fairytale; Prague, 1924). Among her remarkable books of verse are *Stikhi k Bloku* (Poems to Blok; Berlin, 1922), *Razluka* (Separation; Berlin-Moscow, 1922), *Florentinskie nochi* (Nights in Florence; Berlin, 1922), *Remeslo: kniga stikhov 1921–1922* (Craftsmanship: A Book of Poems 1921–1922; Berlin-Moscow, 1923), *Posle Rossii: stikhi 1922–1925* (After Russia: Poems 1922–1925; Paris, 1928), and *Lebediny stan: stikhi 1917–1921* (The Swans' Camp: Poems 1917–1921; Munich, 1957; published posthumously). She also contributed to Russian literary journals, newspapers, and poetry anthologies.

Marina Tsvetaeva's literary reputation had been established in Russia prior to her emigration to the West. During the Russian Civil War, while her husband, Sergey Efron, fought in the counter-revolutionary army in the south of Russia, she voiced her positive attitudes toward the White movement and the White Guard in *The Swans' Camp*. Her poetic universe is spacious, sonorous, even noisy, filled with mythological heroes. With her impetuosity and her restless *Streben*, she was an incorrigible romantic, surrounded by Hellenic gods and proud heroes, medieval Western European and Russian folkloristic men of great strength and courage, and by the works of Goethe, Byron, Pushkin, Blok, and Anna Akhmatova. She learned her *métier* from the "grand style" of eighteenth-century Russian poetry, as exemplified by Derzhavin (her rhetorical archaisms sound very much like the baroque style of his odes). The popular tradition of the heroic or lyric folksong was another source of poetic inspiration for her; a third influence came from ancient Russian myths and folk motifs, and perhaps from the early poetry of Boris Pasternak, whom she resembles in her romantic temperament, as well as in her expressionistic technique. Her powerful verse has tight syntax, elliptical imagery, a discordant sound pattern, and a rigid metrical scheme. At times, she seems to soar like a "classical eagle" or a "romantic albatross."[2] There is swift movement forward and upward in her poetry, and she intentionally stumbles in her frequent divisions of words into syllables. The dynamics of her verse are of a heroic nature, as are her virtues—the nobility and magnanimity of spirit manifested in her expressions of love, hatred, jealousy, and anguish. Marina Tsvetaeva selected words by shape, sound, and meaning; paronomasia became in her poems an integral part of her thinking, not merely an artistic device. Her blend of binary and ternary meters is unique, and her imposition of hyperprosodic stresses is both daring and beautiful. The gift for verbal creativity and colloquial diction, her ability to exhaust an image, theme, or symbol, and her predilection for the tragic pun are among the most original traits of Tsvetaeva's art. Her rhythmic originality manifests a persistent tendency to create new meters as much as to make new rhythms on the basis of traditional meters.

Marina Tsvetaeva's poetry focuses on the poet herself; her work is profoundly feminine, but this femininity is neither meek nor passive. Her visions of love and life are conveyed through exalted figures from biblical and Christian traditions, through historical or legendary personalities: David and Saint George, Phaedra and Hippolytus, Don Juan and Chevalier Des Grieux (*Manon Lescaut*), Pushkin and Byron, Napoleon and Marina Mniszek. She always viewed life with primitive and barbaric simplicity, using sharp masculine rhymes that torment the ear and the heart alike. Although she is difficult to emulate, some of Andrey Voznesensky's and Joseph Brodsky's poems approximate her emotional intonations, her basic stylistic marks, and her special rebellious fanaticism.

In prose, too, Tsvetaeva proved herself a skilled and original artist; here again she transforms people and events into myths and legends. Love and the cruelty of life are conveyed with equal eloquence in the haunting lines of her prose and her poetry. She left remarkable reminiscences about her childhood, her love for Pushkin, about Andrey Bely, Maximilian Voloshin, Anna Akhmatova, Valery Bryusov, Osip Mandel'shtam, Mikhail Kuzmin, and many other writers of St. Petersburg and Moscow. She also wrote literary evaluations and sketches on art; but she was most effective in creating vivid and concrete portraits of her eminent contemporaries. Like Boris Pasternak's fiction, her prose is poetic; its substance is lyrical, and many thoughts are expressed as striking aphorism.

Today, Marina Tsvetaeva has many fervent admirers, both in the West and in the Soviet Union. Many years ago the German poet Rainer Maria Rilke was delighted by the poignant power of her art and its sense of tragic irony. Unfortunately, before 1939, the Russia émigrés in Paris, seduced by the quiet and restrained "Parisian note" poetry, shunned Tsvetaeva's art and her eccentric personality. Her deepening isolation became intolerable, and, as Zinaida Schakovskoy records in her book *Otrazheniya* (Reflections; Paris,

1975, p. 167), Tsvetaeva felt that toward the end of the 1930's she had no place to go: "The Russian *émigrés* are driving me out . . .." Tsvetaeva committed suicide in Elabuga, near Kazan', in 1941.

NOTES

1. See more about Tsvetaeva in an article by P. Antokol'sky in *Novy mir* no. 4 (1966), and in Simon Karlinsky's book *Marina Cvetaeva: Her Life and Work* (Berkeley: Univ. of California Press, 1966).

2. Yury Ivask, "Poeziya 'staroy' emigratsii," *Russkaya literatura v emigratsii: sbornik statey* pod redaktsiey N. Poltoratskogo (Pittsburgh: Univ. of Pittsburgh Press, 1972), p. 50.

POEMS

The three poems cited below are from *Izbrannoe* (Selected Poems; Moscow: GIKHL, 1961). "My regards to the Russian rye" and "The Knight on the Bridge" were published for the first time in *Posle Rossii: stikhi 1922–1925* (After Russia: Poems 1922–1925).

My regards to the Russian rye,
To the fields, where the peasant woman makes her way . . .
My friend! Rain falls beyond my window.
Troubles and whims — upon my heart.

You're in the drone of rain and misfortunes
As Homer is in the hexameter.
Give me your hand — forever in that world!
Here — both of mine are full.

May 7, 1925

THE TAPER

So close to the Eiffel Tower!
Come on! Climb up!
Yet I say that each of us beheld,
And to this day beholds,

Such sights, that your Paris
Seems homely and dull to us.
"Russia, my Russia,
Why do you burn so brightly?"

June, 1931

98

THE KNIGHT ON THE BRIDGE

Pallid
Guard above the splashing of an age.
Knight, knight
On watch above the river.

(Oh, shall I find there
Rest from lips and hands?!)
Sen-tin-el
At the post of separations.

Oaths, rings . . . Yes,
But as stones into the river—
How many—of us have vanished
In four centuries!

Into the water there's passage
At will.—Let roses bloom!
I'm abandoned—I'll jump!
There's revenge for you!

We'll not surrender
—While yet we have passions!—
Avenging ourselves with bridges.
Spread yourselves widely.

My wings!—Into the mud, the foam
—As onto brocade!
Today I won't cry
For my sins upon bridges!

"From that fateful bridge
Venture—down!"
I'm tall as you,
Knight of Prague.

Is it sweetness or sadness?
Only you can see,
Sentinel knight—
Into that river of days.

September 27, 1923

99

MY PUSHKIN

FROM: *Proza* (Prose; New York: Chekhov, 1953).

In the red room there was a locked bookcase.

But even before I was aware of this locked case, there was something else: there was the painting in mother's bedroom—The Duel.

Snow, the black twigs of small trees; two dark figures lead a third, held under his arms, to a sledge—and still another his back toward us, retreats into the distance. The one being helped—is Pushkin; the one retreating— D'Anthès. D'Anthès had challenged Pushkin to a duel; that is, he'd lured him out into the snow and there, among the black, leafless trees, had killed him.

The first thing I ever knew of Pushkin was that he'd been murdered. Then I found out that Pushkin was a poet and D'Anthès—a Frenchman. D'Anthès despised Pushkin because he himself couldn't write poetry, and challenged him to a duel; that is, lured him outside into the snow and there, with a pistol, shot him fatally in the stomach. So, from the age of three, I was firmly aware that a poet had a stomach, and—as I recall all the poets I've ever met—I've worried as much about the poet's *stomach*, which so often was empty and in which Pushkin had been shot to death, as about his soul. Because of Pushkin's duel there awakened in me the feelings of a nurse. I will go even further— there is something sacred to me in the word "stomach"—even mention of a simple "stomach-ache" fills me with a wave of shuddering sympathy, devoid of any humor. With that shot we were all wounded in the stomach. [. . .]

Pushkin was a Negro. Pushkin had sideburns (which were worn only by Negroes and old generals); Pushkin had hair that stuck up and lips that stuck out, and black eyes with bluish whites, like a puppy—black, despite his being clearly depicted as blue-eyed in his numerous portraits. If he's a Negro—then he must be dark.[a]

Pushkin was a Negro just like the Negro in the Alexandrovsky Arcade, the one next to the white bear standing above the eternally dry fountain, where my mother and I would often go to see whether it would strike up or not. Fountains never strike (and how could they, anyway?).[1] A Russian poet— who was Negro, a poet—who was a Negro, and this poet—was killed. [. . .]

The monument of Pushkin was not the monument *of* Pushkin (in the genitive case), but simply Monument-Pushkin slurred into one word, though (whether merged into this single word or taken separately) they were both incomprehensible to me. That figure, which eternally, in rain or snow—oh, how I still see those shoulders, weighed down with snow, those African shoulders burdened and overpowered by all Russia's snows!—with its shoulders in the dawn and the snowstorm, whether I was coming or going,

---

[a] Pushkin was blue-eyed and fair-haired.—M. Tsv.

running away or running toward, it would be standing with its eternal hat in hand—is called Monument-Pushkin.

Monument-Pushkin was even my first unit of measurement for distance: from the Nikitsky Gates to Monument-Pushkin—was a *verst*,[2] that same eternal Pushkinian *verst*, the *verst* from "The Demons," the *verst* from "A Winter's Road," that *verst* from all of Pushkin's life and our childhood anthologies, striped and sticking every which way, incomprehensible and yet forever accepted without explanation.[b] [. . .]

From Monument-Pushkin I also derive my insane love for black people, which has remained throughout my life; to this day my whole being is flattered when, accidentally, in the car of a tram or anywhere I find myself next to a black person. My white wretchedness side-by-side with his black divinity. In every Negro I love Pushkin and recognize Pushkin, the black Monument-Pushkin of my as yet unschooled youth and of all Russia. [. . .]

. . . Because it pleased me that, regardless of whether we came or went, he would always be standing there. Covered with snow or falling leaves, at dawn or twilight, in the murky milk of winter—he would always be standing there.

Sometimes, though seldom, we rearrange our gods. For Christmas and Easter we dust off our gods with a rag. But he is washed by the rains and dried by the winds. He—has always been standing there.

Monument-Pushkin was my first vision of inviolability and immutability.

"To the Patriarchs' Ponds or . . . ?"

"To Monument-Pushkin!"

There were no patriarchs at Patriarchs' Ponds. [. . .]

One day Monument-Pushkin came to visit us. I was playing in our cold white hall. I was playing—meaning that either I was sitting under the piano, the back of my head level with the tub holding the philodendron, or silently running from the chest to the mirror, my forehead level with the pier-glass table.

The bell rang and a gentleman passed through the hall. From the living room, where he had gone, mother immediately came out and softly said to me, "Musya! Did you see that gentleman?" "Yes." "Well, that's the son of Pushkin. Surely, you remember Pushkin's monument? Well, that's his son. He's an honorary chairman.[3] Don't leave and don't make noise, and when he goes out—look at him. He looks very much like his father. You do know about his father?"

Time passed. The gentleman didn't come out. I sat and was quiet and

---

[b] There, a fantastic *verst*
Stuck out before my eyes . . . ("The Demons")
(Pushkin is speaking here of the marker itself.—M. Tsv.)
Neither fire, nor dark huts . . .
Only wilderness and snow . . . I
Come upon
Striped *versts* alone. . . ("A Winter's Road")

watched. Alone on the Viennese chair, in the cold hall, not daring to stand, lest suddenly—he'd walk through.

He passed me—distinctly and without warning—but he wasn't alone, he was with father and mother, and I didn't know which way to look, and so I looked at mother. But she, intercepting my glance, angrily motioned it towards the gentleman, and I managed to catch sight of a star on his chest.

"Well, Musya, did you see Pushkin's son?"

"I saw."

"Well, what did you think of him?" "On his chest he had—a star." "A star! As if there weren't lots of people with stars on their chests! You have a certain special talent for looking in the wrong place at the wrong thing . . ."

"Well, see that you remember, Musya," my father chimed in, "that today, at the age of four, you saw the son of Pushkin. Some day you will tell your own grandsons."

I told those grandsons right away. Not my own, but the only grandson I knew—my nurse's: Vanya, who worked in a pewter factory and had once brought me a silver dove, made entirely by himself, as a present. This Vanya would visit on Sundays, and due to his cleanliness and quiet ways and also out of respect for my nurse's high position, he was allowed into the nursery, where for hours he would have tea with doughnuts. And I (out of love for him and his little bird) wouldn't leave his side, said nothing, and swallowed whenever he did.

"Vanya, the son of Monument-Pushkin visited us." "What, little mistress?" "The son of Monument-Pushkin visited us, and Papa said I should tell you this." "Well, if he came, he must have needed something from your Papa . . . ," Vanya answered in confusion. "He didn't need anything, he simply came to visit the master," my nurse interrupted. "After all, the master himself is a full 'zheneral.' You know the Pushkin on Tverskaya?" "I know him." "Well, that's his son. He's already on in years, his beard's all gray, combed in two. His Most Revered Excellency."

So, because of mother's slip of the tongue and my nurse's chatter, and because of my parents' order to look and remember—just as the white bear in the Arcade, the Negro above the fountain, Minin and Pozharsky, and so forth, were tied in my mind only with objects but not at all with people, and since even the Tsar and John of Kronstadt (whom they had once shown me by raising me above the crowd) were also related not to people, but to holy objects—this event also remained, in my mind, linked to an object: the son of Monument-Pushkin had come to visit us. But soon even the vague individual attributes of the son were lost—the son of Monument-Pushkin became Monument-Pushkin himself. Monument-Pushkin himself had come to visit us.

And the older I grew, the more fixed this became in my consciousness: I had seen the son of Pushkin—that gentleman who had already become a monument because he was Pushkin's son. He was, for me, a double monument to his glory and his blood. A living monument. That is why, now, even after all these years, I can calmly say that to our house on the Three Ponds, at the turn of the century one cold white morning, Monument-Pushkin came.

Thus, even before I read Pushkin, before Don Juan, I had my own *Comendador*.

Thus even I had my own *Comendador*. [. . .]

I read the thick volumes of Pushkin inside the bookcase, my nose stuck in the book and sitting in the case itself, almost in darkness and almost totally pressed against the book, even a little smothered by its weight, which hit me right in the throat, and practically blinded by the proximity of its tiny letters. I read Pushkin right into my breast and right into my brain.

My first Pushkin was "The Gypsies." I'd never heard such names: Aleko, Zemfira, and also Old Man. I knew only one old man—one-armed Osip in the poorhouse in Tarussa, whose arm had shriveled up because he'd killed his brother with a cucumber . . .

Once, gathering my courage, with a sinking heart and swallowing hard, I announced:

"I can tell a story about Gypsies."

"Gypsies?" The nurse said distrustfully, " 'bout what sort of gypsies? Who'd write a book 'bout them, 'bout those beggars, those money-grubbing hands!"

"Not that kind. These—are different. This—is a camp."

"Well, so what if it's a camp. They always stay near an estate in a camp, and then one comes to tell fortunes—a young she-devil, 'Let me, little mistress, foretell your lot in life . . .' while the old she-devil steals the laundry right off the clothesline, a diamond brooch from the mistress' dressing table . . ."

"Not that kind of gypsies. These are different gypsies."

"Well, come give her leave to tell us!" My nurse's friend said, sensing tears in my voice, "maybe there really is another kind . . . Go on, give her leave to tell us, we'll listen."

"Well, there was this young man. No, there was this old man, and he had a daughter. No, I'd better say it in verse. 'The gypsies in a boisterous crowd—Through Bessarabia roamed—Today above the river—In tattered tents they sleep—As gay as freedom is their camp"—and so on—without one break for a breath or any pausing commas—up to *"The ring of the field anvil,"* which perhaps I took for a musical instrument, or perhaps simply—accepted it.

"She recites well! Like a real poem!" exclaimed the seamstress, who loved me secretly but wouldn't dare show it, because this nurse—was Asya's, and not mine.

"A be-ea-ar . . ." the nurse pronounced reproachfully, repeating the single word which had reached her mind. "That's really true—a bear. When I was little, the old men used to tell of it—the gypsies always had a bear on a leash. 'Hey you, Misha, dance!' And it would da-a-ance!"

"Well, go on, then what happened?" (The seamstress.)

"Then, the daughter comes to the old man and says that this young man is called Aleko."

The nurse: "Whaat?"

"Aleko!"

"Well, how can they call him that! There isn't any such name. What do you say he was called?"

"Aleko!"

"So, Alyeka-Kaleka!"[4]

"But you're—a fool. It's not Alyeka, but Aleko."

"That's what I'm saying: Alyeka."

"You're saying 'Alyeka'; I'm saying 'Aleko': e-e-e! o-o-o!!"

"Well, all right: 'Alyeka—is Alyeka!"

"Alyosha, that's what it is in our language," the nurse's friend said, trying to reconcile us. "Let her say what she wants, you fool—after all she's saying it, not you. Musen'ka, don't get mad at the nurse—she's a dummy, uneducated, but you're literate, and you should know."

"Well, the daughter was called Zemfira," I said loudly and threateningly. "Zemfira—and this daughter tells the old man that Aleko is going to live with them because she found him in the wilderness:

> I found him in the wilderness
> And bade him sleep in camp.

And the old man was glad and said that we will all travel in the same wagon: 'In one wagon shall we go'—ta-ta-ta-ta, ta-ta-ta-ta—And visit the villages with the bear . . ."

"With the be-ea-ar," the nurse gasped.

"And so they traveled, and they all lived very well, and mules carried the children in baskets."

"How can that be—in baskets?"

"Like this: 'The mules in saddle baskets—Carried the romping children—Husbands and brothers, wives, maidens—Both old and young followed—Cries, noise, gypsy songs—The clanging of the bear's chains.' "

The nurse: "That's enough about the bear! What happens to the old man?"

"To the old man—nothing, he had a young wife Mariula who left him for another gypsy, and this one too—Zemfira—left. First, all she did was sing, 'Old spouse, terrible spouse! Fear you I do not!'—She sang this about him, about her father, and then left him and sat with a gypsy on a grave mound while Aleko was sleeping and snoring horribly, but then he got up and also went to the grave mound, and then stabbed the gypsy with a knife, but Zemfira fell down and also died."

Both at once: "Ah-h-h! A murderer! So he stabbed him with a knife? And what about the old man?"

"The old man—nothing, the old man said, 'Leave us, vain man!' And he left, and they all left, and the whole camp left, but Aleko stayed behind alone."

Both at once: "That's what he deserved. Killing—without anyone attacking him! You know in our village we also had one who stabbed his wife—now don't you listen, Musen'ka," (in a loud whisper), "he found her with a lover. Killed him and her at the same time. Then went to hard labor. Vasily was his name. Yes-s-s . . . what misfortune doesn't exist in this world! And her only crime, love." [. . .]

NOTES

1. Tsvetaeva here conveys a child's misunderstanding of the several meanings of *bit'* (to strike, beat). The fountain does not spew forth *(zabit')*, and this is logical to the child. For, indeed, how can a fountain "strike" anyone?

2. Here again, Tsvetaeva conveys the child's viewpoint by retaining the child's logic. A *versta (verst)* was both the abstract unit of measurement for distance and the striped marker used to indicate this distance.

3. Probably Chairman for the Preservation of Pushkin's Historical and Literary Legacy.

4. The nurse pronounces the name with a Russian accent and makes a rhyme with "kaleka" (cripple) to show how silly it sounds to her. There ensues an argument between the child, who pronounces Aleko correctly, and the nurse, who cannot hear the distinction in the foreign pronunciation of the letters "e" and "o."

Nadezhda Teffi (1872–1952)

Nadezhda Alexandrovna Lokhvitskaya (pseudonym N. Teffi), a younger sister of the poet Mirra Lokhvitskaya, was born in St. Petersburg. She distinguished herself as a writer of belles-lettres and journalism, poetry and prose, the comic and the serious. Tolstoy's *Childhood* and *Adolescence* and Pushkin's fiction were the first works she read as a girl. The first samples of her poetry appeared under her maiden name in the journal *The North*, in August, 1901; in the same year the literary journal *The Fields* published her first story, "Den' proshol" (The Day Has Passed), also under her maiden name. Several of Teffi's feuilletons in verse were printed in the journal *The Star*, and in the Sunday issues of *The Stock Gazette*. She also submitted many poems and humorous short stories, in Chekhovian style, to Russian periodicals such as *The News, Russia, Theatre and Art, Discussions, The Native Fields*, and *The Bard*. In the years surrounding the abortive uprising of 1905, Teffi's stories evinced marked political overtones against the Tsarist government. She contributed to the first legal Bolshevik journal *The New Life*, the editorial board of which consisted of Social Democrats and liberal members of the literary avant-garde, including such colorful figures as Zinaida Hippius and Maxim Gor'ky. In November, 1905, Lenin took control of the journal, converting it into a party organ. At this time Hippius, Teffi, and other representatives of Russian belles-lettres withdrew from its editorial staff.

Teffi's most significant work was done for the comic-satirical journal in St. Petersburg, *The Satyricon* (later *The New Satyricon*), and for the popular Moscow newspaper *The Russian Word*, to which she regularly contributed feuilletons. Among her many collections of poetry are *Sem' ogney* (Seven Fires, 1910), *Sol' zemli* (The Salt of the Earth, 1910), and *Passiflora* (Passiflora; Berlin, 1922). Her short story collections include *Yumoristicheskie rasskazy* (Humorous Stories, 1910–12), in two volumes; the primarily serious stories *Nezhivoy zver'* (The Lifeless Beast, 1917), later reprinted in emigration under the title *Tikhaya zavod'* (The Peaceful Backwater; Paris, 1921), and *Chorny iris* (The Black Iris; Stockholm, 1921); *Vecherny den'* (The Nocturnal Day; Prague, 1924), *Gorodok* (The Small Town; Paris, 1927); *Vsyo o lyubvi* (All About Love; Paris, 1930), *Kniga Iyun'* (The Book—June; Belgrade, 1933), *Ved'ma* (The Witch; Berlin, 1936), *O nezhnosti* (About Tenderness; Paris, 1938), *Zigzag* (The Zigzag; Paris, 1939), and *Zemnaya raduga* (The Earthly Rainbow; New York, 1952). Some of these volumes contain pieces published earlier in Russia. In addition, she wrote a novel, *Avantyurny roman* (An

Adventure Novel, 1932), a volume of memoirs, *Vospominaniya* (Reminiscences, 1932), one-act plays, *Pyesy* (Plays; Paris, 1934), and many other works.

The October Revolution ended Teffi's creative work in Russia. Although she greeted the February Revolution with enthusiasm, in the manner of other liberally minded Russian intellectuals, Teffi turned away in horror from the Bolshevik *coup d' état* in 1917. She left St. Petersburg in 1919 via Istanbul, and in 1920 she settled in Paris and contributed short stories to the Russian newspapers there, *The Latest News* and *La Renaissance*. Her work *Shamran: pesni vostoka* (Shamran: Songs of the East) appeared in the journal *The Theatre* (Berlin, 1923). Teffi's stories and plays, written in Russia, reveal her keen sense of observation, wit, and gentle humor. Her target is not so much the human personality as the humdrum of everyday life—gray, dull, uneventful, and therefore all the more dramatic in its static nature. Human beings appear against this background as pitiful, intimidated, weak, often ridiculous, and always unhappy. Teffi does not mock or satirize them. The critic Anastasiya Chebotarevskaya compared Teffi's stories, "highly benevolent in their elegiac tone and profoundly humanitarian in their attitudes,"[1] to the best stories written by Chekhov. Their plots are diverse, taken from various paths of human life, psychology, political situations, and the social milieu. There are no fantastic elements; the language is lucid; the portraits are drawn in distinct relief; the wit is exquisite, and the dialogue is striking in its sincere gaiety, which is at the same time tragic or gloomy.

The stories written abroad portray the Russian *émigrés* in France and their pathetic, frequently ludicrous attempts to adjust to a new, foreign country. Fusing irony with bitterness and criticism with pity, Teffi depicts the vulgar, mundane existence of the Russians in Paris and their little tragedies. Among her frequent themes are the memory of a happy childhood and the longing for love which is always unattainable, a thirst for some exciting experiences in life as relief from its incomprehensible void and cruelty.

Teffi's pre- and post-emigration comic plots present the emptiness of man's existence and his attempt to escape this life through beautiful dreams and illusions. The writer tears the veil from these ideals and strivings for a more beautiful world. As in her earlier works, Teffi's *émigré* characters conceal their shallow and unresponsive natures both from themselves and from others by pretending to be something more than they are. Some of these works deal with the problems of human interrelationships and the meaning of life. Although often funny, they display a mood dominated by pathos, and even by hopelessness and despair. In Teffi's later narratives this weary tone gains the upper hand over her former biting wit. Earthly existence is empty and meaningless; as with the Russian Symbolists, Teffi's "real reality" lies elsewhere. It exists only as a dim reflection on earth and is always distant and inaccessible. Man can never detach himself completely from the dead and mechanical world of finite experience. The longing for the beyond remains a mirage for him—a mirage which, though meaningful and beautiful, is at its core nothing but the banal and boring reality of the empirical world. Nonetheless, this world of treacherous but sweet illusions is superior to the dead and empty life on earth. In exposing the oddities of this life and the bewilderment and suffering of Russian exiles, Teffi reveals an affinity with Mikhail Zoshchenko's artistic method. In many ways her writings are the *émigré* equivalents of the latter's short stories depicting the Soviet citizen's everyday life and his inability to adjust to his new Soviet, and therefore alien, surroundings.

Reminiscences and *An Adventure Novel* differ from Teffi's one-act plays and stories. In the former, she uses the hyperbolic grotesque to relate her escape from the Bolsheviks in 1919. *An Adventure Novel* is written as a series of short chapters with rapidly unfolding action. There are many unexpected and intriguing epigraphs from Heine, Goethe, Anatole France, and Dostoevsky, and the entire work is written in brief, energetic sentences.

Teffi has remained one of the most popular writers in the Russian language. Her books received favorable reviews in all influential periodicals abroad, just as they had in Russia prior to the October Revolution. Unfortunately, her writings have been neglected in the USSR. Soviet critics disapprove of her humor, her artistic method, and her prevailing mood of boredom and anguish. Her major fault in their eyes, however, is her indifference to a conscious political platform and to a "vital pathos of struggle"[2]—omissions which, they mistakenly believe, impeded her development as a powerful satirist.

NOTES

1. Anastasiya Chebotarevskaya, "Teffi. I stalo tak . . . ," *Yumoristicheskie rasskazy*, St. Petersburg: Izd. Kornfel'd (1912), *Novaya zhizn'* no. 7 (1912): 255.
2. "Teffi. *Tango smerti: sbornik rasskozov*," *Na literaturnom postu* no. 4 (1928): 87.

A MODEST TALENT

From the Repertoire of the Petersburg Liteyny Theatre

FROM: *Pyesy* (Plays; Paris: Vozrozhdenie, 1934).

DRAMATIS PERSONAE
IGNAT MECHTALIN—An elderly actor, rake, and gambler.
GURTOVNIK—A provincial type, part-time barber, part-time salesman in a

perfume store. Dressed chicly and incongruously, mustachios twirled; he has an indefinable accent. Swiftly changes from a servile to an insolent tone.

FIRST LADY

SECOND LADY—Both are typical club types and lotto players; both are bedecked with necklaces and tucked here and there with brooches, constantly looking into their pocket mirrors and wiping powder from their noses.

THE LACKEY

The dining room in a club. Little chairs, a bar with hors d'oeuvres, behind it a bartender. A door into an anteroom; a door into a gambling hall. There is nobody on the stage. The exclamations of the players are heard from the adjoining room: "Place your bets, deal. Place your bets, deal. Sixty in a round. Pass . . . Your bets . . ." *and so on.* MECHTALIN *comes out, dishevelled, flushed, sweating all over, completely distraught. He comes out onto the middle of the stage, looks around dully, pulls a handkerchief out of his pocket, then a box of matches, and then turns his pocket inside out, shaking it. From the other he takes out gloves, turns it inside out, and shakes out papers and crumbs.*

MECHTALIN. *(Dazed)* Not a kopeck. Everything's gone out the window. *(He suddenly begins to tug at his ear and keeps repeating.)* Why did I bet against Sasha! Why did I bet against Sasha! Why! Why! You see the man's having luck, yet you jump in. *(He shouts)* Nikolay! Some Seltzer! Ignat Mechtalin needs Seltzer!

THE LACKEY. *(Rushing up, in a whisper)* Ignaty Ivanych, I am sorry, you have debts there . . . the bartender has asked me to remind you . . .

MECHTALIN. Liar! Your bartender will never get anything. You can take Ignat Mechtalin's word for it. Get me that Seltzer water. *(The lackey runs off.)* Explo-i-t-e-rs! *(From out of the doors leading into the anteroom,* GURTOVNIK *appears. He looks around timidly, straightens his tie, stretches his neck, and clears his throat as if preparing to sing.* THE LACKEY *is bringing* MECHTALIN *the water.* GURTOVNIK *stops* THE LACKEY.)

GURTOVNIK. Pardong! This is the dramatic circle?

THE LACKEY. It sure is.

GURTOVNIK. *(Seizing his heart)* Oi! You don't say! *(To* THE LACKEY*)* Pardong, you would be so kind as to tell me—the famous artist Mister Mechtalin is here?

THE LACKEY. He sure is.

GURTOVNIK. Oi, my God, how excited I am! *(To* THE LACKEY*)* Please be so kind as to convey to them[1] that Mister Gurtovnik, Faddey Efimych, longs to see them. Be so good as to inform them that I ordered visiting cards, but they're not ready yet. Tell them on Saturday they'll be ready.

THE LACKEY. They're sitting right there—why don't you tell them yourself?.

GURTOVNIK. *(Seizing his heart)* Oi, my God! That's really them, then? *(Again clears his throat, tidies himself, and approaches* MECHTALIN.) You would do me the favor of addressing to my modest figure five minutes of your attention? I have so much craved to see you I just can't find the words . . . Literally, as they say, in my boots is my heart. Such dreams I've dreamed, so much I've striven, and suddenly—bang! Here I am in the very bosom of my divinity. If you would only afford me . . .

MECHTALIN. *(Looks at him fixedly and says suddenly)* Give me five roubles until Thursday!

GURTOVNIK. Oi, my God! And I'm just so . . . so happy! But why do you need five roubles when tomorrow, now that we're together, several million we can earn?

MECHTALIN. What nonsense! Where are you going to get these millions?

GURTOVNIK. I don't have them yet, but very soon—I'll get them tomorrow. With my dramatic talent I'll get them. All I have to do is get on that stage somehow, and you'll have them, I guarantee you.

MECHTALIN. So you think you'll get on the stage?

GURTOVNIK. Of course, I realize I need a solid preparation, and I therefore intend . . .

MECHTALIN. Just look at your legs. Why, you're bowlegged.

GURTOVNIK. To be truthful, only one is, but I have anticipated that. Troosers I have ordered from Tsyrkin the tailor. A forty-rouble style. Brown checked . . . Very snazzy . . . The tailor Tsyrkin says in these troosers I shall literally have no legs.

MECHTALIN. Just give me five roubles until Thursday.

GURTOVNIK. Five roubles? So fatally happy you've made me! Be so kind as to take five roubles. (MECHTALIN *takes the money and goes into the hall.*) I shall wait a while. I shall wait a while. *(He remains alone. He looks at his legs, shakes his head, strikes various poses.)*

MECHTALIN. *(Returns, panting)* The devil's own luck! You still here?

GURTOVNIK. I request you once again to afford me five minutes of your time. I wish to unfold before you several moments of my life. My life, I must tell you, is like a real novel. My father owned a drugstore in Berdyansk and there I received my first inspirations. I have to tell you, I have dreamed of the stage. I am not so much attracted by material gain as seduced by the thought of glory and applause.

MECHTALIN. Do you by any chance have ten roubles?

GURTOVNIK. *(Not listening, with enthusiasm)* Since my very youth I have with all my being felt an unusual upsurge of talent, but alas, condemned I've been to languish amidst the dry and pedantic scientism of the drugstore milieu, whereas my soul has sought the life of another order . . .

MECHTALIN. Listen, I just need it 'til Tuesday. I'll give it back Friday.

GURTOVNIK. *(Not listening)* Life has surrounded me with external smiles, but the soul within me is sad. Women find me no less pleasing than any other brunet, despite the contrary hue of my outward appearance.

MECHTALIN. Does that mean that you are refusing Ignatius Mechtalin ten roubles?

GURTOVNIK. But I knew that only one person in this world would understand . . .

MECHTALIN. *(Cries out)* Ten roubles! Do you hear me or not, devil take you?! Give me ten roubles!

GURTOVNIK. Oh? *(Dazed)* Certainly, I'll be glad to. I just wished to tell you further. . . (MECHTALIN exits. GURTOVNIK *sinks into a chair, speaking rapturously.)* What a man! What power! What strength! Oi! *(He points a finger upwards.)*

(Two women enter and sit at a table near the buffet.)

FIRST LADY. If Vereshchunin comes, he will certainly play for me.

SECOND LADY. Wipe the powder off your nose.

FIRST LADY. Only don't you go crawling off to him. Call your own Peter Ivanych. (GURTOVNIK *looks at the ladies, coquettishly screwing up his eyes and clearing his throat.)*

SECOND LADY. Peter Ivanych is never really on the ball.

FIRST LADY. Likin—now he's the best player there.

GURTOVNIK. *(Getting up)* Pardong. I, it seems, have disturbed you. *(The two ladies silently exchange glances.)*

GURTOVNIK. It seemed to me upon your dress I trod.

FIRST LADY. Very clever. We can't speak to you; we haven't been introduced.

GURTOVNIK. Ah, Madame, beauty never needs an introduction. Take, for example, the Venus de Milo: complete in itself, and all can approach it and look at it and, if I may so express myself, even touch it—but about introductions no one cares, hee-hee.

SECOND LADY. What a comparison . . . Wipe the powder from your nose . . .

GURTOVNIK. I have, by the way, ordered myself visiting cards. Saturday they'll be ready. Eighty kopecks a hundred. Not even an itsy-bitsy bit expensive. On Saturday, if you so wish, I shall present you with one.

THE SECOND. *(To THE FIRST)* Do you suppose he could play for us?

THE FIRST. *(To GURTOVNIK)* Why aren't you playing?

GURTOVNIK. I'm not playing yet, but already I've decided to and have taken steps, as I have within me a great superfluity of aspiration.

THE FIRST. Then what are you waiting for? Go and play!

GURTOVNIK. As hero and conqueror I wish to enter that sacred shrine. That great artist, Ignatius Mechtalin, will take me over its threshold.

THE SECOND. Oh, that means Mechtalin's promised to take him in hand.

GURTOVNIK. So tell me, do you play then too?

THE SECOND. A little.

GURTOVNIK. Oi, my God! What lucky little ones you are then. Nevertheless, I immediately perceived in you something special. 'Pon my word, from the first glance!

THE FIRST. *(Taking offense)* What nonsense.

GURTOVNIK. 'Pon my word! I assure you! It leaves a familiar stamp on a person in a teeny-weeny way. You can deny it?

THE SECOND. *(To* THE FIRST*)* What impudence!

GURTOVNIK. There, then, I knew I was right.

THE FIRST. Firstly, we very seldom play. They used to allow women before, but the police cracked down on it.

GURTOVNIK. What's this you're saying?! How could they manage even a teeny-weeny bit without female personnel? Oi, my God!

THE SECOND. Of course, playing was much more animated with ladies around, and there were many more spectators.

GURTOVNIK. How right you are there! I can see it in my mind how you played. I imagine the public threw many benefits for you, literally carried you off in its arms.

THE FIRST. Why should they carry us? I just don't get it. You're really a strange one.

GURTOVNIK. You've got my word, this is not a compliment even, but the most simple, personal opinion. And you are now completely devoid of the means to be in this walk of life?

THE FIRST. No, it is not entirely impossible. Of course, not personally. We allow certain of our male acquaintances to stand in for us, when we wish to participate . . . But, of course, some of them do let us down.

GURTOVNIK. Oh, I would not have let you down. I would have fulfilled your role so well that you would have licked all my little fingers. 'Pon my word! Ah, if it could be quicker! If only the great Mechtalin more quickly would take me in hand, imbue me with his technique, reveal to me all the secrets of his art. Then I'll show you what I'm fit for.

THE FIRST. What? What's this you're saying? Does Mechtalin have some special techniques?

THE SECOND. Good heavens! Good heavens, is it really true?

THE FIRST. But remember, they say he was supposed to have been involved in some sort of scandal in Nizhny. Remember? Evidently, it's true.

THE SECOND. And he promised to reveal his tricks to you?

THE FIRST. That's simply awful!

THE SECOND. No. All the same, I just don't believe you. If that's so, why is he always such a loser?

GURTOVNIK. Who's a loser? Mechtalin, a loser?

THE SECOND. Sure he is! Never has a cent.

GURTOVNIK. Well, you really bowl me over. In the provinces they clapped so much, a disaster it was. 'Pon my word, they beat their little palms to a pulp for him.

THE SECOND. How did they clap? Whom did they clap? Him?

THE FIRST. Hands? Clapped on him? What are you talking about? (MECHTALIN *flies in, even more distraught than before, and looks around perplexedly.*)

GURTOVNIK. *(To* MECHTALIN) Well, now I can count on your five minutes already . . .

MECHTALIN. Oh, it's you again, good grief! He's still here. Well, what is it you want of me?

GURTOVNIK. I wish to unravel but a few more sketches of my modest past . . .

MECHTALIN. See here, I'm telling you straight: you'd better beat it, while you're still in one piece.

GURTOVNIK. This, pardong, I cannot do, for I really am unable to. I intentionally liquidated that drugstore of mine, the one I got as an inheritance, to spend all of the two thousand on developing my talent with your help.

MECHTALIN. *(Brightening)* You've got two thousand?

GURTOVNIK. A little less. It became necessary to tear away from the arts two hundred for traveling, for buying cuffs, for visiting cards. Four ties I've also acquired, of various *couleurs*.

MECHTALIN. And you've got the rest on you?

GURTOVNIK. I've got it on me.

MECHTALIN. And he says nothing! What a strange fellow!

GURTOVNIK. But you keep refusing to give me an audition. I have not had the opportunity to declaim. As I was about to speak, off you went right away into the other room to fulfill some higher purpose.

MECHTALIN. Now we'll decide straight away what you should do with this money.

GURTOVNIK. It's already decided! As the poet hath said: "Now it is adjudged in the highest council, the will of heaven it is, I am yours." All this money I've assigned to preparing for the stage.

MECHTALIN. Forget it! I'll tell you seriously, you'll get nowhere on the stage. With bandy legs like that . . .

GURTOVNIK. Only one, I assure you; only one.

MECHTALIN. Your physique's a joke, your accent borders on Portuguese, you've got oatmeal in your mouth. Now, don't be angry. Believe me. There are times one can put one's faith in Ignatius Mechtalin.

GURTOVNIK. On the stage I can pretend I have no accent. A Russian accent I can mimic; an artist can do everything.

MECHTALIN. Forget it! Look, what sort of talent can you possibly have? You'll only be throwing away the money. Give me the money instead, and I'll put on such a performance that you personally will thank me.

GURTOVNIK. Your participation is just what I have dreamed of. Only I wanted to play myself and not entrust it to you. I, after all, am no woman. I can do it myself.

MECHTALIN. No, there you're wrong. They won't allow you to play. After all, you're not a member of the circle!

GURTOVNIK. But I was counting on you to go through some speeches with me, you know, give me just a very limited series of lessons. Any price you like you can name, as I have assigned my entire inheritance to pay you for my dramatic development.

MECHTALIN. My dear fellow! Why didn't you say something before?

GURTOVNIK. You wouldn't even give me a teeny-weeny moment to speak.

MECHTALIN. Well, we'll soon set that straight. It's easy with your talent. Now, don't let's lose time: declaim something for me that you may better progress.

GURTOVNIK. Won't I disturb the ladies?

MECHTALIN. Not one bit. They'll be glad. *Mesdames!* This is the artist in training . . . the artist . . .

GURTOVNIK. *(Shuffling his feet) Artiste*—Faddey Gurtovnik.

MECHTALIN. Well, get on with it. Don't lose time! Such an appropriation will be eminently suitable in there right now . . .

GURTOVNIK. *(Strikes a pose and clear his throat)*
> Before the noble Spanish lady
> Their vigil two knights keep.
> Their ears apart, their legs like bows,
> They stand as though asleep.
> Hay smells in the meadows
> And peasant women, with their forks, they beat . . .

I am sorry; from nervousness my speech faltered a little. I'm better at something else. There's one thing I do very well now that I remember; it goes something like this:
> When I was a young attorney
> I passionately loved a Greek maid.
> The charmer caressed my steed,
> A Jew knocked on my door with contempt.
> His gold I took, I cursed him, and he went,
> Now sorrow devours my untrammeled soul.

I've cut this down a bit for speed's sake.

MECHTALIN. Not bad, not bad at all! For a start, maybe quite enough.

GURTOVNIK. Just you give me directions. Should this be slower? *(Declaims)*
> Throw open my cell,
> Give me day's light,
> A black-maned maiden,
> A black-browed steed.

MECHTALIN. *(Interrupting him)* Splendid! You're a terrific fellow. Listen, young man, we won't practice any more now. You must preserve your voice. The voice, in general, is a tender, fragile instrument. It's easy to break one's voice, and then there's just no cure for it. You can believe it. Ignatius Mechtalin says it. There are times, young man, one can put one's faith in Ignatius Mechtalin.

GURTOVNIK. You would perhaps be interested in my prose? I could recite a further piece for you . . .

MECHTALIN. What's the matter with you? For heaven's sake, preserve your voice! For the artist, his voice is the most important thing. No, no! Not a word! My dear fellow, preserve your voice! With tears I beg you—preserve it!

GURTOVNIK. *(Whispers)* So I'm silent already. Long ago I shut up.

MECHTALIN. Well then, to work. They have, of course, already notified you that I collect in advance for voice instruction and hmmm . . . guidance in general. From you, with your unquestionable talent, I won't take much— just . . . hmmm . . . two thousand . . .

GURTOVNIK. Heavens! Such money I don't have. I've got at most about sixteen hundred and fifty-two roubles, and thirty kopecks.

MECHTALIN. Well, fine then, God be with you! Give me the sixteen hundred and fifty-two roubles. You can keep the thirty kopecks.

GURTOVNIK. But my troosers? Forty roubles I've got to keep to pay for them.

MECHTALIN. All right then, pay for your "troosers" and give me the rest. Oh God, how tiresome you are!

GURTOVNIK. *(Hands over the money)* I'm overjoyed! But tell me, I will have to continue long under your tutelage?

MECHTALIN. What's there to practice? You've had your lesson for today. The biggest thing now is to preserve your voice. You're a full-fledged artist; you could even go on the stage right away. Heavens! You've still got that forty. Wait—don't go away, just in case. I might still like to borrow some more.

GURTOVNIK. You'd still like to borrow some more?

MECHTALIN. *(To the ladies)* Here, *Mesdames*, I recommend for your attention the famous artist Gurmotnik.

GURTOVNIK. Gurtovnik, Faddey Gurtovnik.

MECHTALIN. A young rascal of striking genius, thus speaketh I, Ignatius Mechtalin, and there are times one can put one's faith in Ignatius Mechtalin. *(He runs off.)*

GURTOVNIK. Oi, such a man of genius! As for me, I'm just a modest talent. *(Self-contentedly preens himself)* Well then, sweetie *Mesdames*, I have the honor to present my benefit performance.

THE FIRST. You're really going on the stage, are you?

GURTOVNIK. Already I'm there.

THE SECOND. So you're an artist? Seriously?

GURTOVNIK. Yes, I'm an *artiste* unto myself. I have my own modest talent.

THE FIRST. Who would have thought it?

GURTOVNIK. If you really coax me, perhaps even your roles I'll play.

THE FIRST. How's that?

GURTOVNIK. Women's roles. I have a great deal of tenderness in my carriage, they all say so. I'd play a woman's role just a teeny-weeny bit better than a man's. Take, for example, Tat'yana's letter. Do you know, when I read it, they simply can't contain themselves? It's just awful what it does to people.

THE SECOND. What does it do to them?

GURTOVNIK. It's impossible to describe it.

THE SECOND. Well, what does it do?

GURTOVNIK. I've told you already, I can't describe it. How can I undertake a description when it's impossible?

THE FIRST. Why do you keep pestering him? He's said it can't be done, so shut up about it. *(To GURTOVNIK)* Declaim a little for us.

GURTOVNIK. *(Declaiming)* "Here, I am writing to you. What more can I say? What more can I add? Well? Now I know."
I shall declaim no longer. I must conserve my voice a little bitty.

MECHTALIN. *(Runs in, speaking quickly, perplexedly)* Quickly, quickly, give me the other forty, quickly, for God's sake!

GURTOVNIK. *(Struck dumb)* What . . . how can this be? What about my troosers? Oi, my God!

MECHTALIN. What do you need that nonsense for? You have a classic talent: you'll play Hamlet in tights, King Lear in a robe, Ophelia in a jacket . . .

GURTOVNIK. *(Indecisively)* This is really true?

MECHTALIN. And I'll give you the money back in half an hour in any event.

GURTOVNIK. *(Indecisively)* I'm glad, then. Here you are.

MECHTALIN. Thanks, friend! You're a regular trooper! Take it from Ignatius Mechtalin. *(He exits.)*

GURTOVNIK. *(Pensively)* There's something not quite right about all this. So quickly I've made my career, but it's getting sort of sickening in the pit of my stomach. That tailor Tsyrkin is quite some guy . . . hmm . . Ye-s. Somehow a dramatic career doesn't particularly please me. Too many pitfalls, I see.

FIRST LADY. So give up the stage, if it doesn't please you.

GURTOVNIK. You know what?! You've said it! I think I'll give it up. Oi, 'pon my word! You just keep putting out the money. It's so distressing.

MECHTALIN. *(Flies in)* See here, my little friend, don't you have a little money?

GURTOVNIK. *(Horrified)* I've thirty kopecks left only!

MECHTALIN. You must be lying! Rummage around your pockets thoroughly. Surely you must've put something aside for the cabman, didn't you?

GURTOVNIK. No, I didn't.

MECHTALIN. What a dummy! How could you not have put aside some money for the cabman?

GURTOVNIK. *(Timidly)* Mister Mechtalin. I cannot . . . I fear I have a most modest talent, but I've spent so much on it and even severely overdeveloped it . . . Mister Mechtalin, I no longer can . . . I no longer feel an upsurge in my body . . .

MECHTALIN. Then don't push your luck at it! Well, just think for yourself, what sort of an actor are you?!

FIRST LADY. So he's not an actor, is he then? He just butted in here to make our acquaintance.

THE SECOND. And while you were assuring him that he was an actor, he said all sorts of nasty things about you.

MECHTALIN. Him! About me?

GURTOVNIK. I? About him?

THE SECOND. Yes, there's no way you can get out of it now. No way. He said that you're a con-man. No way, no way!

MECHTALIN. Wha-at?!

THE SECOND. He said that you, so to speak, promised to teach him various tricks, and that they almost jumped you in the provinces.

GURTOVNIK. Oi, my God! Sweetie *Mesdames*, what is this . . .

MECHTALIN. (*Advancing toward* GURTOVNIK) So, it's like that?! I exalted you, whereas you have maligned me! I dealt with you, my cursed little Guntorshchik-kins, like my own dear brother, so to speak, went halves on everything . . . and this is what you do. For you, Ignat Mechtalin is a thief?!

GURTOVNIK. I'm on my way already! Oi, my God, I don't understand a thing! (*He keeps moving backward towards the door.*) A long time I've been on my way, already I'm not here.

MECHTALIN. Be gone from here! Base soul! Nikolay, run him out into the street!

GURTOVNIK. (*Desperately, behind the door*) But my troosers, then? Oh, I've gone already, I'm no longer here!

MECHTALIN. (*Wiping his forehead, magnificently*) I'll not give the money back to that scoundrel. This is my moral right, in this you can believe Ignatius Mechtalin unconditionally. (*Striking himself on the chest, he goes into the hall.*)
CURTAIN.

DIAMOND DUST

From the Repertoire of the Petersburg Liteyny Theatre

DRAMATIS PERSONAE:

MI—A young singer
THE THIEF
THE BANKER
THE POET
THE MUSICIAN
THE MAID

A well-furnished room in a hotel. On the right there is a large window hung with a lace curtain. Deep in the interior is a door; on the left, an alcove. Everywhere are trunks, cardboard boxes, large baskets with flowers, garlands, and ribbons. In the middle of the room there is a large table. It is laid for supper. At the table sit MI, THE BANKER, THE POET, *and* THE MUSICIAN.

THE MUSICIAN. (*To* MI) In my opinion, you sang even better than yesterday. I give you my word on it.

THE BANKER. Oh? Always excellently! What of it!

THE POET. Well, I would have said . . . you always have such a metallic sound—in the best sense of the word . . . But today your voice was . . . still more metal . . . metallic.

THE BANKER. Hah! That's because it's composed of the basest metal. Ha! Ha! Ha! Isn't that true?

MI. (*Sits sideways on her chair, her arms on the back of the chair, her head lowered*) How bo-o-oring!

THE MUSICIAN. How can one be bored after such a success? Success gives one wings. When I went out with you onto the stage and heard them raving with delight, I was ready to weep my eyes out from happiness. And His Excellency! You saw what a state he was in? Ha! Ha! Ha!

THE BANKER. He couldn't take his eyes off her.

THE POET. It's torture! I don't like it! (*Naïvely*) Why did he stare so?

THE MUSICIAN. You're still so melancholy! Well, that's enough of that! Are you tired? Give me your little hand. (*He wishes to kiss her hand.*)

MI. (*Pulling back*) How bo-o-oring!

THE BANKER. That's odd! Why so bored? We've come at the very height of the season. Five hundred bathers in the sea. More than a hundred rheumatikky patients. And many with sick stomachs. I just don't see what there is to be bored about. Oh?

THE POET. (*To* THE BANKER) Here; it looks like there's still a little wine left in the bottle. Let's have some. Thanks! Mi, I drink to your eyes, long and dark like two nights of love . . .

THE BANKER. Oh?

THE MUSICIAN. How you sang today! There's still some more wine? I like it with pears.

THE BANKER. I imagine winter here would be boring. The spa closes, everyone goes home. All that's left is a putrid little town. It's disgusting!

MI. No, it's wonderful! I know. I was born here . . .

THE BANKER. Oh?

THE MUSICIAN. I drink to Mi's birthplace. So you know everything around here?

MI. No. I haven't been here for eight years. Everything's changed a lot since then. The spa was quite small then. There was no Grand Hotel . . .

THE MUSICIAN. Eight years ago! You'd be a pretty small girl then, wouldn't you! Give me your hand.

THE BANKER. Ha! Ha! He flings out a compliment, then demands his payoff right away! Ha! Ha! Don't give him your hand, don't let him work up credit. Ha!

MI. Well, that's enough of that! I was fifteen years old when the baron took me away to town to study singing.

THE POET. At fifteen! At fifteen! (*He covers his eyes with his hand and sinks into thought*.)

MI. How strange that they suddenly invited me here . . . Like a fairytale.

THE BANKER. Well, how can it be a fairytale when it's the truth? Oh? If it's the truth, then that means there's no way it can be a fairytale, because a fairytale is not the truth but something invented. Isn't what I'm saying true? One must know how to judge things properly!

THE MUSICIAN. (*Gets up and looks at the basket of flowers*) What luxury! An abyss of taste! This is probably . . . from His Excellency?

MI. No. He sent me nothing.

THE MUSICIAN. Strange! That surprises me! He kept on looking and looking at you . . .

THE BANKER. He gazed and gazed but never a cent he raised! Ha! Ha! (*To* THE POET) Is that what they call poetry in your line of business? They give you money for it, but I can do it just so, for free. Ha! Ha! He gaped and gaped but not a cent he gave. Oh, I've messed it up! It came out better before somehow. (*He lights a cigar and goes to* THE MUSICIAN.) You keep on smelling the flowers? They were not intended for you. Ha! Ha! I'm joking.

THE POET. (*Quietly to* MI) Won't they go away soon, these boring people? Mi, my dear! You have golden eyebrows! You have golden hair! I shall throw you on the red silk of the pillow, I shall throw you down on the pillow like a handful of golden coins! . . . Mi! Can it be . . . Just think a little! Here I am, like a black slave, I follow you everywhere . . . I breathe the dust of your sandals . . .

MI. What? The dust?

THE POET. But I hear only "No"! A black "No" with steel hooves. Mi! Why then do you sing? Why do you sing? Then don't dare sing!

MI. Why indeed! I have a contract!

THE POET. (*Covers his face with his hands and keeps on standing thus*)

THE MUSICIAN. (*In an undertone to* THE BANKER) I am happy that the conversation about this bouquet has brought us closer together . . . has more firmly united us . . . that is, what I wanted to say was . . . I, in general, value . . . (*Quickly*) Can't you oblige me with a small sum for a short time? The very shortest, I give you my word!

THE BANKER. (*With vexation*) I just don't understand you at all, young man! This shows such a lack of tact . . . Here, in the presence of a lady, you allow yourself . . . No, absolutely no! (*He hastily moves away to* THE POET.)

MI. (*Going toward* THE MUSICIAN) You're upset about something?

THE MUSICIAN. Oh, no! It's still the same thing. I love you, Mi!

THE POET. (*Not taking his hands away from his face*) Don't sing! I entreat you for only this mercy . . . Why do you sing?

THE BANKER. Oh? When did I sing?

THE POET. (*Takes his hands down and looks around him, surprised*) Oh, it's you! (*Wipes his brow*) I wanted to tell you something very interesting . . .

THE BANKER. About my singing?

THE POET. Hm . . . yes . . . no, you sing . . . Well, yes, couldn't you lend me fifty until tomorrow . . .

THE BANKER. Oh? My dear fellow, why didn't you ask earlier? I've just given your friend everything I had on me! What a shame!

THE MUSICIAN. (*To MI*) If only they'd go away sooner! I should like to be alone with you. You could sing for me. For me alone, Mi!

MI. You know, all this singing and singing is getting me down. You'd think I was no longer a human being, but a canary. It's driving me nuts.

THE MUSICIAN. Mi! Don't talk so! Oh, if only you knew! Yesterday you sang with your hair loosely flowing, your locks swaying like musical strings. It seemed to me that they rang out and sang . . . Your entire being sings out, Mi! Tonight, I shall not sleep at all. I shall write music, a new romance for you, Mi!

MI. (*Pointing to THE POET*) To his words?

THE MUSICIAN. Yes, to his latest verses to you.
    "My ships have sailed away
    Blue in the mist . . .
    (*Sits down at the piano and strikes a cord*)
    They've sailed away . . . sailed away . . ."

THE MAID. (*Enters*) There's a man here from the shop. He's asking for the young lady.

THE BANKER. Oh? What's this? Let's go and take a look. Perhaps we'll have to pay . . . (*All step out. The window opens slightly. Looking cautiously around, THE THIEF climbs in. He sneaks up to the desk, fumbles about, and tries to open the drawers with a skeleton key. Steps are heard, and the voices of people returning. THE THIEF hides behind the curtain of the alcove.*)

MI. (*Leading all. Goes to the mirror. Holds in her hands a large necklace of multifaceted stones.*) See how beautiful it is!

THE BANKER. Oh? Indeed! This is something I can comprehend! What are flowers and all that . . . rubbish next to it! This is a present, what I call a real present! Here, I'll do it up for you. You don't know how. One must know how to handle such things.

THE MUSICIAN. An abyss of taste! I had a feeling His Excellency would prove himself to be a fine connoisseur!

MI. I do not like jewels! I never wear any. If I get them, I always sell them.

THE BANKER. You cannot sell this thing! First, you must certainly wear it tomorrow at the concert. Then, during the *entr'acte*, you must go and thank His Excellency. You must! Otherwise—there'll be a scandal!

THE MUSICIAN. Yes, it's very important for one's career. How chic! Tomorrow the whole town will be talking about it! And the day after tomorrow, all of Europe! What a giddy success! They'll go out of their minds tomorrow from joy! How they'll stare at her! And then—pictures in all the papers, write-ups! And I—I shall accompany her. On the stage—she and I!

THE POET. (*Quietly to* MI) He thinks only of himself! Eternally about himself! Just look at that. Only about his miserable little career . . .

THE BANKER. It's a pity he's going away the day after tomorrow. Perhaps he might have coughed up even more.

MI. (*To* THE POET) Do you like it?

THE POET. Yes . . . Your face could grace even diamonds.

THE MUSICIAN. I think you already wrote that phrase somewhere.

THE POET. Just what do you mean by that?

THE MUSICIAN. Just what I said.

THE BANKER. Exquisite stones!

THE POET. What do you mean?

THE MUSICIAN. I said that you have spoken this phrase many times on other occasions, that is, to other women, and then, perhaps, you even had it printed in a book you dedicated to that disgusting old dancer . . . well, we understand each other.

THE POET. A disgusting old dancer? The one for whom you wrote your *Waltz Legend?*

THE MUSICIAN. Later. Later. We'll speak about it in detail.

THE POET. (*Shrugs his shoulders and goes up to* THE BANKER) What do you think: Was this expensive?

THE BANKER. This little piece? How shall I put it . . . I would have bought it for over two thousand roubles, but they probably took His Excellency for a straight three.

THE MUSICIAN. And I shall accompany you! To the health of His Excellency! Hurrah! (*Clinks glasses with* MI) But you must be merrier. You really must!

THE POET. (*Haughtily*) Where do you get this "must" from? I should like to know.

THE MUSICIAN. From my heart, Mister Poet, from my heart. A fine source, it would seem. MI! You are the queen of this source. In it eternally resounds your upper "do." In it sobs your deep "la." What a pity that he didn't give you flowers instead of stones. I might then have asked for one as a keepsake. But you couldn't ask for a stone. (*Naïvely*) Or could you?

MI. (*Again goes up to the mirror*)

THE BANKER. (*To* MI) Can't you send these two giraffes about their business? It's outrageous! It seems they've settled down for the night here. Oh? Here, let me hide your necklace in my suitcase. It has a secret lock.

MI. Leave me in peace! After all, you didn't give it to me, so there's no need to get worked up. Just for spite I'll keep it myself.

THE BANKER. Oh? But you've got to take it off at night.

MI. I shall simply sleep in it.

THE POET. Just divine! No, you should always wear stones. You should—do you understand?

THE BANKER. I've always said this. How many times have I urged it. I even feel awkward. Everyone knows I'm patron to our fashionable singer, and yet this *artiste* doesn't have even a single stone. This is spoiling my credit. It reflects upon my business. People might even think that I have no money. Well, if she doesn't want to accept it as a present, she could simply wear it a bit, and then I'd hide it. I inherited many fine things from my late wife. From the second one. She had a fortune. I know that if a woman is in love, she doesn't ask for anything; but if she already has things, there's no point in giving her anything more.

THE POET. Mi is in love! Move the lamp over to me. I'm cold! (*He lowers his head*.)

THE BANKER. The electric lamp warms one poorly. You certainly do have a cold. You should spread mustard in your socks . . .

THE POET. (*Huddles up*) Leave me alone! I'm sick! Be quiet! I can't take it.

THE BANKER. Well, yes. It's the cold. (*To* MI) And why don't you wear good stones, real stones? I know that all our stars wear imitations. The majority. They make them so cleverly now. Pure glass. They polish them with diamond dust. From a distance you can't tell the difference.

THE POET. With diamond dust?

THE BANKER. Well, yes. But I would have allowed her to wear the real ones for a while. I would have allowed the reporters to examine them even through a magnifying glass. I might have even invited an appraiser. Huh?

THE POET. Diamond dust . . . How beautiful this is. It flies, glistens, shimmers . . . it covers the glass and it makes a diamond, a living, joyous stone . . . The crowd looks on it from afar, believes in its beauty and value. Ah, gently, gently! Do not shake off the diamond dust! Do not uncover the dark glass! Diamond dust! Beautiful! It makes me weep!

THE BANKER. The wine here is bad, but very strong! Hah-hah! Isn't that true, Mister Musician! (*He winks at* THE POET.)

MI. Why do you keep sitting here? Go away! I want to sleep.

THE BANKER. Our beautiful hostess implies that she is fatigued.

THE MUSICIAN. I'm going. I beg your pardon! Good night.

THE POET. And I have already gone . . . I have gone long ago, and far away.

THE BANKER. Goodbye, gentlemen. With the permission of the hostess, I shall smoke one more cigar.

MI. No, no! I won't allow it. I'm tired. You'll all go away together. I'll call the servant. She'll close the door behind you and light the way. It's already dark downstairs. (*She goes to the bell and rings for a long time.* THE MAID *enters.*)

MI. See them out. Only make sure it's all of them. Don't forget anyone on the staircase. Look around well. And close the door as tightly as you can.

THE BANKER. (*Laughs affectedly*) Ha! Ha! That's amusing! The poet can fly in on wings through a chink in the door. Plug it with a cork. Ha! Ha! (*They go away.* MI *is alone before the mirror. After a short time* THE MAID *returns.*)

MI. They've gone? Look at it! Isn't it nice? I should say so. From His Excellency.

THE MAID. What a beauty! Heavens! It's simply out of this world!

MI. Tomorrow I'll go and thank him, and the day after tomorrow he's going away. Then we'll sell it! We'll sell it! We'll buy all kinds of stuff. You'll get a new blouse.

THE MAID. I'd rather have some pinafores. They sell such nice ones around here! Everything puffs out, and there's a little bow at one side.

MI. On one side? Well, fine then. I'll buy a pinafore. We'll just have to sell it for a little more.

THE MAID. You'll get a pretty penny for such a piece.

MI. You're right there! It'll bring in ten thousand maybe . . . Perhaps even twenty.

THE MAID. Oh!

MI. Well then, go to bed. I don't need anything. You can clean up tomorrow.

THE MAID. Good night! (*She exits.*)

(*For several moments* MI *walks around the room and looks in the mirror. Then she goes over to the alcove and pulls the curtain. She cries out, rushes to the bell, and wants to ring it, but* THE THIEF *rushes out, seizing her by the arm and pressing his hand against her mouth, while snapping the door shut and locking it. For a few moments they struggle silently.*)

THE THIEF. Quiet! Quiet! . . . Just try it! . . . I'll! . . . aha! . . . I'll kill you on the spot, you wretch! (MI *suddenly ceases to struggle and, having lowered her arms, stares intently at* THE THIEF.)

THE THIEF. That's it, that's it! Don't be a fool! (*He lets her go.*)

MI. You! It's you! . . . No, it can't be. Wait . . . Your eyes . . . Nikas! Nikas! Well then . . . take a look at me, just take a look at me!

THE THIEF. (*Surprised*) N-no . . . I don't know you.

MI. Ha! Ha! Ha! You haven't recognized me yet? Well, think back! Just think back, my dear! Look at my hair! The hair! It hasn't changed, Nikas!

THE THIEF. To the devil with you! I don't know you. I tell you, I don't know you.

MI. Well then, think a little more! Remember the fence in the square? The green fence with the wicket gate. Well? Do you remember, three girls used to sit on it . . . a long time ago . . . eight years ago . . . One was Erli, the other . . .

THE THIEF. So, it was like that, was it? How can I remember all the girls who ever sat on fences? You made it all up. So you sat on a fence then, did you?

MI. Yes! Nikas dear! I'm Mi, don't you see? Long-legged Mi. I had such long legs then, but now . . . I'm petite. Just see how I look, Nikas.

THE THIEF. Mm . . . You're not tall at all now. But now you've made it rich. And we had fun together then, didn't we? I seem to remember . . .

MI. No, we didn't! You didn't even want to look at me. You were so proud! You were the locksmith's apprentice, and you wore an apron and a piece of leather around your head . . . You used to fight with all the strongest boys. You remember, in the square with the shoemaker's son? He socked you in the eye. God, how I cried! It seems as never before in my life! . . . Do you know, Nikas, I really was stuck on you then. I was just out of my mind about you! More than anyone else in the world! I used to sit on the fence and dream . . . I'll grow up and become a beauty, the most beautiful of all; I'll be stinking rich. I'll come to you, no—I'll drive up to you in a carriage. You'll be surprised—"Who is this?" "It is I, Mi, whom you used to know!" And you'll say—"You're even more beautiful than you were on the fence." And—you'll kiss me . . . Ha-ha! It's really funny!

THE THIEF. So you're rich now?

MI. And you know, as I was coming here, I kept thinking the whole way, surely I'll see Nikas! We've already been here a few days. I took a quick turn around the streets and looked for you in all the old familiar places. I was so stupid! As if you'd be sitting around there until now, these eight years! Ha! Ha! I asked about you in the shop on the corner. The owner didn't know me, but said that you hadn't been around for a long time. The old laundress is dead. I just didn't know where to poke my nose next. And suddenly, here you are—right here. Ha! Ha! How happy I am, to be sure! Just think: I was looking for you, and suddenly you come thieving right to me! Just like a fairytale! Downright amazing.

THE THIEF. So what! I've been lots of places. It's always possible to run into someone. Once I ran into an agent of the criminal investigation department. He was, can you believe it, dressed up like a merchant and gave himself out to be a rich man. Well, I went up and sat beside him . . . We began to talk, and then I . . .

MI. No, it really is a fairytale! You know, I would never have dared tell you about this before . . . Well, to put it bluntly, I'm stuck on you. Just think how I've dreamed of this moment! And then it suddenly all came to pass! It happened! Nikas! Look at me!

THE THIEF. I've already looked, damn it! Where did you get the money and the other loot from? Well?

MI. You're simply amazing, Nikas! (She looks at him rapturously.) How many

124

people have I seen in these years! How many educated, important, famous people! They chased after me! They made passes at me! But, Nikas, believe me, this is the truth—there was not one like you, not one like you! Seriously! They were handsome, young, all sorts; but they just weren't you. They didn't have your style. You have such style, Nikas, such style!

THE THIEF. Well . . . so they say. Great. But tell me how you've managed to live it up, and why they give you presents like this nice piece of work? *(He touches the necklace.)*

MI. Oh, of course you don't know! I'm a singer. I sing marvelously! You know, they simply cry when I sing, I do it so well. They say they just can't help but love me when I sing . . . Listen, Nikas, I'll sing to you, for you . . . Dearest! I want to . . . *(She runs to the piano.)*

THE THIEF. *(Seizes her by the hand)* No, no! You are a big fool! Bawling at night! They'll all come running. What an old hen! Doesn't understand anything. I must tell you, sweetie, that the owner here and I don't exactly hit it off together.

MI. Oh? How so?

THE THIEF. Well, because of certain items. Two fur coats and a gold watch . . . mainly. In a word, it would be kind of unpleasant to run into him after our little disagreement.

MI. Well, he won't come here. I have the right to sing whenever I have a mind to.

THE THIEF. A lot you know. I don't even want to listen. At night, listening to singing is . . . bad for my nerves. I'm a tender plant.

MI. What a pity!

(THE THIEF goes up to the table. He takes two spoons and hits one against the other.)

THE THIEF. Silver?

MI. No; second-rate stuff. *(THE THIEF throws away the spoons, takes the half-empty bottle, and pours the rest of the contents into his mouth. He takes a bit of pie.)*

THE THIEF. Well then, they pay you for singing, do they? Hmm! Do they pay you much? Who taught you?

MI. I was just singing one day, and the old baron heard me and asked my grandmother if he could take me to the school in town. He died, but they kept on training me.

THE THIEF. *(Goes to the table, touches some boxes)* Do you have money? I want to borrow some.

MI. Of course. How much do you need? *(Takes her purse from the table)* Here then, take it all . . . two . . . three . . . eight! . . .

THE THIEF. You're joking. It's the big stuff I'm after. How much have you got? Do you have your whole fortune with you?

MI. Yes, there you are—eight.

THE THIEF. Stupid little fool!

MI. Word of honor! My impresario will pay me only after I've returned to town. Here the banker has taken all my expenses on himself. I have nothing more, Nikas!

THE THIEF. God damn it! You've done it now! Well, have you got your jewels around here?

MI. I've got nothing! Can you take my dresses? Nikas! Don't be angry. I have such expensive dresses! You can sell them. Take all of them, all! Leave me only the simplest one. They'll give you a lot of money for them. They've never even seen their like around here!

THE THIEF. Oh, what a goose! I'll go to the bazaar with those rags so they can jump on me right away! Do you really think I could sell them here? I'd have to take them God knows where on the steamer and get rid of them somewhere far off. I just don't have the time. I'm desperately in need of money. Tomorrow there's a big card game. A card shark is coming. Well, you just don't understand at all.

MI. What a pity it has to be tomorrow . . . If you could only wait several days, or 'til tomorrow evening; I'd get it out of the banker.

THE THIEF. Gosh, what next! As if I have time to wait! Tomorrow they'll bring millions into the casino! I'll fix myself up, look sharp, dress up fit to kill—you little idiot! Then if I can knock around there half an hour or so, I'll make a fortune. When they play, they really go crazy. Just like turkey cocks. It's a cinch to dip into their loaded pockets. Only I can't do a thing in these clothes. And there's none to be got anywhere. I've wasted a whole darn night because of you.

MI. Ah, don't talk that way. It hurts me! I would do anything for you.

THE THIEF. Give me the necklace.

MI. What?

THE THIEF. Yes—the necklace. There's a man I know here. He'll get rid of it for me in another place and give me the money. So hand it over. Well?

MI. Ah, the necklace! I completely forgot about it. It's a marvelous piece of work, isn't it? A present from His Excellency. I wasn't proud at all when he sent it to me; I couldn't have cared less. But now I'm glad. I'm proud that you see me as such an important person. Just think: His Excellency himself sent it to me! That surely means something! Now you'll believe I'm somebody special. You see how everyone loves me! And not at all just because I'm the rage. You know . . . I . . . you alone . . . Yes, yes, I'll give you the necklace, only not today. Today I can't. Wait, don't be angry! Don't you see, I just have to put it on when I go to thank His Excellency. Otherwise I can't. Understand? Etiquette. Come tomorrow night—and I'll give it to you. Nikas! Dearest! Can't you see my position? Can't you just see! But tomorrow, after the concert . . .

THE THIEF. She just keeps talking rubbish! I'm telling you straight: I've got to get myself looking really sharp before evening.

MI. Well, what's to be done . . . Nikas, just wait. Afterward you'll come and stay with me in town. I'll give you money, lots of it . . . all that I have. You'll see! It's so fine there! I have such beautiful rooms. My whole life glitters, like precious stones. We'll be together . . . I'll get rid of the banker. I know they'll all hang themselves from grief. Let them! Well, look at me! Am I not beautiful? You bet your life I am! Look at my hair . . . You see? A certain man said that my locks were like golden strings, that they sing.

THE THIEF. Hair? Hair sings? *(Bursts out laughing)* That's a lie for sure! So, you're not going to hand over the necklace? Well, I've had it, I guess.

MI. Nikas! Don't you want to kiss me even once . . . Nikas, dearest! You simply don't know how fine it'll be for us in town. There, you're not looking at me again. *(Embraces him)* Just once! Just one teeny little time! You see how I am all golden. You'll lay me on a red pillow . . . like a handful of gold coins . . .

THE THIEF. Ha-ha! She's made it up. *(He kisses her and, quietly undoing the necklace, hides it in his pocket.)* It's time for me to go then! If someone should come . . .

MI. No, no, no one will come. After all, you yourself locked the door . . . Again, Nikas, once more . . . after all, I've waited for you all my life . . . I've been kissed before . . . but you are the first I have ever kissed myself . . .

THE THIEF. If they find me—then I'm lost. Do you hear that or not?

MI. You are my one . . . my one and only! I sang so well only because I was expecting you . . .

THE THIEF. Let me go, now . . . After all, I'll come again. *(He embraces her with one hand, while putting his hand behind his back, and presses the button of the bell.)*

MI. This means you love me! Dearest, darling . . . Again! *(There is a knock at the door and the voice of THE MAID.)*

THE MAID. Here I am! Here I am! What's up?

MI. No, no, it's nothing! Why have you come? *(THE THIEF tears himself away, makes a sign to be silent, and jumps out the window.)* You're coming back then? Yes?

THE MAID. You rang . . . What's going on there? I'll go for help!

MI. *(Opening the door)* What's the matter with you?

THE MAID. What d'ya think? I hear a ring, I come running, I look, the doors are locked. I knock—you're whispering something, but you don't let me in. Oooh, my knees are still knocking.

MI. Rubbish! You imagined all of it. I didn't even think to ring . . . Help me undress . . . Let my hair down . . . Wait—undo the necklace first, or everything will get tangled . . . Ah!

THE MAID. The necklace? Where is it? You've taken it off.

MI. *(Smiling perplexedly, shakes down her dress, glances beyond the chairs and, suddenly hitting herself on the forehead, begins to laugh loudly.)* Ha! Ha! Oh, you stupid little idiot! Well, the necklace is gone and that's all there is to it.

Perhaps someone just had to have it . . . See—it doesn't bother me one bit! Well, what are you staring at? Didn't we look for it together—yet it's nowhere around. It's gone and that's all there is to it. Ha! Ha! It jumped out of the window!

THE MAID. Ah, my God! What a misfortune! And how can you laugh at it? Somebody stole it! Lord save us! Such a valuable thing! It's not even mine, and it nearly kills me. His Excellency himself sent it. The messenger who brought it from the store said such a thing is beyond all price! Made of French gold, he said, the very purest, and not one single plain stone . . . everything is artificial. There you are!

MI. What? What did you say?

THE MAID. Ah! So now you must really be sad!

MI. Artificial . . . counterfeit . . .

THE MAID. Only I don't know what artificial means . . .

MI. It means . . . it means that he will never come back. *(She covers her face with her hands and cries.)*

CURTAIN

TALENT

FROM: *Literaturnye voprosy* (Literary Questions, no. 6 (Moscow, 1975).

Even while a student at the institute, Zoin'ka Millgau exhibited an exceptional talent for literature.

Once she described, in a German rendition, the sufferings of the Maid of Orleans. Her words were so vivid that the teacher became agitated, got drunk, and couldn't come to class the following day.

Then followed a new triumph, which forever secured Zoin'ka's reputation as the institute's best poetess. She achieved this honor by composing an elaborate poem on the arrival of a trustee, which began with the words:

> "Here, at last, has come our time,
> Your visage we view among us enshrined . . ."

When Zoin'ka graduated from the institute, her mother asked her:

"What will we do now? A young lady ought to be well-prepared either in music or in painting."

Zoin'ka looked at her mother with amazement and answered simply:

"What good is painting to me, when I'm a writer?"

And that very day she sat down to write a novel.

She wrote diligently for an entire month. But in spite of all that, she produced not a novel, but only a short story—a result which was somewhat amazing, even to her.

The plot was exceedingly original: a certain young lady fell in love with a

128

certain young man and married him. The work was entitled "The Riddle of the Sphinx."

The young lady was married on approximately the tenth page of a standard-size sheet of writing paper. What to do with her from then on, Zoin'ka simply did not know. She pondered three days and then composed an epilogue:

"With the passage of time two children were born to Eliza, and she was, to all appearances, happy."

Zoin'ka pondered another two days, then recopied everything neatly and took it to a publishing house.

The editor turned out to be a man of little education. During their conversation it became apparent that he'd never even heard of Zoin'ka's verse on the arrival of the trustee. However, he took the manuscript and requested that she return for an answer in two weeks.

Zoin'ka blushed, paled, curtsied, and returned in two weeks.

The editor looked at her with embarrassment and said:

"Well, well, Miss Millgau!"

Then he went into the other room and brought out Zoin'ka's manuscript. The manuscript had gotten dirty, its corners curled in various directions, like the ears of an alert borzoi. In general it had a forlorn and disgraceful appearance.

The editor held out the manuscript to Zoin'ka.

"Well, here it is."

Zoin'ka didn't understand what was happening.

"Your little piece isn't appropriate for our outlet. Here, if you'll look . . ."

He leafed through the manuscript.

"Here, for example, at the beginning . . . mmm . . . 'the sun gilded the treetops' . . . mmm. You see, my dear young lady, ours is an ideological journal. At present we are advocating the rights of the women of Yakutsk to have community meetings; so we literally haven't the slightest need for the sun. That's how it is, miss!"

But Zoin'ka still did not leave. She looked at him with such defenseless trust that the editor got a bitter taste in his mouth.

"Nonetheless, you, of course, have a gift," he added, intently examining his shoe. "I would even like to advise you on making certain changes in your story, which, undoubtedly, will serve to benefit it. Sometimes the entire future of a work depends on some trifle. Well, for instance, your story literally demands that you put it in a dramatic form. Do you see? A dialogue form. You have, for the most part, brilliant dialogue. Over here, for instance, mmm . . .' "Goodbye," she said' and so forth. Well, that's my advice to you. Rework your little piece into a drama. And don't hurry, but think about it seriously, artistically. Work a bit on it."

Zoin'ka went home, bought a bar of chocolate for inspiration, and sat down to work.

In two weeks she was back, sitting before the editor, while he wiped his forehead and stammered:

"It's useless to have hurried so. If one writes slowly and thoroughly reasons out everything, the work turns out better than if one doesn't reason at all and writes quickly. Drop by in a month for the answer."

When Zoin'ka had left, he sighed deeply and thought:

"Maybe this month she'll suddenly get married, or go away somewhere, or simply give up all this nonsense. Miracles do happen! There is such a thing as good luck!"

But good luck happens seldom, and miracles not at all. In a month Zoin'ka arrived for an answer.

Seeing her, the editor nearly fainted, but immediately regained his composure.

"Your little piece? Ah yes, an exquisite thing. Only you know what—I must give you one brilliant piece of advice. The thing is, my dear young lady, you should, without the slightest delay, put it to music! Eh?"

Zoin'ka, offended, pouted.

"Why put it to music? I don't understand!"

"What don't you understand? Put it to music, and you'll have, you little fool, an opera from it! Just think—an opera! Then you'll come and thank me yourself . . . Look for a good composer . . ."

"No, I don't want an opera!" Zoin'ka said decisively. "I'm a writer . . . and you're suddenly on to an opera. I don't want it!"

"My pet! Well, you're really your own enemy. Just you imagine . . . suddenly they're singing your piece! No, I simply refuse to comprehend you."

Zoin'ka's face assumed a bulldog's expression and she answered emphatically:

"No, absolutely no! I don't wish it. Before you ordered me to redo my piece into a drama, and now you have to publish it, because I've adjusted it to your taste."

"And I'm not arguing with that! The little thing is charming! But you didn't understand me. Strictly speaking, I advised you to adapt it for the theatre, and not for publication."

"Well then, pass it on to the theatre!" Zoin'ka smiled at his stupidity.

"Mm, yes, but you see, today's theatre requires a special repertoire. *Hamlet*'s already been written. Another one's not needed. But our theatre is sorely in need of a good farce. If you could . . ."

"In other words—you want me to rework 'The Riddle of the Sphinx' into a farce? You should have said that."

She nodded to him, took the manuscript and, with dignity, walked out.

The editor stared after her for a long time and scratched his head with a pencil.

"Well, thank God! She won't come back anymore. Still, it's too bad she was so offended. Just as long as she doesn't end it all."

"My dear young lady," he said in a month, looking at Zoin'ka with his gentle blue eyes. "My dear young lady. You've taken on this venture for nothing! I read your farce and, of course, remain an admirer of your talent as before. But, unfortunately, I must tell you that such subtle and refined farces have no success with our crude public. For this reason the theatres accept only very, how shall I put it, very vulgar farces, whereas your piece, forgive me, is not at all titillating."

"You need something vulgar?" Zoin'ka inquired in a businesslike tone and, on returning home, she asked her mother:

"*Maman*, what do you consider the most vulgar thing?"

Maman thought for a moment and said that, in her opinion, the most vulgar thing in all the world was naked people.

Zoin'ka scribbled with her pen for about ten minutes, and on the following day she proudly held out her manuscript to the stunned editor.

"You wanted something vulgar? Here it is! I reworked it."

"But where?" the editor seemed confused. "I don't see . . . everything seems just as it was . . ."

"What do you mean, where! Right here—in the *dramatis personae*."

The editor turned the pages and read:

Dramatis personae

Ivan Petrovich Zhukin, Justice of the Peace, 53—naked.

Anna Petrovna Bek, landowner, philanthropist, 48—naked.

Kuskov, country doctor—naked.

Rykova, doctor's assistant, in love with Zhukin, 20—naked.

District police officer—naked.

Glasha, the maid—naked.

Chernov, Peter Gavrilovich, professor, 65—naked.

"Now you have no excuse to reject my work," Zoin'ka gloated caustically. "I think this should be sufficiently indecent."

1911

NOTE

1. Gurtovnik means to say "him." The plural pronoun used in place of the singular conveys servile respect for one's superior. The lackey's response in using the form is ironic.

Ivan Shmelyov (1875–1950)

Ivan Sergeevich Shmelyov, the son of a rich Moscow merchant, received his legal training in Moscow. He was raised in the Russian Orthodox tradition. His first works were printed by Gor'ky's publishing house, *Znanie* (Knowledge). He also participated in the Moscow literary society *Sreda* (Wednesday), which was attended by Chekhov, Bunin, Alexander Kuprin, Leonid Andreev, Boris Zaytsev, and other writers. Following the October Revolution he lived in the Crimea, where he suffered from starvation and witnessed the bloody executions of the Russian intelligentsia by the Bolsheviks. He managed to leave Russia only toward the end of 1922 and became a leading *émigré* writer in Paris. His famous story "Chelovek iz restorana" (The Man from the Restaurant; Moscow, 1912) is a humanitarian work about an insignificant waiter; *Neupivaemaya chasha* (The Inexhaustible Cup; Paris, 1921) is a poetic tale of a miraculous icon. The Bolshevik terror of the Russian Civil War is described in *Solntse myortvykh* (The Sun of the Dead; Paris, 1926). His other works include *Istoriya lyubovnaya* (A Love Story; Paris, 1929), *Leto gospodne* (The Summer of the Lord; Belgrade, 1933), *Bogomolye* (The Pilgrimage; Belgrade, 1935), *Nyanya iz Moskvy* (The Nanny from Moscow; Paris, 1937), and *Puti nebesnye* (Heavenly Paths; Paris, 1931–38). Shmelyov traveled extensively throughout Europe at the invitation of various literary circles and periodicals—in France, Switzerland, Czechoslovakia, Latvia, Estonia, and Germany. He corresponded with many eminent writers, among them Thomas Mann.

The Russian Orthodox religious tradition forms the most important theme of Shmelyov's oeuvre. In his artistic technique he was a disciple of Leskov, in that he used "skaz" most effectively and was well versed in the innumerable nuances of Russian folk speech. He himself recognized the Russian folk language as his forte in fiction, and his deft manipulation of it was very powerful. The reader is actually able to hear the speech of a naïve, excited fictitious narrator in his immediate environment—affectionate, anxious, depressed, resigned, or angry. Shmelyov's narratives are marked by a rhythmical and declamatory melodiousness which resembles Gogol's *Evenings on a Farm Near Dikan'ka*, some of Turgenev's short stories, and perhaps Lev Tolstoy's *Childhood* and *Adolescence*, as suggested by I. A. Ilyin.[1] Shmelyov's style reaches the level of lyrical and epic contemplation, or the "spiritual" style, in *The Summer of the Lord*. "Delicate colors, refined designs, and spiritual fragrance"[2] are inherent in this work.

The composition of Shmelyov's longer works (*Heavenly Paths*, for example) is often weak and rather disjointed. He was a writer of large proportions and schemes, but he lacked a sense of measure and moderation and was sometimes too flamboyant. He was also guilty of an occasionally uneven style. But in his short stories he demonstrated perfect control of his material. This is especially true of *Vyezd v Parizh: rasskazy o Rossii zarubezhnoy* (Arrival in Paris: Stories about *Emigré* Russia; Belgrade, 1929), his collection concerning the new Russian *émigré*, who has barely escaped the horrors of Bolshevism and is still pursued by vivid recollections of them. At this time Shmelyov was very interested in the theme of the simple Russian's encounter with Western Europe. Despite its excited tone, the short story "Shadows of Days" is an interesting example of Shmelyov's "dream-logic technique," linking him with Dostoevsky, whom he greatly admired as a man and an artist. Many of Ivan Shmelyov's works have been translated into German, French, Italian, and Dutch. In comparison with the subdued and quiet novels of Boris Zaytsev, Shmelyov's fiction is impassioned and boisterous, except for his novels and short stories depicting the religious life of Muscovite Russia amidst the radiance of the Russian Easter and the tolling of church bells.

NOTES

1. I. A. Ilyin, "Khudozhestvo Shmelyova," *Pamyati Ivana Sergeevicha Shmelyova: sbornik*, ed. V. A. Maevsky (Munich, 1956).

2. *Ibid.*

SHADOWS OF DAYS

And into the silent sphere of visions and dreams
Bursts the foam of howling waves.

F. Tyutchev

FROM: *Vyezd v Parizh: rasskazy o Rossii zarubezhnoy* (Arrival in Paris: Stories about *Emigré* Russia; Belgrade: Russkaya biblioteka, 1929).

I

I seem to be on the Place de l'Etoile in a crowd. Whether it's evening or night—I don't know. The sky, black as soot, has become threatening, oppressive. Not a single star can be seen. Beneath the mournful Arc at the Tomb of the Unknown Soldier, the wind tears at the inextinguishable flame. The pale lights of the taxis recede uneasily, peering about with red eyes. Streetcars depart in haste. Everyone is anxious, awaiting something. No faces are seen, only heads and hats; everyone—is leaving for *there*. But the flame already blazes, hurling itself beneath the arches of the Arc. Billows of smoke—heavy, black, as from oil. The lights from the billboards grow dim, glowing crimson and sooty with smoke. Someone says the oil reserves have caught fire . . .

I'm waiting for someone. I watch the flame—a mournful fire. I know—the reserves are around here somewhere, on Presnya.[1] There is a graveyard there, and the oil from there, from beneath the ground, is thick. The flame is fed by that oil. I'm terrified; I want to leave, but it's difficult. Grief stricken, I stare—to the right, below—the Champs-Elysées, spacious, deserted, in flames; the light is pale and sad, with milky-dull globes, as in Moscow during the frost. I must go there, but why—I don't know. There—is peace.

Someone shouts:

"Let me thro-ou-gh . . . !"

The voice is piercing, strained.

I realize—he's making his way through to me, and I wait in alarm.

It's a little old man. The face is familiar, but who he is—I can't recall. He's short and frail, wearing a hat in the style of a priest, with watery eyes and a scraggly beard—like a beggar. He has tucked a red bundle under his arm, as if to go into a bathhouse; yet the bulge is not linen, but communion bread, or apples. How happy I am at his arrival; a kinsman, a fellow from back home. I want to ask him something important. But he winks and urges:

"Let's go, let's go! . . ."

He knows something. They're making way for us. He whispers:

"From the Place de la Concorde . . . Through Berlin, then from there to the right. The last train . . ."

My heart skyrockets. Tickets, visas . . . ? We'll never make it.

He runs, clutching his coat flaps. I realize that this is our cabby, "one of the good ones," but very old. They sent him to get me . . . But somehow he's so strange—his unbelted cloth coat flows like a *sarafan*, and sweeps the floor; silvery baubles edge the armholes in a straight line; his cap resembles some sort of beaver fur, with a little cushion and small corners, and an edging of fox at the neck—like coachmen wear.

I walk in trepidation—we won't make it; it's the last train. It would be better in a cab—through Berlin, then on to the right, it's close. Even without a visa it's possible.

We're running across glazed asphalt. It's slippery. Not a soul around. Behind are bursts, explosions, I turn around and look back—the flame is higher, the Arc shimmers with puffs of smoke, fiery and black. A fire? . . .

Running, I feel my pocket—my *carte d'identité*. What about money? . . . How will we leave? . . .

The little old man is running, waving his small bundle. It seems that he knows *everything*. Visas are being sold on the Place de la Concorde, in some sort of booth. Who exactly is he? He's so familiar . . . Alexey, our coachman? But Alexey was taller, and had a black beard . . . and died when I was a student. He died, yet he lives—it's not strange.

The Champs-Elysées recedes endlessly, down below, in the cold light of lusterless, milky-dull globes. They're strange lights, different. The earlier ones were all greenish, and like small pails. Yet these are like whitish globes—where had I seen them before? In my childhood, in the theatre hallways, at the entrances? The lights of bygone days.

The distance had frozen black like a river. The sullied ice dreamily flows and shines, like smoothed asphalt. Pale lights are moving toward us; taxis speed alarmingly to the Etoile; all of them are empty. On nearby streets, the lights have gone out; there is blackness there. I recall an avenue of lights, windows, automobiles, and hotels—where is all of this? Dark, blind houses. It has all passed by. Now there's one road—straight ahead into the ghastly, cold lights. Soon even they will go out.

I'm running in anguish. The Champs-Elysées, my final road.

I hear everything being deserted behind me; glass is delicately shattering. Did they turn off the globes? Still running, I glance behind. A scarlet glow in back of the lusterless glass, then nothing. I hear how the globes become emptiness. There's a lantern. I run and reach it—then it fades; the red coal has gone out. But ahead they still flicker. I shout, and point to the lamp—and it fades.

"They're going out! . . . Why are they going out?!"

Because of smoke off the Etoile . . . ?

The little old man—it seems to me he's a priest—shouts indistinctly: "The Elysian Fields! . . . the end! . . ."

————————

Something's tapping on the asphalt behind us, hopping like a grasshopper. I sense—someone back in the shadows, on crutches, is catching up. I hear how heavily he breathes, I want to make out his face, but it's not visible. The service cap is pulled down to his nose; his head is bent down, his thin military overcoat beats against the crutches as he runs. I know that he's one of ours, poor devil. I feel so sorry for him. I want to call to him . . .

From out of the darkness—a wagon with hay is coming, enormous, dim. Swaying, it presses down on us, sputters . . . then blocks the road; in a split second all is dark. A peasant's voice from beneath the earth is shouting:

"Stead-dy . . ."

It buries us, falling upon us like a mountain. I tear through, scattering the

135

mound all over—the road, quiet, empty, illuminated; the one on crutches—
behind us.

"Look, look! . . ."

Is the peasant under the hay?! . . .

The avenue is jammed with mounds of straw—a hayloft. The mounds
tremble and move—the peasant digs himself out from under the hay. Behind
the hayloft, the sky is blazing—the fire is raging there. Against the sky, the
Arc quivers. A black pillar of puffs; above it, a cloud, its underside orange,
slips down to the right. That's burning oil. I see how the sparks scatter into
the hay. It will catch fire!! . . . Look, fool, why bring your hay here? . . . It
will all be lost!

The peasant jumps up on the hay and flails his arms.

We run. From the black streets—voices, rumblings. *Has it begun?* . . . The
lights have gone out; the glow provides light.

———————

A dim, empty square. Houses with no windows. In the darkness, little
boys whistle and whoop; they run—pattering. Black trees. Crooked, tangled
twigs against the crimson sky—thrown together in the patterns of a crow's
nest. Behind the somber hill of the Grand Palais, the sky is ablaze—is Les
Invalides burning? . . .

A bridge span blazes on the right. Beyond the bridge, beyond the winged
horses, against the flame—is a cast iron dome. Above it, a glimmer. Across
the scorched sky whirlwinds and smoke. It occurs to me—Les Invalides has
caught fire.

The one on crutches follows me. He points to the dome with his crutch:
"This cast iron . . . is getting sooty! . . ."

I hear a shout:

"Hurry! . . ."

It's a familiar voice. He can hardly be seen because of the fire—he's waving.
I know—he'll *take me away*. That thought is both joyous and terrifying. *There*,
I'll meet . . . my past reaches back to there. *There*—is peace.

But I have to get out of here.

Place de la Concorde, the last train. What's there . . . ? I see—like a
crimson patch, all aflame. Bonfires? I hear a distant noise.

I hurry, afraid to stay. *He* knows this. He looks at me so tenderly:

"It's nothing . . . don't be afraid, son."

He winks. I want to remember—who is he?

"Here, take it . . ."

And he takes communion bread out of his kerchief.

I recognize it—inexpensive communion bread, from out of my
childhood—the bread of poor people. Like a small temple, or pillar. A

rose-colored cross on its tiny dome. Joyfully I take it, and in it—there is that distant, bright, and holy childhood of mine. I look into the little bundle. There are apples, pears, little trifles! I look into his eyes. They're familiar, twinkling with tenderness. Wrinkles, an emaciated face, pointed beard . . . My God! I've remembered . . . It's the old psalm-reader from our alms-house's church! Nikolay Arsentyich, psalm-reader from back home. He came to get me.

He whispers:

"Faster, it's the last one . . . from the Place de la Concorde . . ."

Both happiness and the grief of loss—like a flash—at the moment of realization.

I feel how I need him. I love him, as I did in my childhood—for his wrinkles, his tender hand, for the tapered candles he placed in front of the icons, for the strange words—I don't know them, yet they caress me—for he is like the icon.

He has come for me!

In a flash I see it all.

There were times when he would stroke my head, would give me communion bread (in the shape of a little temple much like this), would lead me to the altar, and show me the book spotted with wax, with the scent of God, his eyes twinkling tenderly. Before the Savior he'd place some tiny paradise apples, delicately streaked with crimson, and tickle them with the holy anointing brush . . .

Everything in me begins to soar as sweetly as in a dream.

I'm recalling *my* beloved icons. They occur only in childhood, and everyone has *his own*—alive only to him. The old man shakes his head, he reads . . . The candle flickers with sleepy nods and drips wax onto his fingers, onto the little old book. From the icon, the same sort of little old man looks down, squinting tenderly. I recall his tinkling voice; I hear his incomprehensible words ". . . and sorrowful is my soul . . . all this day have I lamented . . ." which flow with an enigmatic sadness. Yet my soul becomes so bright, so peaceful.

Through the windows—snowdrifts, stars are visible. Already he's reading: "And for all time and for each hour . . ."—slumberous words, words of the night. The candles go out. The nocturnal street grows blue. The snowdrifts swell into curving banks; you sink into them. It had been falling heavily all day. Sheaves of grain in snow-covered rows. It's so quiet on our little street, so silent—everything filled with the snow. One can hear how the snow shovels crunch; how they dig in, and the thud of clumps of snow . . . A cart slips by as if on snowy down; a shovel stands stuck in the snow.

A cabby drifts by noiselessly; at the corner the little horse snorts—the horse is pleased: he kicks up the powdery snow from under his legs. On the posts, on the fences—piles of snow. They are soft, like gossamer. Small lanterns under the snow glow sleepily; the dogs dig in it with their noses. Beyond the rail fence, in the birch trees, a crow croaks hoarsely—foretelling more snow—without waking. The windows throw a radiance over the snow, and over the windows—a rosy glow from the icon lamps. You enter—it's warm and cosy, the stove-perch is being warmed for the night. You sit on it under the light of a little green-shaded lamp—with a cherished new issue of *Around the World* and a crusty heel of black bread. You read for a long time; the roosters are calling. Through the frost-covered windows—the twinkling of stars, the silvery Nicolas the Supplicator in the corner, a little icon lamp casting patterns . . .

That dear, wrinkled face brings everything back. Joys, losses—all pass by in one flash of realization.

They sent him after me . . .

But, didn't he die? . . . How can he . . . be in Paris? With me?

He died, yet he lives. Not strange.

He's walking, moving along with his little bundle. And I follow behind.

———————————

The glow is covered by a shadow—it's some sort of palace; it's dark. The sky, above the blaze, is turning pale rose. The roofs are becoming black.

The forest with its black trees. Beyond the thicket, in the depths of the forest—the horizon glows with a smoky crimson. A suburban house? There's a greenish light in the trees. Strange. The lights have gone out everywhere else, but . . . ?

The trees recede, I see fiery letters—*Restaurant*.

A glass wall. Mirrors, crystal garlands, and stars are shining. The place is shining with silver; it sparkles resonantly with crystal, it shimmers with frost. And sultry flowers in vases . . .

A restaurant? . . . Don't they know the lights have been turned off . . . ?

In the brilliance, I see a rosy figure—shoulders, breasts, the starched, snow-white flounces of a woman's skirt, heads with bald patches, naked arms entwined, the glimmer of dress coats. I smell the warm, intoxicated aroma of wine and powder, flesh and flowers. I see how the faces, thrown back, cling, and drift languorously in the lights. They lounge in straight-backed arm-chairs, holding goblets, sniffing cigars. The waiters advance, then stand, immobile and decorous, along the walls. Yet no music is heard. It's strange. It seems to me they're *alien*, from another world—as though not even alive. Something like . . . Americans?

A strange restaurant.

Among the trees a reddish glow. I see charred little columns, the bloody reflection of glass in the lanterns. The Great Obelisk is flickering.

Place de la Concorde, the last train.

A rumble is heard. Carts, wheels, horses, mountains of trunks—a camp of rabble? . . .

The sky is ablaze with the cupola of Les Invalides. Two turrets, like two nuns, dressed in sharp little hoods, stand against the sky, one next to the other, filled with anxiety. The trees behind the Concorde, the chambers, the Obelisk—everything in a bloody hue.

How can we get through it? . . .

By the pedestals—frenzied horses, manes streaming in the wind like flames, their bared teeth crimson. The ditch is behind them . . . I run across, I see . . . feet in buckles, stockings, camisoles, swollen faces, wigs . . . I hear shouting:

"They've crushed a lot of people . . . !"

Khodynka Steet, Presnya Street? . . . Crushed people in pits . . . *Here*?!

I'm alone, I'm afraid.

Bonfires smoking. Gypsies beating on basins; they're playing cards. Cauldrons are swirling, the horses shake their heads. There's a rumble as if from a tambourine . . . played by buffoons? Some sort of people . . . in jersey sweaters with collars rolled—maybe thieves?—are dragging fur coats along. In wide baggy pleated trousers, a slick face, like a rabbit in a cap—a rogue—is following me. I feel both disgust and terror. With scarves on their necks, the scoundrels—they're doing indecent things to a young lady. She's wearing a plush blue coat; she flails her arms and shoves back. The cloak has flown open; her swollen stomach is helpless; around her neck dangles a small watch on a little golden chain. They drag her into a corner, paw her . . .

"Let us pass," they shout. They're dragging someone off, though he tries to stand. People on horses are threatening. Somewhere . . . have I seen this before? . . . In the bloody light, *something*—with posts . . . Executions? . . . On new show wagons, in the depths—solid black with people. Young boys latch on to trees; they are waiting.

The Great Obelisk looms over it all. The red stone. Its thousand years have awakened; they blink at the fire, and flow in streams. The morose chambers, the windows, the lamps on the arches—everything flickers. From the balconies, showmen wail above the camp.

I'm looking intently—so where is the train? It should be near the gardens. I won't be able to pass straight through. I see trunks and a scuffle over them. People with wolfish eyes, in ragged scarves; Apaches, in leggings, with hidden knives; fat women with mustaches; young tarts, rabble . . . snatching fur coats, and dragging them away.

I try to get through. Snowy flounces, tail coats . . . a restaurant? . . . Next to the tail coats—women, with naked shoulders, stand close together. They've surrounded them; they're robbing them. They tear off the tail coats, the pearls, the bracelets. Young wenches in tatters cluster around; the ladies fight back. With gaping lips, a cross-eyed man strokes their bodies . . . Reeling, with his hare-like mug, he plays with a fat one, tickling her armpits. A fat man with a cigar looks on dully, sweating. The one with the hare's mug tears at him by his coattails, shaking him out of the coat, as out of a sack. They're beating the tall American: oh my God!

I'm . . . *outside*. I've got to make the last train.

They wave from the balconies. Faces on every floor, as in a gallery. Wailing:

"Victo-o-ry! . . ."

The one in the foreground—the short one, is like a gnome. He has a little black head, like a wedge. He's dressed in a fur coat—with a sheen like the apron of a woman baking communion bread. A stole of fox fur down to his elbows. His eyes bore into you. His mouth is askew; he squeaks—but his squeak, like an awl, bores right into the skin.

Another man is heavy set. A cap like a tower, a coonskin coat like a mountain—ears like an elephant's. The coat of an archdeacon, and his moustache . . . like a Romanian cymbalist's—like two screws.

There is yet another—a beetle-like one. With a pendulous moustache, a nose like a nail, a sour mouth—as though he were sniffing something. He has a stolen polecat fur. Behind him, a man with no forehead, and a big mouth; his moustache, "for piquancy," is arrow-like; his greatcoat, with a red lining and a beaver collar, is slung on one shoulder; his shirt is smeared with oil.

Beyond them are hordes—caps of otter, doggie-like hats, overalls of wolf or skunk fur, camelskin garments, loose capes, half-length coats, plaids, and hoods . . . They thrust their fists toward the Obelisk; they make their appeal . . . to drag their victims off somewhere farther away. It seems to me that this stone—is theirs, this thousand-year-old aspergillum of the rabble, the god of the nomads. They drag it over the earth eternally.

Down below some people shift from one foot to another, confusedly—holding books, poorly dressed, with nervous faces. They argue, whisper, quarrel. Their movements are indecisive, impotent. Some agree, but others protest in silence. There is a rustle of papers, a glint of spectacles . . .

I know—any minute they'll drag them away. Behind them, in prison—a clanging. Snout faced, waiting in animal skins—now they'll be let loose . . .

There is blood on everything—on the Obelisk, the sky. Glowing red in the glass of the lanterns, streaming over the sidewalks, flowing onto the trees.

I cannot pass. I make my way to the Obelisk. A peasant with a sack is gaping at me. A pot-bellied little horse, and a cart. Under the cart there is hay—he is feeding his horse. I ask where the train is. He doesn't listen, but looks ahead to the balconies. They're tossing clothes and fur coats to the crowd. I understand—he has come for them.

At the stone, in prison, there are little old men in smocks and turbans, multicolored—Magi,[2] it seems. Their faces can't be seen; they are all on their knees, their heads together—they're examining something on the ground. I look with horror—a little yellow fire like a tongue. The inextinguishable flame? . . . The oil, even here?! . . . They practice witchcraft, they fan the flame . . . Magi? . . . Is it fires they are fanning . . . or—*light?* . . . In silence, with heads together . . .

The gypsies beat on the basins. The mounts neigh. The tambourine seems to thunder. The cauldrons smoke with fumes, and there is the smell of meat. The smoke is fusty, sickening.

A subterranean staircase. The metro, where a train is standing. A little door, barely luminous. Visas? . . . A woman at a counter, stacks of banknotes. It's a bistro, yet the banknotes appear to be visas. The woman throws down the note "Maryland" and receives three francs in change, our gold ones. I run, the gas burner flickers—a corner, tables piled to the ceiling, like a partition. In the corner—anguished faces, young, with a death-like misery in their glance. Our martyrs! I cry out, "It's the last train, get going! . . ." They're silent, as if dozing. I can't get to them. I throw the gold coins, and I hear their sound. I run—to pass them from behind. Walls. I knock, as if into a void. Where are the doors? Boards everywhere, new ones, the smell of pine. Stairs, stairwells, holes. I'll crawl along the ties, the crosspieces, beams. I see through the holes—down, far below—only lights, bonfires, and smoke. I'm terrified—I'll fall into the gap. The steps have collapsed, there's no railing. I hear . . . the crutches . . . behind me. I turn around—there is *that man*, the one on crutches. He's walking on the beams.

I crawl out onto the landing. There is no escape—it is the final landing, the size of a board. There's nothing for me to hold on to; I fear I'll fall down . . . The sky is blue; there are stars. Glowing lights and bonfires—dots—in the terrifying depth. In the distance, there is a glow, and a dome like a five-kopeck piece. Two small towers like a pair of nuns in their sharp-pointed hoods or—two small sticks in the horrible distance.

I hear a familiar voice: "Hur-r-ry . . . !"

I run down along the small planks, in the wind. It is fresh and frosty. The engines are enveloped in white clouds. There is a platform, and boxes. It seems to be snowing lightly. The train is strange—the benches in the cars are along the walls. I see a small old man waving at me. I am so glad—I run to the cars, but then I think—where is my hat? . . . I've lost it. And my luggage . . . I don't remember. *All* my belongings were there . . . The train will leave in a minute; it's too late. In the car, below me, an orchestra is playing. Bismarck is traveling with us, on his way to a congress.

A whistle. I look—from far away, like a bird, a man waves; he is on crutches, his light military coat billows out in the wind. He is catching up with the train; he has jumped onto it! I'm glad; I cry out from happiness. Who is he? A relative of mine? I cannot see his face.

We are moving. The crystal stars are so bright! The pines lash against my legs. There is the snow, the forests. The music plays—gently.

"We have passed Berlin!"

A peasant's voice: it sounds like—"By-yar-lin!"

The birch trees, with stars peeping through. It looks like Kuskovo. Long barracks under the hillock. The cell windows are fogged over; the melting snow is muddy. A small old man is running to the bathhouse. What shall I do? . . .

It's snowing; there is a platform. I am . . . alone. Now what? It won't look right to be without a hat. I look intently through the window—there is a yellow lamp. I look—Am I . . . *here?* Facing *that* horror? . . . I stand there. From the darkness a lantern slowly appears. Through the window I can see the hall of the railroad station, an empty cot. Someone is standing at the door . . .

A hoarse voice from out of the darkness: "Come in. We're closing!"

Snow has piled up at the door. I see a bell and a rough rope. The snow lies on the bell like a stripe. As I stand, I grow cold. I keep on trying to see everything. There is a bar, a sleeping man; *someone* is waiting behind the door . . . I shall enter immediately . . .

II

I'm from Paris—I'm somewhere near Moscow, traveling.

Nighttime. Snow falls heavily. A deserted, empty station. Not a single car. Everything is covered with snow; even the tracks are invisible. There are no steps on the platform—everything is smooth and clean. Not a single person in sight. The snow is somehow lifeless—it doesn't crunch; it's like cotton. Yet everything around is as always—barns, front gardens, and birch trees. There are lights in the railway station windows.

I look around. How lonely I am! . . . Where I'm going and why—I don't know. I have neither a hat nor any luggage with me. The snow is clinging and heavy as in March. The dim light of the lanterns shines through it. A dog is barking behind the station—an anxious barking—it listens, then barks a little into the void. Then again it listens. It is dark there.

How can I get out of here? Through the station? Without a hat—it just won't look right. Through the garden? There is a coachman somewhere . . . railings everywhere. A sharp anguish—why am I here? I am trying to remember . . . what is it . . . a bathhouse? . . . How many years without a bathhouse! Everybody is in the bathhouse now. There is no one to be seen. Tomorrow is a holiday.

The small station is low, made of boards, and covered with the wet snow. I am trying to make out what's written above the entrance—is it "Moscow"? The small windows look like squares; they are foggy, and the light scarcely penetrates. I look intently . . . Heavens, am I *here*? Indeed, how have I come . . . here? I'm in anguish; I want to return; my legs are weak. The falling snow is wet; the dog is barking—there is no escape.

I look with disgust—a dark hall; the stove is turning black, footbindings are drying . . . in a shaggy hat, a man is asleep . . . greenish smoke from cheap tobacco, a dim lamp in the lantern, its soot meandering like a thread. *Someone* is behind the door . . . I'm so disgusted, I can't go in!

I hear a voice. Is somebody there? He clears his throat viscously, like a sick person. The little lantern dangles, its fireguard sputtering as it touches the snow. I am a slave again . . . to be muddled, confused, to fill out vile questionnaires . . . It's so disgusting!

A hoarse, dull voice from the darkness: "Come in, we are closing up."

I'm thinking—I ought to smoke . . . Should I tell them I am from here and simply taking a walk? . . . I feel for my cigarettes—*Maryland*. They might see the brand . . . I have no matches.

I make my way, as if I were a native here. I try to whistle, but my lips won't obey. In my pocket, there is a *carte d'identité*! . . . The wet snow lies in a drift by the door. No one has walked here for a long time. I pull the handle on the door, but can't open it . . . The small lantern is dim. I see the bell, a frozen rope with a small knot, and the snow on the bell like a stripe. I am cold from standing, but I want to see distinctly. There is a bar, a man . . . is he asleep? *Someone* is behind the door. I feel an itching exhaustion in my legs—should I run away? . . .

I shall enter immediately.

———————

High barracks; on poles—a flour shop, sort of. A dark wall stained from a leak; an arch on beams. A lamp is glowing yellow in the emptiness. It is disgusting to walk—a sticky and slippery floor. The strong stench of a train car filled with bulls; I'm nauseated from the sweetish odor of rot. I can't . . .

I look around—where is the exit? *There* . . .

I see an enclosure in the depths of the hall, a turnstile. Some shadows are moving. I feel both abomination and a strong desire—*to see. They* are hiding.

I know—they cannot do it *here*, because here it is "Europe," a special place—*outside*.[3]

Empty tables between the partitions, as if these were boxes. Some sort of peasant. He's lying on the bench under the window. A blind window. His long-waisted coat is lined with lambskin; he wears a crimson sash, boots with cleats, and a cap. His fist is in his pocket . . . He has an aquiline nose, a swarthy face. Is he a gypsy horse trader? I'm alarmed—if he wakes up, "Europe" will be lost.

I examine the bar. It is a small trough; in it, something like gelatine; it looks terrible—like a yellowish lard. Behind the bar, there is someone looking at me, taking a ladle, and getting into the gelatine with it. I recognize it as a *garçon* from Motte-Picquet, and in horror I wave him away from me—I don't want him! He spoons out some gelatine and carries it to a small table. Pointing at it with his finger, he says, "Eat!"

Behind me, a partition; other people are sitting there. The dishes clatter, the noise is like restaurant noise. A waiter with a napkin is looking. Do they really eat *such things*? . . . I am nauseated, yet wish to placate him . . . He appears to be an Italian, in an imperial. He peeps out from behind the wall—to make sure I'm still here. I play the foreigner—it is "Europe" here—so I say to the *garçon* from Motte-Picquet, wishing to placate him: "*Voilà, monsieur* . . ."

I give him a five-franc note. "Here is some foreign currency . . . I am from Paris and presently will return there . . ."

He looks at me impudently and says to me in Russian: "It's all the same—you must *sign your name*. On all questionnaires, on all fourteen of them! I'll be back in a jiffy . . ."

He disappears. I am alarmed. A head peeps out above the wall—to see if I'm still here. I understand it and move away, where "Europe" is. There I walk like a foreigner. *There* a waiter appears, pointing at me with a note. I see a door which is slightly ajar . . .

I recognize the railroad station—the Vindava one. There is the red broadcloth, the glasses, the chandeliers, the valises. It is the first- and second-class waiting room. *They* are there.

All of them are masked, and wearing fur coats. A train leaves for Riga, another one for Paris. I see a small man with his head erect, dressed in a woman's coat with its fox collar reaching his elbows. There are other people with him; they support and lead him—respectfully. He pokes his finger toward the door, at me. I am terrified, yet I hold myself back at the door handle—it is "Europe" here. All people here appear to be foreigners, and all of them are going—to Europe. I notice that everything on them—except their valises—is foreign. They themselves appear foreign, though dressed in Russian fur coats. At the exit . . . there are our fools, in their cloth caps and red stars. They look around in a servile manner, watching.

I see the fox collar . . . coming toward me! . . . I slam the door and run . . .

The platform is empty. A long train. I see a man: "To Paris?"

He rummages in some kind of bag.

"It's not going."

Somebody is waving his hand at me. A machine greaser—smelling of oil. He leads me somewhere. There is no longer any train, but a field. He whispers: "Straight ahead, straight ahead . . ."

His voice is familiar to me; however, I can't see his face—it's dark.

We walk along a deep corridor; the boards bend beneath us. The cracks in them blink and show golden beneath our feet—below us is an illuminated hall, and an uproar. I step carefully and look through the cracks—the people below us move around in confusion; they slam the doors and search . . . I know—it is *that* man himself among those wearing fur coats.

"Here is the exit . . ."

He is my friend, my relative—perhaps even my late father. I wish to embrace him . . .

I am alone. The door is bolted; the brick is rumbling. I see clean snow, and I swallow fresh air.

Long barracks, a bathhouse. Wet windows with some shadows beyond them. In the ditch there is water; it smells of a bathhouse. The walls are made of logs, of thoroughly rotten wood—the bathhouse is rotten throughout. I look on intently . . . it is so crowded; there are bodies standing, close to each other, densely packed. Bony shoulder blades, ribs, and necks. They are enveloped by the steam; there is the typical bathhouse fizzing noise, the clatter of washtubs. It is too full to enter. I search for a door—there isn't one. I am frightened—how they are squeezed together, how their bodies rub! . . . It seems to me that the steam is coming from them, for the bathhouse is cold. I shout:

"Le-e-t me in! . . ."

Their heads sway, close together—like a ripple. I am afraid that the bathhouse may give way at the joints, that its walls may burst apart . . .

Night. It is snowing. I wander along the alleys. The snow is whitish—there must be a moon in the sky. Dead houses, closed gates. I am confused; I don't know where *my* house is . . . There is an alley, but I cannot ask anybody, for no one is here. What city is it? There are blind alleys and lanterns with oil. Is it Klin? . . . Or Ryazan'? . . .

A coachman is crossing one alley after another, like a shadow. I hear the muffled sound of his sledge on the notches. The manure shows dark. There are vegetable gardens. Where am I? . . .

It seems that it is the Sukharyovskaya Tower by the eye of its clock. Of course, it's Meshchanskaya Street. It is quarter to . . . seven! But why don't I see anybody?

Oh, my Lord, where am I? . . .

Sadovaya Street? It's empty; there are no gardens. Only fences. Everything is upside down. How can it be . . . so forsaken?! . . .

Another coachman drives noisily into an alley. Here, perhaps. It is Zhitnaya Street? A blind alley, a fence . . .

I see—a church. Is it that church? . . . No, this one's shorter. The one in which I was baptized was tall, its dome was green. But the church porch was the same. Of course, it has aged . . . I recognize Nicolas the Supplicator . . . in the snow. The fence. The vestibule of the church. Yes, it is the same church. It is locked.

I press against the door with my aching chest. I kiss the bars of the fence. There is so much snow in the vestibule! The baptismal font used to stand here . . . the white font always stood here. How often I used to climb the steps and look past the bars! It stood, the white font, on its heel. The old font, *mine*. I remember, how into it . . . I press against the door and weep. There is no font. A *single* sharp sensation pierces . . . through me and through the church. The white font . . . We are tied together. I shout from pain through the bars, into the darkness. Oh, my Lord! . . .

Night. It is spring. I am in my patron's study. I am wearing tails . . . I must go to the Regional Court for my defense.

The strict, peaceful, and decorous study is so pleasing to me. Dark curtains. A deep leather divan, armchairs, the bookcases with green blinds, the bronze faces of sages. I see Cicero's even skull and the Tsar-Liberator with his tuft of hair. Codes of Laws. Wise Statutes on the table. The long table is by the window. A candle is burning. The window is open. The wind slightly sways the portière. There is the smell of greenery and night from the garden. The lilac is blossoming. I see its bunches. The candlelight falls on them, on their dark, lusterless leaves. It's quiet. The street lantern pours its light onto the poplar with its small whitish leaves.

"Let's discuss it . . ." my patron says, lighting his cigar off the candle.

He is good-humored and calmly impressive in his words. I am pleased. I know—he is dead, but this does not mean anything, for he exists—in *another* way.

I say: "But how are you *now*? You have the same study, things are in the same order. Even the Statutes? They haven't touched you? . . ."

"They can't," he replies impressively. "*They* don't know. All of this . . ." he points around the study and the garden, "is '*outside*'! The Law . . ." he takes the Statutes and leafs the book like a fan, "you know, already at the time of Justinian . . . with his 'dangling inheritance'?"

I recall something—yes, Justinian? . . . With his "dangling inheritance"? He continues in the same impressive manner: "Well, let's discuss it. The 'dangling inheritance' . . . Don't confuse it with 'escheat'! . . ." He wags his finger, "Don't! For I *know*. When the lawful successor is unknown, or when his whereabouts are unknown," he points somewhere beyond the garden, "but he . . . *exists*! This is only a presumption . . . that he exists somewhere . . . so to speak, po-ten-tially. Let's discuss this special case . . ." he points beyond the garden. "This special case, when a huge inheritance is dangling, so to speak, awaiting its lawful successor, *id est, momentum juris*.* Is this clear? But here," he points at the bookcases and at his peaceful study, "here is—guard-ian-ship! It is an elusive, moral, or better to say, spir-it-ual guard-ianship, *tutela spiritus*.† That's why . . . they are *unable*! Let's not discuss the right—they cannot do it for all intents and purposes! *Impotentes*.‡ It is inaccessible to *perishability*. *Ergo: victores sumus*.§ This is obvious. Do you follow me?"

I understand him completely. We understand everything. I believe, and I am confident that *there is* such guardianship. My patron knows all about it. They *cannot*. That's why this study, this table, these Statutes, this lilac behind the window, the janitor beyond the fence, and the small dome of the Church of the Assumption somewhere there—that's why all this is so firm. Because there is a "dangling inheritance" and guardianship. Yes, indeed.

All of a sudden I realize:

"*Carte d'identité* . . . Do I need . . . my personality? . . ."

He catches the meaning of my words at once. He looks at his watch—his watch is a rarity, a chronometer; he smoothes his small light brown beard and scratches his forehead.

"We'll arrange it. Let's go to the Kamergersky Theatre—Chekhov is playing tonight. Aren't the guardians there . . . on the walls in the hall?" He blinks, "From there you'll emerge with full rights. The law exists! . . ." he repeats, pointing at the volumes.

I understand—there is such a law. My patron knows everything.

*That is the moment of truth
†Spiritual guardianship
‡Impotent
§Therefore: we are victors.

I feel so well that I wish to see the small dome of the Church of the Assumption. I look through the window, but I cannot see—the poplars obstruct my vision, they have grown so large. It seems as if the moon has come out—there is a thin light in the garden. Beyond the fence—are measured steps. The lawyer's caretaker and parlor maid are there. I can hear their quiet laughter.

Then I hear a rustle behind the bushes.

"It is my dog Milord . . ."

I know—the parlor maid is walking Milord. I am at peace.

"Shall I spend the night here? . . ." I inquire.

"Naturally. Let's go now. Bismarck is there . . . And if Bismarck . . ."

I understand—if Bismarck! . . .

My patron goes out to change his clothes. I am dozing.

Why is Milord barking? A truck roars, there is a knocking at the gate. What is it? Do I hear voices in the garden? . . . It's *them*, they have come to get me . . . I know. I extinguish the candle, scurry across the study in the dark. The window can now be seen more distinctly in the moonlight. The trees and the wind are whispering. I hear steps below the windows. I can hear them snatching at the window sill. They are climbing up . . . I can distinguish their cloth caps, I can see their heads in the window . . . I seize something and shout, shout . . .

———————

Milky stripes; dusk. I don't grasp the words, but a joyous voice resounds in my ears: "*Marchand d'habits . . . et peaux-o-o! . . .*"[II]

Paris?! . . . I am in Paris . . . There is a *marchand d'habits*, a junkman with his skins, in our small street. I recognize the milky stripes—they are shutters. The rattle of barrels—the trucks are driving the garbage away . . . it is morning. All shadows have disappeared.

I remain lying for a long time, collecting myself. I am sad at heart. I am in Paris, far away . . .

Throughout the day I am not myself. I touch my head—so much is contained in one man! Everything. From the first ray, until—death. His entire life, a great treasure of lives. Yet, here, *marchand d'habits*—is this my last treasure? My last joy? Dirty rags and skins? . . . His shouting tears away, yet covers—*everything*. As the clarion call at dawn used to do.

It's strange.

Paris; February, 1926

[II]A rag and bone man . . .

CHRIST'S VESPERS

I read in the newspapers:

"In the Russian Boys' Dormitory (Cheville, rue Mulçot), N. N. Kedrov's quartet will sing vespers on Saturday, January 29, at 7 p.m."

I love vespers—they complete the day and calm the passions. You enter the church, stand in a tiny, semidark corner—and those quiet strains of singing, in which are mingled the sadness, the reconciliation and the fatigue of that day, begin to lull the soul. And you sense that beyond this restless, trivial, and at times bitter life there exists another, shining one—life in God.

"The Lord has prepared His Throne in the heavens,
And His Kingdom encompasses all!"

And so I went.

It was a pitch-black autumn evening, rainy; it's like autumn here all winter long. The train traveled from Sèvres, along the heights. In the black valleys, studded with the dim and infrequent lights of unseen villages, the golden threads of trains rushed along and were extinguished. I gazed through the small black window. What darkness! Somewhere here, in the blackness, is Cheville and rue Mulçot—there, just recently, our teenage boys found supervision and shelter—Russia's unfortunate youth.

I peered out into the deep black valleys, at the quiet lights in the rain. Unfamiliar, dark . . . yet somewhere vespers will be celebrated, and a wonderful Russian quartet will sing to those Russian children. Even now it's traveling somewhere, moving through the blackness to Cheville.

I recall these humble, warm Russians. Recently they had sung in London, in Berlin, Madrid, Geneva, Paris, Brussels—throughout Europe. They will be going to America, Australia. They had sung for kings and lords, for the great of this world, in palaces and fabulous halls, in the salons of millionaires, in cathedrals and under the sky, before tens and hundreds of thousands, for the masses and for the elite—they had charmed all with Russian song and prayer sung from the Russian soul. And now they're searching in the gloom for a poor Russian orphanage to sing vespers for the children.

"I glorify Thee, O Lord!"

Here is Cheville. Beyond the station—darkness and mud. It reminds me of a godforsaken backwoods Russian village. Rotting fences along the slope, your feet slip and stick. How can it be here . . . rue Mulçot?

Someone shuffles heavily behind me. A gas burner barely gives off light. I can vaguely see a limping man with a bag. He's poorly dressed. Probably an old laborer.

"Rue Mulçot"—he searches his memory. "I haven't heard it before . . . Mulçot? . . . The orphanage . . . a refuge? I don't think I've heard of it."

He points out the way to town—they'll show me there.

He walks in the middle of the street—it's more level. He shuffles along in the dark. With difficulty I walk along the sidewalk. Potholes, stones stuck in the dirt. It's better to walk in the roadway like the old man. He glances back to see whether I'm still there. He stops, waits—he's afraid I'll get lost. I thank him: "Don't trouble yourself, please . . . I'll find it!" Finally he goes off.

I walk and think: "What a nice old man! Coming from work, tired, and still he tries to help me find rue Mulçot! And who am I to him?!"

The street is better lit here. An intersection. The old man is standing in the mud, waiting for me. A real laborer—his hands are covered with soot; tools bulge from his bag. He stopped just to show me the way. He's already made certain where Mulçot is.

"Ah, I remember! Under the viaduct, and then to the right."

There is still tenderness in people. Who am I to him, bumping into him in the darkness?! True, he's old, a man *of the past*. I wanted to take his sooty hand and tell him many things. He'd understand. I'd tell him that on rue Mulçot live Russian children, barely teenage boys, who had already endured much in life; that we have a great many such homeless ones . . . that goodness had not yet vanished from this life; that here he was—a good, sensitive person, and how nice it would be for us to meet again sometime and speak more intimately; that on this very rue Mulçot right now vespers will be sung, a night service as we used to have them, with the most wonderful prayers of bygone times; that at this very minute astonishing singers are coming here, the likes of which he's never heard before and will never hear again . . . the delight of all in Europe, sensitive Russians, and they're coming here, to his dark Cheville, to sing vespers for the children. The old man would understand all of this. He would understand a great deal without my even speaking. Ah, Russians? . . . He's heard something of them. The old man, sensitive, a man *of the past*.

Here's Mulçot, and the house. In the dark its outline is broad. Many of the windows are lit, on several floors. A small group is huddled near the gate.

"I think it must be here. Yes! . . . This is *onze*!* I heard the Kedrovs will sing . . ."

"But they're at the Châtelet today, they have a concert . . ."

"That doesn't mean anything . . . Once it's been announced, they'll come."

We enter. On the porch—teenage boys. In little jackets, stiff collars, ties—the uniforms are Europe. But the faces are ours.

It's crowded in the rooms. It's past seven. Father Georgy has already arrived from Paris. The quartet is still not here. That's understandable—

*eleven

today they had a daytime concert, the famous "concert of Pillars," at the Châtelet.

"They promised to come directly from the concert."

Half past seven. It's crowded in the rooms, people are pressing against each other. They've come from Cheville and the outlying areas. They've traveled from Versailles, from Paris.

Here is where they will celebrate vespers.

There are three windows in the room. By the back wall—a platform. Above, under the Russian banners—"Lord, save Russia!" is written—gold letters on a light blue background. An ancient, dark icon of Nicolas the Miracle Worker—over three hundred years old. The greenish icon lamp, lit for the night, sadly glimmers. Here it is, a temporary Russian chapel, the cathedral of the poor—in a French house, by the road.

"It is made lofty by having attained humility,
Rich—in its poverty!"

Beyond the windows, black as if smeared with soot, Paris and Versailles sparkle in the thunder of the train. The tiny flame in the icon lamp shudders, the only living thing here. Shadowy, Nicolas fades, grows clear, and fades again.

The boys form rows. But—the quartet?

They're here. Straight from the concert at the Châtelet, from the concert.

A delicately perceptive bass resounds. A broad, corpulent figure—N. N. Kedrov, the leader himself, the chief. With him—his singers: K. N. Kedrov, I. K. Denisov, T. F. Kazakov. These four comprise the quartet. From the road, out of the darkness, from the rain. All of them—as befits a formal quartet from Paris—with snow-white collars and chests, a splendid black luster. Their faces are . . . well, our faces.

Nicolas looks at them. And shining in gold from beneath the Russian banners—

"Lord, save Russia!"

Shoulder to shoulder. Four of them. The quartet. They've stood up. They leaf through the music.

I look at them. They've come, our famous ones, these fine fellows. From a hall filled with many thousands, from all that brilliance—to this poor room, to the image of Nicolas, to Russia. Direct—from Paris, to Cheville, for vespers. Wonderful! I know they love the peaceful, the blessed, that which is *ours*. I know that Europe is enthralled with them. They bring the miracle of their songs, they sing Russia.

"Lord, save Russia!"

Glittering Paris has just heard them. And here—Cheville, the peaceful icon lamp, the crowded room, the boys.

151

Ivan Shmelyov

> "Ble-ss my soo-ul,
> O-o-o, Loo-oo-rd . . ."

Vespers commence.

> "Peaceful light,
> Holy praises
> To the Immortal one . . ."

Vespers go on and on. I stand in my tiny corner and shut my eyes tightly.
Vespers go on. Russia, in Moscow, in the cathedral . . . in Novgorod . . .
Kiev . . . Vladimir . . . Suzdal' . . .
The sixth Psalm. K. N. Kedrov reads. How he reads! . . .

> "Renew, like an eagle,
> Your youth . . ."

Vespers go on. Distant Moscow, distant past . . .
I open my eyes. What simplicity, what poverty! The sorrowful icon lamp,
the boys by the black windows. In each one of us, each of us had in the
not-too-distant past—how much! Paths, always paths—and yet pathlessness. And all of us on the road. Homeless. And the children . . . For now,
Mulçot . . . But in the future? . . .

> "Praise the Lord's Name,
> Praise it, servants of the Lord . . ."

The hushed strains of the quartet. Vespers go on, transfiguring the heart.
Praise Him! Poor Russian children, praise Him ceaselessly. God—is with
you. And poor Russia—with you—the Russian colors on the banners. And
Nicolas—with you. On the road, always on the road. He leads. And—he will
lead us to it.

> "He is forgiving . . .
> He is eternally beneficent!"

Vespers go on . . .

> "From the Gospel according to John . . . the reading . . ."

And each word is—the Light. Is this not a sign—this miraculous Word of
John, for a new day? For this day?! Yes, this truly is a sign, the Gospel for this
day, Chapter 21, from John. It is—Christ's reappearance.

> "My children, have ye any meat? They answered Him: 'No.'
> And He said unto them: 'Cast the net on the right side of the ship, and ye
>   shall find . . .'
> Therefore that disciple whom Jesus loved saith unto Peter:
> 'It is the Lord!'
>
> And they recognized Him: 'It is the Lord!' "

My heart aches, swells. What's wrong with me? I see the boys, standing quietly, bowing their heads; the black windows; beyond them, pathlessness. A room in a strange house, the icon lamp glimmers.

"And none of the disciples did ask Him:
'Who art Thou?' Knowing that it was the Lord."

He came in answer to the singing and summoning. And it is Him the prayer triumphantly praises:

"Glory to Thee, Who has shown us the Light."

And it is to Him, our dear One, that they, these voices of the night, quietly sing:

"We praise Thee, we sanctify Thee . . .
We bow before Thee, we bless Thee, we thank Thee . . ."

This is no longer singing—it is a sweet, fragrant whisper, a prayerful conversation with the Lord. He—is here, in the room by the road, in the Cathedral; the singing has been transformed into the Word, into the Word of God.

They have felt this, our sensitive singers. And they have sung—to Christ Himself, Who has appeared here to the children, by the road, in this unfamiliar Cheville.

And He is speaking to the children, as once long, long ago He spoke to those other children, by the Tiberian Sea.

He spoke to these unfortunate Russian children, in the tiny room of this unfamiliar house by the road:

"Children! Have ye any meat?"

And that which the singers felt, that which I and the others present felt, Father Georgy loudly proclaimed, with the Life-transfiguring Cross in his hand, with joy and faith:

"Can we not all feel, hearing this blessed singing, this gift given to the children, that Christ has truly been here with us? Children . . . He came to you. To whom else should He have come—in this place? . . ."

The icon lamp shined. The banners glistened.

"Lord, save Russia!"

And the four—the Church choir—sang with *new* voices:

"To the Chosen Leader,
The Victorious prayer! . . ."

I was present at Christ's Vespers. There was a miracle, for the Lord touched our souls. He appeared to the soul in the sounds of those miraculous, life-transfiguring prayers.

153

Can one communicate—what is impossible to communicate? Such things must remain within the heart—a burning and trembling.

Sèvres; January 17/30, 1927

THE LITTLE EGG

For Konstantin Dmitrievich Bal'mont

It is spring. But then where is the fresh air, our fresh springtime air, the melting snow, the lilting call of the roosters, the ditches babbling beneath the ice in the morning? Where is the joy which fills one's heart—a joy as if from nothing in particular? . . . A joy in the chirping of the sparrows in the naked trees, in the gleam of the barely oozing buds, in the gleam of the first pebbles on the roadway, and in the first puddles, and in the sound of bells tolling warmth, a melting, springlike sound.

The chestnuts blooming like "little candles" cannot replace for me the fluffy pussywillow, the wild birch crackling in the wind. Such stiff trees, they weep with soot. Can this be spring? Rainy—like autumn? No awakening, no bright smile, as we have—

> "The bright smile of nature
> Meets the morning of this year through a dream."

I'm searching for something. The land is unfamiliar, the sky . . . even it is different. Or are my eyes . . . different? . . .

From the depths of my soul, where lie the shadows of the past, I evoke my sky. Bright, bluish, like the curtain overhanging my little bed, always bathed in radiance. Are those the wings of white doves against it, the crosses of bell towers upon its brilliance . . . and what of this transparent snow, is it a tiny cloud? My sky streams through the windows, vigorous, fresh; it floods everything with the *new*, even those remote corners where the gloomy cold of winter yet remains, where there is still the scent of starry nights, of frozen crackling.

My native, my vibrant sky.

In the shop windows—piles of chocolate eggs, dark. They're bulky, tied with ribbons, mute. Behind the windows, a bistro. On the bars, covered with wine spills, I see pink eggs in bowls. An echo of something? Forgotten.

My faraway past, in fragments.

A fresh scent—like that of damp paper, or the rustling of nanny's gray dress. Festive, still brand new, it scratches my cheeks. The breeze from outside is miraculous, fresh. The tolling of bells is gay. The curtains over my

154

tiny bed tremble, draw back, and the blue sky peeks in with its brilliance. And in it—a little egg, suspended from a tiny gold ring, on a small red ribbon, alive!

A little sugar egg. Here it is, with me. It has neither faded, nor been broken, on the tiny gold ring, in my heart . . . Transparently grayish, like that transparent snow.

The Holiday ends. Spring passes, summer. Stormy nights arrive. They beat on the windows. At any moment the little icon lamp may go out, and my eyes, frightened by the black night, are searching . . . Where is my little egg? . . . There it is, my blessed one, by the icon case. And I am no longer frightened. There is a glow from the egg, and the Angel looks tenderly into my heart.

When in my childhood I felt grief, I would come to the icon case, and look.

Behind the blue and pink Immortelle, in a clump of moss, in the depths behind the little pane of glass, I saw—surrounded by a brilliant aura, with a radiant banner, Christ arising from the Grave. I would stare at this tiny scene until I wept with joy—and this would fill me with light.

I remember, my nanny would say:

"Look through the little pane of glass, very carefully . . . and you will see."

"But what shall I see, nanny?"

"A tiny angel. Look for a long, long time, and you'll see a tiny live angel."

I looked for a long, long time. Something flickered in my eyes, the little flowers danced, and in the depths, behind them . . .

"I see it . . . I see a tiny live angel!" . . .

In my sad moments I would go to the icon case—and look.

My wondrous, distant past.

Paris; April, 1925

NOTES

1. A street in Moscow.
2. The priestly caste in ancient Media and Persia.
3. "Outside"—i.e., beyond Soviet authority.

Boris Zaytsev (1881–1972)

Boris Konstantinovich Zaytsev was born in Oryol. He studied at the Imperial Technical Institute in Moscow, the Institute of Mines in St. Petersburg, and the Law School at the University of Moscow, but never graduated from those institutions. He began to publish in 1901, and several of his short stories appeared in the Merezhkovskys' journal *Novy put'* (The New Direction). His first book, *Rasskazy* (Short Stories; St. Petersburg, 1906), written in an impressionistic, lyrical manner, was published soon after his debut in this journal. Zaytsev's first novel was *Dal'ny put'* (A Distant Journey; Moscow, 1912). From 1921 to 1922 he was chairman of the Moscow Union of Writers, and in 1922 he was allowed for reasons of poor health to move to Paris, where he became one of the leading *émigré* writers. He published many works in exile: *Zolotoy uzor* (The Golden Pattern; Prague, 1926), a novel; *Anna* (Paris, 1929), a love story set in Russia; *Dom v Passy* (The House in Passy; Berlin, 1935), a description of the Paris life of Russian *émigrés*; *Puteshestvie Gleba* (Gleb's Journey; Berlin, 1937), an autobiographical account of the author's boyhood in the country; and his reminiscences, *Moskva* (Moscow; Paris, 1939); *Tishina* (Silence; Paris, 1948), *Yunost'* (Youth; Paris, 1950), and *Drevo zhizni* (The Tree of Life; New York, 1953). Zaytsev also published three literary biographies: *Zhizn' Turgeneva* (The Life of Turgenev; Paris, 1932), *Zhukovsky* (Paris, 1951), and *Chekhov* (New York, 1954). He translated Dante's *Divine Comedy* into Russian in 1961. He contributed to many Russian literary journals, almanacs, and newspapers in Paris. Among his favorite writers were Valery Bryusov, Bal'mont, Fyodor Sologub, Leonid Andreev, Vladimir Solovyov, Nikolay Berdyaev, Baudelaire, Verlaine, Maeterlinck, Emile Verhaeren, and the Belgian fiction writer Georges Rodenbach. But the somewhat feminine sadness of Zaytsev's manner of writing stems from Blok, Lermontov, and especially Zhukovsky. His works resemble diaries and may be regarded as semi-confessions written in a monastic tone. He seldom laughs in his stories and novels—his subdued tone results from a preoccupation with the inner life of his heroes, who lack stormy passions, artificial poses, and angry words.

Zaytsev's early stories and novels are in the tradition of Turgenev's novels of manor life. Their underlying mood is nostalgic and lyrical; the manner of exposition is delicate and sensitive, and the style, extremely personal. His mode of writing has often been compared to a portrait done in watercolors.[1] Although his later works acquired mystical tendencies, he remained even then an artist sensitive to the exterior forms of beauty. His style in these works is transparent, the arrangement of sentences is rhythmical and melodious, and their most frequent image is that of a person at odds with material reality and the people surrounding him. In the pursuit of higher spiritual goals, the hero is a confirmed individualist who proclaims no utilitarian or social ideals and is incapable of realizing them in his own life. Inner freedom is his most precious earthly treasure, for he is perfectly aware of his intrinsic likeness to the Divine Image, as well as of his future eternal life. Zaytsev is a writer of melancholy and quiet resignation, the latter resting on his protagonist's joyous faith in God and desire to come as near to Him as possible.

The details of everyday life are absent from Zaytsev's *émigré* fiction. They do not interest him. His works, however "incorporeal and spiritualized,"[2] are marked by gentle humor; his men and women, ordinary people, are often caught unprepared or confused by the incomprehensible situations with which life has beset them. Whenever Zaytsev presents prosaic details, he poeticizes them by changing the position of an epithet, or imparting an unusual, dactylic meter to a sentence which heightens its emotional effect. The "prosaic" movement of speech thus changes into a metrical, verse-like arrangement. The lyrical, impressionistic tendency and a proclivity toward stylization are characteristic of all of Zaytsev's works, including his literary biographies. Another distinguishing feature of his narrative technique is his device of frequently transforming the authorial narration into an indirect inner monologue. The angle of vision shifts from one person to another, creating a picture of "impressionistic fragmentation."[3] This technique is used, though unsuccessfully, in *Gleb's Journey*. Zaytsev's images of nature, though often stylized, are invariably beautiful—for example, the snows of Paris blanketing streets and squares.

Another of Zaytsev's stylistic talents is shown in the folkloristic flavor of some of his writings. This quality is apparent in the stories "Avdotya—Death" and "The Heart of Abraham," included here. The folk atmosphere is produced by vivid, repeated physical descriptions, by characters suggesting an abstract principle, by roles played by animals and the deceased, by subtly stylized speeches and epithets, and by certain supernatural events: e.g., mystical guidance into another world; a journey in search of a mystical essence; objects and forces of nature which determine one's fate.

Among Zaytsev's excellent nonfiction works are *Italiya* (Italy; Petersburg-Berlin, 1923), several lyrical and plotless short stories about Raphaël and the Emperor Charles V, and a short play about Don Juan. A collection of sketches about Moscow captures its pre-revolutionary spirit as well as its life in the throes of the revolution: *Ulitsa sv. Nikolaya* (The Street of St. Nicolas; Berlin, 1923). His *Prepodobny Sergy Radonezhsky: zhitie* (The Life of St. Sergius; Paris: YMCA, 1925), springing from Zaytsev's pilgrimage to Mount Athos, is most characteristic of his later period, with its pronounced religious and mystical moods. To this genre belong several other works which he wrote at various times: "Alexey Bozhy chelovek" (Alexey the Man of God; Paris, 1925), *Serdtse Avraamiya* (The Heart of Abraham; Paris, 1925), *Afon: putevye zapiski* (Athos: Travel Notes; Paris, 1928), *Valaam: putevye zapiski* (Valaam: Travel Notes; Tallin, 1936), and a story about two archimandrites, "Reka vremyon" (The River of Times; New York, 1968). These works, too, often resemble "poetry in prose" and are imbued with music and mysticism.

NOTES

1. Alexander Afinogenov, *Literatura v izgnanii* (Belgrade: Novoe vremya, 1929), pp. 31–33, 36.
2. M. Tsetlin, "Boris Zaytsev. *Dom v Passy*," *Sovremennye zapiski* 59 (1935): 473–75.
3. *Ibid.*, pp. 473–75.

AVDOTYA—DEATH

FROM: *Tikhie zori* (Tranquil Dawns; Munich: Tovarishchestvo zarubezhnykh pisateley, 1961).

I

The snowfall made it seem brighter indoors. Instead of going over bumpy, frozen ground, the wide sledges slipped along through the now whitening chill. The scent of snow pierced the air so sharply that it brought tears to the eye, and the leadlike distances seemed painfully mournful. Two days after the snowfall an old woman appeared in the small village of Kochki at the house of Commissar Lev Golovin. Lev, a huge man, flabby, with a hernia, a big nose, and a reddish beard, was no longer surprised by anything whatsoever. He was puttering around by the low, wide sledge, arranging its shaft in a different way, when a tall skinny peasant woman called to him.

"That's me all right," Lev answered, with effort, tugging with all his might on the loops of the rope. "And who might you be?"

"What's this, dearie, don't ya recognize me? Matyushkin's widow, he was one of yours, from Kochki. And seein' as I'm now without any support, and besides havin' a blind grandma in my care—Lord bust her—and dumb little Mishka too, we got nothing to shove in our mouths; you struggle like a little fish just to survive . . ."

This woman hardly resembled a little fish; she spoke with a husky, almost masculine voice, but sobbed with sincerity . . .

158

"That's why I moved here and dropped by . . ."

"So that's how it is . . ." Lev scratched himself indifferently. "Matyushkin's widow? Did he really live in our village? I don't think he lived in our village. He was always bummin' around in town."

"What do ya mean bummin' around? You've forgotten everything, dearie; ya don't even recognize me, Auntie Avdotya . . ."

"What do you want?"

A knapsack hung from Avdotya's shoulders. She was extremely thin. Leaning on a long stick, she struck the ground with it and moved a few steps closer.

"What d'ya mean? No doubt ya all took the master's land, but I'm a part o' this place too, strugglin' like a little fish, just to survive, with a blind grandma and dumb little Mishka . . ."

The situation was clear, despite the profusion of unnecessary words. She wanted him to parcel out a plot of land for her. Lev realized this right away, but at first gave the impression that he didn't understand. However, when it became impossible to misunderstand any longer, he commenced explaining half-heartedly that, although it was true that they had confiscated the land from the master, the amount available had by now become even smaller. Lev Golovin was deeply convinced of the truth of his words. But still, it wasn't easy to impress this on Avdotya. For his every word she had ten: her pale lips would tremble, her masculine voice would wheeze its own variation; she'd whack her stick and press against Lev more closely.

"Well then, we'll need a 'comminity' meeting . . . whatever the 'comminity' decides, so be it."

Lev understood this "then" to mean: "If you're going to be such a bastard that I can't get rid of you, then let the community convince you."

And no matter how melancholy, indifferent, and slowed by his aching hernia Commissar Lev Golovin was, toward evening he still had to call a meeting and present the situation. No one was overjoyed at the prospect. But Matyushkin actually had once lived in Kochki. They even discovered some relatives of his. Like a stray dog, Avdotya sat on the steps and gnawed a piece of crust.

"There I am, adjusting the shaft," the Commissar related slowly and sadly, "and there she is . . . Where'd she come from? Popped right outta the ground! Or maybe she got blown to our town by the wind, down the road right along with the first fall of snow?"

"You just try and blow her," a crooked little fellow, Kuz'ka, said. "She looks to be a pretty good walker. I saw her. I spoke with her, too. Gosh . . . she sure breathes fire. She's a regular racehorse."

"Since her late husband was actually from our Kochki, we cannot avoid giving her a small plot of land. We must take action now, at this meeting," briskly stated a puffy man with a scarf around his neck, the former steward,

159

now a well-to-do peasant, Fyodor Matveevich. And with that the affair was decided.

It was resolved to give her just enough land for a single person. She would be settled in the former dairy of the manor. When Avdotya found out, she crossed herself and bowed deeply to the peasants. Taking her stick, she walked, taking gigantic steps along the newly snow-covered road to the station—to get Mishka and the grandma.

"See how she gallops," said Kuz'ka. "You couldn't catch her on a gelding."

Avdotya quickly disappeared into the haze.

II

"The former dairy of the manor" designated a rather small dirt-floored hut where once the separator had hummed. Its handle was then turned by Masha Golovin. She also filled Nikolay Stepanovich's containers and sent them to the station. From these past endeavors, as from the romance between Masha and Permyakov, little remained except the hut itself. The peasants of the tiny village of Kochki had long ago collected the master's cows, and with great distress they, too, had been obliged to surrender them to the village soviet. The separator was sold somewhere. Nikolay Stepanovich, so enamored of propriety and order, up and died, still wearing his spectacles and the old double-breasted jacket of his uniform. And out of the large main house, from the second floor of which could be seen the pond, a corner of the linden grove, and the hillock blocking the horizon before one's eyes, Varvara Andreevna (not by her own choosing) moved into what had formerly been the guest wing. Yet it was precisely she who had changed the least. Although she controlled only a strip of land (being considered a member of the Kochki community), she still ceremoniously and calmly received Commissar Lev Golovin in the kitchen just as before, addressed him in the familiar, and with her beaver hat, fur coat, and cane slowly and commandingly went about her former properties, dropping in to the granary, half of which—as a reward for military services—Red Army soldier Fil'ka had carried off in the spring. She continued feeding the chickens and the hungry old men who had taken over a part of the main house, selling some of her old possessions to the neighboring miller, and ruling, as before, with unquestioned authority. During this time Liza had lost her husband. She returned to the refuge of her birthplace, and in the tiny room of her former youth taught the children of Kochki. Everything remained as of old.

When one fine day Avdotya with her blind grandma, Mishka, two cocks, a trunk, and various pitiful bags and boxes burst onto the estate, Varvara Andreevna was not surprised. She was generally reserved. During these last years her old, once very beautiful eyes had become used to accepting everything as a necessity.

"We've received yet another bawder," she said to Liza, surrendering the key to the hut to the Commissar. "She'll be living in the dairy." Varvara Andreevna pronounced "border" with a French accent, as she had once been taught in Petersburg, at the *pension* of Mme Cheminée. But Avdotya possessed little resemblance to Varvara Andreevna's former associates.

"Just think, perhaps even this Avdotya was once young . . . Perhaps she loved someone and considered marrying . . ."

"Well, that means nothing whatsoever. You know how men are—they just need a worker in the house. It's the bride who looks to see what kind of property the groom has."

Varvara Andreevna was generally skeptical. She treated most of what excited or enraptured Liza with indifference. Liza had grown so accustomed to her mother's continual living for others—for her father, for Liza herself—and it was so clear to her that this rather small old woman was an irreproachable model—that she had long since accepted her characteristic coldness. Likewise (although it saddened her), she had grown used to her mother's indifference to faith.

Avdotya, however, did not indulge in subtleties or niceties. She seethed. It didn't matter to her whether her blind grandma believed in God or not. But the old woman's "gorging" grieved her, drove her crazy.

"Hey you, the braggart tear you up, the devil eat you," she screamed in her masculine voice. "Why should I worry about you, why should I run around collectin' charity for an old mare? I run here, run there, beggin' from decent people. I've run my legs off, and all she does is gobble and gobble, you know, she shovels it in, oo-o you poisonous bastard . . ."

Without answering, the bastard sat on the dirt stoop, stared with her tearful cataract-blinded eyes, and waited for her daughter to box her ears. In this she was not disappointed. Avdotya only pulled Mishka by the ears, but she beat the old woman with her fists, and sometimes with a stick, right across the face. The old woman groaned—because of her age she couldn't cry out loudly. The next day her face was covered with green blotches.

Liza happened to stumble upon one of these beatings. As she had done as a child when confronted with the sight of such cruelties and outrages, she turned white and immediately felt nauseous.

"What are you doing, Avdotya . . ."

Turning around, Avdotya saw the "young mistress"—and herself became frightened: not by the threat of what this mistress could do, but by the fact that, in spite of everything, she was still "the mistress."

And she jumped away from the old woman.

"But, dearie, I was only doin' it a little . . . just to teach her . . . ooo, she's poisonous . . . ya don't know her, mistress."

"But she's your mother . . ."

"All she does is gobble from morning 'til night, and I've worn off my poor little feet . . . Hey creep, whadda ya lookin' at," she shouted at

BORIS ZAYTSEV

Mishka, who was staring with curiosity at his grandmother's "lesson."
"I'll tan your bottom, you'll bounce 'round here like a wheel, ya bitch's
cat . . ."
"Bitch yourself . . ." Mishka dared to say, being beside Liza, and, snivel-
ing, made a beeline for the wing of the manor house.
Liza felt she could no longer speak or else she might weep—and in disgust
she went to the guest wing.
Varvara Andreevna approached the matter much more calmly.
"You're very tenderhearted, and have always been so. You must control
your nerves better with them. They're all like this. Do you think the others
are different? They don't feel things the way you do . . ."
"Ah, mama . . . the woman is old, blind. She beats her with such fury
. . ."
"Indeed, that is so! Indeed, no one would condone this! When she comes to
me, I'll give her such a reprimand . . ."
Avdotya came that very day, at dusk. A burst of steam and cold rushed into
the kitchen when, abruptly pulling open the door with her long arm, she
came in from the frost. In her hand she had a long stick. As always, she wore a
tattered sheepskin coat; her eyes were whitish from the frost, and uneasy.
"I appeal to your kindness, my benevolent mistress. The thing is, behind
your wing here there's one little teeny birch . . . what use is it to you? And
I'm simply freezin', I ain't got the teensiest bit of strength left, the floor's cold,
the old woman's complainin'."
Varvara Andreevna was standing in the middle of the kitchen near the
wooden stove and watching the kasha boil.
"No, no, I won't allow you to take the little birch. That's just spoiling you.
Cut down the brushwood in the ravine. There's as much as you could want.
And there's something else—if you continue to brawl on my estate, you
better watch out . . ."
"What are ya talkin' about, kind mistress, what brawlin', I never brawled
since I was born, I'm a peace-lovin' gal."
"If you continue to cause a scandal with your old mother, don't show your
face around here . . ."
Avdotya continued to assure her that she was a most peaceful gal. But in
deference to the mistress, she was even prepared to abstain from "teaching"
her bastard. And in the ravine, of course; one could certainly go and cut
brushwood in the ravine . . .
Varvara Andreevna's tone had its effect. Possibly it seemed to Avdotya that
if the mistress spoke so commandingly, it meant she also had the power to
have her evicted from the dairy. She couldn't imagine that it would be far
easier to chuck Varvara Andreevna and Liza out of the guest wing, than to
remove her from the dairy. However that may be, whether due to a vestige of
fear, or in the hope of some paltry handouts—they gave them in the kitchen
all the time—Avdotya left submissively.

She humbly made her way home with her gigantic steps. Lost in thought, Liza looked out the window in gloomy disbelief.

After dinner her mother dealt out Patience in the dining room under the hanging lamp. Liza said:

"You know, when she walks like that, with that stick . . . well, she looks just like Death. Like a skeleton, with its bones rattling, and a scythe over its shoulders."

From behind her pince-nez Varvara Andreevna raised her stern, beautiful eyes to her daughter.

"How can she be Death? She's just a beggar. Everything seems like something else to you."

III

Nikolay Stepanovich lay in the graveyard beyond the church under a white birch cross. The winter evening fluttered the delicate peels of birch bark, built up a snowdrift, covered over the dry flowers, and with its light snowy dust sang an eternal song full of sadness and the transience of things. Liza sometimes visited her father. With difficulty, she'd make her way along the tiny path half-covered with snow; she would stand there, rake around the flowers, fix the crosspiece, cross herself, and just as devoutly and slowly walk home. There was a hint of something monastic in her.

Near the fence of the park, from behind the gate, a long thin figure emerged as if from the bottom of the sea, with a stick and a knapsack on its shoulders.

"Ah, benevolent mistress, I'm runnin' to Alenkino, they say they brought materials, they're dolin' out pieces over a yard long . . . I'll get there in a flash, be back by dinner . . ."

"To Alenkino . . ." Liza slowly walked home. "Ten *versts* there, ten back, back by dinner . . ." And the usual depression and heaviness caused by such a meeting with Avdotya weighed on her heart.

At the same time, as if she were on stilts, Avdotya clambered up the hill behind the river from which could be seen the church, the park, and the two-story "manor" house. If she had turned around, she would also have seen the cross of Nikolay Stepanovich. But she had no time to turn around— before her lay the fields, white and cold, distant, with piercing grounds winds flying and howling along the frozen snow-crest in icy streams. She saw how they twisted, first blowing a drift around a little fir tree, then sweeping everything away from the icy bald spots till they were completely bare! One minute she'd be walking, almost gliding, along the road; the next she'd suddenly sink in practically up to her knees. There'd be little enough time to return before nightfall, but along the road in Kuneev you can get a bit of bread . . . although only a crust; she was hungry, not to mention Mishka's complaining all the time, and the grandma . . .

163

"O Lord, take them from me, those cursed devils! They've made me a prisoner, those accursed ones!"

After Varvara Andreevna's "reprimand," Avdotya behaved more quietly. But then she grew clever, beating the old woman no less enthusiastically, but silently, and locking her in the hut until the bruises were gone. She beat her for everything—for the cup she broke because she was blind, for wetting herself, for not closing the door. In these actions a certain strength emerged, which had nestled itself in Avdotya's wry body—the same strength which drove her ten *versts* through the snow for a tiny bit of chintz, or a chunk of bread for that same "bastard." She fought, rushed about, pestered everyone—this constant seething was life.

Then came the day ordained for the old woman to rest from war and battle. Avdotya was, at the time, roving far away. Mishka, though, listened curiously, in solitude, to the old woman's groaning, moaning, and absurd hiccupping. Taking advantage of his mother's absence, Mishka flew out of the dairy barefoot with a shout of victory, marching back and forth along the road. This seemed to him daring, outstanding.

When finally he burst into the hut, the old woman no longer was hiccupping. Mishka touched her sleeve; she didn't move. He became frightened and ran to the mistress.

Early the next morning Avdotya came to Varvara Andreevna.

"Mistress, allow that little pine there, ma'am, above the pond, to be cut down by the peasants. That'll make a good coffin for my old one—oh, she was born long, Lord forgive me . . ."

Avdotya was gloomy and anxious and again dissatisfied—indeed it was true, the old woman had grown so "long," practically half a pine would be needed for the coffin . . . Also, she worried whether the peasants would cut it down, and then about getting the priest . . . Ah, life is backbreaking!!

"Yes-ss," Lev Golovin said that evening with his eternal lethargy and melancholy, to the carpenter Grigory "the Softy," who was sawing boards for the coffin with Kuz'ka. "She's gotten rid of the old lady. Now she'll be after us. First it'll be give her a cart, then cut her some wood, then they'll start dying, and you won't have enough trees to make coffins for 'em."

"I reckon you're right," said "the Softy," gloomily.

"You wait, spring'll come, you'll have enough of plowing her place. You'll hafta give her more land, let her use the horse to till . . . you'll give her everything, but she'll keep twirlin' you just like an evil spirit. Here today, tomorrow in Alenkino, and then watch out—she'll reach all the way to Strakhovo . . ."

Lev Golovin sighed.

"How was it she came, like she'd popped up out of the ground . . . Or like the wind blowed her in?"

The hungry priest performed the old woman's funeral quickly in the unheated church. The old woman lay frozen in the coffin. The bruises on her forehead and cheek had yellowed. And what had once carried the name Elena and sung songs, and perhaps loved, was now all shrunken, bony, and very long. On pieces of torn gray Holland cloth her body was lowered deep into the earth, next to Nikolay Stepanovich's. Liza was the first to throw a clump of earth on her. And Avdotya began to howl—that was the custom in the village, and perhaps she did it not only because of the custom . . .

Mishka was completely absorbed in where they were putting the old woman, but since early morning he had been bothered by a cough. Mishka felt chilled and trembled. Returning from the burial, he dozed off on the stove-perch, where the old woman used to warm herself.

"Oo-o, parasite, look how he's clambered up on the stove-perch!"

Avdotya rattled the dishes, scrubbed, cleaned them, apparently greatly upset, as though she herself wasn't sure whether she should curse or cry. Just in case, she gave Mishka a slap so he wouldn't cough. But he hacked quite loudly all night. Avdotya at times heard his cough even through her dreams, and with rage she would turn over—won't he let a person sleep, the devil! The whole thing was somehow depressing and nasty. She dreamt about the cold—the fields, the whistling of the wind, the white serpents of the blizzard . . . The wind blew fiercely into the hut from the windows and the floor.

The next day Mishka didn't get up. Avdotya was about to get angry, but when she noticed that he was all feverish, coughing, and his eyes were dull, she didn't touch him. She covered him with the grandmother's sheepskin coat and went herself "to the mistress" for help.

"He runs barefoot in the street—what did you expect?" Varvara Andreevna said sternly. "Watch out that pneumonia doesn't set in."

"What can I do, mistress dear, what can I do with the little bastard? I've already told him: 'I'll lock ya in, ya bitch's cat; stay home, I'll tear off your ears' . . ."

"No, no, you will please be quiet. This is not a tavern."

Liza visited Mishka several times.

"How horrible it is in their hut," she said to her mother afterward. "The air . . . the filth, a kind of gloominess, the cold . . . I'm actually afraid of this Avdotya."

"You were always such a nervous person. But especially now, after the death of your husband . . . Fear Avdotya!? She's a despicable peasant woman, nothing more."

Liza decided that was true—it was shameful to fear rather than love. She ought to pray for her. And from that day she began, in every one of her prayers, while naming those near and distant, to add the name Evdokiya. When, kneeling in the darkness, she mentally named her, it seemed that Avdotya was not entirely the same person. Evdokiya was somehow better, finer looking, than Avdotya-Death. And later on, when she'd thought it over, Liza was even embarrassed that she had called her Death. "Lord, the saints have kissed the lepers . . ." She shuddered. Imagine kissing Avdotya's white lips, the bony bared teeth with their smell of decay, of the grave, with the phosphorescent sparkle of her half-starved eyes . . . No, it was clear that she, Liza, was unworthy!

They gave Mishka what they could find in the old pharmacy—quinine and aspirin. But he coughed continuously. He would toss about, wheeze, and even Avdotya suddenly became downcast and walked more quietly on her stilt-like legs. Still she connived to "run off" to the neighbors, over two *versts* to the miller, to Kozlovka, to see Aksyusha "the Kind One."

Once, on a cold night before the Christmas holidays, after covering six *versts*, she was returning home at twilight, dragging some kind of food on her shoulders in a knapsack. As usual, the dogs in Kochki barked at her; as usual, the birches rustled along the ditch around the estate. The only thing which seemed strange was a tiny weak flicker in the dairy window. "I hope you're not burning it, you devil . . ." And she quickened her pace. With a bony hand, she quickly opened the door. Mishka was lying on his back, very still, his little red hands crossed over his chest. A small candle burned near his head. And Liza. A Psalter in her hands.

Avdotya did not comprehend the scene immediately. A cold gust ripped in behind her—she hadn't managed to slam the door. She stopped and stared vacantly at Mishka's sharp little nose, at Liza—pale, with a moist gleam in her eyes—and suddenly, as she stood, a howl, hoarse and wordless, pierced the stinking air. Avdotya collapsed with her stick and her knapsack onto the cold little hands of her son.

"You—my handsome falcon, my golden eagle, my beloved child . . ."

IV

Her child departed having tasted little in life. The coffin was not large, made from the very same pine tree, the work of those same old hands of Grigory "the Softy." Mishka was laid beside the old woman, several steps from Nikolay Stepanovich.

"Well, now she'll be a little more 'freed,' " Lev Golovin said, when he had returned from the cemetery, "she doesn't have two extra mouths now. That's a lot more 'freed'!"

But the little old peasant Kuz'ka remarked with skepticism:

"You'll see, Uncle Leon. Now she'll be so lonely, she'll hang 'round us all the time. You'll have to take the cart to town for her; in the spring, you'll have to plow her place . . . No, we'll have no peace from her . . ."

Avdotya, it was true, was now more free. She no longer had her two devils—nor anyone else in this world. No reason to worry, no one to beat, no one to complain about. But also no one to say a word to at home.

One time, meeting Liza, Avdotya snivelled:

"Mistress dear, this is all I got now . . . I been cleaned out all at once . . ."

At home Liza, sitting with her mother at dinner, suddenly said:

"Still, I feel sorry for Avdotya."

Varvara Andreevna turned her delicate profile toward her and looked at her with those dark, beautiful eyes:

"But that's just what she wanted. How many times did she say so? Besides, in reality, she slaughtered the old woman."

"Yes, but still . . ."

Liza persisted.

"You were always, since childhood, softhearted . . ."

The conversation was just a conversation; it vanished without a trace, like everything else, into time's abyss. The days ran by, flew. The men of Kochki worked; the women were busy with their pots and stoves. Liza taught; Varvara Andreevna managed her affairs; Avdotya, as before, rushed everywhere. Seeing this wiry peasant woman with her knapsack and stick tirelessly marching through the snow, it sometimes seemed the wind itself carried her . . .

The New Year came. The icy sun arose in a milky-rose mist; from the east came the wind, burning like a flame; the snow in mounds glistened like fish scales, piercing one's eyes—you hadn't the strength to look, but could only cover your eyes and turn your head into the calm of your raised collar. But what a squeal the sledges make! Such a melody of swishing, squeaks, and whistling!

The melody is different during days when there are blizzards. Then a mighty bass drones, and echoes, and beats. Against the guest wing, where Liza and her mother were sheltered, a whole mad horde would suddenly charge, knock, rattle the roof, bang in the chimney. The blast would die down for a moment, giving way to the following one, and by morning would pile such a drift at the stoop that the door could not be opened. They'd have to dig out.

On such a day Avdotya was returning from Alenkino. She had left right after dinner. It was white, snowy-misty, though not very cold—she had set out on her stilt-like legs, but in an hour she started to tire. She dropped in on auntie Agafya in Vyselki to warm herself a little and rest. Agafya even gave her tea. When she had drunk it, she felt revived. And even though it was getting dark, she decided to go on.

"I'll get there in one try, dearie . . . I'll run through the little grove, then it's easier to run down the hill, and the wind'll help me."

It was fairly easy to get through the little grove, which had been recently cut down and was now overgrown with delicate little asps, nut trees, and oaks. The blizzard raged along the treetops; it tore and scattered the little brown leaves (which had survived on the oaks) across the whole field. It whistled in the bare branches; it piled drifts by the stacks of firewood in the clearing. But in the open field it showed no mercy. Avdotya, still frisky and stubborn, walked downhill. There, two *versts* below, was Kochki. The tiny forest quickly disappeared, and the wind somehow beat on her from several directions. The snow glued her eyes shut and at times even took her breath away. Suddenly it came up to her knees; the next step was up to her waist. She tried to turn around. Several solid steps— and again she lost the path. Here, there, everywhere it was really deep. She tried a while longer, but couldn't find the path and decided to take the way completely to the right, to the small ravine. And from the ravine straight to Kochki.

She got as far as the bush and was pleased—well, now the ravine, and everything would be clear. She fell into the ravine beyond the bush—that's as it should be, perfect. It became somewhat calmer, but there was so much snow . . .

That same night, before going to bed, Liza stood praying. It was dark; the blizzard roared outside the window. Liza bowed and prayed for her murdered husband, her mother, herself. She prayed for both Mishka and the old woman. Coming to Evdokiya, she suddenly saw—a small hollow entirely covered with snow, and white whirlwinds and serpents, a tall figure, emaciated, with a stick in its hand, a knapsack on its shoulders, desperately fighting, wading through the snow in the ravine. And in white, surrounded by such an unusual light, Mishka and the old woman suddenly appeared. They took the figure by the arms and all went off somewhere . . . Lord, intervene and save!

This time Kuz'ka complained in vain. The citizens of the village of Kochki no longer had any worries, and no more trouble with Matyushkin's widow Avdotya.

Paris, 1927

THE HEART OF ABRAHAM

Published for the first time in *Strannoe puteshestvie* (A Strange Journey); Paris: Voz-rozhdenie, 1924).

Abraham was a peasant from the Rostov region. From his youth he had been strong. He hunted bear with a boar spear, could lift five hundred pounds of oats, ran his household with zeal and success—he lived in prosperity. But he had difficulties in life, and he saw little joy in it—because of his troubled soul. It seemed to him that nothing was as it should be. The neighbor's hut was better, his harvest richer, and he worked less. The miller ground the grain the proper way for the others, but he cheated when weighing Abraham's. Others had stately, beautiful wives, whereas his Mary was not only thin, but pale as well, and not at all attractive. He was strong, whereas she was weak. "She always tries to push everything off on me." He felt his wife was lazy and a spendthrift, that she profited through the sweat of his own hairy black arms.

And he made life hell for her. He forgave not one accidental mistake, until she became quite ill from this bitter life. When death was approaching, Mary began to weep and said to her husband:

"Don't rage against me anymore. I'm leaving you. If I've somehow caused you annoyance, forgive me. I've been a faithful wife to you and have loved, and love, only you. And if God doesn't object, I'll beseech Him to ease your heavy heart."

And with that she died.

Abraham felt great pity for her and grieved, but, although he saw that other women were prettier, he didn't marry again. Things became even more difficult for him. "Other people's wives don't die, but mine did. How can I live as a bachelor now?"

He was pious. He prayed and asked for a sign, but none appeared. When finally he was sick to death of his home, his household, his farming, he went to see an old hermit who lived in a little cave in the forest. This old man ate only berries, drank only spring water, and had a long gray beard.

He looked at Abraham, thought for a moment, and said:

"Your strength is great, your shoulders are like a bear's, your arms are covered with hair, but your heart is rough. Your heart is hard; it is envious and dissatisfied with everything. As long as you cannot master your heart, you will not be happy."

"What should I do, old man?"

"Travel throughout the world. Serve God; only if He crushes your heart will you find yourself."

Abraham sold his house and herd, took a knapsack and a stick, and traveled the world.

He begged for alms by the churches, worked as a farmhand, and at last came to be a novice in a long-forgotten monastery in the forests around Lake Peipus. But even while begging at the church, the miserliness of people always enraged him. As a fieldhand, he was angered because they profited so well from his work. Even in the monastery, where he baked bread, worked as a cook, and chopped wood, he could find no peace—he didn't like the monks. This one was fat, that one thought solely of how he might gorge himself more, a third one only pretended to be praying.

And Abraham left the monastery.

He wandered for a rather long time and prayed to God to crush his heart, so that he might be cleansed of envy and wrath. He recalled his deceased wife, and now thought of the time he had spent with her—that time had indeed been happy; it had indeed been good.

Abraham began to turn gray. But still he had achieved no peace.

"Lord," he once prayed in a forest on a lakeshore in untamed Galicia. "Why do You persecute me, a wanderer?"

He fell on the ground beneath a tall juniper bush and sobbed. When he arose he saw, some ten steps away, a small hare—a gray one, standing on his hind paws and wiggling his ears, as though bowing to him. Abraham approached the hare, but it gently hopped along the path, constantly looking back at Abraham and making a sign with his little ear, as if to say, "Follow me." In this way they went neither a long nor a short distance, when suddenly they came to a small clearing, and in it a tiny chapel. The little hare bent both his ears crosswise; this meant:

"Here you are, Abraham!"

And, turning to the side, he disappeared into the forest.

Abraham walked over to the little chapel. He grew terrified; something seized his soul. No one was around. The chapel was overgrown, deserted. A swallow flew softly out from under the roof. Dampness and silence. Entering, Abraham noticed a darkened icon of the Mother of God. He knelt and prayed a little. It seemed to unburden him somewhat.

"How strange," he thought, "why this hare and this chapel—whose icon is this?"

But he liked the place. He took some bread out of his knapsack, sipped a little water from the nearby stream, and didn't notice the evening approach. It was far to any human habitation, so Abraham decided to spend the night there. He tucked the knapsack under his head, lay down by the entrance, and fell asleep. His dreams were tranquil. He saw his deceased wife—something in her features reminded him of the icon, so much so that Abraham couldn't tell whether the image he dreamed was that of Mary whom he had persecuted and reproached in life, or whether it was the other. But she said to him:

"In the morning you will take the icon, go down to the lake, and sail across with it. Take it to that monastery, the one where you lived as a novice. It has been here long enough."

Morning was misty and warm. Abraham took the icon and began to walk, but he didn't know where the lake was or which way to go. Suddenly a swallow flew out from under the roof and kept hovering over him. Then he understood—he was to follow. And, in fact, there was a boat at that very place. Abraham sat at the stern, took the oar, and pushed off. He placed the icon up front, facing him. On a tiny board at the bow sat the swallow.

So they sailed on the mirrorlike surface. A scarcely visible mist drifted over the water and softly, like muslin, enveloped the forest along the shores. Although he was strong, Abraham rowed weakly. A silvery, gently murmuring stream, like the chasuble on the image of the Mother of God, stretched behind the stern of the boat.

When they had sailed to the middle, it seemed to Abraham that the world was ending—the land had disappeared. Only the mirrorlike water, the mist, and the silence remained. He felt excited and moved to tenderness; he put down the oar and bowed before the icon.

"Do not fear, Abraham," he heard a voice, so reminiscent of his late wife's.

"I am the Mother of God and Consoler of Hearts. Because of certain of your prayers and your own anguish, I have taken pity on you. I am taking your heart."

Sweetness, but also terror, seized Abraham. He fell even lower before the icon. The swallow twittered. Abraham felt his heart smolder slowly and searingly, as if an invisible mill were crushing it. And as less of his former self remained, his tears flowed more abundantly.

When this miracle was over, he arose. The icon still stood as before. But with the most profound amazement Abraham noticed that it now glowed with clear yet delicate colors. The boat sailed along by itself. The swallow took off and flew to Abraham.

"Greetings, blessed Abraham, reborn to love and gentleness. From this day on you have been given the cross of preaching God's Word and the glory of the Mother of God among the pagans and unbelievers. Bring the icon to the monastery."

Abraham lifted the icon and brought it to the same monastery where he had lived before. He was again accepted as a novice, and afterward took the vows of a monk. But now nothing angered him, nothing called forth envy or anguish. He felt himself unworthy and the lowliest of the low, he rejoiced in everything, and he prayed for everyone. Daily he begged forgiveness for his harsh persecution of his meek wife, Mary.

When he had spent some time at the monastery, with the blessing of the Father Superior, he went with the miracle-working icon deep into the forests and founded there the monastery of the Mother of God and Consoler of Hearts. And when enough brethren had gathered there, he went further into the forest and again established a monastery in the name of the Most Blessed Virgin. Later he organized yet another monastery, all for the glory of the Immaculate One. Wherever he appeared with the icon he had miraculously found near the lake, there wafted a soft breeze of purity and grace. Throughout that untamed region, inhabited then by pagans, Abraham became the prophet and preacher of the most luminous truth of Christ.

Thus through anguish, prayers, and compassion the former Abraham died and a new one emerged. And even now on the lake there remains that bright silver stream, made by the miraculous boat where the new heart of Abraham was born.

A CONVERSATION WITH ZINAIDA

*De profundis clamavi**

Published for the first time in *Novy zhurnal* (The New Review) 50 (New York, 1958).

You came to our solid country home like a whirlwind. You literally galloped in on your horse—it was autumn of the first war—rushing in from the estate of our neighbor, your cousin. Tall, slender, with a face quite broad, and somewhat delirious eyes. You chattered without a pause and enthusiastically kissed my mother, my wife. Everything was boiling and seething inside you. It was hard for you to sit still.

Those were strange times, menacing times. They're recalled in cold, autumnal dawns, in wailing winds and the roaring birches at the entrance to the country estate, in the fatal dusk of Europe's approaching night.

There was always boldness and daring in you. So much strength, and such vigor! You couldn't simply ride a horse. You had to gallop at a mad pace. And so your horses were always frenzied. Once, at dawn, flying out from our country estate, you fell off your sidesaddle—the horse had shied away from a jumping dog. You slammed against the ground—but nothing happened— you jumped up, overtook the horse, and galloped away again.

Do you remember? We even galloped together on horseback throughout the neighboring countryside.

"No, I really can't go at a trot! If I ride, I must ride!"

The race would take place in the sunset's crimson glow, along the border of the Rytovka woods. We called this race "the flight of Charles the Bold after the Battle of Nantes."

"I haven't even the slightest notion of who this Charles the Bold is, but if you say that he's bold—well then, I really like him!"

Within a thousand *versts* from us, in the direction of that bloody sunset, battles were raging and many bold men were dying. It hadn't reached us yet. Fate had, as yet, only brought us to the theatre—for the time being we hadn't taken part.

But you couldn't sit for long in that remote Tula region. *There* it was thundering loudly. We pranced a little while about the fields and the edges of the Kashirian forests. That very same wind that whistled through the old birches at the entrance to the country estate carried you off into hell itself— you went to the war as a nurse.

You've been gone for a long time. But that means nothing. I still see and

*Out of the depths I cry to Thee.

hear you, and here I am, talking to you as you were many years ago, a crazy little country girl; later, my friend in a foreign land.

So listen to what I say. Directly before me, beneath the Crucifix on the wall, there are two small, metallic icons—St. Serafim of Sarov and Christ the Almighty. You left these for us, remember?—an everlasting keepsake of you, of Russia; a Russian soldier, dying in your arms, entrusted them to you at his hour of death. I know those hands; I know your heart. The "Unknown Soldier" removed these icons worn next to his body and entrusted them to you—as to a sister, a true sister. And he was not mistaken. Your moist, green eyes gazed upon him, and he was not mistaken. He entrusted them to the right one. And on these simple icons a martyr's blood has been secretly imprinted. I feel you, Russia. Meek and nameless Russia.

I follow your path, Zinaida. I see you in the hospital, as tempestuous and indomitable as you were on your horse, as you were in our conversations.

On the street beneath your windows there lies a little old wounded general. There is gunfire. They're firing at the hospital; must the general lie and wait for them to finish him off, as well? Who will volunteer to help? He needs those gray-green, delirious eyes—and here they are; they are found. Only a woman like you could have leapt out from behind the hospital doors and, under fire, quickly reached, dragged away, covered, and saved the old man. "I can't just trot!" A full gallop is needed here. For this act the Order of St. George was pinned to your chest.

In the darkness of the Civil War I lost track of you; I see and comprehend nothing. I don't know what steppes you roamed with your field hospitals, whose moans you heard, to whom you said goodbye.

"But do you know that I was married in Kiev? Oh, it's better not to recall! He was killed within a few months."

I had, in fact, known all of this. Yes, she's gone; but it's as if I can still hear her voice—still the same, swift and rapturous. This is indeed a dialogue with a shadow—in this shadow there is a portion of the past life, the past charm. Back then, you appeared not as a shadow but, simply, as Zinaida—from Yugoslavia—in Paris of the twenties. You were just as crazy as before, as you threw yourself on our necks and smothered us in your embraces. Ten years had tempered you. You had experienced the hell of war, revolution, civil war, the life of a refugee. No longer were you that carefree young girl from a gentry family who galloped with me across the Tula-Kashirian fields. Your hands had grown callused. With these hands you could now make hats, print scarves with designs, sew, clean, and cook.

You know all this yourself. But I want to recall aloud, and so I speak to you.

Yet it's possible that you didn't know of this at the time—of an imperceptible poison already inside you—the evil poison of illness, stimulating, yet venomous, inflammatory, debilitating—a slight cough, laughter, a flush, excitement, fatigue.

You dashed around Paris, too, as you had across the Russian fields. Did you truly fall in love with someone? The colonel had, by then, been gone for a long time. You got married in Paris to a friend of yours from the Zagreb days—one of the "marksmen of the Imperial Family." A good man, simple and easygoing, weak. He had a small beard, like the Emperor and everyone else in his regiment had worn. But now he ran a garage. Russian chauffeurs would park their cars there. Among them was even the Commander of the Army at the Western Front.

———

Did you live well with your marksman here? I don't know. So-so, I would suppose. I don't know about your actual romances and infatuations, but I think you had a great many of them. Well, eternity's line has surely separated you from all "such concerns" by now.

However, at times you were wildly jealous of your marksman, and would fly into rages at him. Completely true to your nature, you played pranks—after a quarrel you were perfectly capable of leaving in the morning for the entire day, having locked his shoes in the dresser. Let him sit around at home! And so the marksman, with his little imperial-style beard, would sit and spend the whole day at home, in an impotent rage (this is only a stupid trifle I just remembered from your stormy life).

Here, in Paris, as on the fields of battle, as in the field hospitals, you were always helping someone, rushing around, lending support, getting excited. Still, strength is needed even for the hats over which you pored, for clarifying opinions, for love, for throwing tantrums. You were coughing badly. Did you notice yourself? I don't know. In cases like yours, the ill are inclined to be optimistic. Yet you were losing weight, while your greenish eyes became brighter and burned more painfully. As before, you continued to smother in your embraces those friends whom you had known since Russia, since youth. But your youth was apparently waning.

And so, finally, you were sent away from your crowded little apartment with its unfinished hats, the mannequin in the corner, strewn scraps of material, and its dingy atmosphere—there where you coughed, bending over your work—to a sanatorium, far away, on the Italian border.

The marksman was left alone. You stayed in the mountains; here is a vestige of that life, a photograph—you with a girlfriend from the sanatorium, standing on a cliff, the same enthusiastic eyes, long legs, prominent cheekbones, fir trees in the background encircled by savage mountains. It was all so like you! It fitted you so well! You might just edge out onto that sheer cliff, verdant with forest; you might just leap down below—out of bravado, just to prove something to somebody. God only knows what you were capable of. Most likely, you'd do something wholly out of character.

In your fate, as in your eyes, your long legs, and quick movements, there was always something unusual. You had been singled out by your strange, wild flight and Russia's boundlessness.

Meanwhile, the marksman lived alone. In his solitude he would fire a practice shot or two now and then, if only good-humoredly and innocently at first. Of course he'd go to the garage but, even more often, out to drink. Evenings he played cards and entertained women. He fell into a circle of risqué acquaintances. Money, money—money was needed for everything. Little by little he became weak, undisciplined—and degenerate. Sometimes you even came to Paris, but not often and not for long. Did you notice the change in him? You said nothing, not even to those who were close to you.

The cloud, blackish-green, was approaching. While you were coughing, breathing in the mountain air on the Italian border, the cloud was growing, closer and closer. Finally it came.

It devoured all of your still youthful life, and left no vestige. Once a sudden realization, a flash, transfixed you there, in your mountain refuge, and you ran out headlong and dashed to us—not as before, on a horse, yet in the same bullet-like way. In our apartment you lay half-delirious, feverish, but there was no longer a marksman—because of the money, cafés, and vodka. His own money was insufficient; so, he ended by spending someone else's. He didn't embezzle much. But he could no longer replace it, and he could not endure the disgrace. Gas lifted the disgrace away from him and carried him into eternity. The marksman with his little, imperial-style beard fell asleep in this gas.

Sitting in your Brianson sanatorium, you suddenly felt it: something had happened. Who was there to go to in Paris? You had neither father, nor mother, nor sister. You pressed against my wife as if to your own mother; having embraced me, you sobbed. But there was love surrounding you, and not only ours. Others came, also embracing, kissing, consoling you. Mostly women—women's hearts have more room for others.

Life is terrifying. Your marksman had been lying unnoticed for three weeks; no one had looked in on him. Only when it smelled of gas on the staircase did they suspect something. How is it that the building didn't blow up? All the same, there was no explosion. What remained of the marksman was laid to rest in the Roman earth.

You went back into the mountains. The affair with your husband—it was like hundreds of others in Paris, in France, in all the world. They also cried a bit and then calmed down. You lived there alone again. Alone there, amid the half-doomed strangers, amid the rocks, savage mountains, wild fir trees along the slopes, breathing in air the likes of which we can't even imagine here.

Perhaps once again you climbed the steep slope with your chance friend, as you had done there earlier, and sat, with tears of laughter, and wrote us enthusiastic, desperate letters.

I'm looking once more at the little icons bequeathed to you by the soldier. And once more you, Russia, the soldier, all flow into one—into a moan, a prayer for all who suffer, just like you, yourself, dying lonely in that Brianson sanatorium. From this loneliness, "appealing from the depths of your soul," you wrote to us: "You are my family. You are, for me, both Russia, and father and mother. I have no one else."

Yet we were over a thousand *versts* away when finally, one day, the blood gushed from your throat like a fountain, with all the storm and impetuosity of your entire life. Your blood could not be stopped; no, it couldn't be stopped.

Your humble friend, having returned from there, though only half-cured, brought me this piece of news about you. I accepted it. I know that you are lying alone in Brianson, in its mountainous earth, but we cannot forget you. Yes, you are always with us. In the Apostle's words, "Death is vanquished by victory."

Paris

Mark Aldanov (1882–1957)

Mark Alexandrovich Landau (pseudonym Mark Aldanov), born in Kiev, studied chemistry and law at the University of Kiev. In 1919 he left Russia and settled in Paris and America. He acquired an international reputation with a series of novels topical in content but historical in form. His major historical works include the tetralogy *Myslitel'* (The Thinker): *Devyatoe Termidora* (The Ninth of Thermidor; Berlin, 1923), *Chortov most* (The Devil's Bridge; Berlin, 1925), *Zagovor* (The Conspiracy; Berlin, 1927), and *Svyataya Elena: malen'ky ostrov* (St. Helena: A Small Island; Berlin, 1926), all dealing with the French Revolution and the reign of Napoleon. Perhaps Aldanov's most successful books are *Desyataya simfoniya* (The Tenth Symphony; Paris, 1931) and *Nachalo kontsa* (The Beginning of the End; Paris, 1939; English translation entitled *The Fifth Seal*), dealing with the Spanish Civil War and the gloom and fatalism which preceded World War II in Europe.

Aldanov also contributed essays and articles on Russian literature to Russian periodicals and newspapers in France and the United States. Together with M. O. Tsetlin, he was a founder of *The New Review*. His obituary on D. S. Merezhkovsky appeared in no. 2 (1942) of this journal, and his own reminiscences, under the title *Armiya obrechennykh* (The Army of the Doomed), appeared posthumously in New York in 1969. Aldanov's short stories were also published in American journals such as *Decision*, *The New Leader*, and the *American Mercury*, and his works have been translated into twenty-six languages. Some of his political studies were written in French or Italian: *Lénine* (1919), *Deux révolutions: la révolution française et la révolution russe* (1921), *La politica estera dei Soviets* (1922), and *L'Enjeu des neutres* (1939).

Aldanov's historical novels are urbane and cultured, with much philosophical commentary on the elemental nature of history. For him, the role of chance in history is fundamental, and he published extensively on the philosophy of history. Aldanov's novels are constructed as a series of memorable scenes and episodes, each episode existing as a separate unity, and all of them arranging themselves in a large mosaic panel, but never merging. This compositional device is one of the salient traits of his prose. In analyzing Aldanov's fiction, Georgy Adamovich gave the following pertinent characterization of his novels: "About *The Conspiracy*, the best of his works, one could say the same that usually is said about Goethe's *Iphigenie auf Tauris*—it is overloaded with virtues. Everything is successful. Not a single slip, not a single weak page. [. . .] Furthermore, Aldanov is not concerned with the

Russian tradition of 'falls' and 'soarings.' He proceeds confidently and uniformly, remaining on a high level without becoming fatigued. [. . .] We tend
to consider Aldanov a skillful, sober, multi-experienced 'describer,' and
nothing else. This judgment is extremely nearsighted. Aldanov's fastidious
dislike of cheap 'animation' is combined in his works with a rare gift for vivid
portrayals."[1]

To the peculiarities of Aldanov's art may be ascribed a greater interest in
people than in historical events. His emphasis falls on the irony of fate, and
the "vanity of vanities" is presented as the *leitmotif* of the entire history of
mankind. His skepticism comes from Voltaire, Ernest Renan, and Anatole
France; his pessimism, from the philosophy of Ecclesiastes. According to
Vladimir Weidlé, Aldanov adheres not to the tradition of the Russian
novel—not even to that of Tolstoy, although he professed to be his pupil—but
to the French tradition. Tolstoy and Dostoevsky were engrossed in the
individuality and inimitable personality of man, whereas Aldanov sought the
typical. People interested him not so much in their uniqueness, but in their
impersonal aspect, as types. Weidlé suggests, therefore, that Aldanov's novels
should not be compared with Tolstoy's works or with others written in the
Russian literary tradition, but with first-class French and English writings,
such as *Les Thibault* of Roger Martin du Gard, or *Point Counter Point* by
Aldous Huxley.

To Aldanov's artistic deficiencies belong his occasionally long and tedious
passages, a lack of continuity in certain of his intellectual discourses, and
heroines who are psychologically rather flat. On the other hand, one must
admire the structure of his works, his subtle irony, his freedom from bias in
the presentation of historical—and especially contemporary—controversial
issues and events, and, finally, the portrayal of his major and secondary
protagonists. In his essay "O romane" (About the Novel),[2] Aldanov describes
the basis of his aesthetics in a way which can hardly be improved: in the novel
he sees the manifestation of the "freest form of art, including poetry, drama
(the dialogue), journalism, and philosophy." These characteristics well describe Aldanov's own works. To them we may add the tensions created by an
organic synthesis of the elements of an adventure novel with the author's
erudition and careful research.

NOTES

1. Georgy Adamovich, "Literaturnye besedy," *Zveno* no. 1 (1927).
2. *Sovremennye zapiski* no. 2 (1933): 436.

TAMARIN'S MILITARY MISSION

Published in *Novy zhurnal* (The New Review) 2 (New York, 1942).

I

For a long time Konstantin Alexandrovich could not fall asleep in the house of the Soviet agent. He kept trying to put his first impressions of Spain in order. He wondered if he'd forgotten anything important or said anything superfluous. "No, everything seems in order. What sort of impressions can one get from one day, from a ride in an automobile? It seems to be a wonderful country, and the people are wonderful. They could live splendidly if they weren't knifing each other. God only knows why they have this Civil War. Maybe they don't even know themselves? Or maybe they do know, but we don't understand. After all, do they understand anything in Europe about our Revolution? Or can one really understand what's happening in China? Though I've read the papers daily for several years, even I've remembered only two names, Sun Yat-sen and Chiang Kai-shek. And there's also some 'Christian general,' who seems the biggest bandit of all. But that is none of my business; my job is to study the situation at hand and present a report to Moscow. Of course, studying the situation won't be easy for me, not knowing Spanish. Still, there was something interesting in what the comrade with the loose tongue was saying. No, I don't think I told him anything I shouldn't have," thought Tamarin in his bed. "An absurd war, what else is there to say. People of the same blood, one language, the same faith, are slaughtering one another because of ideas which don't interest nine out of ten of them in the least. And now even ours have gotten involved." (He again recalled "C-comrades and citizens!" at the border.) "Without them, these things wouldn't be happening. Yet I'm working for them . . . It's somehow very cold in Spain. Have I already caught a cold on the trip? Some vodka at a comrade's house would be very nice" . . . Tamarin remembered his dinner with Nadya in Paris and sighed. "Where is my dear Nadya? I didn't even get to say goodbye. I have to send her a postcard from Madrid. My mission's secret, but with God's help Nadya won't tell General Franco about it" . . . He was already dozing, when a wild shout was heard outside. "*Sereno!*"—someone yelled with delight. "What the hell? What's that? Are they asking us to go to bed? 'Sereno' means 'quiet.' That's a nice way of calling for silence for the night," Konstantin Alexandrovich thought, smiling. "Really, that's very, very sweet. Right out of *Carmen* and the 'Musical Drama' . . ." The night watchman was already yelling rather far away. Immediately after his directive, the noise of the street increased. The trucks rumbled past. So, with a smile, Tamarin too went to sleep.

He was awakened not at five, as he had arranged, but at quarter-past six.

He washed, trying not to make noise, and pulled his uniform out of his suitcase. It was wrinkled and smelled faintly of moth powder. This annoyed Konstantin Alexandrovich—whatever the case, he still represented the Russian army here. He took his English razors, selected the best, a "Tuesday," and shaved very carefully. It turned out to be harder to pull on his boots than it had been before, in Russia: he was out of practice. [. . .]

Despite the early hour, breakfast was prepared for Konstantin Alexandrovich. An elderly Spaniard, the one who had served dinner the night before, brought it to him on a tray. A basket with provisions for the journey was also prepared. [. . .]

He went out, holding himself even straighter than usual—almost like his best days in the Guard. Due to his robust figure even the baggy overcoat sat well on him. At the entrance stood a large automobile, a new, very nice Buick. Two men jumped out and saluted with clenched fists, one standing at attention, becoming a statue. The one who remained at ease was still just a youth. "Ah, that's the Spanish bodyguard!" Konstantin Alexandrovich surmised, restraining a smile. He'd never in his life seen a better-armed man: the youth had a rifle, hand grenades on his belt, a saber, two pistols, and a dagger. [. . .] The young man looked at him enthusiastically. Despite his weapons, there was nothing military in the young Spaniard's facial expression. Whereas the chauffeur, an unnaturally light blond, around thirty, with red stripes on his sleeve, was a genuine soldier. Even his clenched fist salute was according to military regulations. Tamarin, not without pleasure, glanced at his petrified figure. "Yes, he's a German!" he recalled. [. . .]

The sight of the republican army did not inspire him with the greatest confidence. About three times they overtook military units walking along the road. Konstantin Alexandrovich observed them intently. He was unpleasantly surprised by the disparity of uniforms—here there were the multicolored uniforms of the royalist era, khaki shirts, blue blouses, leather jackets, African burnooses, and even some sort of oddly draped, frivolous capes. Their weaponry was just as diverse. The soldiers were marching improperly; both the Commander and the chauffeur looked with disapproval at them. [. . .]

There was actually little order. By the tortured and angry faces of the soldiers passing him, Konstantin Alexandrovich surmised that they'd been marching for a long time and that they were poorly fed. At the small station where the road intersected the railroad tracks, there stood a great number of empty wagons, and some wagons with soldiers. Again, by various signs not apparent to civilian eyes, it was clear to Tamarin that this was not the first day these wagons had stood here, nor the first week even. [. . .]

He also thought about his report. "Ascertain which of the two sides has more chance of victory! But how to ascertain this? Let's suppose that in Madrid they'll permit me to obtain materials pertaining to their own strength. They, as is customary, will exaggerate; I, as is customary, will make adjustments for this. Of course, I'll visit all the fronts they allow me to visit. But what about data on their opponent's strength?" [. . .]

He didn't like the Spanish landscape. Everything was bare, sun scorched, colorless; there were only various shades of gray. The sky was just the same—whitish-gray, murky like a mixture of water and milk, sometimes—with the rare emergence of the sun—changing to a hue of yellowish-gray; such a landscape, in Tamarin's opinion, properly belonged in Africa, not in Spain. But, unlike Africa, it was cold. "Maybe there's some *couleur locale*, but there's really little that's Spanish here," thought Konstantin Alexandrovich, gathering everything he remembered of Spain. He'd retained very little: *Carmen*, castinets, mantillas, *dueñas*, rope ladders, and a statue of the *Comendador*. "It ought to be sunny here. This is against the rules. If you're really in Spain, then there ought to be sun . . ." He felt very cold in his buttoned overcoat. He didn't want to eat yet, but it would be nice to warm up with a strong drink. More and more often, Tamarin glanced at the basket of provisions. "What might be in there? Had that fellow thought to pack some sort of small bottle? Who knows, maybe fortunately he did?"

At eleven o'clock they arrived at a settlement which could have been either a large village or a very tiny town. The chauffeur stopped at a garage, showed yet some other paper, also folded very neatly, and demanded gas. The attendant was not overjoyed at this demand. He grimly submitted, however. While the car was being filled, Tamarin took a walk, stretching his legs and trying to warm himself. On the square there was a tightly locked little church. "It looks like the old and noble style," he thought, hesitating—architectural style was an obscure subject for him. "Perhaps Cervantes used to come here or, what's his name, Lope de Vega . . . There was such a man, but what he wrote, I don't know. I haven't read much, it's a pity . . ." [. . .]

The chauffeur told him that he was born in Magdeburg, was the son of a government official, a doctor of philosophy from Berlin University, that he had held a good position in the Social Democratic party, had worked in several of its departments, written for the press, and in the next election would have had a strong chance of moving into the *Reichstag*.*

"My candidacy had already been carefully considered within the party, but because of Mr. Hitler I had to flee, although I am in origin a one hundred percent Aryan. There is not one drop of Jewish blood in my veins . . . Of course, I am no anti-Semite," he added quickly, "I have close friends who are Jewish. I am only stating a fact."

"Here you hold the rank of sergeant?"

"I was wounded, recommended for an award, and should have already received an officer's rank three months ago. But because of the state of affairs here promotions have been delayed," the German answered gloomily. By his

*German parliament

tone it was easy to understand that he had the very lowest opinion of the procedures here. [. . .]

The Spaniard related something about the war, rather confusedly, partly because of the nervousness which a Soviet General's presence produced in him, and partly because of his insufficient command of the language. However, he spoke French skillfully, with an amusing but less offensive accent than the German's. It came out in the conversation that he was the son of a worker from Irun, had been employed in a workshop from age twelve, had at first joined the anarchists and only later realized this had been a serious error, that the anarchist group was not, in fact, proletarian, but petit-bourgeois.

"Isn't that so?" he respectfully addressed the Commander.

"Yes, of course," Konstantin Alexandrovich emphasized energetically, mentally pronouncing unprintable words.

"I joined the party two years ago," continued the Spaniard. Subsequently he spoke of the Communists as simply "the party," in the same way English ministers, uttering the words "the government of His Majesty," have in mind only the British government, and not the cabinets of other monarchies. "After the anarchists I came close to joining the Trotskyites. That too was a grave mistake." "I joined, I joined . . . Eh, young little fool!" Tamarin thought with pity. [. . .] Almost from the beginning his contact with these people, as if his equals, brought him a certain sort of satisfaction, surprising even to him. The Revolution and the Soviet social structure notwithstanding, experience told him that such contact between a general and the lower ranks was harmful and not permitted. "It's true, they're Spanish and class-conscious . . . But then as soon as my soldiers in 1917 became class-conscious, everything went to hell . . ."

The chauffeur inquired of Tamarin if he had known Lenin. At that moment it seemed to Konstantin Alexandrovich that the German wanted to confer some sort of title even on Lenin: "Did you know, Your Excellency, His Excellency Lenin? . . ."

"No, I never met him."

"And Stalin?" the bodyguard asked, excitedly. His eyes began to sparkle.

"Don't know him either," answered Tamarin. Both of his companions were visibly disappointed. The conversation grew stale. [. . .]

II

Dusk had already set in when distant artillery fire was heard. Even Konstantin Alexandrovich himself didn't think that those sounds would affect him so much: "Here I am, after twenty years, again a witness to war!" In the last few years the thought had occurred to him more than once that essentially he was not by nature a military type, that if in his time he had not been sent to the corps, but to high school, he might very well have become a professor of physics or history. This thought did not please him. Now, after hearing that distant, dull boom, unlike any other sound, Tamarin experienced joyous excitement.

From the hill, according to the German, one could acquaint himself with the general picture of the Madrid front. Tamarin got out of the automobile, took his notebook and field binoculars. He couldn't see very much. Nevertheless, he jotted down something like a plan. The bodyguard looked at him enthusiastically, as the young aides-de-camp must have looked at Napoleon on the eve of Austerlitz: their faces expressed a conviction that here they were witnessing the conception of ideas of genius. So as not to disillusion him, Konstantin Alexandrovich continued to draw the plan a bit longer than necessary. The chauffeur checked the gas, swearing under his breath.

The number of guards increased. Controls became more and more strict. At intersections and bridges, officers in khaki examined their papers more and more carefully. They sullenly questioned the bodyguard—obviously not entirely pleasant questions, since he would flare up, turn around to look at the Commander, and then, in embarrassment, explain evasively that they were asking about various trivialities. [. . .]

When they arrived in Madrid, it was already completely dark. The firing diminished. The Buick, maneuvering slowly, passed along the way to a strange, zigzagged barricade. Tamarin, having already studied the layout of Madrid while still in Paris, at first tried to orient himself, but in the darkness he could distinguish nothing. He was chiefly excited by the military rarity of the situation—a besieged capital. "And this darkness! I've never seen such a city! . . ." Only rarely did they come across burning lanterns; the auto would pass illuminated oases, and again all would plunge into darkness. It was really impossible to comprehend how the chauffeur managed to drive. [. . .]

The automobile stopped on a very short, narrow street with a lamp at one end. Tamarin saw a long, three-storied, rather gloomy house. Sandbags surrounded the walls at ground level. "Here it is," the bodyguard said, jumping out. He ran to the porch and knocked on the door. A bluish light flashed, and a woman with a pocket flashlight appeared on the porch. The bodyguard took off his cap, bowed, and, after showing the order, explained something in a low voice. The woman nodded her head and, smiling, began to speak very quickly. "Thank God! Does that mean there's a room?" Konstantin Alexandrovich asked, getting out of the auto. Something crackled and crunched unpleasantly beneath his feet. The sidewalk was covered with fragments of glass. The windows with shattered glass were curtained off or taped. Half torn-off shutters dangled on two windows. [. . .]

Tamarin looked with satisfaction at the quiet decent though rather small room. "This is just fine. *Merci. Gracias,*" he said, trying to recall how to thank someone in Spanish. The woman also spoke unusually fast, with a prevalence of the sounds r-r and h-h. "If she'd only shut up; it's awkward to listen and not answer a single word," he thought, smiling helplessly. "Kutuzov would have immediately taken this Micaela by the chin . . ." Perhaps at another time Konstantin Alexandrovich might also have acted as Kutuzov had, but now he only wished that Micaela would leave him in peace. He had a headache. [. . .]

He put on his pajamas and got into the bed, which turned out to be rather hard. He covered himself with the blanket, stretched out delightedly, and with even greater delight relaxed. "Yes, indeed, even with these Spanish girls, there are in one's old age blessed moments." [. . .]

A loud crash awakened him. Konstantin Alexandrovich jumped up, "What's that?" Cries resounded from the street; below it seemed that a mass of people were running. Tamarin groped for the light switch, with some trouble found it, fumbled with his hand along the wall, and turned it on. The lamp did not light. It was totally dark, even darker than in the evening. The cries from the street grew louder. Suddenly a strong explosion reverberated. "A bombing!" His heart began to pound. "I've lost the habit! . . ." With a slightly trembling hand again he turned the switch sharply, several times, as if from the force of his movement the lamp would light—and then he realized that the power station must have turned off the current. Konstantin Alexandrovich searched for his slippers with his feet, didn't find them, and then, barefoot, carefully began to feel his way along the stone floor to the window, sticking his left hand in front of him and orienting himself more by the current of cold air. He stumbled and almost fell, but caught his balance and pulled aside the curtain. It grew hardly any lighter. The shouts came from somewhere to the left. Apparently people were running and hiding. The terrifying explosion resounded again; a long rumble, seeming still closer and merging with it, increased in volume until it was unendurable, then a woman's shout, a howl, and weeping. Tamarin realized that somewhere, very close, a house had collapsed. "Maybe this will be death! . . ." He crossed himself, looked at the ceiling, and at last began to consider calmly just what could occur. "It won't crash on me—I'm on the upper floor . . ." A third explosion resounded, after it a fourth, a fifth. The blows followed, one after another. [. . .]

The cries outside subsided and changed. Gay voices were heard, as if those who were saved were congratulating each other. Still another dull blow resounded, but it was already far away. Suddenly the bulb lit in the room, outside something weakly flooded with a very pale bluish light. [. . .]

From the street familiar voices called to him—his traveling companions. "How about that! Even you're here?" said Tamarin joyfully. [. . .]

"Tonight a major battle is expected," the bodyguard said, lowering his voice, "I was just informed. We are going to attack the clinic in the University complex. It's in the hands of the Fascists. This is top secret." "I won't tell anyone. Is this University complex close?" "Extremely close. From Puerto del Sol trams 22 and 12 go there." Tamarin could only gasp—a clinic, a major battle, the tram travels on a battlefield! "For the attack of a clinic my strategic knowledge is not necessary . . ." [. . .]

He put his broadcloth robe on top of the covers and lay down again. He thought it would have been nice to put something more on his feet. Even a feverish shiver was almost pleasant in itself—if only one knew that one could be like this for a long time, a very long time—for eternity. Tamarin now felt as physically and spiritually exhausted as if he were a hundred years old. "God grant that I don't become seriously ill here! There's not a single soul here!" he thought with terror, shaking his head. "It's good that I wasn't really frightened at all. The only terrifying thing was the sound, especially of the house collapsing. Artillery fire is a different matter—there's greater danger, but the sound impression isn't the same." He was pleased that he again found himself in the midst of a war, but now that feeling was considerably weaker in him than several hours ago. [. . .]

Suddenly, somewhere below, music was hard. Tamarin, dumbfounded, listened intently. "A guitar?" They were playing something very familiar. A voice joined the instrument, a rather pleasant little tenor, singing in Russian: ". . . I would return at dawn. Always was gay, drank vodka," the little tenor sang. "What a miracle! . . ." "And at gypsy school—Educa-education I received . . ." Someone laughed gaily. "So there are still Russians here! And I thought there were only Cheka agents! Obviously they're officers," Konstantin Alexandrovich thought joyfully, although this actually was not at all logical. ". . . Flying half-drunk in a troika/ I remember you. / And down my rosy cheek / A tear will—a tear will roll from my drunken eyes . . ." Unexpectedly, there also appeared a tear on Konstantin Alexandrovich's cheek. "A very nice voice! And he sings exactly like we used to sing . . ." He suddenly recalled another night, long, very long ago, a celebration of the Alexandrovsky Regiment. Almost fifty years had passed. ". . . Who's that in Hungarian mourning clothes / Whose visage is full of miraculous charms? / I recognize you, immortal one . . ." Tamarin saw before him the hall of the gathering, the table covered with bottles, the crowd of officers singing, the merry face of the future tsar, waving his arms in time to the music. "If a sorcerer would have predicted then, what a prophetic Oleg he would have been! Why did this happen? Who needed all of this?"

The singing broke off. Harsh Russian cursing was heard, after it laughter and the tinkle of a smashed glass. "Probably they know my name. Should I go down?" Konstantin Alexandrovich thought. "No, it's impossible; my mission's a secret. Of course, they'll know my name. So what—in three years or so no one will know it on this whole earth. On the whole earth!" "I recognize you, immortal one!" "I don't recognize; and I am not immortal; and I don't understand a thing: how did I get from *there* to *here*? It's as if my reason and will never once took part in all this! And indeed they didn't. And of course it's the same with everyone, except perhaps certain extraordinary people: you go in one direction, and wind up in exactly the opposite . . . No, certainly I can't drop in on them. Only in the extreme event that I'm terribly ill. But I'm *already* ill! In fact, haven't I already contracted typhus?" [. . .]

Tamarin got up, poured himself some wine with his shaking hand and drank it down in one gulp. "Maybe I can still fall asleep. It's strong wine . . . I'll read a little for the night . . ." He looked at the books on the bureau. There was one volume of a collection of Clausewitz. [. . .] Again he lay down, waited several minutes to warm up, didn't warm up, and opened the book with an effort. Or, more accurately, the book opened up at a bookmark. And again, but with even greater anxiety than before, in Paris, Konstantin Alexandrovich read: "He said to me, 'Be calm / Soon, soon you'll be worthy / You'll be in the Heavenly Kingdom. / Soon to these earthly wanderings / Of yours will come an end. / Already the Angel of Death has prepared / A sacred wreath for you."

III

Like this, trembling with fever, with open eyes and labored breathing, he lay there a long time—three, perhaps four hours. Several times he lit the lamp, peered intently at the clock's hands to determine the time, but was always mistaken. The light irritated his inflamed eyes, and he quickly extinguished it. "I'm ill, I'm really ill," he thought with anguish, considering what should be done. "I no longer have any close people anywhere in this world; behind me are only the graves of people once close to me. And here I haven't a mere acquaintance who knows even remotely who I am . . ." Toward the end of this long night his thoughts became tangled. He realized he had a high fever. "Probably about 39° or maybe even 40°?" For a long while he tried to remember by what scale this was: by Celsius or Reaumur? But he couldn't remember and was very disturbed that he couldn't. "Who was this Celsius, after all, I don't remember . . . Reaumur—Yes . . . as a child, I was terrified of the word *gangrene*[1]; what gang? what green? . . . This hasn't the slightest connection with what's going on here. I have a fever, typhus, perhaps, but there is nothing at all to cause gangrene." [. . .]

"Franco has battleships; this must be noted in my report . . . I wrote in my book that as yet it is impossible to predict the result of a battle between the naval fleet and the air forces; there is no data . . . and it's of no concern to me," muttered Konstantin Alexandrovich, who was not in the habit of talking out loud to himself. [. . .]

"Maybe I should go outside, eh?"

Konstantin Alexandrovich was quite pleased with this thought and hurriedly started to dress. "I have a pass and can go where I wish, see what I want. The door downstairs there was bolted, without a key . . . I might suddenly see more battles! Yes, certainly at night there are battles!"—this pleased him even more. The exhaustion had been lifted from him as if by a magic wand. But his reasoning was getting worse. "That wine has warmed me . . . Yes, I must send a postcard!" The postcard to Nadya, as before, was lying in the pocket of his overcoat. When he had put on his coat, Tamarin tiptoed out of the room. A typewriter was still pounding. "Could that be a hallucination? No, never in my life have I had hallucinations of any kind. In any case, that would be a strange hallucination." [. . .]

It was very cold; the streets were empty; lamplights were few and far between. At one of these a sort of high pedestal struck his eye. He didn't surmise at once that this was a mailbox, but finally he recognized it. Konstantin Alexandrovich dropped his postcard in—"Of course, this is a mailbox; there can't be the slightest doubt"—and he felt great relief. Even in his normal condition, unsent letters disturbed him a little. Now, however, he sighed so joyfully, as though finding a mailbox in this big city were an uncommon piece of luck. "It means I won't be lost! . . . Yes, there is a triumph of evil, and I am taking part in it all, a fool in the service of evil-doers. However, the others are no better than they, nor smarter than I . . ."

Not far away a cannon shot was heard; after that another, and then a third. Tamarin was terribly happy. "That's it, I've got to get over there!" he said to himself, and quickened his pace. More and more often he came across destroyed houses. "It's strange that there are so few of them! If the Germans were bombing for real, there would be nothing left of the city." On the left, a high pillar with a globe on top came into view. "A monument? It was erected to someone, and for no reason. There's no great harm if it's smashed. And then you'll demolish their monuments, and that will also be excellent," he advised someone or other. Konstantin Alexandrovich was even more pleased when he saw a poorly lit café with a partially torn off door. He went in, muttered something, and poked his finger into the first bottle he came upon. Light came from the grill on which fish were being fried. The old barkeeper poured the patron a shot, paying not the least bit of attention to his overcoat. "He'd probably pay no attention if Hitler himself dropped into his place in a German uniform," Tamarin thought. "Now, there's a wise man!" He swallowed one shot, demanded another, and paid. Again shells thundered, machine guns crackled. "The University complex?" Konstantin Alexandrovich joyfully asked, recalling approximately what his bodyguard had called this place in Spanish. The old man nodded his head indifferently and turned the fish over on the grill. Only now did Tamarin sense the strong unpleasant odor of the fish. With the disgust of a sick man, he ran out of the inn.

And it was as if life wanted to surprise him for the last time—the moon came out from behind the clouds, casting reddish light across the dying city. Konstantin Alexandrovich exclaimed in amazement: "Enchanting, enchanting!" He muttered: "That seems the right thing to say, 'enchanting'? If you want, you could make out a sign. If not in the moonlight, then in the lamplight . . . It appears there are even more lamps here. *Peluquería*, hairdressers!" he read happily. "*Confitería*, *Camisería*—I understand them all!

Carpintería What's a *Carpintería? Asegurada de incendios.* 'insured against fire.' Each house has this sign, 'insured against fire' . . . That's *asegurada* for you. Russia was also *asegurada de incendios.* As were we all."

At the corner the sentry was hesitantly about to motion toward him; but, seeing his uniform, he saluted and didn't stop him. Tamarin came out onto a great square. Everywhere ruins were bathed in moonlight. On the right, a large building was burning. Konstantin Alexandrovich began to laugh. "Indeed, even there at Velasquez there was light from the smithy's fire. A *Kunststück*! Here life has performed a *Kunststück*! . . . *Cine 'Las Flores.'* But it's insured! It's insured!"

Ahead of him a narrow road descended, from which crooked paths rose along the other side up onto the hill. Only now did Tamarin notice that on this rather small hill stood large asymmetrical buildings. He surmised that this, in fact, was the University complex; quickly crossing the road, he began to climb the path. Above his head a shell burst. "It looks like I've come upon the attack," he thought. People with rifles pointed were running to the building. "Eh, fools! How they go! Look, they'll be killed by the gunfire! . . ."

In front of the people attacking, a man in a leather jacket, with unusually quick, distinct movements (as though in a movie), had—unlike the rest—clearly grasped the essence of such a war. Running about twenty steps, he'd then turn around, shout something, and fall to the ground. Not all of them did the same thing. At that very second machine guns began to explode. After waiting a minute, the man in the leather jacket, stooping, rushed ahead, zigzagging, throwing back his right hand holding a grenade. Several people running after him fell. Tamarin gasped and ran after them, grabbing a saber on the run. "Boys! . . . *Todos para uno!* . . . *Lenin dos-dos!*"† he shouted in a voice not his own. A huge explosion. Tamarin was flung to the side, dropped the saber, raised both his arms, and fell. The bursts of explosions, fading, merged with the gunfire.

†All for one! . . . Lenin two, two!

NOTE

1. In the original Russian the words are *Antonov ogon'* (Anton's fire, gangrene). As a child, he thought the words referred to a real person.

Mikhail Osorgin (1878–1942)

Mikhail Osorgin (pseudonym of Mikhail Andreevich Ilyin) was born in Perm'. As a young lawyer, he took an active part in the 1905 revolutionary uprising, was arrested and jailed, and was subsequently coerced into self-imposed exile in Italy, where he became well known as an Italian correspondent for *The Russian News* and a contributor to various literary journals abroad. In 1916 he returned to Russia and lived under Bolshevik rule until 1921, when he was again arrested and jailed as a self-styled anarchist, nonconformist, and proponent of the free press. Sent again for a brief exile in Kazan', he was finally deported to Germany in 1922, together with other Russian writers and scholars. He first lived in Berlin and in Italy but then moved to Paris, where he contributed to more than twenty *émigré* journals and newspapers, chiefly *Contemporary Annals*. In the latter he published fiction and book reviews, primarily concentrating on Soviet belles-lettres, with which he was well acquainted. He also printed many idiosyncratic and controversial journalistic writings in the newspaper *Days* and later in *The Latest News*. Imbued with his political irreverence, his engaging, instinctive sense of humor, and his wryly ironical attitude toward himself, these works also included topical comments on *émigré* life and politics; some were signed with the facetious pseudonym "Robky chelovek" (The Timid Man). His stories are light, pleasant, buoyant, often derisive in tone; his jokes are neat and exact.

Osorgin's first book published abroad, written in Moscow before his deportation, was a collection of sketches on Moscow during the first revolutionary years, *Iz malen'kogo domika* (From a Small House; Riga, 1921). His book *Tri povesti* (Three Novellas) had come out earlier—in Moscow in 1917. During his final exile he published five novels and five collections of stories and articles. Four more collections were published posthumously (three others had appeared before 1921, in Russia). Among Osorgin's most successful works are his novel *Sivtsev vrazhek* (1928; issued in English translation under the title *Quiet Street*, 1930) and *Povest' o sestre* (1930; published in English as *My Sister's Story*, 1931). Nothing else by Osorgin had appeared in English until the recent publication by D. M. Fiene of several stories and articles in *Russian Literature Triquarterly* (1972 through 1979) and of a collection of short works spanning Osorgin's entire career, *M. A. Osorgin: A Reintroduction: Selected Stories, Reminiscences and Essays* (Ann Arbor: Ardis, forthcoming).[1] Other books by Osorgin which were well received include the

189

novels *Svidetel' istorii* (An Eyewitness to History, 1932), its sequel, *Kniga o kontsakh* (A Book of Endings, 1935), *Vol'ny kamenshchik* (The Freemason, 1937), and a volume of short stories, *Chudo na ozere* (Miracle on the Lake, 1931). During the 1930's Osorgin often vacationed in the village of Ste Geneviève des Bois, near Paris, where he owned a small cottage. Here he conducted a campaign against contemporary urban civilization, urged a return to the bosom of nature, and wrote feuilletons about gardening and the beauty of the Russian language. Some of his feuilletons on these topics, which appeared originally in *Contemporary Annals*, were later published in the collection *Proisshestviya zelyonogo mira* (Events of the Green World; Sofia, 1938).

Osorgin's later stories and novels, especially *Quiet Street* and *An Eyewitness to History*, are written in a lyrical impressionistic style. Elements of the old-fashioned Russian language blend curiously with contemporary cinematographic effects. Virtually all of Osorgin's works contain and are enhanced by his humor and irony, although his philosophical discourses and commentaries within the text may seem ponderous at times. Osorgin's propensity toward non-conformism combined with his anarchistic political philosophy led his compatriots in Paris to view him as an artificial poseur. This artificiality alienated those who did not know him well. His Italian sketches, included in the collection *Tam, gde byl schastliv* (There Where I Was Happy, 1928) and *Miracle on the Lake* and elsewhere, resemble Boris Zaytsev's reminiscences about Italy. In *The Freemason*, Osorgin's manner of narration is quite original: the author plays with the plot and style; he inserts his own ironic comments into the narrative fabric and incorporates elements of "constructivism" (that is, by using the meanings and the stylistic role of Masonic symbols and terminology). Gleb Struve perceives in this novel the influence of Zamyatin and of the Soviet "neo-realists,"[2] as well as Osorgin's own attempt at stylization in the eighteenth-century spirit. What is of most interest about *The Freemason* is that it is a humorous account of a typical (non-intellectual) Russian *émigré* trapped between Russian and French cultures in Paris, who tries, largely in vain, to make sense out of life through Freemasonry.[3]

Mikhail Osorgin was an expert on Russian literary style, usage, and grammar, and on old texts of all kinds, especially those of the seventeenth and eighteenth centuries. Many of his essays dealt with various Russian styles and old Russian manuscripts. For two years beginning in the spring of 1934, he published nearly every week one "story of bygone times" *(starinny rasskaz)*; they are dissimilar in their fictional content and are loosely based on actual events, primarily from the eighteenth century. Beautifully written, each in its own style befitting the content, time, and place, these stories are light and humorous. Osorgin owned many books and manuscripts from this period, was acquainted with the holdings of the Turgenev Library (of which he was one of the directors), and subscribed to the journals *The Russian Past* (which ceased publication in 1918) and *The Russian Archive* (which ceased publication in 1917).

Osorgin's novels, short stories, sketches, reminiscences, and articles were read with pleasure by Russian *émigrés*, for they tended to avoid (at least in the author's final decade) contemporary and frequently tragic issues. His irony and humor were pleasing to them; furthermore, his mode of narration was neither rhetorical nor authoritative, but picturesque, vivid, sincere, warm, and humanitarian. Although Osorgin's stylistic games at times bewildered his Russian readers, his great erudition, his thorough familiarity with the Russian past and Italian treasures of art, and his good-natured yet ironical smile made up for that which was uneven or unpolished in his mode of story-telling.

Osorgin was also widely read outside the tight circle of Russian intellectuals in Paris. For example, his *Quiet Street* went into two editions, and it was a best seller in its English translation. The Western reviews of his works were very positive. Indeed, he was one of those few Russian *émigré* novelists who achieved, before 1930, a greater distinction in exile than even such writers as Bunin, Aldanov, and Vladimir Nabokov.

Like the Merezhkovskys, Osorgin remained in France during the German occupation, dying in November, 1942, the village of Chabris, where he and his wife lived as refugees after the fall of Paris.

NOTES

1. D. M. Fiene's translations in *RLT* are as follows: "The Original Chess-Playing Robot," *RLT* 3 (1972), with an introduction that includes a translation of the interview "How M. A. Osorgin Lives and Works"; "The Anniversary," *RLT* 14 (1976); "Contradictions," *RLT* 16 (1979), and an article by D. M. Fiene entitled "M. A. Osorgin—The Last Mohican of the Russian Intelligentsia (On the One-Hundreth Anniversary of His Birth)," *RLT* 16 (1979).

2. Gleb Struve, *Russkaya literatura v izgnanii*, p. 274.

3. In 1924 Osorgin joined the Paris Masonic Lodge *Severnaya zvezda* (L'Etoile du Nord), a Russian-membership lodge founded by N. D. Avksentyev and under jurisdiction of Le Grand Orient, one of the two main lodges in France (the other being La Grande Loge de France). A second Russian lodge subordinate to Le Grand Orient was *Svobodnaya Rossiya* (La Russie Libre), founded by E. S. Margulies. (Its second Russian member was V. A. Maklakov.) In 1938 Osorgin became Worthy Master of *Severnaya zvezda*; among his closest friends in the Masonic order was Mark Aldanov. Osorgin's *Events of the Green World* reveals some of his philosophical preoccupations as a Freemason, such as the enlightenment and education of the masses and some other, ethical, problems. For more information, read D. M. Fiene's "Life and Work of M. A. Osorgin, 1978–1942," II, 427, and his *M. A. Osorgin—A Reintroduction*, p. 189.

THE CHOOSING OF A BRIDE

"Et la postérité refusera d'y croire . . ."

FROM: *Povest' o nekoey devitse: starinnye rasskazy* (A Tale about a Certain Maiden: Stories of Bygone Times; Tallin, 1938).

With dainty slippers on her bare feet, it was Natashen'ka's, that is, Natalya Kirillovna's, custom to go down to the pantry cellar in the morning. She went there with three of the servant girls, but she herself would undo the lock and step down the cold and slippery short staircase onto the ice, where in rows stood earthenware milk pots, wooden pans of sour milk, vats of home-brewed ale and beer, small tubs of pickled preserves, and a week's supply of freshly slaughtered meat. The smell of mold and the piercing cold which seized the young *boyaryshnya*[1] was actually pleasant after sleeping in the stuffy chambers of her uncle's manor. With her exquisite snow-white hands she would pass various supplies up to the servant girls, selecting as much as was needed for the table and the household. For her efforts she would take for herself a small pickled apple—she loved to eat them in the morning before anything else. At this point two of the servant girls would leave for the kitchen. The young mistress and the third girl would then go down to the deeper cellar, where the wines and brandies were kept—there, too, to obtain the daily supply. And as they were crossing the yard, the chickens, geese, and lopsided ducks would scurry and fly to them from all corners and accompany them to the porch.

After changing into something pretty but modest, befitting a gentlewoman, Natalya Kirillovna would hurry to the parish church in the village of Zhelchino, which was right next to Aleshnya. There she had her very own place—by the wall—beneath the right side of the choir section, out of sight. She prayed fervently, but about what—that was her affair. They called her the Zhelchino nun and were amazed that she had no inclination for merrymaking or dancing and was so devoted to her prayers. The young neighbors, gentrymen of the Korobyin, Khudekov, Lyapunov, Ostrosablin, and the Kaznacheev families seldom and with difficulty lured her into the general merrymaking. But when they did succeed, all the other girls around her somehow paled and faded, as it were, and no one paid attention to any of them—they all looked at her. Such attention embarrassed her—she'd stay a short time and then go home, where there were always many household duties awaiting her, because her uncle (her father's brother), an extremely wealthy *boyar*, relied solely on her for everything and lovingly called her "my dear little niece Kirillovna."

*And prosterity simply won't believe it . . .

192

This was the spring of her life, the threshold of the future. The future appeared to her to be very straightforward: her rich relatives would arrange a marriage to a man of equal (though not especially notable) rank—a man of dignity. And then she would have her own household and her own family.

Natashen'ka was very pretty—from her youth she had always been tall, well-proportioned, fair, with dark eyes under shapely brows and long, luxuriant hair. She had an obliging nature, a humble appearance, and was affectionate. But what was in the soul of this girl, neither her parents nor her friends knew.

An edict was issued from Tsar Alexey Mikhaylovich to all regional capitals and other towns: "Authorized persons from the court *boyars*, or the noblemen and deacons, under the watchful gaze of the vice-regents and provincial governors, are to conduct a survey of all the young maidens of the region, from among the *boyar* as well as the common classes, title notwithstanding, and information concerning such maidens as are especially beautiful and by all criteria healthy is to be sent to Moscow. Once the very best have been selected, they should be brought for the Tsar's inspection, and should stay in Moscow at the houses of relatives with respectable women, where they will be given further instruction."

The Tsar had been widowed; a tsar cannot remain unmarried. The choosing of a bride is not a frivolous matter—it is not simply a question of the Tsar's happiness, but of a mother for the Tsar's future children. In earlier times they would have herded at least fifteen hundred selected maidens to Moscow; now they'd accept only those who had been carefully chosen, and who bore the enthusiastic approval of the local administration. Those proving to be especially fine would be taken to the upper chambers of the palace for the Tsar's perusal, and those not appealing to his taste would still receive a reward. Whoever was the best—would be the Tsaritsa.

From November to April, Moscow was filled with beauties. Of these the leading ones were Oksinya, daughter of Golokhvastov of Ivlevo; Marfa, daughter of Demskoy of Smirnovo; Marfa, daughter of Vikentyev of Vasilyevo; as well as Anna Kobylina, Ovdotya daughter of Lyapunov from L'vov, and Ivan Belyaev's daughter—the novice. Perhaps a prettier maiden than she could not have been found, had there not also been Natalya Kirillovna, the daughter of Naryshkin, who had been sent from the country and was living at the house of the *boyar* Artamon Sergeevich Matveev, the Tsar's prime minister.

Tsar Alexey Mikhaylovich did not hurry his review; he visited the upstairs quarters only three times a month to evaluate one maiden in each of six chambers. One can't decide such things immediately. The *boyar* Bogdan Khitrovo, an expert on feminine qualifications, aided him by pointing out whose arms were skinny, whose shoulders bony, whose face had even one blemish, whose legs were not well formed, whose hair was dull. The *boyar* was keenly aware of all these criteria. Doctor Stefan, a learned German, was expert in his own area: whether the pelvis was sufficiently broad, the breasts well-endowed, and the blood healthy—all this in consideration of future children. The midwives took care of the other necessary details. So there wouldn't be any mistake.

However, the Tsar's concerns were not centered on his future wife alone. He was also involved in renovating the Kremlin Palace. Previously Russian masters had worked on it, practicing their simple carving. Now the Tsar had brought in Germans and Poles, who covered the walls with gilded leather; the carving became intricate; in the Banquet Hall the stars' heavenly movement was depicted; in the future Tsaritsa's quarters the green satin was removed from the walls and the ceiling, and instead they were covered with fabric panels and whitewashed; in the passageways the corners and walls were decorated with Flemish wall hangings, and glass beads adorned their green background; the renowned icon painter Simon Ushakov was in charge of the wall and floor décor.

The Tsar's night chamber was being readied also. They workers exterminated the proliferation of bedbugs, thirsting for the royal blood, with flowers of sulphur. A new bed was installed, a carved walnut one, in the German style (large enough for four people), with wooden pedestals ending in the shape of a bird's claws; the carved designs of the upper and lower frames of the bed were gilded—these were of open fretwork depicting human masks, birds, and grass. The sides were decorated with a colored border, and all around the border silver trim was attached with copper nails. Above the bed was a gilded carving of a nude woman: in her right hand was a sword, and in her left, her attire. In the corners, four golden-winged birds sat on four apples. The mattress was of down, the border of the bedclothes was of a heavy silk, deep crimson trimmed in white, yellow, and green; the pillowcase was of crimson satin. The large and thick bed curtains were striped; the sable blanket was backed with satin, adorned with plants and grass of silk on a silver background; the crest was of gold satin framed in crimson silk, embellished with white, azure, and green. The center bed curtain was a special material from Kizylbash—on its smoky background birds and grass made from various silks were sewn, and it was lined in green taffeta.

Yet this bed was not even the most splendid one, nor this blanket the one of greatest value. For the future Tsaritsa a blanket of the finest gold silk had been prepared; it had bands of ermine on it; the crest was of crimson satin edged with pearls. On the crest were twenty-two emeralds and among them two large green faceted stones. To sleep under such a blanket was impossible— one would be crushed by its weight. But the sight of it alone would enchant even the most demanding.

With these domestic concerns in order, the "Most Gentle" Tsar arranged the inspection of the maidens for that evening in the upper quarters in groups of six (but one at a time). Among them was Natalya Kirillovna, daughter of Naryshkin.

Natashen'ka endured all sorts of torment and every kind of maidenly embarrassment. This was already the third month; the senators had been secretly evaluating her, as well as the *boyar* Khitrovo, the German doctors, and the midwives. At last she was taken to His Majesty's Palace, with two women servants and her nurse. They lived in a rather small room decorated with broadcloth; the bed was large and kept very tidy; the servants and the nurse slept on benches along the walls. They lived there one week, then another, and still the Tsar found no time for his inspection. The maiden had already become accustomed to the place, and she slept sweetly at night in her well-heated room beneath a light cover. But on the appointed day she was given neither a cover nor a nightgown, and the room was now even warmer. She was put to bed early. The servants and the nurse stood at the foot of her bed beginning in the early evening, speaking softly. Natashen'ka was ordered to sleep as soon as they put her to bed—and may God prevent her from stirring during the inspection! So she lay there as if on fire, in silence and practically unconscious from fear.

The "Most Gentle" Tsar loved to dress in the German fashion on formal occasions, but for everyday he dressed simply—over his shirt and regular *kaftan* he wore a common light homespun coat; in his hand he held a staff inlaid with horn. It was his custom to go up to the inspection dressed like this, accompanied by the doctor, his old father confessor, and two servant girls each carrying a stout candle. Before each inspection he would pray fervently not only that God would give him wisdom and that his judgment would not be impaired by any extraneous feminine charms, but also that he would view all of the candidates with sensible attention, choosing not a lover but a spouse for the rest of his years. But of course, being human, he did not always escape joyful excitement while visiting the chambers of the really exquisite maidens selected by his experts. It often happened that each new maiden seemed to him better than all those he had seen before, and even more beautiful than he had thought possible. He was sure he could not endure his painful widower-hood a moment longer. However, he would contain himself and continue his inspections, recalling some of the maidens in minute detail for a longer time after.

In the chambers, with broadcloth upholstery and carpeting, the Tsar's footsteps were hardly audible. When the Tsar and his retinue entered the rooms, the women in charge would bow deeply without a word, the servant girls with the candles would stand at each side of the bed, the doctor and the priest would place themselves at the door and await the Tsar's summons, should the need arise. The "Most Gentle One" would approach alone with a calm and kindly face, not permitting himself any improper haste or precipitous emotions, without embarrassment, as if fulfilling his duty as Tsar or selecting a valuable gem for his crown. Without bending over or touching her, respectfully stroking his beard, he would carefully examine all the attributes of the supposedly sleeping maiden with a gaze neither brazen nor offensive, but masculine and experienced, without any superfluous hypocrisy. When he had concluded his inspection, he would silently turn and leave, and the servant girls with the candles would run ahead. If, however, the scene he had beheld had particularly pleased him—in a soft voice he would order Doctor Stefan to check all the specific details of the maiden and record and retain this data.

Naryshkin's turn came on the first day of February. That evening she cried and moaned; they washed her face with cold water three times. Though she calmed down later in the evening, she again became flushed, as if from a fever, and totally exhausted her servants and nurse. They were barely able to get her to bed by the appointed hour and arrange her decorously and beautifully, allowing her best features to show, but not exposing too much, and leaving her exquisite face directly toward the viewer, so he might see the graceful arch of her brows and the outline of her lips.

If this picture was not good enough, then the Tsar would have to continue the search not in his native land, but somewhere beyond the sea. Perhaps there he might find something better.

The Tsar entered in his usual fashion, and the servant girls with their candles cast light upon the beautiful maiden. No one knows what might have been, had Natashen'ka not disobeyed the warning against opening her eyes. She didn't actually open them completely, but made only a tiny slit in one eye, scarcely blinking. However, when through this tiny slit she saw before her the Tsar's beard and his two eyes looking right at her, she became so embarrassed that she could no longer contain her maidenly modesty. As it is told, she squealed slightly and covered herself as best she could with her "twain arms."

This was an unheard of act, a clear insult to the Tsar! Her servants and her nurse rushed at her to pull away her arms, but she would not allow this. The Tsar, having seen even more than usual, himself began to laugh in embarrassment and hurried to leave, firmly striking the floor with his horn staff. And there was grief among those left alone in this chamber, because the women were firmly convinced that from this day onward all their hopes were ended. The maiden could have become Tsaritsa, but now she'd be driven away in disgrace.

It is further related that on the same night the Tsar saw two more maidens. One of them was the novice Ovdotya Ivanovna—the daughter of Belyaev, who had been guarded and prepared by Egakova, Ivan's adopted sister, and the old woman Iraida. This novice was truly beautiful, and she lay there just as they had placed her—immobile and totally still, as if she were really sleeping. But for some reason the Tsar looked at her, as well as at the other girl, absent-mindedly, as though pondering or recalling something totally unrelated. He scarcely noticed her real beauty.

The Tsar observed his possible brides many times until of April. In the middle of the month all the maidens who had been gathered together were allowed to return to their homes with presents, whereas the *boyar* Artamon Matveev was told to detain his guest for a little while—the Tsar wished to see her once again at the *boyar's* mansion. When he saw her, Natashen'ka was not as she had been in that chamber, but was dressed in a heavy robe of green satin thickly encrusted with gold and sable skins. Her cape was decorated with crimson circles embroidered with gold and silver silk. She was, they say, in no way worse than she had been in that chamber; she did not avoid the Tsar's gaze, but nevertheless blushed with the glow of her youth. The Tsar gazed at her incessantly, and not as a tsar, but as a star-struck bridegroom, unwontedly abrupt and youthful, unbefitting his age.

It is further known that Natalya Naryshkin became Tsaritsa of Russia, and thus rose above all others and was remembered throughout history for bearing for the Tsar a son, and for the Empire—Peter the Great. And so it turns out that in his choice of a spouse the "Most Gentle" Tsar Alexey Mikhaylovich did not err.

NOTE

1. *Boyar* is a member of the early Russian nobility, often with a special, privileged relationship to the monarch. *Boyarynya* is the wife of a *boyar; boyaryshnya* is their daughter.

Georgy Adamovich (1894–1972)

Georgy Victorovich Adamovich, the most prolific and perhaps the most influential critic of the Russian emigration, graduated from the Faculty of History and Philology of the University of St. Petersburg in 1917. He began to publish while still a student. His first short story, "Vesyolye koni" (Merry Horses), appeared in 1915 in *The Voice of Life* no. 8, edited by D. V. Filosofov with Zinaida Hippius's untiring assistance. In 1916 Adamovich's first volume of poetry was published by The Hyperboreus in St. Petersburg, with the title *Oblaka* (Clouds).

Although he admired the poetry of Alexander Blok, Adamovich was closer to the Acmeist school of Nikolay Gumilyov and Anna Akhmatova. (The latter frequently visited Adamovich's sister Tanya in their apartment.) Adamovich often met with Akhmatova in the St. Petersburg Bohemians' night club *Brodyachaya sobaka* (The Stray Dog). Poets, painters, musicians, and dancers would gather there in the evening to discuss the latest events in art and literature, to amuse themselves by performing various tricks, or to listen on occasion to Akhmatova, Bal'mont, Bryusov, Blok, Esenin, and Igor' Severyanin reciting their latest poems. The famous ballerina Tamara Karsavina danced for them one night.

In 1915 Adamovich joined the Acmeist Guild of Poets (1911–16), organized by Gumilyov and Sergey Gorodetsky. In 1918, Georgy Adamovich and Georgy Ivanov organized the Second Guild of Poets (1918–20). During 1920–22 Adamovich attended various literary gatherings and poetry *soirées* of the Russian writers housed in St. Petersburg's *Dom iskusstva* (The House of Art), formerly the elegant Villa Rode, a wealthy merchant's mansion. Following the Revolution, during those years of hunger, cold, and disorder, it served as a shelter for St. Petersburg writers, critics, artists, and musicians: Victor Shklovsky, Nikolay Klyuev, Fyodor Sologub and his wife, Anastasiya Chebotarevskaya (herself a poet and translator), Remizov, Olga Forsh, Irina Odoevtseva, Mikhail Zoshchenko, Osip Mandel'shtam, Mikhail Gershenzon, Vladimir Pyast, Vsevolod Ivanov, Evgeny Shvarts, L. Ya. Bilibin, Mikhail Slonimsky, and others.

Emigrating to France, Adamovich first settled in Nice, but then moved to Paris (1923). There he published works in all the Russian *émigré* journals, reviews, newspapers, anthologies, and collections. Together with Mikhail Kantor, the former editor of *The Link*, Adamovich organized a journal under the title *Encounters*. Between 1937 and 1939 he wrote essays and articles for

Russian Annals, Russian News, The New Russian Word, and *Russian Thought*, and for literary journals and almanacs such as *The New House, Experiments, The New Review, Bridges*, and *Aerial Ways*. His major works are the following: the aforementioned *Clouds*; a second volume of poetry entitled *Chistilishche* (Purgatory; Petrograd, 1922), *Na Zapade: stikhi* (In the West: Poems; Paris, 1939), *L'autre patrie* (Paris, 1947), *Odinochestvo i svoboda: literaturnye ocherki* (Solitude and Freedom: Literary Sketches; New York: Chekhov, 1955), *L. N. Tolstoy* (Paris, 1960), *V. Maklakov* (Paris, 1959), *O knigakh i avtorakh* (On Books and Their Authors; Munich-Paris, 1966), *Edinstvo: stikhi iz raznykh let* (Unity: Poems of Various Years; New York, 1967), and *Kommentarii* (Commentaries; Washington, D.C.: Kamkin, 1967). Adamovich was also the author of the brochure "Vklad russkoy literatury v mirovuyu kul'turu" (1961), which was later translated by Dmitry Obolensky and published at Oxford as "The Cultural Achievements of the Russian Emigration." Adamovich lectured on Russian literature from 1950 to 1960 at the University of Manchester, and for one semester (1960–61) at Oxford University. In 1971 he undertook his first and only trip to the United States, where he lectured at Harvard, Yale, and New York University. He died in Nice on February 21, 1972.

From the mid-1920's until the late 1930's, Adamovich was one of the most important *émigré* critics. A literary movement in Paris, sometimes known as the "Parisian note," was shaped and determined by him. His main suggestions centered on ascetic simplicity, the rejection of all forms of experimentation in versification, and the recommendation of eschatological subject matter: truth, loneliness, suffering, death. According to Adamovich, the works of Anatoly Steiger express the essence of the "Parisian note" best of all.

Adamovich was a thoughtful though inconsistent critic. But his artistic flair and feeling for language were excellent, and he was brought up in the best and most refined traditions of Russian and Western European culture, whose historical past he knew quite well. He admired Pushkin, Lermontov, Blok, and Tolstoy (though he felt distaste for the latter's moral preaching), but disliked Fet. He also did not care for Chekhov, especially as a playwright, because his portrayals of everyday life as dull, mediocre, and vulgar obscured the questions of eternal significance. It seems inconceivable that Adamovich, an erudite and perceptive critic, should have rejected the young writer V. Sirin—though, in his defense, it should be noted that he was supported in these attitudes by Georgy Ivanov and Marina Tsvetaeva. In Adamovich's opinion, Dostoevsky was a dangerous metaphysical writer, and he did not approve of Tsvetaeva's "loud poetry" and her experimentation in rhythm, meter, and rhyme. The poems fiom Boris Pasternak's *Doctor Zhivago* also met with Adamovich's severe criticism. In general, Adamovich resembled Aldanov in his rather skeptical remarks about belles-lettres and poetry-writing. "All of this leads to nothing!" he reiterated at his meetings with other younger Russian poets at Montparnasse. These novices in poetry and the many readers of Adamovich absorbed his views, grew with them, and formulated their own literary tastes and aspirations with his *Commentaries* in view. Among them, Adamovich approved of the poems of Anatoly Steiger, Lidiya Chervinskaya, and Igor' Chinnov.

Adamovich was not a prolific poet. His poems, particularly in the collection *In the West*, are refined, concentrated, and free from everything superficial and accidental. He was gifted with a feminine suppleness of style, straightforward and melodious. There is no trace of overexertion, cumbrousness, or artificiality in his verse. He was forever enchanted by the image of Lermontov's Angel, bored by the songs of the earth that for him could never replace the sounds of Heaven. In his essay "The Impossibility of Poetry," presented in excerpts below, Adamovich claims that real lyrics are quite seldom written, and then only as a few accidental lines, since poets cannot sing like the angels. The music inherent in Blok's poetry captivated Adamovich for the rest of his life—in it he detected those motifs from Wagner which Nietzsche called "*die Musik der Zukunft*."[1] This dynamic music, perceptible in Blok and also in Georgy Ivanov, in some rare moments can transfigure the entire world, if only as a transient illusion. A similar musical quality is occasionally reflected in Adamovich. His poems, brief and highly polished, revealing rare simplicity and refinement, can easily be held in the memory.

NOTE

1. "The music of the future." See Yury Ivask, "Poeziya 'staroy' emigratsii," in N. Poltoratzky, *Russkaya literatura v emigratsii*, p. 52.

POEMS

FROM: *The Anchor: An Anthology of Emigré Poetry*.

A moonless evening, a hotel, we two
On coarse sheets, as usual, drifting . . .
Dreamer, where is your world? Wanderer, where is your home?
Isn't it late for an artificial paradise?

A heavy autumn rain pelting the window.
The wallpaper moving before unmoving eyes.
Who is this woman? Why is she so silent?
Why does she lie beside me now?

An autumn evening, God knows where, we two
In perfume and clouds of smoke . . . we suffocate,
Pondering death. And our lives.
And the horror of all this. And that it's irreparable.

———————

The patron stares over the bar, groggy as always.
The *garçon* counts the dishes at the stand . . .
Insistent, importunate, unflagging,
One with the other—fire and smoke—they struggle on.

One doesn't love for the sake of love, or get drunk from wine.
What does a man know, who can't call himself his own?
He grins at his emptied glass,
Utters something, shakes his head.

"To her who hasn't come! And the end of separation.
To this fireside evening, to arms around one's shoulders
And to the angel, as well . . . And those other sounds . . .
Who flew at midnight . . . and to heaven, and to everything!"

He lost the game—he took the consequences.
Time to be leaving. There isn't any hope.
—And white without mercy, implacably bright,
Day begins as an icy streak.

———————

Under branches of rotting lilacs,
Deaf to flattery and abuse,
Far from all, having all forgotten,
At last he sleeps in peace.

The quiet graveyard deserted,
The quiet firmament spacious,
And each day the air is fresher,
Each day a deeper sleep.

But you, with your worrisome hand,
Bringing flowers here—
Why deceive yourself
With a blasphemous dream?

———————

Speak to no one. Don't drink.
Leave home. Leave sister and brother,
Leave people. Your soul must
Feel it—no return.

You must unlove the past. And then
Unlove nature,
Grow more indifferent, day after day,
Week after week, year after year.

And slowly your dreams will die,
And all will be dark. In this new life
You'll clearly see
A wooden cross and a crown of thorns.

THE IMPOSSIBILITY OF POETRY

FROM: *Kommentarii* (Commentaries). First published in *Opyty* (Experiments) no. 9, 1958.

Beginning—that's the most difficult part: how to start? with what? I some-times envy people with "one-track minds," those to whom this difficulty is unknown, not to mention those unembarrassed by the kind of stereotyped, meaningless "journalese" which sticks one word to another in readymade phrases, those who take up their pens and write:

"In this present work, I assigned myself the task of . . ." and so on, coping with this "task" without revisions, in one or two hours—the article is ready, all that's left is to hand it in for publication. Berdyaev, for example, wrote like that. [. . .]

As to the title, "The Impossibility of Poetry," there should be a subtitle. Something uncontrived, something in the nature of "from my memoirs," or "from letters to 'X,' " though it's clear to everyone that there never was nor is there any "X" on this earth. It would be good to add "For the Select Few," as Zhukovsky did, if it weren't that, in circumstances other than Zhukovsky's, it might sound pretentious. When one thinks of it—this is "For the Select Few": I and "the select few" are one and the same. I am, as you see, one of these few.

"We alone understand such poetry"; "we are the chosen, the initiated, the special," "*nous autres, les* madmen,"* as Poplavsky once laughingly said—a rare, unforgettably clever man. No, "For the Select Few" is not suitable, and my essential point, perhaps, does not even concern itself with the fact that this essay is addressed to them. The essence lies elsewhere. In Annensky, in one of his "Books of Reflections," there are several lines about a person who has been standing for quite some time in a queue at a box office, who little by little makes his way to the front of the line and is already quite close to the cherished little window. The tickets being distributed at the register are special, not for entrance into the world, but for an exit out of it; that is, for those for whom a return to God is impossible, à la Karamazov, however much they might want to do so . . . In Annensky this is very convincingly depicted with that exceptional ingratiatingly venomous insistence of his, and I can't conceive of a better way to describe meditations on poetry.

Such an approach would be suitable, because the individual who has essentially only written or thought about poetry wants once and for all "to take stock on himself," wants to come to some resolution, to make things add up. One thing was said to no purpose, another—so much for the sake of rhetoric that it is embarrassing to reread it; here he hurried past, made a mess of it, there flippantly repeated, without verification, what he heard from Khodasevich or from Zinaida Hippius—and so forth. The "total" (why should he delude himself) is meager, while that little window is indeed quite close, and ahead, above the shoulders of those standing in line, the lowered face of the cashier appears for a moment, and one can see how she smiles or frowns as she tears off the little tickets one after another. "It's time, my friend, it's time." Let's talk a bit about poetry, seriously, perhaps for the first and, who can tell, perhaps for the last time in our lives. [. . .]

Movement, development and (even more so) "innovation" in poetry are accompanied by a certain amount of vanity and by a deviation from everything that can be called the poetic idea in the Platonic sense.

No matter how marvelous it appears at first glance, movement disperses thoughts, thins the emotions, and in this way from the very outset leads ultimately to apostasy.

But what can the poet do? Mark time? Content himself with the stylization of the classics? Twelve smooth little lines, four-foot iambs, love, and blood? No, that is no solution, no way out. It's difficult to find a way out. In the past there was movement; otherwise we couldn't even "mark time." The historical understanding of movement, development, is irrefutable, and its legality

*we, then, are the madmen

203

seems beyond all doubt. It's obvious, however, that not all periods are identical in this regard; so it is appropriate at this point to paraphrase a famous dictum of Leontiev: "It is necessary to freeze poetry so it won't rot."

Very likely this is *our* discovery, and for it we must thank not our own special perspicuity, but (as it turns out) only those fortunes which placed us in a special, unprecedented set of circumstances, and moreover in an epoch when novelty (in whatever form) became almost the slogan of certain influential artists. Our historical destiny was contemplation of the purest, least adulterated kind, inasmuch as there were no fields for our active participation, no arenas—not to speak of our naturally rather weak inclination toward active pursuits. And having grown rigid, having come to a standstill—historically and socially—we discerned that "something," elusive to others. To take pride in this would be foolish. To rejoice would be as unfounded. Least of all would there be any basis for making some kind of obligatory and invariable principle out of that which was confided to us within an exclusive arrangement, as if privately, with Fate—"spiritually," and not to be divulged. "Long live the triumphal procession of art toward new, bright horizons! Long live all forms of avant-garde art!" enthusiasts are inclined to exclaim in the normal historical state of affairs. Indeed, let them find even more refined expressions for their aspirations than those which I in mockery have advanced. Well, so then let's agree: Long live art! Why, in fact, should we not wish a long life for art? Nowadays, the continuous renovation, the continuous alteration of styles is extolled. This trend had been sanctified by Baudelaire, who called for a "dive into the depths of uncertainty in the search of that which is new"—a feeble, internally barren line by a great poet. And so, long live art! Yet one could find five or six people who would undoubtedly say: we will not exchange this, our unexpected revelation, for anything; and no one, not by any arguments, not by any references to whatever authorities, will convince us that our revelation is just an annoying consequence of "the circumstances of emigration," a result of the loss of living ties with reality, or simply impotent snobbish grumbling. Yes, our involuntary, historical pause, our exit from a prolonged engagement on a stage now stripped of its scenery, has had its effect. Nevertheless, it was worthwhile, more than worthwhile, to lose everything considered part of the usual historical surroundings so that in the ensuing void, as if through a distant, narrow crack, a light might glimmer . . . For the affirmation of the unattainability of poetry is ultimately its great glorification, an obeisance to the earth, a declaration of eternal love, though it be love for a phantom. Yet the phantom is so wonderful that, once having glimpsed its features, one will not wish to gaze upon anything else. "He had a single vision" . . .

The West and Western poetry are undoubtedly against us, and the entire Western poetic experiment, in this sense, is refuting us. There can be no question whatsoever about the "impossibility" of poetry in the West; especially in France, which, in the assertions of certain critics, is now experiencing a poetic flourishing the likes of which it has never known.

One could raise many objections to this, especially from the Russian point of view; for example, that in poetry the West is no authority for us; that because of our deep mutual heterogeneity there is hardly anyone in the West from whom we might learn; that we had Pushkin at a time when Victor Hugo shone, glittered, and reigned in France—and the question of which of them was the barbarian, which the poetic infant, would be absurd even to argue. Even if we remain within these local boundaries which are alien to us, it would be valid to observe that the present "flourishing" was probably engendered in France not so much by the upheaval of creative forces as by the abolition of everything which had only recently compromised the formal foundation and fabric of poetry. At present "everything is allowed" in French poetry, and when creation begins and empty chatter ends, no one is certain . [. . .]

If poetry is coupled with life and, as a constituent part of life, it more or less satisfactorily moves within the general stream; if its purpose lies more or less in furnishing spicy, piquant, unexperienced sensations, in distracting, gladdening, comforting, or triumphing over daily tedium; if a successful, daring figure of speech alone, an "image," justifies poetry's existence, then of course the Western poets are right—in their own way; and in their own crude, serenely coarse condition even many Soviet poets are right—and we are not.

But very likely the Russian tendency toward extremes makes itself known: all or nothing. If I cannot achieve "all," I do not want any sort of intermediate stage. I choose "nothing," or almost "nothing"—for we will manage, nevertheless, to save some tiny fragments . . . Yet in my misery I do not envy these pseudo-Croesuses, even those of the fascinating Dylan Thomas type, and I reject any games in common with them.

I have no objections whatever to an innovation which would limit itself to formal investigations. The only trouble is that in poetry—and this is especially obvious in Russian poetry, where unmistakeable metropolitanism goes hand in hand with that ineradicable Mirgorod [Gogolian] sort of "hick town" effect—the only trouble is that formal innovations in poetry are usually combined with a particular literary pose, with a challenge, a "thrust forward." Theoretically, this combination is not at all necessary; yet in practice it is the first thing to reveal itself, and our "Mother Russia" does not forgo the opportunity to flaunt herself, brilliantly scintillating with all that is laughable and pitiable within her (about which Turgenev wrote with such bitterness in *Smoke*). [. . .]

The transposition [of this "thrust forward" attitude] to poets, especially to Russian poets, is quite distressing;

"I don't give a damn

about ten-ton[1] bronzes,
I don't give a damn
about marble slime . . ."

This is taken from Mayakovsky, from the most celebrated of his verses, "In Full Voice." In the introductory article to a collection of his works lying before me, the author makes the enthusiastic and servile observation that Mayakovsky "was fearlessly breaking established canons," while further on follows the sort of prattle so familiar to us, since so many use it that it doesn't even amaze us anymore. One has to make an effort to come to one's senses and, having come to one's senses, ask oneself: "What is this, what is this? What sort of nonsense is this? Where is all of this leading?"

Mayakovsky was an extraordinarily talented person and could have become a very great poet. I don't think that, after Nekrasov, there was anyone in Russian poetry whose tragic notes sounded more clearly. In Mayakovsky's voice there was bronze, there was tempered steel, and although his earlier whimsical tunes were not quite compatible without their creator—the Ill-fated Wretch—and were closer to futuristic melodrama than to futuristic Aeschylus, subsequently it seemed that he had to free himself from his extreme exaggeration of coloring. "A Cloud in Trousers" was a rare poetic promise. Yet the very title of the poem (that is, the character of this title, its internal composition) was enough to engender apprehensions, and these apprehensions proved justified.

Let's forget "Except like in Mossellprom," since Mayakovsky himself did not consider these exercises as poetry. However, even that which he did consider poetry makes one despondent: undue familiarity, boisterous laughter, the absence of "a little word conceived in simplicity"—even if only a single little word, his steadfast certainty that precisely in these features is revealed the progress of art and the destruction of canons; that this destruction is necessary, beneficial; that together with it poetry advances in triumph . . . You become despondent, and if one were roused to object, to persuade, to argue—one would have to begin with the very beginning: two times two is four.

Mayakovsky was correct in his fundamental conviction that, one hundred years after the death of Pushkin, one must not write verses exactly as Pushkin did. However, together with this formal conclusion from an indisputable premise, he carelessly and hastily drew an emotional conclusion on the basis of the public's momentary, foolish response, the noise and success. And he not merely ruined himself, but also allowed a poetic demagogue-like monster to rise within him. Mayakovsky brought Russian poetry to the brink, almost to the abyss, though steadfastly remaining brilliantly resourceful in his combination of words and all other types of verbal contrivances. What alienates one is not his ends, but his means. Why are the bronzes "ten-ton"? Oh, this "ten-ton"! Not only the neologism itself, but also its ponderous, caddishly negligent, emotional coloring, the essence of which finally becomes obvious beyond any doubt by the phrase following it: "marble slime." "Oh, what are you there; look at us, we're wearing our hearts on our sleeves, we're good fellows, you'll get to know us!"

The foreigner "will not understand nor will he notice,"[2] of course, what is hidden behind these words. They might be appealing to the foreigner, even to the highly knowledgeable foreigner. It is necessary to be Russian in order to be able to say to oneself with a shudder: this is she, our motherland, our "autocratic Russia, homeland of Orthodoxy," as Bunin's merchant-patriot (and, of course, potential pogrom-maker) Rostovtsev says, close to tears. This is she, even in her Soviet garb, strangely retaining her former Russian brigand features; it is she who gave birth to it in her depths, and nurtured it. Forgive her, then, if her sons do not find other words, except the phrase from Rozanov which I remember—"I part with eternal parting,"[a]—to describe her image.

With Marina Tsvetaeva the matter is more straightforward. Often enough I hear reproaches that I do not appreciate or understand her. My lack of appreciation is possible. But there is nothing in Tsvetaeva to misunderstand.

She was, of course, a real poet, and, of course, in her poetry there are brilliant strophes, melodic and melancholy, feminine, and unique to her. The reverie, the semi-somnolent and melodious intonations, the quiet, somnambulant pace of several of her verses to Blok, or of the early poems about Moscow, are unsurpassed. But the creative pretensions of Tsvetaeva little by little turned out to be in discord with her powers. I maintain this as an obvious truth, although I realize that I remain alone in this observation. Yury Ivask, for example, one of her faithful, unwavering admirers, was even reminded of Derzhavin, saying of her that she possessed a lofty poetic style, a lofty spiritual nature, pathos, splendor, magnificence. This is a portrait, a characterization, but not a proof. We disagree, based on our own readings, as to whether there was in Tsvetaeva enough "combustibility" for a continuous flame. (Or did she, for the most part, blaze illusively, mechanically, in pace with her inertia, as did her kindred spirit Bal'mont in much of his work?) It is possible to argue this point. Yet to argue that in her patter, in her lamentations and exclamations, in her rhythmical convulsion there is no artistic novelty—

---

[a] Once I happened to speak for a long time with Mayakovsky—in "The Hall of Comedians," at night, when word of Rasputin's murder spread. Everyone was agitated; for several hours the usual partitions between literary groups and subgroups disappeared. From Rasputin the conversation, naturally, passed on to poetry. Mayakovsky was unusually restrained and wise, infinitely wiser than his ever-assumed pose.

that is, indications for further development—in my opinion, is impossible. Tsvetaeva belongs to those with whom the epoch ends, and only the spirit of opposition with which she was obsessed, the spirit of artistic "defiance," prevented her from making this confession. Even to herself.

More significant—formally and intrinsically—is Pasternak, although he has none of Tsvetaeva's "charm." But did he search for it, did he desire it, was he inclined to be tempted by it? Hardly—just as Pushkin would hardly be tempted by the qualities which we sometimes like in Fet.

Pasternak—together with Khlebnikov—is our only poet of the "innovative" type who does not consider his laboratory experiments in any way connected with the tendency to oppose oneself to the rest of mankind in self-indulgence and a display of one's personal genius. This alone should inspire us with confidence in him, even if his poetic images were devoid of other features, rare and outstanding. However, his experiment itself not only fails to refute our doubts about the future "possibility of poetry," but unexpectedly brings new evidence to support those doubts by its own example, with all of its own improvisational arbitrariness.

In Pasternak, the word went mad for the first time in Russian poetry. The word ceased to be a logical unit, restricted in its movements by logical meaning and incapable of being treated in such a way that the logical links between concepts could be replaced by some other links. Pasternak does with the word everything that comes into his head and forces it to change its meaning wherever he wishes. For Pasternak, it is not important that the sky is the sky, or that a tree is a tree. What is important is only the given line or stanza as a unified conception; and within the line or stanza the "sky" can lose all those heavenly connotations which had been deemed implicit up to that moment. Is this liberation a step forward? At first glance, it seems to be—"the destruction of canons." But if this is indeed a liberation, then it is accompanied by an improverishment, a diminished effectiveness—because, even before, in the works of perceptive poets, the word never, under any circumstances, appeared exclusively as a denotative sign. In the word there was that which Pasternak exalts in it, plus the logical meaning—and there was the deep, let us say, even almost metaphysical, substantiation of the certitude that the logical content necessarily remains the primary essence of the word. "In the beginning was the Word . . ." The defense of logic was almost the main aspiration of Khodasevich, while earlier—that of Gumilyov, who, as I remember, especially insisted upon the necessity of the visual verification of metaphors. In Pasternak's work, metaphors often appear as completely nonsensical; it is partially this quality which allows him to generate verbal whirlwinds in which he is tsar and god, bound by no one and nothing. The whirlwinds are undeniably full of inspiration. Yet this inspiration is a personal gift of the poet which he cannot transmit to anyone else; whereas, while transmitting his method and style, he instigates a renunciation of prose, a fear of it, in place of its subjugation. Precisely in this lies the root of the whole problem, of all the hopes, dreams, all the "impossibilities," all creative impasses and dramas: prose must be realized in poetry, it must enter into it and dissolve within it. Poetry must rise above prose, after it, and not meekly to the side, as a cowardly flight from confrontation, without agreeing to risk anything. A line of Pasternak is a line of least opposition, with all its external, purely syntactical or stylistic complexity; the formal scheme of his poetry hides within it a foreboding (one would like to say, an omen) of "impossibility," but instead of breaking his head against the wall—or at least risking this!—Pasternak seeks out roundabout paths, even furnishing them with small benches on which to rest. All this may appear as an intentional, preconceived distortion of Pasternak's position: imagine, he, the most difficult of the difficult—and yet the least opposition! In Pasternak's justification, diverse conclusions arise: in the first place, he does with the word what other poets in the West were doing long ago, which means that he moves on a level with the vanguard of Western culture, contrary to the majority of his countrymen. Second, our Euclidian-rationalized world has collapsed beneath the blows of science, so how is one to know if Pasternak's imaginary chaos does not correspond more precisely to the true reality than does three-dimensional poetry? Is not the sharp, intuitive contemporaneity of Pasternak revealed in the Lobachevsky-Rimanovsky perception of reality? I've already come across this second argument somewhere, and I believe it may successfully attract people who have, in essence, a weakness for Modernism. But this argument is false. Conjectures, even if scientifically indisputable, that our thinking is subjected to laws—which are not at all obligatory for the universe—do not take us away from this earth, do not change anything in the structure of our brain; and no sort of relativity, whether it's annoying to us or not, affects poetry—if it is really poetry, and not a pleasant pastime with the newest wonder-playthings. Playfulness in Pasternak is invariably felt—in contrast to the works of Blok, who, among the new Russian poets, was least susceptible to it. Yet it is strange—the aftertaste of Pasternakian poetry is bitter. Liberation brought us nowhere; it led nowhere. Pasternak remains in the void, and sees only mirages around him.

"Impossibility," however, he strengthens in other ways. You read Pasternak, and from the very first line you know, you feel, that there is being offered to you something artistic, poetic, and new. Indeed, there is little that dampens one's ardor more powerfully than intrusive high artistic value or, more precisely, the obviousness of artistic intentions. An icy shower! True, in Pasternak these pretensions are of good quality and are not the same as those in another fiction writer who writes, for example, "The sea's silver tablecloth was embroidered with quivering pearls . . ."[3] and in his antediluvian naïvete thinks that he is writing "artistically," whereas if he were to write that the moon was reflected in the sea, then this would not be done "artistically"! No, Pasternak, of course, is on another level; but his intentions, that is, his "seams," are still visible. Pasternak presents poetry—"poetry" in quotation marks. And when pastry is given to a starving man, he's inclined to say, "Give me a piece of bread." You cannot satisfy poetic hunger with cream.

In these attempts to pinpoint finally the very crux of the disagreement, the thought emerges: Isn't the essence of poetry the perception of the vanity of vanities? Does not our hunger come from the fact that the vanity of vanities is not nourishing? You read the verses, you see how tightly and harmoniously they are constructed—and you are perplexed: *for what purpose* are they created? Why? Poetry should answer this question or cancel it out, discard it. But all the means accessible to poetry are only approximate, and in the light of our bewilderment, our "why?," their lack of substance is revealed. The golden bird of paradise will flit away, no matter what. At best, a parrot with red and green feathers will remain squawking in our hands.

What, then, is to be done?—you ask yourself for the hundredth time. What is to be done in the name of "image and likeness"? For the sake of encouraging "better words," what sort must one find in oneself? The attempt to remove all ornamentation, all kinds of trinkets—not just the pretty ones, but also those of excellent make, high quality—little by little will lead to a blank page. No kind of honey tasted quite right, and "here I lay dying," even though with a blissful feeling of righteousness and faith. (A little like in Annensky's monologue of Famira after the match with the Muse . . . How well this is done in his poem! Yet who remembers this monologue? Five, perhaps, six people. Whereas millions remember the "ten-ton bronzes.")

A danger lies in wait and is worse than an empty page: a natural, even (in a certain sense) healthy aspiration to free oneself from the tyranny of "impossibility"—without, however, agreeing to step onto the path of placid entertainment, in the spirit of the "lemonade" of which Derzhavin spoke, of course, in jest. This aspiration can lead to the writing of verses no different from those which the imitators of Mayakovsky wrote, listless, pale, not even dead but as if not having yet been born, as yet in a state of limbo. The subjugation of prose can actually become the realization of prose, and even its triumph. If there is no response in answer, there is no one else to blame—you yourself are guilty; you must start again, from the beginning.

We have a poet in emigration, still comparatively young, who is akin to my theme, although I don't know if he would agree with such an allegation—Igor' Chinnov. A certain lack of attention accorded to him is the result of his apparently extreme "chamber quality." And it is true, reading him you at times recall Paul Valéry's witty remark, typically Gallic in its explicitness—"*Ecrire en moi naturel. Tels écrivent en moi dièse.*"† Chinnov writes in "*moi bémol*,"‡ he muffles the tone with that same obsession with which Tsvetaeva or Mayakovsky were boisterous in their poems. But his most refined, stylistic

---

†Write to me in white [keys]. Such people write to me only in sharps.
‡In flats

finds, the iridescent mother-of-pearl nuances of some of his epithets were inspired, it seems to me, by a dual repulsion: from feeble imitation and from splendor, behind which one can pull off anything on the sly. Like the tightrope-walker on the wire, here he'll take a step; there he'll stop, pausing for a breath—yet he'll never lose his balance. Not a single break.

Again I think of Valéry: "Will there be something great in Europe again," or "Will there be a twenty-first century?"—as one of our Russian writers recently asked himself.

Bewilderment is related to creative work, though in our "atomic" age it is possible to interpret it more widely and alarmingly. The sensation now being spread is sometimes compared with that prevalent during the decline of Rome, imprinted in the famous Verlaine sonnet—"All has been drunk, all has been eaten, *plus rien à dire*."§ But obscurantism—a great, black barbarism—was imminent for Rome, which harbored a strength no less than that belonging to classical antiquity. Now here is light in the world: everything is clear, everything has been calculated, obscurantism has no place from which to emerge. But the headlong acceleration of technical progress has proved so infectious to art that in the last hundred years it has changed its form more, repudiated more, become carried away by various momentous considerations, proclaimed or conceived a hatred for more; in a word, it has manifested impatience and restlessness more than in the two previous millennia. Traits common to Pushkin and Horace, for example, are more obvious than those common to Pushkin and Khlebnikov, or to Pushkin and the French Surrealists. And this impatience, this restlessness, is still gathering strength . . .

In the first mischievous Futurist years there was a man by the name of Vasilisk Gnedov, considered a poet, although it seems he wrote nothing. His only work was entitled "Poem of the End." During literary *soirées* people shouted to him, "Gnedov, give us the poem of the end! . . ." "Vasilisk, Vasilisk!" He would walk up, somber, with a stone face, that is, "in the manner of Khlebnikov," and would remain silent for a long time; then slowly he'd raise a heavy fist—and say in a low voice, "That's all!" In the future, more talkative poets will very likely be found, but this "That's all!" from nearly half a century ago now presents itself as symbolic. How to continue, how to develop poetry? And what if development is impossible; will life be retained in poetry? "Will there be a twenty-first century?"

At present, our better verses are not being written but are being polished. Georgy Ivanov virtually does not write, but polishes, skillfully blending the

§And there is nothing more to say.

final fragments of feelings, hopes, and thoughts. This is being done without, thank God, concessions to some kind of Modernism. Yet he, one must believe, does not flatter himself with the possibility of developing his artistic devices.

———————

The glorification of the past to the detriment and scorn of the present is a banal and laughable position, especially if it is based on the criterion of age. It doesn't even pay to talk about it, this—"It's your generaion, *you try!*" Still, even the assertion that all epochs are identical, and that the trace left on art by each generation is of equal worth to all others, is no less erroneous.

In the Russian past there was much that was good, as well as much that was weak. However, in concluding these remarks—in which so much is left unsaid!—and as much in commentary on these observations as a key to them, and even a justification for them, I cannot refrain from bringing from the past a short poem—six lines of Boratynsky:

> Tsar of heaven! Calm
> My painful soul.
>
> Let forgetfulness
> Of worldly delusions come.
>
> And for Your austere paradise
> Grant strength to my heart.

In speaking of verses which are well liked, one usually says "Amazing!" "Wonderful!" There is nothing of the "wonderful" in these verses! Yet you will find few verses in all of Russian literature that are purer, more steadfast, more precious, freer from poetic roguery—this is, precisely, the return to the altar of that which man received from above, the clear reflection of "image and likeness." Neither irony, nor tears, nor picture-painting tinsel—no symptoms at all of dilution of will. Economy of means, that is, the beginning and end of mastery, is brought to perfection—the entire verse is held together, of course, by one word, "austere." But this word is filled with enough substance for dozens of poems in the vein of some unfortunate "Inoniya,"[4] and the whole is flooded with the illumination cast by this one word back over the lines.

After everything that has swept through my memory up to this point, it is indeed "impossible to heed without agitation" such words. And I want to say, "Evgeny Abramovich, you were not the first Russian poet, but our first teacher in poetry; for the coldness which surrounded you, for your condescending approval—even though with some reservations—of Belinsky the Babbler (who led you to believe that you were a backward person, while he thought himself progressive and felt, therefore, he had the right to teach you some sense), for everything that we have since come to, for human baseness, for 'ten-ton bronzes,' for your staunchness, clairvoyance, and grief, allow me to give you my compliments, 'to kneel humbly,' as it was said by another poet, 'teacher, before your name . . .' "

Or in other words—it is as if drunken Marmeladov,[5] with an empty bottle in hand, were to turn to poetry with the plea: "May your kingdom come!"
But it never will.

NOTES

1. Adamovich appears to have been exasperated with Mayakovsky's neologism *mnogopudye*, which is analogous to the existing Russian word *mnogopolye*.
2. Reference to one of Tyutchev's poems.
3. Reference to Maxim Gor'ky's style of writing.
4. Reference to one of Sergey Esenin's poems.
5. Reference to Dostoevsky's novel, *Crime and Punishment*.

Vladislav Khodasevich
(1888–1939)

Vladislav Felitsianovich Khodasevich, a prominent poet, biographer, essayist, translator, and critic, was born and educated in Moscow. He first published in Russia in 1908 as a symbolist poet, but his more distinctive work was done in emigration. His poetry, witty and ironic, deals with the soul's imprisonment in the material world. His verse collections are *Shchastlivy domik* (The Happy Little House; Moscow, 1914), *Putyom zerna* (By Way of the Grain; Berlin, 1920), *Tyazholaya lira: chetvyortaya kniga stikhov* (The Heavy Lyre: A Fourth Book of Poems; Berlin, 1923), *Sobranie stikhov* (Collected Poems; Paris, 1927), and *Sobranie stikhotvoreny: 1913–1939* (Collected Poems: 1913–1939; Munich, 1961; published posthumously). He was a regular contributor to *La Renaissance* and *Contemporary Annals*, and his poetry appeared in various Russian anthologies and literary journals. His three other publications, *Derzhavin* (Paris, 1931), *O Pushkine* (About Pushkin; Berlin, 1937), and *Nekropol'* (Necropolis; Brussels, 1939) are very important critical pieces. Khodasevich, an intelligent skeptic who hated his own skepticism, had a romantic, passionate vision of some future miracle taking place in the realm of art—of beautiful music suddenly resounding in poetry. In his own poems, however, there was no music—only the sensible word, irony, and tormenting anguish. His poetry incorporates a struggle between irony and music; he hoped for the victory of music, but irony always gained the upper hand. Andrey Bely heard in Khodasevich's verse the poetic sounds of Boratynsky, Tyutchev, and Pushkin[1]; and D. S. Svyatopolk-Mirsky, who was fond of paradoxes and biting formulations, referred to Khodasevich as a "small Boratynsky from the Underground, the favorite poet of those who don't care for poetry."[2]

Khodasevich's language is clear, his style simple, and his craftsmanship precise. While he acquired this method from the Acmeist school of poetry, the deep thought in his verse can be traced to the Symbolists. His sarcastic attitude toward himself and the world around him recalls the second period in symbolist poetry, with its characteristic disappointment in the mysteries of the universe, and the persona's loss of former ideals and aspirations. Khodasevich's dependence on the poetry of Boratynsky and Tyutchev reveals itself in doubts, anxieties, and convictions that everything on earth is transitory, illusory; Khodasevich, however, sees the world in its concrete, everyday, colorless outlines. He prefers the genre of elegy: sad reflection, complaint, and maxims. Like Boratynsky, he uses negative epithets beginning "without," "no," "half," and so forth. In Boratynsky these negatives have a deep metaphysical meaning; in Khodasevich they are less philosophically charged. His intonation is even smoother and more down-to-earth than that of his famed predecessor in versification. From Pushkin, Khodasevich learned careful craftsmanship—precision, transparency, perfect harmony and proportion of stanzas, and intonation. No exaggeration, no adornment, no artificial solemnity in tone or expression, and no rhetoric is found in Khodasevich's verse. His mastery of the alexandrine and iambic tetrameter and pentameter was also acquired from Boratynsky and Pushkin. But he has created his own magnificent grotesque, a desert of despair, as psychologically contemporary as "The Waste Land" of T. S. Eliot. The poet, both as man and as artist, has abandoned his normal sense of perspective and rationality. Thus, using the vocabulary of the Russian Symbolists from the second, desperate, and disillusioned period and employing the versification of the nineteenth century, Khodasevich has constructed an eerie universe where the persona loses his personality and the world loses its concrete form and proportions. Metaphysically this world is absurd, frightening, and grotesque. There is no longer rationality and logic in this material world—prosperity and disintegration are one and the same; chaos and destruction are pervasive.

Having reached these conclusions in his verse, Khodasevich lapsed into silence as a poet. He continued writing critical essays and books about Russian writers, poets, and Russian literary life in general at the beginning of the twentieth century. In 1925–26 he published critical articles and reviews in the newspaper *Days* and from 1927 until his death he was in charge of literary criticism for *La Renaissance*. He was a sober and perceptive critic, thoroughly acquainted not only with eighteenth- and nineteenth-century Russian literature, but also with Soviet fiction. In *Necropolis* he reminisces about Valery Bryusov, Alexander Blok, Andrey Bely, and Nikolay Gumilyov, as well as about the atmosphere of various literary circles in St. Petersburg and Moscow. Like *Derzhavin*, this book is written with a profound understanding of Russia and the *Zeitgeist* of the period.

NOTES

1. "Tyazholaya lira i russkaya lirika," *Sovremennye zapiski* 15 (1923): 378, 388.
2. *Vyorsty* no. 1 (1926): 208.

POEMS

FROM: *Sobranie stikhov* (Collected Poems).

God is alive! Wise, but not abstruse,
I wander through my poems,
Like a stern Father Superior
Among his humble monks.
I tend my obedient flock
With a prosperous staff.
The keys to this secret garden
Jingle at my waist.
I am hopeful and voice this hope.
Perhaps only the angel, prostrate before God,
Can sing beyond logic and sense—
Or the cattle, unaware of Him,
Can bellow and roar without meaning.
But I am neither radiant angel,
Nor vicious serpent, nor stupid bull.
As a gift from generations
I love my human speech:
Its severe freedom,
Its tortuous laws . . .
Oh, if only I might clothe my dying moan
In a lucid ode!

1923

———————

All is stone. Into a stony passage
The night retreats. In doorways, at gates—

Like sculptures—couples stuck together.
A heavy sigh. The heavy odor of a cigar.

A key clinks against stone, a bolt groans.
Walk along the stone till five,

Wait: a sharp breeze will blow through the ocarina—
Across chinks of cumbersome Berlin—

And another vulgar day will rise behind the houses,
Above this stepmother of Russian cities.

1923

FUNERAL: A SONNET

FROM: *Sobranie stikhotvoreny: 1913–1939* (Collected Poems, 1913–1939), ed. N. Berberova.

Brow—
Chalk.
Casket—
White.

Priest
Sang.
Shots
Sound—

Day
Blessed!
Tomb
Blind.
Shadow—
Into Hell!

1928

DERZHAVIN

(ON THE HUNDREDTH ANNIVERSARY OF HIS DEATH)

FROM: *Statyi o russkoy poezii* (Essays on Russian Poetry; Letchworth: Prideaux Press, 1971).

Derzhavin died on July 8, 1816. If today, on the hundredth anniversary of his death, he would arise and appear among us—how angry he would be, that obstreperous and fidgety old man, at his books being simply entitled (minus his Christian name): *The Works of Derzhavin*, for in his estimation:

217

"There is only one God, and one Derzhavin!"
What a scene he would make, how wrathfully he would draw his robe about him and pull his nightcap down over his bald pate, at the realization of the change in his reputation—a reputation attained through years of work, anxiety, disputes, at times even humiliation—and of divine, poetical soaring. With what disappointment and bitterness could he, this Russian Anacreon, "in the frost, and by the hearth"—he who had celebrated Plamida, Vsemila, Milena, Chloé, utter the words of another, later poet:

And where's the joy, when someday
The bearded rhetorician chooses your works
As a lesson for his students!

Sitting on our school benches, we all memorized "God" or "Felitsa"— memorized them, it would seem, so that we might forever divorce ourselves from Derzhavin and never willingly return to him. We are compelled forever to bear in mind that the works of this glorifier of Felitsa are a classical example of Russian pseudo-classicism, i.e., an essentially artificial, superfluous, and unjustified phenomenon, something of the sort, which (thank God) has ended, disintegrated, become "history"—and to which no one will ever return.

Here lies a great injustice. They labeled this phenomenon pseudo-classicism—and with this laid it beneath a gravestone, as it were, from under which it can never arise. Meanwhile, in the poetry of Derzhavin a spring of creativity pulsates and foams, deeply exciting, intense and alive, i.e., by no means artificial. Derzhavin's poetry is united with life by the most durable ties.

The eighteenth century, especially its Petrine beginning and its end under Catherine's reign, was a creative and victorious age in Russia. Derzhavin was one of Catherine's collaborators, not only in the propagation of enlightenment, but also in the area of governmental organization. During Catherine's reign these two areas were closely linked as never before. Every cultural activity, poetry included, had a *direct* part in the formation of the government. It was necessary not only to mold exterior forms for Russia, but also to breathe into them the living spirit of culture. Derzhavin the poet was as much an indirect architect of Russia as was Derzhavin the administrator. Therefore one could say that, in its essence, his poetry was not merely a *document* of the age, or a reflection of it, but an actual part of its substance; it is not that Derzhavin's epoch was *reflected* in his poems, but that they themselves, in a number of various ways, *created* that epoch. In those victorious days the cannons resounded in concert with victorious poems. Derzhavin was a peaceful fighter; Suvorov, a warring one. They accomplished a single, general task, although sometimes trading weapons. I doubt whether many people know that not only did Derzhavin dedicate poetry to Suvorov, but Suvorov did the same for Derzhavin. Moreover, Derzhavin in his time had even fought against Pugachyov. And I would venture to say that the difference between the victories of the latter and the creative achievements of the former is smaller than it would seem at first glance.

Even in intensity their labors have much in common. Always remembering that "the victors are not judged," Suvorov was victorious wherever and whenever possible. An administrator as well as a poet, Derzhavin worked indefatigably. "The beautiful" was one of his weapons—and not as a fawning courtier, but as a great poet. He cast with a generous hand his diamonds of beauty, caring little about the motivations prompting his generosity. He knew that beauty was immutable and eternal. His inspiration was set aflame by the tiniest spark:

> Empty houses, empty groves,
> Emptiness in our hearts.
> As if deep in the night,
> Silence slumbers in the wood.
> All nature is dismal,
> The gloom of fear invades,
> And terror walks behind;
> And if it weren't for the singing of the winds
> And the gurgling of the streams,
> We might see the image of death.

It is unimportant that these verses were written "On Her Majesty's Departure for Belorussia." They are included in the ode only incidentally. Genuine terror, the genuine and terrible sensation of death mysteriously pervading nature, arose in the poet not at all in connection with the absence of the sovereign (whose journey, in fact, was brief and profitable). What is important is that this terror did arise, and that it was expressed with such force. The inclusion of these majestic lines in an "official" ode was an act of Derzhavin's poetic generosity—and that alone. To say that they were intended as some sort of "court" poetry is naïve and shortsighted.

Historical commentary harms many of Derzhavin's creations, insofar as they should be taken solely as an artist's creation, and not as historical documents. It harms them not in the sense that it diminishes them in our eyes, but because it relegates their main and most valuable content to a less important level. For accurate artistic interpretation it is often necessary to cast aside the motivations for the origin of this or that piece. "Felitsa" is *beautiful* not because of the occasion or event for which it was written, or because it depicts such and such historical *personages*, but because of the portrayal *itself* and its very *nature*. When Derzhavin subsequently wrote that he was the first "to dare praise the virtues of Felitsa in light Russian verse," certainly he took pride not in his revelation of Catherine's virtues, but in the fact that he was the first to use "light Russian verse" for this purpose. He realized that his ode was the first artistic incarnation of Russian *everyday* life, that it was the embryo of our novels. And, perhaps, had "the old man Derzhavin" lived to read the first chapter of *Onegin*—he would have heard in it echoes of his own ode.

Pre-Derzhavin lyrics were almost completely conventional. Both the exterior world and the poet's own private emotions were depicted in an ideal, rather abstract, quiet, pure, and simple form. They could not mix colors and were unaware of half-tones. Derzhavin was the first to begin depicting the world as it appeared to the artist; in this sense he was the first genuine lyric poet in Russia.

He was the first Russian poet capable and, more important, desirous of expressing his personality as it was—of painting his own portrait in a lively and authentic sense, undistorted by any conventional pose, unconstrained by classical trappings. Not without reason did he, bard and dignitary, in certain of his portraits decide to pose for posterity in his nightcap and robe.

During his life he was a reliable servant of tsar and country. Because of his excessive adherence to the law, truth, and forthrightness, he was often "a nuisance." For this reason his service career was a long series of ups, downs, and new ups. Occasionally he suffered, but he never relented. In anger, he once said to the Emperor Paul himself a word which even today must be replaced by dashes in print. Many lines in the works of Derzhavin are devoted to forthrightness and honesty. For us they are somewhat boring and seem elementary; but it is impossible not to value their forcefulness. The ode "To Tyrants and Judges" echoes the mighty speech of a genuine poet:

> Arise, O God of the Just!
> And hear their prayer:
> Come, judge, and punish the deceitful,
> And alone be the Tsar of earth.

In "A Monument" he is proud, moreover, that he has "spoken the truth to tsars with a smile." He underestimated himself in these lines, for he did possess the ability to speak the truth to tsars not only with the cautious smile of an honest servant, but also with the wrath of a poet.

Alongside this somewhat dry and severe image we can visualize yet another image of Derzhavin: the dignitary in his private home life, resting from his duties, a lover of the Muses and hospitality, conscientious in household affairs, a benevolent master to his own servants, a landowner, and something of a sybarite, able to forget everything on earth "amidst wine, sweets, and perfume." He loved his home with the love of a true pagan. Not without pride, would he invite his friends and benefactors to dinner. He was equally satisfied with his family prosperity and the abundance of his table:

> Sheksnin golden sturgeon,
> Kaymak[1] and borsch already set;
> Punch and wine entice from their decanters,

> Shimmering with ice and sparks of light;
> From the censer wafts a delightful scent,
> The fruits piled high in baskets smile,
> The servants dare not even breathe
> Around the table, awaiting you;
> The hostess, young and stately,
> Prepares to extend her hand.

Here, among the groves and fields of spacious and fertile "Zvanka," he preferred with bliss this "solitude and peace" to the troublesome court of the tsars:

> Breathing innocence, I drink the air, the moisture of the dew,
> I gaze upon the crimson dawn, the rising sun,
> I seek out lovely places among the lilies and roses . . .

And in the house were those "worldly adornments" precious to him; he admired his possessions, could describe—and loved to describe—objects, pictures, crystal, "various pieces of linen, cloth, fabric, patterns, the designs on the napkins, tablecloths, rugs, and of the lace and crocheting." He delighted in the view which opened before his windows:

> Where from the stables, apiaries, aviaries, and ponds
> I see now gold in the butter and honeycomb, under the branches,
> Now the purple of the berries, the velvet down of the mushrooms,
> Now silver, flickering from the bream.

The doctor and church elder report to him on the conditions of the peasants' life. Then

> The noon hour strikes; the household hurries to serve the table.
> The hostess leads her guests to the feast with the surging chorus—
> I survey the table—a garden of various dishes,
> All in a pattern.
> The red ham, the green shchi with egg yolks,
> The rosy-yellow pie, white cheese, red crayfish,
> Pitch-black and amber caviar, and over there with a blue feather,
> A rainbow pike—exquisite!

Before dinner he liked to play cards—without excitement, of course, without any uproar, only uncomplicated games—"Fools or faro, for penny stakes, and without paying off losses." He was cheered by the distribution of pastries and cookies to the children of the manor, by his amateur theatre, by chess, archery, and the picture projector in the evenings—the whole dear routine of rural life. And nature, enlivened by human activity, beguiled his enamoured gaze. With delight he would watch the return of the men and women harvesting the grain, listen to the singing that floated up from the river, and hunt joyfully, far afield, with several neighbors. And one can scarcely begin to enumerate Derzhavin's joys in the bosom of nature. Above this quiet, placid, healthy life he stretched his blessing hand. He truly loved the earth deeply and wisely—and, on this earth, his prosperous and solid home. So chaste, so majestic was this love that one wishes to bow before it.

It is here, in this circle of contentment, peace, and inspired indolence, that yet a third Derzhavin reveals himself to us: Derzhavin the lover.

His amorous affairs were expressed for the most part in his translations of Anacreon and his imitations of classical lyrics. We do not justly value Derzhavin's Anacreontic poetry, which is exquisite in its somewhat heavy grace. It is no longer a creation of the young Derzhavin; one senses in it the awkward precariousness of an old man dancing. Finally, it possesses a faithful and subtle sense of antiquity, a feeling for the jolly and slightly shameless eroticism of paganism.

Incidentally, in Derzhavin's love one senses a slight coldness—a legacy from the voluptuous, though not passionate, eighteenth century. The pathos of tragic, omnipotent, and miraculous love never occurred to Derzhavin. He was guided not by mysterious Eros, but by playful Amour. Derzhavin would never forget the surrounding world for the sake of a woman he loved. On the contrary, he sought in the conditions surrounding him those delicate features which corresponded to his own tender emotions. A connoisseur and lover of tangible beauty, an admirer of Tonchi and Angelica Kaufman, sculpted by Rachet, "the skillful sculptor," he searched for a beautiful, tangible frame even for his love. He created his own unique world, within which flowed the events of his love—the decorations of a pastoral ballet, here merged with the living pictures of northern nature. He replaced the shepherds and nymphs with rosy-cheeked peasant girls, and not without a challenge inquired of Anacreon himself:

> Have you seen, Bard of Tiisa,
> How in the spring calf's meadow
> The Russian girls dance
> To the pipes of the shepherd?
> How bowing their heads they step,
> Tapping their shoes to the beat,
> Gently moving their hands and their gaze
> And speaking with their shoulders? . . .

Even in his attitude toward his beloved Derzhavin displayed as much the admiration of an artist as the voluptuousness of a lover, and perhaps even more admiration. His beloved is seldom alone; more often she appears surrounded with companions equally frolicsome and rosy. She resembles at one and the same time a fragile eighteenth-century shepherdess and the exquisite Princess Nausicaa.[2] There is in her the charm of a Russian girl, languorous, light-brown-haired, and sweet.

I envision Derzhavin the lover as a benevolent, gay, quick-witted old man surrounded by young maidens. He celebrated many in poetry—Lisa, Lila, Chloé, Parasha, Varya, Lyubusha, Nina, Dasha, and numerous more. His love intoxicates and fizzes like wine. He has no particular preferences; he had an equal liking for both lovers and wine:

> Here's rosy-red wine,
> Let's drink to the health of rosy women.
> How it delights our hearts
> To be kissed by its crimson lips!
>> You, too, are rosy and pretty:
>> So come and kiss me, my sweet!
>
> Here's dark dusky wine,
> Let's drink to the health of the dark-eyed ones.
> How it delights our hearts
> To be kissed by its purple lips!
>> You, too, are dark and pretty:
>> So come and kiss me, my sweet!
>
> Here's golden Cyprian wine
> Let's drink to the health of the fair-haired.
> How it delights our hearts
> To be kissed by its exquisite lips!
>> You, too, are fair-haired and pretty:
>> So come and kiss me, my sweet!

And so on. There is a unique and enviable wisdom in the simple logic of this refrain. The placement of the colon is delightful in its simplicity and expressiveness—"You, too, are pretty: so come and kiss me."

But dark or fair, pale or rosy, mature women or young maidens, all of Derzhavin's females resemble each other, although they are all and always flesh and blood, alive and corporeal. Not one of them, it appears, ever seemed to him unattainable, otherworldly—a dream. All of them were only the best blooms from his garden, where he strolled, gracious host, dignitary—Gavril Romanovich Derzhavin . . .

And suddenly . . . In the midst of this solid, luxurious world, breathing with prosperity and contentment, which he so loved and so keenly sensed with his entire being, the thought of death must have been terrible. True, at times he (like Anacreon) dismissed it with a wave of his hand, but sometimes it must have terrified and tortured the old man. Why? To decay, to disappear, no longer to be part of this exquisite, blossoming earth in any way? No; death had to be conquered—conquered not somewhere there, "in the heavens," but here, on this very earth. And this task belonged to no one but Derzhavin himself.

A singer, he clutched at his only weapon, the lyre. It had to achieve for him

223

real immortality. The miracle of poetic creation had to carry the singer away from the stagnant, decaying world. He believed—as had Horatio:

> I, with unusual soaring,
> Detach myself from this decaying world.
> With immortal soul and songs,
> I rise in the air like a swan.
>
> . . . .
>
> The tomb will not keep me,
> Among stars I'll not turn to dust,
> But like a songbird
> My voice will resound from Heaven.
> And, lo, I see already a feather cloak
> About my figure is drawn;
> Down on my breast, a winged back;
> I shine with the snowy whiteness of a swan.
>
> . . . .
>
> Away with the funeral, glorious and splendid,
> My friends! Chorus of Muses, do not sing!
> My spouse, clothe yourself in patience!
> Don't wail for the man you suppose has died.

His poetical "soaring," which attains surges and sweeps of a kind perhaps found in no other Russian poet, served him as a faithful pledge of approaching immortality—not only mystical, but historical as well. The latter was for him, creator and devotee of earthly joys, I would say, more highly prized than the former. And he desired that his voice should "resound" anew "from Heaven"; that his word should always be heeded by that same earth he loved so well. His word must remain eternally on this earth as a real part of his being. His carnal link with this earth must not be severed.

But what of his soul? Already meditating on his soul's final separation from everything earthly, he compared it to a swallow that, "freezing in winter like ice," will with spring again be resurrected to life:

> My soul! You are a guest in the world:
> Are you not this winged creature?—
> Glorify immortality, my lyre!
> I, too, shall arise, shall arise—
> Arise—and in the chasm of ether
> Shall see you, Plenira!

He feared the eternal cold and emptiness of interstellar space, wishing once again to fill it with his dear images of the earth. Even in immortality, "in the chasm of ether," he yearned once again to see the image of his most enduring

224

and deepest love—Plenira, his earthly wife. Eternity itself, if he desired it at all, was only a means to prevent his ever being separated from this earth, to once and for all secure his ancient, spiritual union with it.

Not without reason did he begin that poem about his immortal soul with the words:

> O, *home-loving* little swallow,
> O, dear, silver-gray little bird!

Immortal and yet forever tied to this, his earthly home, Derzhavin is one of the greatest Russian poets.

Cocktebel, 1916

INFANCY

FROM: *Mladenchestvo: otryvki iz avtobiografii* (Infancy: Selections from My Autobiography; *Vozdushnie puti* [Aerial Ways] no. 4 [New York, 1965]).

One of my characteristics is extremely important—impatience, which has caused me much unpleasantness in life and torments me constantly. Perhaps it springs from the fact that I was, as it were, born late, and from that time on it's as if I've always unconsciously tried to make up what I'd missed. The eldest of my brothers was a whole twenty-two years older than I, whereas the sister closest to my birthdate was eleven years older. When I was born, my father was approaching his fifty-second year, and my mother, her forty-second. [. . .]

My late arrival hindered me even in literature. Had I been born ten years earlier, I would have been a contemporary of the Decadents and Symbolists—three years younger than Bryusov, four years older than Blok. I, however, came to poetry just when the most significant of all the contemporary movements had already begun to exhaust itself, but before the time had come for a new one to appear. Gorodetsky and Gumilyov, my equals in age, felt the same as I. They tried to found Acmeism, which, essentially, came to naught and of which nothing has remained but its name. So Tsvetaeva (who is, by the way, younger than I) and I myself, emerging from Symbolism, had nothing and no one with whom to identify, and remained forever "renegades," alone. The literary classifiers and compilers of anthologies don't know where to stick us. [. . .]

All these pre-conscious events seem to me prehistoric. To these also belongs the story of the first word I ever spoke. My sister Zhenya, then twelve, was pushing me, like a doll, in a wicker carriage on wooden wheels. At that moment a kitten came in. Seeing him, my eyes popped open, I stuck out my hands and distinctly uttered: "Kit, kit!"

According to legend, the first word spoken by Derzhavin was "God." This, of course, is far more majestic than in my case. All I have left to console me is that, in general,

> . . . there certainly is a difference
> 'Twixt me and Derzhavin,

and that, what's more, in the last analysis, when I said my first word I understood what I was saying, whereas Derzhavin didn't.

A love for cats permeates my entire life, and I'm glad that I enjoy a reciprocal feeling on their part. I like to make fleeting acquaintances with them on the street; and I confess my ego is flattered whenever a stray, wild cat comes to me when I call him, presses against my legs, purrs, and follows me. Several years ago, late in the evening, I made the acquaintance of one such creature at Pont de Passy. After conversing a short time, we walked together, at first along the sidewalk, then along the avenue Bosque. He didn't lag behind me even on the rue Ste Dominique, where many people were coming out of an art exhibition. Like true Parisians, we stopped at a bistro and had a drink: I, a shot of cognac; he, a small saucer of milk. Then he escorted me home and, judging by all signs, would have stayed with me, but unfortunately I was living in a hotel.

There exists a popular opinion to the effect that cats cannot grow accustomed to man, and to the effect that they are stupid. They are compared with dogs. I am not fond of these childish considerations. Of course, it's pointless to speak of small and dull minds in animals. To find such a mind all you have to do is visit your friends, since even the dumbest of our acquaintances is still smarter than the smartest dog. Cats do not like to condescend to an exhibition of mere quick-wittedness. They can't be bothered with such things. They are not smart; they are wise—another thing entirely. Squeezing his eyes shut, my Nal' lapses into a mysterious reverie, and when he returns from it—the reflection of some other existence, where he has just sojourned, can be read in his eyes.

Cats are disposed toward philosophizing and dreaming. They are impractical, and do not always consider their circumstances. Therefore their bravery is foolhardy. When I frighten a two-month-old kitten, he doesn't take flight, but rather springs into attack. They're proud, independent, and love to rely on themselves alone. Their friendship is therefore devoid of stormy displays and shows no hint of fawning. When offended by you, a cat can very well sulk for whole days and pretend for entire weeks not to notice you. The cat decidedly has no desire to guard your house, because he is not your servant. But he likes to be your companion in conversation—silent, purring, or mewing—always in a different way. He loves sports and likes you to share his enthusiasm. The late Murr would come to me at any hour of the day or night and shout (somewhat nasally), "Let's play! Let's play!" until I'd agree to play hide-and-seek with him. He'd rush from one room to the next, hiding behind the furniture and the curtains, and forcing me to look for him—and he was prepared to continue this amusement ad infinitum, although my legs already shook from exhaustion. But, for all that, there is nothing more touching than feline friendship. It makes itself known in particular when your circumstances are bad or your spirits down. I can positively confirm that I had only to be downcast in order for a cat, who had until that very moment paid no attention to me whatever, to approach me immediately to be caressed. This feline sympathy always fills me with deep and tender emotion. And, even now, when my dear friend, little Hippety-Hop, upon meeting me on a sad Boulogne night, runs after me along the street, bitterness leaves my heart and it begins to seem that life is pleasant for me and it doesn't hurt to breathe. [. . .]

The Paris Exhibition of 1889 gives me the opportunity to date an extremely important event in my life. That summer my sister Manya arrived from Yaroslavl' with her husband Mikhail Antonovich, of whom I was deathly afraid and whom I despised with all my soul for his attempts to instruct me in good manners. Subsequently, I realized that he was a good and fine person, but of pedagogy he hadn't the minutest comprehension. He trained me like a small dog. That wasn't the problem, however. I clearly recall a summer morning and a small bench on the tiny path leading from the wicket gate to the terrace. Manya and I are sitting on the little bench; my sister is teaching me to read. I already know the letters (when and how I learned them, I don't recall), but I can't master the syllables. In the alphabet book which we're studying (even now I could recognize it from a thousand others), as is customary, little pictures are printed, and under them, the corresponding words: there is a drawing of an ear—under it appears "EAR"; a drawing of a sledge—under it, "SLEDGE." I had quickly realized that it wasn't worth it to labor over recognizing the words, if one could read simply by looking at the little picture. We had already gone through sledge, and ear, and house, and many others, when my trick was suddenly revealed—while, glancing at the next picture, I unthinkingly read "horse." However, that wasn't what was there—it was not a horse, but a giraffe. That alphabet book was replaced by another, without pictures, and I had to learn to read for real. At about four I was already a speedy reader and soon began to consume book after book. My brother Misha gradually compiled a whole library for me, made up of fairytales and morally educational stories published by the Society for the Distribution of Educational Books. I quickly learned "The Hunchbacked Pony" by heart and loved it very much. (I love it to this day.) The little books were very thin, in multicolored jackets. They sold for one or two kopecks. Shortly thereafter I also began to receive as gifts more expensive books. I received Pushkin and was assured that it was very good; it seemed to me, however, that after "The Hunchbacked Pony" Pushkin's fairytales were insignificant. I was also given Lermontov, but for many years I was afraid even to open that book—the small picture, depicting a skeleton on a bed (an illustration for "The Boyar Orsha"), inspired real terror in me. I dreamed about it at night.

I became aware of death very early, though no one in our family had died. I was afraid of the dark, dead people, and especially—hell, when God dispatches sinners, so the devils can torture them there. I also knew that devils sometimes appear on the earth, at midnight, and fall back down there at dawn. So when my brother Stasya "fell down" in his exams, he began to seem to me a rather suspect creature, the more so since at home everyone scolded and shunned him. This suspicious attitude increased especially when Stasya entered medical school, and I learned there exists on this earth a horrible place—the *anatormental* theatre—where there are dead people and they cut them up. I understood very well why the theatre was called *anatormental*—people who catch *tormentulosis*[3] wind up there, a dreadful disease for which (I had heard) there was no cure and after which there was only one direction—to the fires, to hell. I was very afraid I too would get tormentulosis. I tried to be good, so I would not catch such a horrid thing.

But then the following event took place: one fine day I was informed that I would be taken that evening to the theatre. I began to yell at the top of my lungs and yelled like that right up to evening. Finally they told me we were going not to the theatre, but to nanny's house in the country. I agreed, but not without apprehension. They brought out the coachman. I was carried out, bundled up to my head. We got in and started to move. This was my first time outside at night. Great Dmitrovka Street, illuminated by occasional lanterns, in which red flames danced and flickered, seemed to me an abyss into which we were sinking. At last we arrived. Nanny's country cottage seemed to me a beautiful and elegant place. There was a lot of gold on the walls. Crowds of people thronged at every level on balconies, along which stretched black tubes. On the top of the tubes stood bright gold flames—in those days the Bolshoy Theatre was still illuminated with gas. Suddenly the flames became blue; all around them it grew dim. Then to my right, far away and beneath me, a spacious, well-lit clearing was revealed, like the altar in a Catholic church. Some amazingly agile and nimble people were jumping and dancing there, sometimes alone, then in pairs, then in whole rows. Some of them were pink, like me, others—black, like Negroes. I thought they were naked, because they were dressed in tricot, and very tiny as a result of their distance from me—almost as tiny as the fireman who walks on the fire tower across from the Governor General's house. Amazingly, I wasn't aware of the music at all, and it has slipped from my memory. Then suddenly, where they were dancing, it all went dark again, while around me it became bright, and at the same moment I heard the sound of a downpour. But there was no rain and, looking around, I realized that the sound was coming from many people clapping their hands at the same time. Then there was something else, a kind of mixture of flames, people, and horses; then we found ourselves at home, and I had to confess that I was very pleased with nanny's cottage and that I wouldn't mind going back again right away. I was told that we would soon go again, when "The Magic Pills" would be there. Today we had seen "The Cyprian Statue."

From that day on, my entire youth was colored with a passion for the ballet, and I can't recall it except in connection with this. The ballet constituted a decisive influence on my whole life, on the subsequent formation of my tastes, partialities, and interests. In the final analysis, it was through ballet that I came to art in general, and to poetry in particular. The Bolshoy Theatre was my spiritual birthplace. With reverence and gratitude, I recall its splendorous majesty, its ceiling decorated with clouds and mythical scenes, its elegant gilding, the crimson velvet of the pit, the purple damask of the curtains in its loges, the severe and majestic emptiness of the Imperial box, in the mysterious darkness dimming the mirror's glow; on festival days heavy gold candelabras were lit. I remember to the minutest detail the semicircular corridors of the theatre, the polished steps of its stone staircase, and the entirely unusual, unique, rather sweetish smell of the spectators' hall—it seemed to me a mixture of chocolate, perfume, and broadcloth. [. . .]

After a short time, without outside help, but aided only by the power of my attention and love, I learned to distinguish from one another not only the ballets, but also individual artists and even the subtleties of their exquisite profession. Geyten, already quite aged and about to retire from the stage, I confess I remember hazily. However, I can vividly picture the lovely Roslavlyova, with her softly inspired dancing; the fragile Jurie, with her needle-like movements; Fyodorova the Second (the one who later went into acting); and the first successes of that rising star—Gel'tser.

During the early years of my balletomania the scenery division was in the hands of the "machinist and decorator" Val'ts. Later real artists were attracted to it. With the appearance of Klodt, and especially of K. A. Korovin, the scenery and costumes improved greatly, in an artistic sense. Korovin's "Esmeralda" was an event. But I must confess that at times I wanted to grieve because the Val'ts tradition had been suppressed. The productions of Val'ts were tasteless in some respects, but there was in them so much talent and magic—there was in their very lack of taste so much delight, and in their naïve naturalism such inadvertent and exquisite convention that one couldn't help calling them enchanting. In 1921 in Petersburg I had the chance to see "Raymonda," staged in the faded, "pre-reform" scenery of that very style—it was uncommonly beautiful. [. . .]

In 1918, when the Bolsheviks were possessed by a mania for monuments, for some reason they put up a monument to Heinrich Heine in our playground (in the Alexandrovsky Garden). A consumptive, bearded gentleman sat in an armchair, and at his feet, caressing him, nestled a half-naked female with flowing braids—maybe a Lorelei, or maybe his Muse. The monument was made of some kind of white plaster and was hollow inside. In the winter of 1921 I happened to pass by it. Heine's nose was completely black, the back part of the Lorelei had been broken off, and the hole left in its place was filled with dirty paper, tin cans, and all sorts of garbage. There were no children around, not even any crows in the bare trees.

Once, when I was going home with my nanny and we were about to cross the street, a policeman stopped us. At that very moment along the tracks for the horse-drawn trams, right at the fence of the garden, an open carriage passed by three steps in front of me. A fat coachman was driving a pair of black horses, moving at a slow, heavy trot. In the carriage, closer to me, sat a lady, all in black, and beside her a man in military uniform. Someone nearby said: "His Majesty!" Nanny pulled off my little hat. I distinctly saw and have forever recalled the face of Alexander III, turned toward Her Majesty, with his evenly trimmed beard, a face which seemed kind and good to me in its massive, fleshy softness and in the heavy glance from beneath its firmly knitted brow.

I liked His Majesty very much. That very day (or the next) nanny and I went to see him at the square in front of the governor general's house. The crowd awaited his exit and roared "Hurrah!" for a long time, when a group of military men came onto the balcony; I couldn't make out His Majesty among them. In the evening on Great Dmitrovka Street burned strings of colored lanterns. From lantern to lantern on thin wires hung oblong multicolored lamps, and on stone posts along the sidewalk, oil pots were ablaze, sputtering and giving off smoke. Their dancing flames gave terrifying faces to the passersby, and the shadows cast by flags, flying from houses, also seemed terrifying to me. [. . .]

It is often interesting to follow from the window all that's going on outside. In nanny's room I had put a little footstool on the window box and was sitting upon it. Nanny was ironing the linen. It was spring. The window was open, and I was sitting in the window box, as if in a theatre box. Beneath me was a sloping iron roof—part of the shed above the staircase leading into the yardkeeper's lodgings, which were in the basement. On the roof stood pots of hyacinths—from one Easter to the next Mama saved their bulbs. We ourselves wouldn't be going to the summer house for a while yet, but over there some lucky people were leaving already; the movers were loading the furniture onto a cart—they would probably break it all. They carried out a parrot in a cage. I craned my head, leaned out—and suddenly the courtyard, which had been beneath me, swung swiftly upward, everything was turned topsy-turvy, then something hit my skull, dirt fell on the back of my head, and I myself, looking up at the blue sky, was slipping down along the roof, feet first. Beside me—a rumbling: a flower pot rolled along, too. It disappeared over the edge of the roof, but I caught myself with my heel in the rain gutter and stopped. Then nanny's scream and nanny's huge leg in a white stocking with a red garter under her knee dropped down above me. She grabbed me by the arms, and we got back into the room through the very same window. No one was home. Nanny dressed me, and we went by coach straight to Iversky Church. Nanny lit a candle and prayed for a long time, and kissed all the icons and made me kiss them. If I hadn't latched onto the rain gutter, I would've fallen down a whole floor and could have seriously, if not fatally, broken my neck. At home nanny told all this to Mama. Mama cried and scolded her, and me. Shouting. Everyone was crying, everyone was hugging me. Then I was made to stand in the corner. [. . .]

Like many children, I often wondered whether I was adopted, and I was filled with ardent self-pity. At times, after some unpleasantness, I would find joy in aggravating this wound with all my might. I would lock myself in the most remote corner of the apartment (off limits to me) and there, in the darkness, lit by the last bit of a candle, I would indulge in terrifying reveries. I had visions of heart-rending family scenes, evoked by my reading of Dickens and Spielhagen. In them I played the martyr's role, so miserable and so noble, as only one can imagine oneself. At these times I thought of myself in the third person, "he." Each time the scene ended with "he," after uttering the most heart-rending and self-sacrificing speech in the world, making peace with all, settling everything and making everyone happy, falling victim to all those sufferings he had endured: "When he had finished speaking, he put his hand to his heart, staggered, and fell over dead." I would further imagine the wailing at my coffin—and would start to cry myself. Those were sweet tears, though, cleansing, like all tears shed over imagined happenings. Pacified and with a softened heart, I would abandon my strange sanctuary with a certain spiritual elation, and would promise myself to be, in the future, exactly as good and kindhearted as I had imagined myself.

The attacks of these tragic experiences were especially frequent when I was about eight and already attending school. Gradually they began to find an expression and, partially, a release in poetry, which I created, by the way, under the influence of literary patterns of a very special sort. But at this point I should like to go back a little, to the origin of my literary experiences.

I was about six when I wrote my first couplet, expressing the very essence of my feelings at that time:

> Who is the one I really love?
> Well, you know—it's Zhenichkov.

One must not think this couplet completely devoid of rhyme. At the basis of the rhyming of "I love—Zhenichkov" there is a very accurate feeling for rhyme and rhythm. I recall only one instance in printed poetry of a rhymed pair of words of a masculine line with a dactylic ending—"antrashá" and "professorshá" in Andrey Bely's "First Meeting." However, this rhyme scheme often occurs in folksongs, from the oldest to the most contemporary. It would be much more difficult for me to defend another poem that remains lodged in my memory. It was inspired by the pussywillow market, which at that time was set up on Theatre Square and only a few months later was moved to Red Square:

> Spring! The first storm window is taken out—
> And the sounds have rushed into my room,
> And the Easter bells of the nearby cathedral,
> And the mumbling of people, and clicking of wheels.
> The square is terribly crowded,
> And many balloons are sold,
> And gendarmes are riding along,
> And all carry their willows home.

The deficiencies of the second quatrain are obvious. The first, as the reader has already noticed, I took from Maykov—not because I wanted to steal anything, but because it seemed to me completely natural to use an already prepared selection which expressed my impressions accurately, as no other lines could better do. I had experienced Maykov's quatrain, just as I had my own. There's nothing amazing in this. A certain contemporary poet for the very same reason considers Lermontov's "Cossack Lullaby" to be her own *first* poem.

After this I tried my hand at writing plays. Symmetry, it appears, seemed to me the basic architectural law of play construction. Therefore I counted out the pages in a thick oilcloth notebook, divided them into four equal parts, and in the appropriate places marked: "Act One," "Act Two," "Act Three," "Act Four." Then the notebook was filled with the text of what I imagined to be a comedy, "The Nervous Old Man"—an imitation of some comedy by Myasnitsky, which my brothers were at that time rehearsing for an amateur theatrical. After the comedy there followed a drama, "The Shot." The pages were counted out, as they had been the first time; but nothing after the first scene ever turned out. That's why I remember that scene in detail: "The living room in the house of Madame Ivanova. Madame Ivanova, Madame Petrova. Before the curtain is raised, a shot is heard backstage.

MADAME PETROVA. Ah, what's that? I think it's a shot!

MADAME IVANOVA. Please, don't be alarmed. That was only my husband shooting himself."

One passes through this youthful stage quickly. Soon I began to write much more meaningful poetry. There were quatrains and sextets of a moralistic nature, in the vein of Dmitriev's fables, but, of course, extremely naïve. (By the way, even Dmitriev's fables betrayed naïvete; Pushkin and Yazykov had reason to make such fun of him). At last, from fables I passed to pure lyrics, in which I tried to communicate my heart-rending and harrowing emotional experiences. Novels formed the basis of the content. I had to borrow the form from another source. My sister, my brothers, and the young people who frequented our house sang romances now and then, sometimes real gypsy ones, sometimes drawing room versions. "Dark Eyes," "While

Gazing at a Ray of the Purple Sunset," and works similar to these became my literary models. A romance which began with the words

> When we said farewell,
> When we parted,
> Tears flowed like a river,
> But soon we shall
> Forget our grief,
> The moment we meet again

seemed to me the height of poetic perfection. I began to compose amorous romances with maximum doleful content, and at times, while writing, I would even shed a tear. Someone gave me a whole package of *carnets de bal**; they were pieces of multicolored, glossy pasteboard folded in two. On the second page there was printed in gold a list of dances, but the remaining three pages were blank. From each of these little notebooks on a pink or blue silk cord was hung a slender little lacquered pencil, also pink or blue. With these tiny pencils I wrote, covering the blank pages of the little notebooks with languorous verses in which were inevitably depicted such poetic phenomena as night, sunset, clouds, the sea (which I'd never seen), and so forth. My "poetry" had a distinct drawing room or ballroom flavor, whereas I imagined myself to be a languorous, pensive, and unfortunate youth, ready to die of love and consumption. Tuberculosis actually threatened me. [. . .]

My health was poor. In the summer of 1895 it was decided I should be taken not to the summer house on the outskirts of Moscow, as usual, but to the Volga, outside of Yaroslavl', where my oldest sister lived. Mama and I settled eight *versts* from Yaroslavl', at the Tolgsky monastery, which had been founded on the banks of the Volga in honor of the miraculous icon of the Tolga Mother of God. We lived in the monastery's hotel, which was rather deserted, with wide, vaulted corridors smelling always of black bread, and spacious rooms which were vaulted as well. I was extremely fond of the Volga and steamships. At the arrival of every steamship (only one of these, the "Prince Mikhail Tverskoy," had two levels) I ran to the airplane pier, where each time a prayer service would be held. Right by the hotel there was a small cemetery with its gravestones overgrown with moss and pressed into the earth. Beyond the cemetery began the large monastery park, filled mainly with groves of cedars. I would go there to walk, and little by little I became acquainted with the monks. One of them, emaciated Father Alexander, the monastery's iconographer, with hair as red as fire and an aquiline nose, was especially fond of me. He fashioned a tiny boat with a sail from cedar bark—I let it go on the small lake inside the park. Occasionally the Father Superior of the monastery himself would appear in the alley of trees. I would approach

*dance-cards

him for his blessing. He sometimes took me by the hand, and together we'd walk for a while.

At the end of the summer John of Kronstadt came to Tolga. After dark a crowd of people met him at the shore and escorted him to the monastery. The following morning he said mass—the other children and I were put up front. That same day, at about four o'clock, I ran, as usual, into the park. Father John was walking with the Father Superior and Father Alexander. He blessed me and asked my name. His manner was unusually simple, and he was considerably less portly than many of the other monks I knew. His face was also as simple as his manner—it seemed to me very feminine and peasantlike, and I thought it strange that he was accorded such esteem. Toward evening he left. A crowd of people again gathered at the shore with icons and church banners. The steamship cast off; it was windy and cool. Father John stood alone at the stern, the wind ruffling his cassock and his hair. So it was till the steamship had gone quite far. The crowd didn't move. It was so quiet that the splash of the water running to the shore could be heard, and so wonderful and sad that I cried.

NOTES

1. A cheese made from baked milk.

2. Nausicaa, in Greek legend, daughter of Alcinous, King of the Phaeacians on the island of Scheria (*Odyssey*, VI, 15–315; VIII, 457). When Odysseus swam ashore to Scheria, he was found by Nausicaa. She supplied him with clothes and took him to her father's palace, where he was hospitably entertained.

3. Khodasevich is relating a word play of the sort a child would make when he has misunderstood or misinterpreted. In the original, the child replaces *antonov ogon'* (gangrene; literally, "Anton's fire") with his own invented term "anton-fagon," which is why he thinks that those who die of the disease go to burn in hell. And therefore these dead bodies lie not in an *anatomichesky* (anatomical) theatre, but an "*anton*ichesky" theatre.

Don Aminado (1888–1957)

Don Aminado (pseudonym of Aminad Petrovich Shpolyansky) is one of the best Russian poet-humorists. In Paris he contributed feuilletons in verse to the newspaper *The Latest News*. These contained humorous comments on the everyday life of Russian *émigrés* and their political and ideological *mêlées*. Prior to his exodus to France, Don Aminado had already published *Pesni voyny* (The Songs of the War; Moscow, 1914) and was a contributor for many years to the famous journal *Satyricon* (St. Petersburg, 1908–13; *The New Satyricon*, 1913–18). His other publications include several volumes of poems, *Dym bez otechestva* (Smoke Without the Fatherland; Paris: Sever, 1921), *Neskuchny sad* (The Cheerful Garden; Paris, 1935), and *Nakinuv plashch: sbornik liricheskoy satiry* (Putting On One's Cloak: A Collection of Lyrical Satire; Paris: Neskuchny sad, 1928). Shortly after World War II Don Aminado published his memoirs, *Poezd na tretyem puti* (The Train on the Third Track; New York: Chekhov, 1954); many of its pages are devoted to the Russian exile period. His usually refined irony and benevolent ("lyrical") satire in the last volume at times acquires a sharp and even caustic character, as when he speaks, for example, about D. S. Merezhkovsky. But the book has much valuable, informative material about Mother Maria, Lyubov' Stolitsa, Marina Tsvetaeva, Vera Inber (with her "mincing poetry"), Mikhail Osorgin (whom he criticizes for the occasionally ponderous philosophical insertions and commentaries within his texts, as well as for his frequently artificial pose), Teffi, Dovid Knut, Antonin Ladinsky, Lidiya Chervinskaya, Anatoly Steiger, Alla Golovina, Mikhail Struve, P. N. Milyukov, I. N. Golenishchev-Kutuzov, Leonid Zurov, M. V. Kuleshevich, M. L. Kantor, *Contemporary Annals*, and the Merezhkovskys' Green Lamp. The book abounds in humorous scenes and events; for example, on p. 296: "The Serbian King Alexander invited to his palace Z. N. Hippius and D. S. Merezhkovsky and, to the harmonious sounds of a balalaika [sic] orchestra, fastened on them the Order of St. Sava of the first degree,[1] accompanied by swords and bows. They really deserved this honor." On p. 307: "The young poets recited their own poetry to one another and, having achieved fame, appeared at the *soirées* of The Green Lamp, and Zinaida Hippius scrutinized them through her lorgnette, while Adamovich wrote flattering testimonials about them."

Don Animado also tried his pen at purely lyrical poetry, but apparently he did not think much of himself as a lyrical poet. Marina Tsvetaeva recognized him as a true poet and encouraged him to write verse. In a letter dated May

31, 1938, she urged him to display his talents as a poet: "You are quite a remarkable poet . . . far more a poet than all those poets, young and old, who are publishing their works in thick journals. In just one of your jokes there is more *lyrical power* than in their entire seriousness. [. . .] Your very essence is poetic; your essence is that of a poet, which you disregard; but in disregarding it you are a greater poet than those who pray to this essence in themselves. Some of your humorous poems are actually on the verge of *real* poetry." In all deference to Marina Tsvetaeva, it should be stated, however, that "lyrical" satire and feuilletons in verse were really Don Aminado's forte; in that area he was invariably original, resourceful, and observant. Some of his lyrical poems, though, did turn out well ("Uezdnoe" [The Provincial] and "Siren' " [Lilac], for example). He possessed an indubitable poetic gift, evident at times even in his political verse.

Don Aminado was familiar not only with Russian life in Paris, but with the French world as well, and was well acquainted with several French humorist writers. Often he viewed the tragic qualities of life in exile through the eyes of these writers, and this additional perspective added depth and attractiveness to his works. In Zinaida Schakovskoy's words, "he taught us to smile at our bleak life."[2] But at the same time he was the most severe—and the most understanding and good-natured—judge of those whom he, like Nadezhda Teffi, showed in the "distorting mirror" of his writings. "They were the mob law of Russian *émigrés* directed toward themselves,"[3] says Schakovskoy.

Don Aminado also excelled in aphorisms. Some are printed in Russian calendars even today, for example: "Hairs are like friends: they turn gray and thin," "Test friendship with red-hot iron—not with a precious metal," "We must live without glancing behind, but . . . looking around." The works of Don Aminado will most certainly provide future historians of Russian literature in exile with perceptive, curious, and rich material.

NOTES

1. Z. N. Hippius's Order of St. Sava is in the possession of Temira Pachmuss.
2. Z. Schakovskoy, *Otrazheniya*, p. 228.
3. *Ibid.*, p. 233.

I
TO THE STARS! AND BACK.
ABOUT BIRDS

There is one thing in this world of which I am certain:
> The birds have undone us.

Stormy petrels. Seagulls. Falcons and ravens. Cocks crowing before the dawn. Nonexistent albatrosses, invented in the most shameless fashion. Soaring gerfalcons, soaring unfailingly. Dying swans. Evil kites and silver doves. And, finally, wounded mountain eagles—regal, proud, and implacable.

> "I sit behind bars, in a damp dungeon.
> A young eagle reared in the wild . . ."

What are we to think of this! We have bared our heads, shaken our bushy manes, and reached out toward the bars—in orderly columns, closed ranks, a well-knit society insuring the people's sobriety.

Meanwhile, the time was such that, let us say, should a fourth-year student die from scarlet fever, the entire high school would sing:

> "You fell a victim in destiny's struggle . . ."

Indeed, already quite sensitive and under the spell of the eagles, we wandered about like madmen.

The eagles, for the most part, inhabited cliffs and earned their keep by permitting themselves to be wounded right in the heart, or right in the chest, and, invariably, with an arrow.

On certain especially solemn occasions the arrows, at the public's request, were tipped with deadly poison.

Even the hardest of hearts could not endure this infamy.

The eagle would flap his mighty wings, shed bloody rubies into the verdant valley, inscribe as many circles as he was able, and . . . fall.

It should be added that he never fell in the usual way—but just as if shot though the heart.

The story with the eagles went on for some time, and who knows when it would have stopped, had the great leader not appeared—in his Russian side-fastened shirt, with the madness of the brave.[1]

Having coughed, he burst out in his Nizhny Novgorod bass:

> "Above the gray abyss of the sea
> Proudly hovers the stormy petrel,
> Black, like a bolt of lightning . . ."

237

Everyone, deeply impressed, could only sigh.

And, truly, this bird was first-class—hovering, soaring, and going about his business in general.

We drank Kalininsky beer, traveled to the Sparrow Hills, and looking askance at the good-natured raspberry-red policemen, declaimed in voluptuous whispers:

"The zest of life's battle
For these loons is inaccessible"

And roaring, we added: "They shy from the very rumbling of its thunder . . ."

But the loons won out in the end. Those very loons.

Then, instead of Kalininsky beer, we began to use a solution of carbolic acid, potassium cyanide, shot ourselves in the right temple, and left about fourteen pages of a letter to our friends, saying, "They don't understand us—Europe and Martha."

At that same time there appeared:

The most sinister Raven since the creation of the world and a white seagull, a decadent, incomprehensible, solitary bird.

The Raven croaked, "Nevermore!"[2]—and vanished.

He was a foreign character, offensive, and unfit for melodramatic declamations.

So it was the seagull, who made for herself a completely headspinning career.[3]

Maidens with breaking hearts, with languishing eyes, with incomprehensible anguish, maidens with orchids and a tragic smile—they all would wring their hands, fold their fingers across their bony knees, and say:

"I long for fairytales . . . I long for caresses . . . I am the seagull."

Then they took it into their heads that Kommissarzhevskaya was a seagull, and Hippius was a seagull, and almost that Maxim Kovalevsky, too, was a seagull.

"See, the morning is blazing open. The waters are glowing rose.
A poor seagull is winging over the lake . . ."

But in all good conscience one must admit that nature has not yet created a bird more voracious, insatiable, and insolent than this most unfortunate seagull.

However, you saw it yourself . . . For seven or eight years there was no salvation from seagulls.

Only very seldom would you chance upon some provincial dying swan or bluebird, or the autumn cranes would accidentally fly over—circle a bit and then return to their home.

But these brought no real pleasure.

Oh, how the years roared past, how they rushed on! How quickly decades flashed by! What fervent bitterness filled our penance! We have paid a high price for these wild ducks, these bluebirds and eagles, gerfalcons and falcons, ravens and white seagulls, and even more so for the stormy petrel.

> "There was the peasant, but we spoke—of grace.
> There was dung, but we—played the timbrel!
> So by melodramatic declamations
> Are destroyed even nations,
> Like weeds."

AFTER EVERYTHING

Well now, gentlemen pessimists,
Elegant cynics, skeptics,
Disgorgers of words, soothsayers,
Radicals with your scoundrel doings, critics,

Palmbearers of the coming public,
Bullies, dancers on graves,
And darlings of the most esteemed public,
Contented now, aren't you?

Didn't you insist, the truth
Would shine forth like a blazing sun
Over the icy tundras of the North,
If, there on the tundras, pre-parliaments were convened?

How brilliantly you envisioned it all,
You efficient, strutting pigeons,
Talleyrands from the city of Vinnitsa,
You lodgers and eternal summer guests!

Rejoice, you prophets,
You players of intricate pipes,
All the poor of Russia drift
With no soul, no family, no kin.

Only walk through the streets more quietly,
Stop your chatter on trams, in bakeries,
Pretend you're Brazilians or Czechs,
Just don't let on that you're Russian! . . .

For three or four days ago
We at least had the ghost of a Homeland,
And because of the dim outlines of our peninsula
The concierges and their wives tolerated us.
But today . . .

Oh, Righteous Lord!
Of one thing I beseech you!.
Grant that I no longer may hear the laments
Of those who babble melodious speech.

For more bitter than the stupidity of our foes
Is the scandalous vulgarity of our fellows!
For if there is no salvation from these friends
Your Sovereignty does not exist.

A POEM ABOUT NECKTIES

Glass and bronze. In the flickering of store windows
Nameless silks sing out.
In them are gathered secret desires
And every hue! Frivolous aquamarine.
Ruby, the fire of smoldering ashes.
And deep blue—the cyclone's favorite color.
And rose, the color of Burgundy wines.

Orange, like a light maraschino.
And bronze, like a withering tree.
Green, like the blessed Campagne,
And ash gray, like the silver of aging hair,
Black, the sad color of ignorance.
Oh, neckties, wordlessly singing,
Shedding fiery sighs!

The bustle, the corruption of my age,
Its whine of grenades, its din of society balls,
All things, created and crumbled into fragments,
Sing without words and shower us with sighs.

And I, coming from a northern land
Now stricken from the European map,
I see you in your murderous excitement,
But know you are also doomed.

So that it may sweep away your taunting beauty,
And trample down your magnificent sin,
You'll be rounded up by Heavenly Justice,
Which makes equals of us all.
And you'll be burned in some Vendée,
When they've leveled the mound with September's earth,
And those well-scrubbed necks will then be clothed
In a noose of rope available to all.

A LULLABY

> "Sleep, my little boy,
> Sleep, my little dove"
> Sasha Cherny

Sleep, Danilka. Sleep, my dove.
Here we've come to Paris,
And, think whatever they may,
We were lucky to come.

Here we can live and wait
Without trembling or fear.
Here we have both the kind *Sainte Vierge*,
And the concierge with his wife,
And the gendarme with his big feather,
And a republic besides.

This, my boy, is not Moscow
Where grass grows over the streets.
Here there's asphalt, an inset lawn,
And a reason for everything.

See, in the very center
The metro laid out so skillfully,
How it rushes, clangs, and screeches,
Halts, and takes off again.

So here there's nothing to grieve us.
We'll wait and we'll live.
But how? Well now, my dove,
That's what Paris is for, after all,
This luminary city, this city of light.

The Russian Committee is here,
The Employment Bureau besides.
We'll go there together
And say, "The babe and I
Have come to Paris.
We'd both like to eat.
What have you here in Paris?"

Well, they'll write down how and what.
And I'll sell my coat
And buy for you bananas,
A sabre, whip, and drum.
The day will pass. And two. Then five.
We will live and wait.

We'll lament aloud:
That flesh is stronger than spirit,
That God is high above,
And Russia—far away,
That Danilka and I
Are two sand grains of existence,
And very soon somewhere
They'll lay us both to rest
Not just for an hour, but all eternity,
At the Employment Bureau's expense.

"Here lie the father and babe,
They'll inscribe: 'Look, Paris!
Inseparable friends
Two sand grains of existence,
Two bits of dust, two tears,
Two droplets of rain from a wicked storm,
Which raged across a land,
Both wretched and evil.' "

NOTES

1. The reference is to Maxim Gor'ky.
2. Reference to Edgar Allan Poe's poem "The Raven."
3. Reference to Chekhov's play *The Seagull*.

Nikolay Otsup (1894–1958)

Nikolay Andreevich Otsup, a younger friend and disciple of Nikolay Gumilyov, was born and educated in Tsarskoe Selo. A talented poet and important member of the Acmeist *Tsekh poetov* (Guild of Poets), he emigrated from Russia to Berlin in 1922, and then to Paris. He studied at the University of St. Petersburg and the University of Paris. The following are his collections of poetry: *Grad* (The City: Petrograd, 1921), *V dymu* (In the Smoke; Berlin, 1928), *Zhizn' i smert': stikhi 1918–1958* (Life and Death: Poems 1918–1958; Paris, 1961) in two volumes, and *Dnevnik v stikhakh: 1935–1950* (A Diary in Verse: 1935–1950; Paris, 1950). He also published the long poem *Vstrecha* (The Meeting; Paris, 1928), which actually consists of several separate poems; a novel, *Beatriche v adu* (Beatrice in Hell; Paris, 1939), and his reminiscences, *Sovremenniki* (Contemporaries; Paris, 1961). *Contemporaries* and *Life and Death: Poems 1918–1958* were published posthumously. Ostup's literary activities included translations of Russian poetry into German and the editorship of *Numbers* (1930–32). Arrested by the Germans during World War II and confined to a concentration camp, he escaped and participated in the Italian Resistance. Upon his return to Paris after the war, he completed his studies at the University of Paris and there defended his doctoral dissertation on Gumilyov. He became a professor of Russian language and literature at a college in Paris, published selected poems of Tyutchev in French, and compiled an edition of the poetry of Gumilyov in Russian under the title *N. Gumilyov: Izbrannoe. Predislovie i redaktsiya N. Otsupa* (N. Gumilyov: Selected Poems. Edited and with an Introduction by N. Otsup; Paris, 1959), which appeared after his death.

Interested in the ideology of art, Otsup put forward a concept of "Personalism"[1] to counterbalance the Soviet formula of "Socialist Realism." In his long essay "O personalizme" (About Personalism), published in *Borders* in 1957, he defined it as a movement which is "based on the freedom of art and the Christian experience of God, personality, and freedom." As a poet, Otsup gave much thought to the formal aspects of his poetry. In the first volumes of his verse he paid much attention to the principal behest of Gumilyov—to write poems without "mystical haze" and "mystical allusions." In his later works, however, there appears an image of some mystical "Beauty," a feminine spiritual leader, purifying the poet's soul and elevating it to the high plane of mystical Christianity. Allusions to the Beauty are found in *Beatrice in Hell*, *A Diary in Verse*, and in his drama *Tri Tsarya: drama v stikhakh* (Three

Tsars: A Drama in Verse; Paris, 1958). The last two works, as well as the poem *The Meeting*, reveal Otsup's growing interest in the "large form" toward the end of his life. *A Diary in Verse* is especially valuable to the student of Russian literature in exile, because it contains perceptive observations on the literary life of the Russian community in Paris (1926–39) and characterizations of various poets; e.g., Boris Poplavsky.

In his artistic evolution, Otsup proceeded from Acmeism to the traditions of Lermontov and Innokenty Annensky. His poems—airy, precise, lyrical, expressive, yet rather cold—are on the whole composed in strict adherence to the rules of prosody. But his occasionally nebulous words and allusions create effective stylistic shifts which, in turn, enhance poetic expressiveness. His constant manipulation of temporal and spacial planes is another characteristic of his aesthetics. Otsup's love lyrics, Italian poems, and languishing songs have clearly resulted from their author's uplifting artistic inspiration and experience. The imagery is vivid, and the rhythm restrained and dignified. The manipulation of sound is a dominant feature of the poems dedicated to Tsarskoe Selo and its "tsars and poets," Puskhin, Gumilyov, Annensky, and Akhmatova. Otsup's lyrics have a profound, pure sound. As a master of versification, he may one day stand next to Adamovich and Georgy Ivanov in the history of Russian poetry.

NOTE

1. Otsup's "Personalism" was not invented by him, but reflected that version of "Personalism" popularized by Berdyaev.

ON POETRY AND POETS

FROM: *O poezii i poetakh* (On Poetry and Poets; *Numbers* no. 6 [Paris, 1932]).

New outbursts of that destructive energy which first made its crude appearance after 1914 are occurring right now in the air of Europe and throughout the world. We can already forsee their ultimate effects:

> And the final, most horrible, age
> Both you and I shall see,
> A foul sin engulfing the sky,
> Laughter freezing on lips,
> The anguish of nonexistence.

Perhaps all this has already come to pass; but if not yet, the wait for it will probably not last much longer, judging by the continual decrease in fresh air and the increased difficulty in breathing.

In conjunction with this general state of affairs—though perhaps even independently—the small but complex world of the Russian *émigré* writers seems to go through such a period, when solitude, mutual alienation, and the cooling of their passions seem particularly distinct.

Even five years ago *émigré* men of letters behaved quite differently. It was as if they were called upon to divide some huge legacy: the intrigues and machinations of a small group were linked with events of a worldwide scope, and a struggle—hardly noticed from the outside, but obvious from within—took place over this imaginary pie, over this invented right to occupy the attention of Russia, Europe, the world.

Having intrigued sufficiently, having thoroughly quarreled among themselves, and having become disenchanted with friends and allies, but most importantly with their purpose in this world, these men of letters have now found themselves surrounded by a sad and healing solitude, with the sober realization of their very humble and therefore, perhaps, especially burdensome and honorable mission.

There was a time when any self-respecting representative of the golden youth couldn't help but publish a book of decadent poetry. There was yet another period, when hundreds and hundreds of poetry writers were registered in the professional unions of Moscow and Petersburg. If of the former it's been justly said that "They were frantic over nothing," then the latter had one extremely serious justification: an identity card from "a professional union," even one such as the poets' union, made it easier to procure bread.

But now, here in emigration—within that group which has had the air pumped out of them as though to facilitate more expediently the precision of some sort of scientific experiment being conducted on them—shouldn't these germs, which produce the disease of authorship for the sake of boasting and vanity and, especially, for the procurement of bread, have died out without a trace?

Isn't their most remarkable love for literature superfluous? Isn't their stubbornness terribly costly?

Indeed, are these poet-*émigrés* the real crux of the matter? Do they not represent only a more convenient clinical sample for observation? Is not every poet—no matter where or when he might live—a being doomed to voluntary deprivation, on whom life vents its crudity and evil?

I think Rimbaud's whole secret was his urge to answer crudity with crudity, a blow with a blow. A poet, whatever he might be ("Olympian" or "damned"— the difference is in the strength of his opposition), endures all of life's insults for himself and for everyone else. [. . .]

Gumilyov had a "golden dream" about the role of the poet in society:

> The earth will forget the insults
> Of all its wars, all its victims,
> And, as of old, the Druids
> Will teach from the verdant hills.

"The poet must know how to do everything," said Gumilyov. "The poets of the future are the natural and sole rulers of free peoples."

Need I remind you how far all this is from our present reality?

The fate of Lamartine was a lucky accident. Basically Goethe was fortunate in finding a patron—that's all there is to it.

In the overwhelming number of cases the poet is forgotten, humiliated, alienated from everything, or at least for a great deal in the "non-literary," active sphere of life.

One would have to be a Christian to demand nothing better for the poet than that which he is given.

Gumilyov was no Christian, though he crossed himself at every church.

Blok was a Christian, although he wrote blasphemous poetry.

Blok demanded no rights for the poet whatsoever. He never said one word about any kind of power in governmental affairs. What kind of Druids have we here—the poet is lower than the shoemaker.

Blok wasn't upset about that. An otherworldly reward awaited the poet. Just as for Baudelaire the crown of the poet was made of the most immaculate rays, for Blok the death of a poet—be it even under a fence—was nevertheless an uncommon death.

> It is God who covered me with snow,
> And the blizzard who kissed me.

Rimbaud wanted no heavenly reward; he wanted it here on earth—in the form of power and money. Gumilyov was convinced that power and respect were proper to the poet. Without any special effort, he managed within his own circle to attain both.

Blok probably wouldn't have felt quite right if poets had been held in esteem. Blok generally disliked powerful people.

With this autumn, 1931, ten years have passed since the deaths of Blok and Gumilyov. Many more decades will probably pass before one of these two names—the second, of course—moves away an immeasurable distance from the other. Meanwhile, however, they are joined more firmly than any other two names in new Russian literature.

It isn't fitting to belittle Gumilyov's poetry. It simply had an unfavorable fate. It had to endure comparison with Blok's poetry, as if both "adversaries" were equal. The lives and fates of Gumilyov and Blok resemble two opposite, but equally valid solutions to the problem they held in common. Their poetry is not of identical quality.

It is very probable that the victory of Gumilyov's principle would have been in the history of poets' lives—a victory over their fate. It is a different matter that this is essentially impossible. But a great number of contemporary poets are almost justified in "fashioning themselves after Gumilyov." His masculine courage was not invented. The recollections of those friends who had seen him in his house slippers change nothing.

I do not agree with one of our most astute critics, who recently wrote that Gumilyov was only a "poetic dabbler" and that they made him a powerful man and warrior only after he was already dead.

I also had many opportunities to see Gumilyov "in his natural size" with all his weaknesses. But knowing, as an eyewitness, to what extent the legends about Gumilyov distort and exaggerate the truth about him, I still think the very inaccuracies of these legendary notions about him, can properly communicate the true substance of his life.

So what if his hunting feats in Africa were not so dangerous and his deeds in the war not so remarkable? Nevertheless, both in these instances, and especially in his private life, Gumilyov was a hero.

> And I, relative to the hippopotamus,
> Arrayed in my armor of sacred treasures,
> Walk straight, triumphant,
> Fearless amidst the wilderness.

These lines, translated from Gautier by Gumilyov, could be used as his epitaph.

There was only one thing he truly feared, one thing about which he was "cowardly": pitiful, gray, mundane reality. In that struggle his strength was not equal to Blok's.

Gumilyov escaped from reality into his elaborate exploits, into the exotic, his dream of the Druids, his visions of the mightiness of people.

It's really strange, but for so long no one was able to discern in Blok, beyond the clouds of the romantic, the average man and citizen.

If Gumilyov could read the poetry which has been written in emigration, he would probably be quite satisfied. *Emigré* poetry has reached what he valued most of all—a consistently high level of craftsmanship. Although there is almost nothing extraordinary, there is so much labor and so much (if not very obvious, certainly indisputable), success. The question of who needs these successes is a different matter. Blok would answer, "No one." Which would have meant above all: "This poetry hasn't the power to change anything at all in this world." Well, what about Pushkin's poetry? According to Blok, it should "brand the heart," "probe with its harmony." By what sign can such poetry be recognized? Blok demonstrated many times that it was easy for him to recognize this, if the subject was Pushkin or another of the great poets. Concerning his contemporaries, his judgment was poorer. From among those poets younger than he, he most often encouraged the weakest, those in whom he found the echo of a "serious theme."

"Listen, listen to the music of the revolution!" He caught the music in the poetry of Nadezhda Pavlovich and therefore valued her weak poetry. But toward Mandel'shtam he was cold.

As "the organizer of group efforts" in the creation of poetry, Gumilyov was the sole figure for the last decades. Even Bryusov did not accomplish as much in this area. Whereas this was totally foreign to Blok . . .

Among the authors whose new books have not yet been noted in *Numbers*, three at least have a good grasp of their craft.

They're already almost *maîtres* of poetry.

They avoid careless, impromptu words of the type abundantly included by novices in the field so as to accelerate their ascent "on the wings of inspiration."

Most likely, they have not included everything they've ever written in their collections. One divines selectivity. One senses culture, control.

It is clear to these authors that the more faultlessly they communicate each sound, the more effectively their voice will reach unknown ears. They concern themselves with polishing the technique of their poetry, just as a radiotelegrapher would carefully maintain the perfect and powerful functioning of his apparatus for signaling into space. Fortunately, they are not occupied with the means of communication to such an extent that they forget the substance of what they wished to express.

I am speaking primarily about A. Ladinsky, V. Smolensky, and D. Knut. P. Bicilli has written about the last one very sensitively and justly in *Numbers*. I direct those who are interested to his review.[1]

If A. Ladinsky should be reproached for anything in connection with his new book,[2] it should perhaps be for his inability, or more accurately his lack of desire to be miserly with the stanzas. Some of his poems could be imagined in shorter versions (I doubt whether this is merely an error in my imagination); only then would they be faultless.

There are poets who are able to communicate, in one line or stanza, the tension of an entire poem. In this sense Tyutchev knows no equal in Russian poetry.

Ladinsky's gift is undoubtedly not of this nature. He is incapable of conserving his power for one decisive blow. In a sampling of Ladinsky's especially remarkable lines, you will find not one compressed and expressive to the maximum. But if Ladinsky's poetry seldom "strikes the heart," it soars above us, carries us away, and captivates us. The magic of *A Northern Heart* is not contained in its separate lines—it is in the totality of all the poems which make up this book.

However strange it may be at first glance, the poetry of Ladinsky is very masculine. The poet sees himself as the guardian of everything ethereal, heavenly, feminine, theatrical.

He has to conceal with his very breath, to protect with concern and a caress this fragile, helpless life. He wants no contact with the crude, blood-soaked world. There no one needs his sympathy.

He is a knight, a protector of woman and of her always slightly theatrical charm.

Here are some of Ladinsky's especially captivating lines on the soul:

> And it sadly answered:
> "I'm not yet fit for life in Paradise,
>
> I haven't yet burned in fire,
> Nor sobbed myself weary in silence,
>
> Nor learned to live,
> I must yet live with people."

Poetry can replace any activity for an author. Perhaps, if Smolensky hadn't written *Sunset*,[3] he might have perished. But instead, fortunately, he wrote a book of poems. Everything in the book is devoted to a fatal exhaustion, everything is permeated with it, and everything in the book is at least partially subjugated to the mood of the author. Much in *Sunset* is not due to borrowing from this or that poet, but is taken from the poetical dictionary of our time.

No such dictionary (not only of words, but of whole phrases, terms, intonations) has been compiled by anyone; but it is always within the reach of a cultured writer. One need only have a good ear and a good memory.

But even when recognizing in Smolensky the clichés of that catastrophic Esperanto, one cannot but sense behind these sincere and conventional phrases his own breathing, his own fate. This is the poetry of an extreme individualist, who essentially loves no one and nothing but himself. He poses a little with his slow demise and his sensation of being superfluous. He expresses love for women without passion or enthusiasm. Death, especially his own, moves him to emotion.

"There a person has burned to ashes."

Blok's phrase suggests burning for the sake of someone or something, but not for himself. The poetry of Smolensky is blatantly egocentric. He pities no man and would not lose his soul for anyone or anything.

In Smolensky—not because he writes about death, but because of how he writes it—the whole world is saturated with the sweet, suffocating odor of decay.

But how fine, precise, succinct are several of his poems! How clear and accurate his diction! How successful his art often proves!

In saying "almost *maîtres*," rather than *maîtres*, I had in mind that distance, already slight for Ladinsky and Smolensky, which separates literary adolescence from maturity. Their powers are not yet absolutely tested; something hasn't settled, something will be added, and then these poets will completely master their poetic universe. But the essential thing is already present—both Ladinsky and Smolensky are poets.

This cannot yet be said about Anatoly Steiger.[4] There is in his poetry good taste, a knowledge of the craft, an awareness of others' poetry, and his own helplessness—it is difficult to say which of these elements is most prominent. There is even a trace of what's called the personality of the poet. But perhaps because of Steiger's nature, perhaps because he hasn't the will to perfect his poetry, all this is neither good nor bad. That is to say, it is good on the surface, in its absence of crude errors and in the subtlety of the way he draws the images in various poems. But the author must do much more before his poetry will be memorable and exciting.

For the present, as an epigraph to *This Life* we can choose two lines of Steiger:

> And from the sky a voice is heard,
> Indistinct—neither yes, nor no.

It is difficult to judge authors on the basis of two or three pieces published in almanacs. [. . .]

Yu. Mandel'shtam probably has an unconscious conception of what the "most perfect" structure of a poem should be. He knows where a line should be cut off, where the voice should be raised. He strives for, and very often achieves, exterior effects. He too is almost a *maître*, like Ladinsky or Smolensky. But up to now, unfortunately, Mandel'shtam has displayed nothing but delight in the game of poetry.

He has learned the mainspring of poetry, its technical nature, but has not yet meditated on the emptiness of even the most skillful word game.

Still, it seems that, even taken by itself, this game he plays is not at all demeaning.

But if Mandel'shtam is destined to become a poet (which in my opinion is entirely possible), such a transition will be more torturing and painful for him than for those poetry writers who are technically helpless, and in whom the knowledge of poetry's "mainsprings" is subjugated more and more to their growing need to express themselves as best they can.

POEMS

FROM: *Numbers* no. 4 (Paris, 1931).

> All will be destroyed; in the meantime
> We love, defying death,
> The toes of children's feet on a summer beach
> And a pigeon's small claws in the clay.
>
> And many other things . . . And yet too few
> Are these charms of earth
> To suppress the more powerful lure
> Of that dimness beyond our lives.
>
> There we've long been straining to seek
> An aim and explanation for the world,
>
> But have learned only day by day
> (Not cutting the knot with one blow)
> To be content that—we live,
> But with no certainty
> That we should, that this is not all in vain.

———————

> His parcel swinging,
> His lusterless umbrella open . . .
> Dressed rather carefully,
> In no special rush.
>
> Behind him a hurried mincing
> A homely man, slouching, in glasses,
> And further, next to a young man,
> On sharp spike heels

251

A woman passes. Behind her
A rosy-cheeked soldier.
The whole day, hundreds of days,
And thousands of days, back and forth,

Walking side by side or separately
These, or others, wherever they happen to be . . .

Not a single human, no people
(Yes, alive, but who, and what),
Just so many gestures and objects,
Grimaces, topcoats, umbrellas.

———————————

FROM: *Numbers* no. 1 (Paris, 1930).

In a life which can only torture,
In a sky which is only a chasm,
What is there beckoning man,
As if promising freedom and peace?

You've never wished to meet in the coolness
Of the fields or in evening haze,
You've never looked for your own grave?
But why, unable to pray

And unable to break our languor,
Do we embrace delusions again and again,
And imprudently search once more
For tenderness, friendship, and light on earth?

———————————

Death matters to us
Not just in the final hour.

It's ever-present
Wherever the bottom gives way,
And even in shallower places
We see its shadow.

And even I, alas, I, like all the others,
Am in terror of turning to nothingness!

Yet if this world were not wrapped
In the breathing of death
Then, perhaps—
Life would not be worthwhile.

NOTES

1. This reference cannot be verified.
2. A. Ladinsky, *Severnoe serdtse* (A Northern Heart; Berlin: Parabola, 1931).
3. V. Smolensky, *Zakat* (Sunset; Paris: Ya. Povolotsky, 1931).
4. Anatoly Steiger, *Eta zhizn'* (This Life; Paris, 1931).

Yury Fel'zen (1895–1943)

Nikolay Berngardovich Freydenshteyn (pseudonym Yury Fel'zen), a young *émigré* writer and poet, the son of a St. Petersburg physician, wrote psychoanalytical novels without plots: *Obman* (Deception; Paris, 1930), *Shchastye* (Happiness; Paris, 1932), and *Pis'ma o Lermontove* (Letters about Lermontov; Paris, 1935–36). He also contributed to Russian-language journals and almanacs in Paris. Zinaida Hippius was very fond of Fel'zen because of his ability to discuss the "metaphysics of love" and because of his pleasant character, education, culture, and erudition; she affectionately called him "Sparzha" (Asparagus) because he was tall, slender, and blond. This sobriquet became his "everyday name" among the Russians in Paris. He died in a German concentration camp after the Nazis arrested him, his father's German descent notwithstanding.

On the surface, Fel'zen's short stories and novels may appear tedious—his characters are weak, nearly spineless, refined, fatigued, and meditative. They engage in endless discussions on love and death, the insanity of life and human endeavor. Frequently in love, their feelings are not reciprocated; or, like Lermontov, they do not wish "to love for a moment, and to love eternally is impossible." These attitudes, as well as his melancholia, clarity of vision, stream of consciousness, and *monologue intérieur*, stem from Marcel Proust, James Joyce, Virginia Woolf, Valery Larbaud, and other European avant-garde writers of that time. However, Fel'zen's works lack Proust's "black humor," pathos, and cruelty. His style is uneven, "gracefully careless,"[1] often even grammatically incorrect. One enters a labyrinth of long and complex subordinate clauses without hope of seeing the light of an exit. This mode of writing is reminiscent of Proust, but Fel'zen's preoccupation with his inner "I," his excessive interest in its complexities, ultimately leads to the "I's" gradual reach beyond its restrictive boundaries, as Yury Terapiano has suggested.[2] Written in the form of a diary or letters and addressed from the "I" of the novel to his beloved Lyolya—whose love is difficult and even tormenting—the novels develop almost endlessly along an inner plane. In reality, though, each word is justified within the framework of the novel, for each sentence has its own inner content. The emotional intensity of Fel'zen's narrative can hardly be rendered in a smooth and polished style. Interested solely in the inner life of the "I," he follows in great detail every ramification and scarcely perceptible transition into an opposite emotion. He is successful in finding adequate expressions for the spiritual and emotional intricacies of

254

his "hero." Fel'zen's novels are difficult to read, requiring great effort and attention from the reader. Fel'zen nonetheless succeeds in conveying the essence of his vision in his literary experimentation.

The theme of love and jealousy is developed against the background of the author's insightful philosophical considerations, instructive commentaries on art and literature (as in *Letters about Lermontov*), and versatile generalizations concerning human nature and man's endeavors in general. Yury Fel'zen's novel is outside the traditional Russian literary form. He was an original writer, whose work assimilated and surpassed Western European experiments in prosody. He entered the Russian literary scene in the 1930's neither imitating nor resembling any specific writer, for he had found his own style. His essays, short stories, and novels captivate the reader with their emotional and philosophical profundity and the novelty of their artistic method.

NOTES

1. Georgy Adamovich, "Literaturnye besedy," *Zveno* no. 8 (1928).
2. For more details, see Terapiano's review of Fel'zen's *Happiness* in *Numbers* nos. 7–8 (1933): 268.

THE SEVENTH LETTER

FROM: *Pis'ma o Lermontove* (Letters on Lermontov).

There is a joyful force, which seems to uplift us, in the realization that we—capriciously and groundlessly—have singled someone out and then have concentrated all our affection on that person, all the heroism and attentiveness of which we are capable, all our expectations for reciprocal gratitude, all our hopes, our entire stake in the future. It's pleasant to do something nice for someone accidentally and effortlessly (from this feeling there arise in us hypothetically inspired conversations, a sweet and, very likely, deceptive interrelationship with that person); but it's inexpressibly more pleasant to do something nice for someone we have decided to consider and, in fact, do consider to be the only one whom we shall constantly spoil with our attention, favors, and help—this being very important for him and sometimes difficult for us. We often forget the primary reason for our sensitivity (the fact that we have manifested our will, that we have touched a chord within ourselves), and we desire only one thing: to be constantly charitable and to believe in an understanding gratitude. And indeed, the more generous we become, the more our constantly sacrificing help becomes arbitrary and unearned: and perhaps the further removed from reality our imagined friendship, our charity and responsiveness become, the more stubbornly our imagination likewise retreats—not only from reality, but even our own perception of reality. This duality, this incompatibility between our strivings and perceptions, between our convenient imaginings and our sobering, disillusioning instinct, remains with us always and is apparent in everything, and at every moment—smashing (as is its fate) against reality—we spiritually disfigure and cripple ourselves. A similar willfully stubborn preference, a similar concern, pleasant and necessary to us, a concern arising only from our self-love, our own, as it were, special choice, and our own absolutely irreplaceable worries about other people—all this is not only related to love (what you're suspecting, I am now hinting), all this is related also to our feelings for children. Recall how we indulge some children, load them with toys, tease them half-affectionately, want to hug and pet them, and the more we manage to cuddle them, the funnier and sweeter they seem to us. We may forget ourselves, our preference, and the reason for our caresses and presents, but we shall never in any way deceive our chosen one. There's even something akin to this in our literary "romances"—however, I am unmistakably aware of your poisonous, destructive objections, the grimace at each one of my (in your opinion) artificial and irresponsible statements, and even now I can easily imagine you reading my letter, while in your eyes and on your furrowed brow there is the unreal shadow of doubt: "Now what's this about fabricated romances, why so much talk about them—and, what's more, so senseless and unclear?" You torture me so with your ill will and lack of faith, you hold such unintentional power over me that I'm usually ready to admit I'm wrong and to agree with whatever you want, if only you would value our beneficial union and consider us as of one mind in all things. True, my compliant nature does not predispose you toward good will and trust, and I, of course, know that in the final analysis I am hurting myself. But there are certain occurrences and relationships in which every silence as well as every word inexorably harms us, and I have many times been reduced to the point of seeking out peace, if only for the next ten minutes. Fortunately, now that you're far away, I have involuntarily calmed down and gained strength, and I will not yield to you in this argument about "romances." I, perhaps awkwardly (though for my part correctly) labeled a romance as that infrequent, prolonged condition which has always been evoked by some writer or poet; but in that condition—not just briefly exalted, but precisely prolonged and reliable—there is the basis and many of the characteristics of an arbitrarily one-sided infatuation. At this point I am thinking of Lermontov, and immediately—without any searching or striving—various signs of my love occur to me: in his name there is for me (as I've already written you) something which uniquely and magically inspires me; in his appearance, his poetry, his statements (as in the words of one's beloved) there is a special, indefinable "touch of uniqueness"—and only a very few unexpected things, a certain assuredness, well-being (what the French call *securité*) in him, indeed unchanging and undeceiving, for which I have a responding gratitude, sometimes boredom and, as usual in these sadly unequal relationships, a morbid curiosity about everything incidental. Likewise, if you only knew how simply the boundaries of time, death, and the possibilities of mutual understanding are smashed, what amorously thoughtful conversations I, for countless hours, have carried on with myself in order to shock you, you would not frown and make fun of me—you see, how well one can explain in a letter what can't be said aloud (but this is only true of me with you—because of my fright, because of your seemingly deliberate, alienating, and contemptuous impatience with me).

All the incidental information about Lermontov, the diaries, the letters of his acquaintances (recently published in a single volume which I devoured in a few evenings), all that excites me just as if—remaining concealed and unpunished—I were spying, eavesdropping, sneaking behind someone I love on whom I'm gathering new and forbidden information, which is gradually merging with him, which is becoming irrefutable and seemingly eternal, forcing me to love him even more. Through his poetry, through his letters and the recollections of others, I am amazed by Lermontov's own capacity to love, his spiritual richness, his preparedness, initially indistinct, but then linked with his image, pale, dissembling, always able to divine and already inevitably lonely. Varen'ka Lopukhina—apparently a victim of tuberculosis, the unfortunate Vera in "Princess Ligovskaya," and "Princess Mary" (in one of his diaries she is spoken of, probably with exaggeration, as "rather young, intelligent like daylight, and in the fullest sense exquisite")—was a sixteen-year-old maiden whose friends good-naturedly and fondly teased her, "Varen'ka's got a mole, Varen'ka's a freak." For some reason, for Lermontov, as for so many remarkable people, it turned out that his Varen'ka was married to someone else; and in his defiant, secluded work he tried to justify and give meaning to his outwardly pointless, unsuccessful life, whereas inwardly he was, like very few people, faithful and had preserved his integrity. Indeed, in his persistent attention he often was merely deceiving women—he must have more than once fancied he saw "the feature of another," and Lermontov could have applied to more than one instance his famous lines:

> When, at times, I look at you,
> And penetrate your eyes with a lingering gaze,
> My heart continues a secret dialogue,
> But not with you.

The last witness was his naïvely touching *cousine*, who recalls a similar "conversation"—on the day of the death, the murder of Lermontov, of that "eternally grievous duel" (as the son of the murderer inadvertantly expressed it).

I believe that even Lermontov (like all other dreamers, great and small) had his own "romance with a poet," perhaps several. The main one among these was not Byron (as would be most natural to suggest), but Pushkin. Furthermore, I feel, no one loved Pushkin as much as Lermontov (who, even with his hussar understanding of honor, felt nevertheless that everything should be forgiven Pushkin), and no one sacrificed so much and was punished so mercilessly for his love. I also must confess that not only did I myself love (and I'll no longer be "polite" and keep stoically silent about this), but that I even love all other loving people, every kind of love, my own and others', and especially love in vain, not reciprocated by anyone or anything. Because of his hopeless, consciously hopeless, loyalty, Lermontov is exquisite and comprehensible to me, and I often find myself in a kind of frozen, inexplicable terror (like that which follows a miracle) in those moments when I have stolen through that intelligent, bitter hopelessness into the living stream of his life—completely carefree, yet difficult, self-esteemed, rejecting the easy and simple solution, ready to answer for everything, in perilous defiance of both well-being and vulgarity.

Is it not true that every emotion must attain a period of maturity, even one of old age—what La Rochefoucauld calls *"la vieillesse de l'amour"** and to which he attributes only sufferings? I think this is the most wonderful, the most humanly significant time of love, a time of patience, clairvoyance, the absence of distortion and disenchantment. Occasionally it lasts until the very death of the loving one. You see what a naïve and incorrigible enthusiast I am, although even I myself wouldn't call the ardor of my trustfulness "enthusiasm," and I will try somehow to divorce myself from it in front of you. Let's say, for instance, that such an "old age of love" had come and our love hadn't passed—certainly if we had earlier found some sort of false values, these would have already been revealed; if instances of betrayal and obvious insufficiencies had alienated us, we would have become aware of them, too; yet all these discoveries had not killed our love. Then what would kill it, and for what eventuality would we not be prepared? Therefore we have learned a kind of fearless honesty, produced an inexorably accurate evaluation of the person closest and most curious to us, about whom it is especially difficult to judge and reflect dispassionately. Such a period of "amorous maturity" (keeping in mind of course the difference between real, palpable, and powerful love and artificial "literary romance") came to me with regard to Lermontov, and I not only admire him but even offer a possibly dispassionate appraisal, an appraisal synonymous with admiration, in truth no longer blind, and free from initial misconceptions and unreliability.

It seems I realized only recently what precisely in the writer (and indeed, in people generally) is close to me, and why this, and not some other thing,

*the antiquity of love

startles me and becomes for me an inexplicably noble achievement. I have only recently gained an understanding in this confusion (according to my own, though probably borrowed, goals), and no longer err; only it's odd for me now, having grown up and matured, to condone what once uncontrollably attracted me, as has happened to me with Lermontov. I am firmly aware that no "game of intellect," no cleverly phrased questions—even though concerning transient and otherworldly considerations—no inventing or disputing of "new ideas" seems to me at all worthy or even creative, and I, unwavering, detect it when the tense, slow, fearful human endeavor taking place in the dark is replaced by something easy, unplanned, and irresponsible. I am disgustedly indifferent to "contortionists—male and female" of all sorts in art, and I love people who think diligently and carefully, who are conscientious and serious to the point of naïvete. If they are fortunate, if their slow inspiration resembling torment or self-torture, like separate consecutive suicides, can, as it were, tear away and express this or that essence, a fraction of the essence, a "grain" of their sacrificial lives (so that the whole of their creation resembles "clots of spiritual blood," halted and deadened—since these are only "clots" and blood no longer flows within them, but they [these "clots"] are seized and passed along in this instantaneously frozen state alone), if such a "fragment of essence" is found and passed along, I wish for nothing greater and will believe nothing else. For that which is unobserved, unexpressed, simply does not exist for us, just as an unknown person in an unfamiliar and unknown city or a pebble on a faraway shore does not exist for us. Every form of revelation, prophecy, grace is always both conjectural and disputable, whereas those incarnated spiritual forces, captured in words, can be tested by each of us in his own way, can be judged real or false and are certainly—though one-dimensionally—tangible. Of course, faced with the strangeness of our fate, even this immeasurably difficult tension in people who have prepared themselves, as if unconsciously, to alter their own nature, and then in their creative agitation to express themselves, turns out to be useless and to lead nowhere (and for us it's better not to live or to live ignoring everything around us and hiding everything without a trace from ourselves), but even this vain and useless tension is not an attempt to lead us into deception and does not appear to be the result of a deception. If to those few of us the striving to discover everything new not only outside us, but also within ourselves is granted, then another way very likely needn't be sought. For me, just such eternally conscientious and righteous creators are Tolstoy and Proust; whereas Dostoevsky posited ultimate questions and heaped confused, unlikely situations on us, Tolstoy and Proust always tried—occasionally poorly and unsuccessfully—to hint, to illuminate, to explain. It seems to me that Lermontov was in Tolstoy's vein and was "serious to the point of naïvete" in his unceasing desire to illuminate, express, and clarify something of his own self (some day, if I can cope with my laziness, I will painstakingly prove this to you with the texts). Such intrinsic integrity within him—a hussar, a society type, a poet of probably fortuitous and quick inspiration—is for me most unexpected and appealing.

Besides, hussar, "scoundrel," society type—this was nothing but Lermontov's outer pose, which was far more noble and exhibited his great readiness to pay and answer for his transgressions, than those high "tragic" poses assumed by many, even famous people, who assess their rivals and friends according to the degree of their "wealth" or "sense of tragedy," in addition to taking anyone at their word and themselves speaking in extremely loud tones about their own sense of tragedy, surveying the silent and, therefore, wealthy ones with condescending complacency. Lermontov was both wiser and more conscientious than all these frivolous tragic squawkers—and how much more he, continually risking his life, being misunderstood, unloved, and lonely, and at the same time, like a man of the world, indifferent and reserved, never complaining to anyone, how much more worthy and somehow, in human terms, dearer, was he!

Pavel Muratov (1881–1950)

Pavel Pavlovich Muratov, a former artillery officer, was a very gifted and erudite writer. He was brought up in the best traditions of Western European culture and art. Prior to the Revolution of 1917, he was chiefly known as an art historian, and later as the editor of an excellent but short-lived literary journal, *Sofia*. In exile after 1922, he continued writing about the history of art, published a book on the Russian icon, and republished his earlier book *Obrazy Italii: putevye zametki* (Images of Italy: Travel Notes, Berlin, 1924), which was held in great esteem by the public. Muratov was also a military historian, publicist, and fiction writer. He published his essays on art and his short stories in *The Will of Russia, The Window, La Renaissance,* and *Contemporary Annals*. As a fiction writer, he published a novel entitled *Egeriya: istorichesky roman* (Egeria: A Historical Novel; Berlin, 1922); several collections of short stories, for example, *Tri rasskaza* (Three Stories; Moscow-Berlin, 1922), *Morali* (Morali; Berlin, 1922), and *Magicheskie rasskazy* (Stories about Magic; Paris, 1928); a book of historical studies entitled *Geroi i geroini* (Heroes and Heroines; Paris, 1929); and two comedies, *Priklyucheniya Dafnisa i Khloi* (The Adventures of Daphnis and Chloé; Paris, 1926) and *Mavritaniya* (Mauritania; Paris, 1927).

Muratov's stories—many of them using Western European plots—and his historical novel *Egeria* are characterized by swiftly developing action, unusual plot collisions, and an intentional lack of psychological situations. The influence of Henri de Régnier is evident throughout *Egeria*—it is a stylized work, distinct from the historical novel or the psychological work in the manner of Mark Aldanov. Muratov's plays likewise stand outside the tradition of Russian drama.

He spent World War II in England and died in Ireland in 1950. Together with his Irish friend W. E. D. Allen, a historian and collector of Russian icons in Dublin, he wrote (in English) an analysis on the strategy employed in the Soviet-German War and a book on the military history of the Caucasus in the nineteenth century. Muratov's travelogues reflect his erudition, his love for Italy, and his subtle artistic method in portraying a multitude of intimate details of historical and cultural significance, as can be seen from his *Images of Italy* and "Poezdka v Apuliyu" (Journey to Apulia), presented in an abridged version here.

JOURNEY TO APULIA

FROM: "Poezdka v Apuliyu" *Contemporary Annals* 24 (Paris, 1925).

I. EN ROUTE

Upon leaving Naples, the roads become bad. All the skill of the guide cannot protect our motorcycle from the ruts. In the lightweight sidecar the two of us, the artist and I, are sitting on one side, rocked in unison by frequent jolts. The badly painted suburban houses finally vanish; the very last chicken makes its determined run across the edge of the road right in front of our wheel; the road, thickly sprinkled with white dust, draws us into its smooth curves. Cutting delicate tracks in this thick layer of white powder is as unnatural for the motorcycle as driving a wooden cart into a snowdrift. Behind us a huge cloud rises, and through this milky fog we leave behind, one after another, the slow Neapolitan carts, in each of which, relying on the lazy pace of his mule, a man lies squinting in the noonday sun, indifferent to the dust and the haste. [. . .]

III. LUCERIA

A half-*verst* from Luceria on a bare slope stand the vast ruins of Castello Svevo. The fortress of Frederick II was constructed so soundly that its walls and towers have remained relatively intact. Eighteenth-century travelers saw and sketched the imposing remains of the Imperial citadel which stood within the walls. That building no longer exists—it was demolished; its stones were used to construct a courthouse in the city.

The role played by Luceria in the history of Frederick II is well known. After the suppression of the Arab insurgence in Sicily, the Emperor resettled several thousand families in Italy. Some were assigned to Accerenza, others to Luceria. Later, by the Emperor's decree, all the Arabs were concentrated in Luceria; there were more than sixty thousand of them here. To accommodate the bravest and most reliable detachment of the Emperor's troops, an immense fortress was constructed. Gradually, however, the Arabs took over the neighboring city as well. The Christians abandoned it, and a mosque was erected on the main square. When he came here, Frederick II became that sultan of Luceria which the Pope's accusations had exposed him to be. Within the citadel chambers he maintained a thoroughly eastern court. Magnificent horses were kept here for his amusement, and colorful Arab hunting parties with their falcons and trained tigers were arranged. In Luceria discussions with eastern wise men and the pleasures of the harem awaited the Emperor.

262

All this was not new for southern Italy. Frederick II was merely continuing a tradition peculiar to his ancestors, the Norman kings of Sicily. However, at the height of the Emperor's battle with Rome, all these things caused an absolute scandal. The Sicilian kings had more or less concealed their predilection for things eastern. Frederick II enjoyed them openly, with an unmistakable challenge. In this particular situation, as well as in others, he rushed to occupy the official position of an impenitent sinner. It may be that Luceria was his political blunder. By a twist of fate the Normans, warriors by nature, proved greater diplomats than this Emperor, whose tastes were hardly warlike and yet who was forced to fight all his life. From a purely military viewpoint, the unassailable fortress of Luceria, occupied to the end by loyal Arab troops, was a tremendous source of power, the key to Apulia and even to the whole of southern Italy.

This is obvious from the fear which Arab-controlled Luceria inspired in the enemies of the Emperor after his death. Pope Innocent IV himself addressed the Emir of the Arabs at Luceria with very flattering proposals for allegiance to the Most Holy Throne. The Emir was about to yield to the temptation, but his people remained faithful to the dynasty. On a November night in 1254, under cover of a storm which concealed him from Papist troops, Manfred appeared here, triumphantly met by the Arabs. With their help, he set out to regain the crown. The Arabs formed the main body of his troops. Embarking on his decisive campaign, which ended outside Benevento, Manfred left his young wife, Helena Epirus, and his small children in the Luceria fortress. But when news of his defeat reached her, Helena panicked. She fled to Trani, where she thought she could board a ship. There she was captured and turned over to Charles of Anjou. Her youngest son, Henry, died a blind old man in the Neapolitan Castile del Ovo in 1318, after fifty-two years of imprisonment.

After Manfred's defeat, the Arabs of Luceria submitted to the victors. But two years later, as soon as the news arrived of the campaign of the last Hohenstaufens into Italy, they revolted. Anjou besieged the Luceria fortress in vain. He was forced to abandon the siege in order to march against Conrad's troops. After his victory and the execution of his northern seeker of the throne, Anjou again appeared before Luceria. The Arabs defended it desperately, but Anjou surrounded the fortress and took it by starving out the defenders. This time the King spared their lives. However, he abolished the Arabs' privileges. Charles I installed his garrison in the fortress; he ordered that the mosque on Luceria's main square be razed and a cathedral built in its place. Half the city was given to settlers sent from Provence. The final reprisal against the infidels was delayed until 1300, that very Anno Santo to which Dante was a witness. Suddenly, in the midst of a secure peace, an entire army besieged Luceria. The city was taken by storm and its whole Arab population was slaughtered, down to the last soul. Two years later the new cathedral was triumphantly consecrated, and in the new Luceria the memory of the Moslem colony of Frederick II and Manfred was supposed to have vanished.

But this memory will not vanish completely while the excellently constructed towers and walls of Castello Svevo remain standing. Something in this structure eloquently expresses how great an epoch for southern Italy was the era of Frederick II. Apulia then lived an international life. In this dull little provincial town—where today the visit of three travelers constitutes a real event—do not the memories of those Moslem warriors and German knights, of Helena Epirus and Charles of Anjou, of the Arab builders of its fortress and the French architect of its Gothic cathedral give proof of that fact? The will of a strange man, the most fantastic of the Emperors, was needed to blend east and west, north and south, on this deserted clump of earth.

In his excellent book *La Grande Grèce*, which remains the unsurpassed model for travel books, François Lenormand tells of his encounter with a flock of Pythagoras' cranes at the site of ancient Cotrone. "I was always singularly lucky," he says, "in having meetings with those living beings who provided me with a live commentary on the classical tradition. I'm not speaking of the little owls at the Athenian Acropolis, with their tenderly doleful call; there are always so many of them there that not a single traveler has missed the sight of them. But I saw the large, red kites of the goddess among the ruins of her temple at Karnak in Egypt, the Livonian turtledove among the cedars at Ihden, and Zeus' eagles soaring above the three still remaining columns at the temple of Nemesis. I heard the cawing of Apollo's ravens at the beginning of winter on the terraces of his temple at Delphi, and the springtime call of the cuckoo in the woods near the Heraeum in Argos, where Zeus assumed the form of this bird to carry his sister Hera away and make her his bride. In the grass at Epidauris I picked up the grass snake of Aesculapius. I came upon a large sea turtle, sleeping on the waves near the shores of the Aegean, and a school of dolphins in that very same place, where one of them had once carried the poet Arion of Methymna on his back" . . .

That day at the walls of the castle at Luceria we were as happy as that author of the best of books on southern Italy had been—we saw Arabian hunting falcons nesting in the clefts of the wall towers, and in the distance above the plain we saw the imperial eagle flying toward the sea. Had Frederick II been concerned with providing a landscape similar to that native to the warriors of the prophet he settled here, he could have found nothing in all Italy more suitable for them. It is the landscape of wilderness, a landscape for war, a landscape for men who are protectors, nomads, shepherds, and horsemen. Like straight and delicate white lines, white roads stretch from the hill at Luceria toward the Apennine Mountains, toward Foggia, toward Troy. They are apparently the only features which, throughout the many centuries, civilization has managed to bring to the wild steppes of Tavoliera. [. . .]

IX. BARI

There is nothing stranger than these two Bari, the new and the old, placed virtually side by side, right next to each other—which nevertheless have not a single feature in common and even live completely separate lives. The new Bari is young; it has lived through a little more than a century, having been begun in the brief (and, for northern Italy, happy) years of Murat. From the 1860's and 70's, its construction has assumed an American tempo, and the growth of the city has not ceased even today. Now it is a network of wide streets crossing each other at straight angles, lined with houses resembling, more than anything else, the houses along the densely inhabited streets of some new section of Rome. Generally, it is like the average capital of a South American state or of any small country. It is very lively, very business oriented, very unspectacular, not too dirty and, fortunately, has no particular pretensions to luxury of the kind which has so successfully ruined the elegant sections of the new Rome and Naples.

Right next to this industrious and peacefully vulgar city is the old Bari—a labyrinth of narrow alleys, of the most picturesque courtyards falling into ruin from the decrepitude of their palazzos, of ancient little shops, of dark and severe medieval church walls, of arches with peeling crests, of clotheslines with linen tangled by the sea breeze, of twisted balconies strung with bunches of yellow pumpkins and red tomatoes, of romance, poverty, indescribable filth, old rags, the life of the seventeenth century side by side with the twentieth. For a painter, old Bari is a windfall, and our artist, struck by such an unexpected find, quickly found nourishment for himself—a group of dark-haired women sitting in a small circle in straw chairs, a magnificent exterior staircase dramatically encircling a stinking yard, garlands of drying vegetables under a boldly constructed vaulted marble arch. Leaving him, I wander further along the blind alleys and loops of tiny streets, walk out toward the sea which, from this perspective, seems suspended above the small fishing port now below me. It is already growing dark, and I want to manage a visit to the Cathedral of St. Nicolas, a huge Romanesque basilica— its nave rising high above the beehive of the old city, which has parted for it in deference—it is precisely a nave, a ship, as it is quite accurately called in Russian architecture as well. Inside there is total darkness, not a soul. His slippers shuffling, an old church guard hurries toward me. His joy at seeing me attests to the rather small flow of visitors. Is that true? The old man sighs and shakes his head; the times have changed greatly. He suggests I come tomorrow morning.

The next morning I return to St. Nicolas. Again, there is no one in the church. In the crypt, Mass is being said above the grave of the Saint; two or three old women kneel by the ancient benches, which have been highly polished by the touch of previous visitors. In the vestry, the attending priest is selling small icons and vials of healing manna, sealed with wax. There are

265

neither buyers nor donors. Where are the pilgrims, where are the Russian palmers, where are those pious Slavic people from the other side of the Adriatic, where are the fishermen who seek protection and aid from their Saint, the patron of travelers, and sailors, and captives?

What is this—an accidental error, a deceptive, unreliable impression? I can't believe the fate of the cathedral is indeed so intrinsically joined with the fate of old Bari. Life is over there, on the streets of that new city, so totally devoid of all personality, in the shops and offices, at the port and the prefectory, in the newspaper publishing houses, in the public schools, at the post office, at the central station, in the Camera di Commiercio. Here there is only history, only the past, fading, essentially vanished, but still majestic in its stones, its singing, its religious beliefs, and the words of its prayers.

Those who have in the last several years been speaking of a rebirth of the Church should be advised to come out of their closed little intellectual circles, where this or that judgment is all too glibly formed, and look for impressions at the very site of historical sacred events and places. The common crowd has withdrawn from the church walls, left them, and settled somewhere farther away, just as new Bari has left old Bari, just as new Rome is settling somewhere totally independent of St. Peter's. The people must live the life of our times, a life about which they were not even consulted while it was being adopted. Is it their fault that there is no longer room in this life for either Saint Peter or Saint Nicolas?

Saint Nicolas—patron and protector of fishermen on the Adriatic—it was he who replaced Poseidon. But not many years will pass before motors begin to putter on the calm surface of the Adriatic and the Ionian Sea. The eye of the fisherman will cease to search for the wind along the horizon; the sail, given life by the breath of the sea, will become a memory. Still another link between man and nature will be severed; still another myth will yield its place to the price of fuel and the level of horsepower. For those generations growing up faced with such obvious, such vital mechanical power, what meaning can a myth about the great sea deity and a legend about the great Christian Saint have?

Nearly nine hundred years have passed since the day when the enterprising Apulian sea travelers, imitating the Venetians, transported the remains of Saint Nicolas from Lycian Myra to Bari, to the place where, under the Norman kings, a grandiose cathedral—the model for all the Romanesque cathedrals of Apulia—was erected. Nine hundred years—what depth, what a pool of history! And one senses this depth so strikingly here, precisely because beside the old Bari, nestled around its cathedral, there has settled a new Bari, as separate as if it had been cut off with a knife. Let us examine it with no less attention—for indeed this is also history, our own history. Fortunately, we are not granted the power to see the present with as much daring as we can see the past—for whose clarity of vision would not be obscured by the sight of our terrible, cursed age? [. . .]

Alas, our return to the contemporary world holds little joy. Good Lord, what has become of Salerno, where I hadn't been for fifteen years! Where has this Newcastle soot come from, these coal-covered, back streets, these huge, ugly, boxlike houses—and, what's more, with pretensions to the "modern style"? Can this be called the progress of the city? How wonderful the coastline used to be here, wide, smoothly rounded by the curve of its shore—with cozy, provincial cafés, where, sitting at a small table, one could hear the lapping of the sea and gaze at the stars, rocking among the riggings of the fishing boats. At this same site greed has forced the construction of a row of crudely attractive, multilevel houses, to fence poor Salerno from the sea with a high wall, which seems to have been transplanted from the most banal of Berlin's streets. The Salerno we loved has forever ceased to exist. Perhaps there is someone who feels that civilization has achieved a victory here. However, those who refuse to fall into ecstasy over these pitiful triumphs of civilization should not despair. Civilization presses us; we retreat. Just now, returning from the seacoast of Apulia, from the slopes of Monte Vulture, from the mountain passes of Basilicata, we know that unfathomable Italy is still wonderful and great . . .

Vladimir Weidlé (1896–1979)

Vladimir Vasilyevich Weidlé, art historian, critic, essayist, and poet, was born in St. Petersburg. He graduated in history from the University of St. Petersburg in 1916, lectured on history there from 1916 to 1918, and taught history of West European medieval art from 1921 to 1924. In 1924 he left Russia and settled in Paris, where he contributed to Russian literary journals and newspapers. But he had begun to publish long before his move to Paris. In St. Petersburg his article about Marcel Proust appeared in the journal *The Contemporary West*, two poems and several critical reviews were published in the journal *The Russian Contemporary*, and in the almanac *Tomorrow* (Berlin, 1923), he published his first literary essay about Alexander Blok and a poem entitled "Oda" (An Ode).

From 1932 to 1952 Weidlé was professor of Christian art and Western religious history at the Russian Theological Academy in Paris. He then became director of programming at Radio Free Europe in Munich, 1953–58. Later he was appointed professor at the European College in Bruges, Belgium. He lectured at the Institute of the History of the Arts at the University of Munich in 1964–65, and subsequently at the State University of New York in New York City (history of Russian art, 1968), and at Princeton University (theory of poetry, 1970). He gave lectures and papers on the history and theory of Russian and Western European art at various congresses and conferences in Oxford, Rome, Florence, Athens, Amsterdam, Brussels, Paris, Vienna, Salzburg, Munich, Hamburg, Basel, and Ascona.

Weidlé is the author of many erudite, outstanding studies of Russian and Western European art and culture. His major works include *Poeziya Khodasevicha* (The Poetry of Khodasevich; Paris, 1928), *Les Abeilles d'Aristée: Essai sur le destin actuel des Lettres et des Arts* (Paris, 1954), *Les Icônes Byzantines et Russes* (1940), *La Russie absente et présente* (Paris, 1949), *The Baptism of Art* (London, 1950), *Vecherny den'* (The Twilight of Day; New York, 1952), *Zadacha Rossii* (The Task of Russia; New York, 1956), *Les Mosaïques Vénitiennes* (Florence, 1956), *Bezymyannaya strana* (The Nameless Country; Paris, 1968), *O poezii i poetakh* (On Poets and Poetry; Paris, 1973), and the reminiscences "Pokhorony Bloka" (Blok's Funeral) in *The New Review* no. 65 (1961): 270–76. Weidlé's verses have appeared in many collections of poetry, among them *Concord* (Washington: Kamkin, 1966), pp. 89–96, the almanac *Aerial Ways*, and *The New Review*. His poems about Rome and, especially, about Venice, and the blissful Italian blue of the Mediterranean Sea and neighboring regions are intense in their evocative power and aesthetic appeal.

La Russie absente et présente, translated into German, Spanish, and English, was awarded the Rivarol Prize. The Russian version of *Les Abeilles d'Aristée* appeared as *Umiranie iskusstva* (The Death of Art) in 1937 and came out in a new German translation as *Die Sterblichkeit der Musen* (Stuttgart, 1957); it was translated into Japanese in two separate editions. In 1957 Weidlé received the UNESCO Prize for his article "La Biologie de l'art," in the journal *Diogène* no. 18.

Sensitive to sound, rhythm, and the variety of possible arrangements of details, Weidlé became, after 1958, a writer of artistic prose—not, as he insists, to be confused with belles-lettres. According to him, Russian literature (in comparison with Western European literatures) lacks this genre. He planned to entitle a collection of his nonfiction artistic prose with one of Pushkin's lines, "Prezrennoy prozoy govorya" (Speaking in contemptible prose). As early as 1912, fascinated with this type of writing, he subscribed to various French publications, among them *Nouvelle Revue Française*. Some of his later books in Russian are written in this manner. Their style is clear and straightforward, devoid of eccentricities and whimsy, but it abounds in humor and manifests great vividness in exposition.

Weidlé's place in Russian *émigré* literature is determined principally by his refined and perceptive literary critique and his erudition in the history of art. His works in these two areas have become one of the most precious achievements of Russian literature in emigration. To the sophisicated and experienced reader, his essays are masterpieces in enlightenment and a revelation in scholarship.

SUNDAYS IN LONDON

FROM: *Vecherny den'* (The Twilight of Day; New York: Chekhov, 1952).

Every Saturday at precisely eleven o'clock in the morning a street organ, harnessed to a little mare, travels to an awkward-looking house on an uninhabited street in a little town not very far from the capital. A bearded man in a jacket with an upturned collar is turning the handle sullenly, and a crackling waltz rattles, zealously cutting the bleak, dreamy silence. The roller revolves, laboriously spitting out the crumpled sounds of a wornout melody. These sounds, skipping away from the machine, the little horse, and the bearded man, spread out, grow bolder, fill the entire street, press against the wall, and creep up to the topmost floor. There in a glass cage under a glass roof a clerk, writing behind a desk, raises his head, exchanges a glance with his neighbor, and puts down his pen for a moment: Strauss' "Blue Danube" is proclaiming freedom to him. In an hour, in a solid crowd of clerks, accountants, and writers, he'll push his way through a gateway jammed with bicycles, go out into the street, now unrecognizably busy, stop home for a little while, and, having managed to grab a bite, will once again make his way with the crowd to the station to stand in line at the ticket window where they sell round-trip tickets—until Monday morning he, like everyone else, is a free man.

The train has left and is already winding among the reddening hills, the naked trees, and the December fields washed by rain. Halfway along, you can see rails and still more rails, brick walls, chimneys, angular factory complexes, working men's settlements with their strict lines of houses, where the same identical sooty little balconies, roofs, and window-sash frames flash by.

While the steam engine makes its way to the city through these endless suburbs, rain will begin to fall and twilight will descend. Under the glassy railroad station sky, pale lanterns are lit. After the deafening roar of the wheels, the sounds of the city seem more distinct. A string of old-fashioned taxis stretches alongside the entrance; but it's better to pass them by and go out onto the square, immediately plunging into the damp London fog which smells of stone and iron. Although it is not yet dark, the day is already forgotten; Saturday evening—the night before Sunday.

The rays of lanterns pierce the drizzling mesh of rain; the shop windows gape with a glow into other worlds; they're selling flowers in the motley electrical twilight; multicolored posters praise winter in Egypt and early spring in Sicily; on a slimy brown wall a bay shines blue; the hotels of Monaco sparkle, and the world-famous gambling casino gleams with its paper marble. You plunge into the streets, and the streets carry you away; the farther you go, the faster and faster you're carried along. A five-story building will, like a whirlpool, suck the visitor into a restaurant with music; having satisfied him, it will turn him out again onto the wet pavement where his steps will, of their own accord, direct him to a nearby movie theatre or to the theatre district's Shaftesbury Avenue, glaring with its unbearable lights. Exhausted, he returns after midnight to his far-off dwelling, walking down endless streets, accompanied by innumerable lanterns. How palely they glimmer; they speak of such loneliness to the passerby, so much so that he would like to extinguish them and wander forever into the impenetrable, into the hellish city of darkness.

You awaken—and how striking is this measured silence, the decorous desolation of the streets. A porch with columns, three steps, and then, wherever you look beneath the sober morning sky—everywhere the same brick-red three-story houses, the same stairs and columns and doorknobs, the same entirely first-rate but identical coziness. These well-to-do apartments are no richer in imagination that the poor ones, and for all of them there is set aside one and the same seventh day, rather empty, but proper and dignified. Everything is closed—museums and drugstores, libraries and confectioneries. All you can get is a stamp or some cigarettes, and that only by putting money in a vending machine; only by strolling all morning along the clean-swept Sunday streets can you understand the meaning of this vast pile of human dwellings arranged not by the compass and slide rule, nor by the will of a great architect, but by the monotony of necessities established over the centuries, by the alternation of lives, by layers of death. If you don't get lost in the streets, each one just like the next, if you don't confuse the squares—a rectangle of trees, framed by a rectangle of houses—you can go from west to east, passing over the oases of parks and the lagoons of circular clearings, passing by thousands and thousands of lowered Venetian blinds and silent, superfluous billboards, and come at last to the very heart of this holiday wilderness. Until tomorrow it's dead. The high priests have abandoned the bank and the stock market, the praying of the typewriters has fallen silent; the crowd, which only yesterday had been eating the bread and wine of those numbers that they write on the board with chalk, wipe off, and write again, is gone. Instead of those huge buses the color of bull's blood, only little boys, the sons of dignified doormen, scurry on roller skates along Lombard Street. Soon even they will disappear; only the granite façades along the emptied sidewalks will stare at each other until evening; and the dark lights of their mirrorlike windows will gleam unhappily.

Today there are no writers at the blackboard; rather, with his white hand, a preacher is sketching the firm pattern of universally acknowledged moral laws. In St. Paul's Cathedral of Westminster Abbey these elevated, instructive words echo solemnly. Preceding and completing them is the harmonious singing of the choir. They sing in the same manner everywhere, in both Catholic and Protestant churches of all persuasions. The churches are almost completely filled, but for a latecomer people gladly move along on the bench and let him glance into their prayerbooks, if he has left his own at home. There is satisfaction in the fact that everyone around is quite obviously in such a magnificently cheerful mood, although one can't help realizing that for many of them the meaning of their presence here is entirely limited to the attainment of this good feeling, as is evidenced by the efforts of the preacher to refrain from disturbing this centuries-old custom of Sunday piety and well-being. True, even if they don't pray very ardently in Westminster Abbey, the ancient cathedral itself, always and for all, raises a prayer on high—through its past, its architecture, each of its gravestones. There is no similarity whatever between it and the Christian Science meeting hall recently constructed in Chelsea, which resembles a movie theatre. Here too—without a cross, without a single Gospel text on the walls—there is a service going on, although somewhat later and with greater comfort than anywhere else. Well-dressed women distribute programs and seat those attending in plush folding chairs, upholstered in crimson velvet and arranged in ascending rows. On the platform there are two rostra—from one a man is reading texts from the Holy Scriptures; from the other, a woman, alternating with him, reads selections from the writings of Mrs. Eddy. Listening to all this and joining in with a final chorale are unusually venerable voices, which belong to individuals entirely capable of spending quite substantial means in order to find (without any "passage through the eye of a needle," and with all their belongings intact) a cure for themselves, as well as inheriting the Heavenly Kingdom by the most expedient path.

Before noon, with the conclusion of the church service, the streets become busier. Our visitor, if he doesn't go to listen to vagrant orators in Hyde Park, will inevitably come in his wanderings upon one of the many processions of those groups who, at that hour, are moving across the city in all directions. The firemen and constables march; organizations of citizens who have been wounded for the Motherland pass by; women with babies in their arms, attracted by the uniforms of the Queen's Guard, stream to Whitehall; and right there, in a long line with music, flags, and flowers, a detachment of the Salvation Army—old spinsters, school girls, energetic young women in uniforms corresponding to their ranks and ages—is moving in the direction of the war memorial. On Trafalgar Square a rather dense crowd is listening to a preacher, who has clambered onto the pedestal of Nelson's Column. He waves his arms, shakes a Bible, screeches, and stamps his foot, speaking about his own sinful life and repentance, calling on all living Christians to repent. The listeners shrug their shoulders, but he flares up all the more. "No, no," he shouts, "don't play with the Devil; sin is not simply spitting and wiping it off." At this point he actually spits on the black cover of the book of Scripture and wipes the spit off with his sleeve. A chuckle passes through the crowd, but he, unembarrassed, continues his sermon on the square. Now he has finished, and an automobile is already carrying him away to some other square, to another crowd, perhaps to where there is not a single soul, but the smell of the fish market has not yet disappeared; or farther, where some fans of military music have lined up along the sidewalks to meet an approaching band. The sticks of the drummers are raised high; the strident, piercing sound of the flutes resounds; the uniforms pass in endless colors; the officer waves his baton, and then at last, spreading out, the soldiers march along the blackened street, near the Tower.

At one o'clock the museums open. Behind the National Gallery with its faded colonnades, whose basilica is derogatorily nicknamed "the pepperbox," treasures and wonders are revealed; there are paintings, majestic paintings, jealously guarded by gleaming glass, in which the Sunday visitor too often finds the reflections of conceited Sunday faces etched in boredom. He will wander, lost even more, in the gigantic halls of the Victoria and Albert Museum, where there is a restaurant like a railway station buffet, and where there are Persian rugs and reproductions of Raphaël, Meissner statuettes and Chinese silks, Bodhisattvas and Crucifixes. But most likely he prefers once again to frighten the pigeons under the black portico of the British Museum. On winter days, when there's insufficient sunlight, the milky-dim electric globes are lit and the marble pieces from the Parthenon begin to seem transparent, lifeless, so abandoned and gray that, if you didn't resurrect them within your own spirit by the power of imagination, you would think that they had turned into their own copies, into pale fragments of their greatness. No, better to go away into the foreign section, to Egypt or Babylon, or farther yet, going up to the second floor, to plunge into the gritting of teeth or the lamenting of primitive witchcraft or cannibalism. Only solitary gawkers wander in this terrifying world of strange faiths and strange arts. They shudder involuntarily, seeing in the showcase, among grimacing masks cast in gold and the snakes of Quetzalcoatl sprinkled with emeralds, an unforgettable, triumphant, disgustingly transparent skull of rock crystal, gleaming through its eye sockets and the gap of the nose.

A little bell rings; the doors close squeaking; soon the day will end. But the hour that has now come is the best, the most significant of all. Was it not this hour which the silly music of yesterday foretold? There is nothing more wonderful and sad than this twilight glow which transforms the city. At four o'clock in Petersburg, along the embankment during the winter a shadow falls over the rosy snow, the sledge runners noiselessly slip along, the lanterns scarcely flicker, and in the windows of the Winter Palace, as in each oncoming face, shines the glow of the fading sky. The rays of the sunset pierce Paris above the river; the clouds disperse, the sharp-peaked gables grow dark, the bridges arch their backs, the towers take on a dull red tone, and it seems both banks, one after the other, will weigh anchor and sail away into the very depths of the sunset. But this merciless stone world is even more deserted and gigantic, and the smile of the sky is even sweeter right here, among the sparse trees of Leicester Square. Dense flocks of sparrows chirp on the bare branches; if you tap on the tree trunk with a stick, they'll rise in one flock, sprinkling the paling airy blue with black spots, and a minute later fly back. While you walk along Piccadilly, a weak light still streams from above, with a certain shy caress, onto the cumbersome boxes of the houses. In a moment it will go out, and then all that's left is to stroll to the station, creep into the darkness sitting on the train bench, think about the gateway with the bicycles, about the office under the glass roof, and for the whole week (or maybe for one's entire life) to cherish in one's soul these tender twilights of London.

THE CHARM OF ITALY

Lanky Englishwomen with little red books in their hands stand at the crossroads like lampposts, and their steep shadows fall on the uninhabited Pompeiian streets. Others, having already absorbed their lessons from the very same little books, with expressions of duty fulfilled on their faces, crumble rolls for the pigeons on St. Mark's Square. A third group, tossing their heads back on the wooden spine of a bench and practically dislocating their necks, admire the ceiling of the Sistine Chapel and wonder aloud about that strange name—Michelangelo. In July at midday some brash Bavarians, dripping with sweat, ascend the Palatine or crawl along the roof of the Milan Cathedral; they wear thick woolen jackets, the same type of socks, shoes with taps, and green felt hats with little coquettish cock feathers. In Florence, above the Ponte Vecchio, in the corridor which joins the Pitti and Uffizi galleries, a bearded man in new galoshes desperately searches for something in the Phillip's tour guide and, meeting a countryman, entreats him to explain exactly where around here is "that much praised Baptistry of theirs."

Many are familiar with scenes and encounters of this sort, especially those who were in Italy during those idyllic prerevolutionary, prewar years. In those years, even among us, a trip to Italy had become the obligation of everyone who respected himself and who was even partially literate. Through Vienna, through Berlin, and even by sea from Odessa at times there stretched out hordes of tourists, sometimes with families, sometimes alone, students—male and female, bookkeepers, Volga merchants, retired military men, industrialists from the Urals, dignitaries, public school teachers, and even priests (God knows from what provinces they came), carrying teapots so at the stations they could get boiling water. By that time it had long since been established that, of the Italian cities, the French were particularly fond of Venice, the English of Florence, the Germans of Rome; the Russians found no one place especially reserved for them. So July and August, the most inappropriate months for touring Italy, were christened the "Russian season." Then began the mandatory tours of museums, palaces, and churches, the purchase of souvenirs, the writing of post cards depicting a cemetery in Genoa or a fisherman from Capri. Many ridiculous things began—but it would be even more ridiculous if, behind these trivialities, we had failed to perceive things of significant and substantial value. Written in those years were Blok's "Italian Verses," Rozanov's "Italian Impressions," Muratov's "Images of Italy," Zaytsev's "Faraway Land," and numerous other books, poetry and paintings, related in one way or another to their authors' Italian travels. One of the finest Russian traditions which had somewhat lost its vitality toward the end of the century—the tradition linked to the names of Batyushkov, Tyutchev, Turgenev, expressed in the paintings of Sylvester Shchedrin, in those days of Boratynsky in Naples, by Gogol' and by Alexander Ivanov (who were both bewitched by Rome)—was renewed and gave promise of expanding . . . The revitalization of this tradition and its fruitful development was a token of the European essence of Russia, for every country in Europe possesses its own series of Italian travelogues and its own kind of love for Italy.

"*Je n'ai pas le Heimweh, mais le Herausweh*,"* Tyutchev would say; despite all his Slavophilism, Russia at times annoyed him to the extreme. However, his words can be understood in another sense, less scathing and more suitable to European national feeling. A man of European culture exhibits precisely this characteristic state of a rather unstable equilibrium between *Heimweh* and *Herausweh*, between homesickness when he has stayed too long in a foreign land, and a longing for things foreign when compelled to endure an uninterrupted stay in his native country. The first of these feelings is universal; the second apparently constitutes a unique peculiarity among Europeans, and led to Europe's "opening" the Old and New Worlds, whereas nowhere else in the world could another Columbus be found to open Europe. Within European culture, this peculiarity also plays a very constructive and unifying role. Thanks to it, the mutual attraction of European countries manifests itself perhaps even more deeply and actively where it is characterized not by proximity or similarity, but by contrast. Business, commercial, and (depending on these) even cultural ties between Italy and the rest of the Mediterranean coast of Europe are ancient and enduring; but there is not that special spiritual and emotional attraction to her, as one sees, for example, in the Scandinavian countries. A border of mountains, in former times almost impassable, divides Germany from Italy; yet from the heroic tales of Theodorich[1] to the insane politics of the Hohenstaufens, from the tragedy of Dürer and all the German art of his time, scorched by the Italian sun, to the Roman happiness of Goethe, to the picturesque dreaming and failures at the beginning of the last century, to Burkhardt, to Wagner, to the Turin madness of Nietzsche, the same attraction for Italy has continuously mutilated and revived again and again a contradictory German culture. However, it is even easier to show the entire force of this magnetic power by the example of another country enraptured by Italy: the classical, clear example of England.

Toast with five o'clock tea, changing for dinner, tennis, golf—all this and even more the English have spread to the ends of the earth, not only to Italy. But to nowhere but Italy have they carried such a greedy curiosity, such burning and unselfish love. The old spinsters with guidebooks in hand at

*It is not homesickness I suffer from, but a longing for the beyond.

275

Pompeii, Venice, and the Vatican are only one of the humorous and, in the final analysis, touching symbols of this love. One can obtain an especially distinct notion of the strength and prevalence of these feelings in the 1930 London exhibition of Italian art. One must envision the crowd thronging from early morning to a gray building on Piccadilly, walking up the staircase, filling hall after hall—a rapt, almost prayerful crowd. One needn't know Italy to dream of her, and it's enough to be an Englishman to believe in Italian art. However successful the two previous London exhibitions devoted to Flemish and Dutch painting had been, they certainly weren't surrounded by such attention, such solemnity, such universal ecstacy. After all, these two had demanded a certain special preparation, whereas practically every Englishman was acquainted, if only through hearsay, with those wonderul Italian works, for the sake of which he would have traveled to Florence (if he could afford it)—but now could simply go to London. The trip there, from the most remote corners, was made, to be sure, by all those who had, if only once, seen a reproduction of a Botticelli, who had at any time glanced at a book of Ruskin or simply admired the palaces of the doges in the showcase at the railroad office. What joy this wonderful event held for all of them, when hundreds of those little stars from Baedeker were transferred to the London sky; that is, something happened akin to the Coliseum being moved to the Square of Westminster Abbey, and St. Paul's Cathedral being crowned with the dome of St. Peter's.

To tell the truth, it was a little sad to look at these canvases sent to spend the winter in the north. The halls of the Academy were stuffy, crowded, and dingy for them—especially after dark, when the boring, round lamps were lit, their reflections repeating in endless rows in the glass case of "Venus Rising from the Sea." Everything grew somehow deathly then, and in this temporary graveyard of paintings one was left to reflect on their dimmed charm, or else to watch the crowd, moving in deep rows along the walls on which hung "slices of Italy." Passing from painting to painting, stringing them one after the other to the point of utter exhaustion—indeed, any one of them demands full attention; any one desires the best you can give—every onlooker, to the extent of his capacities, tried to absorb this five-hundred-year-old, this profound, full, truly human life of Italian art. Not without reason does the National Gallery in London have the best collection of Italian paintings outside Italy. Not without reason have the English long since considered Italian art not simply a "school" among other artistic schools, but as the definition of art itself, as the yardstick and symbol of all art. Not without reason have so many Englishmen been raised on the centuries-old tradition of Italian travel, generation after generation their offspring are the ones who have now come to look at those Italian trophies earned by their ancestors. Each sees what he can, receives what he deserves, judges according to his own understanding; but all feel that before them is something not merely wonderful yet foreign, but a part of their national heritage, won by history and adopted through persistent love. The Puritans usurped the Bible (although even Cromwell didn't sell off the Italian paintings of the executed King); their heirs and secret enemies created Holy Scripture from Italian art. It is certainly no accident that they chose precisely the country where painting had so closely merged with life, where art was so vital a human concern and, simultaneously, such an eternal celebration. The charm of Italy is explained by the motivating force of contrast.

England is attracted not by any single special feature of Italian artistic forms, nor even by the externally apparent perfection of Italian art as a whole, but by something more profound. It is precisely that southern, pliable, physical feeling for life, so contrary to the English temperament, which has remained throughout the passage of so many centuries the inexhaustible source of Italian artistic creativity. The direct influence of Italian painting or architecture on English painting and architecture often turned out to be not particularly productive—as evidenced, for example, by the pseudo-Italian buildings of Oxford, very touching and sweet, which nevertheless cannot be taken entirely seriously, or the even less successful "supposedly genuine" Italian-style painting of the nineteenth century. In this type of painting, as in the classical forms of Queen's College of Bodleian, there is, not without reason, something deeply literary. Literature has long since been the main, practically the only expressive feature of English life; and it is precisely in literature that the Italian influence is most forcefully revealed.

It would be as impossible to imagine English literature devoid of dreams of Italy as it would be to think of the works of Shakespeare without his Roman tragedies, without *Romeo and Juliet*, without *Othello*, without *The Merchant of Venice*. The traditional comparison between the sightless world of Milton, hovering in a fog beyond the grave, and the blindingly clear vision of *The Divine Comedy* is entirely valid; but, obviously, even the great Puritan poet, doomed to blindness as if in fulfillment of his own poetics, somehow needed this Latin tangibility and visualness. He, too, had traveled to Italy. He, too, like many of his contemporaries, wrote Italian verse. During the Elizabethan era a uniquely refracted adaptation of Italian art, and, what's more, of Italian life itself, was one of the major stimuli of dramatic creativity and set the stage for its unprecedented flowering. The Puritan revolution struggled against (what is considered) this pagan poison; it introduced into the English language a distorted version of the name Machiavelli, as one of the names of the devil, but was unable to eradicate a whole series of words invented by Englishmen according to Italian models, although unknown to Italians. The temporary ebb of Puritanism elicited a new wave of attraction for Italy. That wave never completely subsided during the intellectual eighteenth century and was stimulated anew, with enormous strength, by the poetry of the resurrected Romantic movement. Byron's Italian years cannot be erased from

English literature, and no one thinking of Italy will forget that Keats went there to die, that Shelley expired on Italian shores, that Deandra and Browning spent the longest and happiest part of their lives in Italy.

This tie has never been broken; it is not severed even now. It was precisely in Italy that Lawrence searched all the more persistently—traveling on foot through Sicily, Sardinia, and the high-lying Italian valleys after he had written *Lady Chatterley's Lover* in Florence—for that primordial naturalness, that physical-spiritual wholeness which he tried so feebly to express in this hardly successful book, and for which in somewhat different (but nevertheless Italian) models even the Elizabethan playwrights had been seeking. Against the background of this centuries-old interest, every client of Thomas Cook and Sons on a three-day tour of Rome encounters a meaning incomprehensible to himself, yet still undestroyed even through lack of understanding. One wants to greet this old sorrow, this true love for that faraway southern land, not with the shadows of Pompeiian Englishwomen, but with something entirely different—with the memory of violets, for instance, blooming at the pyramid of Caius Cesti on the grave of Keats, or that of the lonely Englishmen's graveyard behind a fence of cypresses, behind a tall stone wall floating off into the sky like a fragile little island on some faraway Florentine square.

NOTE

1. Dietrich von Bern.

M. Ageev

Not much is known about M. Ageev. He sent three of his manuscripts to Paris from Constantinople: two excerpts from his planned novel *Roman s kokainom* (A Novel with Cocaine) went to the editorial office of the literary journal *Numbers*, and "Parshivy narod" (Wretched People) was directed to *Encounters*. "Povest' s kokainom: po zapiskam bol'nogo" (A Tale with Cocaine: Based on the Notes of a Sick Man), much admired by Georgy Adamovich and Vladimir Weidlé, appeared in *Numbers* no. 10 (1934); "Wretched People" saw print in *Encounters* no. 4 (1934). *A Novel with Cocaine: Based on the Notes of a Sick Man* was published as a separate edition in Paris two years later.

The novel portrays the gradual disintegration of the narrator, the fifteen-year-old high-school student Vadim Maslennikov. It portrays the constant struggle of good and evil in his mind and heart, and the influence of narcotics on Russian adolescents. In its preoccupation with pathological psychology, its portrayal of sex, and its emphasis on the pernicious effects of drug addition, *A Novel with Cocaine* is strangely in tune with contemporary interest in these themes. On the other hand, Ageev's *exposé* of ethical antinomies and subconscious conflicts links him with Dostoevsky, in that both writers reveal the complexity of human nature.

Ageev's portrayal of sex and the pathological mental condition caused by abuse of the sexual drive reflects the same crude advocacy of individualism and bold treatment of sexual themes found in the works of Boleslav Markevich and Ieronim Yasinsky (pseudonym Maxim Belinsky). Their works, indulging in the bacchanalia of pornography in Russian belles-lettres, were unpalatable to the Russian literary taste at the turn of the century. Some later writers—Anatoly Kamensky, Sergey Sergeev-Tsensky, Lidiya Zinovyeva-Annibal, Fyodor Sologub, Mikhail Artsybashev, Mikhail Kuzmin, and Leonid Andreev—also became engrossed in the portrayal of sexual life and a variety of perversions. In many respects, then, these writers paved the way for the interest of Ageev and Georgy Ivanov[1] in sexual entanglements and pornography, much in vogue in the modern literature of the West.

Despite its general pathological trend, *A Novel with Cocaine* is well written, its style more restrained and polished than in the works of those writers mentioned above. There is no indulgence in sexual vagaries or pornographic pictures for their own sake. The compositional design is well conceived. Basing his assessment on only those excerpts of *A Novel with Cocaine* which had been published in *Numbers*, Georgy Adamovich referred to Ageev as a "true fiction writer." Unfortunately, Ageev made his appearance in the pantheon of Russian literature with only these works. Nothing is known about his future artistic evolution, his literary career, or his personal life.

NOTE

1. See Georgy Ivanov, *Raspad atoma* (The Splitting of the Atom; Paris, 1938).

HIGH SCHOOL

Burkevits refused.

FROM: *Povest's kokainom: po zapiskam bol'nogo* (A Tale with Cocaine: Based on the Notes of a Sick Man).

1.

Once, at the beginning of October, I, Vadim Maslennikov (I was then going on sixteen), leaving early in the morning for school, forgot the envelope my mother had put on the dining room table the previous evening, which contained the money I was to bring in for first semester. I remembered the envelope when I was already standing in the tram, when—from its gathering speed—the acacias and pickets of the boulevard fence were transformed from needle-like flashes to a solid stream, and the gravity weighing on my shoulders pressed my back even closer to the nickel-plated bar. However, my forgetfulness didn't bother me in the least. I could bring the money to school tomorrow as well, and there was no one in the house who would steal it. Besides mother, there was only my old nurse Stepanida, who had been part of the household more than twenty years and lived in the apartment as a servant—and her sole weakness, perhaps even passion, was her constant and noisy whispering, like the cracking of sunflower seeds, with the aid of which (and for lack of companions) she carried on long conversations with herself, and at times even arguments, often interrupting herself with loudly voiced exclamations such as "Well, yes!" or "Of course!" or "What nonsense!" When I got to school, I completely forgot the envelope. That day I had not thoroughly studied my lessons (which, by the way, did not happen often at all), and so I had to prepare them partly during recess, and even partly while the teacher was in the classroom. This burning state of anxious attention, during which I assimilated everything with such ease (although with the same ease I'd forget it all the next day), greatly favored the exclusion of everything extraneous from my memory. Only when the long recess had begun, when, because of the cold but dry and sunny weather, they let all of us outside and I saw my mother on the lower landing of the staircase, did I recall the envelope and realize that, apparently because she couldn't bear to leave it there, she had brought it with her. My mother stood alone on one side, in her moth-eaten fur coat and silly hood, with strands of her gray hair hanging out (she was then already fifty-seven) and with noticeable anxiety, which somehow intensified her already pitiful exterior. She peered helplessly at the crowd of high school students running past, several of whom glanced at her with a smirk and said something to each other. As I approached, I had the urge to slip by unnoticed, but my mother, catching sight of me and immediately lighting up with an affectionate smile, not gay but resigned, called to me—and I, although I was terribly embarrassed in front of my classmates, went up to her. "Vadichka, my dear boy," she began in an elderly, dull voice, handing me the envelope and with her small, yellowish hand touching the button of my overcoat timidly, as though she'd been scalded. "You forgot the money, dear boy, and I thought you'd be frightened, so here—I have brought it." Having said this, she looked at me as if begging for charity. But in my rage over the shame done to me, I countered in a hateful whisper that these silly displays of affection were not proper for us in public, and that if she was so unable to bear it and just had to bring the money, then she should pay it herself. My mother stood quietly, listening without a word, her tender old eyes lowered guiltily and mournfully—and I, after running down the already deserted staircase and opening the tightly shut door which noisily sucked in air, turned and looked at my mother. I did this not from the slightest twinge of compassion, but wholly from fear that she would burst into tears in such an inappropriate place. Mother was still standing on the upper landing; sadly bowing her ugly head, she followed me with her gaze. When she noticed that I was looking at her, she waved her hand and the envelope, like they do at train stations. This movement, so young and vibrant, showed even more vividly how old, ragged, and pitiful she was.

Outside, several of my classmates came up to me. One asked, who was that clown in the skirt I'd just been speaking to. Laughing gaily, I replied that she was an impoverished governess, that she'd come to me with letters of recommendation, and that, if they wished, I'd introduce them to her: they could court her not without "success." After I'd said this, not so much because of the words I'd spoken as from the responsive laughter, I felt that *this* was too much, even for me, and that saying this had really been uncalled for. When she had paid the money, my mother came out and passed along the small asphalt path to the gates, looking at no one, walking hunched over, as if attempting to shrink even smaller, and as quickly as she could, tapping her worn-down, completely crooked heels. I felt anguish for her in my heart.

This anguish, which so deeply inflamed me for the first instant, lasted a very short time. Moreover, its disappearance was rather distinct, and so my

281

full recovery from this pain occurred in two phases, as it were. When, returning from school, I walked into the entry hall and passed along the narrow corridor of our poor, small apartment, smelling pungently of the kitchen, to my room, the anguish, though it had already ceased to hurt me, still somehow reminded me that it had hurt an hour before. And later, when I went into the dining room and sat at the table, and before me sat my mother ladling the soup, not only did this pain no longer bother me, but I couldn't even imagine that such anguish could have troubled me in the first place.

But as soon as I felt relieved, a multitude of malicious considerations began to upset me: that such an old lady should understand that she actually disgraced me with her clothing; that there was no excuse for her to come shuffling into the school with that envelope; that she forced me to lie, and that she deprived me of the possibility of inviting my classmates over. I watched her eating soup; I observed how, while lifting the spoon with her trembling hand, she spilled part of it back into the bowl. I looked at her yellow cheeks, her nose reddening from the hot soup; I saw how after each gulp she licked the grease off her lips with her whitish tongue, and I sharply and keenly loathed her. Sensing that I was watching her, mother as usual glanced at me tenderly with her fading brown eyes, put down her spoon, and, as if compelled by her own glance to say at least something, asked: "Is it delicious?" She said "delicious" with a childish coyness, while shaking her small gray head at me with a questioning affirmation. "Dee-lish-us," I repeated, neither affirming nor denying, but merely mimicking her. I pronounced this "dee-lish-us" with a disgusting grimace, as if I would at that very moment vomit, and our glances—mine cold and hateful; hers warm, revealing her innermost self, and loving—met and merged. This lasted for a long time; I distinctly saw how the expression in her kind eyes grew dim, becoming bewildered and then sorrowful. But the more apparent my victory became, the less perceptible and comprehensible seemed my feeling of hatred toward this loving and aged person by whose destruction this victory was achieved. This is probably why it was I who couldn't endure this any longer, and I was the first to lower my eyes, pick up a spoon, and begin to eat. But when I again raised my head, having calmed down inside and wishing to say something just for the sake of conversation, I could no longer speak. Involuntarily I jumped up from the table. One of my mother's hands lay on the tablecloth holding a spoonful of soup. Her other elbow was propped on the table, and on the palm of that hand she had lain her head. Her thin lips had stretched across her cheeks, distorting her face. From the brown sockets of her closed eyes tears flowed, like fans accentuating her wrinkles. There was so much defenselessness in her small, yellow, aged head, so much forgiving yet bitter sorrow, and so much hopelessness from that vile old age which had made her now useless to anyone. Though still frowning at her, I said suspiciously, in a rude voice, "Don't weep," "Here, stop it," "You've got no cause." I actually wanted to add "Dear Mama" and perhaps even go to her and kiss her, when at that very moment my nurse, balancing herself on one felt shoe, burst with the other one through the door and carried in the second course. I don't know for whose benefit or why, but right at this moment I banged the plate with my fist. Absolutely convinced of the correctness of my actions in this case—by the pain of my wounded hand and my trousers covered with soup; the justification for which was somehow vaguely strengthened by my extreme fear of my nurse—and cursing threateningly, I went to my room.

Soon after this my mother got dressed, went somewhere, and returned only just before nightfall. Having heard her clatter straight from the entrance hall along the corridor to my door, knock, and ask, "May I?" I rushed to my small writing table, quickly opened a book, and, with my back toward the door, said in a bored tone, "Come in." Crossing the room and hesitantly approaching me from the side, while I, seemingly engrossed in my book, noticed that she was still wearing her fur coat and her silly black hood, my mother pulled her hand out from under her arm and put two crumpled (as if in their shame they wished to make themselves look smaller) five-ruble notes on my desk. Then, patting my hand with her gnarled little hand, she said softly, "Please forgive me, my son. You're good, I know." And she stroked my hair and hesitated for a moment, as if she wanted to say something more. But saying nothing, my mother tiptoed out, ever so quietly closing the door behind her.

2.

Soon after this I fell ill. My first rather large fright was, however, immediately calmed by the businesslike gaiety of the doctor, whose address I had chosen at random from among the advertisements for specialists in venereal diseases, which filled practically an entire page in the newspaper. Examining me, he looked exactly like our teacher of literature when he had just received an unexpectedly good answer from a really poor student—he widened his eyes in respectful amazement. Then, slapping me on the shoulder, he added in a tone not of consolation but of calm certainty in his ability, "Don't fret, my young man; in a month we'll have you all fixed up."

When he had washed his hands, written the prescriptions, given me the necessary instructions, and ignored the ruble coin I had put down awkwardly askew, which therefore rolled with increasing velocity and finally clattered as it came to rest on the glass-topped desk, this doctor, deliciously picking his nose, dismissed me, warning meanwhile with an uncharacteristically gloomy concern that the speed of my recovery, as well as my recovery in general, depended entirely on the faithfulness of my visits, and that the best thing would be for me to come daily.

Despite the fact that I soon found out that these daily visits did not seem the least bit necessary, and that the doctor had the usual desire to increase the jingling of my rubles in his office, I nevertheless went to him every day— simply because it gave me pleasure. There was in this squat-legged, rotund little man, in his small, succulent bass voice that sounded as if he'd eaten something delicious, in the folds of his greasy neck, which reminded me of bicycle tires stacked on top of each other, in his gay and cunning little eyes, and generally in his whole demeanor toward me, something comically praiseworthy and approving, and in addition something hard to capture, but pleasantly flattering. This was the first time that a man of years, and consequently "an adult," saw and understood me from exactly that perspective in which I wished to present myself. I went to him daily, not because of my illness, but because of the man himself; not as a doctor, but as a friend. The first time I even awaited the appointed hour with impatience, dressing for the occasion as for a ball, in a new double-breasted jacket, trousers, and patent leather lofers.

In those days, wishing to establish a reputation as an erotic *Wunderkind*,* I related the nature of my illness in class (I said that the disease had been cured, when at the time it had only just begun). In those days I was totally confident that, having made known such a thing, I had gained greatly in stature in the eyes of those around me. In those days I committed a terrible act, the result of which was a crippled human life, and perhaps even death.

About two weeks later, the outer signs of the disease had subsided, though I knew very well that I was still infected. I went outside, intending to take a walk or go to the cinema. It was an evening in the middle of November—that amazing time of year. The first fluffy snow slowly fell over Moscow, like splinters of marble in blue water. The roofs of the houses and the boulevard flowerbeds swelled like light blue sails. Hooves didn't clop, wheels didn't clatter, and in the calmed city the squeaky-clean bells of the trams excited visions of spring. In an alley I overtook a girl who had been strolling in front of me. I overtook her not because I wanted to, but simply because I was walking faster than she. But as I came abreast of her and was passing, I fell into some deep snow—she looked around, and our glances met, our eyes smiled. On such a warm Moscow evening, with the first snowfall, when one's cheeks are berryred, and the wires are like gray steel cables in the sky; on such an evening, where could one get the strength and sullenness to walk away silently, never to meet one another again?

I asked her name and where she was going. Her name was Zinochka and she wasn't going anywhere in particular, "just out walking." At the next corner stood a trotter; the sledge was huge, shaped like a wineglass, and the gigantic horse was covered with a white horsecloth. I offered a ride; Zinochka, flashing her eyes at me, her lips forming a button, nodded again and again, like a child. The cabby, with his side facing us, had dived into the fore-carriage, which was shaped like a question mark. But when we came up to him he came alive a bit; following us with his eyes, as if aiming at a moving target, he shouted out hoarsely, "Please, please, I'll drive you." Seeing that

*a child prodigy

he'd made a hit and that it was necessary to retrieve his game, he slipped out of the sledge. One-legged, green, and majestically huge, in white gloves the size of a child's hat and in a cut-off Onegin-like top hat complete with a buckle, he approached us and added, "Would you like to drive with a frisky one, sir?"

Then began my agony. To go to Petrovsky Park and back into the city he wanted ten rubles. Though this "sir" had in his pocket five and a half in all, in those years I would have ignored that fact and gotten in, considering any swindle less shameful than the necessity of haggling with a cabdriver in the presence of a lady. But Zinochka saved the situation. Screwing up her little eyes in outrage, she firmly informed him that that was an unheard of price and that I wouldn't dare to give him more than five rubles. While saying this, she took me by the hand and dragged me forward. She pulled me away, and I, though moving, resisted slightly, as though with this resistance taking the guilt from myself and transferring the full embarrassment of the situation onto her. It looked as if it didn't matter to me and as if I was ready to pay, whatever the price.

Having gone about twenty steps, Zinochka glanced past my shoulder with the stealth of a robber. Noticing that the cloth was being quickly taken off the horse, she nearly squealed with delight. Turning in front of me and standing on her tiptoes, she whispered triumphantly, "He's agreed, he's agreed" (she began to clap noiselessly), "he'll give us the ride right away. Now see how clever I am" (she kept trying to look me in the eyes), "see, it's true, aha!"

This "aha" sounded very pleasant to me. It seemed as though I was an elegant debaucher, rich and profligate, whereas she, an unfortunate and impoverished young girl, controlled me in my extravagance, certainly not because these expenditures were beyond my means, but merely because, in the narrow perspective of her poverty, she—poor little thing—could not comprehend the admissibility of such expenditures.

At the next intersection the cabby caught up with us, passed us, and, restraining the lunging trotter by pulling the reins like a rudder, right and left, and leaning to the back of the sleigh, he unfastened the sleigh robe. Seating Zinochka and slowly (although I wanted to hurry) going to the other side, I climbed into the high and very narrow seat. After placing the tight velvet loop over the metal hook, embracing Zinochka, and firmly—as if I intended to fight someone—tugging at the peak of my cap, I said haughtily, "Drive on!"

A lazy smacking sound resounded, the horse barely tugged, the sledge slowly glided along, and I still felt everything trembling inside me from this coachman's mockery. But when after two turns we'd emerged at Tverskaya-Yamskaya, the cabby suddenly tightened the reins and shouted an "e-e-e-ehp," during which the sharp and steel-like "eh" piercingly rose upward before it struck against the soft obstruction of the "p" which halted its progress. The sledge lurched frighteningly; we were thrown backward with our knees up in the air and then instantly forward with our faces in the quilted backing before us. The whole street then rushed toward us; yet snowy ropes lashed our cheeks, our eyes. A few times trams we had barely missed signaled at us, and again "ep, ep," but severely and abruptly like a whip, and then a joyfully evil bleating, "baloooy," and the black flashes of the oncoming sledges with the torturing possibility of an unexpected shaft in the chops, and clop, clop, clop, the spurts of snow from the hooves rang out against the metal front of the carriage, and the sledge trembled, and our hearts trembled, too. "Ah, how wonderful," beside me whispered a childlike, ecstatic voice in the wet, lashing sleet. "Ah, how marvelous, how marvelous!" And to me it seemed "marvelous," too. Only as always, with all my strength, I resisted and opposed this delight which had burst open in me.

When we had passed Yar and the tram station tower, the boarded-up confectionery stand became visible. At the crossing to the circle the cabby laid his back toward us and, tightly reining in his horse, abruptly sang out in a gentle, womanish voice, "pr . . . , pr . . . , pr . . ." We entered the crossing at a walk. The snow stopped right at that moment and listlessly floated around the single yellow lantern, but it didn't fall to the ground; it was as if someone was shaking out feathers over there. Beyond the lantern in the black darkness stood a signpost and next to it a fist with pointing finger and a cuff with a part of the sleeve, crookedly nailed to the tree. A crow was walking along the finger, scattering snow.

I asked Zinochka if she wasn't cold. "I feel marvelous," she said, "it's true, this is marvelous, huh? Here, take and warm my hands." I unglued my arm, which was aching at the shoulder, from her waist. Water flowed from the peak of my cap onto my cheek and down my collar; our faces were wet; our chins and cheeks were so stiff from the frost that we had to talk with our faces immobile; our eyebrows and eyelashes were glued with frozen icicles; our shoulders, sleeves, chests, and lap robe were covered with an icy crackling crust; steam rose from us and the horse as if everything were boiling inside us, and Zinochka's cheeks looked as if someone had pasted red apple peels on them. On the deserted circle everything was white and light blue, and in this white and blue, in their napthalene-like glistening, in this motionless, almost indoor, silence, I saw my anguish. I remembered that in several minutes we would be in the city, that I'd have to get out of the sledge, go home, bother with my filthy disease, and tomorrow get up in the dark. It all ceased being marvelous for me.

This was the strange thing about my life. While experiencing happiness, it was enough simply to think about the brevity of this happiness for it to end exactly at that moment. The sensation of happiness would end not because the exterior circumstances which had given rise to this happiness had abruptly ceased, but from the mere realization that these exterior circumstances would very soon and inevitably cease. As soon as this realization came to me, at that very moment my happiness was already gone; whereas the exterior circumstances which had created this happiness, and which were not yet destroyed, were now only irritating. By the time we had driven out of the circle back to the highway, I already wanted only one thing—to be in the city as quickly as possible, to get out of the sledge and pay.

Driving back was cold and boring. But when we'd reached Strastnoy the cabbie, turning around, asked whether we wanted to go farther and, if so, where. I, glancing questioningly at Zinochka, suddenly felt my heart stand sweetly still (as it customarily did at such times). Zinochka looked not at my eyes, but at my lips, with that fierce, senseless gaze, the meaning of which I knew well. Getting up, my knees trembled with happiness. I whispered into the ear of the cabbie that he should take us to the Vinogradov.

It would be entirely false to say that, during the several minutes it took to get to the house of our rendezvous, I was totally undisturbed by the fact that I intended to infect Zinochka. Pressing her to me, this was actually the only thing I constantly thought about; but while thinking of this, I was horrified not by my own sense of responsibility, but only by the unpleasantness which others could heap upon me for such an act. However, as almost always happens in such situations, my dread did not prevent me in the least from the accomplishment of the deed, but only prompted me to carry it out so that no one would discover the culprit.

When the sledge had stopped at a reddish house with caulked windows, I asked the cabbie to drive inside. In order to get through the gates, the sledge had to be backed toward the boulevard fence; but when we were already inside the gates, the hissing runners cut into the asphalt, and the sledge stopped across the sidewalk. During these few seconds while the horse was stuck and then with a jerk pulled us into the courtyard, the passersby who happened to be there walked around the sledge and looked us over curiously. Two even stopped, and this visibly affected Zinochka. She somehow became instantly aloof, removed, and upset as if offended.

After getting out of the sledge, Zinochka walked away into a dark corner of the yard. I, settling accounts with the cabbie (who stubbornly demanded a tip), recalled unpleasantly that I had only two and a half rubles left, and that if the cheap rooms were occupied I might be short fifty kopecks. When I'd paid the cabbie and approached Zinochka, I already sensed, by the way she repeatedly tugged at her bag and anxiously shrugged her small shoulders, that right now she wouldn't budge from that spot. The cabbie had already left, and from the steeply turned sledge there remained a flattened circle. The two curious passersby who had stopped at our arrival had now walked into the yard and were standing at a distance, watching us. I stood with my back to them so Zinochka wouldn't see them, embracing her small shoulders and calling her my tiny one, my little one, my baby girl. I spoke words to her which would have been totally devoid of meaning if they had not been pronounced in an unctuous voice, the sound of which somehow became, of itself, sweet like syrup. Sensing that she would submit, that she was becoming the former Zinochka—though not the one who so passionately (as it seemed to me) had gazed at me on Strastnoy, but the one who had whispered in the park, "Marvelous, ah, how marvelous!"—I clumsily and confusedly began to explain to her that I had in my pocket a whole hundred-ruble note; that they wouldn't make change here; that I needed only fifty kopecks; that I'd return them to her in a few minutes; that. . . . But Zinochka, not allowing me to finish, with frightening speed opened her little old imitation alligator bag, pulled out her tiny change purse, and dumped the contents into my palm. I saw a small pile of silver five-kopeck coins, the kind that were apparently somewhat rare, and cast a questioning glance. "There are exactly ten of them," she said reassuring. Then squirming pitifully, as if in explanation, she added with embarrassment, "I've been collecting them for a very long time; it's said they bring good luck." "But little one," I uttered in noble confusion, "spending these would be a shame. Take them back, I'll make do without." But Zinochka, growing really angry now, was frowning from the effort of shutting my palm with her fragile hands. "You must take them," she said. "You must. You'll offend me."

Will she go or not? will she go or refuse? That was the only point that troubled my thoughts, my emotions, my entire being as I nonchalantly led Zinochka to the hotel entrance. She took the first step and stopped, as if regaining her senses. In anguish she glanced at the open gates where those two passersby stood, just like obstructing guards. Then, as if in parting, she looked at me and smiled pitifully. Lowering her head and sort of hunching over, she covered her face with her hands. Stepping higher, I grasped her arm right under the armpit, pulled her up the stairs, and pushed my way through the door obligingly held by the doorman.

When we reappeared in an hour or so, while still in the yard I asked Zinochka which way she had to go. Then I could say my house was in the other direction and part with her forever right there at the gates. That's what I always did when I left the Vinogradov.

But though I was usually motivated to part thus by a feeling of satiated boredom and sometimes even disgust—emotions which (though I already knew I'd regret them in a day) prevented me from believing that tomorrow I might again desire this young girl—now, sending Zinochka off, I felt only chagrin.

I felt chagrin because, in that room behind the partition, the Zinochka whom I had now infected did not fulfill my hopes. She continued to be exactly as delighted and sexless as she was when she had said, "Ah, how marvelous!" Undressed, she stroked my cheeks, repeating, "Ah, you're my beloved, you're my little sweety pie!" in a voice which rang with childlike, innocent tenderness. And this tenderness—not coquettish, but spiritual— embarrassed me and prevented me from presenting myself as *totally*, as they say, shameless. (Although even this is inaccurate, for the primary and fervent charm of human depravity is the victory over shame, and not the absence of it.) Although not realizing it herself, Zinochka prevented the beast from overcoming the man; so now, experiencing frustration and chagrin, I labeled all the foregoing with one word: "pointless." I had pointlessly infected this silly girl. I realized and felt this, but I understood and felt this as "pointless" only because it was as if I had consummated an act not only not terrible, but which, on the contrary, seemed to me a sacrifice—something I had offered expecting pleasure in return, and which indeed I had not received.

Only while standing at the gates when Zinochka carefully tucked away the scrap of paper with my supposed name and first telephone number; only when, after she'd thanked me and said goodbye, Zinochka started to walk away—yes, only then did a voice speak within me. (But not that self-confident and insolent one with which, lounging on the couch, I would imagine myself deliberately addressing the outer world; rather, a quiet and gentle one, which I used for conversing with and addressing only myself.) "Ah, you," this voice said bitterly, "you destroyed this silly girl. Look, over there, she's walking there, that baby. And remember how she said, 'Ah, you're my beloved!' Why did you destroy her? What had she done to you? You miserable creature!"

It was an amazing thing—that figure receding into the distance, the figure of an unjustly insulted person departing forever. There was in her a certain human impotence, a certain pitiful weakness which begged forgiveness for itself, which called out, which tugged at you. There was in that figure receding into the distance something reminding one of injustices and insults one had to speak of once more, of someone to whom one had to turn once more in farewell, and it was necessary to do this quickly, immediately, for the person was leaving forever, and much pain would remain within her which would continue to cause torment, and perhaps would even prevent one from sleeping at night in one's declining years. Snow was falling again, but now it was dry and cold; the wind caused the street lamp to flicker, and along the boulevard the shadows of the trees wagged in a friendly way, like tails. Zinochka had long since turned the corner; Zinochka was long since out of sight, yet again and again I recaptured her in my imagination, let her go to the corner, and watched her receding figure; and again, for some reason with her back toward me, she would fly back to me. Finally, while unconsciously slipping my hand into my pocket, I jingled her unused ten kopecks' worth of silver coins, and at that moment recalled her lips and her childish voice when she had said, "I've been collecting them a long time; they say, they're good luck." It was like a lash across my wicked heart, a lash which forced me to run, to run after Zinochka, to run across the deep snow in the sort of enervating tearfulness you feel running after the last train as it is already moving, and as you run, you know and you feel that you'll never catch it.

That night I wandered along the boulevards for a long time afterward; that night I swore to myself that I would save Zinochka's five-kopeck silver coins till the end of my life. I never again met Zinochka. Moscow is large and has many people.

3.

The main leaders of our class were Stein, Egorov, and, as I wished to appear then, I myself.

I was friendly with Stein, all the while sensing with a constant uneasiness that I would instantly loathe him the moment I ceased to force this friendship within myself. Towheaded, without any eyebrows, and already balding, Stein was the son of a wealthy Jewish furrier and was the best student in the class. The teachers very seldom called on him, having over the years ascertained that his knowledge was irreproachable. But when the teacher, after glancing at the class rosters, said "Shshshtein," the whole class fell silent as though expecting something special. Stein, tearing himself from the desk as noisily as if someone were holding him there, quickly stepped out of the row of desks and, practically toppling over on his long, skinny legs, stopped far from the rostrum. He stood slanting so awkwardly toward the floor that, had a straight line been extended upward from his toes, it would have come out the top of his narrow skinny shoulders, on which he had reverentially folded his huge white hands. Standing slouched with all his weight on one foot, the toe of the other one hardly touching the floor (as if this leg was shorter), like a peasant woman, clumsily pretentious, but not at all comical, his voice indicated—in his response—a haste which seemed to hurl him forward, as though from the sheer abundance of his knowledge, and, while listening to the questions put to him, a careless condescension. He would brilliantly drone through his answer, expecting a favorable "sit down," and he always tried to look past the class out the window, while seeming to chew or whisper something. Then, rushing across the slippery parquet just as he had approached, he'd quickly return to his seat, noisily seat himself, ignoring everyone, and immediately begin to write something or to rummage in his desk until the class's general attention was attracted to the next student called on.

When anything funny was said during breaks and the laughter reached Stein at his desk, he would toss back his head, close his eyes, and wrinkle his face, to indicate how he suffered from this laughter—meanwhile banging his fist very rapidly on the desk, as if this would suppress the laughter inside him. But that laughter simply smothered him—his lips were compressed and emitted not a single sound. Then, waiting for the others to laugh themselves out, he would open his eyes, wipe them with his handkerchief, and say, "oofff."

His hobbies (which he told us about) were the ballet and the "house" of Maria Ivanovna in Kosoy Alley. His favorite saying was that "One must be a European." He used this expression constantly, whether or not it was pertinent. "One must be a European," he'd say, arriving and by his watch indicating that he'd come precisely one minute before the reading for prayers. "One must be a European," he'd say, when telling us he'd attended the ballet the night before and sat in an expensive theatre box. "One must be a European," he'd add, hinting that after the ballet he had gone to Maria Ivanovna's. Only later, when Egorov really began to plague him about it, did Stein lose interest in his favorite expression.

Egorov was also wealthy. He was the son of a Kazan' timber merchant, very well groomed and perfumed, with a very straight white part all the way to his neck through yellow hair slick and gleaming like polished wood which, had it come unglued, would have come off in one complete layer. He would have been handsome if only his round and watery eyes—the glassy eyes of a bird—did not take on an expression of fear and amazement whenever his face turned serious. During his first months in high school, when Egorov was still something of a hick, even calling himself Yagorushka, someone nicknamed him Yag for short, and this nickname remained with him.

He was already fourteen when he was brought to Moscow, and was therefore assigned automatically to the fourth-year class in our high school. The supervisor brought him to us in the morning even before the lessons began, and immediately proposed that he read the prayer while twenty-five pairs of attentive eyes stared fixedly at him, anxiously seeking any food for ridicule.

Usually the prayer was read in a monotonous patter, to which we responded with the customary necessity of rising, standing for half a minute, and, after rattling our desks, sitting down. Yag, however, began to recite the prayer distinctly and with unnatural emotion, while crossing himself (unlike all the others, who would merely wave a fly from their noses, so to speak). He spoke fervently, closing his eyes, while bowing theatrically—and again throwing back his head, his insipid eyes sought the classroom icon hanging high on the wall. Just then the chuckles became a chorus of laughter, except for Yag, who, having broken off the words of the prayer, looked at all of us with his chicken-like, frighteningly amazed expression. The class preceptor, however, was completely unnerved; he shouted at Yag and all of us that, if anything like this happened from now on, he would take the matter to the council. Only a week later, when we all learned that Yag was from a very religious family, a family of former Old Believers, one day after classes were over the same class preceptor, blushing like a young fellow although already an elderly man, suddenly went up to Yag and, taking his hand and looking aside, haltingly said, "Egorov, please forgive me." Saying nothing more, he quickly jerked away his hand and, slinking down the corridor, he made motions with his hands as if he were snatching something from the ceiling and harshly hurling it to the floor. Yag walked to the window and, standing with his back toward us for a long time, blew his nose.

But this was only at first. In the more advanced classes Yag greatly deteriorated (in the headmaster's words), and began to drink heavily and frequently. Upon coming to class in the morning he made a deliberate circle, went up to the desk occupied by Stein, and, having belched threateningly, fanned all of it, like smoke from an expensive cigar, toward Stein's nose. "One must be a European," he explained to the onlookers. Although Yag lived alone in Moscow, rented expensive quarters in a mansion, apparently received a great deal of money from home, and was often seen riding in cabs with women, he nevertheless studied regularly and quite thoroughly and was considered among the best students; only a very few were aware that he used a tutor for practically all his subjects.

One could say that the rest of the class was attracted to us three—Stein, Yag, and me, the head guys (as we were known)—like a horseshoe set against a magnetized bar is attracted by its two ends. At one of its ends the horseshoe was joined to us by its very best pupil; receding along the horseshoe's perimeter in accordance with the students' falling grades, then again returning, it rejoined us with its other end, at which was the very worst student and loafer. We head guys combined the basic traits of both the former and the latter—though having the grades of the best, we were always considered by the administration in the same category as the worst.

From the best of the students Eisenberg was attracted to us. From the worst of the loafers—Takadzhiev.

Eisenberg (or, as he was called, "the meek one") was a modest, very studious and very shy Jewish boy. He had an odd habit: before he'd say anything or answer a question, he would swallow his saliva, help it along by inclining his head, and, when he had finished swallowing, say "mte." Everyone considered it a must to taunt him about his sexual abstinence (although no one could truly establish the veracity of this abstinence, he himself confirming it least of all). Often during recesses a crowd would surround him, demanding, "Well, Eisenberg, show us your latest lover," and attentively examine the palms of his hands.

When Eisenberg spoke with any of us, he unfailingly tilted his head down and to the side, cast his nettle-colored eyes away, and covered his mouth with his hand.

Takadzhiev was the oldest and tallest in the class. This Armenian enjoyed universal admiration for his amazing ability to transfer the butt of a joke from himself entirely to whatever nasty grade he had received. Unlike the others, he never felt any malice toward the teacher, but enjoyed the joke himself more than anyone else. Like Stein, he had his own favorite little saying, which had arisen in the following circumstances. Once, during the distribution of our corrected notebooks, the literature teacher, a good-natured scholar named Semyonov, while handing Takadzhiev his notebook and slyly casting daggers with his small eyes, explained that although the composition was excellently written and there was merely one insignificant error in the composition—a misplaced comma—he, Semyonov, was compelled by precisely that paltry error to fail Takadzhiev. The reason for such an (at first glance) unfair grade was apparent in the fact that Takadzhiev's composition coincided word for word with Eisenberg's composition; likewise—and this was especially mysterious—the misplaced commas coincided. Adding his favorite expression, "A falcon is recognized by his flight, and a brat by his snivels," Semyonov gave Takadzhiev his notebook. But even after receiving his notebook, Takadzhiev continued to stand at the rostrum. He once again asked Semyonov—Was it possible that he had understood him? And how was it conceivable that these misplaced commas should coincide so completely? Receiving Eisenberg's notebook for comparison, he leafed through for a long time; with ever-growing amazement on his face he compared something, searched it through, and finally—now in utter disbelief—first glancing at us, all ready to burst into laughter, he turned his eyes very slowly, bulging with amazement, and looked straight at Semyonov. "Whot a clearin-cidence," he whispered tragically, shrugged his shoulders, and lowered the corners of his lips. The failure was assigned, the price was, as it were, paid; and Takadzhiev, who actually had an excellent command of Russian, had simply used this instance to amuse his friends, himself, and even the literature instructor, who, despite the cruel severity of his grades, loved to laugh.

Such were the points of our contact with the ends of the class horseshoe, along which all the remaining students seemed more distant and therefore lackluster in accordance with their position in relation to the center of the horseshoe, as a result of the old struggle between twos and threes.[1] There in the far-off, unfamiliar milieu was Vasily Burkevits, a short, pimply, and shaggy fellow. At that time an event occurred involving him, which was extremely unusual for the firmly and peacefully regulated life of our old high school.

4.

We were in the fifth class, during the German lesson taught by Volkman, a completely bald fellow with a red face and a white Mazepa-like moustache with reddish hairs in it. At first he questioned Burkevits (he always called him Burkewitz) from his seat, but when someone kept prompting him, Volkman got angry. The carrot color of his face immediately became beet-red, and after ordering Burkevits to leave his seat and stand at the board, growling "*Verdammte Bummelei*,"† he tugged himself lovingly by the brake of his ill will, his whitish-red moustache. Standing at the board, Burkevits was just about to answer, when suddenly something exceedingly unpleasant happened to him. He sneezed, but sneezed so unexpectedly that the spray flew out of his nose and, dangling, hung practically to his waist. Everyone chuckled.

"*Was ist denn da wieder los?*"‡ Volkman asked and, as he turned around and

† damned lounging around
‡ Now, what is the matter?

saw, added, *"Na, ich danke."* § Burkevits, blushing in embarrassment and then immediately turning pale to the point of greenness, fumbled in his pockets with trembling hands. But no handkerchief was procured. "My dear friend, you ought to pluck out your oysters," remarked Yag, "God is kind, but we still have to eat today." "Whot a clearincidence," exclaimed Takadzhiev. The whole class was already roaring with laughter, and Burkevits, confused and terribly pitiful, ran out into the hall. Volkman, banging his pencil on the table, kept shouting, *"Rrruhe,"*‖ but in the general clamor all that was heard was the growl of the first letter—a sound, amazingly illustrating the expression of his eyes, which bulged so that we experienced terror not so much for ourselves as for Volkman himself.

The next day, however, when we came to the German lesson, Volkman, this time being obviously well disposed and, having decided to have a little laugh, again called on Burkevits. *"Burkewitz! Uebersetzen Sie weiter,"*# he ordered, adding with feigned terror, *"aber selbstverständlich nur im Falle, wenn Sie heut 'n Taschentuch besitzen."***

What was wonderful about Volkman was that only by knowing the preceding events could one have guessed whether he was coughing or laughing. Now—catching sight of how, after he had uttered those words he opened his mouth wide and emitted from it a gurgling, hoarse, and bubbling stream; how the little reddish tips of his moustache rose slightly as if a terrific wind were blowing out of his mouth, and how a lavender vein swelled as thick as a pencil on his now raspberry-red bald spot—the whole class began to laugh wildly and uncontrollably. Stein, his head thrown back with his eyes shut tight in agony, smartly rapped his white fist against the desk. Only after everyone had calmed down did he wipe his eyes and emit his "oofff."

Only several months later did we realize to what extent this laughter had been cruel, unjust, and inappropriate.

The fact was that when this unpleasantness happened to Burkevits, he didn't return to class, but on the following day he appeared with an unfamiliar, wooden face. From that day on the class ceased to exist for him; it was as if he'd buried us. Probably we too would have forgotten him a short while later, if in another week both we and the teachers had not noticed something exceedingly odd.

This oddity consisted in the fact that Burkevits, the Burkevits who always got twos and threes, suddenly began unexpectedly and persistently to move away from the center of the class horseshoe—at first very slowly, then more and more quickly, to move along it in the direction of Eisenberg and Stein.

At first this migration occurred slowly and with difficulty. It goes without

§Well, no thank you.
‖Qui-et
#Continue translating
**But only in that instance that you happen to have a handkerchief today.

saying that even in his marking system a teacher is usually guided not so much by the knowledge a student exhibits at the moment he is called on, as by the reputation for knowledge which that student has built for himself over the years. Occasionally, although very seldom, the individual answers of Stein or Eisenberg would be so weak that, had Takadzhiev been in their place, he would have received an unconditional three. But since this was Stein or Eisenberg, recommended by years of fives, the teachers, though perhaps with reluctance, would give a five. To accuse the teachers of unfairness in this would be just as fair as to accuse the entire world of unfairness. For it's already happened quite often that recommended celebrities, these "A" students of the fine arts, have received from their critics rapturous reviews even for works so weak and careless that, had they been produced by some other unknown, given even the best of circumstances, they would have been ranked at the level of Takadzhiev's three. Burkevits' main difficulty was not his anonymity, but something much worse: his reputation had settled over the years at the average three level, and now this reputation for mediocrity greatly hindered his progress and stood before him like an indestructible wall.

But, of course, all this was only for a short while. In general, the psychology of the five-point system was already such that moving from a three to a four was like swimming across an ocean, but jumping from a four to a five was just a short hop. Meanwhile Burkevits was pushing forward. Slowly but persistently, not giving an inch, he moved along the curve, closer and closer to Eisenberg, closer and closer to Stein. At the end of the school year (the story of the sneeze took place in January) he was already close to Eisenberg, although he was unable to draw abreast of him during this short time. But when, still with the exact same wooden face and bidding no one goodbye, Burkevits walked from the last examination into the cloak room, none of us ever supposed that we'd become witnesses to a difficult struggle, a struggle for supremacy, which would be set in motion from the very first days of the next school year. [. . .]

NOTE

1. Based on a five-point system, in which a five is the highest grade.

Boris Poplavsky (1903–1935)

Boris Yulianovich Poplavsky, one of the younger Russian poets in exile, created a sensation in the literary circles of Paris. He is remembered chiefly for the verse collections *Flagi: stikhotvoreniya* (Banners: Poems; Paris, 1931), *Snezhny chas* (A Snowy Hour; Paris, 1936), *V venke iz voska: chetvyortaya kniga stikhov* (In a Wreath of Wax: A Fourth Book of Poems; Paris, 1938), and *Dirizhabl' neizvestnogo napravleniya: stikhi 1924–1935* (The Dirigible of an Unknown Destination: Selected Poems 1924–1935; Paris, 1965); the last two books were published posthumously. Poplavsky's novel *Apollon Bezobrazov* (The Formless Apollo; *Numbers* nos. 2–3 [1930]) allegedly described the personality of Alexander Ginger. The two were great friends, although Poplavsky admired French culture, whereas Ginger was a confirmed Buddhist.

Russian readers in Paris were wonderstruck and carried away by Poplavsky's apocalyptic visions of perishing Europe and by his grotesque portrayal of a new, huge, and doomed Babylon—the clamorous Paris of sinister servants, beautiful ladies, portentous sunsets, and otherworldy music heard by a "dirty angel." Many saw Poplavsky as a Russian Rimbaud, a talented *poète maudit* who overpowered his listeners with tremendous imagination and delirious visions. He became the legendary hero of Russian Montparnasse; some were attracted by his vagaries, and others were repulsed. For he was at one and the same time a drug addict, a friend of criminals, and a mystic immersed in the works of Ste Thérèse and Jakob Boehme. He appeared in "Russian Paris" like a meteor, with some "fiery traces" noticeable in his poetry; however, the memory of his sensational appearance and disappearance has been clouded by the legend surrounding his bizarre, almost insane phantoms, a legend given credence by his poems (which resemble the spiritualistic record of a romantic visionary) and by *The Formless Apollo*, which today would be described as an "anti-novel." He was torn between debauchery and purity.

Poplavsky considered himself an heir to Blok's mystical poetry, to the verse of Lermontov and Pushkin, and to the prose of Rozanov and Dostoevsky. To a certain degree, he may have been right—if we add that there were also echoes of Mayakovsky in his verse. His main influences, in fact, came from Baudelaire, Nerval, Rimbaud, Laforgue, Apollinaire, and Breton. His craftsmanship, however, was deficient in many respects—monotonous rhythms, slipshod style, even vulgarisms in expression, stress on normally unstressed syllables, awkward rhymes, poor word choices, and other imperfections. On the other hand, his impetuous and boisterous verse contains dazzling flashes of genuine poetry. Poplavsky is an innovative poet because he enriched the poetic vocabulary, freed the language from its habitual associations, disrupted logical ties and sequences, and introduced new, bold, and unexpected metaphors. There is much music in his verse, in which he comments on his own existence; his poetry completes his dreams, thoughts, doubts, and spiritual transports. Freedom and whim—the two most characteristic traits of Poplavsky's poetry—impelled him to use airy and shining imagery.

Poplavsky has often been referred to as the "first and last Russian surrealist poet." In fact, he was fond of surrealistic images reminiscent of hallucinations. He liked to use metaphors formed from two or more contrasting concepts, rather than from existing analogies, and he often employed personal, accidental associations. Poplavsky captivated his audience, lovers of everything new and spectacular, with his "inimitable magic world" and with the basic melodiousness of his poems. As Adamovich remarked after the appearance of *Banners*, Poplavsky's "sentimental demonology"[1] charmed everyone, even though it was neither fully understood nor completely accepted. Gleb Struve is of the opinion that Poplavsky's surrealistic world is created by "unlawful means"[2] (namely, by borrowings from the paintings of Chagall) and that Poplavsky is actually not a musical but a visual poet. Like a painter, Poplavsky was keenly sensitive to visual detail; his poetry abounds in such images and colors as "a lilac skeleton," "dawn in her costume of crimson frills," "a sky-blue horse," or "the dark city flees to the green hills." But with his careless choice of words, banal meanings, half-formed images and rhythms, he often bore little resemblance to Blok or Rimbaud; rather, he might be compared to Igor' Severyanin and to Fofanov, with their *Effekthascherei* (stylistic adornments to cover up their stylistic deficiencies). Gleb Struve further maintains that Poplavsky's prose, which is lyrical and musical, is more successful than his poetry; it abounds in unique observations and appropriately selected words. Poplavsky reveals his visions and dreams more fully and with greater artistry in his fiction than in poetry. The atmosphere of Russian Montparnasse is forcefully conveyed, with its dominant mood—as in the "Parisian note" poetry—of complete and hopeless loneliness.[3] Poplavsky's prose displays many artistic defects—mainly because the historical scope of Western culture was alien to him, as was a sense of simplicity and sincerity. Nevertheless, *The Formless Apollo* is a curious experiment in Russian prose in Paris of the 1930's.

NOTES

1. "Literaturnye besedy," *Zveno* no. 4 (1928).
2. Gleb Struve, *Russkaya literatura v izgnanii*, p. 339.

3. For more information on Poplavsky, see Anthony Olcott's article "Poplavsky: the Heir Presumptive of Montparnasse," and Simon Karlinsky's miscellany "In Search of Poplavsky: A Collage," both in *The Bitter Air of Exile: Russian Writers in the West 1922–1972*, pp. 274–288 and 311–333, respectively.

POEMS

FROM: *V venke iz voska: chetvyortaya kniga stikhov* (In a Wreath of Wax: A Fourth Book of Poems).

You are sunstroke at midnight;
Without harm.
You are gray water in the sea,
You are not water.
You are incomprehensible noise in the house,
And I dance.
An incredibly painful dream.
You are a wheel:
It clatters over the stones on the roof,
Buzzes, like mice,
Slowly circles inside the flame,
Trembles in ice,
In silent depths of the water
You pass by,
And in the heights, in all the gardens,
In every form,
And for this there is no cure.
In sleep, in dreams,
A lilac skeleton, floating
And on the moon
Dancing to the quiet sounds
Of fatal waters.
And arm in arm I dance with him,
With death, and devil.

FROM: *Flagi: stikhotvoreniya* (Banners: Poems).

DOLOROSA

Dawn in her costume of crimson frills
Was out on the terrace in tears.

Evening, slender, in tails,
Hovered in vain.

But then above the lace of the grating
She rose to him; at once,
Emitting a short streetcar moan,
He flung down his greenish corpse.

Then into the streets, the square,
To the limpid gong of the corner clock,
A sky-blue horse rushed out,
A carriage of azure glass.

Loudly slamming the musical little door,
Autumn jumped out while still in motion,
Clasping her band to her ailing heart,
And screaming the scream of sinners in hell.

Responding from air and darkness,
Crowds of white roses began to float,
And winter, under Cancer's strange sign,
Came out in the sky to shower the frost.

And, dancing beneath the lantern ball,
Sagging into abysmal silence,
Death began singing all in vain,
Above the prostrate Madonna.

1926–27

FROM: *Dirizhabl' neizvestnogo napravleniya* (The Dirigible of an Unknown Destination).

MEMORY

In the forest there was the sound of garments falling
The sacred soul is in sick water
All naked, autumn bathed in the dew
All reflected, it quickly shut its eyes
In the forest an incredible noise in the water
The soul was in the azure and nowhere.

THE EVENING WALK

Above the statue the sunset held
Its rifle atilt. I watched from the boulevard.
A pair, exchanging greetings, walking toward me:
A poet's soul and, it must be, a demon.

They flowed into the café through the window.
The moon followed them, sprawling beside.
On an island, like vowels in a strophe,
People thronged, drawn by a parade.

The moon squatted like a soldier in need,
But, lo, the river's far bank is already up in the sky.
And welcoming, as always, a misfortune,
Seismographers have solved a brand new rebus.

Lightning fell, the billboard lit up in smoke,
Someone's daughter cried out insanely,
A shadow broke out of a storeroom to freedom.
And the twelfth night began.

The player piano of the soul
Is always ready to burst into a harsh tune.
So dance, you crowd of elect!
Crumble the lime in this subterranean crypt!

THE TEACHER

Who is your teacher of singing?
The one who walks in a circle.
Where have you seen him?
On the boundary of the eternal snow.
Why don't you wake him?
Because he would die.
Why don't you weep for him?
Because he—is I.

FROM: *The Anchor: An Anthology of Emigré Poetry.* "The Rose of Death" was first published in *The Link* no. 5, dated May 1, 1928.

THE ROSE OF DEATH

In a black park we'd meet the Spring,
The bow of a cheap violin would softly tell lies,
Death would descend atop a balloon,
Touching lovers on the shoulder.

The evening is rosy, the wind carries roses,
In the fields a poet is drawing a sketch.
The evening is rosy, the roses smell of death,
And green snow falls on the branches.

A dark breeze scatters the stars,
Nightingales are singing, echoing engines,
And in a stall above the green sea
Tuberculous gas is blazing.

Ships sail into the starry sky,
Spirits wave hankies from the bridge.
And glittering through the dark air,
A steam engine sings on the viaduct.

The dark city flees to the hills,
Night clatters at the dance hall,
And soldiers, quitting town,
Drink thick beer at the station.

Swinging low, brushing past souls,
The lunar globe floats over the puppet theatre,
And from the boulevard, to fragile organ music,
A carousel waves to the ladies.

And spring, flushing infinitely rosy,
Smiling and retiring to her fortress,
Opens her deep-blue fan
With a clear inscription: death.

THE FORMLESS APOLLO

CHAPTER ONE
which precedes the seduction

The rain fell unceasingly. It would drift away, then again come close to the earth; it gurgled; it gently rustled; it fell slowly, like snow, then pelted headlong in light gray waves, pressing against the glistening asphalt. It fell this same way on the roofs, the eaves, and the roofs' undulations; it flew into the most minute projections of the walls and floated for a long time to the bottom of enclosed courtyards, the existence of which had escaped many of the residents of the house. It fell as a man walks on snow, majestically and monotonously. It descended like a writer who has lost his appeal, then flew way up high above the world, like those irretrievable years when there are as yet no witnesses in a man's life.

A kind of intimacy arose among the drenched people gathered under the store awnings. They glanced at each other in an almost friendly way, but the rain would treacherously abate, and then they would part.

The rain fell in the same way in the public gardens and over the suburbs, and even where the outskirts ended and the real fields began—although that was somewhere inconceivably far, a place where, no matter how one tried, one would never arrive.

It felt as if rain were falling on the whole world, as if all the streets and all the passersby were united by its gray salty substance.

The horses were covered with splotchy blankets and, precisely as in ancient Rome, the poor scurried along, their heads covered with sacks.

On the side streets the streams washed away bus tickets and orange peels.

But the rain also fell on the flags of the palaces and on the Eiffel Tower.

The crude beauty of the universe seemed to melt and dissolve in it, as in the passage of time.

The periods of its swelling and subsiding were uniformly repeated; it endured and abided and seemed as dense as cloth.

But if one stares at the wallpaper in one's room for a long time without moving, or at the adjoining bluish wall on the other side of the yard, it suddenly strikes one that at a certain imperceptible moment twilight mingles with the rain, and the world, now washed out by the rain, is absorbed with redoubled speed and vanishes into the twilight.

Everything changes in the room on the top floor; the pale yellow glow of dusk dies abruptly, and the room becomes almost totally dark.

And then the edge of the sky again frees itself from the clouds, and a new white twilight illuminates the room.

Meanwhile time passes, and the workers return from their offices; far

302

below the street lights are lit, and their reflection shines transparently on the ceiling.

Things go on and time is hopelessly lost.

The huge cities continue to suck in and breathe out their human dust. Innumerable encounters of eyes occur, and certain of them always try to conquer, or else they surrender, look down, crawl past. No one dares approach anyone else, and thousands of dreams scatter in all directions.

Meanwhile the seasons change, and spring blossoms above the rooftops. Way up above the streets it warms the rosy squares of the chimneys and the delicate gray metallic surfaces, to which one clings so pleasantly in one's utter solitude, shutting one's eyes; or, finding a comfortable nook, reads books forbidden by one's parents.

High above the world, in the darkness of night, snow falls on the roofs. At first it is scarcely visible, then it accumulates, forming an even and monotonous presence. It darkens and melts. It disappears, never once seen by human eyes.

Then, when everything is almost brimming with snow, with a sudden unexpectedness and no period of transition, summer arrives.

Gigantic and azure, it majestically reveals itself and hangs above the flags of the public buildings, above the corpulent verdure of the boulevards, and above the dust and the touchingly tasteless suburban summer homes.

But in the interim there are still certain strange days, translucent and murky, full of voices and clouds. They shine in an unusual way and slowly, very slowly die out, reflecting on the rosy plaster of some remote little houses. And the trams somehow jangle curiously with a long drawn-out squeal, and the acacias scent the air with their sweet, heavy odor of decay.

How mighty is summer in the deserted cities, where everything is half closed up and people move slowly, as if through water. How marvelous and empty are the skies above them, which resemble the skies of jagged mountains, those skies breathing dust and hopelessness.

Dripping with sweat, my head lowered, almost unconsciously, I descended along the huge river of a Paris summer.

I unloaded trucks, looked after the racing gears of machine tools, and with an hysterical flinching lowered hundreds and hundreds of dirty restaurant dishes into boiling water. On Sundays I slept on the parapet of the fortifications in my cheap new suit and my odd yellow shoes. After that I simply slept on benches and, during the day when my friends went to work, I slept in their rumpled beds, in the depths of their hot, gray, tuberculous rooms.

I shaved and combed my hair carefully, like all beggars. In the libraries I read learned books in cheap editions with idiotic underlinings and notations in the margins. I wrote verses and read them to my roommates, who drank cheap green absinthe the color of gas and sang, in falsetto voices but with undisguised pain, Russian songs—the words of which they could hardly remember. After that they would tell anecdotes and laugh in the mist of cigarette smoke.

I had arrived recently and had only just parted from my family. I was hunched over and my whole exterior expressed a kind of transcendental humility which I couldn't seem to shake, like a skin disease.

I wandered around the city and visited my acquaintances.

I'd immediately regret my arrival, but would remain nevertheless. With humble politeness I would carry on endless boring and listless *émigré* conversations, interlaced with sighs and afternoon tea from poorly washed dishes.

"Why do they all stop brushing their teeth and walking with their backs straight, these people with their yellowed faces?—" the Formless Apollo would say, ridiculing the *émigrés*.

Dragging my feet, I had left my family; dragging my days, I had lived to the age of twenty-four.

During those years the clothes I wore wrinkled of their own accord and shrank; ashes and bits of tobacco covered them. I rarely washed, and I loved to sleep without undressing. I lived in twilight. At dawn I'd fall asleep on someone else's rumpled bed. I drank water from a glass that smelled of soap and stared at the street for hours on end, puffing on the butt of a cigarette thrown away by the landlord.

Then I'd dress, slowly and dejectedly examine the soles of my boots, turn my collar to the wrong side, and carefully part my hair, displaying that special coquettishness of the poor who try to show by this and other pitiful gestures that nothing at all has changed.

Then, stealthily, I'd go out onto the street at that unusual hour, when the vast summer sunset still burns and has not yet consumed itself, and the street lamps in yellow rows like some kind of huge procession already usher out the dying day.

But what actually has taken place on the metaphysical plane, just because millions of people have been deprived of several Viennese couches of dubious origin and a few paintings of the Dutch school by little-known artists, undoubtedly copies? And because, in addition, they've been deprived of their cakes and featherbeds, the kinds of things which literally compel one to fall into a deep after-dinner sleep, almost deathlike, after which one awakens completely disgraced? "Aren't they charming," the Formless Apollo would say, "all these crumpled, faded *émigré* hats, sitting like dirty gray and half-

dead felt butterflies on poorly combed and balding heads? And those shy pink
holes which appear and disappear at the edge of a worn-down slipper (at the
Achilles heel), and the absence of gloves and the subtle touch of neckties?

"If He'd been born in our time, wouldn't Christ have gone without gloves,
in run-down shoes and with a half-dead hat on His head?

"Isn't it plain to you that undoubtedly Christ would have been banned
from many places, that He would have been bald, and had dirt under his
fingernails?"

But I didn't understand any of this then. I was deathly afraid of going into a
store, even when I had enough money.

I blushed like a petty thief when speaking to the police. I was absolutely
tortured by everything, until suddenly I'd cross the boundaries of poverty.
With a certain sinister Christian pride I would begin proudly to display my
ragged and water-logged shoes, which sloshed at every step.

But especially in the summer I would often become even more indifferent.
I'd eat bread right on the street, not even bothering to brush the crumbs off
myself.

I'd read papers I had picked up off the street.

My shirt wide open, I would proudly exhibit my narrow, hairless chest and
look at the passersby with an absent and dreamy expression, resembling an
air of superiority.

My summer happiness freed me from all hopes, but I gradually began to
find that this hopelessness was sweet and that unheroic death was a very
common experience, that sometimes there was in it a bitter and actually
almost classical greatness.

I began assuming ancient poses, i.e., poses corresponding to the weak and
narrow-shouldered philosopher-Stoics, striking in their frankness, probably
due to the special features of Roman clothing which reveal the anatomy . . .

The Stoics also shaved poorly, I thought, but they washed themselves
well.

And once, truly, right from the bank I went swimming naked in the Seine
at night.

But all this came to me with difficulty.

My soul searched for some presence which would at last free me from
shame, from hope, and from fear; and my soul found it.

Then began a special ominous poverty-stricken paradise which led me and
several others to an insane fear of losing that subterranean black sun which
(like an infertile Seth) illuminated it. My weak soul sought refuge. It sought a
cliff, from the shade of which it might be able to survey the dusty, sunny, and
hopeless world. And be able to doze in its shadows in the sunny wilderness,
with an insane feeling of gratitude toward that rock warmed by the sun,
which isn't even aware of the soul's existence . . .

Just such a man appeared, for whom there was no past, who scorned the
future and always stood facing some landscape scorched by the sun, where

nothing moved, everthing slept, everything dreamed, everything appeared as if in the vision of one asleep.

The Formless Apollo existed entirely in the present. His existence was like a golden wheel with no top or bottom, revolving to no purpose, away from the world's perfection, unstructured and unrewarded, supporting an unseen person carried away from the world by his own terrifying happiness.

In his presence everything turned to stone, as if he were the Medusa.

The world seemed a vast, scorched, stony landscape, one of those scenes from the mountains of Atlas reminiscent of Hell, over which swept Simon Magus. But Simon wasn't cruel. The tiniest bit of grass could grow in his presence and birds could sit on his hands, he was so oblivious. Moreover, he was somewhere far, far away, beyond the sunrises and sunsets, where both time and eternity, day and night, Osiris and Seth, and all those living and all the dead, all future generations, and all hopes, and all voids, exist together and never depart and never fall silent, and from there descend into life with tears in their eyes.

CHAPTER TWO
*in which is discussed how I first became acquainted
with the Devil*

Sometimes you travel around the city, sometimes through the virgin forest. Passing through a hundred tram lines, stopping at a multitude of corners, I came to the river, left it, and again returned to it. The sun was setting over the brown trees of the bank which it had scorched, over the soft lilac asphalt and the souls of the people filled to the brim with that warm and vague, wonderful, and hopeless fatigue of the city forest. On the orange water, in a small boat right by the shore, sat a still human figure who seemed extremely small from my position on the bridge. I don't know how long I stood on the bridge, but each time I turned my eyes in that direction the small figure continued to sit motionless, carelessly and persistently, at first seeming to me useless, then awkward, then finally quite provocative.

All fishermen are dreamers, I thought, but this man wasn't even a fisherman, and consequently he had no justification for his defiant immobility. Finally, after what must have been an entire hour of enduring this mockery, I suddenly wanted to go down there and force this man to get up or turn around, or at least simply to show him by my expression that he had absolutely no right to such behavior, except the right of an utterly obtuse or at least sleeping man, or at very least the right of those beggars who, with amazing physical tenacity, sit frozen in undoubtedly uncomfortable positions on the benches in public parks. At last, having lost all patience, I went down there, awkwardly stepping along the huge stones like a conspirator, and approached the flat-bottomed boat. It was about a yard from shore and was moored by an iron chain; in it that mysterious man had already been floating, and yet not drifting, for probably several hours. At first I passed by him with feigned timidity, but then, seeing that he paid no attention whatsoever, practically in despair I stopped before the boat and stared at his unusually determined profile—a mixture of rudeness and tenderness, beauty and ugliness.

At first glance this profile had an almost comic expression, but there was in it something that completely forbade any urge to laugh, even for an inveterate prankster. It was quite obvious that the man had long since noticed me. He even hesitated a moment, as if debating whether he should turn his head in my direction; but, concluding that any improvement would be the enemy of good, he decided, with enchanting conservativism, to continue examining the fiery hair of the sinking sun, splendorously scattered across the sky. His clean-shaven face seemed forged from bronze, and his eyes had that special expression, more common among women, which appears on the faces of high society folk when they see something perfectly well but think it better not to take notice. Finally I took two steps back and, with the unusual dexterity of an attack of hysteria, jumped into the boat. This strange act can be explained by the fact that for several minutes everything had been very strange—everything was sailing on the open sea of the uncommon, an uncommonness, however, which seemed self-propelled, self-developing, the uncommonness of dreams and the most important events in the kingdom of recollection, which also happen as if of their own accord, and are likewise propelled by some sort of fair wind of predestination, of fate and death.

———

The seated man smiled slightly, remaining motionless, as if he'd expected this. He continued to sit, having barely cast at me that sort of inexpressive glance people give when they are willingly but ironically inviting one to sit down. Now his face was distinctly visible, fully illuminated by the majestic fading of the cooling sky. This face was so common and at the same time so strange, at once so banal and so distinctive, that for a very long time I seemed immersed in it, as if struck blank by amazement, although it was impenetrable. I had completely forgotten the unusual manner of my appearance on the boat.

Under his smartly cocked cap, which seemed transported here from Twentieth-Century Fox Films to depict the life of bums in New York, small wide-set blue eyes gazed steadily, sternly, and even good-naturedly, eyes which had a certain peculiarity that I realized only a good while later and which is extremely rare among Europeans, this uniqueness owing to the fact that they expressed absolutely nothing whatever. From the very first I attributed a sense of amiability to them, though it was certainly possible to

307

attribute to them any feeling you wished. God forbid, dear reader, that you
should ever meet such amiability, for it is precisely that amiability which may
have been the Formless Apollo's most terrifying feature.

At last this man exchanged his comfortable position for another, apparently even more comfortable one which would probably have taken me a
whole hour to find and which, afterward, I would have been unable to bear
for more than five minutes. He leaned back on his left elbow and with his
right hand pulled out a pack of yellow cigarettes and flat matches. Then he lit
up and threw the match overboard, observing during this ritual such artistic
simplicity and economy of movement that, although in the depths of my soul
I'd begun to cower, at its upper levels I re-experienced the most intense
wrath. Just then the Formless Apollo turned his eyes from the cooling sky
and with a mocking expression looked at me. His eyes were not in the least
like the eyes of a hypnotist—they didn't glitter, nor were they mysterious or
languorous; they didn't grow dim, but more accurately rotated together with
his face. They were not like living things, but like the thick lenses of those
beautiful acetylene torches that sit in lighthouse towers. Yet these eyes were
not at all glassy; it was more as if their transparency was clouded by
something, like those of Europeans under the influence of the tropics, or of
opium smokers. And yet these eyes were not at all sleepy; they were neither
asleep nor awake. They were average eyes, completely void of expression.
They were absolutely unique eyes. The Formless Apollo had now been
looking at me for a rather long time, and apparently the examination had its
own phases, one gradually replacing another. Probably my image was passing through shadow and light. I could attribute many professions and
philosophies of life to him, and yet obviously none of them remained very
long with him, because the Formless Apollo, having never been mistaken
about people, loved to vacillate, loved simultaneously to confirm and deny,
loved to preserve contradictory evaluations of a person for extended periods
of time, until suddenly, like the instantaneous process of crystallization, there
would emerge from the dark laboratory of his soul a distinct and firm
judgment, which would additionally include that moment of proof henceforth eternally inseparable from the person, like leprosy or the scar from a
bullet wound. This process betrayed a certain special, purely intellectual
ethic of his—or, more accurately, his extremely ethical attitude toward his
thoughts, as if they were living beings, in relation to which he remained
entirely passive, as if refraining from forcing their development in any way.
"What do you think about N.?" I once asked him about a certain person, who
had long become boring to us and had finally died, and thus certainly could
add nothing further to the complex of recollections linked to him. "I can't say
anything about him now, but I'm waiting," he answered, referring to himself
as if he were a river or a waterfall along which something would have to float
past from somewhere. But I guessed all these transmutations of my existence
in his eyes only much later, when I noticed that the Formless Apollo treated

me as if, in reality, I were simultaneously both a fool and a genius, both weak and strong, affectionately interesting to him, yet infinitely removed from him. On that memorable day (or, more accurately, evening) that examination seemed to me entirely useless, like examining the pattern of the wallpaper, and therefore offensive; so immutable, frank, and exceedingly banal was the Formless Apollo's expression, like the expression of Giaconda or the glass eyes in the store windows of optometrists. It seemed utterly impossible to extract by this glance anything from a being; and although the Formless Apollo essentially ignored the conversation of his companions completely, he nevertheless gleaned the hidden meaning of their words through the imperceptible movements of their hands, their eyelashes, knees, and insteps, and in this way unerringly discovering what the speaker actually wanted to express or, more accurately, what he wanted to hide. But basically the Formless Apollo's glance wasn't even condescending; it didn't even deign to allow us the privilege of being offended; it simultaneously slipped away and yet remained, it was at rest and ineffaceable, like a reflection in a window. Then the Formless Apollo suddenly arose slowly and, with the gesture of Xerxes commanding the sea to be churned, threw the half-smoked cigarette into the water; afterward, in the same graceful and economical way in which he did everything, he took off and then replaced his cap right down to his eyes and prepared to jump out of the boat, but changed his mind, pulled it in by the chain, and calmly got out of it with several rather old-mannish squats on one leg. The Formless Apollo had the somewhat narrow but completely straight shoulders of a Greek youth and uncommonly slender hips, giving him the appearance of an Egyptian bas-relief or an American sailor. He was a rather lightweight, graceful athlete, and his entire body seemed chiseled from the yellowish wood of an orange tree, although he hadn't at all the appearance of a strong man.

Then I, too, leapt awkwardly out of the boat (for some reason he suddenly stepped out, whereas I leapt out) and followed him, firmly resolved to lag not a single footstep behind this man until he either fought with me or allowed me to penetrate his circle. For he was always surrounded by a seemingly invisible and perfect circle, as impenetrable to those he embraced as to those he slapped in the face; although I noticed that during conversations with the most common people—sailors, circus acrobats, or women—this circle would disappear, perhaps precisely because the circle did not exist for them, and he would become almost warm, for the Formless Apollo always tried, to the limit of his strength and idleness, to hide his profession and education and would become quite angry and avoid anyone who, having long accepted him as a pleasant and limited person, would suddenly change that opinion of him.

309

He thoroughly studied and artistically mimicked the insignificant gestures of very simple people, their way of wearing a hat, of greeting each other, of lighting a cigarette. Indeed, even Christ had come incognito, he once said, and therefore it was certainly not shameful for us, mere mortals, to protect ourselves against those impolite and tastelessly inquisitive glances which are flung at any man we have reason to believe is highly intelligent and who, in our presence, avoids interfering in a heated argument. The Formless Apollo gracefully moved forward, then suddenly turned around and, frowning, returned to the boat. We sat in that boat yet another hour, during which my exhaustion, boredom, feeling of rivalry, desire to leave and yet to remain, desire to mock the Formless Apollo and finally almost to attack him with my fists, reached such a degree that for me that moment is unforgettable for its torturing poignancy. But apparently the Formless Apollo had something to think through, to experience fully. He completely forgot about me, being wholly immersed in an intellect-destroying contemplation of the water and the sky, which were constantly changing, growing green and blue, crimson and then remaining unchanged. Along the bank, as slowly as the lights of a funeral procession in the rain, the green gas lamps began to burn. Over there the automobiles flew past, the trucks rumbled, and the dusty trees swayed to the beat of music, shrill and remote. It was the night of July fourteenth, and somewhere firecrackers were already popping and children squealing; just above the river the moon was rising, and perhaps it was precisely for it that the Formless Apollo had waited. Huge, dull orange, like a sun sinking into the smoky, earthly atmosphere, like a sun finally surrendering to earth's gravity, like a drunken sun, like a mendacious sun, it gazed with its solitary and still warm pupilless eye, pressing the warm tin roof and far-off low islands with its enormous ponderosity. Then it rose a little higher and grew lighter, and, like the trembling hands of one awakening from a stroke, spread the white line of its reflection along the water toward us. Meanwhile, remote shots of rockets cracked from the opposite side of the river, and like low-growing bushes the mystical flora of the fireworks began to blossom and fall, blaze and disintegrate. Slowly they'd rise above the river, burst and fade, leaving behind ashen images in the air. Finally the last burst resounded confusedly, like the awakening of someone from a dream, and already the singing of the horns and violins became clear, the squeaking of the clarinets and the frequent funereal clashing of cymbals. Now the sky was dark blue, the water black, the moon white, and our faces leaden. The Formless Apollo suddenly waved his arms in the air, as if he were swimming out of something. Then the movement turned into the efficient stretching of a pleasantly tired man, and we stood up, climbed out of the boat and up to the bridge.

So, like Don Quixote and Sancho Panza, like Dante and Virgil, like two enemies, like two friends, like two undistinguished strollers, we walked along the uninhabited streets, across the deserted squares and boulevards, until suddenly we fell into a crowd of dancing people, a crowd of boisterous and rosy people who, having scattered from the dance floor the moment the music ended, stared at us with half-open mouths, as if they were seeking confirmation of, let's suppose, the fact that today was a holiday and everything was fine, and, not finding it, immediately turned away. The farther they played into the night, the redder and gayer became the musicians, as if they grew fatter before our eyes. They drank beer, puffing and blowing and spilling it. They swelled out and continued playing with incredible exertion and the same sort of endurance. It seemed a horse would have burst into tears from exhaustion, shrugged its shoulders, and left, but they kept on playing, although they looked ready to drop dead. Occasionally two orchestras would try to outplay each other; in one there were saxophones and a trombone; in the other, identical old men trying to make as much noise as possible. Of course, the former won.

Soon we came to the Boulevard St. Michel. We walked along it and, like two conspirators, began to approach the Montparnasse quarter, where the international Bohemians, though consisting almost entirely of people who despised France, were nonetheless shouting and celebrating more than all the others on this July fourteenth. But the Formless Apollo and I had long since grown used to this spectacle and, finding a little table covered with spilled beer at the very edge of the dancers and the night, we sat down, as if we belonged here, to watch these foreign dances. [. . .]

Gaito Gazdanov (1903–1971)

Georgy Ivanovich Gazdanov, born in St. Petersburg, was another writer of the Proustian school. He was the author of several novels, many short stories, and critical articles. His three most important works are *Vecher u Kler* (An Evening at Claire's; Paris, 1930), *Istoriya odnogo puteshestviya* (The Story of a Certain Journey; Paris, 1938), and *Nochnye dorogi* (Nocturnal Roads; New York: Chekhov, 1952).

Gazdanov, the son of a forester, first entered the Poltava Cadet School, then attended the Kharkov High School. When he was fifteen, he joined the Volunteer Army and was assigned to an armored train. For a while he stayed in the military camp Gallipoli (in the Dardanelles), which housed the remnants of Baron Wrangel's army until 1921. From there he moved first to Constantinople, and then to Bulgaria, where he graduated from the Sumensky Russian High School in 1923. In Paris he earned his living as a factory worker, then as a taxidriver, and later he enrolled at the University of Paris. During World War II he became a member of the French Resistance and worked for a Russian underground newspaper intended for Russian prisoners of war. In 1953 he was invited to work at Radio Station Liberty in Munich, where he stayed until his death.

An Evening at Claire's and a short story, "Vodyanaya tyur'ma" (A Watery Prison; *Numbers* no. 1 [1930]), are autobiographical works, but in them Gazdanov succeeded in transforming reminiscences into art. He acquired his manner of writing from the works of Proust, who was extremely popular among younger Russian writers in the late 1920's and early 1930's. He is linked to Proust by his method of conveying an impetuous wave of memories while emphatically assigning them all to the past, by the rhythmical qualities of his sentence structure, and by long paragraphs which connect a multitude of heterogeneous subjects as separate units of a single recollection. Even Gazdanov's humor resembles Proust's, in that he pays attention to the multiplicity of minute details. But he has his own distinct *Weltanschauung* and describes the world in his own manner. Gazdanov was a skeptic, cynic, and lover of paradox.

Leonid Rzhevsky calls Gazdanov's writing "meditative prose."[1] His narratives contain many reflections which, accompanying the author's impressions, overpower the objective portrayal of plot situations. These reflections succeed one another like the separate links of a chain. Gazdanov's writing is partly Western European in nature, but the lyricism of his meditations is purely Russian. Despite their seething abundance, his minute details are clear and drawn in distinct relief. Though definitely an innovative writer among the younger Russian generation in Paris, Gazdanov lacked the gift of artistic imagination in plot construction, and therefore wrote many works which were rather poor. Some of his sentences contain obvious grammatical errors or French calques. Adamovich, with some justification, refers to this characteristic as "a mixture of French with the Nizhegorodsky dialect, or ultra-French influences combined with those from the Soviet language."[2] Disturbing is Gazdanov's unnecessary loquacity; such loquacity is also typical of Yury Fel'zen, another disciple of Proust in Russian Paris. Fel'zen's language is diminished not so much by his grammatical mistakes as by the loss of its organic structure and superficial, excessive articulation. Both Gazdanov's and Fel'zen's sentences may appear artificial, scattered, and verbose, with weakened syntactical ties. Nevertheless, both of them attempted to enrich and enhance the nuances of the word, to imbue prose with intellectual content, and to improve the rhythmical qualities of fiction. Their organic fusion of humor and lyricism is another appealing feature. In his later stories, Gazdanov achieved a firmer composition and better artistic distance from his protagonists. Elements of the psychological novel, the adventure novel, and the novel of manners are equally evident in his works. The compositional design of his short stories, however, has always remained superior to that of his novels.

NOTES

1. L. Rzhevsky, "Pamyati G. I. Gazdanova," *Novy zhurnal* no. 106 (1972): 291.
2. Georgy Adamovich, "Literaturnye besedy," *Zveno* no. 5 (1928).

A WATERY PRISON

> *"Quand nous sommes seuls long-temps, nous peuplons le vide de fantômes."**
>
> Guy de Maupassant

The hotel not far from the Odeon, to which I had returned (having spent a year on the other side of Paris), had not changed at all in my absence. As before, a gramophone thundered in the student's room (he was Greek); as before, my other neighbor, a young man from Vienna, was quiet and drunk—the same as last year; as before, the proprietor of the hotel played

*When we are alone for a long time, we people the void with phantoms.

cards in a nearby café, shuffling them quickly and daily losing the small sum of money his wife had given him. The proprietress had become somewhat plump and had aged a bit, but she still remained just as nervous and sensitive a woman, and, as before, all her leisure time was devoted to discussing the possibilities of some unpleasant act or other on the part of her tenants, whom she constantly suspected. Most of all she feared that one or another of her tenants would unexpectedly not pay her for the room, although this had never happened and everyone paid exactly on time. Even should someone not pay, it wouldn't have ruined her (she was rather well off)—however, this thought didn't pacify her at all. Her perpetual anxiety was extremely valuable to her because it sustained within her something akin to a spiritual tension and provided her with the energy needed to arrange everything in the most fortuitous manner and, through a series of varied and thoroughly conceived means, to attempt to protect herself from that horrible event—that is, should one of her boarders unexpectedly not pay the rent on time. This goal became a compulsion for her; she thought only of this, worried, sighed, and was always discussing similar occurrences from the experiences of her friends, likewise proprietors and proprietresses of hotels and furnished rooms. Deprived of this peculiar spiritual sensuality, her life, most probably, would have lost all meaning.

"Listen, Jean," she said to her husband, "I've decided to keep a close eye on apartment seventeen. Something's happened to him—he's been so strange lately. Keep an eye on him."

But the proprietor, being an extremely reckless gambler, was to all other things completely indifferent. The cards had devoured him whole and dominated his imagination, so much so that even through lunch or dinner he thought only of playing cards; if the soup was tasteless, this instantly called to mind the losing hand in spades he'd held yesterday; and vice versa, at the sight of a delicious ragout, that marvelous set of diamonds which he had put together on Saturday of last week sprang into his memory—the proprietor always reacted to his wife's remarks with doubt, regardless of whether they were, in fact, valid or not. He answered the proprietress with her own words, simply rearranging them and adding to them a hint of perpetual reproach—and he never thought before answering.

He replied: "Apartment seventeen is strange? I don't think so. It's you who are strange, my dear . . ." He would answer mechanically, and this became for him as customary and necessary as moving his chair back to get up from the table, or opening his napkin. He once even told the proprietress, after she had remarked on apartment seventeen's again returning at four o'clock in the morning:

"Apartment seventeen? It was you who came at four o'clock in the morning," although the proprietress usually went nowhere and never retired later than eleven. Sputtering angrily, she started to tell him that if the hotel was still solvent, it was only thanks to her; but the indefatigable proprietor again

314

answered: "It's you who are obliged to all of them, my dear," and went to play cards. The only person who sympathized with the proprietress about her imagined mishaps was a little old man who often visited her and who was distinguished by a stentorian voice completely incongruous with his height; but the words of this man held no weight, because he had no personal opinions—only an inexhaustible supply of enthusiasm and grandiloquence, without, however, the slightest trace of individuality. Not one thought had ever occurred to him that had not been first suggested by someone else, and the process of thinking was completely out of the question for him. He was unable to form even the simplest opinion if it necessitated any mental effort at all, but in lieu of this he possessed the ability to be instantly aroused the moment anyone expressed any opinion whatever in his presence. He would support that opinion and say in his thunderous voice:

"But, my God, that's precisely the truth! But, Madame, you are entirely correct! Whom can one trust? No, Madame, I see that what you say is the truth, the whole truth, and nothing but the truth."

"Oh, if only everyone understood me the way you do," the proprietress would reply.

As the little old man left, the husband of the proprietress would accompany him and, while walking beside him, would whisper in his ear: "Don't you pay attention to Louise; she's nervous and because of this, I must tell you the truth, with each day she gets more stupid. What can one do, it's just her age."

And the voice of the little old man would instantly thunder: "But, my dear Jean, you're entirely right, I always knew this. I agree with you. Yes, I agree with you—she's a rather nervous woman. And that's because of her age, as you put it so well . . ."

At the corner the little old man would take leave of the proprietor and drop into the café to drink a little red wine, and the café owner, also an old friend of his, would ask him: "Did you visit them again? Oh, you do have great patience, old man. How can you chat with such idiots? Both he and Louise are idiots." "No one doubts that," the little man would shout, "and if I tried to argue with you I'd be wrong."

He wore in his buttonhole the ribbon of the Legion of Honor, which he had received for his fecundity—he had fourteen living children. He was respected for this ribbon—it seemed a symbol of a mysterious, but indisputable, grace bestowed upon him; and if any of his acquaintances had said that the little old man was simply stupid, they would have been ridiculed. The old man was always meticulously dressed and wore only black suits. His face was red and wrinkled, but his eyes were huge and beautiful. They had the ability to assume two expressions—the first, an unusual vividness which appeared each time he spoke, and the second (and entirely unexpected), a human and elderly sadness which (incomprehensibly) sometimes seized this chatterbox. It appeared that nature had created these eyes to be sad, but her creative powers were insufficient to raise this Chevalier of the Order of the Legion of Honor to an understanding of this sadness. The little old man never knew that in his eyes was remorse, an awareness of death, and a profound sorrow for his own insignificance; had he understood this, he could have been the Don Juan of his time and a master of hearts. But such a thought never entered his head.

The first night following my arrival, I opened the window to see whether the old beggar with the shaven head was still living opposite me on the floor above, as before. I knew that at eleven o'clock the dull little lamp would be lit in his small hovel, and the shadow of his bumpy skull on the ceiling would scurry and tremble till four in the morning. Glancing out the window, I was reassured that everything was in order; nothing could change this beggar's long-term habit, and if one fine day I had noticed that the light in his room was not lit, I'd have known that he had died or was dying. I couldn't conceive of what he was doing for those long hours on end—whether he was working, or reading; but he was so shockingly poor and so weak that all notion of work would cancel itself of its own accord. Several times during the day I had seen him on the street, and I always watched him with morbid curiosity and pity. He trembled constantly, had trouble standing, and was dressed in terribly inhuman rags. An old navy cap covered his head; he pulled it over his forehead, so his eyes couldn't be seen. He was very old and so pitiful that his appearance forced all to turn around to look, even the dealers, insensitive and heartless women; and only once a young Greek banana peddler, a stocky man with dark eyes and a narrow forehead, said after him: "People like that should be drowned." A passerby, a heavy lady dressed in fashionable stockings, the kind with black heels, jumped to the beggar's defense. Smiling radiantly, she spoke with conviction: "You just wait; when you're old, you'll be just the same," and suddenly enraged, she added: "but you should be drowned right now, instead of waiting until you're old." This didn't bother the Greek in the least, however. And the old man, swaying and trembling, walked into a cheap restaurant. He bought himself a bowl of fried potatoes, a bit of greenish-gray cheese resembling soap, and a piece of bread; then, chewing on the way, he returned to his fifth-floor room. It took him a quarter of an hour to walk up the stairs.

Downstairs, in the evening, the numerous visits to Madame Mathilde would begin. She owned a rather small public house; on its frosted glass doors and windows beautiful swans and flowers were drawn. The visitors conducted themselves gaily (within reason), maintaining their propriety, and only on one occasion did a drunken sailor, totally unaware of how he had come to the door with the swans, force his way in and shout: *"Je veux la patronne!"*† Two young fellows with sad physiognomies quickly and noiselessly led him out. But he didn't give up—again he began to shout; when

†I want the concierge!

the door opened and one of the young men asked him, "What do you want, Monsieur?" a sudden surge of propriety took control of the sailor and he answered: "I would appreciate a few minutes of private conversation with the directress of your institution." But then the desire for this inaccessible woman was reawakened in him with its former vigor, and again he plaintively cried: "*Je veux la patronne! Je veux la patronne!*" Finally Madame Mathilde herself appeared at the doorstep. Huge tears welled up in her eyes; she held her perfumed handkerchief to her face. She was pale, determined, and sad. She spoke to the sailor in a tearful voice: "My dear baby, you know this is impossible"; the sonorous, light clouds of the two gigantic gramophones playing in the salon drifted through the marvelous body of Madame Mathilde and hung in the air around the sailor; his sad frenzy knew no bounds. When the door closed against him for the final time, he shouted weakly, no longer hoping for any response: "*Je veux la patronne!*" and went staggering away, disappearing into the darkness of the night, where the four-cornered lamps suspended from poles were gazing with their greenish-white flames as though staring into a well.

When I moved back to my hotel, I began to lead the same life as I had a year ago; as before, I did nothing and had no idea of what would become of me the next day; my pockets were empty; in my ears constantly, ceaselessly, murmured mellifluous waves of a faraway sea, which I'd heard long ago and in so many places. I loved to imagine I was living at the seashore. Lying on my bed, I'd envision a swaying hammock strung miraculously over the bay, the grayish-blue surface of the Bosphorus, beautiful villas, rising right from the water's edge, white sails drifting as if through a dream, birds, and the wavy mirrors of the currents—this complex spell would suddenly debilitate me; my body would grow relaxed and fatigued, as if I'd spent the night with a woman. Struggling not to close my eyes, I'd watch all the objects which filled my room come to life and take on their own existence; I'd watch a mysterious light run across my wardrobe mirror, the pages of the books on the table flutter, the marble ship of the washbasin float in the darkness; and from the oval grating between the hot and cold water faucets would flash the white face of a watery prisoner, whom I had left there a year ago and whom I found, as before, in his watery prison, when I returned. Even during the day, whenever I happened to glance at this tiny oval window, which reminded me of a porthole with a grating, I'd see (so it seemed to me) a small figure grabbing the bars of the grating with his fingers and watching me pleadingly.

I always felt that the life I was leading in this hotel and which consisted of the necessities of eating, dressing, reading, visiting, and conversing was just one of the numerous aspects of my existence which went on simultaneously in different places and under different circumstances—in the air and under water, here and abroad, in the snow of northern regions and on the hot sands of ocean shores. I knew that, while living and moving there, I was affecting many other beings—animals, people, and spirits. I could scarcely imagine some of them; I could only visualize them flying with soft black wings, made of some miraculous substance which I could never touch. I saw others before me; they accompanied me everywhere; I had long been used to them and even to the fact that, by some law incomprehensible to me, they were endowed with the gift of silent speech by which they communicated with me apart from words and thoughts, which would have been too heavy for them, like air saturated with moisture before a storm—too heavy for those transparent insect wings, after which the black swallows dive in the air. Sometimes these beings, as if sensing the danger of madness threatening me, would suddenly appear before me like close relatives at the bedside of a dying man—and their legions, made up of a barely perceptible quivering in the air, became my protection. They would swarm in the darkness, constantly appearing and disappearing, and someone's forgotten eyes (which they suddenly called forth from my memory) often compelled me to breathe heavily with excitement. Glancing from the depths of my bed, which had suddenly acquired an unusual, otherworldly softness, I could see the pale, pleading face of the prisoner, and I would slip into a deep sleep.

In the morning I'd put on my pressed suit, carefully comb my hair, and after breakfast go to Mlle Tito, with whom I was involved in several trivial business arrangements which brought in a trifling income. I researched information she required concerning the stage in ancient France, collected quotations for her from Flaubert, Anatole France, and Balzac, and explained to her why she ought not to overuse indented lines, which she was extremely fond of doing.

Mlle Tito's profession was not quite clear to many because, while having no personal fortune, she lived in a very fine apartment, spent a great deal of money, treated her visitors to champagne—admittedly, rather bad, but all the same, champagne—and ordered expensive clothing for herself. Also, she was relatively pretty and comparatively young, and these qualities were sufficient to insure that her circle of acquaintances would not shrink. She spoke French with mistakes and a slight Russian accent; she spoke Russian with a French accent, and also with mistakes. She had no native language, although she was Jewish by descent. On the walls of her rooms hung a number of portraits with long dedications—in English, Spanish, French; when asked, "Who is this?" she'd reply, smiling dreamily: "Oh, that's my old, old friend. He knew me when I was still a virgin." She meant to say "a young girl," but she couldn't perceive the difference between these two concepts. Such an answer sounded even more ambiguous, as Mlle Tito had never been married. When one of her guests, a Russian critic, a harsh and sarcastic man, retorted following such a reply: "Most likely, that was a rather long time ago?" she didn't understand his rather rude irony and naïvely said that it was. The largest portrait depicted a Spanish general in full dress uniform. The general was old and had a gray drooping mustache, and his simple, manly face was somewhat reminiscent of Taras Bul'ba. On the portrait, in bold letters, was a quotation from

Lamartine (of whom the general apparently knew), although from the portrait one would never imagine so. It said: "*Et sur les ailes du temps la jeunesse s'en va.*"‡ But, finding these words insufficiently expressive and, perhaps, by dint of his military habits and peculiar demands on literature, which included the requirement that every quotation must sound approximately like a tune played by a regimental band, the general, on his own initiative, affixed to this melancholy statement three plump exclamation marks, which imparted an entirely different and comical meaning to Lamartine's words. However, both the general and Mlle Tito were especially pleased with the photograph, which had accurately captured all the intricate details of the general's parade dress, as well as with this quotation with its deafening addition—although it remained unclear why, strictly speaking, the general had fallen into such a pathetic state and over whose youth he was grieving. The other portraits were somewhat smaller, and the faces depicted in them were far from achieving the dignity of the general's; however, for some reason, there were more Spaniards than any others. But, when I asked Mlle Tito if she had lived long in Spain, she said: "Only two weeks in all." Then I mentioned the portraits, and she explained to me her clear preference for Spaniards by stating that she was very fond of the Latin race. However, her understanding of the Latin race was rather unique; for some reason she did not include Frenchmen, for example, under this classification. I didn't dare question her further, and she added that I wouldn't understand anyhow; so I surmised that, in all probability, there existed some sort of physiological difference between Frenchmen and Spaniards, imperceptible to the average human understanding but completely obvious to Mlle Tito—like the difference between related types of insects, to the layman completely unnoticeable, but immediately perceptible to the scientist.

Mlle Tito's apartment was rather well furnished; every object was directly connected with some recollection or other. The harp, standing between the window and couch, rattled melodiously every time a truck passed along the street. It had belonged to a deceased friend of Mlle Tito, a girl who had died quite young and who had, before her death, asked Mlle Tito to keep it. I had no notion of what this friend was like, but according to Mlle Tito's stories, she was an extremely refined and very talented woman. "*Elle était sur le point de mourir,*"§ Mlle Tito would say, mixing Russian expressions with French, "and she said to me: 'You can spit on everything else, but not the harp.' I answered her: '*Ma pauvre petite, tu peux être tranquille.*' "‖ The piano had been given to Mlle Tito by a certain Italian count, who was very poor; so, having bought the piano on credit, he only paid for the delivery and made the first payment, and then left for either Milan or Genoa and never returned.

‡And on the wings of time youth departs.
§She was on the point of dying.
‖My poor dear, don't worry.

Nevertheless, Mlle Tito continued loudly expressing her surprise every time the collection agent for musical instrument sales and accessories called on her after the usual lapses of time, invariably demanding the next payment and verbosely apologizing for the disturbance.

The care of Mlle Tito's library was assumed by a certain prominent figure, the name of whom Mlle Tito for certain reasons could not reveal; later I found out that the library was compiled by a certain senator who was, in fact, rather well known, and that the reason Mlle Tito did not wish to reveal his name was that he had already spent half a year in jail for the embezzlement of public funds and the forgery of a signature on a bank draft. By the way, the library, which at first consisted of French classics, was supplemented by Mlle Tito herself, who acquired with her own money Nadson, Turgenev, and the novels of Dekobra, whom she sincerely considered the best contemporary writer and—for entirely incomprehensible reasons—a pupil and disciple of Anatole France.

Mlle Tito was deeply convinced that she was a rather spoiled society woman, corrupted by Parisian snobbishness, weary of beauty and art, and charming in her treatment of people. She unwittingly nourished this delusion in herself by reading French novels, in whose heroines she invariably discovered a resemblance to herself; the more wonderful the heroine, the more she resembled Mlle Tito. But she considered Diana—some character from Dekobra—to be the truest depiction of herself.

"When I asked him," Mlle Tito would relate—she was acquainted with all the prominent people or, more accurately, thought she was acquainted with them; and whenever any one of these people, in reply to her deliberately careless bow, which she considered most fashionable, looked at her with obvious amazement, she would say addressing her companion: *"Regardez-moi ça, c'est un peu fort quand même."*#—"When I asked him: 'Tell me, am I really called Diana?' he smiled and said: *'Peut-être bien!'* Oh, *il est très fin,*** I really understood him perfectly."

She always said: "You don't think that I really understand this," as if all her listeners expected her not to understand, and as if her comprehension would be for them one of the surprises which she so dearly loved. These surprises consisted of the most diverse things, but always had a somewhat odd character, which called forth sincere delight only from Mlle Tito herself.

She received two to three people every evening. "I like to have gatherings of a small number of people," she would say, *"des gens qui se comprennent bien, quoi,*‡ and who all belong to the same milieu." The Abbé Tétu and the poetess Raymond, who carried on long conversations about Catholicism, Buddhism, and Mohammedanism, were her most frequent guests. Mlle Tito was an

#Just look at me, it's really just too much.
**Yes, you could be! Oh, he is very nice!
‡people who understand each other

ardent Catholic—it was precisely Abbé Tétu who turned her toward religion; he was a bald and smiling fellow in a long soutane, who was very fond of Russian tea and consumed an incredible number of biscuits. The Abbé was always perfumed and smiled constantly. When I looked at him for a long time, I suddenly had the impression that the Abbé had been surprised by a hit on the head, that he had stopped thinking, and on his face a beatific smile had appeared, which would remain until that torpor caused by the blow had passed. But the Abbé never stopped smiling; only the curve of his lips varied according to the type of conversation. The nuances of his smiles were numerous; even when the conversation turned to very sad events, the Abbé would raise his eyebrows, assume a mournful expression, but nevertheless would smile, and this could only be interpreted in the following way: "These poor people killed Mlle Tito's brother in battle, but could they really have known, could they really have understood what awaited him in heaven?" Thus everything turned out so politely that no one was shocked. Usually, however, the Abbé's smile was condescending and benevolent; it seemed to produce the feeling that the Abbé knew and understood all, that he was gently poking fun at human weaknesses and was surprised by nothing. And indeed, it was impossible to catch the Abbé off guard—no matter what was said, he maintained the appearance of one to whom everything had long ago become transparent, and he held the most exact and infallible opinions concerning everything—whether it be a question about the Second Coming, or Balkan temperaments, or the usefulness of raising rabbits in enclosures with clay soil, as the poetess Raymond had once remarked, though she knew absolutely nothing about rabbits and mentioned them only because, in her own words, she loved all of nature. When the Abbé spoke out—and he expressed himself only on matters pleasant for all—it appeared that he, though making no real point at all, was doing a favor to those around him: he didn't speak, but took upon himself the task of uttering several sentences, accompanied by the most varied and gracious of smiles; it seemed that inside he was nevertheless sorry to waste his Catholic, all-encompassing wisdom on these simple people. "All the same, the Abbé didn't snatch the stars from the sky," as the Russian critic said of him, himself also a frequent guest of Mlle Tito, a man of thirty or thereabouts, whom she revered for his wonderful grasp of French. But the critic visited Mlle Tito not because of her charm, as she thought, but for reasons more mundane—he had given her an idea for a play which she was writing, and he showed up either for money, which she never wanted to pay him right away, or to discuss the details of the next act. The shallow mind of the Abbé was fond of special turns of speech, which seemed exceedingly effective and remarkable to Mlle Tito but were, for the most part, rather tiresome and ludicrously naïve. "*Oui*," he would say, "*nous vivons entourés de mystère et c'est toujours nous qui entourons l'inconnu.*"‡‡ Or: "*que le*

‡‡Yes, we live surrounded by mystery, and it is always we who surround the unknown.

321

ciel descende jusqu'à la terre, Dieu ne descendrait pas jusqu'au ciel." § § He had an entire collection of such expressions, and when he repeated any one of them, he would listen to the silence which would descend on the room, and invariably add: *"et d'ailleurs, qu'en savons-nous?"*‖ ‖—which plunged Mlle Tito into a state of complete ecstacy. The poetess listened to him with the same attention; she even slightly opened her mouth with the look of a capricious child, but only so much as to still remain polite.

Just as Mlle Tito in her own estimation was a society woman, attractive and intelligent, so the poetess imagined herself to be a darling child who had preserved the freshness and fascination of youthful charm. Therefore, giggling and trembling, she spoke with a peculiar childlike (so she thought) voice: *"Oh, que vous êtes méchant!"* ## and then slightly puckered her lips. All poetry was for her something akin to a garden where children played; she once even expressed it in approximately this way and was offended when the critic shrieked with laughter—imagining, as he explained, Victor Hugo with a little sand shovel, Verlaine and Baudelaire pretending to be little horses, and Oscar Wilde in short pants, rolling a hoop in front of him. But the specialty of the poetess was moonlight, which she described in each of her poems and which appeared one time in a sky that seemed "to be marble, like Hellenic columns," once "in the living room, which resembled a greenhouse," and once in a garden. In all these instances the moon "danced and cast spells," sometimes resembling the face of a forsaken mistress, sometimes a giant pretzel, and sometimes the "eyebrows of the East." Indeed, it seemed that if there were no moon, the life of the poetess Raymond, deprived of all these eyebrows of the East and faces of forsaken lovers among Hellenic columns, would have lost all meaning. The poetess believed in life beyond the grave and was convinced that after death she would turn into a tiny star with a wistful glow. "But how much do you weigh?" the critic suddenly asked. She shrugged her shoulders and turned to the Abbé, looking for sympathy; the Abbé smiled, inscrutable as the sphinx, and one never understood what he was thinking—or indeed if he was thinking at all, or whether that smile concealed a sinister emptiness, in which floated only snatches of sentences on the mystery encompassing us and about the unknown which we ourselves encompass.

Mlle Tito was very economical. Her dinners consisted most often of ingeniously prepared vegetables, but for this paucity of food she substituted an abundant quantity of wine. Her favorite and most frequently served dish was carrots. Because of these carrots there even occurred a small rift between Mlle Tito and the critic, who, in answer to an invitation to dine made in the

§ §Let heaven descend to earth, God will not descend even to the sky.
‖ ‖and furthermore, what do we know of it?
##Oh, what a bad boy you are!

322

presence of the Abbé and the poetess, replied in Russian: "Look here, you're probably going to prepare carrots again, right? You know, I'm not a rabbit that feeds only on carrots and cabbage. You buy some meat, then I'll come." Mlle Tito looked at him (as he himself expressed it) with a completely pseudo-classical look; however, he paid not the least bit of attention to this and again repeated: "Buy some meat, then I'll come," and began discussing the stage decorations of the most recent revue at the Folies-Bergère.

The day after I had moved back to my former hotel I went to Mlle Tito's and found an unfamiliar young man with her, whom she introduced as a Spanish playwright. This Spanish playwright—a short man in a checked suit—sat on the couch and continuously laughed somewhat anxiously. I kept expecting him to speak; but he said not a word, and since, at times, his eyes suddenly held an expression of tortured awkwardness, I concluded that he probably wasn't sufficiently fluent in French. That was rather far from the truth—the Spanish playwright literally did not know one single sound in any foreign language, whereas Mlle Tito, as it became clear later, spoke no Spanish. Although, stealthily glancing at me and addressing the playwright, she would occasionally utter several strange and unfamiliar syllables in a mysterious language, somehow hoping the Spaniard would understand her, nothing came of it. The playwright, after laughing for a whole hour—he apparently considered such conduct among people who knew no Spanish to be the most polite and inoffensive—left, having come to no agreement at all, although he had come, as was later revealed, regarding the translation of his play into French. He squeezed my hand strongly as he left and suddenly smiled a smile so sincere that it immediately became clear how deeply he understood the absurdity of his situation during the entire course of his visit, and how glad he was when that visit had finally ended.

When he had left, Mlle Tito began speaking to me in Russian and told me that she had that morning nearly become the victim of an automobile accident, because her taxi—when she spoke in Russian she pronounced it "tak-see"—collided with another car. Then she began to talk about her remarkable memory and facility in languages—she had lived in France for fifteen years, had left Russia while quite a "virgin," and yet spoke Russian so wonderfully and fluently that no one would take her for a foreigner; what's more, she spoke French even better. As proof, she read for me one poem of Blok and one of Baudelaire, not always comprehending the sense of the words, mangling the stress in Russian, and pronouncing the French "*je*" as if it were the Russian sound "zhe."

Then, at last, she showed me her manuscript, which I was to correct; laying the papers on my knees, I immediately set to work. Meanwhile, Mlle Tito wound up the gramophone, put on *Nocturne en ré-bémol* as performed by Helman. Glancing at her now and then, I noticed that she was biting her lower lip, grimacing, and generally behaved somehow strangely. When I asked her what was the matter, she put a finger to her mouth, then quickly said: "*C'est l'inspiration,*"*** and began to wave her long fringed scarf and jump around the room. She stretched her arms in various directions and threw her head back with such a strong jolt that I was afraid she would fall. "*La danse nocturne,*" she whispered and was about to lower her head to her bosom, but then raised it again and once more began to jump around. Fortunately, the record soon ended, and Mlle Tito stopped dancing. "Do you understand art?" she asked me and, not waiting for a reply which didn't interest her in the least, continued: "I understand it much better than others *et j'en souffre, j'en souffre.*"\†\†\† I recalled that Mlle Tito had once attended junior high school—which she called preschool—and that her education had not gone beyond that humble educational institution. "But I understand everything," she said suddenly, as if guessing my thought, though that would have been unlikely. In answer to my questioning glance, she explained to me that she really knew how each person should achieve wealth in life. Wealth was, in actuality, the only thing of value to her, and art itself, of which she spoke so much, could not exist without this prerequisite condition. Art must be preceded by fame; fame, by wealth. Mlle Tito would never have even started to read the manuscript of a novel of Tolstoy or a poem of Pushkin, had they not already been famous and prosperous people. She reacted to poor and unknown authors with scorn. Regarding the Spanish playwright she immediately asked his translator, "What does he have?" "I understand everything," Mlle Tito repeated, came up to me, patted me on the shoulder, and said: "*Du courage, du courage,*" as if she wanted to console or calm me, meaning that this all-embracing knowledge of hers did not threaten me with any personal trouble.

That evening, as always, her usual guests gathered—the Abbé, the poetess, and the critic; I wasn't able to leave, no matter how much I refused to stay. I wasn't sorry about this, though, because the evening was very lively and gay. It had even occurred to me that this was quite unexpected, when suddenly a major conversation erupted over the cauliflower—and the conversation ended in a tremendous scandal. Supper was going quite well, until they brought on the cauliflower—in a gigantic covered dish. Mlle Tito, smiling and sparkling, said to the Abbé: "*Et voilà une surprise spécialement pour vous*"\‡\‡\‡—and the Abbé gallantly bowed his bald head. I noticed, however, the critic's dissatisfied look. The lid was raised, and the cauliflower appeared before the Abbé's eyes. It was covered with bread crumbs and floating in golden butter. It seemed to me the Abbé was not overjoyed by this surprise, but he quickly said:

"*Que c'est charmant, que c'est charmant, mais vous avez un don mystérieux de*

***It is inspiration.
\†\†\†I am suffering, I am suffering.
\‡\‡\‡And here is a surprise especially for you.

deviner toujours ce qui est le plus désiré par tout le monde. Mais c'est merveilleux, je ne trouve pas d'autre mot pour définir toute la délicatesse avec laquelle vous avez su nous surprendre d'une facon tellement fine et agréable."§§§ The poetess clapped her hands and seconded the Abbé, saying that she was in ecstasy over the two delights of this dinner—the fortunate union of the Abbot's eloquence and the culinary charm of Mlle Tito.

"*Et bien,*" she said, "*tout le monde en est ravi. C'est fin, c'est délicat, c'est tout ce qu'il y a de merveilleux, comme l'a déjà dit monsieur l'abbé.*"‖ ‖ ‖

"Everyone fell silent; it seemed to me that in Mlle Tito's eyes and on the bald pate of the Abbé happy, transparent tears appeared. But just then, the critic turned in his chair and said:

"*Et moi, je trouve que tout ça, c'est tout simplement bête. . .*"###

"*Comment bête?*" **** Mlle Tito inquired in a low and courteous voice, and she felt that everything was lost. "*Comment bête?*" she shrieked, desperately and unexpectedly, forgetting the presence of the Abbé and the poetess. "You came to eat meat and my cauliflower . . ." "I haven't eaten your meat," replied the critic, but she didn't hear him. "And what's more you create a scandal? *Je vous déteste, ingrate!*"†††† her face reddened, her gaze wandered. She grabbed a plate from the table and hurled it at the critic; the plate shattered against the wall. Then she began to sob and started to grimace in almost the same way as when inspiration had seized her. "I must tell you," the critic continued, "that you're always skimping and serving rubbish. That baldy will, of course, eat anything, because he's French, but I, thank God, am Russian, and I don't intend to eat just any kind of cabbage and weeds. You're always poking your unusual 'charm' and other nonsense at everyone, but you still haven't paid me my money, by the way. What sort of charm is that? . . ."

"Scoundrel!" screamed Mlle Tito, who had stopped sobbing. "*Gredin! Vipère!*"‡‡‡‡ At the word *vipère* the Abbé paled and rose from the table, and for the first time in his life stopped smiling. "*Mademoiselle,*" he said softly. "*Je m'en fiche!*" §§§§ screamed Mlle Tito again and rushed at the critic, but fell and bit his leg. There was complete confusion. The maid ran into the dining room, holding the Abbé's cane in her hand, and attacked the critic and the Abbé at the same time; but with unusual agility the Abbé jumped on a chair and stood there, his hands raised threateningly. From the adjoining room

---

§§§How charming, how charming, but you always have an uncanny talent for guessing what is most desired by everyone. But it is marvelous, I cannot find any other word for defining the delicacy with which you are capable of surprising us in such a fine and agreeable fashion.
‖ ‖ ‖Well then, everyone is delighted with it. It is fine, it is delicate, it is the most marvelous thing, as the Abbot has already said.
###As for me, I find all that is just plain stupid . . .
****How, stupid?
††††I detest you, you ingrate!
‡‡‡‡Idiot! Viper!
§§§§I don't give a damn!

were heard the sounds of the gramophone, turned on by the poetess, who had left the dining room as soon as the conversation with the critic had assumed a menacing tone. For several seconds there was a violent uproar in the dining room; then the critic succeeded in fending off Mlle Tito and her maid. He made his way to the entry hall and, seeing me, said: "Well, now we can go home." I left with him and crossed the Passy bridge. Paris was lit up for some holiday or other, boats from which fireworks whistled were floating along the Seine, and the people, standing along the banks, shouted and waved their hands.

When I entered my room, I was struck by the greenish twilight which came from the window and permeated everything; all the objects which made up my furniture also seemed green — and the room suddenly reminded me of the cabin of a sunken ship. All around was silence; only now and then the passing horns of automobiles from St. Germain Boulevard could be heard; or suddenly through the air, which had for a second become metallic, a streetcar jangled as it passed, and the rustle of its rollers against the wire quickly crept into the darkness, hissing now louder, now weaker. Perhaps it was streetcar number nineteen, going to Henri Martin, the best avenue in Paris. The first time I went there I decided that, without fail, I would live in one of those private houses hidden in the tall trees — and because the streetcar was going in that direction, I felt regret.

The greenish air, through which I moved while undressing for bed, possessed a strange density uncommon for air, and in the darkened mirror things were reflected differently from the usual, as if they'd been sunk in water a very long time ago and had by now submitted to the inevitability of existing underneath it. I suddenly felt wretched and uneasy; the appearance of my room again reminded me that I'd already been living too long as if my hands and feet were tied — and that I could neither leave Paris nor exist any differently. Everything I'd done was unsuccessful — I was moving just as if I were under water — and until now I had not understood this with complete clarity. But now that I realized this, I could hardly breathe for grief — and I dozed off only after a long while. Whenever I turned, the thought torturing me disappeared and was replaced by another, no less unpleasant. When I finally closed my eyes I saw myself transported into a huge, dark house, which I immediately recognized, since my dreams often took me there, and I remembered the carved wooden columns of the house and its high ceilings and its rooms, fashioned from the softest material which would change appearance with each moment — one time an aquarium, where crocodiles with human arms were swimming, then a fountain, then a person, then a cloud, then a bird with yellow plumes, and then the recollection of an event which had occurred long ago. This time I saw that the rooms were submerged in green water with long strings of seaweed growing along the walls; high up, just beneath the ceiling stood, quite still, the bald head of the Abbé Tétu with unmoving, unsmiling eyes. Then Mlle Tito floated by; her body was covered with inscriptions. I recognized from afar the exclamation marks of the Spanish general — and realized that these inscriptions were the autographs of her numerous friends and acquaintances. Mlle Tito's friend, the same girl who had left the harp, was sitting below on a tall stool and playing the piano. Each time her finger pressed a key, a small crystal bubble of air would appear; it would rise with a faint gurgle, reminding me of the sounds circus musicians produced from their numerous bottles, filled with water to various levels. Mlle Tito's friend was playing a tune unfamiliar to me, and the silvery accompaniment of the tiny bubbles made it especially delightful; the little bubbles popped out and slowly floated away one after the other, making a glimmering necklace of marvelous white amber. Hanging onto a life preserver, the sailor who was in love with Madame Mathilde floated into the room, and the black letters on his life preserver repeated his distraught cries — *"Je veux la patronne!"* But the sailor's wish now, in this watery prison, suddenly took on an evil meaning not inherent in it, sounding like the threat of an all-powerful tyrant from whom Madame Mathilde would never escape.

Suddenly, strong currents passed through the room. The Abbé's head began to rock — and I saw a person in a white robe whom I immediately recognized as my watery prisoner, although he had grown a hundred times larger, and his black eyebrows floated separately from his face with its pleading eyes. "Director of the Watery Prison" was written on his chest. He stopped in the middle of the room, as though he intended to go to the surface, but remained still. The glassy eyes of the Abbé looked at the director with terror; in place of Mlle Tito a gigantic green lizard appeared. But the music played on — and I felt that now I would never leave this watery prison and would remain here forever (like my prisoner) in the porthole, behind the grating of the washbasin. The water began to flood my throat; the piano sounded more and more remote; the little bubbles became more dull — and I fell into a deep swoon. Then a light breeze began to blow across a field of rye, coming from somewhere unknown. I gradually became aware of what was happening to me, heard the sound of slowly falling rain — and remembered that I had left the window open the evening before, after returning home from Passy, where I had been a guest of Mlle Tito.

Ivan Lukash (1892–1940)

Ivan Sofontovich Lukash, prose writer and essayist, graduated from the department of philology at the University of St. Petersburg and settled in Paris after the October Revolution. He came to Paris via Constantinople, Bulgaria, Germany, and Latvia. Earlier he had written a collection of prose poems, *Tsvety yadovitye* (Poisonous Flowers; St. Petersburg, 1910), and from 1912 on he participated in the Ego-Futurists' publication *Peterburgsky glashatay* (The Petersburg Herald). He also contributed short stories to the newspapers *Speech* and *The Modern Word*. In exile, Lukash was a faithful contributor to *Russia Illustrated*, *La Renaissance*, and *Russian Thought*. He published a collection of essays, *Goloe pole* (The Bare Field; Sofia, 1921); a collection of stories, *Chort na gauptvakhte* (The Devil in the Guard House; Berlin, 1922); and *Bel-Tsvet* (White Flower; Berlin, 1923) and *D'yavol: misteriya* (The Devil: A Mystery-Play; Berlin, 1923), among many others. The novella *Graf Kaliostro* (Count Caliostro; Berlin, 1925) was followed by a collection of stories on historical themes, *Dvortsovye grenadyory* (The Palace Grenadiers; Paris, 1928), and the novels *Pozhar Moskvy* (The Burning of Moscow; Paris, 1930) and *Sny Petra* (The Dreams of Peter; Belgrade, 1931). In 1934 a film, *Sergeant X*, was produced from a scenario by Lukash (Serzhant Iks; Paris, 1933). It focused on the tragic fate of a soldier serving in the French Foreign Legion.

Lukash's father, a guard soldier in the Imperial Household Finnish Regiment, participated in the Turkish War of 1876–77 and was awarded many military decorations, including the highest war distinction, the Order of St. George. After his retirement as a lance-corporal, he became a janitor in the Art Academy of St. Petersburg. Despite his rather meager finances, Lukash's father gave each of his seven children a university education with stipends from the Russian government. For his military accomplishment he was granted the title of Russian Honorary Citizen.

During World War I Ivan Lukash joined the Imperial Army as a volunteer. His personal war experiences and impressions gave him rich material for his later stories, novellas, essays, and novels. Among those of his works which received general recognition are the novels *Vyuga* (The Storm; Paris, 1936), concerning the paradoxical nature of the Russian Revolution and the mentality of its participants, and *Bednaya lyubov' Musorgskogo* (The Unfortunate Love of Musorgsky; Paris, 1940), written in the tradition of Dostoevsky and Tolstoy. His other works are marked by a valid psychological delineation

328

of the simple Russian soldier and his inborn feeling of duty, loyalty, and sacrifice to the Russian Emperor. These portrayals, reminiscent of Lev Tolstoy's military tales, and presented against the background of important historical upheavals, are sometimes of a fantastic nature, but are always set forth in a clear yet captivating manner. Moreover, Lukash was able to capture the *Zeitgeist* of the period. It should be mentioned, however, that at times his excessive sensitivity and admiration for the unbounded spaciousness, beauty, and past military glory of Russia result in unnecessary sentimentality. Though he was very talented, his works occasionally reveal a lack of literary culture—a proclivity for a rather primitive symbolism with mystical coloration (especially in *The Devil: A Mystery-Play*), annoying abuse of pathetic tone, and *Effekthascherei*. Zinaida Hippius[1] and Gleb Struve[2] were critical of these and other artistic faults in his work. Their criticism is especially justifiable with regard to his pretentious *Dom usopshikh: poema* (The House of the Deceased: A Poem; Paris, 1922). Its plot concerns a Soviet sanatorium in the Crimea, the residence of some Soviet officers. The novelist's heavy-handed attempts at a psychologically accurate depiction of their characters and political convictions, along with his artificial style, resulted in a complete artistic failure. In some of his other works, however, Lukash excels in his impartial presentation of historical or military events. His restrained and polished style is reflected in his short story "Noch' na 28 fevralya v Zimnem dvortse: ocherk (The Night of February 28 in the Winter Palace: A Sketch; St. Petersburg, 1917), to cite but one example.

NOTES

1. Temira Pachmuss, *Intellect and Ideas in Action*, pp. 394, 419.
2. Gleb Struve, *Russkaya literatura v izgnanii*, p. 180.

THE NIGHT OF FEBRUARY 28 IN THE WINTER PALACE: A SKETCH

"They gathered together in this time of foul weather . . ."

The evening of February 27th . . .

The huge Winter Palace was dark and deserted. A black gloom slept in all its windows. The slender silhouette of the Alexandrovsky Column cast a ghostly shadow on the Winter Palace Square. Above the Square a frosty mist was rising . . .

Before seven o'clock the Preobrazhensky and Pavlovsky Regiments and the

Guard crew had been in the Winter Palace, but they'd all left, they'd all abandoned it . . . They had gone over to the People. It was rumored that a Provisional Government had been created, that the troops were going over to the People, regiment after regiment.

The Winter Palace was dark, and it seemed as if the massiveness of its crimson red colonnades, the semivaulted arches of its entrances, and its black windows all stood guard. Will anything happen here? . . .

In the courtyard, on the small square between the striped sentry boxes of the guardhouse, a single lantern burned dimly, casting a yellowish circle of light. That same day, ever since morning, a platoon from the Petrograd Regiment had been standing guard at the Palace guardhouse.

In the offices located on the lower floor, with their windows facing the Winter Palace Square, the guards on duty were sitting on ancient wooden benches. They wanted to leave it all and go home . . . Many pressed their faces against the cold panes of glass. They were listening. In the darkness, beyond the snowstorm, machine guns crackled somewhere nearby. The tall bronze steeds above the arch of the Ministry of Finance were distinctly outlined against the sky—now red from the far-off glow of a fire.

Everyone knew the Peter and Paul Fortress had already been taken by the People. And what if cannon shots should suddenly start to pound the Palace from over there? What if they should suddenly start attacking it; in the attack who would separate the innocent from the guilty, foe from friend . . .?

From nine o'clock on, the telephone began ringing in the offices. General Khabalov was calling the Commander of the Palace Guard.

"I wish to conduct my troops into the Palace . . . Prepare yourselves."

The Commander of the Guard, Prince Ratiev, did not reply immediately. He managed to speak with the Commander of the Palace Administration, General Komarov, who phoned Count Nirod. The call to Nirod did not go through, and the Prince decided to act without the Commander. He answered Khabalov.

"I consider it impermissible for you to bring your troops into the Palace. The Palace is a historical building, not a fortress."

Khabalov seemed to agree. In an hour the phone rang again, and again they carried on negotiations. Khabalov was insistent. One of his Generals—the former Commander of the Pavlovsky Regiment, General Zankevich—was adamant in support of his requests. At midnight the phone rang again for the Commander of the Guard. Khabalov had decided.

"I have declared Petrograd in a state of siege . . . Be so kind, Prince, as to place yourself under my command . . . I will conduct my troops into the Palace."

He designated the password upon which the Palace Gates were to be opened for the troops, and said the officer leading the troops would have his, Khabalov's, calling card. Prince Ratiev tried to object, but Khabalov hung up.

The Night of February 28 in the Winter Palace: A Sketch

The dark red masses of the Winter Palace were turned into the final fortress of the Autocracy. That night the guard on duty at the Palace was Danevich. Like all the Palace guards, he realized that Khabalov's attempt to make a final stand in the Palace was both terrifying and pointless. The People had already won . . . And their attack would be terrible. In the heat of the battle millions of the People's money invested in every armchair, statue, in each candelabrum and porcelain vase of the Palace would be scattered and blown to the wind . . . but now it was too late—Khabalov had decided.

Prince Ratiev had gone to speak with the ailing Komarov—Danevich remained alone. He was almost in tears from his grief at the fate of these high white halls, this crystal, and the ancient darkened landscapes on the Lyon velvet and damask-covered walls. The same feeling is shared by all old museum guards who deeply love those antiques around which flow their quiet lives . . .

At close to one o'clock in the morning a hollow rapping was heard at the iron gates of the garden, from the Neva Side.

Hatless, tripping in the snow, the guard ran through the dark garden to the gates. That night was icy and windy.

"Who's there?" he shouted through the wind.

"Loyalty," answered a hollow, hoarse voice. That was the password designated by Khabalov.

The guard didn't let them in; he demanded the calling card. Through the iron scrollwork they shoved the card. Frozen and lashed by the wind, Danevich searched out Prince Ratiev with this visiting card.

"The troops are coming . . . They gave the password, here's the card . . . The troops are coming . . . What shall I do?"

"What can I, what can we all do?" the Prince said. "They'll come in anyway." In the meantime, the infantry had made their way from the Neva through the garden, which was buried in snow. They had already come into the Palace through the Saltykovsky entrance.

Their chains rumbling, fourteen pieces of artillery entered the Winter Palace from the square through the Main Gates. Behind them came more than a thousand infantrymen and a company of policemen taken from the streets and dressed in soldiers' uniforms.

These were all the troops which still remained loyal to Khabalov as of the 27th of February.

Immediately the Palace offices became noisy and steamy. Here gathered Khabalov, the War Minister Belyaev, General Balk, the former Mayor of the city—Commissary Vendorf, and the Police Generals. All were pale, nervous, and perceptibly confused. Not one of them took off his overcoat. Everywhere was heard the tinkling of spurs and French mixed with Russian curses.

At one o'clock Prince Ratiev and Danevich carried the ailing and paralyzed Commander of the Palace Administration, General Komarov, from his room in their arms.

Together, they pushed the sick man's chair through the long dark suites of the Palace galleries and halls. In the darkness, the lengthy journey seemed confused and labyrinthine. Reflections flickered in the dark windows; the glimmerings of crystal vases and the edges of gilded frames sparkled. In the Romanov Gallery, they were haunted from every corner by the faces of the darkened portraits of the Tsars.

How many of them were here! . . . Farthingales, wringlets, the camisoles of Catherine's era, parade uniforms with the propped-up collars of the reigns of Alexander and Nikolay. Old men, children, women. In the semidarkness their faces appeared phantasmagorical, their expressions evil and menacing . . . The small wheels of the chair squeaked across the slippery parquet.

They stopped in a huge room next to the elevator.

Ratiev and Danevich hoped that Komarov would persuade Khabalov to leave the Palace. Danevich rushed downstairs to the offices and asked Khabalov to come up. He curtly refused. He had no desire to listen to the paralyzed old man.

"We are staying . . . Tell them there, upstairs, that we are staying."

Belyaev and Khabalov had decided to entrench themselves in the Winter Palace. They didn't want the officers to be quartered on the lower level with the windows facing the Palace Square—when the battle with the People began, the artillery from the Square would destroy these rooms first.

They demanded a safe, concealed area for their headquarters.

They were conducted through the Palace. The Generals glanced out the windows, conversed, waved their hands in refusal. The Generals were not pleased with this area, either . . . Finally they were shown into the small and narrow rooms near the Saltykovsky entrance, with their windows facing the Palace Garden. The Emir of Bukhara always stayed in this red, yellow, and white suite, the so-called fifth guest section.

Here it was quiet and remote. Here the red brick fence of the Palace Garden would protect them from the wrath of the street. Khabalov's entire headquarters were transferred to this section.

The General Command—over thirty in all—began to fill the room. Still in their overcoats, they lay down on the couches and beds, slumped in the chairs, and someone had even stretched out and was already asleep on the floor, which was covered with a coarse wall-to-wall carpet . . .

At two o'clock in the morning Grand Duke Mikhail Alexandrovich arrived at the Winter Palace. He was very pale. He didn't remove his overcoat, but passed hurriedly into the so-called Ladies' Quarters, where the Japanese prince had resided during his visits.

This was one of the cozier Palace refuges. It was filled with green, pale rose, and bluish landscapes—the kind found in sitting rooms. Airy Japanese screens with herons and flamingoes, fragile porcelain.

Ratiev, extremely upset, approached the Grand Duke.

"Your Highness, there are troops in the Palace . . . History will not forgive us for turning the Palace into a fortress. It is shameful to fire from the Palace . . ."

"Shameful," confirmed the Grand Duke and added, "the troops must be removed."

The order was relayed to Khabalov. The Grand Duke remained alone in the silence of those nocturnal rooms, having requested a glass of tea.

Komarov and Prince Ratiev sent Danevich to inquire whether the troops were leaving. Danevich again ran downstairs.

The gigantic and echoing lower corridors. Rifles stood in racks. On the stone floor, soldiers were lying or standing, helter-skelter, though many still moved about like shadows. The electric lights glowed dully in the oily, damp mist. Cigarette smoke hung like a wall in Khabalov's headquarters. No one had any intention of leaving; many were already asleep . . .

In the offices Danevich was met by startled guards. The order had been given to remove all window frames. Since early morning they'd been bringing machine guns into the Palace. Machine guns . . .

It had been decided to put the machine guns in the White Hall. The walls of the lofty hall were hung, from ceiling to floor, with gold and silver dishes. Many of the dishes bore large diamond-studded monograms.

And it also had been decided to put machine guns in the Gold Reception Hall. In that same famous Reception Hall, where the sculptured walls were overlaid with gold, where the tables were made of the most delicate, ancient mosaics, where stood the world-famous mirror fireplace with one of the rarest of landscapes by Rinaldi.

The innumerable treasures of these huge, lofty halls.

What was the purpose of this?—this thoughtlessness, this cruelty, this torture?

It was as if the People had volunteered to destroy all their own treasures. Even at a glance the number of valuables collected in these halls, where it had been decided to put the machine guns, was obvious.

There was the huge clock made of dark silver—the "*At mg nio*,"[1] apparently the only one of its kind in all the world, groups of cast silver statues, marble, huge crystal candelabra, crystal vases, bowls, fragile porcelain, ancient masterpieces on the walls, and chandeliers. In the halls, among these chandeliers, there was a massive bronze one weighing 2,700 pounds, and a silver one of 828 pounds . . .

It had been decided to station the machine guns here . . . Who knows, perhaps on the 27th of February they still had faith that these dark little steel beasts, greedily howling, might disperse the waves of the attacking crowd. Indeed, they had become accustomed to suppressing the People's wrath, the People's sorrow and pleading, with machine-gun fire.

But, in fact, at the very first cannon shots from the parapet of the Peter and

333

Paul Fortress, at the very first gunfire from the Palace Square—everything in these halls would be scattered into millions of smoking splinters and piles of twisted and melted metal.

Moreover, in the Winter Palace there was an infirmary. These machine guns seemed all the more horrifying when one remembered the Palace infirmary. At night, when they were choosing sites for the machine guns, the last machine gun was stationed at the very partition, the wooden partition which separated the halls of the Palace from the wards of the infirmary. Also, the infirmary windows partially looked out onto the Palace Square . . .

During the attack, is it possible that the muzzles of the cannons and the narrow throats of the machine guns would stop to choose where they'd send their iron blows?

Perhaps they hoped that the People's wrath would spare the infirmary, that, protected by it, they might entrench themselves in the Palace and shower the city with bullets while awaiting reinforcements? Perhaps they were confused and had simply forgotten about the wounded? It's not our place to pry into their souls. But it was horrible . . .

Horrible. Because that night five hundred and thirty-five wounded men and gravely ill soldiers lay in the Palace infirmary. More than five hundred helpless people lay there, people who had no suspicion that, behind the wooden partition, next to their cots filled with suffering, it had been decided to station machine guns.

At dawn the bronze window frames were ordered unscrewed; the huge windows were taken out—so the machine guns could be set up everywhere.

Danevich, shaken, returned to Prince Ratiev. The latter hardly heard his entire report before he rushed into the Grand Duke's suite. When he returned, he hurriedly ordered Danevich:

"Go downstairs immediately . . . Summon Khabalov and Belyaev . . . Tell them the Grand Duke demands their immediate presence."

In a few minutes the following procession climbed up the dark staircase to the "Ladies' Quarters": in front walked the guard Danevich and behind him, marching ponderously, the two Generals. Khabalov had already removed his overcoat downstairs, but Belyaev threw his onto a chair only after he'd entered the suite. The Generals straightened their uniforms and morosely went in to Mikhail Alexandrovich.

In fifteen minutes both Generals returned . . .

The troops had been given the order to evacuate the Winter Palace immediately. In the lower corridors they'd begun awakening the exhausted soldiers. The butts of rifles banged against the stone slabs with hollow echoes, voices were heard, the clinking of spurs, the shouts of orders . . . At dawn the troops began to leave. The machine guns were carried out.

Soon after, the Grand Duke also left the Winter Palace. And at about six o'clock in the morning the dark red masses of the Palace again grew silent and deserted.

Thus, on the night of the 28th of February, the Winter Palace was saved from the sweeping attack of the People.

NOTE

1. Illegible.

Irina Saburova (1907–1979)

Irina Evgenyevna Saburova lived, until 1915, in Riga (Latvia) and on her father's estate on the River Dniepr. In 1917–18 she resided in Finland, and then returned to Riga, where she stayed until 1943. During World War II she fled to Berlin and finally settled in Munich, where she lived until her death. She graduated from both Russian and German high schools and enrolled in the French Institute in Riga. Her first husband, Alexander Perfilyev, was a poet and journalist. Her second husband, Baron von Rosenberg, an officer in the Russian Imperial Navy, died in 1958.

Saburova began writing when she was eight years old; her first short story was published in the Riga newspaper *The Lighthouse* in 1923. After that she contributed short stories and translations to various Russian periodicals in Riga, among them *The New Fields, A Small Flame,* and the newspapers *The Russian Word* and *Today* until the Soviet occupation of the Baltic states in 1940. From 1933 to 1940 she edited the weekly journal *For You* and translated books for various editions. After 1953 she was a regular contributor to the newspapers *The New Russian Word* (New York) and *Unity* (Melbourne), and she worked as a translator at Radio Station Liberty in Munich (1953–73). Her publications are voluminous. Among the most important are *Ten' sinego marta: sbornik rasskazov* (The Shadow of Blue March: A Collection of Stories; Riga, 1938), *Dama tref: sbornik rasskazov* (The Queen of Clubs: A Collection of Short Stories; Munich, 1946), *Korolevstvo alykh bashen: rozhdestvenskie skazki* (The Kingdom of Crimson Towers: Christmas Fairy Tales; Munich: Posev, 1947), *Razgovor molcha: sbornik stikhov* (A Conversation in Silence: A Collection of Poems; Munich, 1956), *Kopilka vremeni: rasskazy* (The Strongbox of Time: Short Stories; Munich, 1958), *Korabli Starogo Goroda: istorichesky roman iz zhizni russkoy Baltiki 1924–1944* (The Ships of the Old City: A Historical Novel from the Life of the Russians in the Baltic Countries 1924–1944; Munich, 1963), *Shchastlivoe zerkalo: rasskazy* (A Happy Mirror: Short Stories; Munich, 1966), *O nas: roman* (About Us: A Novel; Munich, 1972). *The Ships of the Old City* also was published in German, under the title *Die Stadt der verlorenen Schiffe* (Heidelberg, 1951) and in Spanish as *La ciudad de los barcos perdidos* (Barcelona, 1958).

In 1960 Saburova recited her works at the Literary Circle in Bern, Switzerland; in 1946, 1968, and 1973, she was invited to give readings and lectures in New York, Washington, Philadelphia, Ottawa, Toronto, and Urbana, Illinois. At these gatherings her poems, put to music by the composers Z. Zubkovich, Avenir de Monfraid, and A. Karpovich, were sung by various Russian and American singers. Among her favorite Russian writers were Alexander Grin, Mark Aldanov, and Mikhail Bulgakov, but she was also very fond of Hans Christian Andersen, Selma Lagerlöf, Henrik Ibsen, Jack London, O. Henry, Oscar Wilde, Erich Maria Remarque, and Ortega y Gasset, to name only a few. Within her own works, Irina Saburova expresses a deep personal affirmation of life even in its apparent absurdity. She seeks to exhort her reader to fight for the realization of his dreams, though their ultimate attainment may seem impossible; she reminds us that the greatest treasure guiding our personal fate is the human heart. She was especially successful at writing fairytales. She claimed that "fairytales survive millennia," whereas culture, civilizations, nations, and states invariably perish. Medieval Germany yielded its place to romantic Germany, which fell before the Germany of music, science, religious doctrines, and arts; then came the Germany of Bismarck, Kaiser Wilhelm II, and Hitler. Yet underneath this chaotic conglomeration is a constant quite independent of, and even indifferent to, the flow of time and its transient vogues in philosophy, customs, and habits—the constant of the fairytale world.

Saburova claimed that man's life is full of "miraculous" events and phenomena: ancient city walls, cathedrals, castles, bridges, various monuments from chivalrous, feudal, and romantic eras inexplicably survive the human destruction of war. In her short stories, she points to these "miracles" with artistic skill and moderation. At the same time, her stories concern our contemporary life as well, with all its incomprehensibility and its absence of love, understanding, and sympathy. Although she portrays only a few traits in the development of her heroes, they are nevertheless well delineated and show great depth. Their language is individualized, and the mode of their thoughts and actions is often quite amusing. Saburova's plots, her characters' relationships and psychological entanglements reveal the author's sense of subtlety and artistic proportion. Her works may be viewed as a curious amalgam of the fantastic and of empirical reality with its dreams, disappointments, and fears. The material is presented with concentration, pensive sadness, and gentle humor, all of which create the emotional tone and aesthetic form unique to Saburova.

IRINA SABUROVA

BECAUSE OF THE VIOLETS

FROM: *Kopilka vremeni* (The Strongbox of Time). "Because of the Violets" was first published in *Ten' sinego marta: sbornik rasskazov* (The Shadow of Blue March: A Collection of Short Stories).

Fima and the Fairy lived in one and the same house, bordering the five-cornered square. The house formed one of these corners: greening walls, rusty patched tile on an angular roof. The upstairs windows were built very large; they were probably installed recently, and therefore they appeared bright and looked like patches, as did the tin on the honeycake-like edging of the tile; below were rickety, corroded doors with yawning snapdragons on the pediment.

Everyone affectionately nicknamed her the Fairy, though her real name was Felicita and she scarcely resembled the princess of elves. Only her hands and her eyes, the shade of drowned violets, were beautiful. Artists and those delicately exciting ladies of ancient country estates must have had such hands. However, the Fairy's country estate had long ago drowned in the high tide of the Revolution, and now she worked in a bookbinder's shop. Her artistic inclinations found their expression in this activity alone.

She went to the bindery early in the morning. It smelled of various kinds of paper and almond glue. Printing presses whined laboriously, and from the gray overcoat of the foreman (who gilded the letters) there fell the minutest gold dust, as though from the delicate wings of a moth.

They gave all the most refined work to the Fairy: she bound the small and graceful volumes of poetry in Moroccan leather and moire silk, selected the brocade binding for fairytales, and covered huge historical volumes with suede. She knew how to embroider book covers with beads and how to adorn them with variegated inlays, how to burn brown letters through the velvet, and how to make small copper corners. In general, she was proud of her work. A beautiful book can give a great deal of consolation, especially if, raising one's eyes from it, one looks out through a high window at the colorless sky, knowing only too well that, when this sky grows dark, one must go home and so complete this day and many more to come. Yes, a book is always a consolation.

At home there was her husband, short and fat, in large spectacles, rosy-cheeked, and plodding. He worked as a bookkeeper, entering with precision the rows of figures; at home he'd don his neat lounging jacket and rearrange the books on his favorite bookshelf in similar rows. He took a great interest in the history of the arts and was reputed to be a real authority on the Pre-Raphaëlites.

In life, he occasionally revealed a certain sentimentality—he saw to it that on the green, tiresome desk of each employee, on his or her name day, a rose would appear (wrapped up in a curved piece of paper) together with cheap

338

flowers of the season, preferably those "with a meaning." On Sundays he went to the movies, often to matinées, when the air there was cleaner and the film was unreeled more slowly.

The Fairy's sister was responsible for the household. She was younger and more contemporary. After cleaning their small kitchen until it shined, she would put her lipstick on very carefully and go to the university. She studied more out of vanity than from inclination; actually, she was building her future on a cautious flirtation.

In essence, the Fairy was pleased with her life, and only at times did she feel that something was missing. These sensations of impending emptiness, propelling her somewhere into an impetuous chasm, became more frequent, especially from the time when Damian first appeared at their place.

Under the stairs in the basement, the windows of the lower apartment faced a tiny shed in the yard, crowded by the old walls. There it was always dark and damp, and it smelled of cats.

Fima lived in one room and rented out the second one. Whenever there was swearing behind the wall, she'd bang threateningly with a broom. Fima was large, clumsy, and looked rather stout because of the blue apron wrapped over her coat. Her hands were rough like splintered wood, and her face was flat and completely colorless. Her lips were pressed into a thin thread; she had white eyebrows, and indomitable and rebellious eyes like small dots that could have been daubed with cheap cerulean by an artist from a local fair.

A while back, Fima had been married; her husband had called her Fimushka, or more frequently Fimka. He drank a lot, beat her severely, and cursed her, inventing new words in his frenzy. Fima did not know his present whereabouts and secretly hoped that he either had become an inveterate drunkard or was in jail. When questioned, she snapped back, and she did everything silently and distrustfully—she had once and for all severely censured life.

Fima derived a certain pleasure from sweeping the stairs and the potholes in the narrow sidewalk in front of the house. The largest part of it was occupied by the wooden hatch of a rubbish bin, where a thin stream of sticky dirt oozed out from under its heavy lid. She liked this work, and in winter she'd solemnly pull on her gray gloves with the fingers cut off—to give her a better grip on her broom. The pentagonal square was her real household—she knew it by heart. She knew where and when the sun would shine into each small corner, and how the square would change, responding to people who crossed it at various times of the day.

Upstairs, in their home, lived a female bookbinder, apparently of former nobility. Once she stopped on the stairs while putting on her gloves, and Fima saw her hands—so pale they seemed to glow in the dark. Every morning Fima could hear her small heels; then again as she would return at lunch, go back, and return in the evening. In the twilight, her face became older, tired, and expressionless; her eyes moved without seeing anything.

339

She was probably thinking about her own special affairs—such useless thoughts.

Her sister was always all dolled up; a stupid, vain girl, she painted her lips like a cannibal; she was no better than the restaurant wenches. The husband of this one upstairs was an orderly person, and their small flat was very nice. One day Fima dropped in on them to repair their waterpipe—she was also the janitor of the house—and saw how clean their apartment was. There was a piano in the dining room and a large picture covering the entire wall: some park was painted there, but under the paint the canvas showed through.

Recently Fima had become interested in everything happening in the upstairs apartment, because Damian began to visit it almost every day. Fima had to know everything about Damian.

Every day at about five o'clock Fima would go to the restaurant, which formed the second corner bordering on the square, to wash the dishes in the kitchen, to wipe up the ash-darkened puddles on the small marble tables with wet rags smelling strongly of beer, and to sweep all the cigarette butts into a heap. There were no clean people here—they mostly wore traveling caps or crumpled hats; their faces were unshaven. They'd come in at night and make a row until morning.

Fima was well acquainted with this blue smoke, the odor of wine, the abominations and restaurant filth, drunken tears and songs. Only now she would come in earlier and, pursing her lips, would stop at the inner glass door with a rag in her hand, as if waiting to enter. Behind the door, at the black piano, sat Damian—he was so thin and pale; it was probably no fun for him to bang on the piano all night, either.

Damian behaved very independently—during the day he studied at the conservatory, and he played in the restaurant from evening till morning. Furthermore, he did exercises for his health, beautifully starched his own shirts, and almost every day painstakingly ironed his only decent suit, because otherwise he would feel like a lost soul.

Dress him in a colored dress coat with lace cuffs and a foulard kerchief around his neck, and any artist could have used him as a model for a portrait of a marquis of the 1830's! Damian, however, limited himself to the love of music, women, his own pride and youth, and firmly believed every day was good because it could be miraculous.

Besides, he was very lucky. An acquaintance, a bookkeeper, who lived across from the restaurant, courteously offered him the use of an old, but remarkably melodious Steinway; moreover, the bookkeeper's wife, a woman always slightly misty-eyed and with the poetic name of "the Fairy," had critical appreciation for his playing. Damian often played duets with her. She would accompany him softly and fluidly, merging her tone pleasantly with his. He loved to watch her hands on the keys—hers were not simply hands, but a pearlescent poem.

340

Her sister had only bright lips; the rest of her was a colorless chill. Damian was indifferent toward her, but he loved to sit with the Fairy at twilight, engaged in long conversations. He liked a certain frailness in her; what was more, she read many books and gave him valuable advice. In the area of beauty Damian was very serious and learned everything.

When the clock struck eight, he would quickly rise, button up a superfluous button and, kissing her hands picturesquely, descend the stairs quite erect and gay. It was time to cross the square and sit down at the discordant, ghastly instrument which he scornfully called a *shkapa*.

Damian politely but resolutely rejected the wine glasses offered him—the stench and numbed, stupefied faces around were sufficient. Toward dawn, when the customers were insensible to everything, Damian sometimes allowed himself some enjoyment, modifying the requested melodies in such a way that even on this *shkapa* they began to sound good.

Fima listened to him at these moments. She knew that Damian was not his given name, as many thought. She had looked through the church calendar, and the rarity of the sonorous "Damian," instead of the ordinary "Demyan," somehow confused her. With pain, she once noticed that a button had been torn off his cuff and feared that he, so neat and clean, must have felt uncomfortable because of it, yet had no one to sew it on.

Fima avidly devoured all the fragments of others' conversations in which his name was mentioned. She would not, of course admit it to anybody; even she herself could not quite understand why this handsome young man was so pleasing to her. He was young enough to be her son.

This fact, however, was not the crux of the matter. And even the fact that he probably had never even noticed her, with her face flattened against the glass door and a wet rag in her hand, was unimportant. He did not know that later, after his departure, she would carefully wipe the black and white keys of the instrument with a clean scrap from her old dress. But what if he ever did decide to stay and even speak to her—what about, oh Lord?! Conversations—they were for that one, upstairs—Fima had seen them standing at the window together. That woman was a match for him, or perhaps some other, a better one still.

The crux of the matter was different entirely—Fima once suddenly felt her lips break into an affectionate, imploring smile; she hardly had time to compose herself and snap at the approaching waiter: "Why are you wasting time? Kick these drunkards out! They've guzzled enough; it's already light out. That dandy over there might bang away till noon yet. Why should I stand and wait till he finishes?"

Damian came in the evening to talk, but he would come in the morning if he had to practice one piece or another. The Fairy was at the bindery; her husband was in the office. The Fairy's sister, in the kitchen, would listen indifferently to his passages. That's how it had been today.

Coming home for dinner, the Fairy went into the dining room and stopped in amazement: in a low, small milk-glass vase which sometimes served as an ashtray, a small bouquet of large, dark lavender violets was unfolding its wide, round leaves. The Fairy liked violets very much, and especially these autumnal ones, so large and dark, without fragrance; they were as mysterious and crepuscular as poetry. Who had brought them?

"Who brought the violets?" asked her husband when the Fairy passed through into the kitchen to wash her hands. He was standing there, attentively watching the preparation of the mustard.

"It was the Fairy," her sister answered quickly, "I saw her myself."

The Fairy looked at her sister in bewilderment—she had been about to thank her sister for the violets.

"You?" the husband asked with surprise. The round lenses of his spectacles flashed with distrust. Her sister smiled faintly, lowering the corners of her painted mouth. Her sister never bought flowers, considering it old-fashioned. The husband presented her with flowers only on her name day. Nobody else had entered their apartment that day, except Damian . . . Was it really possible that Damian had brought these violets?

"Oh yes, I bought them yesterday—I had some change," the Fairy said quickly, blushing slightly, and walked out of the kitchen.

Why hadn't her sister said that Damian brought the flowers in the first place? What was so remarkable about that? He came so often to see them . . . it was an expression of his attention, a courtesy, but the sister had lied and had wanted the Fairy to corroborate the lie—why? Because the husband mustn't know this? He might think that . . . what, exactly?

The violet bouquet on the table suddenly became mysterious and exciting. How sweet he was! He had brought it himself, placed it in the small vase himself . . . secretly, to give her pleasure. He'd probably deprived himself in everything.

They dined in silence. The husband was businesslike and withdrawn. He was preoccupied with something, and the Fairy felt guilty. Why not tell the truth? But already she knew that now she wouldn't do it. Let these violets remain just as dim and tender as her conversations with Damian. Not for other people, but for herself.

She also kept his smile for herself, to recall afterward when she was alone—so infectious, a little sly, and triumphant, as if it weren't forbidden, and couldn't be, because everyone could take what he needed. And how emphatically and beautifully he kissed her hands! Perhaps, the next time they met, his kiss would be longer still?

"I am so grateful, Fairy, more than you can imagine," he did not finish his sentence when leaving. But perhaps this inexpressible something was now expressed—through the violets?

The Fairy had married late. She had kept hoping that someone would come, someone handsome and daring. There had been infatuations and disappointments. One day it suddenly dawned on her that there was nothing more to wait for. The four years of her marriage passed unnoticed—work, books, home. All of this was, of course, far from important, even unnecessary; but through the trifles one can forget how life slips by. From the moment when Damian first appeared at their place, she began to think about this more often—his smile was almost too dazzling. And how much more radiantly he would smile for the one he really loved!

The day was over. The Fairy had smoked for a long time, watching the violets grow darker until they became completely black. The smoke moved around the room, merging with the dying light of a gloomy day. Each item, each trifle, including the Fairy's gray dress, seemed fragile, hopeless, enveloped with the sort of fatigue that makes one's eyes lose their luster and one's shoulders droop. However, perhaps later the Fairy might laugh triumphantly and exultantly and—allow not only her hands to be kissed.

Walking out to the stairs with her sister, the Fairy suddenly recollected: "Why did you say that I had brought the violets?"

"Didn't you? . . . Who did, then? Truly, I was convinced . . . oh, Damian begins to court you quite seriously."

"What nonsense!"

"Do you think I'm blind or something? It's enough to see the way he kisses your hands. A real marquis! Congratulations! Personally I don't like him. A marinated aesthete. But this is the sort of thing you like. Do you remember that . . ."

"Stop! It's nothing of the sort!"

"Then why are you so excited? You can't fool me, Fairy. Besides, you yourself know perfectly well that it's true . . ."

"I simply think that Damian himself likes violets very much . . ."

They went farther without noticing Fima, who was standing under the stairs. She was on the point of going outside with her dustpan and a broom.

"Viol-its," Fima repeated to herself and smiled condescendingly. "Just imagine . . . like a real fancy lady. He plays music and loves violits. A funny fella."

She stepped out, followed the departing figures with her eyes, and began to scrub the pavement.

The square was beautiful at this moment. The twilight enveloped the corners with a mist, and through it shone the orange lights of the lanterns. The people were passing quietly, unhurriedly. Furs hung from the women's shoulders, their perfume floating like the clouds, their escorts murmuring in self-confident, gentle bass voices . . .

"Buy some violets! The violets are good!"

A peddler was returning from the market. There were crushed asters unsold in her large basket, and a heap of small, lavender bouquets. She wished to get rid of them quickly, because they would wither before tomorrow; it was not reliable merchandise. The asters would be all right—you could even comb them with a brush. But the violets could fade at any moment.

Fima heard the peddler's voice even from her distant corner and frowned. Was she really crazy, or what? Should she throw her money away? Better to slip it to a beggar, though even they're all idlers and frauds.

However, when the peddler approached, having shouted to no avail, Fima, frowning sternly, lifted up the flap of her coat, took out a fat old purse and, digging in it for a long time, pulled out a silver coin with her stiff fingers.

"Here you are. Well, give us that one, won't you. After all, they shouldn't go to waste."

The peddler looked at her with surprise, and Fima felt herself blush up to her ears.

"Be on your way, this ain't no market place," she grumbled and, grabbing her broom and stooping, as if she'd done something shameful, she dove under the stairs. Her hand squeezed the tiny violet bouquet. Fima looked at it under a yellow, flickering lamp, spreading her fingers wide to protect the flowers and not crush them.

"How pitiful they are, these little bitty flowers. You can crush 'em in a flash. His soul's just so delicate, a real young 'un. Everybody needs his toy . . ."

Fima dumped some torn-off buttons onto her chest of drawers, and also some mislaid needles. She kept them carefully in an old icon lamp made from thick cherry-colored glass with a broken base. She had pasted up the hole with some wax, and in its place had bought a new white icon lamp for herself. But this broken one could stand on the chest of drawers—it could be used for some other purpose.

Now Fima carefully washed the ruby-colored icon lamp, wiping the round dents of its pattern with the hem of her apron. She had to hurry, so that they wouldn't notice her in the restaurant. They would laugh at her.

"I forgot my dust rag on the 'strument," Fima said peevishly, sticking out her apron with one hand and pushing aside the waiter, who was leaning against the lintel, with the other. "Has that dandy come yet?"

"He'll be here in a minute. See that you don't leave your rags around here. He's strict."

"I know, I know."

Fima approached the piano sideways, grabbed an invisible dust rag, and, looking around, took the icon lamp with the violets from under her apron and put it atop the piano. She stepped back, admiring it. The small vase was at its best, shining brightly. She was ready . . .

The glasses clinked at the bar. Fima slunk through the door, wheezing and blushing and, out of habit, even grumbling as she walked.

She did not sleep the entire night, tossing fitfully and listening intently to the bed's squeaking and to the irksome groaning of the drunken tenant behind the door.

"Perhaps it's sinful to put flowers in an icon lamp? But putting in needles—isn't that a sin? And what if somebody saw her leave the violets, or if Damian began asking questions—wouldn't all of them in the kitchen grin at her?" As for them, she knew how to fix their wagons. If she had to, she'd even give them a sock in the teeth. She'd make short work of it.

But while he's playing, he'd now and then glance at those violets—he loved such flowers. He'd surely realize there weren't only drunken mugs around him. Perhaps he would even drop in on her to thank her . . . that was almost ridiculous. But perhaps? He'd sit down here at the table; she would cover the table with a clean tablecloth, would set out the samovar. She even had one little jar of preserves; she'd made it herself as an indulgence. She didn't like vodka—it was filth she could do without, for even without it her head was whirling, and she could scarcely catch her breath. Oh Lord, she wouldn't even know where to stick her hands! What would she say to him? Her words were like a broom—scratchy and chafing.

"I am grateful to you, Efimiya Ivanovna," Damian would say. "You shouldn't have done it; still, the whole night as I was playing, I would look at the violets, would play and look at them, and think, 'Who could it have been?' No one but you. I noticed you long ago. You're a working person, and so am I. There isn't any sin in that, Efimiya Ivanovna. All of us live a hard life."

A hard life! At this point she would tell him everything, everything . . .

That evening the Fairy returned from the cinema. A woman on the screen, ridiculously and awkwardly dressed, whose husband was primarily interested in a roast turkey, found herself (after a strange chain of events) in the palace of a real prince in a small German principality. She put on a Parisian dress and immediately became better looking, even blossomed. She dined with the prince at the same table, but later in the morning she left him again—returning to her former life.

The actress wasn't particularly beautiful, but the Fairy was startled by her eyes—by her glance as she was leaving; these were the eyes of one taking leave of a fairytale. She left in silence, and the Fairy felt like screaming because of this silence.

As always after the movie, it seemed to the Fairy that thousands of eyes were looking at her. She moved lithely and even began admiring her hands, now swiftly rearranging the dishes on the table and carefully caressing the small, low vase with the lilac-colored bouquet.

Her husband, sitting opposite, watched her attentively.

"So then, it was you who brought the violets, Fairy?" he asked with a slightly ironic smile.

345

"Yes, of course. But why do you ask?" The Fairy tried to control her voice, making it sound unruffled.

"Because it was I myself who bought them as I walked home from the office. Lately you've been sad for some reason, and I wanted to make you happy. Why did you lie, Fairy?"

That night the Fairy cautiously wept in the darkness, pretending that she was smoking. Her tears streamed, incessant and weary, and she controlled her breathing, making it regular so as not to awaken her husband.

How could she think it was Damian? . . . Oh, yes, he valued her very much as a friend—but one doesn't bring violets to one's friends, doesn't make provocative intimations. That small lie, which had filled her entire being with an expectation as yet unbetrayed, suddenly appeared to the Fairy as a great lost happiness.

One always hopes that something may, something must happen; suddenly a small trifle—like this small bouquet of violets which Damian had failed to give her—mercilessly reveals that there is nothing more to expect, that one's life has already slipped by, and that one must manage to exist till the end somehow, reconciled with that final loss. Everyone ought to have happiness in life—but many never do.

The drunken crowd stayed till morning. It grew quite light at six o'clock. Their faces were yellow like beer; the tables were yellow, even the piano keys were yellow, and blue smoke hung in the room. There were dark circles under Damian's eyes; finally he rose, stretching a bit and cracking his knuckles. Got to get home quickly, take a cold shower, and get to sleep. Then again a shower, exercises, and later, a date with Helen.

"Volga, Volga . . ." resounded from the street, the last customers' yellow voices still droned. Arranging his music, Damian nearly tipped over a small, absurd, red vase which had suddenly appeared on top the piano. Who put it here? Half-shriveled, smoky violets (they too hadn't slept all night) drooped in the dull red glass. Damian smiled for some reason and walked to the door. He stopped on the stairs, blinking his eyes. The sun was rising from behind the sharply outlined roof of the house.

"You have forgotten your bouquet, S-S-Sir. It was a present for you," the waiter giggled, lisping like an old-time servant and, catching up with him, shoved a small grayish-lilac lump into his hand. Damian raised his eyebrows slightly in amazement and grabbed it with disgust. He turned the wet, weak, drooping stalks in his fingers and looked around. A stout, ridiculous peasant woman who was sweeping the street stood close by, staring at him. He often chanced upon her and sometimes wondered—how could such a person live? Yet those blue dots on her whitish face also looked at the sun; perhaps they even thought about something.

Damian turned around and obligingly tossed the small bouquet into her large dustpan of gray tin, spattered with dirt. At least she wouldn't have to pick it up from the street; this would be a help to her. He felt that he had performed a good deed and, smiling, he walked down the street, squinting at the sun.

That day he himself bought a small bouquet of violets—large, dark lavender, very delicate. At first Helen wanted to pin them to her dress, but then she changed her mind and left them on the table.

"I love violets, but just the Parisian kind—you know, the ones made of silk. At least they can be perfumed, whereas these have almost no fragrance, especially in the fall, and they wither so quickly."

Helen's hair was golden, her face a delicate rose, and in the rouged little heart of her lips her small teeth sparkled. Damian carefully helped her on with her cape trimmed in fluffy fox. He could not afford any silk Parisian violets for her. He loved her very much and thought she might understand and forgive his inability. Her words were very painful to him.

Georgy Ivanov (1894–1958)

The poetry of Georgy Vladimirovich Ivanov, the husband of the poet Irina Odoevtseva, belongs to the St. Petersburg school of versification, to the Acmeist movement. His first publications appeared in 1911 in *Apollo, The Contemporary*, and other literary periodicals in Moscow and St. Petersburg. His earliest collection of poetry was *Otplytie na ostrov Tsiteru* (Departure for the Island of Cythera; St. Petersburg, 1912); it was followed by *Pamyatnik slavy* (The Monument of Glory; St. Petersburg, 1915) and *Lampada* (The Icon Lamp; Petrograd, 1922). In 1923, Ivanov emigrated to Paris. He published many collections of poetry abroad, among them *Veresk* (Heather; Berlin, 1923), *Sady* (The Gardens; Berlin, 1923), *Rozy* (The Roses; Paris, 1931), *Portret bez skhodstva* (Portrait Without Likeness; Paris, 1950), and *Stikhi 1943–1958* (Poems: 1943–1958; New York: Novy zhurnal, 1958). His fiction works include a "risqué manifesto" (Roman Goul') *Raspad atoma* (The Splitting of the Atom; Paris, 1938), and a book of literary reminiscences entitled *Peterburgskie zimy* (Petersburg Winters; Paris, 1926).

Georgy Ivanov was a true master of melodic verse. Deep despair and celestial music are simultaneously audible in his poems. He continued Lermontov's and Blok's poetic tradition, with its basic musical intonations, but rejected the latter's romantic illusions and expectations. Together with Adamovich, Ivanov participated in the Second Guild of Poets. Not an imitator of his predecessors, but merely inspired by their music, Ivanov had no hopes for any kind of salvation for man—he simply considered music to be a miracle in its own right. A romantic attitude, curiously fused with nihilism, is conveyed in many of his poems, where he derides and rejects everything around him with irony and despair, in defiance of the nebulous, rosy illusions of the Russian *émigrés*. He inherited Blok's dynamic syntax, based on verbs of motion and forceful sounds, as well as his imagery (snow, dust, stars, roses, dark willows, and the icy sea wind), and the preponderance of black and hazy blue colors. He transformed the personal disappointment and anguish of distant exile into magical music, with "no," "nothing," "nowhere," and "no one" sounding like "nightingale warbles" (Yury Ivask). Ivanov's melancholia invokes freedom, spaciousness, and blue stars shining in an icy void. He is at once a skeptic, nihilist, cynic—and a lyrical poet, grieving over a life and an eternity seen as hideous and meaningless. Poetry is equally meaningless, but it is redeemed by being beautiful, bewitching, mysterious, and victorious in a world of absurdity and frigid nothingness. His manipulation of vowels

348

and consonants creates a harmonious, perfect design of parallels and repetitions, with vowels dominating the entire scheme. Ivanov's verse is light and sonorous, creating the effect of poetry sung. Melodiousness appears to be his poetry's metaphysical substance, as is the case with the poems of Zhukovsky, Fet, Polonsky, and Alexander Blok. But Ivanov's melody is excessively sweet and alluring, in spite of its tragic nature. As Yury Ivask sees it, Georgy Ivanov translates "the horror of wolves into the language of nightingale warbles" and hears "Divine music in the universal void." This music is the music of Death, of the spiritual demise of St. Petersburg and Russia. The themes are always the persona's leave-takings and separations. Ivanov's entire oeuvre may be characterized as a funeral dirge for the Russia which has been, but is no more—receding slowly into the dusk of non-being. This world is still and silent, covered by snow and ice, on which some quaint, squirming phantoms are grotesquely scattered. This is the essence of Ivanov's poetic universe.

His skill in poetic composition is elegant, and his rhythms are intricate. From the Acmeists (in particular, Nikolay Gumilyov and Mikhail Kuzmin) he inherited an exterior expressiveness of detail, figures of speech, and his cold, precise, and beautiful lines. Ivanov's poetic vocabulary is intentionally sparse and monotonous, as is his arrangement of strophes. His syntax displays an elliptic reticence. Occasionally he employs surrealistic grotesque images: for instance, trousers made of wax, music, or grass. His verse is a curious, organic combination of Verlaine's rhythm and melody, of scarcely perceptible impressionistic attributes (halftones, allusions, unfinished thoughts)—and a classical clarity of style reminiscent of Pushkin. In Ivanov's works we may find even the "prosaisms" of Vasily Rozanov and Innokenty Annensky. The fascination of his verse rests on this integral confluence of romantic moods and attitudes, inherent melodiousness, and a classical transparency of expression sprinkled with occasional "prosaisms." He resolves difficult poetic problems with ease and virtuosity by employing thematic contrasts and semantic antitheses; by his "ring-like" verse composition, emphasizing dramatic collisions between the beautiful vision and the ugliness of the temporal, empirical world; by lexically contrasting parallelisms and oxymorons; by stylistic clusters of poetic, caressing, "russified" foreign words, or Old Church Slavicisms, with prosaic and colloquial expressions, and other poetic devices. Moreover, Ivanov uses the so-called lyrical grotesque—the alternation of dream and reality, the ridiculous and the frightening, melody and satire, beauty and deformity, fear and courage, cynical laughter and lyrical song. The effect of *Verfremdung* (alienation, defamiliarization) is another important component of his system of versification—the persona receives letters from his dead friends; in a tender embrace, people waltz in their life beyond the grave; the sepulchral voice of hell sounds in the twitter of a bird. All sense of reality and normal proportions disappears in the vortex of the absurd and fantastic. Like Gogol's St.

Petersburg, Ivanov's Northern Russian capital dissolves in a "misty fog." Only a shadow walks noiselessly along the lanes of the Summer Garden. People, objects, and concepts move, change forms, and disappear. The world lacks all stable qualities—"it is merely a fit of atomic hysterics."

The subject of the gradual death of art has interested many Western European writers, among them Thomas Mann. Ivanov develops and amplifies this theme in his poems and in *The Splitting of the Atom*. Here, his former aestheticism transforms itself into anti-aestheticism—his music becoming primitive and rough. Instead of displaying the former St. Petersburg refinement, this work employs rude street language. The vocabulary is saturated with vulgarisms, puns, sarcastic observations, and crude colloquial expressions. The theme, content, and meaning likewise become coarse and primitive. *The Splitting of the Atom* is entirely *terre à terre*, without spiritual or religious considerations. The author reaches here a "dark pit" of philosophical indifference and torpor with regard to all aspects of human existence— here and beyond. It seems that the atom bomb had actually exploded within the human heart years before it exploded over Japan in 1945.[1] *The Splitting* is a natural consequence of the evolution of Russian Modernism in belles-lettres—art is hell; it is a monstrous inferno. The artist is eternally suspended between a precipice and an abyss. Despite these gloomy findings, the work is a valuable literary illustration of the latest phase in the history of Russian modernist fiction.

In *Petersburg Nights* Ivanov has also captured the inner rhythm of the twentieth-century *Zeitgeist*, mirrored in his own loneliness, the loss of his former ideals, his anguish and skepticism, and his craving for personal happiness. Ivanov's lyrical persona protects the image of Beauty from the devastating triviality of the new world—inane and vulgar. The thematic range of Georgy Ivanov's work is narrow, but this self-imposed limitation is assumed in order to render in greater relief his *Weltanschauung*.[2] Like Paganini, he was able to captivate his audience by playing on a single string, and like a magician, he materialized his remarkable, beautiful poetry out of Nothing.

NOTES

1. Cf. Vladimir Nabokov's play, *The Waltz Invention* (Paris, 1937–39), about Salvador Waltz's monstrously destructive invention which gives him unlimited power over other men.

2. For more details, see Irina Agushi, "The Poetry of Georgij Ivanov," *Harvard Slavic Studies* 5 (Cambridge: Harvard Univ. Press, 1970), pp. 109–158.

POEMS

FROM: *The Anchor: An Anthology of Emigré Poetry.* First published in *Rozy* (The Roses).

Passion? And if there is no passion?
Power? And if there is no power
Even over oneself?

What am I to do with you?

Only don't gaze at the stars,
Don't mourn, don't fall in love,
Don't recite melodious poems
And don't cling to happiness—
There's no happiness, my poor friend;
Happiness slipped from our hands,
It sank like a stone in the sea,
Splashed like a tiny goldfish,
Floated south like a chunk of ice.

There's no happiness, we're not children.
So, we must choose—
Either live like everyone else in the world
Or die.

———————

A bluish cloud
(A chill at the temple).
A bluish cloud
And still more clouds . . .

And an ancient apple tree
(Perhaps I should wait?)
An innocent apple tree
Blossoms anew.

It's somehow so Russian—
(Smile and squeeze the trigger!)
This narrow cloud,
Just like a boat with children.

351

GEORGY IVANOV

And especially the blue
(On the first strike of the clock . . .)
Hopeless horizon
Of endless forests.

FROM: *Sady: tretya kniga stikhov* (The Gardens: A Third Book of Poems).

I won't ask for love, nor sing about spring,
But that only you alone should heed my song.

Would I have the strength, O judge for yourself,
To glance into this snow and not go insane?

An average day, an average garden,
But why the pealing of bells all around

And nightingale songs, and flowers in snow?
Oh why, please answer, or is it you don't know?

Would I have the strength, O judge for yourself:
To glance into your eyes and not go insane?

I don't say believe, I don't say listen,
But I know even now you are gazing into this same snow

And over your shoulder, my love is watching
That snowy paradise surrounding you and me.

1921

FROM: *The Muse of the Diaspora: Selected Poems of Emigré Poets* (1920–1960), ed. Yu. Terapiano (Posev, 1960). First published in *Stikhi: 1943–1958* (Poems: 1943–1958)

To Roman Goul

In Russia there remain not even cherished graves,
Perhaps there were—but I've forgotten.

There is no Petersburg, Kiev, Moscow—
Perhaps they were, but I forgot, alas.

I don't know the borders, the seas or the rivers.
I know—there remains there a Russian man.

Russian in heart and Russian in mind,
If we were to meet, I'd know him

Instantly—half a word . . . And then I'd begin
To discern in the mist his country as well.

FROM: *Rozy* (The Roses).

I hear—history and mankind,
I hear exile or native land.

In books I read—goodness, deceit,
Hope, despair, belief, disbelief.

And see the gigantic, frightful, and tender,
Thoroughly frozen, hopeless forever.

And see frenzy or torment where forever
All things have lost their meaning.

And see, outside time and space—
Above the wretched earth, an unearthly radiance.

Irina Odoevtseva (1901–)

Irina Vladimirovna Odoevtseva (pseudonym of Iraida Gustavovna Heinecke), poet and novelist, was born in Riga. A member of the acmeist *Tsekh poetov* (Guild of Poets), she published a collection of ballads, *Dvor chudes* (Court of Miracles; St. Petersburg, 1922). Together with her husband, Georgy Ivanov, she emigrated from St. Petersburg to Paris in 1923. There she wrote several novels: *Angel smerti* (The Angel of Death; Paris, 1927), *Izol'da* (Isolde; Paris-Berlin, 1931), and *Zerkalo* (The Mirror; Paris, 1939). Since World War II Odoevtseva has published the collections of poetry *Kontrapunkt* (Counterpoint; Paris, 1950), *Stikhi, napisannye vo vremya bolezni* (Poems Written During an Illness; Paris, 1952), *Odinochestvo* (Solitude; Washington, 1965), *Desyat' let* (Ten Years; Paris, 1961), *Zlataya tsep'* (The Golden Chain; Paris, 1975), *Portret v rifmovannoy rame* (My Portrait in a Rhymed Frame; Paris, 1976); the memoirs *Na beregakh Nevy* (On the Banks of the Neva; Washington: Kamkin, 1967), containing reminiscences of Gumilyov, Anna Akhmatova, Arthur Lurye, Andrey Bely, and others; and the novel *Ostav' nadezhdu navsegda* (Abandon Hope Forever; New York, 1954).

Odoevtseva was known in Russia for her grotesque revolutionary ballads about the hungry and cold city of St. Petersburg. *On the Banks of the Neva* deals with the same period. She was a disciple of Nikolay Gumilyov and has retained some of his rules in versification, even in her current poetry. Its form is refined, the epithets are fresh and always to the point, the meter and rhyme are well controlled without hampering the free flow and suppleness of verse. Her pathos never becomes disturbing or annoying, because it is always subdued by playful irony. Some of the old clichés in poetry, like Lermontov's "I skuchno, i grustno, i nekomu ruku podat' " (I am bored, and sad, and there is no one to whom to extend my hand"), Odoevtseva has revived in good humor: "Ochen' mne i 'sku,' i 'gru'."[1] Her feminine, light, graceful, and delicate poetry relates both the tragic and the festive manifestations of life in their organic complexity—sadness and gaiety are interwoven. The world acquires the semblance of a mirror reflection, yet is completely free of the Symbolists' vagueness and reticence. Hers is a perfect sense of measure in poetic expression, and she carefully avoids verbosity and repetition.

As a poet, Odoevtseva requests little from life—only some fragments of happiness or peace, and she expects nothing from heaven. Her occasional references to paradise are striking in their "earthly" appearance: there are red and golden apples, the familiar fragrances of bird-cherry trees and luscious green grass. But there is also a certain tendency toward "Gothic ballad" features—black ravens, apparitions, forebodings, and prophetic dreams. This curious confluence of tragic atmosphere with fantastic and fairytale elements is Odoevtseva's contribution to poetry. Moreover, her verse, although always constructed as a short story, reveals through its exterior epic texture the persona's genuine lyricism combined with a poignant feeling of irony. This quality, too, indicates the originality of her poetic talent. Her only artistic defect, perhaps, may be found in the lack of deep concentration in her lyrics—her attention is scattered among diverse, emotions, details, visions, considerations, and omens.

As a novelist, Odoevtseva uses a different artistic method, even though a certain "feminine" quality remains in her fiction as well. Cleverly and wittily written, her novels resemble movie scripts. They lack complex psychological situations, truly dramatic collisions, and stylistic innovations. The well-to-do heroes have no particular aspirations other than the enjoyment of daily life. In their mediocrity and ordinariness, they are neither good nor evil; instead, they are simply too uninteresting to attract the reader's attention. Odoevtseva wrote only one "ideological" novel, *Abandon Hope Forever*, in which she attempted to solve some serious ethical and political problems; it is a complete failure from an artistic point of view. But her reminiscences *On the Banks of the Neva*, "About Teffi," and other chapters from the manuscript "Na beregakh Seny" (On the Banks of the Seine), on which she is working now, are attractively written with regard to the portraits and the manner of narration, at once ironic and sympathetic.

NOTE

1. Something like "Boy, I've got the 'slows' and the 'lows.' "

POEMS

FROM: *Odinochestvo* (Solitude).

> The heart of another (yours, reader?
> Yours, dreamer?
> Yours, stranger?)
> Beats in my breast,
> Growing heavier, more unrhythmical,
> Night and day and even in sleep,

Repeating over and over—
Something I don't understand.

On the wall, the floor, the window—
Silvery moonlight flecks;
And the ringing nightingale song
Of full moon delirium,
Swarthy mugs in the mirrors,
And enchanting, delicate faces—
Blur in the trembling of moon,
Though these are my own reflection,
None resemble me,
But beyond, in the mirrors, like a backdrop,
Terror scatters in sparks.

—Help me! Help!
Far away on the Island of Crete
A labyrinth, a bloodthirsty Minotaur,
And Ariadne's guiding thread.
There are other threads too—
They will lead you to me—
Seek, oh seek them out!

FROM: *Zlataya tsep'* (The Golden Chain).

Asleep and wide-awake
I live in utter joy.
—I.O.

In an alien land,
An alien family,
An alien auto. . .
Why am I here?. . .

Well yes, of course, even I
Once had
My land,
My home,
My family,
And my very own black poodle Krak.

All this is true.
But then
When February thunder crashed—
Destruction

nostalgia

and collapse,
A refugee's grief and
Seas, no, oceans of tears . . .
And the fatal question
Why didn't we stay at home?
By now just a bore—this story
Of us.
　　　　　Crushed under history's wheels.
It's useless to recall
What was. It was, now it's past,
Overgrown
　　　　　With weeds of oblivion . . .

The crystal air of the Pyrenees.
Still more rashly, tenderly
Sighs my heart,
Three thousand meters high,
Where the snow is heavenly blue
Life seems magically new
As when I was nineteen
On the banks of the Neva.

From the cliffs an eagle silently
Winged upward,
And flew up
Surely
To the throne of God.

—Stop, moment!
Oh stop and slide
Backward:

　　　　To Russia,
　　　　　　　To youth,
　　　　　　　　　　To Petrograd!

Cry of my heart,
So banal,
Devoid of magic,

For indeed I know
This moment won't stop,
Or slide backward,
And they won't return to me—
My country,

IRINA ODOEVTSEVA

My family,
   My home,
      My black poodle
      Krak.

FROM: *Portret v rifmovannoy rame: stikhi* (My Portrait in a Rhymed Frame: Poems).

I don't live only in poems,
I also live truly, for real,
And it's not hard to see me—
Look me over, critique me in print,
So as to tell others later
About me, as I was
In those years when I lived here
               Together with you
               On this earth.
But, of course, like all eyewitnesses,
You won't remember a thing.

With this I send you regards from Nice
And a present for Christmas—
My portrait in a rhymed frame—
Keep it for luck.

                                        1960–75

I can't forgive myself—
Though the others I've forgiven all—
That in your pernicious fate
I changed nothing,
Helped you in no way,
Failed to protect you from death.

All that your soul requested,
All that it loved here. . .
I was unable. I could not.

So little warmth on the earth,
So much coldness—and evil!

It seems early to die,
Although there's nothing to live for,

358

Nothing and no one.
A surrounding, shoreless ocean
Of my despair—
Despair triumphant.

My tears—not water and salt,
But tears of a widow—blood and pain.

It's frightening to be alone
But still more frightening—to be with others—
In this gyration of nonsense—
More frightening. More unbearable.

In the transparent silence of night,
Resound, barely audible,
Poems you dictated before death.

Tenth wave of despair.
      Darkness.
            And a lapse into unconsciousness—
            Till tomorrow.

                                        1958

oxemora — 2 contrasting properties put together

Anatoly Steiger (1907–1944)

Baron Anatoly Sergeevich Steiger, a Swiss citizen, was born on his father's estate near Kiev. After the Revolution of 1917 he went to Constantinople, where he lived with his sisters and brother Sergey in the Mennonite orphanage for Russian children. Via Prague, the Steiger family arrived in Paris, where Anatoly Steiger discovered a friend and mentor in Georgy Adamovich. He was also very fond of V. Sirin (whom he came to know in Berlin), of Boris Poplavsky and Georgy Ivanov. Steiger died of tuberculosis in a Swiss sanatorium on October 24, 1944.

Among his collections of verse are *Etot den'* (This Day; Paris, 1928), *Eta zhizn'* (This Life; Paris, 1931), *Neblagodarnost'* (Ingratitude; Paris, 1936), and *Dvazhdy dva chetyre: stikhi 1926–1939* (Twice Two Is Four: Poems 1926–1939; Paris, 1950; published posthumously). Steiger participated in the Merezhkovskys' Sunday salons; Zinaida Hippius, who liked Steiger's personality and poetic gift, considered him a talented and engaging writer. Steiger's correspondence with Marina Tsvetaeva was published in *Experiments* no. 8 (1957).

Despite his incurable illness, Steiger was very active in the literary life of "Russian Paris" and loved life, jokes, and gaiety. He was constantly engaged in literary discussions, especially with Adamovich at Montparnasse, concerning the artistic "Decadence" of St. Petersburg; later, politics would be discussed. (He even joined the party of *Mladorossy*, Young Russians.) He urged Georgy Ivanov "to tell him everything" about Anna Akhmatova, Vyacheslav Ivanov, Fyodor Sologub, Osip Mandel'shtam, and other poets of Russia's Northern capital. During World War II, while gravely ill, he became a journalist and conducted an open campaign against German propaganda, for which he was denounced in the Nazi press.

Anatoly Steiger's works expressed the essence of the "Parisian note" best of all. However, the lyrical purity and simplicity of his short verses surpassed the restrictions of Montparnasse's aesthetics. His poems are quiet, restrained, precise, profound, and sincere. Innokenty Annensky, Anna Akhmatova and (to some extent) Georgy Ivanov were his predecessors. Yet his poetry is original—he has his own intonation, style, and manner of lyrical expression. He treats many themes in his "diary-like" verse, uses aphoristic sentences, and conveys his feelings in concise, compressed, often unfinished lines. Digressions, the interplay of light and shadow, a lack of melodiousness and color are also among the formal characteristics of his poetry, which is devoid of artificial poses, abstract thought, splendor, undue familiarity, and wit.

These characteristic traits of Steiger's poetics underlie and accentuate the leitmotifs of his verse. Adamovich was of the opinion that Steiger's poetry originated from his craving for love, as well as from his sensations of pain. Perhaps, Steiger's craving for love even resulted in sensations of pain. Furthermore, the "muffled intonations" of the persona's voice extend beyond itself, to create a resonance akin to someone speaking in an empty room. This effect amplifies the persona's sense of relative isolation and alienation from human society, nature, and God.

This quality is apparent in the poem, "Actually, how very little," which appears below. The persona asks for "Love, a forsaken house, / The moon above an old pond, / And a rose bush by the porch." The accumulation of the images evokes a mood of nostalgia which, paradoxically, cancels the possibility of ever realizing such wishes. This, in turn, emphasizes the ironic tension of the poem, when we consider that these "very little" requests are actually quite enormous. Yet it is this very intrusion of irony which saves the poem from tones of pathos, shrillness, and affectation.

Elements of the passing of time and a prevalent mood of elegiac sadness combine in Steiger's poetry with an intense search for love and ultimate truth beyond the apparently incomprehensible and insipid surface of reality. These disparate strands are interwoven into a single, though multi-faceted, poetic texture which reveals a richness of thought and feeling beneath its seemingly simple, polished surface.

POEMS

FROM: *Eta zhizn': kniga vtoraya* (This Life: Book Two).

> Actually, how very little
> We ask of God for ourselves:
>
> Love, a forsaken house,
> The moon above an old pond,
> And a rose bush by the porch.
>
> That the roses bloom and bloom,
> The nightingales sing in the night,
> That those dark eyes of yours
> Not disappear from earth . . .

ANATOLY STEIGER

How little? But you're asking for years,
While the green water flows
As always, into the Seine,

And from the sky a voice is heard,
Indistinct—neither yes, nor no.

Mahrisch Trübau, 1930

We know—love occurs,
We know—there is happiness,
It's just that one heart doesn't know
How to break the news to another.

In some faraway land,
Or maybe right here beside us,
Are others, also awaiting
A sign, a voice, and their allotted hour . . .

But we pass by for years,
Not seeing them.
And allotted hours scatter, unseen,
Like sand from Your hands.

Kreuzborg

The priest is leading newlyweds.
The bridegroom is looking perplexed.
The bride, in translucent gauze
Like a cloud, is serene.

All is subject to decay. Of course,
In a year she'll betray him.
But with what will this boy replace
All he doesn't value today,
All he is yielding to her?

POEMS

FROM: *Dvazhdy dva chetyre: stikhi: 1926–1939* (Twice Two Is Four: Poems, 1926–1939).

AUTUMN

We will leave—and no one will notice,
We'll arrive—and no one will greet us,
No one will extend us a hand,
No one will look into our eyes,
Departing, forgiving, or greeting . . .

Across the sky floats the waning
Moon. The flowers are dying,
The leaves lie still.

And autumn, fallen onto its knees,
Beats its head on the step.

Vienna, 1930

Lidiya Chervinskaya (1907–)

Lidiya Davidovna Chervinskaya, like Anatoly Steiger, wrote poems in the spirit of the "Parisian note." Her verse is diary-like, very personal, with muffled intonations, phrases expressing the persona's perplexity and queries concerning the world of finite experience. Unexpected aphorisms impart a certain affectation to her style, as does the use of parentheses, dashes, and disconnected syntactical units to form many subordinate clauses. As in Steiger's poetry, there is little melodiousness; the *leitmotif* of her verse is approaching death. The emphasis is on the persona's experience of love—or, rather, "not love, but merely a shadow of the shadow of that love known as earthly." Hers is the poetry of belated regrets, pangs of conscience, and the domination of merciless intellect. Everything in these poems is subjected to the persona's analytical, inquisitive mind. They often sound like pieces of rhythmically arranged prose, expressing a call for silence—one of the foremost prerequisites of Georgy Adamovich's aesthetics. Chervinskaya's artistic technique reveals control and prowess, and there is charm, a joyous smile, and a fluency of poetic speech when she speaks about flowers, small insects, dreams, music, the tolling of church bells, and books. Her manner of expression is deceptively direct; her meaning is often complicated by ambiguous or obscure references. In comparison with Steiger's verse, hers—though also short—is not as compressed.

Chervinskaya's poetry excludes descriptive portrayals; the exterior world—nature—is also absent. Here and there scant, incomplete hints at the presence of an urban landscape do appear. Chervinskaya's gaze is always directed toward herself; contemplation, dusky moods, and a "muffled" voice are constantly in the foreground. Seldom do any bright colors enliven her poems; her favorite material is Indian ink, black and white halftones. She also avoids the musical tonality of verse, paying more attention to conversational intonations. To achieve a greater vividness, authenticity, and variety in these intonations, she frequently breaks the quatrain, ending her poem sometimes as a sonnet, or introducing a new line, or stopping in midsentence for an unexpected effect.

Chervinskaya's verse conveys the moods of an "urban heart." Her poetic universe is populated by shadows, and she attempts to convey to the reader this world of half-shadows, half-light, with its vagueness of outlines, diffusion of moods, and incompleteness, indefiniteness, or even duality of feelings, as in the lines: "I know—not knowing. I love—not loving./I remember—not remembering you." She often avails herself of incomplete, ambiguous, and paradoxical epithets; for example, "unintentional happiness," "unrealized fatigue," "an uncomplicated inaccessibility of the heart," or "clarity which is very inexact." Many of her epithets are prefixed with the negative particle "ne" (not)—"a strange, unfamiliar Eastern garb," "not a single sincere word," "not hypocrisy, not indifference"—expressions which are also indicative of an inner vagueness of the poet's sensations and experiences.

Chervinskaya's poems are irreproachable in artistic taste; there are neither declamations nor shortcomings. Hers is the poetry of allegories. The value of her work is unquestionable, for in it she conveys the atmosphere and poetic "jargon"[1] of Russian Montparnasse in prewar "Russian Paris."

Among Chervinskaya's major works are the following collections of poetry: *Priblizheniya* (Approaches; Paris, 1934), *Rassvety* (Dawns; Paris, 1937), and *Dvenadsat' mesyatsev* (Twelve Months; Paris, 1956). Her verse and critical essays appeared in various Russian-Parisian literary journals, newspapers, and anthologies.

NOTE

1. Yu. I. [Yury Ivask], "Lidiya Chervinskaya. *Dvenadsat' mesyatsev*," *Opyty* 8 (1957): 136.

POEMS

FROM: *The Anchor: An Anthology of Emigré Poetry.* First published in *Priblizheniya* (Approaches).

In May the doubts are calm . . .
I know—even this is poetry,
I feel—this is Spring.
I believe—sins will be forgiven
For those needing pity . . .

The rain is again light gray . . .
Sometimes it's hard to speak,
So why speak?
I know one must understand,
I think—one must love . . .

It's fearful to utter: forever . . .

LIDIYA CHERVINSKAYA

Somewhere the years are passing,
Somebody's years are ending,
Brightly they melt, no trace—
The music, the rain, the man . . .

If you haven't always followed
The waning moon without sorrow,
If you haven't always kept silent,
If you're not weary—not very weary,
Stay awhile with me.

Let's be more rational, sterner, attentive . . .
(Though why, and of what shall we speak—till dawn?)
A passerby smiled—at us?
We must seem very happy . . .
Goodbye. My time has also come.

FROM: *Sbornik stikhov, IV* (Collection of Poems, IV; Paris: The Union of Young Poets
and Writers, 1930).

> "In a wreath of violet flowers,
> In a silver kimono . . ." L.K. [Lazar' Kel'berin]

Blue, blue sounds—and you
In the gold of your beloved, thick hair . . .
He is merciless, your god of beauty,
Your unheard-of "Chinese" Christ.

In strange, unfamiliar Eastern garb—
Pale—and conscious of you alone—
He sojourned in your toy house—
Intricate, ornamental, essential to him.

A guest, discontent with his fate,
Having singled you out from countless souls
Returning to earth, he merged with you.
Mute ink has turned into sound.

. . . Stern child, solemnly evil,
Your beauty's a riddle to me,

366

Etched by a delicate needle, it's terrifying to me,
The image of this unforgiving Christ.

Paris, 1930

FROM: *Rassvety* (Dawns). First published in *Numbers* no. 10 (1934).

It's almost like an awareness
It's almost like a confession—
That from this offense my blood is raging.
Perhaps, it's an unintentional deception,
Perhaps, joy—tormenting, elusive.
Perhaps, it is—love.

I know—not knowing. I love—not loving.
I remember—not remembering you.

The sun is cold, happiness lies in dreams,
The white sky in my high window . . .

Maybe what churns inside me is—birth
Of new sorrow.

Perhaps, this is only again the reflection
Of this ultimate, languishing clarity.
Of this haughty disgraceful muteness—
Of being silently true to You.

FROM: *Dvenadsat' mesyatsev* (Twelve Months).

April: The early sun behind the red curtain.
The solar ray penetrates the window
in contrast with life which is
cold, narrow, dark.

In contrast with the ray—the inevitability
of approaching death, separation, the end . . .
My passionate tenderness—in contrast
with stinging pity at the sight of a dear
face, no longer young.

To separate so, without a single word . . .
This I shall never understand.

367

While loving, we didn't have time to notice
how enmity arose between us.
A pure, bright morning in April . . .
Where was it? When?

October: What is death like? I don't know: a flight
          or a fall . . .
                  A flame or night . . .
          A pain or oblivion . . .
                  Snow or blood . . .
          I only know that, when your hour comes,
          I will not die with you, I shall not be of help . . .
          For what, then, is my love?

December: Such silence encircles,
          as if the world were mortally ill
          and sunk in a heavy, yet sensitive dream.

          In the distance, in the brilliant snowy wadding,
          clocks of hazy bell towers
          like Christmas decorations . . .

          For what now are the empty dreams,
          when the hour of judgment is so near
          and you remember only atonement . . .

          As if by a hypnotic force
          the golden hands twitch
          on the bright blue clock face.

                                    Zurich

Dovid Knut (1900–1955)

David Mironovich Fiksman (pseudonym Dovid Knut), an *émigré* poet in Paris, was born in Orgeev near Kishinev in Bessarabia. Together with Boris Bozhnev, Alexander Ginger, Boris Poplavsky, and Serge Charchoune, he organized the literary group *Palata poetov* (The Chamber of Poets) in 1922.[1] He wrote several collections of poetry: *Moikh tysyachelety* (Of My Millennia; Paris, 1925), *Vtoraya kniga stikhov* (A Second Book of Verse; Paris, 1928), *Parizhskie nochi: trety sbornik stikhov* (Paris Nights: A Third Collection of Poems; Paris, 1932), *Nasushchnaya lyubov': chetvyortaya kniga stikhov* (A Vital Love: A Fourth Book of Poems; Paris, 1938), *Nasushchnaya lyubov': chetvyortaya kniga stikhov* (A Vital Love: A Fourth Book of Poems; Paris, 1938), and *Izbrannye stikhi* (Selected Verse; Paris, 1949). Following the liberation, he went to Israel, where he died of cancer. With his wife, Ariadna Scriabin, daughter of the famed composer, Knut took active part in the Jewish Resistance during the German occupation of Paris. The poet's wife was caught and summarily executed by the Germans. Despite this tragedy, Knut continued his anti-Nazi efforts.

The originality of Knut's poetic talent, his inimitably personal intonation, and his fresh, unusual conceptions are obvious even in his first volume of poetry. He was very successful with the trisyllabic meters which he employed in his slow, sorrowful, or exultant poem-meditations on the fate of the Jewish people. These poems were treasured by a devoted circle of sophisticated readers in Paris. Some of Knut's poetry is dedicated to the Jewish-Russian town of Kishinev, where Pushkin conceived his novel in verse, *Evgeny Onegin*. Several of Dovid Knut's descriptions—of the Jewish funeral service, for example—are especially vivid and haunting. He wrote poems in Hebrew as well. His lyrics are, in general, very energetic, emotional, even passionate, loud, and often solemn. Such a Muse, of course, did not harmonize with the "muffled voices and whispers" of the "Parisian note" poetry, or with the majority of *émigré* public. However, "The Dialogue," cited below, may be considered as a mock "Parisian note" poem, with its profusion of elliptical phrases and half-expressed thoughts. Yet beneath this parody of form there lies a deeper and serious thematic intent which constitutes one of the central leitmotifs of Knut's oeuvre—that is, man's persistent alienation from God, the world, and even himself.

To illustrate the salient features of Knut's peculiar stylistic and poetic signature, as well as his views on man and his place in the universe, it would seem necessary to analyze "Apotheosis" at some length. In this poem he employs a series of verbs which are made more emphatic by the imperative tense: "Silence!" "Listen!" "Hover," "Sear," etc. In addition, the disruption of the forms of traditional poetry at times results in lines which contain only a single word. This effect serves to amplify the significance of the sound and even the shape of the word, and also to intensify its underlying metaphysical conception. The use of the imperative, abrupt starts and stops in the rhythmic texture, as well as of powerful images and striking epithets such as "I am/The lowliest nit,/Feeding from Thine udder" aid in creating the impression of speech compressed to the very limit of human endurance—or, rather, speech that is all too conscious of its inability to express the inexpressible glory of God, yet is forced, almost of its own volition, to speak in muted tones and through clenched teeth.

This attitude of man in relation to his Maker is illuminated in the content of the poem itself. Man, even the poet who is blessed with the ability to hear the song of the Lord, considers himself to be "small," "mute," "dumb," "Thy lowliest dog." And yet he is privy to knowledge not only of his Creator, but also of the accompanying "Word," which in this context bears a strong similarity to the concept of "Logos" in Osip Mandelshtam's philosophical world outlook. What the persona experiences, then, is his being reflected against the glory of God's image, which further elucidates why it is that man seems so small and sooty against such a pure eminence of divinity. It is clear that, in this view, man may not aspire to be like God; but he may, if he is blessed with grace, gain a sense of "The Word" which is Knut's evidence not only of a poet's calling but of the Lord's true existence.

Biblical themes, eroticism with biblical overtones, and vigorous diction are also salient traits of Knut's poetics. The pathos and verbal intoxication of his early poetry led to several serious artistic deficiencies—his occasionally bombastic language, pompous garrulity, and rather cheap bacchanalia of erotic fervor and unbridled temperament. But his later works are humane, simple, sincere, and restrained. *Paris Nights* is the best of Knut's collections of verse. Here the cumbrous imagery and "excessive noise and crash"[2] (in Yury Terapiano's words) are absent. In this book Knut displays his mastery of craftsmanship and poetic diction.

NOTES

1. See *Novaya russkaya kniga* no. 2 (1922): 33, for further information.
2. "Pamyati Dovida Knuta," *Opyty* 5 (1955): 94.

POEMS

FROM: *Moikh tysyachelety* (Of My Millennia).

APOTHEOSIS

Silence!
Clamp shut those indecent lips!
Across your crude and unseemly tongue
Be branded a white-hot seal.

In silence,
Unheard of,
Enormous,
Dumbfounding,
Our ears will rise in deference—
To hear.

Lord, look upon me.
I stand,
I am small,
I am mute,
I am dumb.
I am
Thy lowliest dog.

I am
The lowliest nit,
Feeding from Thine udder . . .

Silence!
Melt the soul in silence!
Listen!

And, lo,
In silence
To me
Come the tidings:
Behold.

And, lo,
In silence
To me

371

Comes the song:
Behold.

And, lo,
In silence
To me
Comes the sign:
It is so.

With peaceful light it illumined—
With vernal fragrance it scented—
With empyreal joy overshadowed—

Hover,
And warm,
Thou Beneficent One.

Sear
The infinite
Darkness.

Grant Thy grace
To all, O Lord,
To all, my God,

        —Whose souls dwell in blackest pitch,
        —To creatures, inhuman,
        —Transient, strange,
        —To all these ugly mugs and mutants
        Of Thy net's catch.

O Lord!
I breathe not.
I stand not.
I dare not—

In the heavenly murmur,
In the celestial trampling,

It hovers—
Deepening blue—
The Word.

Ineffable.
Inimitable.
Supreme.

FROM: *Izbrannye stikhi* (Selected Poems). "Get Away" was first published in *Parizhskie nochi* (Paris Nights). "The Dialogue" was first published in *Nasushchnaya lyubov'* (A Vital Love).

GET AWAY

Get away from me, O man, get away—I'm yawning.
With this awful price I pay for my wretched wisdom.
You see my arm lying on the table as if alive—
I unclench my fist, no longer wanting anything.

Get away from me, O man. You can't help.
A barren, oppressive night congeals over me.

THE DIALOGUE

—Oh, if we only knew . . .
        —May I interrupt you?
Say, old chap, what time is it?

—And so we forget . . .

        —Beg your pardon, I know what day it is,
But can't for the life of me remember the date.

. . . And so—every man for himself—and about himself—
In this vicious human fate.

Antonin Ladinsky (1896–1961)

Antonin Petrovich Ladinsky, formerly an officer in the White Army, emigrated to Paris in 1921 and lived there until 1948. He published several books of poetry, including *Chernoe i goluboe* (The Black and the Azure; Paris, 1930), *Severnoe serdtse* (A Northern Heart; Berlin, 1931), *Stikhi o Evrope* (Poems about Europe; Paris, 1937), and *Pyat' chuvstv: chetvyortaya kniga stikhov* (Five Senses: A Fourth Book of Poetry; Paris, 1939). He also wrote several novels, among them *15-y legion: istorichesky roman* (The 15th Legion: A Historical Novel; Tallin, 1937) and *Puteshestvie v Palestinu* (A Journey to Palestine; Tallin, 1937).

Ladinsky was an erudite man and an excellent stylist, especially in his Russian translations of Voltaire and other French writers. In the late 1940's he became a "Soviet patriot" and in 1948 he returned to the Soviet Union, where he published the article "Poslednie dni I. A. Bunina" (The Last Days of I. A. Bunin, *Literaturnaya gazeta* [Literary Gazette], October 22, 1955). Following that essay, he published the historical novels *Kogda pal Khersones* (When Khersones Fell; Moscow, 1959),[1] *V dni Karakally* (In the Days of Caracalla; Moscow, 1961), *Anna Yaroslavna—Koroleva Frantsii* (Anna Yaroslavna, Queen of France; Moscow, 1961), and *Posledny put' Monomakha* (The Last Journey of Monomakh; Moscow, 1966; published posthumously). He did not publish poetry in Russia.

Ladinsky was a serious and original poet. He grieved for the fate of Europe and portrayed his impressions quite vividly, being endowed with a rare gift for rendering artistically the *Zeitgeist* of a historical period. His sketches of the lives of historical personalities were equally successful; for example, Vladimir Monomakh's marriage, his fate, battles, internecine wars, defeats and victories. Although the fall of the Roman Empire and the development of the ensuing Christian world, as well as the Christianization of Russia by Prince Vladimir, are topics of great cultural and historical significance, Ladinsky, like Mark Aldanov, was mainly interested in the sequence of historical epochs and the reflection of the present in the past. His curiosity about cultural and historical themes is evident even in his poetry. Haunted by the vision of the impending spiritual demise of Europe, he wrote *Poems about Europe*, conveying the continent's cultural malaise. Here he is akin to Osip Mandel'shtam and Tyutchev, who also dedicated many poems to these subjects. Ladinsky, moreover, resembles Gumilyov in the "masculine" tonality of his verse and in his love of exotic lands. Ladinsky's poetic world is vibrant with sound and

374

color—it is decorative, festive, romantic, and variegated, and yet at the same time, frail and unstable. It is a sad and magnificent ball, a kind of final celebration of the St. Petersburg era.

Despite the underlying feeling of something drawing to a close, Ladinsky's poetry rushes forward headlong—there is a wild whirling of airborne people, suspended above the earth before the last day, the thundering of the entire world's breakers, or the music of heaven. There is abundant light and spaciousness in his poems, a desire for life, and the sensual enjoyment of earthly existence. Against the background of Steiger's and Chervinskaya's colorless and monotonously flat poems, Ladinsky's poetic universe is strikingly vibrant and musical. In his technique also he is altogether different, being fond of the sonorous iamb and trochee, of metrical accelerations, exclamatory intonations, archaisms, hyperbole, rhetoric, and bold, memorable imagery. Although he wrote poems about Egypt and the Caucasus (including a long piece entitled "A Geographical Poem"), alongside these stylized exotic landscapes Ladinsky created his own personal universe in which snow, ice, blue sky, dark earth, ballet, and the theatre constitute his favorite images.

Ladinsky also tried his hand at lyrical poetry (for example, "A Poem about an Oak") and odes in the style of Lomonosov; here, too, he proved to be an original, gifted poet. However, the dominant theme of his entire poetic work was "Great Russia"—a culture, a way of life, receding into the irretrievable past.

NOTE

1. Formerly *Golub' nad Pontom: istorichesky roman* (Tallin, 1938).

POEMS

FROM: *Stikhi o Evrope* (Poems about Europe).

> A man steps out for a moment.
> And quits this world for good.
>
> Returning home no more,
> Finding rest beneath a wheel in the street.
>
> He probably reckoned on living long,
> Had hopes for happiness, possibly.

Wished to settle all his affairs
Here in our fragile world of glass.

But he failed the Almighty judgment and design,
Couldn't realize His heavenly intent.

Of course, he did his best to breathe
And even shed tears for the beautiful.

But he overlooked the essential
In all his trifling affairs.

1933

———————

How boring
Without the circles of hell,
Without the inseparable Muses,
Without tears, without poetry.

Without lengthy—till dawn—
Sleepless nights in hell,
Without the bitter taste of
Lead in your mouth.

Without music. In sinful
Love without lies,
Without inconsolable
Partings, transformations.

How horrid and dull:
A Sahara of flats
And a well organized
World . . .

Then, in marble,
A grand mausoleum
Inscribed: "Most Glorified . . .
Peace to his dust" . . . Holy oil.

Perhaps there is only
Bland ether then,

Vapid eternity
In blue paradise.

FROM: *Severnoe serdtse* (A Northern Heart).

Languishing absently in your daily cares,
At night you fly away from me,
Then at dawn, from a light blue road,
You return home in tears.

Turning toward you from my desk,
I ask, "Where have you been?
Where have you spent the night? In heaven?
But why have you come back weeping?"

Wringing your hands, hearing someone's call,
Not finding words to reply,
You remember slowly, with effort,
A tall, white house,

Far-away hills,
Hazy trees by the water.
You tell me: "I've seen a land
Like the moon of paradise.

I've seen the snow falling
Onto shores of huge, dark rivers.
I've heard in the frosty silence
Now music, now anguish, sobbing in sleep.

But alas, I cannot recall
Its name—this illusory land,
Perhaps it was Russia, or paradise,
Such a beautiful, sorrowful place . . ."

Vladimir Smolensky
(1901–1961)

Vladimir Alexeevich Smolensky was the son of Alexey Smolensky, a Colonel in the Imperial Army. In 1920 the father was shot by the Bolsheviks on his estate near Lugansk. Vladimir Smolensky was very young when he volunteered to fight in the White Army against the Bolsheviks. His military detachment was evacuated from the Crimea in 1921. First he lived in Africa, in Tunis, where he began writing poetry. In 1923 he moved to Paris, where he worked as a laborer in the automobile and metal industries. Later he received a scholarship, graduated from high school, and finished his studies at the Commercial Academy of the University of Paris. After his graduation from the Academy he worked as a bookkeeper in the wine industry. Throughout his life in emigration he suffered much for his uncompromising hatred of the Bolsheviks, who had forced him into exile and who continued to destroy his beloved Russia. In an attempt to alleviate his anguish, he began to drink. He died in Paris, from cancer—a slow and painful death. The poems written just before his death convey moods of humility and repentance.

When Smolensky arrived in Paris from Tunis, the French capital was already host to many eminent Russian artists and writers. Shalyapin was singing; Anna Pavlova delighted French audiences with her ethereal dancing; Bakst, Benois, and Korovin produced beautiful costumes and scenery for Sergey Diaghilev's Ballet Russe and created their remarkable paintings. There were many Russian newspapers, journals, and almanacs. The young literati formed circles and groups, gathering at Montparnasse, with Georgy Adamovich at the center. Poetry and belles-lettres were discussed at the Merezhkovskys' Sunday *soirées* and The Green Lamp; Vladislav Khodasevich and Ivan Bunin also attracted many young writers to their literary gatherings. Bunin, Hippius, Boris Zaytsev, Mark Aldanov, V. Sirin, Ivan Shmelyov, and many other illustrious writers published their works in *Contemporary Annals* and were responsible for stimulating great creative activity in the arts.

Smolensky, with his attractive, romantic appearance and beautiful voice, became a favorite poet in "Russian Paris." He often recited his works at various literary gatherings, at the request of his sympathetic audience. His lyrics were praised by Khodasevich, a difficult and exacting critic, and by

Pyotr Bicilli, who, in one of his essays, referred to Smolensky as a "true poet," capable of music and "pure lyricism."[1]

Among Smolensky's works are four collections of verse: *Zakat: pervaya kniga stikhov* (Sunset: A First Book of Poetry; Paris, 1931), *Nayedine: vtoraya kniga stikhov* (In Private: A Second Book of Poetry; Paris, 1938), *Shchastye: sobranie stikhov* (Happiness: A Collection of Poems; Paris, 1957), and *Stikhi 1957–1961: chetvyortaya kniga stikhov* (Poems 1957–1961: A Fourth Book of Poetry; Paris, 1962, published posthumously). He was an editor of *Orion: A Literary Almanac* (1947).

Smolensky is a romantic poet, his romanticism stemming from the works of Alexander Blok (of the era of "Snezhnaya maska" [The Snow Mask] and "Strashny mir" [The Frightful World]), Tyuchev, and Lermontov. His expression of rapture in loneliness, pessimism, despair, and death also resembles some of Georgy Ivanov's poetry, though it does not spring from the same philosophical convictions. Smolensky appears more restrained, perhaps more rational, and more complex in his treatment of emotions than does Ivanov.

Death is the favorite theme in Smolensky. Tamara Velichkovskaya[2] maintains that the word "death" and its derivatives form the largest section of his poetic vocabulary. "Love" and "dream" occupy second place; "wings" and "darkness" the third; and "heart," "angel," "coldness," "stars," "God," "soul," and "loneliness" the fourth. He treats the stars and angels not as poetic properties, but as eternal, frightening, unfathomable mysteries. A special place in Smolensky's work is occupied by his poems about Russia. They are serious and tragic in their essence. He remembers his childhood, speaks with his beloved father, and grieves over the destruction of the Russian spirit surrounded by "snow," "ice," "impenetrable darkness," "despair," and "obtuse insanity." Love, God, the light of reconciliation and enlightenment, Christian humility, and faith in God's mercy enter his later poems. In these he did not hesitate to employ a lofty vocabulary and an elevated tone. His personal themes, however, go beyond the usual limitations of personal lyrics, and his craftsmanship clearly reveals the poet's artistic taste and his perfect control of rhythm, color, sound, musicality, and figures of speech.

Tamara Velichkovskaya remembers one of Smolensky's readings of his own poems in Paris, which took place in an old and mysterious mansion. With many precious *objets d'art* in every room, the mansion was romantically linked with the names of Turgenev and Pauline Viardot. Their portraits hung in the large drawing room, which had become so crowded that some of the audience spilled out into the wide corridor. The tall, slender, and very handsome poet recited his verse in a sonorous, pleasant voice—slowly, with a singsong lilt. The perfect merging of audience, setting, figure, personality, and poetry so captivated them that, wishing to hear more and more poems, they refused to let him go. Such was the aura surrounding him.

VLADIMIR SMOLENSKY

NOTES

1. P. Bicilli, "Vl. Smolensky. *Zakat*. Paris, 1931," *Sovremennye zapiski* 49 (1932): 450–451.
2. "O Vladimire Smolenskom," *Vozrozhdenie* no. 142 (1963).

POEMS

FROM: *Sobranie stikhotvoreny* (A Collection of Poems; Paris, 1957). This poem was first published in *Zakat* (Sunset).

They will live crammed—the earth will be crammed like a prison—
They will know there is no God, no hell, no eternity,
They will build houses of concrete and steel, higher than clouds,
And a great airship will reach the farthest planet.

And when the trumpet sounds over the whirling world,
When heaven opens like a door above the earth,
When the lights go out, and coffins open in crypts—
No man will understand anything, no man will believe . . .

1929

Days follow nights,
With lights extinguished indifferently.

Dream floats after dream,
Identical, dark.

The firmament closes in.
I know, O Lord—this is death.

I know, O Lord, it was You
Who led me down this path of destitution,

You, who extinguished the lights around me,
The visions in dreams, the nights, and days,

So that I, in impenetrable dark,
On this empty and icy earth,

380

And destined like all to die
Would have nothing to regret.

———————

This poem was first published in *Numbers* nos. 7-8 (1933); then in *Nayedine* (In Private).

Seven letters, three syllables, a word, a name—you,
Radiance from the celestial darkness.

Seven letters, like a steel chain—cannot be broken;
Seven letters—we cannot write until death.

Three syllables, three wings, raising the dust,
Sail through the heavens like winds.

A single, simple word, but fired,
Like coal, white-hot.

FROM: *The Anchor: An Anthology of Emigré Poetry.* This poem was first published in
Numbers nos. 2-3 (1933).

What's it to me that you live?
What's it to me that you'll die?
I don't pity you—in the least.
For me, you're invisible, deaf, and mute.
Your name, how you lived,
I never knew or forgot,
And should your coffin pass by me,
My hand wouldn't even touch my brow.

Yet I dread to think that I, too,
Mean nothing at all to you,
That my life, my death, and my dreams
Are irrelevant, boring to you,
That everywhere—God is a witness—
I'm profoundly, forever—alone.

Sergey Makovsky (1877–1962)

Sergey Konstantinovich Makovsky, a poet, critic, art theorist, and writer of memoirs, was the son of the celebrated painter Konstantin Makovsky. From 1909 to 1913 Sergey Makovsky edited the St. Petersburg journal *Apollo*, where he printed the poems of his two "discoveries," Anna Akhmatova and Cherubina de Gabriak. While still in Russia, he published several books, including *Sobranie stikhov* (Collected Poems; St. Petersburg, 1905) and *Russkaya grafika* (Russian Graphics; St. Petersburg, 1915). Over a period of several years he headed the publishing house Rifma (Rhyme), which printed collections of poetry by Georgy Ivanov, Yury Ivask, Irina Odoevtseva, Lidiya Chervinskaya, Anatoly Steiger, and other Russian poets. In exile Makovsky published a variety of books: *Siluety russkikh khudozhnikov* (Silhouettes of Russian Artists; Prague, 1921), *Poslednie itogi zhivopisi* (A Final Summation of Painting; Berlin, 1922), *Somnium Breve* (Paris, 1948), *God v usad'be: sonety* (A Year on a Country Estate: Sonnets; Paris, 1949), *Krug i teni: pyataya kniga stikhov* (Circle and Shadows: A Fifth Book of Poetry; Paris, 1951), *Na puti zemnom: shestaya kniga stikhov* (On a Land Journey: A Sixth Book of Poetry; Paris, 1953), *V lesu: sed'maya kniga stikhov* (In the Forest: A Seventh Book of Verse; Munich, 1956), *Eshcho stranitsa: vos'maya kniga stikhov* (Another Page: An Eighth Book of Poems; Paris, 1957), *Na Parnase Serebryanogo veka* (On the Parnassus of the Silver Age; Munich, 1962), and *Requiem* (Paris, 1963).

Makovsky's poetry resembles Tyutchev's later verse. The twentieth-century spirit of experimentation in versification and belles-lettres was alien to him; instead he looked for inspiration to the old and well-tested Russian poetic tradition. Heavy archaisms from the eighteenth century (and from Tyutchev) and a craving for "concentrated solitude" from Pushkin were the two distinguishing features of his poetic world. He accepted life with wisdom and sober gratitude — especially in Italy, where he could meditate on the Old Testament while admiring the ruins of ancient Rome. Makovsky was a writer of great and genuine culture.

POEMS

FROM: *Somnium breve: stikhi* (Somnium Breve: Poems).

To Z. N. Hippius

Beware of phantoms — of shadows, of shadows
    from that land once so dear:
to the heart who has not forgotten it
    shadows will say, "This was."

At the time of repentant anguish, anguish,
    fated and waiting for you,
those misty hosts will move
    and take you along with them.

Into their pools — moving backward, backward
    they will direct your soul,
and sprinkle dead water upon you,
    and bind you in shrouds.

Beware of memory, painful, painful
    languor for ones loved long ago,
and of love, dispersing in ages past,
    like smoke over graves.

Yury Mandel'shtam (1908–1943)

Yury Vladimirovich Mandel'shtam, a young *émigré* poet and literary critic, was married to the eldest daughter of Igor' Stravinsky, Lyudmila Stravinskaya, who died shortly before World War II. Mandel 'shtam himself was deported by the Gestapo and died in a German concentration camp during the war. He graduated from the University of Paris, spoke several languages, and was an expert in French, English, and Russian literatures and cultures.

Mandel 'shtam wrote several collections of verse: *Ostrov* (The Island; Paris, 1930), *Vernost'* (Loyalty; Paris, 1932), *Trety chas* (The Third Hour; Berlin, 1935), *Gody* (Years; Paris, 1950), and a book about Dante, Goethe, Napoleon, Beethoven, Balzac, Mérimée, Rimbaud, Rilke, and others, entitled *Iskateli: etyudy* (Searchers: Sketches; Shanghai, 1938). He was also the author of scholarly, well-written critical articles on Bunin, Andrey Bely, Lev Shestov, and other writers, poets, and philosophers.

A follower of Khodasevich's system of versification, Mandel'shtam polished the exterior form of his verse and tended to impart to it an intellectual, reflective streak. His poetry is erudite and reveals an exquisite literary taste, artistic restraint, sobriety, and a positive attitude toward life with all of its hidden discords and bewildering complexities. Whereas Mandel'shtam's early poems aspire to Neo-Classicism, his later work manifests Romantic tendencies, humane feelings, and a deceptive simplicity of style.

In much of his poetry Mandel'shtam juxtaposes concepts and images such as extravagance and miserliness, "life's desert" and a "bright ethereal blue dream," memory and forgetfulness, and happiness and pain, to name a few. These appositions serve to intensify an undercurrent of philosophical inquiry in his verse. This is especially notable in "Prayers," in which a monk, a soldier, and a poet voice their individual prayers by turn as the choir, "behind the wall singing," serves as a refrain, as a linking device, and as an echo to the traditions of ancient Greek tragedy. What is particularly striking about the content of each of these prayers is that it becomes increasingly evident that each could not avoid committing the very sin he asks forgiveness for: the monk had to doubt in order to find faith; the soldier had to kill, for that is the nature of war and of his profession; and the poet must experience the joy and

pain of sensuality and love in order to create his verse. This progression leads
to a view of the continuity of all life which is further reinforced not only by
the choir, but by their "strange songs," which are, of course, the songs and life
itself, and as such reflect Mandel'shtam's positive and sober attitudes.

POEMS

FROM: *Sbornik stikhov, I* (Collection of Poems, I; Paris, 1929).

PRAYERS

The choir behind the wall was singing
Strange songs.
                    A monk prayed:
"I have known doubt and creeping fear.
Forgive me, Lord—along the dark path
I wavered in deciding to follow Thee!
Forgive me, Lord!
Grant that on my long path
I may hear the victorious: 'Lazarus, rise'—
            Sweet destiny."

The choir behind the wall was singing
Strange songs.
                    A soldier prayed:
"Clothed with my flesh, I have gone through hell—
—Its eternal fire and clatter of demons' hooves.
Lord, forgive me my murders and timid protests!
Forgive me, Lord!
Grant, at times, on my difficult path
I may hear music more tender and miraculous
            Than flashing bullets."

The choir behind the wall was singing
Strange songs.
                    A poet prayed:
"Lord, forgive me—in my twilight years

My eyes watched and my ears listened,
Our arms entwined as did our sinful souls.
Forgive me, Lord!
Grant me, O Lord, on my sorrowful path
Happiness more poignant, pain yet unfathomed,
Sweeter images, more enchanting sounds—
   —The secret boundaries."

The choir behind the wall was singing
Strange songs.

1928

FROM: *Perekryostok: sbornik poezii* (The Crossing: A Collection of Poems; Paris: Povolotsky, 1930). This poem was first published in *Vernost'* (Loyalty).

To Vladimir Smolensky

What's with this world? In it we are so dissimilar:
I am extravagant; you, miserly and poor.
Yet we'll both die of loneliness,
To us the earth's a bore, and noon is pale.

We tire of our flighty friends.
But the closer and more essential each to the other,
All the more do worthless words and people
Divide us like an abysmal sea.

FROM: *Gody: stikhi 1937–1941* (Years: Poems 1937–1941).

Do you see? In life's desert
You've not been cheated.
There rises in the dark-blue night
A bright ethereal blue dream.

Lighter than happiness, snow, or sky
Is this light dream and radiant hour,
With the radiance of mysterious harmony,
With the radiance of unadorned joy.

But by morning you will forget
This fortuitous dream.
So forget. The time will come
To remember all mysteries.

Victor Mamchenko (1907–)

Victor Andreevich Mamchenko, born in Nikolaev, was conscripted into the Imperial Navy and went by ship to Africa in 1920, as a sailor. In Tunis he worked as a longshoreman, a farm hand, and a painter. There he published his early poems in the journal *The Black Lily*. In 1923 he moved to Paris and entered the University of Paris, returning soon thereafter, however, to his work as a builder and painter. Later he taught the Russian language to French adults and edited manuscripts written by his fellow exiles. In Paris he published poems and articles in various Russian literary journals and anthologies, and in Russian-language newspapers. Together with Vadim Andreev, Dovid Knut, Antonin Ladinsky, Yury Terapiano, and other Russian poets in exile, Mamchenko organized and actively participated in the Union of Young Poets and Prose Writers, 1924–1956; Terapiano served as its first chairman. Between 1936 and 1975 Mamchenko published seven volumes of poetry: *Tyazholye ptitsy* (Heavy Birds; Paris, 1936), *Zvyozdy v adu* (Stars in Hell; Paris, 1946), *V potoke sveta* (In a Flood of Light; Paris, 1949), *Zemlya i lira* (Earth and Lyre; Paris, 1951), *Pevchy chas* (The Choral Hour; Paris, 1957), *Vospitanie serdtsa* (The Education of the Heart; Paris, 1964), and *Son v kholodnom dome* (A Dream in a Cold House; Paris, 1975), the latter compiled during his present confinement in a Russian nursing home near Paris, where Mamchenko lives partially paralyzed and mute.

In the early 1920's Mamchenko became very close to Zinaida Hippius. He shared many of her innermost thoughts and ideas, particularly her concept of sublime and spiritual love. She used to call him affectionately her "Friend Number One" among the guests at her literary Sunday salons. In his loyalty and passionate strivings he reminded her of St. John of the Cross. Toward the end of her life, however, Hippius's letters to Greta Gerell[1] repeatedly expressed her disappointment in her once-dear friend, who had begun to drift away from her cherished ideals. Her long poem "Posledny krug" (The Last Circle)[2] was dedicated to Mamchenko as a token of her gratitude for their former spiritual and "brotherly love." The dedication is dated October 26, 1943.

The main themes in Mamchenko's work concern love, life, and death, which he treats in the light of the eternal ethical norm—absolute goodness and absolute morality. Loyalty, friendship, the idea of men's mutual responsibility toward one another, the necessity of performing good, moral deeds and of struggling against all evil and violence—these form the basis of human interrelationships, as Mamchenko conceives of them. His persona does not wish to accept the past and the present because they have been founded on acts of volitional destruction and desecration. Therefore the persona tends to withdraw into his own world of reverie, amidst the beauty of nature's birds, flowers, and the distant, unattainable blue sky. Only occasionally does Mamchenko write lyrical poetry about his childhood and youth in distant Russia. He is fond of Pushkin and Tyutchev, and among Russian fiction writers he favors Dostoevsky and Lev Tolstoy.

Because of the abstract and generalized nature of his poems, it is rather difficult to fathom them completely. As Gleb Struve aptly puts it, Mamchenko is a difficult poet since he is "tongue-tied."[3] At times it is not easy to see what is hidden behind his imagery. Although he is less "tongue-tied" in his later poetry, even here the reader is often hindered in his attempt to re-create the poet's universe because of a certain boundary, as it were, beyond which he cannot move. The air is very thin in Mamchenko's work; it is difficult to breathe the rarefied atmosphere of his domain of reverie, devoid of all concrete outlines. The persona, estranged from the world of finite experience, finds his existence in some distant, indefinite (though not fantastic) realm.

While Mamchenko's versification has been likened to that of Khlebnikov, this resemblance is only superficial, for he avails himself of the so-called synthetic meter.[4] This likeness gradually disappears in his later poems, but his works continue to appear somewhat elusive because of his monotonous rhymes and obscure vocabulary. Often, however, the reader is stunned by the luminous, vigorous, and gripping formulations in his verse—in "Osenny den' vokrug" (The Autumnal Day Is Around) or "O, da, moy drug, ne nado slyoz i strakha" (Oh, yes, my friend, let's be without tears and fright), for example. It is obvious that Mamchenko's poetic universe and craftsmanship are in need of serious study and evaluation.

NOTES

1. See Pachmuss, *Intellect and Ideas in Action: Selected Correspondence of Zinaida Hippius*, pp. 531–639.
2. Edited and with an Introduction by T. Pachmuss, *Vozrozhdenie* nos. 198, 199 (1968): 7–51, 4–47, respectively. Read about "The Last Circle" in Temira Pachmuss, *Zinaida Hippius: An Intellectual Profile*, pp. 287–304.
3. Gleb Struve, *Russkaya literatura v izgnanii*, p. 335.
4. *Ibid.*, p. 335.

POEMS

FROM: *Vospitanie serdtsa* (The Education of the Heart).

NICE

Like eternity in bygone days —
I see you among the rocks;
With a white bird, the azure air
Floats, peaceful, above you;
And the sun glitters on the waves —
Gilding even your feet;
As though sadness and joy like light —
Remain after us — millions of years;
I always recall you this way —
Like the tragic peace in music;
And earth would succumb to evening,
With grassy joy for a bed.

FROM: *Son v kholodnom dome* (A Dream in a Cold House).

THE DEATH OF THE POPLARS

The sick poplars of Paris
Along the sidewalk — delirious,
In the fumes, with fluttering leaves,
They wander, raving, to their homeland.

And the smoky din is shocking
To poplar anguish,
Where a rivulet's murmur is heard,
As it carries sun along the sand.

A clumsy wind blows through the block,
Passing in a pre-dawn wave,
Anxiously shedding white down
On the resonant-stony earth.

Over the roofs a spring shower
Hovers, rosy and cool,
Like the miracle dream of a poem,
Not yet fallen on granite.

VICTOR MAMCHENKO

A SUPPLICATION

In splendorous cathedrals — a celebration:
Somewhere in heaven — Christmas . . .
On the earth, snowless ice —
A sparkle constrained in the night;
The north wind whistles
Time moves on
No one trusts another
Don't knock at these doors —
They'll never be opened
Move on again into the gloom
And freeze in a corner there,
Perhaps you'll dream of brotherhood
Your heart will pound with joy
It's no misfortune to die.
The terrible tears will finish
Describing for the living god
The dead image of Christmas.

A DREAM IN A COLD HOUSE

In the winter sky, low and hazy —
        The yellow moon;
With great effort, I walk in the forest;
        Before me — there is a wall.
I climb up. The time of night
        In snowy silence
Is frozen. There is no power,
        No strength in me.
I'm afraid: I hate,
        And my soul is burning,
Beyond the wall I see a house
        And people in the window.
I see gold and precious things,
        And sumptuous feast and rugs,
The ominous glint of swords in the dark,
        The hours of deafening stillness.
All riches here were snatched
        Through plunder and war,
And many a slave is buried,
        Beaten behind this wall.
Quarrels I hear and shouts

In a foreign tongue,
Words like wild beasts,
      Like the call of wolves.
Obscured by a fog
      — of chilly gray —
"I'll destroy them by deceit,"
      One speaks.
Another says: "We must kill them
      With poison!"
They shout: "Avenge us, O our God,
      With bloody war! . . ."
And they brandish swords and poison,
      Looking toward the East . . .
I see — another house there, close, nearby,
      Like a living flower.
A different house and people —
      Completely different from these.
Their breasts inhale a bright light,
      Their house is completely open
To friends and the world. Their life
      Is striving toward happiness — filled
With all the world, with each small part,
      Like love.
Like golden bees,
      The people there live,
I see — I'm of their kind,
      They call me to come,
United, innumerable,
      And strong in their labors,
Unyielding, like a dam
      Against great waters.
Miraculous the work, and deft the movements
      Of straining arms;
In the shared deeds of their service
      There is no pointless torment.
They possess both swords and boldness
      And fire to consume,
But use those things — for good,
      To protect the people.
Because with wolfish howling,
      Like an ailing monster,
The black house of war, has crushed the people
      With thievery.
I understand: with death and blood

Victor Mamchenko

The black house breathes;
Happiness prompts the luminous house
To live with love.
In the black house — fights and trampling,
The measured clang of steel,
Neither people nor warriors — just robots . . .
See — they are marching out —
This is a dream — I must awake,
I'll never sleep again,
But even in pain my soul rejoices
To see this prophecy.
I know: though sleeping, I must awake,
But through the denseness of sleep
I see the black house and its wall
Consumed in flames, collapsing.

Alexander Ginger (1897–1965)

Alexander Samsonovich Ginger, the husband of the poet Anna Prismanova, wrote rhythmical poems and was engrossed in varied experiments in versification. His style stems from the tradition of Derzhavin, as well as from the Russian Futurists. His Muse, loud and solemn, stands in sharp contrast to the poetry of the "Parisian note." Pathetic and comic elements strangely coexist in Ginger's works, as can be seen even in the title of his third collection of poems, *Zhaloba i torzhestvo* (Complaint and Triumph; Paris, 1939). Similar antinomies appear elsewhere in his work. He is a very original poet, even though at times he seems to be "tongue-tied" and difficult to comprehend, as is Victor Mamchenko. His creation of "words with a twist"[1] is reminiscent of Khlebnikov's artistic method, the difference being that Ginger did not indulge deeply and systematically in this activity. Rather, he "coerced" his language, making it difficult and seemingly ungrammatical. Through this technique he arrived at rather striking patterns of poetry. His oeuvre, however, has not been sufficiently investigated by literary scholars, and it is quite conceivable that one day he will be "discovered" as a poet of impressive craftsmanship and depth.

Such depth and skill in poetic form is apparent in "My father, the sun, with you today," and in "Three passions have, since time untold," both of which are translated below. The former, a solemn invocation to the sun, bears a resemblance to Derzhavin's odes; it demonstrates man's longing for peace and tranquility free from the "vanities of life" which he senses around (and, significantly, within) him. That the sun, a traditional symbol of man's bright consciousness, should play a central role in this poem is likewise indicative of Ginger's close affinity with the classical poetry of Russia's eighteenth century. The latter poem, constructed by means of a series of rhymed couplets, achieves an ironical second plane of meaning that undermines its apparently transparent surface. By imposing attributes entirely incongruous to his subject matter, Ginger creates an illusion of logical and precise thought while simultaneously destroying this illusion with irony and elements of the grotesque. A card game "mocks its foes with laughter," and a six of spades becomes "firmer than swords of steel and stately lances." In style, this poem is once more reminiscent of Russian classical verse and, in fact, is closely related in tone to the mock epic—a popular classical and neo-classical genre.

Ginger produced several collections of poems: *Svora vernykh* (The Gang of the Faithful; Paris, 1921), *Predannost': vtoroy sbornik stikhov* (Devotion: A

393

Second Collection of Poems; Paris, 1925), the aforementioned *Complaint and Triumph*, *Vest': chetvyorty sbornik stikhov* (The Message: A Fourth Collection of Poems; Paris, 1939), and *Serdtse: stikhi 1917–1964* (The Heart: Poems 1917–1964; Paris, 1965). His works also appeared in *The Relay Race: A Collection of Russian Emigré Poetry* and *The Muse of the Diaspora: Selected Poems of Emigré Poets, 1920–1960*, and other volumes.

NOTE

1. Gleb Struve, *Russkaya literatura v izgnanii*, p. 162.

POEMS

FROM: *Sbornik stikhov, I* (Collection of Poetry, I; Paris, 1929).

To the memory of E. A. Boratynsky

My father, the sun, with you today
    I'm face to face—
Drawn to you more lovingly and freely
    Than son to father.

A responsible oath I place
    At your feet—
My father, the sun, protector of paradise
    And the songs of birds.

I'm summoned, though in vain, by the evil will
    Of strangers.
I wish them neither well nor ill,
    I see them not.

What shield can I use to defend
    Myself from myself?
To burn up in you, be reborn in you,
    Loving you.

The lilac of a forsaken garden rings out.
    A bee glistens,

The worries of life recede,
    The affairs of earth.

I'll retreat into impetuous summer
    From the vanities of life.
Remain with me, source of warmth and light—
    O you, my father, you.

FROM: *Zhaloba i torzhestvo: tretya kniga stikhov* (Complaint and Triumph: A Third Book of Poetry).

Three passions have, since time untold,
Destroyed the peace of man's abode.

These are their names, cursed by the Divine:
The flesh of woman, the splash of cards, and the vapor of wine.

Like cures like, save yourself some way,
Mold your spirit in a struggle with your clay.

Abandon woman, think of other affairs,
Wine will bring oblivion to their snares.

But you, wine, friend of the frost of fall,
Transient senselessness of bitter gall,

You will surrender before a woman's arms.
You will surrender to nights of feminine charms.

Though the voluptuous struggles against the wine,
Both are destined to weigh the same over time.

Till the card game makes its triumphant rise,
Sharper than an axe and quicker than flies,

This, the third passion, mocks its foes with laughter.
For in a greedy heart, like a savage pasture,

The Six of Spades takes root, entrances
Firmer than swords of steel and stately lances.

Anna Prismanova (d. 1960)

Anna Semyonovna Prismanova, the wife of Alexander Ginger and poet in her own right, published several volumes of verse, among them *Ten' i telo* (The Shadow and the Body; Paris, 1937); *Bliznetsy: vtoraya kniga stikhov* (The Twins: A Second Book of Poetry; Paris, 1946), *Sol': tretya kniga stikhov* (Salt: A Third Book of Poetry; Paris, 1949) and *Vera: liricheshaya povest'* (Vera: A Lyrical Novella; Paris, 1960). Her poems also appeared in various anthologies, literary journals, and almanacs.

Like the poems of Marina Tsvetaeva, Prismanova's work did not harmonize with the poetry of the "Parisian note." Elements of fantasy as well as concrete detail, of the sentimental as well as the grotesque, are to be found in her remarkable verse. She engaged in bold experiments with language. Her intentional breaking of rules of grammar, emphasis, and meaning serves to heighten the effect of the grotesque; she used such devices unabashedly (and with great success). All of them lead her away from the muffled intonations, elliptical phrases, and half-uttered thoughts that distinguish the poetry of the "Parisian note."

She favored strong, even crude, but completely concrete images, and employed a certain complex system of repetitive, frequently antithetic symbols or signs. This method is especially evident in poems like "The Smith" and "Poison." "The Smith" brings into stark contrast the image of the skeleton and (within the framework of the poem) blood. This apposition leads the reader beyond the image itself to the underlying metaphysical concepts: on the one hand, the bones represent a kind of prison, or a house "without will, without indignation"; while at the core lies the soul of the clerk—his very blood—that leaves this cell, this "duty [. . .] like a stone" to walk among the autumnal bushes and to regain, at least for a moment, the recognition of his former life. By using sets of contrasting pairs—skeleton and blood, pen and wing, clerk and smith—Prismanova achieves a second plane of meaning in her lyrics.

Through the unexpected juxtaposition of antithetical images and their underlying philosophical, ethical, and religious implications, Prismanova's poems gain great power and strength. In "Poison" she dramatically shows how an excess of inspiration may become destructive, even fatal, to the creative person. A series of grotesque images, the persona's allusion to and identification with the mad Ophelia, who mumbles mad snatches of songs and strews plucked flowers, and the connection of this "poison" to the biblical serpent all suggest the inversion of the traditional notion that inspiration stems from contact with the divine or with a Muse. Prismanova indicates that, on the contrary, such abilities are the gift of the devil.

Prismanova's poetry requires a very careful reading because it is intentionally made difficult. This second plane of meaning—so essential for the fathoming of her *Weltanschauung*—is achieved by juxtaposing the concrete with the abstract, the fantastic and grotesque with the real, and a subtle, though crucial use of biblical and mythological allusions. Thus, in her effort to transcend the limitations of pure lyrics, she places "soul" together with "salt," "mushrooms" with "slime." Her "Four spiders on the ceiling weaving one and the same web" strangely resembles a frequent image in the poetry of Zinaida Hippius. Another salient feature of Anna Prismanova's art is the narrative element which is skillfully introduced into her verse. She was particularly successful in those poems where this narrative merges with her own lyrical theme to present a lyrically colored story. These attributes, the emotional ringing of her voice, and the epigrammatic opening lines are akin to the verse of Marina Tsvetaeva, Boris Pasternak, or even Khlebnikov. But Prismanova was less inclined toward experimentation in meter, always preferring the iamb (as did Khodasevich). In this respect her poetry is far from the rhythmically innovative work of Tsvetaeva or Dovid Knut.

Prismanova's poetic universe is strikingly original in its conception and execution, in its avant-garde stance, and in the boldness of its voice and imagery. Unfortunately, her work is even less well known to the Western reader than is that of many other *émigré* poets cited in the present volume.

POEMS

FROM: *Sol': tretya kniga stikhov* (Salt: A Third Book of Poetry).

> Had you come to visit me,
> readers (who love all things strange)—
> you would have seen only skin and bones
> and a soul twisted around itself.
>
> There is usually much salt in such a soul.
> No one has asked me about the salt—
> but I, through great effort of will,
> will put into words all the salt of loving energy.

ANNA PRISMANOVA

FROM: "The Sisters."

. . . .

Maria cooks soup with an axe
and washes the floor in azure dress.
In spring she leaves the house
with lofty summer lightning in her gaze . . .
Her neglected children
sit on the fence in worn-out pants.

In her apartment there is a glow and din.
Rain and snow fall in her apartment . . .
To frighten the neighbors (and the enemies, too)
she goes to bed at three or four o'clock.
The moon sheds its beams at her feet:
she plays, before the moon, on her lyre.

. . . .

She sleeps in the day, squeezing her index finger
in her fist. The night shows
a strange picture to her: together in one pot
Maria cooks both mushrooms and slime.
Four spiders on the ceiling
weave one and the same web.

. . . .

POISON

To Georgy Ivanov

We gave away the whole essence of our soul for a song.
For the sake of his head, Kant crossed out his body.
The artist toward the end lost his vision,
and the perfect musician lost his ear.

And the loss of the heart—even if it's only a part
(but, unfortunately, the largest),
I have achieved, at the mercy of my own words,
working unceasingly with my soul.

My words come to me of their own accord,
in dreams, when I don't call them forth at all.
And I, like Ophelia, with my hair undone,
tear out large roses.

398

And so I live this way, born
countless hundreds of years ago,
the serpent of paradise possessed my poison,
but Orpheus has my narrow frame.

No, it is not paradise I am approaching, but the end
of the life granted me, weeping and singing . . .
I am dying, my friends, of music:
my entire core is being torn out of me.

1938

FROM: *Bliznetsy: stikhi* (The Twins: Poems).

THE SMITH

Only the clerk's bones bend
over the cheerless pages,
but his blood looks out the window
at autumn with her red bushes.

Even if the bush is like a flame beyond the glass,
his duty is like a stone, the culprit of labor. . .
The clerk, with his lustrine wing,
resembles a raven.

He bends his skeleton over dead letters,
without will, without indignation,
but his blood cherishes the trace
of his former life.

The inkwell was empty,
the goose quills flew,
and near the green of a leaf
walked wildness and confidence.

There, with bright embers before his face,
and in a mysterious illumination—
he was a gypsy smith
in a previous incarnation.

Yury Terapiano (1892–1980)

Yury Konstantinovich Terapiano, a Russian poet and critic, was born in Kerch', in the Crimea. In 1911 he graduated from the Alexandrovskaya Classical High School, and in 1916 from the Law School of the University of St. Vladimir in Kiev. Drafted into the Imperial Army, he attended a military school and was assigned to the southeastern front. Toward the end of the summer of 1919 he joined the Volunteer Army.

Terapiano published his early works in Kiev literary journals. In Paris, together with Vadim Andreev, Dovid Knut, Victor Mamchenko, Antonin Ladinsky, and several other Russian poets, in 1924 he organized the Union of Young Poets and Prose Writers and served as its first chairman. His published works include six collections of poetry: *Luchshy zvuk* (A Better Sound; Munich, 1926), *Bessonnitsa* (Insomnia; Berlin, 1935), *Na vetru* (In the Wind; Paris, 1938), *Stranstvie zemnoe* (Earthly Wandering; Paris, 1951), *Izbrannye stikhi* (Selected Poems; Washington, 1963), and *Parusa* (Sails; Washington, 1965). He also published a novella, *Puteshestvie v neizvestny kray: vostochnye legendy* (Voyage to an Unknown Country: Eastern Legends; Paris, 1946), and the reminiscences *Vstrechi* (Encounters; New York: Chekhov, 1953). Since 1955 he had been in charge of the "Literary Criticism" section in the newspaper *Russian Thought*. Among his many perceptive articles and critical essays are the following: "O Bloke, o Gumilyove" (About Blok, About Gumilyov) in *The New Russian Word* (February 17, 1952), "O neizvestnykh stikhakh O. Mandel'shtama" (On O. Mandel'shtam's Unpublished Poems) in *Russian Thought* (November 19, 1955), and "O Bloke i Gumilyove" (About Blok and Gumilyov) in *Russian Thought* (September 7, 1957). With I. Yassen and V. Andreev, Terapiano edited the anthology *The Relay Race: A Collection of Russian Emigré Poetry* (Paris: Dom knigi, 1948), and he was an editor of two journals, *The New Ship* and *The New House*. The anthology *The Muse of the Diaspora: Selected Poems of Emigré Poets, 1920–1960* was likewise edited by Yury Terapiano.

Among Russian poets, Terapiano was especially fond of Derzhavin, Zhukovsky, Pushkin, Lermontov, Boratynsky, Innokenty Annensky, Blok, and Osip Mandel'shtam; among prose writers, Gogol', Turgenev, Dostoevsky, Tolstoy, Leskov, and Chekhov. He also held in high esteem the works of Homer, the Greek tragedians, Dante, Goethe, Balzac, Stendhal, Baudelaire, Verlaine, and Rimbaud. In his own poetry Terapiano reveals the craftsmanship of the Acmeist school, although he never participated in

Nikolay Gumilyov's Guild of Poets. In his subjects he is also akin to Gumilyov (and to the French Parnassian poets as well), in that he is interested in Eastern exoticism and esoteric studies. From the very beginning of his literary career, however, Terapiano aspired toward "simplicity in his artistic method, self-awareness, moderation and purity of expression, and an intense search for God."[1] His poems are precise and clear, even when he expresses his personal anxiety, excitement, doubt, or temptation. His classical and neo-classical training in poetry was evident even when the "Parisian note" was flourishing in Paris, with Anatoly Steiger and Lidiya Chervinskaya as its exponents. Terapiano's verse does not resemble Steiger's "whisper" or Chervinskaya's "muttering," and the range of his poetry is wider than theirs, or even than Vladimir Smolensky's and Boris Poplavsky's. Their indulgence in self-seeking had always been alien to him, and Georgy Ivanov's nihilism, fashionable at that time, did not affect Terpiano's aesthetics. The basis of his *Weltanschauung* is religious; several of his poems are written as prayers to God or the Virgin Mary. Russia, the Crimea, the Civil War, the poet's own war experiences, daily *émigré* existence in Paris, and nature in both its tranquil and stormy states form the subjects of Terapiano's poetic works. In them we can meet a swallow, a medical nurse working in a Russian field hospital, Homer, the apocalyptical Angel of God, and the classical Nausicaa.

Terapiano's book *Encounters*, containing vivid reminiscences of Parisian literary life and graphic portrayals of many Russian poets—among them, Boratynsky—is especially valuable to the student of Russian literature.

NOTE

1. Cf. K. V. Mochul'sky, "Terapiano, Yu., *Bessonnitsa*," *Sovremennye zapiski* 58 (1935): 476–477.

POEMS

FROM: *Parusa* (Sails).

Just yesterday—shadows and chilly gloom,
Now all has bloomed in the silence.
Everywhere, lilacs. Transparent light of spring.
Over the lake the reeds fall silent.

A red-breasted bird fearlessly
Plucked at a worm by my feet.

401

I recalled it all: the sadness of earthly dust
And, like a river, the sound of flowing time.

Spring has arrived, unexpectedly and early,
Though in the Crimea the ice melted long ago,
And slowly, from a verdant barrow,
The herds are descending, the reed-pipe sings . . .

Fragile branches sway
In a damp, weary garden,
The bright summer ends,
The wind foretells misfortune.

I listen to the silence with my heart.
My past has risen from the depths.
Memories, farewells,
And silence, silence.

The gods know love. The burden is heavy, even there.
The all-beatific ones and mortals—equal in the timeless riddle.
The evil prophetic Fates amidst their heavenly realm
Have parceled out love's duration just as stingily.

Curses, tears, and moans to them from the Earth:
"We dream of paradise, but Olympus is hidden by clouds . . ."
How sad, how tragic is love, Antigone,
And Oedipus dies, scorched by eternal fire.

> O, daughter of supreme ether
> O, luminous beauty. . .
>   E. Boratynsky

I still dare not address you,
Death, as "luminous beauty,"

I cannot yet master
The turn of your fatal wheel.

In weakness, exhaustion,
Still ready to bend—
And then, before me—the sudden image
Of quite another existence:

An unearthly dawn, glowing red,
Meets the sail of a ship,
And Eros and Psyche enter
Anew the Elysian fields.

Vladimir Zlobine (1894–1967)

Vladimir Amanyevich Zlobine, Zinaida Hippius's personal secretary beginning in 1916 and a poet in his own right, studied law at the University of St. Petersburg. In December, 1919, he joined the Merezhkovskys and D. V. Filosofov in their flight from St. Petersburg to Poland. In Warsaw he assisted Hippius with the literary section of the newspaper *Freedom* (1920–21; renamed *For Freedom* in 1921). In 1921 he settled in Paris, together with the Merezhkovskys, and continued to work as their secretary. He also lectured on Russian affairs at various literary *soirées* and published his poems and essays in the Russian newspapers and journals which appeared in France. Hippius, who rested her hopes on Zlobine as a possible future associate in her "apocalyptical" Church, wholeheartedly supported his literary undertakings and entrusted him with the preparation of lectures, speeches, articles, and essays on politics, religion, and Russian belles-lettres. She edited his early poems and taught him the art of writing.

Zlobine was on the editorial boards of several literary journals, among them *The New Ship, The Sword, La Renaissance,* and the above-cited newspaper *Freedom.* In 1951 Zlobine published his first volume of poems, *Posle eyo smerti* (After Her Death), dedicated to his former mentor, who had died in 1945. His book *Tyazholaya dusha* (The Heavy Soul), also dedicated to the memory of Zinaida Hippius, appeared posthumously in 1970 (Washington, D.C.: Kamkin). In the fall of 1965 Zlobine was on the faculty of the Department of Slavic Languages and Literatures at the University of Kansas. There he gave a seminar on Russian Symbolism with particular reference to the works of Zinaida Hippius and D. S. Merezhkovsky. Upon his return to Europe he lived in Rome and Paris, writing poems for *The New Review* and various anthologies of Russian *émigré* poetry.

Zlobine's verse belongs to the St. Petersburg school of poetry; it resembles that of Zinaida Hippius, Mikhail Kuzmin, and Innokenty Annensky. In his perfect artistic taste and control, he is a St. Petersburg poet, as he is in his rhythms and vocabulary—clear, expressive, precise. However, in Zlobine there is an altogether different and unexpected motif—a certain wise yet untroubled acceptance of life in all its manifestations. Melancholy is conquered, and freedom is achieved through cheerful poverty and joyous wandering. His intonation, full of playful thoughtlessness and good-natured simplicity of heart, is also new and unfamiliar to the poets of St. Petersburg.

One of his best poems is "Svidanye" (The Meeting), dedicated to Zinaida Hippius and Merezhkovsky.

It should be added that Zlobine disappointed Hippius because of his indifference to matters of paramount significance to her. She failed to find in him support for her religious and socio-political views and activities, and was dismayed by what she felt were his limited achievements in poetry.

POEMS

FROM: *Novy zhurnal* (The New Review) 88 (New York, 1967).

> They severed my head on a block
> And my head rolled off.
> They tried giving it to a dog,
> But the dog sniffed and went away.
> So my head lies on the square,
> Under the fence, in a ditch.
> People walk on, horses gallop by,
> And in all its glory
> A church procession passed.
> While my head lives on and on,
> It sees and understands all,
> And does not fear, for it knows
> That soon Christ will come . . .
>
> Perhaps, even tonight.

To Temira A. Pachmuss

> Oh, these dreams without meaning or name,
>   Which come to me before dawn,
> Never reaching my captive consciousness.
>   What do you wish? I fear you.
>
> I am silent, there's no peace in my soul.
>   It's incomprehensible why
> There lives within me some other,
>   Mysterious being.

405

Friend or foe? What do you try to recall?
　　　Whose mark is on your brow?
It seems to me you wish me well,
　　　Or perhaps not. How can I know?

And again I cast out my nets
　　　Into the immovable sea of dreams,
And again these sounds, again these sounds—
　　　And silence.

FROM: *Russky sbornik, kniga I* (The Russian Collection, Book I; Paris: "Podorozhnik,"
1946).

A MEETING[1]

To D. S. and Z. N. Merezhkovsky

They had nothing,
Could understand nothing.
They watched the starry sky
And slowly walked arm in arm.

They asked for nothing,
Agreeing to return it all,
If only to lie together in their narrow grave,
And never know separation.

To be together . . . But life did not forgive them,
As death could not forgive.
Jealously, it parted them
And covered their footsteps with snow.

Between them are no mountains or walls—
Just the emptiness of universal space.
But the heart knows no deception,
The soul is primevally pure.

Meek, it's prepared for the meeting,
Like a white, imperishable flower,
Lovely. Again they met
At the predestined hour.

Mists dispersed gently,
They came together—forever.

The same chestnut trees above them
Shed their rose-colored snow.

And the same stars still reveal
Their heavenly beauty.
And just as before they rest,
But in the paradise forest of Boulogne.

NOTE

1. Nina Nikolaevna Berberova, poet, fiction writer, and critic, dedicated the following poem to the memory of Zinaida Hippius, who was a close friend of hers for several years in Paris.
FROM: *The Muse of the Diaspora: Selected Poems of Emigré Poets, 1920–1960*

To the memory of Z. N. Hippius

For ten years I haven't opened my old
Box with her letters. Today
I lifted the lid. Once with her delicate hand
She filled these pale sheets with writing,
To my joy.
A stray butterfly was dozing there
Among her poems, among those bewitching words,
Perhaps a year, perhaps ten.
And suddenly, unfolding its wings of orange
(Recalling the rusty color of her hair),
It flew out from the darkness of bygone days
And sped away through the window to the sun,
Into the radiant day, into the azure present.

It was as if I'd rolled away the stone
From the crypt of one deeply sleeping.

For more details, see Berberova's autobiography, *The Italics Are Mine.*

Tamara Velichkovskaya

Tamara Antonovna Velichkovskaya, born in Russia, received her education in Yugoslavia. She began writing poetry when she was six years old but did not show her early works to anyone, for they represented a kind of diary about her unusual personal impressions, experiences, or moods. She greatly admired the poet Andrey Bely, but after her "discovery" of Alexander Blok she became fascinated by the "magical spell" of Blok's poetry for the rest of her life. Later she grew fond of Marina Tsvetaeva's poems and those of Vladislav Khodasevich.

Much to Velichkovskaya's chagrin, she was able to come to Paris only during World War II, in 1942, when the "first, magnificent period" of Russian literature in exile was already over. Living first in Lyon (1927–42) and later in Paris, she became immersed in the cultural atmosphere of the French capital. Bunin, his wife V. N. Bunina-Muromtseva, Boris Zaytsev, Leonid Zurov, Vladimir Smolensky, and many other Russian poets and fiction writers encouraged the young poet in her early literary endeavors. Especially helpful was Yury Terapiano, who invited her to attend his literary *soirées*, at which the younger Russian poets would recite and criticize, under Terapiano's tutelage, their own works. In 1947 Sergey Makovsky suggested that Velichkovskaya join the Union of Russian Writers and Journalists, and since that time her poems, short stories, novellas, translations, and articles on art have appeared in various Russian-language journals. Several of her poems appeared in *The Relay Race: A Collection of Russian Emigré Poetry*, and in *Concord: From Contemporary Russian Emigré Poetry* (Washington, 1966), compiled by T. Fesenko, and in several other anthologies.

Bunin was greatly impressed with Velichkovskaya's poetry; encouraged by him, in 1948 she opened her own literary *soirées*. These were attended by many notable Russian poets and writers, among them G. Adamovich, Georgy Raevsky, Sofia Pregel', Yu. Terapiano, Anna Prismanova, Alexander Ginger, Leonid Zurov, and Professor V. N. Ilyin. Velichkovskaya's *soirées* were discontinued in 1954. In 1952, her first book of poetry appeared in Paris entitled *Bely posokh* (The White Staff), and in the early 1960's she was elected to the Board of the Union of Russian Writers and Journalists, Association des Ecrivains et des Journalistes Russes à Paris, as treasurer.

Tamara Velichkovskaya is a great lover of the Italian Renaissance and has written much about Leonardo da Vinci and St. Francis of Assisi. She further translated Michelangelo's sonnets from the Italian, St. Francis of Assisi's

"Hymn to the Sun," and Paul Eluard's French poem "Freedom." These translations appeared in *La Renaissance* and *Russian Thought*. She also distinguished herself as a literary critic, writing lengthy, perceptive essays concerning Russian poetry.[1] Her novella "Vorony khvost" (The Crow's Tail) was serialized in *La Renaissance* (Nos. 219, 220; 1970) and was highly praised by Terapiano in *Russian Thought*.[2] Velichkovskaya's numerous essays on old art treasures and picture exhibitions are written with expertise, and yet in a vivid graceful style. The poet is also a keen observer of nature's ever-changing moods, which may be observed in her own paintings. Furthermore, she is an excellent musician and talented in many areas of the arts.

In her poetry Velichkovskaya excels in varied rhythmical and metrical patterns, and her mastery of caesura and rhymes is irreproachable. Her stanzas are very successful in conveying the persona's impressions, fears, anxieties, and expectations by means of delicate poetic imagery. Nature, people, thoughts, the interplay of light and shadow—all of these appear very naturally in her poetry, but with her typically refined, profoundly poetic finish. Perhaps some of her strophes resemble Anna Akhmatova's staccato lines, the ineffable and vague expectations of Alexander Blok, or Georgy Ivanov's paradoxical poetic statements. Even Mikhail Kuzmin's affectionate voice may resound in her stanza. On the whole, however, Tamara Velichkovskaya's poetry is unique in its delicacy and poetic expressiveness. These qualities are especially noticeable in *The White Staff*, in which the poet's simple, concrete, and transparent images are very effective in their emotional appeal and aesthetic beauty. The persona seems able to perceive the central essence of the objects, events, and feelings which in Velichkovskaya's poems possess a life of their own; they establish communication with the poet, and her poems are filled with a mutual empathy. This quality lends her poetry a particular freshness. The persona, sensitive to all "unearthly voices," is endowed with keen personal susceptibility and insight. The compositional design of the poems is well conceived. Velichkovskaya's lyrical poetry indeed deserves the attention of reader and scholar alike.

NOTES

1. Read, for example, her essays "O Marine Tsvetaevoy," *La Renaissance* no. 140 (1963); "O Vladimire Smolenskom," *ibid*. no. 142 (1963); "O poezii Materi Marii," *ibid*. no. 205 (1969).
2. Dated April 30, 1970, and June 4, 1970.

POEMS

FROM: *Bely posokh: stikhi* (The White Staff: Poems).

Not all things pass without a trace,
Not all is pointless, accidental . . .
    What is this? — bitterness? — if so,
    Then how unusual.

Behind it, wings flutter,
Behind it, dreams linger,
And unfettered thoughts take flight
Like startled birds.

Transparent, like mica,
The melodies fly away with them . . .
    What is this? — joy? — if so,
    Then how inexplicable.

The skies are open to thoughts,
And each one strives to enter.
And yet a dream, like a white dove,
Suddenly lights on your shoulder.

My heart feels a widow's grief,
Three times it has sung.
Three times it has bloomed with love
And three times widowed.

But after the third
My heart wept hollowly,
Telling my eyes — go blind,
And my ears — go deaf.

Sternly it sealed itself,
Unwilling to beat as before.
But a bird is chirping again,
And my heart is afraid of that bird.
The linden's honey is fragrant;
And that linden frightens my heart.

410

Again in fields, to the right and left,
I met a familiar breeze who knew me . . .
And suddenly he burst into a familiar tune,
As though calling my name.

And we strolled as friends, in harmony,
My winged companion grew calm and hushed.
I spoke to him of my grief,
And he spoke of his wanderings.

The clouds changed guard at heaven's horizon,
The wind and I remembered spring —
He'd never say in company
What he tells me when we're alone.

And he spoke to me of many things,
And in friendship saw me to the station,
He sprinkled my path with leaves
— But the most important thing he never mentioned.

To Sergey Makovsky

Two poplars grow. They
Live like kindly neighbors.
They spend their windy days
In constant conversation . . .

The minutes pass, the days, the years:
Each year it seems more difficult to bend.
The trees grow. Never
To touch.

But there, in the underground depths,
Where the woodcutters cannot reach —
In deepest secret, in silence,
Their roots are forever entwined.

TAMARA VELICHKOVSKAYA

FROM: *Vozrozhdenie* no. 143 (November, 1963).

An autumn night — I cannot sleep;
Last night, cold as ice,
In the garden, a bird in the nutgrove
Moaned through the night,
Her moaning was heard
Until dawn in the autumn bushes,
Like a complaint, an incantation,
A mounting fear.
And with all its foliage
The inclement, long night rustled,
While the bird kept moaning and singing,
As though she'd lost the strength
To endure the wind and the cold.
The darkness echoed plaintively,
That all would grow more and more wretched,
The winter — closer and closer,
And the heart, overwhelmed with darkness,
Would shrink into a small lump,
And spring would return no more;
Or if it did — would be different . . .

Dmitry Klenovsky (1892–1976)

Dmitry Klenovsky (pseudonym of Dmitry Iosifovich Krachkovsky) was born in St. Petersburg. He graduated from the Imperial Nikolaevskaya Tsarskosel'skaya High School (earlier attended by Nikolay Gumilyov). During World War I, while a student at the University of St. Petersburg, he was drafted into the Imperial Army.

Klenovsky spent much of his youth in France before the October Revolution. There he became acquainted with the poetry of Henri de Régnier, de Hérédia, Albert Samain, Coppée, Sully-Prudhomme, and other French writers. He was much impressed with their works and with French culture in general. Among Russian poets, he particularly favored Pushkin, Boratynsky, Tyutchev, Fet, Lermontov, Alexander Blok, Gumilyov, Osip Mandel'shtam, Anna Akhmatova, Innokenty Annensky, Vladislav Khodasevich, and Lidiya Alexeeva. In their works Klenovsky found a reflection of his own moods and *Weltanschauung*. In later years, although he was frequently invited to recite his poetry at various literary *soirées* and gatherings, Klenovsky could not travel abroad due to his chronic illness. Instead, Russian poets, writers, and scholars visited him in Traunstein, West Germany (where he established his residence in a nursing home after World War II), or engaged in a spirited exchange of ideas in correspondence. Among his correspondents were Sergey Makovsky, Nina Berberova, Sofia Pregel', Vladimir Markov, Anna Prismanova, Lidiya Alexeeva, Gleb Struve, Boris Filippov, Leonid Rzhevsky, Nonna Belavina, and Strannik (pseudonym of Ioann, Russian Orthodox Archbishop of San Francisco).

Klenovsky's first book of poetry, *Palitra* (The Palette; St. Petersburg, 1916), was typical of the Acmeist school. After a prolonged silence in the Soviet Union, he published *Sled zhizni* (The Trace of Life; Frankfurt/Main, 1950), *Navstrechu nebu* (Meeting Heaven; Frankfurt/Main, 1952), *Neulovimy sputnik; chetvyorty sbornik stikhov* (The Elusive Companion: A Fourth Collection of Poetry; Munich, 1956), *Prikosnovenye: pyataya kniga stikhov* (Contact: A Fifth Book of Poetry; Munich, 1959), *Ukhodyashchie parusa* (Departing Sails; Munich, 1962), *Razroznennaya tayna* (A Broken Mystery; Munich, 1965), *Stikhi: izbrannye stikhi iz 6-ti knig i novye stikhi 1965–1966* (Poems: Selected Poems from Six Books and New Poems 1965–1966; Munich, 1967), *Pevuchaya nota* (The Melodious Note; Munich, 1969), *Pocherkom poeta* (In the Poet's Own Handwriting; Munich, 1971), *Tyoply vecher* (A Warm Evening;

Munich, 1975), and *Poslednee* (The Last Word; Munich, 1977; published posthumously).

His poetry also appeared in anthologies such as *The Muse of the Diaspora: Selected Poetry of Emigré Poets, 1920–1960*, *In the West: An Anthology of Emigré Poetry* (New York: Chekhov, 1953; ed. Yu. Terapiano), *Literature Abroad: A Collection-Anthology of Works of New Emigré Writers, 1947–1957* (Munich: TsOPE, 1958), and *The Pearls of Russian Poetical Works: Selected Poems from the End of the 18th Century to Our Time* (New York: Ob-vo druzey russkoy kul'tury, 1964; comp. T. A. Berezny). Although totally blind in his last years, Klenovsky continued composing poetry, which he dictated to his wife, Margarita Denisovna Krachkovskaya, and published in *The New Review* and *The Contemporary*, two literary journals which, to the great joy of their readers, had published his works for many years.

Klenovsky was the "last of the Tsarskosel'sky swans,"[1] continuing the tradition of the St. Petersburg school of poetic craftsmanship. This type of poetry is distinguished by exquisite artistic taste, impeccable technique, and philosophical or contemplative moods manifesting the poet's ever-struggling antinomies. In Klenovsky's poetry, Platonic ideas (the earth as a prison of the persona's spiritual aspirations) contend with his sensual joy in earthly existence. The persona's love for life and its varied experiences, and his refined poetic perception of the entire universe, at times attain Eucharistic depths—Christ Who is breaking Communion Bread, Apostles who wander through time and space, and the poet himself, who sends his greetings from *there*. But on the whole, Klenovsky's imagery is restrained and even sparse, lending a sense of spaciousness to his verse. Pastel colors, the rustling sounds of foliage and lizards, the gentle Russian landscape and scenes of Russian still life—these are the salient features of his poetry, with its uplifting simplicity and quiet beauty. There are no turbulent emotions and no intentional disorder in style; all these qualities illustrate the Acmeist manner of writing poetry. It is only natural that after the appearance of Klenovsky's first book of poetry outside of Russia, in 1950, he was immediately hailed as one of the best Russian poets.

NOTE

1. Faby Zverev, "Poety 'novoy' emigratsii," in N. P. Poltoratzky, *Russkaya literatura v emigratsii*, p. 71.

POEMS

FROM: *Pocherkom poeta* (In the Poet's Own Handwriting).

Be thankful for the new blossom
Which opened last night on the balcony,
Be thankful for the sea and the sand,
And the maiden breast beneath your palm!

Be thankful—no, I cannot count
Everything we should be thankful for!
Even the cross inside that low fence—
Which might not have been, and yet is here.

1969

FROM: *Tyoply vecher* (A Warm Evening).

You utter, "No"? And yet
You are waiting, seeking something—
Doesn't it show
That something may be granted,
Even as alms to a beggar?

For you would seek nothing
From those powerless to help you!
Before a stone you'd be mute,
And how could you ask
The grave to grant you life!

But if you still whisper words,
And your heart stands still in excitement,
Then it does exist, it's alive—
That bond between heavenly being
And its image on earth.

1973

In death the passage is frightening
Into the unknown.
How can we comprehend
That place?

How to cross over there,
       Beyond natural law?
How to grope for a path—
       Which is not by land?

Perhaps there is even a stream?
       Though probably
Not like here,
       Only similar?

Perhaps even the trembling
       And rustle of a spring grove?
Not exactly like here, but maybe
       With some resemblance?

I shall adjust to those places
       (However distasteful some!)
If only something is there,
       Something must be!

Or if I find
       Only a void,
Better to make my peace
       With that void!

And, abandoning guesses
       Forever,
Simply plunge into that place,
       And never look back.

As though into a dark pond at night,
       With only this pitiful hope:
Perhaps water nymphs
       Do live there after all?

———————

The bitter almond bud is
Fresh as the sweet.
Its fruit may be bitter
Or sweet—but that is the secret!

Just as flowering love
Is always enclosed in mystery:
Can you ever foresee
The bitterness it conceals?

Remember, as you swallow
Your first chagrin,
Remember then—for all this,
There was first love's bloom.

FROM: *Stikhi* (Poems; Munich, 1967).

In some way we are all wounded
By impetuous fate,
But while one cries out and weeps—
Another bends over him, saying:

"Brother! You too will find
That no wound is frightening,
If carefully cleansed,
Dressed, and forgiven."

1949

Like a kiss through a handkerchief
That maddens all the more,
Like that postscript between the lines,
That essence of letters—

That's how our meeting began
In those days of the past:
Not passion, but all curiosity,
Whim, not delirium.

But fatal was the burn
Of those frivolous joys;
You could not, nor could I
Sever our embrace.

And now, as you see, it's preserved,
And will live through the ages,

Begun so long ago,
As if only a trifle.

1953

———————

From the fresh foam Aphrodite
Emerged, sultry and gay,
Aphrodite replaced that other—
That Greek, the woman who died.

I wandered along the beach with her,
Repeating again and again: that I loved her,
That I desired her even more
Than that best of ancient wives.

I assured her: "Dita, you know,
You're not a bit worse than she,
You melt like foam in my arms,
And your breasts are like marble!"

Not for her, long fallen to dust,
Have we composed verses through time,
Have we been courageous or pitiful,
And sinned in all ways.

But for the silly girl
Who chanced upon our path,
The one who struts her new clothes
And ogles everyone.

O, goddess! There's no deception here!
When, burning in dreams, he hears
Light murmurs from the Aegean's foam
Over shoulders embraced!

1962

———————

THE TRACE OF LIFE

I like to read on the first snowfall
    A hare's tiny footsteps.
Look: here he spent the night,
    Here he skirted danger,

There he sat, pressing back his ears,
    Twitching his whiskers in the wind,
And here he leisurely nibbled
    The sweet young bark of a birch.

My soul has grown warm and pleased,
    And I, with eyes transfixed,
Am reading this hare's naïve
    And capricious tale,

And I think: perhaps Someone
    Is reading the trace in my soul
Of my own indelible years,
    With the same loving care.

And all things that bloomed so gloriously for me,
    That sang sweetly for my heart and mind,
Will probably seem
    As naïve a tale to Him!

Valery Pereleshin (1913–)

Valery Pereleshin (pseudonym of Valery Frantsevich Salatko-Petrishche) was born in Irkutsk. In 1920 he went with his mother, the well-known journalist Evgeniya Alexandrovna Sentyanina, to Kharbin, where he attended the high school of the Lieutenant-General K. L. Khorvat, the commercial college of the Chinese Eastern Railways, and the high school of the Christian Union of Young People, finishing the latter in 1930. In 1935 he graduated with honors from the Kharbin Law School and entered its graduate college, where he also studied Chinese. This institution, along with other universities in Manchuria, was closed by the Japanese in 1937. Pereleshin graduated in 1944 from the only two institutions of higher education still open: the Polytechnical Institute and the Theological School of St. Vladimir.

In 1939 Pereleshin moved to Peking, where he lived until 1943. Then he went to Shanghai (1943–50) and several other Chinese towns; in 1953 he resettled in Rio de Janeiro. In 1973 he visited Paris and Marseilles, and in April, 1974, he represented Russia and Brazil at the International Festival of Poetry in Austin, Texas.

Pereleshin began writing poetry when he was six years old; his first poem appeared in the "Page for the Young Reader" of the Russian newspaper *The Boundary* (Kharbin) in 1928. His short poem "Under our hats—away from the light . . ." was especially popular in the 1930's and was later included in the anthology *The Anchor: An Anthology of Emigré Poetry*. From 1932 on, Pereleshin's poetry appeared regularly in *The Boundary*, in the newspapers *Dawn*, *The Kharbin Times*, *Gun-bao*, and *Churaevka*, as well as in the Shanghai journals *The Phoenix* and *The Sail* and other publications, such as *The Lawyer's Day* and *The Day of the Russian Child*. It also appeared in the anthology *Gumilyov's Collection* (1937), in *The Theological Seminary (1939)*, and even in the pro-Fascist newspaper *Our Path* and the journal *The Beam of Asia*. Pereleshin also translated Chinese poetry into Russian; all of his translations were masterpieces in technique and poetic spirit. He edited the anthologies of Russian poetry *Convolutions* (Kharbin, 1935) and *The Island* (Kharbin, 1946), the latter together with Nikolay Shchegolev, another Russian poet living in the Far East.

Pereleshin's favorite writers are Leskov, Leonid Andreev, V. Sirin, and the poets Pushkin, Lermontov, Count Alexey Tolstoy, Boratynsky, Tyutchev, Fet, Gumilyov, Georgy Ivanov, Khodasevich, Adamovich, Osip Mandel'shtam, and Marina Tsvetaeva; he even attempted to imitate the poetry of Antonin Ladinsky. He refers to himself as a neoclassical poet, in that he avails himself of stories from the Gospel and parables such as the Prodigal Son and the Good Samaritan. In his poetic technique he favors metonymy and such devices which enhance the clarity and continuity of form and style.

He has published several fine collections of poetry: *V puti* (En Route; Kharbin, 1937), *Dobry uley* (The Kind Beehive; Kharbin, 1941), *Zvezda nad morem* (The Star Above the Sea; Kharbin, 1941), *Zhertva* (Sacrifice; Munich, 1944), *Yuzhny dom* (The Southern Home; Munich, 1968), and *Kachel'* (The Swing; Frankfurt/Main, 1971). In *En Route* there is an emotional intensity which resembles Lermontov's. Pereleshin's inclination toward heroic pathos, his psychological interest, striking contrasts, and colorful consonantal sound effects are also akin to Lermontov's. In addition, Pereleshin's verse has the quality of lyrical "chamber" poetry; though, in the apt formulation of Alexis Rannit, it is of a different nature than the "beautiful decadence of the feminine principle underlying the 'Parisian note' (Georgy Ivanov, Adamovich, Ginger, Chervinskaya, Steiger, and later Chinnov)." According to Rannit, Pereleshin is a "poet of masculine tenderness, of the music of thought, or rather—of the music of meaning (with the emphasis on *music*), a type of the so-called 'invariable melody' of a polyphonic work."[1] Rannit has in mind the way in which Pereleshin continues the intellectual poetry of Boratynsky, Gumilyov, Khodasevich, and Bunin—not so much thematically as rhythmically. Intellect is the impetus in Pereleshin's later works. His persona's psychological life is deduced from his "pre-conception" and "pre-intention."[2] The poet wishes to achieve an objective cognition of the world, to believe in the mathematically true order of the universe, and to renounce personal happiness in the name of tormenting freedom in the service of his Muse. The central poem of the volume is "The Admonition," presenting a dual dialogue between (and within) the poet-novice and the romantic-classicist. The intense color and solemn diction of the poem ("torzhestvennaya," "tselomudrennaya," "prikosnoveniya," "prisnivshayasya," and "besnuyushcheysya") create here an effect of rhythmical swinging, in contrast to the didactic nature of a discourse on moderation and the closed character of the composition. *En Route* displays a great variety of rhymes and themes. Its intonation is emphatic, and its decorative character is the persona's youthful restlessness and heroic pathos; its poetic vocabulary is dynamic, and the poetic design is rigorous, with solemn, slow movement and elegance in form and content, both reminiscent of Boratynsky's verse.

Pereleshin's characteristic techniques and themes are noticeable also in his second volume of poetry, *The Kind Beehive*. However, here the poet's religious, mystical, ethical, and aesthetic considerations come to the foreground. There are only a few metaphors, and the imagery is striking in its transparency. In his *Russian Literature in Exile* Gleb Struve criticized Pereleshin for his occasional bad taste in verse. Indeed, his poems sometimes use imperfect rhymes, such as "sosedny-edko," "lechit-navstrechu," "sprosa-prichesok," "tuzhe-Luzhin," and "okno-noch'." Pereleshin's later poetry, however, contains fewer instances of imperfect rhyme, and he introduced in the pentameter of his sonnets a compulsory caesura which had been absent in his early verse (in "Ars Longa," for example). The caesura after the second foot in the pentameter increases the sonorous effect of the sonnets in *The Southern Home*, his fifth volume of poetry. In general, Pereleshin's craftsmanship has greatly improved in his later works; in these, artistic ingenuity is quite visible.

NOTES

1. Alexis Rannit, "O poezii i poetike Valeriya Pereleshina—shest' pervykh sbornikov poeta (1937–1971)," *Russian Language Journal* 30, no. 106 (Spring 1976): 83.
2. *Ibid.*, p. 83.

POEMS

FROM: *Reflections*, November 1, 1935.

> Under our hats—away from the light,
> Into our pillows—away from the noise,
> Away from the wind and the night—
> Wrapped in our collars,
>
> As though into Lethe, we leave,
> We sullenly leave,
> Muttering, shamming uniqueness,
> And writing verse.

FROM: *The Boundary*, April 1, 1935.

> Weep not for your own heart,
> Nor another's grief,
> Nor over open wounds,
> Nor even for whole nations
> Perishing in world evil—
> Weep no more for anything at all.

POEMS

FROM: *The Boundary*, November 20, 1925.

ARS LONGA

Your squeamish hand will convulse
When, disturbing a spider's nook
In a sedately decorous chronicle,
You find a worm in the binding.

Like a hint from out of the distance
You'll realize then—you'll probably pass
Your whole life long over ancient wisdom,
Sucked into bygone ages.

You'll stoop in motionless meditation,
While the worm resumes its toil,
Interrupted but momentarily.

Confess, you eternal bookworm,
Staring into the eyes of your ridiculous fate:
Is one century enough for you?

FROM: *The Boundary; The Kind Beehive*.

OVER A COFFIN

The Angel of Death has light footsteps:
He's like a whip, like night, like fate.
And once again—the murmur of a strange crowd
Surrounds a tight-skinned brow and cheeks.

Once again, at a new funeral,
Coiling, like a slithering snake,
An ineffable fear, an incredible fear
Corrodes the hearts of men.

The psalm flows, and fear intensifies—
Like a shadow on every face.
So many young bodies, so many white arms
Will return to earth at the end!

So many swift legs, so many sharp eyes,
Straight shoulders and tender lips . . .
They say that those who have left us
Were received by the clement Angel of Welcome.

423

And merciful God has consoled them
In His sorrowless realms,
Where they dwell like a sigh, like vapor—
As the old monk assures us.

That is why the monk keeps crosses all around,
And a skeleton in the midst of living men,
Below it the words:
    "Don't forget: Once I was like you,
    And you will become like me!"

May 25, 1938

FROM: *The Boundary; En Route.*

THE ADMONITION

This is the start, believe me! If
Affectionate arms—two arms—
Have appeared in your dreams, then even more fascinating
Temptations await you, my friend!

Evil, we conquer time,
Humbled, we'll see eternity;
My boy, break away from them—from those
Who visit you from the dark.

Break away from the beaten track
Without a backward glance—and seek the narrow boundary,
For love is the start of decay,
And the voice of the flesh—is the voice of lies.

Our solemn flock
Will pray together for you,
That your chaste
And simple soul won't fall.

We will guard you from earthly love
For the sake of that from Heaven
In this incorporeal azure,
With our shoulders, childishly weak.

Yes, but such visions,
Such enticements! You'll discover

424

Her sweetest caresses
And sighs in the dark.

And if . . . we ourselves remember
The burden of raging blood—
With darkening eyes,
Beseeching a woman for love—

Then, woe unto you! Forever
The flame and only the flame,
And the palm of her hand
Will sear through the lids of your eyes.

October 31, 1936

Igor' Chinnov (1909–)

Igor' Vladimirovich Chinnov, the son of a lawyer, bibliophile, and polyglot, was born in Latvia; he graduated from the University of Riga. From 1947 to 1953 he lived in Paris, where he attended the Sorbonne University. From 1953 to 1962 he worked in Munich at Radio Station Liberty, and was in charge of programs on contemporary Soviet, French, and German literature and art. Since 1962 he has been Professor of Russian Literature at the University of Kansas, the University of Pittsburgh, and Vanderbilt University. His first poems appeared in Riga in the Russian literary journal *The Garret*, then in *Numbers*. He was acclaimed as an original poet only after World War II, when the first book of his poetry, *Monolog* (The Monologue), appeared in Paris in 1950. Sergey Makovsky spoke highly of these poems for their "ethereal beauty and glowing reflections." After *The Monologue* Chinnov published the following collections of verse: *Linii: vtoraya kniga stikhov* (Lines: A Second Book of Poetry; Paris, 1960), *Metafory: tretya kniga stikhov* (Metaphors: A Third Book of Poetry; New York, 1968), *Partitura* (A Musical Score; New York, 1970), *Kompozitsiya: pyataya kniga stikhov* (Composition: A Fifth Book of Poetry; Paris, 1972), *Pastorali* (Pastorals; Paris, 1976), and *Antiteza: sed'maya kniga stikhov* (Antithesis: A Seventh Book of Poetry; College Park, Md.: Birchbark Press, 1979). Chinnov also contributed to Russian journals and anthologies.

Chinnov's *Weltanschauung*, as revealed in his earlier works, may be described as purely aesthetic—empirical reality is deceptive; life is merely a flow of events which bring forth diverse associations, connected into an organic whole by the persona's own contemplative sadness. Since the world of senses is drab and boring, the persona cannot help but succumb to vague illusions about some supranatural reality, where all human concepts of space, time, and other categories have no place. It is not surprising, therefore, that the thought of death appears quite often in these early poems—death may enable the persona to catch a glimpse of the other world. These verses convey the most delicate transfigurations of empirical reality into its shadow, its otherworldy, ephemeral existence. Everything on earth is but an illusion, a reflection of some universal, incomprehensible mystery. This theory of associations is akin to Alexander Blok's "music of the celestial spheres," for example, in his poem "The Twelve." Chinnov's elegant imagery and metaphors also point to this music of the celestial spheres, and the enveloping

426

world of material reality teems only with dark shadow of an unfathomable cosmic process.

The formal aspects of Chinnov's early works link him with the "Parisian note" poetry. The verse is very short and may come abruptly to an end; there is a certain reticence about fully expressing thoughts and emotions; parenthetical clauses appear between dashes, or in brackets; there is serenity of restrained epithets; an absence of motion verbs gives a great variety of static, visual images (in Chinnov's poetry, mainly inanimate objects). A tendency to conceal the careful formal polish of the verse, and an occasional hint of irony are also typical. His themes are "eternally important" (also a characteristic of the "Parisian note" poetry): love, death, human solitude, and beautiful nature. These are presented against a background of pensive sadness. No moral, religious, or philosophical questions are raised.

Every sound in Chinnov's poems has its own function in his lyrical variety of emotional sketches. His thought is elusive, consisting of colorful, bright, metallic, and shining fragments of sensations, allusions, and melodies. In this his work differs from the poetry of Chervinskaya and Steiger, with their intentional "colorlessness." It is not easy to reconstruct the unity of Chinnov's pictures or to synthesize his concepts and ideas. Despite the concrete outlines of details and the absence of rhetoric, his poems are extremely difficult to characterize or paraphrase. Valery Pereleshin pertinently observed that they resemble "impervious and permanently unstable clouds which are far more peculiar to his art than his figurative speech."[1]

Chinnov's poetry is fragile and stylistically almost perfect. Seldom does he use outdated or inadequate rhyming patterns, such as "skazat'-opyat'," "polna-menya," "yuda-chuda," or "obryvom-molchaliva." And only occasionally does he indulge in a fanciful, artificial arrangement of words. His "verbal whims," however, may be the outcome of his rejection of hackneyed epithets and other literary clichés, and of his search for original expressions. His decorative "poetic garments" are rich in color, graceful outlines, alliteration, and delicate images.

Chinnov's later poetry is different. It combines grotesque, fantastic imagery and amusing, unceremonious references to the "universal soul" which he calls "Lizaveta Smerdyashchaya" (from Dostoevsky's *Brothers Karamazov*) or Vasilisa-Vas'ka Prekrasnaya; to fate—Duryokha Ivanovna; to hell—the realm of the devil-grasshopper, the devil-cockatoo, and so on. The persona has also changed; instead of striving to penetrate the music of the supranatural world, he speaks with heaven in the Pskov dialect and dreams about his future arrival in paradise in these terms:

> We'd meet with the important angels,
> We'd joke and drink a bit,
> And to the story, which has its end,
> We'd add a heavenly postscript.

This quatrain is typical of Chinnov's later poetry, likewise original and bold, but also weird and pessimistic, with a grotesque, jocular character. He now smiles sardonically at life's enigmas and mysteries. While employing the same system of formal devices as in his early poetry, in *Pastorals* he introduces strong surrealistic overtones. The world is now utterly absurd, life is void of any higher meaning, the universe is essentially cruel and senseless, and the persona can enjoy only sensual perception and purely aesthetic pleasure.[2] Human freedom and an aversion to the mechanization of man in society are Chinnov's primary concerns. His former Neo-Acmeism, with its halftones and crystalline perceptions, has been replaced by a new, fantastic, chimeric world, with an underlying irony and grotesque symbolic static images.

NOTES

1. "Mnogoznachitel'nye namyoki," *Novoe russkoe slovo*, dated March 16, 1970.
2. See more about Chinnov's artistic method in John Glad's article "The American Chapter in Russian Poetry," *Russian Language Journal* 30, no. 106 (Spring 1976).

POEMS

FROM: *Pastorali* (Pastorals).

> *I wish to take in everything with my eyes*
> *From the darkening garden.*
> Innokenty Annensky

It was a southern garden. And birds—semiprecious stones,
Like fireworks, like magnificent rockets,
All but obscuring the sunsets and dawns,

Were gleaming. I admired the feast —
The ruby, emerald, and sapphire,
That living, living, yet incomprehensible world.

The feathered tsar kept calling—in his eastern
Guttural—standing solitary,
Lapis-yellow, bordered in black.

A small bird, rose-blue,
Nodding "yes" with his head,
Vowed repeatedly that he was—from Uruguay.

428

I replied: "I, too, am from far away,
From a place where birch and magpie live
And the snow lies wide and deep;

But I'm forced into a different land,
And so, little bird, I must find swift joy
In this revelry of color."

FROM: *Monolog* (The Monologue).

A luminous sky, and flying birds.
What do I know—of life, of death, of God?
What do we know?—I remember the very same sunset.
I remember the deck, the distance, like a gently inclining shore . . .

A child was traveling with us, sad and blind
From birth, dispassion in his vacant gaze.
He listened keenly . . . to the blue sea murmuring vaguely
At the stern, beyond unseeing eyes . . .

A heart will cringe—a tiny, frightened hedgehog —
In God's invisible, burning palms.

Life's thin thread is like a web in the forest,
A summer dewdrop, a tiny tear, a bead of sweat.

Veins appear on the leaves, like dark hands.
The season of mushrooms, beginning of separation.

Intimate with the forest and God,
A small leaf, like a sparrow, flies to the road.

Here it has fallen, as some say,
Into nature's lap, to its native soil.

A roof, a nest. And, like the stork,
Your time stands motionless, planning its flight.

Soon, in God's invisible hands
A heart will cringe—a tiny, frightened hedgehog.

FROM: *Linii: vtoraya kniga stikhov* (Lines: A Second Book of Poems).

    —Smoking chimneys.
      Coal and road-metal on the pier.
    —The transparent sky
      And the silvery twitter of birds.

    —The smoke is dark and bitter,
      The gray shore joyless.
    —The sun's ray tender and light,
      And a butterfly rests on the heather.

    —Smashed by a storm
      Two boats lie across a gray shallow.
    —The azure sea
      Is calm and the shore—sunlit.

    —Shriveled shrubs,
      And a graveyard—too large for eyes to measure.
    —And the shimmering immortelle,
      Radiance of life and death.

We were in Russia—in the south, in July,
And the wounded struggled in the sweltering car,
On the field we found two shiny bullets —
Like acorns, you carried them in your palm —
Along the line of life, the line of happiness.

Two lizards flashed over a stone,
A dead man lay there, as if asleep.

Wartime, battlefield,
Russia . . . I have forgotten it all—so much more peaceful
Here, a garden—a deep lake beside it.

But if by chance, through the shade and chill,
A boy appears with two acorns in his hand,
Again—the south, Russia, July near the end,
And, as if through the lake or garden,
Disquieting ripples cross my oblivion.

————————

Dim twilight of a hot bedroom.
A raven croaked once in the somber park.
My heart beats in the silence,
Like the spinning wheel of the old Parcae.
They spin the thread quickly.

I know—the yarn nears the end.
In this weather it's boring
To hear their hastening sounds.
It's raining, and dark all around.

And mice nibble nimbly
At life, granted from above.
Now it won't be long,

Till the day when ennui will end
And those sounds, which disturbed our sleep,
Will be silent forever.

————————

Tell me, what has happened to the world?
It looks as though the rain,
With its vague, delicate dots,
Traces a new drawing over the old.

You'll reply: "All is as always.
The same houses across the street,
And the waters flow just the same."

— But all is not as always. On the contrary:
Through the lettering of commercial firms,
Through the rain, through the houses of Paris,
Through the entire nontransparent world —
I glimpse a different drawing.
It is composed of different lines
And different colors.
But unearthly glimpses
Are difficult from the earth.

431

Yury Ivask (1910–)

Yury (George) Pavlovich Ivask (literary pseudonyms B. Afanasyevsky, G. Issako, B. A., and Yu. I.), poet, critic, and scholar, was born in Moscow and graduated from the Law School at the University of Tartu, Estonia. He also studied philology at the University of Hamburg. In 1949 Ivask came to America. He received his Ph.D. degree from Harvard University in 1954, with a dissertation on "Vyazemsky as a Literary Critic." He taught Russian literature at the University of Kansas, the University of Washington, and Vanderbilt University. He is presently professor of Russian literature at the University of Massachusetts in Amherst. His numerous publications include *Severny bereg: stikhi 1933–1936* (The Northern Shore: Poems 1933–1936; Warsaw, 1938), *Tsarskaya osen': vtoraya kniga stikhov* (Regal Autumn: A Second Book of Verse; Paris, 1953), *Khvala* (Praise; Washington: Kamkin, 1967), *Zolushka* (Cinderella; New York, 1970), *Konstantin Leontyev: zhizn' i tvorchestvo* (Konstantin Leontyev: Life and Works; Bern, 1974), the long autobiographical poem *Homo Ludens* (Paris: *Vozrozhdenie* [La Renaissance] nos. 240–242 [1973]), and many others. He also wrote introductions to various editions of published works, for example, "V. Rozanov. *Izbrannoe*" (Selected Works; New York: Chekhov, 1956), "O. Mandel'shtam. *Sobranie sochineny*," Vol. III (Collected Works; Washington, 1968), and many perceptive, erudite essays on Russian poets, including Batyushkov, Boratynsky, Fet, Sluchevsky, Marina Tsvetaeva, Boris Pasternak, Andrey Bely, Georgy Ivanov, Mikhail Kuzmin, Alexander Blok, Anna Akhmatova, and Velemir Khlebnikov. He is the author of an excellent essay on "Poeziya 'staroy' emigratsii" (Poetry of the "Old" *Emigrés*) in *Russian Literature in Exile: A Collection of Articles* (ed. N. P. Poltoratzky). Ivask has contributed poetry and essays to numerous Russian newspapers, journals, almanacs, and anthologies. He was editor of *In the West: An Anthology of Russian Emigré Poetry*, and he edited the literary journal *Experiments* in 1955. Ivask has also published extensively in such American and Western European periodicals as *The Slavic Review*, *The Russian Review*, *The Slavic and East European Journal*, and *Die Zeitschrift für Slavische Philologie*. His favorite contemporary Russian poets are Osip Mandel'shtam, Marina Tsvetaeva, Irina Odoevtseva, Igor' Chinnov, Valery Pereleshin, and Joseph Brodsky. Ivask also favors the Anglo-Welsh poet Dylan Thomas, known for his rich assonance, alliteration, and language replete with rare words; and the French poet Guillaume Apollinaire, who opposed traditional structure in poetry and was a spokesman for artistic experimentation in the first two decades of the twentieth century.

Yury Ivask's early poetry is written in a classical manner. Its basic tenor is quiet; the style evinces simplicity and clarity; the language is restrained, elegant, and somewhat stylized; its archaic expressions are in perfect harmony with the philosophical content of the verse. Ivask writes about the meaning of life and death, "the importance and the rights of the intellect, and the poet's languishing desire to 'resolve all enigmas' and to attain a reconciliation of consciousness with reality"—so Pyotr Bicilli summarizes those "Hamlet-like" inquiries.[1] Ivask also muses upon such concepts as valor, heroic deeds, glory, friendship, and loneliness. Some of these emphases, as well as the classical simplicity and transparency of his style, link his early poetry with that of the "Parisian note." Bicilli traces Ivask's poetry to Boratynsky and Tyutchev, but Ivask's impressionistic technique, together with his excessive interest in the sound of the word (alliteration), his volitional disruption of the regularities of syntax (for example, the absence of punctuation marks), and occasional elements of *"zaum"* (trans-sense) language, put the imprint of originality on Ivask's poetry even at that early stage. Gleb Struve described this mode of poetic creation as Ivask's "aspiration to combine in one line the Russian 'Empire-style' of the nineteenth century with the Russian 'Renaissance' of the twentieth century; Pushkin and Boratynsky with Annensky and Mandel'shtam."[2]

Ivask attained his poetic peak toward the end of the 1950's, when the new style he had been gradually developing, a kind of Neo-Baroque, became quite noticeable. It is a radically new manner of writing, intimate, with highly personal chains of associations fused with sound experiments, neologisms, and elliptical imagery. Ivask himself asserts that his mature style was formed partially under the influence of Derzhavin, the English metaphysical and intensely religious poets John Donne, Richard Crashaw, and George Herbert, and the Spanish poet Luis de Góngera, who delighted in philosophical conflict. Ivask's present style is quite different from that of the "Parisian note."

His almost Dantesque poem *Homo Ludens*—actually a cycle of lyrical octets—is particularly interesting because, although it is autobiographical, the poet's personality does not occupy its center. There are two major images: man at play, living in space but outside of time; and paradise, existing simultaneously on earth and in Heaven. The man at play hopes to bring humanity, now confined to hell, closer to paradise. He cannot save men from evil, however; he cannot open the heavenly gates. There are recondite philosophical and literary references, trains of associations and images, and "sound chains"—all of them creating the strong impression of a game, aesthetic pleasure, poetic imagination, enjoyment of nature, sports, and even Russian peasant food. Ivask conceives all of this as the experience of a paradise on earth without melancholy and despair. The structure of the world and the structural design of *Homo Ludens* are in perfect harmony. The reader himself must participate in the game in order to understand both the content of the poem and Ivask's implicit dictum (as paraphrased by V. V. Weidlé): "Although unwilling to live in hell, we do not accept paradise without a wee bit of Hades."[3]

Homo Ludens is a rich source of material about the poet's life—his early days in Moscow, his adolescence in Estonia, his trip to see the poet Chinnov in Riga, his visits to the Merezhkovskys' famous Sunday salon in Paris, his meeting with Marina Tsvetaeva, his studies in Germany, graduate work at Harvard, subsequent journeys to Mexico, Portugal, Spain, Italy, France, Greece, and other European countries. As E. Rais suggests, *Homo Ludens* is the only successful example of a Russian poem with literature as its central theme.[4] In reality, however, the poet receives his inspiration not merely from reading books, admiring works of art, and musing upon the culture and history of mankind, but also from his enjoyment of nature and the variety of his personal experiences. Ivask's imagery is vivid and original, and the fanciful style of Neo-Baroque is sustained throughout the poem.

Ivask's later poetry, fresh and joyous, is light, carefree, and serene. Its basic moods embrace the persona's love of God's Creation, his firm faith in its fundamental goodness, and curiosity about everything in the sensory world.[5] It is difficult to translate such poetry because the sound texture is lost in translation, and the cement which bonds the content, the stream of personal associations, the playful and discordant sound instrumentation, teasing half-rhymes, extravagant images, and frequent enjambments is easily destroyed in the process. Yury Ivask is a gifted, very cultured, and original poet. His unique *Weltanschauung* and technique hold rich discoveries for the careful and serious student of Russian versification.

NOTES

1. Pyotr Bicilli, "Yury Ivask. *Severny bereg*. Warsaw, 1938," *Sovremennye zapiski* 66 (1938): 476.
2. *Russkaya literatura v izgnanii*, p. 36.
3. V. V. Weidlé, "Zhretsy edinykh muz," *Novoe russkoe slovo*, dated October 21, 1973.
4. "Yury Ivask. Igrayushchy chelovek: *Homo Ludens*," *Vozrozhdenie* no. 240 (1973): 7.
5. Georgy Adamovich, "Igor' Chinnov. *Partitura. Stikhi*. Izd. *Novogo zhurnala*, 1970. Yu. Ivask. *Zolushka. Stikhi*. Izd. zhurnala *Mosty*, 1970," *Novy zhurnal*, Book 102 (1971): 382–386.

POEMS

FROM: *Tsarskaya osen'* (Regal Autumn).

1.

The oaks and maples bend
In shimmering, golden glory,
Coating the slopes in foliage,
Crimson and sacrificial.

Contemporary of the Byzantine world,
Framed in the glow of golden icons,
A silver pontiff
Humbly kneels.

And crowned with glory anew,
Transcending the laws of time,
He raises above us
The radiant Cross of Christ.

A blue-eyed lad—
Like a gentle, heavenly cherub,
Holding a heavy crozier, silently,
Vigilant, follows him.

2.

Oh, so much gold! And yet not wealthy!
No, quite poor! So very poor!
—These golden leaves, the sunsets,
And the silvery glint of graying hair . . .

The crumbling, crumbling of that same Byzantine world.
Well then, crumble: and quickly!
While the winds, like our national orators,
Disrobe their golden tsars.

Tsars—the oaks, and patricians—maples,
And you, tsaritsa—that larch;
The hillocks' summer lighting illumines their slopes,
And the leaves—and poverty—cover them.

435

September, September, the dying of the mighty,
Of the Juliuses and Augustuses of earth.
But behold October, the final radiance has come,
And barbarians carrying axes.

Doomed sovereigns of the garden
Are felled by the savage . . .
But snow falls not; oh, fall, fall . . .
You, impossible, beatific snow!

3.

This—is a gold that glitters, but gives no glow,
Lifeless, heavy—
The lifeless, golden sun of Lethe,
Decrepit Lethe, sinks to the bottom.

Black waves applaud—could this be the rabble,
That rabble, seething around our feet?
So bestial, superstitious!
Why have the tsars not dealt with it in time?

Foxy mugs on the court patricians;
The khaki throng of Varangians bodes evil.
The tsar can't sigh for all his brocade,
Nor raise his head, with its wreath of pearls.

Is it ordained that I endure this hour of shame?
Even the hangman's face is flooded with horror,
Windows flush in humiliation and sorrow,
The brocade is drenched in blood and wine.

I hate sly monks
And the dense, superstitious mob;
The loyalty of the lowly salt pillar I praise,
A loyalty free from senseless fear.

The dead sun is also the sun of glory,
A solitary beloved majesty;
And I bless that extinct, solitary power
With my poor, petrified hand.

FROM: *Severny bereg* (The Northern Seashore).

My glum enemy is silent.
I wait for my radiant friend.
I have fulfilled my duty.
I leave the circle.

A harmonious choir of youths
Gives song to honor the victor.
His gaze grows suddenly dim.
What did you glimpse, proud man?

He has fulfilled his duty. He waits.
Death, where is thy sting?
Today he will lose his mind.
To the victor glory means little.

The enemy is gone.
I know no friend.
Only barren snows.
And unearthly shadows.

FROM: *Tsarskaya osen'* (Regal Autumn).

THE PINES

. . . A man in radiance, in silence,
Trusts his intellect again,
Forgetting nonsense and dreams
Once pleasing to him.

A flighty devotee of obscurantism,
Now he glorifies anew
The bright and mysterious law
Of justice and moderation . . .

The magnificent even lines
Of accessible Hellenic heights,
Extending into the blue distance,
Are mysteriously severe.

This golden geometry!
This azure silence!
The midday searing heat and stillness,
The scales stand at equilibrium.

Index

439

446